ANCIENT CRETE

FROM SUCCESSFUL COLLAPSE TO DEMOCRACY'S ALTERNATIVES, TWELFTH TO FIFTH CENTURIES BC

'Ancient Greece', with its associations of city-states, democratic governance, and iconic material culture, can no longer be envisaged as a uniform geographical or historical entity. The Classical city-states of Crete differed considerably in culture, history, and governance from those of central Greece. In this book, Saro Wallace reaches back into Crete's prehistory, covering the latest Bronze Age through the Archaic periods, to find out why. She emphasizes the roles of landscape, external contacts, social identity construction, and historical consciousness in producing this difference, bringing together the wealth of new archaeological evidence available from the island with a variety of ancient text sources to produce a vivid and up-to-date picture of this momentous period in Crete's history.

Until 2009 Saro Wallace was Lecturer in Mediterranean Archaeology at the University of Reading, having previously held lectureships at the Universities of Bristol and Cardiff. A recipient of a Leverhulme Postdoctoral Research Fellowship and of regular grants from the British Academy and the Institute for Aegean Prehistory, she has published many papers and reviews in the field of Bronze to Iron Age Greece. She currently directs excavations at the Late Bronze–Early Iron Age mountaintop site of Karfi, Crete.

ANCIENT CRETE

FROM SUCCESSFUL COLLAPSE TO DEMOCRACY'S ALTERNATIVES, TWELFTH TO FIFTH CENTURIES BC

Saro Wallace

CAMBRIDGE
UNIVERSITY PRESS

CAMBRIDGE
UNIVERSITY PRESS

32 Avenue of the Americas, New York NY 10013-2473, USA

Cambridge University Press is part of the University of Cambridge.

It furthers the University's mission by disseminating knowledge in the pursuit of education, learning, and research at the highest international levels of excellence.

www.cambridge.org
Information on this title: www.cambridge.org/9781107688414

First published 2010
Reprinted 2011
First paperback edition 2014

Printed in the United States of America

A catalog record for this publication is available from the British Library.

Library of Congress Cataloging in Publication data
Wallace, Saro, 1973–
Ancient Crete : from successful collapse to democracy's alternatives, 12th–5th centuries BC / Saro Wallace.
p. cm.
Includes bibliographical references and index.
ISBN 978-0-521-11204-8 (hbk.)
1. Crete (Greece) – History – To 67 B.C. 2. Crete (Greece) – Politics and government. 3. City-states – Greece – Crete – History. 4. Democracy – Greece – Crete – History. 5. Social change – Greece – Crete – History. 6. Landscape – Social aspects – Greece – Crete – History. 7. Group identity – Greece – Crete – History. 8. Crete (Greece) – Social conditions. 9. Material culture – Greece – Crete – History. 10. Crete (Greece) – Antiquities. I. Title.
DF261.C8W35 2010
939'.1801–dc22 2009033585

ISBN 978-0-521-11204-8 Hardback
ISBN 978-1-107-68841-4 Paperback

CONTENTS

LIST OF TABLES AND ILLUSTRATIONS

TABLES

FIGURES

COLOUR PLATES

Colour plates follow page 6.

ABSTRACT

In today's politics democracy is often presented as a largely self-contained system, able to be introduced abruptly into a variety of social environments with predictable and permanent success. The idea that social collapse (whatever its origins) can be orchestrated and managed to the same end has also gained ground. Against this background, this book's investigation of how far the earliest consensualist states, those of Greece, developed out of specific, regional material and historical conditions following Bronze Age state collapse, and of the role played by cultural practice in structuring them, seems especially pertinent. Interest in regional variance between early Greek state forms has recently grown among archaeologists and text historians. The book is sited within this context: as a comparative regional study focused on Crete it counters teleological/evolutionary notions of a widespread, uniform trajectory of social change towards a single democratic 'light at the end of the tunnel' in early Greece. Between the horizons of east Mediterranean state collapse in the twelfth century and Greek democracy establishment by the fifth, Crete's course of social and political development diverges markedly from that of much of central Greece: democratic systems did not develop there. Analysis of the island in its broad Mediterranean context shows how regional and contingent factors interacted with larger-scale processes and structures to produce Crete's difference, as comparisons are drawn across the ancient world (Cyprus, Athens, the western Greek colonies, the *ethnos* states of north central Greece, Ionia, and Sparta). At island level, the project necessitates writing the first synthetic social archaeology of Crete in the Early Iron Age to late Archaic periods, drawing together a very large amount of good-quality archaeological evidence produced in the last twenty years and a broad range of older data of more variable quality. Archaic and Classical text sources are additionally examined, particularly to illuminate issues around cultural and political identities in Crete by the end of the period covered.

The issue of how far agency, self-consciousness, and choice determined contrasts between regional social systems is an important focus here. However, the book's main argument is that a series of important developments in *cultural* practice, ultimately rooted in the process of Bronze

Age state collapse, conditioned the way states emerged and developed in different Aegean regions. Crete's collapse is shown to have involved a unique degree of planned, preemptive cultural adjustment that, viewed together with macroeconomic and geopolitical factors, helps explain the remarkable degree of social stability in the island during the immediate post-collapse period. The book identifies a horizon of social complexity emerging in Crete in the tenth century BC – much earlier than in most other areas of Greece – showing it to have been closely tied into this earlier cultural history. This precocious development is argued to have played a strong role in producing an especially bounded, oligarchical small state in the island by the seventh century BC. In contrast, central Greek societies were characterized by extreme and long-term instability and tensions after the Bronze Age collapse, and experienced a different rate and scale of economic and political growth in the period prior to democracy's emergence. The book questions the notion of developmental 'progress' or 'success' and its association with democratic outcomes by suggesting that the early development of complex and stable social structures in Crete *limited* the dynamism of the island's participation in international trade and politics and ultimately helped discourage participative political structures from taking root there. Specific local constructions and conceptions of historical, cultural, and ethnic identity also had strong roles in structuring the state and were heavily manipulated to this end: the book concludes by showing how and why Cretan societies took on a status of ideological 'other' for other Greek communities, deeply affecting the way the Cretan states viewed themselves, were viewed, and operated in the perspective of Classical democracy.

ACKNOWLEDGEMENTS

Many organisations and institutions in the United Kingdom, the United States, and Greece have supported the research needed to write this book. I am grateful to them for supplying the resources that allowed me to work with primary data in the field and secondary sources in a range of libraries. I thank them, too, for funding vital time for slow reflection on and improvement of the work at the writing stage. The Institute for Aegean Prehistory, A. G. Leventis Foundation, British Academy, Leverhulme Trust, Greek Government State Scholarships Foundation, and Mediterranean Archaeological Trust have all contributed significant resources, including field research grants for the Karfi Project and the Roots of the Cretan Polis Ceramic Study Project (the results of which have contributed to this book). The British School at Athens offered small grants for a variety of purposes. I would like especially to note the generosity and efficiency of funding from the Institute for Aegean Prehistory and the Leverhulme Trust. The Samuel H. Kress Foundation generously funded the inclusion of the colour plates.

The British School at Athens offered excellent library research facilities between 2001 and 2004. My employment as a lecturer in Greek and Mediterranean archaeology at the Universities of Bristol, Cardiff, and Reading from 2004 onwards offered a salary to live on and access to some internal research grants and facilities that helped the book's production: I must particularly thank Sue Giles at Bristol, Howard Mason and Ian Dennis at Cardiff, and Margaret Mathews at Reading for help in scanning, correcting, and advising on some of the illustrations used here, as well as the holders of copyright illustrations who have allowed me to adapt and reproduce their images. The 24th Ephorate of Prehistoric and Classical Antiquities of the National Archaeological Service in east Crete supported my recent work at Karfi, which has greatly informed this book, with permissions to work at the site.

Another important acknowledgement should go to the individual members of the scholarly community who listened to my ideas with patience, wisdom, and interest, using their own knowledge and experience to refine and improve them. Among them I count many close friends as well as colleagues. The constant moral support of Krzysztof Nowicki, and his incredibly detailed understanding of Crete's ancient landscapes, as well as his permanent readiness to engage in highly informed and passionate debates on Aegean prehistory, had a special role in improving my work, for which I offer many thanks. Donald Haggis (whose work inspired my first studies of the Cretan economy in the Early Iron Age) has been a tireless critic, friend, and supporter of my work; so has Leslie Day. James Whitley is acknowledged here not only for the level of personal support and stimulating discussion he offered me in the years 2002–4, but also for the amount of original and creative thought he has given to the study of the Aegean Early Iron Age generally and the Early Iron Age of Crete in particular. Though I disagree with many of his positions here, if he had not put them forward in his characteristically polemical style, this field would be considerably poorer.

Among the other colleagues who have stimulated my thinking through personal discussion in a friendly and open way, I would like to mention Tom Brogan, Cyprian Broodbank, Jan Driessen, Birgitta Eder, Brice Erickson, Geraldine Gesell, Carl Knappett, Nota Kourou, Irene Lemos, Sandy MacGillivray, Nicoletta Momigliano, Margaret Mook, Cathy Morgan, Laura Preston, David Ridgway, Sue Sherratt, Lena Sjögren, Metaxia Tsipopoulou, and Todd Whitelaw, but there are many others who have helped me in this way, including all those who have kindly given me permission to reproduce their illustrations. I especially thank Chris Mee, who has offered steady and generous support in all my academic endeavours.

Another group of helpers has been the residents of Crete and many other parts of Greece, who have spent hours chatting about their history, environment, and ways of work; have refreshed me with their hospitality; and have shown me the way through their landscapes with such friendliness and humour. There are too many of them to name, but all have played a role in giving Greece the irrepressible spirit and zest that warm me whenever I visit. I would like to mention here only some very particular friends, the Kargiotakis family of Tzermiado in Lasithi. The regular group of staff and affiliates at the Institute for Aegean Prehistory (INSTAP) Study Centre for East Crete, who create a uniquely friendly, stimulating, and dynamic environment for all those working on Cretan archaeology, should be given special thanks, too.

The staff at Cambridge University Press in New York have been most enthusiastic, supportive, and efficient throughout, and I would like to thank warmly in particular Beatrice Rehl and Susan Thornton.

In the United Kingdom, Robin Turner's kind, steady, and quiet support during the early stages of my research career will always be remembered. I would also like to thank Simon Walton and Lada Jamnicky for the entertaining distractions that were so much needed during the various stages of writing. I have very much enjoyed writing this book and hope it will be used by both prehistorians and historians of Greece, who will wrestle further with the questions I have tried to address, and who constantly improve the base of data I have used. All errors, inadequacies, and misunderstandings in the text are my own.

Saro Wallace
Reading, UK
April 2009

PART ONE

Crete between east and west, state collapse and state emergence

1 INTRODUCTION

In a post–Cold War age, as alternative political structures have become weakened, marginalised, or fragmented along ethno religious lines, 'democracy' is increasingly held up as an ideal. At the same time, the concept also seems to be becoming more morally ambiguous, and more controversial: recent years have seen forceful external attempts to introduce democratic regimes to societies voicing active resistance to the concept. The cultural and conceptual attributes of the earliest democratic states, the Classical Greek poleis, have long been appropriated by various nationalisms (particularly Greek nationalism) and most recently by 'Europeanism' in a global context – promoted, for example, as symbols of world peace and friendship during the 2004 Athens Olympic Games and cited as a cornerstone of common European heritage in the draft European constitution (Dunn 1992: vii; European Union 2003; Hamilakis 1999; Hamilakis and Yalouri 1996; Lowenthal 1985: 74–125; Morris 1994; Morris and Raaflaub 1997; Ober and Hedrick 1996b; Simandiraki 2004; Yalouri 2001). More than ever, it seems, we need to review how far we can characterise consensualist/democratic ideologies as a 'natural', permanent, or desirable social outcome. Investigation of the degree to which the earliest known democratic systems developed out of specific material and historical conditions and were constructed, consciously and otherwise, through cultural practice, can help in this, allowing us to trace and evaluate important alternative trajectories in historical perspective (Cartledge 1998).

The exercise takes us back to the end of the Aegean Bronze Age. The period around 1200 BC marks the collapse across the region of Late Bronze Age states (LBA: c. 1700–1200 BC) which had been ruled by highly stratified, regionally centralized elites. Collapse or disturbance occurred at the same time across much of the rest of the east Mediterranean, where related kinds of palace-based state had existed (Gitin et al. 1998; Ward and Joukowsky 1992). By the seventh century BC, a new kind of small bounded state, structured around the principle of participative government by a class of nominally 'equal' citizens, had developed in much of the Aegean, with an extreme form of directly participatory democracy becoming established in Athens by the fifth century.

This was not, however, a standard outcome throughout the region. Crete, for example, contained states with a distinctive type of political structure, which failed ever to take on the democratic characteristics seen in many central Greek regions. Using the island as a case study, I will show that this fact relates to a consistently divergent path of social development in Crete between the twelfth and fifth centuries – that is, the Early Iron Age (EIA: c. 1200–700 BC) through Archaic period (Archaic: c. 700–480 BC). Scholarly interest in the historical reasons for structural variance between Archaic-Classical state forms in different Aegean regions has recently been increasing, but some regions remain neglected (Brock and Hodkinson 2000; Cartledge 2001: 21–39; Davies 1997: 25; Morgan 2003: 1–2). Crete is one of these – often presented as a sketchy template of contrast to central Greek patterns, or as the subject of extreme generalizations, based on isolated elements of the cultural record, about 'continuity' in social structures between the Bronze Age and Classical periods. These inadequacies are recognised (Lemos 2002: 1; Morris 1998: 12–13), and scholars have started to redress the balance by focusing in depth on specific themes relating to the EIA-Archaic period, or by looking at selected parts of that period, in the island (Prent 2005b: 53–84; Sjögren 2004: 3). Still, however, a detailed, accessible, consistent, and broadly based social narrative for the whole period between Bronze Age state collapse and polis emergence in Crete is lacking (Perlman 2000: 59–60).

One reason is that sources of text evidence are patchy: the structure of Classical Cretan states is much less well documented than that of their counterparts in the central Aegean, particularly Athens. Another is the nature and quantity of archaeological evidence: there is both too much, and too little, of it available for the period between the twelfth and the fifth centuries in Crete. A large and complex body of data now available for the EIA, constituting the densest and best-quality coverage for any Aegean region, meets what has long been viewed as a 'gap' in the record for the later Archaic period (c. 600–480 BC). Research has only just started to reveal the partly illusory nature of this perceived gap, suggesting that it has arisen from high levels of selectivity about the kinds of material worth studying (Erickson 2004, 2005; Haggis et al. 2004: 344). For the Classical period, the archaeological record from Crete is simply not well investigated. In particular, no large Cretan settlement site occupied continuously through the Archaic and Classical periods has yet been extensively or systematically excavated using up-to-date techniques.

Because synthesis is so challenging, single elements of the record, or individual sites, are often seized on for interpretation in a decontextualised way that fails to realise their full informative potential. My aim here is to engage with the full weight and complexity of Cretan archaeological data through this period, as well as the insights available from contemporary texts (the latter known only from the eighth century BC onward), to achieve an improved understanding of the long-term social changes that produced the special features of Cretan society through and beyond the rise of the polis state.

The analysis must, I argue, start from the great horizon of state collapse at circa 1200 BC, which I will show to have strongly conditioned the nature of the new state forms established by the late eighth century. In many areas of the east Mediterranean, the collapse was of a dramatic and often violent nature, involving the destruction and/or abandonment of major settlement centres. In Parts Two and Three I show that Crete's collapse process had a special character, involving a significant degree of preemptive cultural and social adjustment. Though the island's social and political structures *were* deeply disturbed, this seems to have occurred in a remarkably well-insulated environment, permitting Cretan societies to accommodate and adapt to changing wider political and economic circumstances more smoothly than groups in some other Aegean regions. In Parts Three and Four I go on to identify patterns of newly emergent social complexity in Crete (directly prefiguring the formation of small states) from the tenth century BC – that is, much earlier than in most other Aegean regions. This phenomenon seems directly linked to the positive way in which Cretan communities had collapsed about two hundred years earlier, as well as to macroeconomic and geopolitical trends in the east Mediterranean as a whole. By the late eighth century, the period at which states are usually considered to have emerged in central Greece, I argue that Cretan societies were already well launched on a particular trajectory of social development that ensured that they never developed democratic structures. That is, the 'successful' nature of social collapse circa 1200 BC was directly linked to the later development of social conditions in which democracy did not/could not emerge. Instead, a range of distinctive cultural and structural features characterised Cretan states between the seventh and fourth centuries. I analyse these, relate them to earlier developments, and compare Cretan state structures to those of other regions in Part Five. Notwithstanding these differences, macroscale factors, operating at the level of the Aegean in some cases and of the whole east and/or central Mediterranean in others, continued to affect Cretan societies deeply. The record shows that they saw themselves as closely tied into a pan-Hellenic heritage and culture. Part Five explores the historical factors producing this outlook, and how the latter was reconciled with local structures of political and economic life.

Because it attempts to cover as broad a range of archaeological and textual data as possible, I have titled this book a 'cultural history'. The phrase has been used recently by Morris (citing Hunt 1989) to describe how different types of ancient cultural evidence can be analysed together to write history in its broadest sense – that is, to explain and interpret change in society over time. The approach emphasises the centrality of culture in embodying, structuring, and reproducing society (Gellner 1983: 37–8). Here I identify and discuss a wide variety of types and levels of interactions among the cultural, social, economic, and political spheres in the long term, while recognising the impossibility of writing a 'total history' (Braudel 1979: 901–3; Febvre 1938: 2–4, 9; Hodder 1987; Trigger 1998: 167–79). The recognition of social change as culturally conditioned, particular, reflexive, contingent, and conjunctural emerges as a major theme. Using the Cretan case, I aim to offer a microcosmic insight into contingent processes of social change *and* a generalizing comparative analysis of the origins, structure, and cross-influence of early small states. In attempting this dual perspective, I return regularly to the questions of how local, particular, and contingent factors interacted with large-scale processes to produce Mediterranean communities that were strongly linked in cultural, ethnic, and political terms, yet retained consistently different social structures, and of how cultural practice conditioned social change repeatedly, continuously, and at a number of different levels. The latter is especially notable in this case with regard to the development of group identity structures linked into a strong historical consciousness. Ancient communities' conceptions of space and place, both at intrasite levels and in the wider landscape, are a particular focus in this connection: I attempt to build an integrated understanding of different fields and scales of cultural activity over time in relation to fixed spatial parameters – including Crete's boundaries as an island, its dissected landscape, and its positioning between the Aegean and Near Eastern geographical regions – as well as to changing social structures.

One of the book's approaches is to assess the relative 'success' (in terms of longevity, cohesive strength, and influence) of different early Greek state forms, nearly all of which incorporated some elements of consensualist/participatory ideology. Investigating the links between 'successful' outcomes and 'alternatives to democracy' seems especially interesting in a present-day political climate where the collapse of political systems is presented as able to be engineered, with defined and predictable consequences, and democracy seen as able to be artificially imposed on a post-collapse 'blank slate' if it does not emerge naturally. Within the limits of its ancient subject matter, the study challenges notions of the historically inevitable emergence of consensually governed states (whether through 'organic' evolution or revolutionary action) and concludes that collapse, though it may be engineered or modified in many and varied ways, has deep, uncontrollable, long-term, and materially embedded political consequences. I highlight the self-consciousness and agency of communities in determining their own political identity and development, but also their vulnerability to broader forces of change. Ultimately, I suggest that the conscious, articulated resistance to adopting democratic systems that seems to have emerged by the fifth century in Crete grew out of a set of historically and culturally framed conditions which could not easily have permitted another course.

At a regional level, too, the book's aims and scope are closely related to the time of its writing – at which the body of archaeological data for Crete has become so rich and varied as to demand a deep and wide-ranging interpretative synthesis. In view of the fact that existing Aegean-wide syntheses have significant gaps, I have recognised an important chance to use a really solid and well-informed body of interpretation from an area with close links to other Aegean regions throughout this period to pose newly angled research questions concerning those other regions. Interpretations based on the Cretan data are used throughout the book as a comparative basis from which to explore aspects of the EIA-Classical record in other regions, including the Cyclades, central and northern Greece, Ionia, Cyprus, Sparta, and the west Mediterranean colonies. Strong contrasts in social and cultural developments between regions, but also some instructive parallels, are highlighted. The depth of comparative analysis varies, depending on the type and quality of evidence available for each region and the perceived value of the comparison in throwing light on the study's main issues of concern. Given the focus of the book on Crete, *all* the compared areas are treated at a much briefer and more superficial level than the island itself. The comparisons are enriched by reference to selected cross-cultural models. However, by the very nature of its approach – that is, to highlight and explain significant regional differences in social patterns, as well as shared features, over time – the book avoids positing universalising models for social change either at the pan-Aegean level or across the whole period covered. Rather, the intention is to contribute to contemporary archaeological and anthropological thought by siting a complex case study within, and using it to engage with and develop, some important perspectives in archaeology since the 1990s (including, for example, approaches focused on agency and on cognitive and symbolic systems). While the study's tendency is to move away from processualist standpoints, not least by deconstructing several influential examples of processual models previously applied to this period, a number of models are developed, and patterns identified, that clearly have wider potential applications in archaeological research. These include, for example, the notion of 'successful' collapse; the recognition of state formation as a partly diffused process, occurring at distinctly different horizons and in different ways, but within a relatively short period; and the recognition of multitype reference to past material culture (including very recent material culture) as a powerful social phenomenon and mover in crisis periods. As explained later, some approaches used here (for example, close attention to settlement patterns and landscapes) diverge from those most often previously used to explore this period in the Aegean. I aim to highlight the value of such aspects of the record by integrating them fully into the interpretative picture: Again, I hope this approach will have resonance beyond the region treated.

One note of caution should be sounded at this point. Despite its intended relevance to general political history and theory, this book is primarily a study of ancient (mainly prehistoric) archaeological evidence, with all the inexactitude that involves. The societies under discussion, which were small-scale, agriculturally based, and technologically undeveloped, are difficult (if not impossible) to compare directly with modern or recent historical societies, and ancient Greek democratic systems differed greatly from those of any modern state (Raaflaub 1997b: 35). Thus, the relevance of this study to modern history and politics can only be stretched so far: In this regard the general conclusions will be of most interest, while the detail of the work is intended to make a contribution in its own right to the study of Mediterranean prehistory and early history.

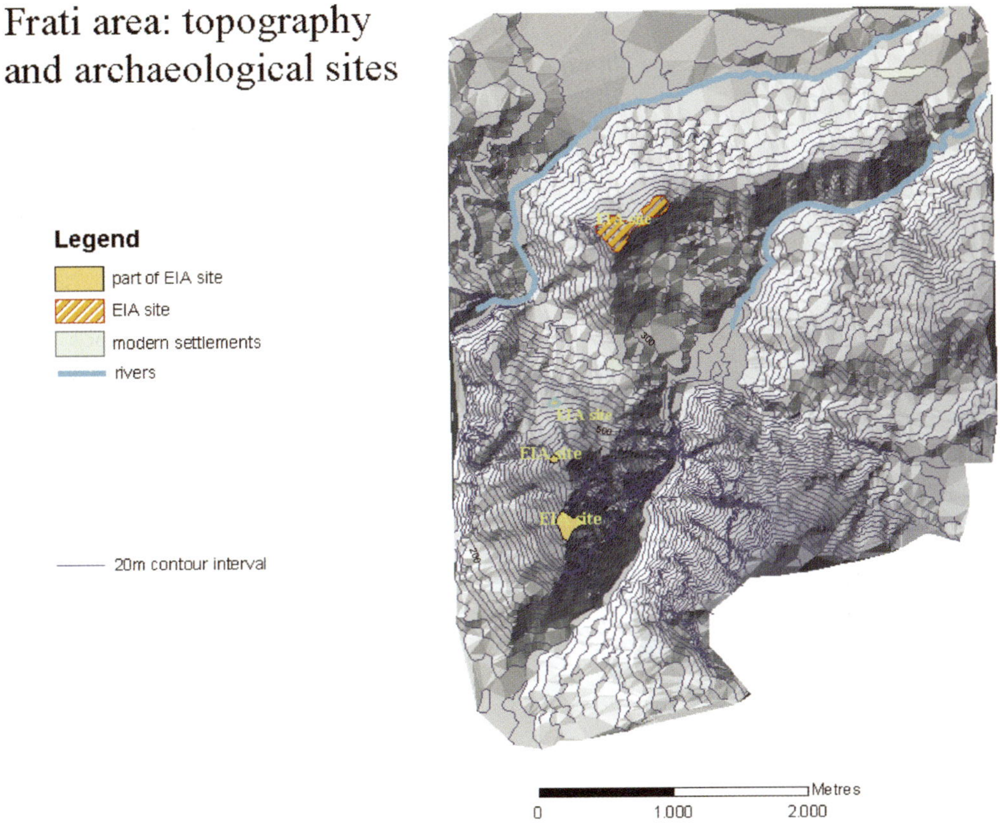

PLATE 1. Relief map of the area around Frati Kefali and Kefala. The sites guard river gorges used as natural routes northwards from the coastal plain to the south.

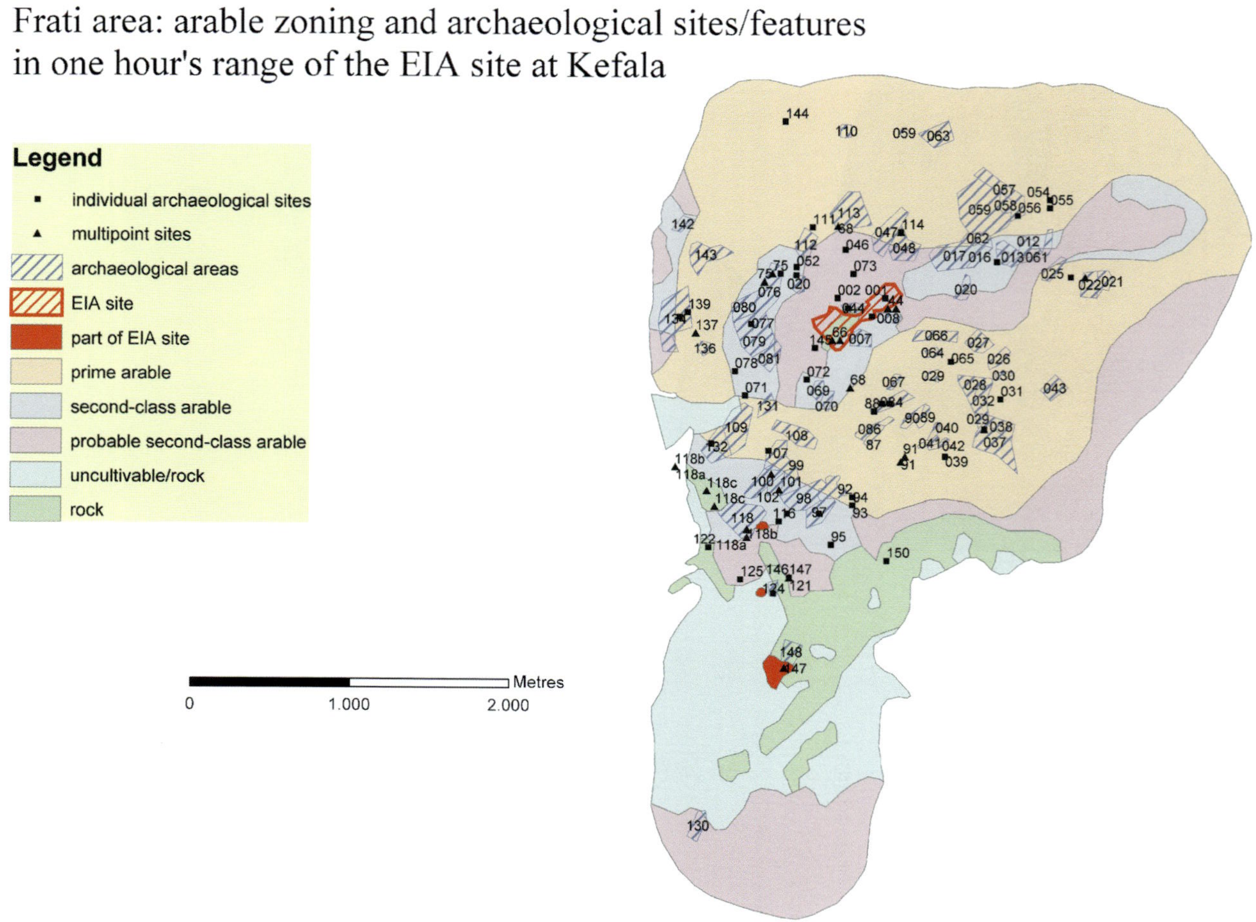

PLATE 2. Plot of arable land quality within a one-hour range of the Frati Kefali and Kefala settlements, showing the clustering of sites of most periods (from prehistory to the present) in the most historically productive and easily cultivable zones.

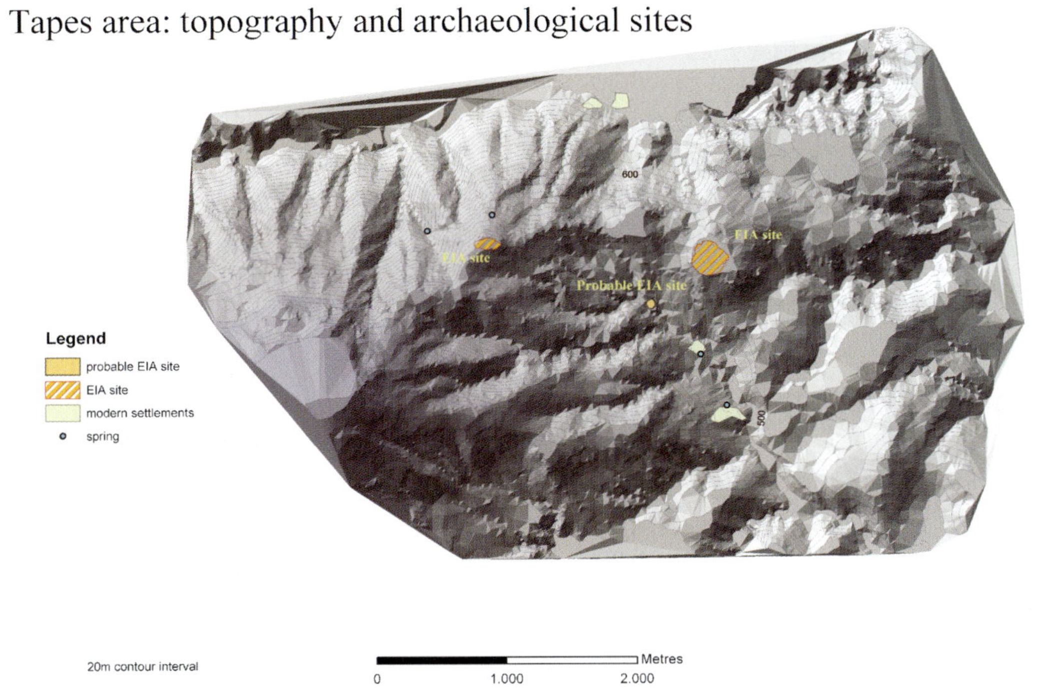

PLATE 3. Relief map of the Tapes area.

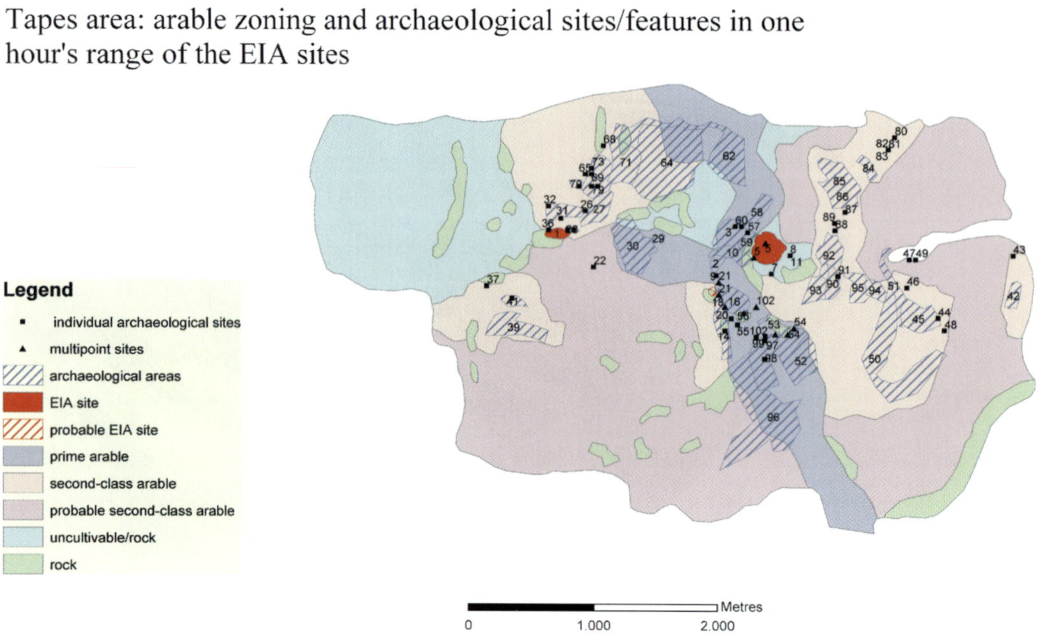

PLATE 4. Plot of arable land quality within a one-hour range of the Tapes Epano and Kato Kastello settlements, showing the clustering of sites of most periods (from prehistory to the present) in the most historically productive and easily cultivable zones.

Vrachasi area: topography and archaeological sites

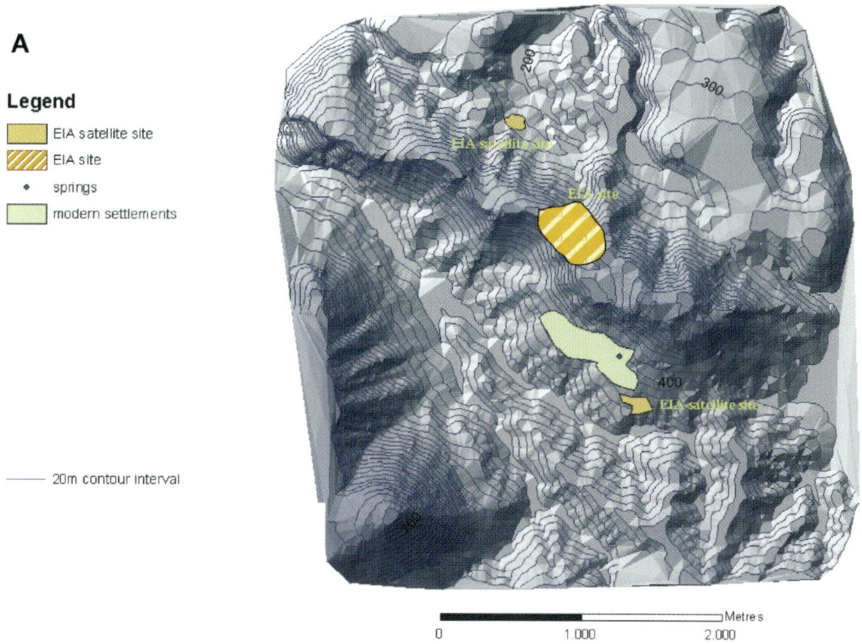

Vrachasi area: arable zoning and archaeological sites/features in one hour's range of the EIA site

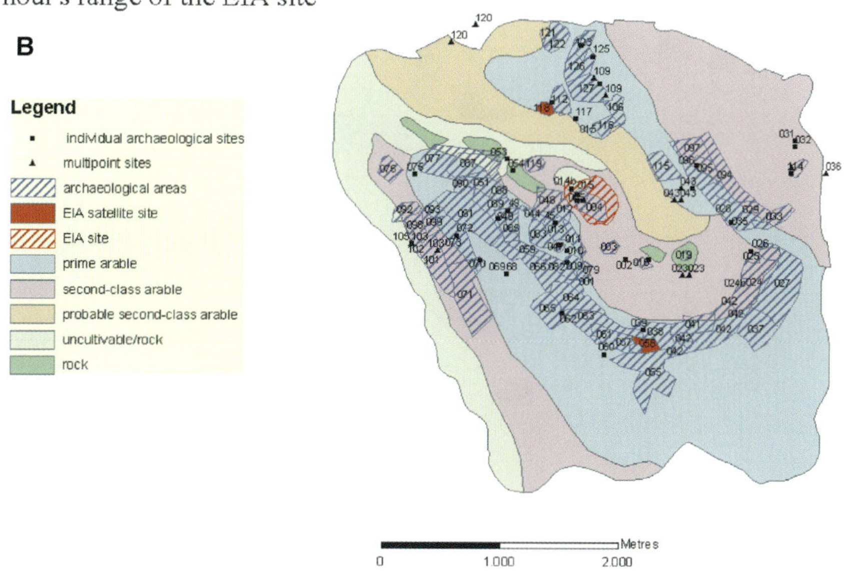

PLATE 5. A) Relief map of the area around the site of Vrachasi Anavlochos; B) map showing hinterland quality in a one-hour walking zone around the site of Vrachasi Anavlochos, and the locations of possible satellite sites of EIA-Archaic date.

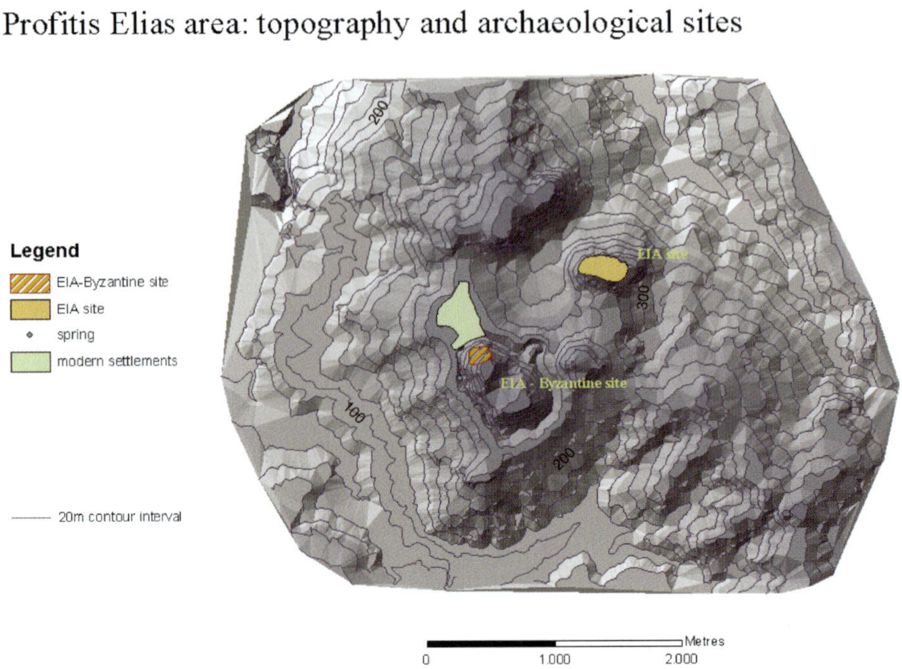

PLATE 6. Relief map of the area around the sites of Profitis Elias Rokka and Korifi.

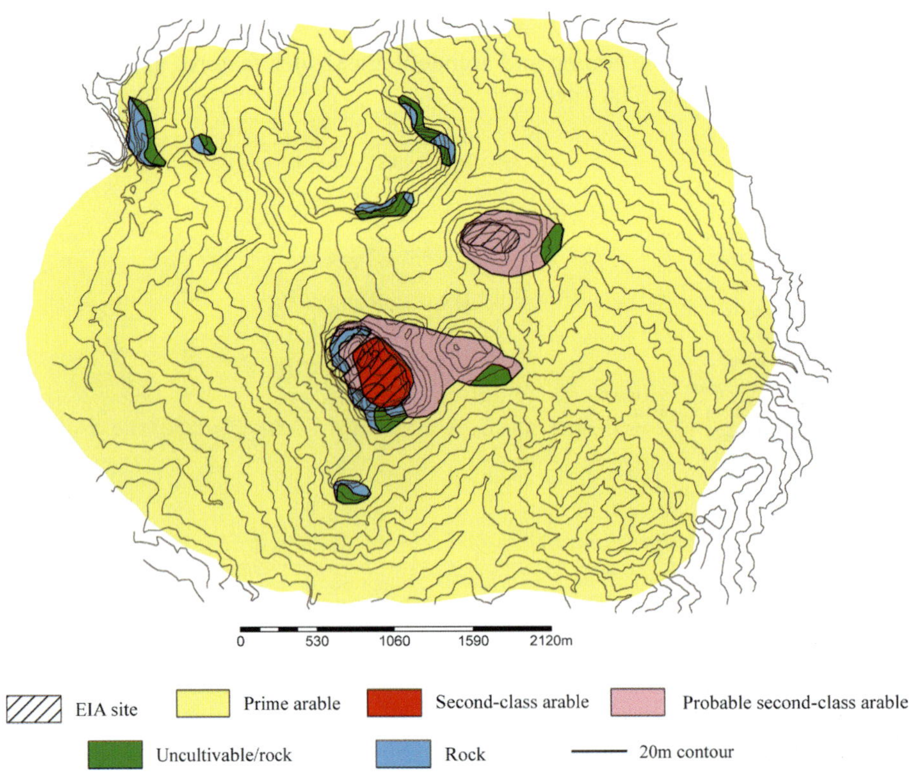

PLATE 7. Plot of arable land quality within a one-hour range of the Profitis Elias Rokka and Korifi settlements, showing the clustering of sites of most periods (from prehistory to the present) in the most historically productive and easily cultivable zones.

2 METHOD AND STRUCTURE

Data sources and data coverage

Given the time span covered, the majority of which is prehistoric, most evidence used here is archaeological. Notwithstanding the comparative richness and diversity of the archaeological record for EIA-Classical Crete, it still contains a large number of gaps. Overreliance on selected *fragments* of archaeological information to support a case can still be a tendency of scholars from a Classics background, but few experienced archaeologists would feel comfortable with this. What I attempt to do here is to build broad general interpretative arguments based on what can reasonably be evaluated as the most representative data sources, avoiding reliance on small or unrepresentative elements of the data to support major points. My view is that interpretations are often more convincingly supported by identification of strong, widespread patterns of lower-resolution data than reliance on one-off cases of high resolution: consequently I often give more weight to the former. For example, in suggesting that the roots of the well-documented interstate conflict in Classical Crete lie in a set of tensions reached from the Early Archaic period onward, I rely more on a broad base of data indicating settlement development and growth by this period to back up my points than, say, the deposition quantities of particular artefacts, such as weapons, in Archaic graves and sanctuaries. Approaches of the latter kind, examples of which are illustrated at several points in the book, often seem naïve, given the plethora of social factors that can affect the way societies deposit goods in the mortuary and ritual record.

The book follows a broadly linear chronological structure, starting with the collapse period circa 1200 BC and ending by considering the Classical polis. This structure, the origins of the study, my own balance of expertise, and the types and limitations of data available, all influence the work's emphases and the types of data on which it relies most heavily. For example, much of the newest, most detailed settlement evidence for Crete dates between the Early Iron Age and Early Archaic periods. A large proportion of it relates to settlement pattern at a very general level, since it has been acquired through intensive and extensive survey. This is supplemented by evidence from settlement excavations of a varying standard and at different stages of publication. Unfortunately, by contrast, we still have no detailed published stratigraphic record of any sizeable Cretan settlement or cemetery used through the late Archaic to Classical period, and thus contemporary with the first detailed textual sources for the island. On mortuary practice, the recent high-quality publication of a large cemetery at Knossos (North Cemetery) offers considerable insight into social and economic developments during the Cretan EIA, but at a single and rather exceptional settlement (Coldstream and Catling 1996). Otherwise, much mortuary evidence (especially for the Archaic period) comes from old research projects, incompletely published, or from small rescue excavations of scattered tombs, without wider context. Cult practice is fairly well documented at settlement level in the Cretan EIA, but the practice of using caves and open-air sites for cult, often without any architectural context and over very long timescales, means that extra-settlement sanctuaries are less well understood. Cult sites of both types have often been particular victims of unsystematic early excavation and damage through looting. Whole areas of potentially fruitful analysis (such as ceramic production) can receive only limited discussion here because of the lack of provenance and technological studies undertaken to date for this period in Crete.

This uneven balance between the types of evidence available has helped us push the study into productive new directions, including a focus on cultural landscapes as a whole, and on the investigation of subsistence and environment as factors in cultural and social change. This represents a move away from the more narrowly mortuary-, architecture-, or artefact-focused discussions of the Greek EIA dominant in the literature, which often cover only a small selection of well-known sites. The latter approach partly reflects the somewhat different character and patchy geographical spread of EIA evidence in central Greece, but also, often, a rather limited breadth of scholarly vision. As noted earlier, I shall show that considering, in a consistent and balanced way, the *full range* of EIA data in Crete (uneven though it is) can help identify productive research directions and develop enhanced interpretative frameworks for other parts of the Aegean in this period. The sheer variety of data sources studied here contributed to one of this book's major conclusions – that very diverse elements of cultural practice conditioned the structure of social and political systems in this period. The picture is further enriched by reference to textual sources alongside archaeological data. However, the study of texts raises additional issues of approach, which I discuss separately later.

Defining the region

The study aims at comparison of 'Crete' with 'other' Aegean and Mediterranean regions, but how are these boundaries defined, and how far can a single book go in drawing such comparisons? Three decades after Coldstream, Desborough and Snodgrass published major syntheses on the 'Dark Age' Aegean, important new primary data about the period have come to light for a number of Greek regions (Coldstream 1979a; Desborough 1972a; Snodgrass 1971). However, the volume of these data, their scattered nature and variable quality (many from rescue excavations), and the expectation today that meaningful archaeological analysis will address data from a number of different thematic and theoretical angles mean that broad yet deep research syntheses in the vein of these earlier works are now difficult – if not impossible – to write. Alternative approaches have recently included the writing of textbooks covering the whole period, and the entire Aegean region, at a fairly superficial level, with a focus on the best-known sites (Dickinson 2006; Osborne 1996; Whitley 2001; Wallace 2009). At the advanced research level, scholars have often chosen to focus in depth on just one part of the period, or some regions only, or to emphasise specific aspects of material culture (Eder 1998; Lemos 2002; Morgan 2003). Edited volumes have made important contributions, often mixing textual studies with archaeological ones and including some valuable new field reports. By their very nature, though, these volumes often lack the kind of synthetic analytical scope needed to integrate different types of research satisfactorily (Deger-Jalkotzy and Lemos 2006; Fisher and van Wees 1998; Kyparissi-Apostolika and Papakonstantinou 2003; Stampolidis and Giannikouri 2004).

If Aegean-wide synthesis with an adequate depth of regional coverage is now difficult to achieve, restricting the analysis of social and economic interactions to the island scale alone makes little sense as an alternative. Thanks to Crete's geographical position, these interactions always went well beyond the island's physical boundaries, while still feeding back substantially into economic, social, and political changes within it (Broodbank 2000: 68; Cherry et al. 1991: 9; Horden and Purcell 2000: 123–73; Knapp and Blake 2005). This recognition informs the present study, which builds partly on approaches to the archaeology of the Mediterranean using world-systems theory developed in the 1990s (Rowlands 1987; Sherratt and Sherratt 1991, 1993) to show how Crete's changing types and levels of interaction with outside regions influenced local developments in multiple spheres – conflict and defence, economic growth, and the construction of community identity.

Analysis even at the island level is sometimes too general to be meaningful, and we need to move down to the level of the small region: Bintliff has recently called for more 'regional, intra-island, in-depth explorations of specific [Cretan] landscapes to get a surer feel for what our general interpretative problems come to at grass-roots level' (Bintliff 1999: 6). One of the most successful examples of this approach for the EIA has been the Kavousi survey and excavation project in the east of the island, with a recent offshoot at Azoria (Day et al. 1986; Gesell et al. 1983, 1985, 1988, 1991, 1995; Haggis 1993: 165; 2005; Haggis et al. 2004, 2007a, 2007b). However, it is much more difficult to define regional political or economic boundaries for the Early Iron Age in Crete than it is for the Late Bronze Age, when a hierarchical organisation of settlement and territory seems to have operated. Interaction between social and economic groups in the EIA can be shown to have taken place within a number of strongly defined, but partly overlapping, identity frameworks. To understand these properly, research needs to bridge the gap between studies of small regions like the Kavousi project or other recent regional intensive surveys (e.g., Hayden 2004, 2005; Watrous et al. 2004), which are limited in the wider generalisations they can make, and scholarship that, in attempting to generalise about the Aegean as a whole, relies on superficial and often misleading summary 'overviews' of EIA Crete as a whole.

In sum, in this book, I treat the island in this period as a valid, but never restrictive, analytical unit. Close similarities in natural environment, ongoing contacts, and strong links in material culture and social phenomena between its regions *do* allow meaningful generalisation. By undertaking synthesis at the island scale, in conjunction with a representative range of external comparisons, I aim to make it much more difficult to arbitrarily select microregional or otherwise isolated aspects of the Cretan EIA data to illustrate arguments about wider Aegean developments which they may not actually support (Morgan 2003: 49–50). When making comparisons with other regions, the Cretan evidence and its interpretation are always used here as the main focus point, reference, and guide. As a result, my generalisations about other regions are often too shallow to cover the full complexity of developments there. I suggest, however, that this superficiality is justified within the corrective scope of this study. Throughout, the regional boundary designations I use outside Crete can vary considerably, depending on the type and level of comparison being drawn.

Structure of the book

The range of cultural fields examined and my interest in cross-regional comparison have led me to divide each part of the book into thematic subsections within a linear chronological framework. However, there is no systematic or repetitive ordering of these sections for each period covered: the work is intended to be neither a gazetteer nor a textbook, but an integrated historical synthesis and narrative. The arguments made often rely on the combined force of several different bases of evidence. Many of the latter have been described at length, and often resummarised, in other publications so it is needless to discuss them here again at any length. The broad diachronic themes investigated, such as the construction of social and cultural identity, relate by their very nature to multiple sets of cultural behaviours. Thus, while evidence relating to cult, burial practice, settlement layout and distribution, subsistence data, and ancient texts is drawn on to support certain arguments, the discussion of it is not always divided into self-contained categories.

Examination of the nature of state collapse in Crete at the end of the LBA, and its comparison with the type of collapse experienced by other areas at this time, is the subject of Part Two. I follow this with a discussion of the island's external relations in the period between collapse and the seventh century, by which time new kinds of small state had emerged on the mainland and in Crete (Part Three). I show that Crete's external contacts continued, yet changed significantly in character, during and immediately after the collapse period and that a major factor in state emergence and development here, and throughout the rest of the Aegean, was a significant growth in the luxury goods/materials trade with the east and west Mediterranean from the tenth century onward. I compare Crete's role in, and response to, this development with those of other Aegean areas, finding unusual features in Crete's case that applied right through into the seventh century and beyond. Part Four moves back again in time to the tenth century, to look in detail at changes within Cretan culture and society from this important horizon onward. In examining why and how a regionally precocious level of complexity was emerging in the island from this time, I show that, although connected with external economic developments, the phenomenon had strong roots in the conditions created by the twelfth-century collapse. In the second half of Part Four the discussion follows the development of large Cretan polities through the period of their consolidation as states by the seventh century.

Part Five discusses the development and expansion of these states and the details of their structure during the period in which written sources become available – the late eighth century onward – and draws comparisons with other Aegean regions in these respects. Texts are referred to extensively here to allow a deeper insight into political and social structures and supplement the relatively thin archaeological record for late Archaic to Classical Crete. However, using them poses particular problems of interpretation, concerning the way in which social identities and power relations were being represented and manipulated through writing. Monumental inscriptions provide fragmentary and narrowly limited information on political structures, and ceramic inscriptions are few on Crete. Literary texts concerning Archaic to Classical Crete are also few in number, are often written from an external perspective, and mostly date later than the fifth century. By their nature, they can never be treated as accurate historical accounts. My strategy in Part Five, then, is to select certain important and distinctive characteristics of Cretan states referred to in, or inferable from, the texts, including the absence of democratic systems, as the focus of exploratory discussion. I assess the origins and interrelationships of these features in the context of comparisons with other Aegean regions, and of the foregoing archaeologically based investigation. In its conclusion, Part Five raises questions about the long-term consequences of Cretan states' intrinsic and perceived difference from their Aegean counterparts and evaluates the main factors that produced this difference in a long-term perspective.

Ultimately, the book is structured so as to provide a bridge between two important historical horizons – state collapse and state emergence – in both a descriptive and an analytical sense. It also aims at explanation of each development in terms of and in relation to the other. I hope that in reading about the developments analysed at the end of the book, the reader will gain a better understanding of those discussed at its beginning, and vice versa.

Straddling a disciplinary boundary

The fact that this work originates in study of Crete's prehistoric (Late Bronze to Iron Age) archaeology has encouraged an approach consistently centred on material culture in its full breadth, even where the analysis covers periods for which texts are available. This consistency is, I believe, integral to constructing a really valid narrative, and notwithstanding the uneven balance of data types across the period studied, the material framework informs all discussion here. Material culture studies offer special angles of insight on issues like social agency, structure, and identity in the ancient past – though not necessarily a more honest or direct picture than that gained through analysis of texts; poststructuralist theory has helped scholars recognise that *all* cultural information is mediated by social structures. In the study of ancient Greece, this recognition has effectively reduced the long-established divide between archaeologists/anthropologists and textual historians to a comfortable working level (rather than the divide's being eradicated by the advent of reliable 'middle-range' predictive theory, as once envisaged: Renfrew 1980; Snodgrass 1987: 1–67). Scholars with roots in either field are now so familiar with the use of analytical frameworks from sociology, history, and anthropology to write broad-ranging, contextualised cultural histories that it is unnecessary to introduce a study of the first-millennium Aegean by explaining the value of 'boundary-crossing' approaches (Finley 1999; Humphreys 1978; Shanks 1996: 169–73; Small 1997b: 217; Whitley 2001: 42–60).

At the same time, given the ever-increasing resolution, specialisation, and volume of archaeological evidence and awareness of its multiply valid readings on one hand, and the variety of types of ancient text and recognition of *their* multilayered meanings and treatments on the other, the field in which my own expertise mainly lies needs to be stated, and the potential for superficiality and imbalance in this book acknowledged. The book does *not* claim to be an in-depth text-based study of the structure and outlook of the Classical Cretan polis. Scholars with backgrounds in text studies continue to make valuable inroads in this field – though they are hampered by the limited number of written sources and current lack of accurate, reliable deep syntheses of the archaeological record for Archaic-Classical Crete on which to draw to enrich and support their arguments (Erickson 2002, 2004, 2005; Guizzi 1999; Perlman 1993, 1996, 2000, 2002, 2004a: 1149, 2004b, 2005). I have used their work to guide me in the present, archaeology-led study, in which I use only a representative selection of textual sources in order to develop and explain the picture of long-term social change. My overarching aim is to contextualise texts and archaeological data broadly in relation to each other, not just at a contemporary level (only possible in the latter part of the period studied) but by moving forward and backward in time.

In attempting this I try to reconcile some small, but significant, interdisciplinary differences of perspective that still exist. From the archaeologist's viewpoint, ancient historians discussing Early Iron Age to Archaic Greek society often overgeneralise about it from a teleological perspective based on what we know of the Classical polis state (Foxhall 1997: 114). Here, by contrast, awareness of the Classical Cretan state form, while informing the study's questions from the outset, is never the starting point for the investigation, or the basis for any interpretative assumptions made. Text-orientated historians can gloss over the uncertainties and variability of the archaeological record, thereby failing to exploit its complex interpretative potential. Concentration on the textually best-recorded events/developments and on individual historical figures can throw only limited light on the long-term social processes behind major shifts in political structure, including the rise of democracy (Morris 1997d, 1998; Raaflaub 1997a: 50–1). These problems are less obvious for the Archaic period, where analysis of the united number of contemporary texts can be convincingly used to flesh out relatively superficial readings of the archaeological evidence. They are nakedly so, however, when the prehistoric Iron Age is discussed in historically based narratives. This is often done in a prefatory way, with little or no attempt to address complexities or internal discrepancies in the archaeological data (e.g., Osborne 1996: 19–40, 70–129). Despite their skills in deconstructing texts, historians still often show a tendency to rely on them too trustingly as outlining basically sound historical facts (references to colonisation and to the origins of the polis state form are two cases discussed here in which straightforward reliance on textual accounts is questionable in the light of what the archaeological record reveals). A different, but related, problem occurs when 'art-historical' outlooks, rooted in the origins of Classical archaeology as a branch of art history, restrict analysis to only a few aspects of material culture alongside textual sources, minimising the importance of deep spatial and cultural context (Morris 1987: 22–3, 1998: 7–8; Whitley 2001: 3–42). I try to avoid these problems by adopting a consistently broad-ranging, contextualised approach to analysing *all* types of cultural data, through *all* the periods addressed.

Turning round to view matters from the text historian's angle, archaeological studies often seem too specialised to be useful, with the sheer complexity and variety of published archaeological material making it difficult to frame clear overarching interpretative questions or draw firm conclusions. These detailed studies (e.g. of pottery) often stop short of addressing big issues that close textual studies around the period in question have brought to the fore, or fail to integrate textual information deeply and thoughtfully enough, citing isolated or simplified aspects of the texts to support archaeological inferences without evaluating them in informed context (Small 1997b). I hope to avoid the latter failing by using textual hindsight to pose specific questions of the long-term archaeological record, *after* analyzing the record on its own terms – the main question being 'Why did the Cretan polis take the unusual form indicated in texts by Classical times?' In this particular case, it is rarely possible to match substantial text data with a good range of contemporary archaeological information. Nor is there space here to give all relevant texts their own detailed interpretative discussion. For this reason, I present Part Five merely as an opening to and stimulus for discussion by text historians and archaeologists alike.

Areas of previous scholarship built on directly

I) MODELLING PROCESSES OF SOCIAL CHANGE: STATE COLLAPSE AND STATE FORMATION THEORY

At its most general level, as a study of social change, this book draws on work in sociology that shows how cultural and social practice transforms social structure (Bourdieu 1977: 8, 72, 82–4; Giddens 1984: 16–25, 244–62). As an archaeological study, it focuses on exploring how this process operates over a very long timescale. Sociological models have already been used in studies of the Aegean at just this period. For example, Durkheim's distinction between organic and mechanical solidarity in modelling structures of social cohesion has been used by Morris to contrast the Cretan and Athenian forms of the polis state (Durkheim 1964: 179; Morris 1997b: 91–2). I show how, despite true and meaningful structural contrasts between these regions, this kind of extreme polarisation can be difficult to relate to preindustrial societies, which all clearly retained a large role for the clan – and thus have links into the 'mechanical solidarity' model. In an interesting discussion on the diversity of early Greek state structures, Morris has also used Gellner's model of 'agroliterate state' growth to position Archaic to Classical Crete and Sparta in opposition to a 'citizen state' model for Athens (Gellner 1983: 9–10, 1988; Morris 1997b: 92–4, 98–100). There are difficulties here too, arising from the generally small scale, and broadly consensualist structures, shared by most early Aegean states, and the significant changes in the relations of these states with their territories that occurred between the eighth and fifth centuries. Such polarisations, while useful thinking tools, tend to minimize the subtle, complex, and widespread variability between regional state forms, and to compress or oversimplify diachronic change. They often perpetuate an Athenocentric viewpoint, indirectly generalizing all other contemporary state forms as 'other' that is ultimately rooted in the ancient literature itself, and that I try to deconstruct here from a Cretan perspective.

Collapse theory offers promising assistance in investigating the period between the collapse of Late Bronze Age state systems and the rise of the polis state (Snodgrass 1991b: 65; Whitley 1993). However, the use of the Aegean Late Bronze Age state collapse as any kind of paradigm in general collapse theory has always been held back by disagreements about the exact circumstances and immediate consequences of the collapse, and by regional disparities in the history and structure of collapse within the Aegean as a whole – which, as this book shows, cannot be easily encapsulated in a general model. Tainter's work, for example, generalises about the Aegean collapse with reference to the mainland states only, and to 'Mycenaean civilisation', with unsatisfactory results; we are not dealing here with a single, wholesale 'civilisational' collapse (Tainter 1990: 10–11). The LBA Aegean and east Mediterranean constituted a multinodal political and economic system, with strong elements of shared culture and technology, in which there was no single preeminent power. In contrast, much of the literature on collapse has dealt with highly centralised systems such as empires. Looking at a regionalised system can give us insight into which types of shared structural feature can promote systemic collapse over a large area, but also reveals how other features – including varying levels and types of previous interaction and interdependency between nodes – limit the evenness of collapse effects.

Explanations including population flight, famine, earthquakes, and disease have previously been put forward to explain the collapse circa 1200 BC, especially with regard to mainland Greece. I will show, however, that the quantity and diversity of data now available illuminate the specific, and *political*, nature of the crisis in the region. The data allow us to build newly complex and sensitive regional models of the Aegean collapse, and of post-collapse societies, that can be used as a rich and instructive comparison and reference point for the study of collapse processes in other areas and periods (Trigger 1998: 167). The study also aims to theorise collapse, and the developments following it, on their own terms, rather than relying on knowledge of the circumstances prior to the crisis to predict its consequences – a somewhat circular approach, criticised by Sherratt (1998: 292), but still quite widely used – for example, by Small (1998). The book finds little support for hierarchical schemes of determination of environmental, subsistence, macroeconomic, force-based, or ideological factors by each other – whether in the collapse process or in the subsequent emergence of new state structures – though such schemes have been a major concern of processual archaeology (Gledhill and Rowlands 1982: 144–5; Shanks and Tilley 1987: 58–9, 176).

The issue of how to identify stimuli to and processes of state formation in ancient societies runs through much of the book. Evolutionary perspectives, positing a tribe-chief-state progression occurring in response to environmental or demographic factors, have sometimes been used both to explain the rise of the polis state and to characterise its structure (Donlan 1994, 1997; Donlan and Thomas 1993; see Foxhall 1997: 114). But other scholars have already noted the inadequacy of such models to explain either the high degree of regional variability in Archaic-Classical small-state forms across the Aegean, or the very specific ideology and tightly bounded structure that characterised so many of those states (Morris 1997b: 94; Shanks 1996: 159; Shanks and Tilley 1987: 58–9; see Shennan 1993). My work extends this critique, with the study of Crete particularly highlighting the role of contingency and of agency (at small-group level) in state formation. I show the focus of community organisation to have moved from the level of the small to the extended kin group during state emergence, with the latter type of group eventually becoming a powerful and strongly incorporated body within the Cretan state. Rather than a discontinuous and unconscious 'progression' from achieved-rank system to chiefdom to state, then, a strong emphasis on kin bonds as a base of social power continued and strengthened over time in Crete, coming to operate at larger and more complex scales, and to be constructed and manipulated through myth, history, and material culture in complex ways.

A much-debated issue in Greek Iron Age/Classical research, relevant to studies of democracy in more recent historical periods, is of how far the consensualist ideologies that famously distinguished the polis state emerged as a resolving measure in social competition – whether through top-down or bottom-up mechanisms – and of how regularly conflict was involved in the process (e.g., Morris 2000: 155–95). This issue ties into much wider debates on state formation in general (Shanks and Tilley 1987: 57–60, 182; Trigger 1998: 179). The tendency of the scholarship to date has been to simplify the picture of EIA social relationships into one of roughly equal competing elites, which by the late eighth century had shifted their basis of competition to a more insulated, institutionalised plane in order to reduce unmanageable frictions (de Polignac 1995: 11–89; Morris 2000: 109–55). In Crete – a geographically clearly bounded, yet externally well-connected region, offering a large quantity and rich diversity of archaeological data – new opportunities arise to study the self-conception and self-assertion of various *different* class/status groups within EIA society, and how tensions between these groups may have pushed forward change in social structures. I am able to identify significant changes in the basis and representation of social inequality over time, particularly through the systematic analysis of mortuary data, not yet undertaken for Crete as a whole in the EIA period (Morris 1987; Whitley 1991a).

Lastly, the role of conflict at various levels in the formation and development of complex societies is an issue that arises at several points in the study of EIA-Archaic Crete. In examining this I have regard to a range of previous hypotheses on the role of conflict in the Aegean in this period, as well as more general scholarship on the importance of conflict in early states (Carneiro 1970, 1981; Earle 1997: 7–9).

II) ECONOMY

My interest in the relationship of settlement, economy, and landscape in the very long term is ultimately influenced by *Annales*-type approaches to history long of interest to prehistorians of the Mediterranean (Bintliff 1991: 1–2, ed, 1991a; Hodder 1987: 2; Knapp 1992; Knapp and Blake 2005; Moreland 1992; Shanks and Tilley 1987: 184–5; Sherratt 1992; Trigger 1998: 159–67). To help avoid the environmentally determinist interpretations of social change typical of traditional *Annales* approaches, I have drawn on long-term social and economic history, and on ethnography, to elucidate the changing nature of long-term relationships of environment, subsistence, and sociopolitical systems/structures, an approach now well developed for the BA-Classical Aegean (Forbes 1992; Halstead 1987, 1992, 1996; Rackham and Grove 2001; Rackham and Moody 1996).

I place great emphasis on the social embeddedness of the ancient trade economy. Despite much written on this subject since Finley's seminal work (Finley 1999), this still seems badly needed. Certainly, in recent studies of Crete's EIA trade there has been too little attention to consumption context in analysing commodity movements: instead, emphasis has been placed on modelling those movements in terms of rather mechanistic supply and demand models grounded in classical economic theory (e.g., Hoffman 1997; Jones 1999, 2000; see exceptions like Crielaard 1999, also Morris 1999, 2002; Sherratt 2003: 860 offers a critique). An important argument made in this book is that the early establishment of a strongly inward-orientated emphasis in the production and circulation of value goods severely held back Crete's economic growth during the period of Aegean colonisation and booming trans-Mediterranean trade 800–400 BC. This boom, and the raising of competitive stakes it entailed, is usually seen as having contributed significantly to the emergence of polis states in the Aegean. I suggest that Crete's unusual mode of economic reaction/participation helps explain the distinctive political structures found in the island by Classical times and invalidates any blanket adoption of secondary state formation models for the Greek polis (Morris 1987: 1). Few scholars working on Mediterranean trade at this period have considered the response or contribution of Cretan societies by using data from the island as a whole, or by comparing different regions of Crete – instead, they tend to refer to just a few well-investigated sites. This reflects a general tendency of scholars using world-systems theory in archaeology to overlook important aspects of social and historical particularity, which I try to move away from here (Cowgill 1988: 251).

III) LANDSCAPE AND SETTLEMENT STUDIES

Attention to the experiential aspects of ancient landscapes, and the functioning of sites in their landscape setting, is another important feature of this study. Recent archaeological research has shown that the experience of natural and cultural landscape features can be central to the structuring of social identity and social memory, though relatively little of this work has focused on the rich archaeological landscapes of Greece (Ashmore and Knapp 1999; Bender 1993, 1999; Bradley 2000; Hirsch and O'Hanlon 1989; Tilley 1982, 2004; Ucko and Layton 1999; van Dyke and Alcock 1998). I suggest that in post-collapse Crete, important symbolic meanings were attached not just to ritual sites, or to recognisably 'antique' sites/features in the landscape, but to other sites, of a range of different types (some of them very recent in date). It becomes clear that landscape was a powerful domain of socially transformative cultural practice at this period. We see, for example, the continued use of long-established open-air cult sites in certain types of natural location through the collapse period, but also the establishment of new cult sites in similar locations and apparently referring to the same kinds of tradition. Widespread settlement nucleation in very specific types of landscape from the tenth century onward is another very deliberate choice, linked to increasing levels of sociopolitical and economic complexity in this period. Also seen are reuse of abandoned *settlements* dating from the collapse period for cult, burial, or feasting during the period of state emergence and expansion (apparently in the interests of political bonding and legitimation), and the targeted, symbolic reuse of Bronze Age tombs for cult and burial at the same period, a phenomenon related to changing constructions of group identity at a number of levels. This rich variety of practices offers us rare and valuable insight into ancient *mentalités* (Burguières 1982). I will highlight parallels and contrasts between these practices and ritual/symbolic uses of landscape in other Aegean areas during the same period. Analysis of the latter phenomenon has often been restricted to the funerary sphere (e.g., Antonaccio 1995; Morris 2000: 24–33; Snodgrass 1982b). Considering the broader variety of evidence offered by the Cretan record offers deeper insight into wider Aegean worldviews, while elucidating the peculiarities of Cretan outlooks and relating them back to the specific history of the island and its physical environment.

This book makes particularly heavy use of settlement evidence, which has become especially plentiful for EIA Crete during the last thirty years. In doing so, various problems are highlighted with existing scholarship on ancient settlement in Crete and other Aegean areas. Like other aspects of material culture, settlement data need to be adequately theorised in their own (landscape) context before being used in generalising interpretations, but this is often not adequately done. Despite the long and impressive history of Aegean field survey, strongly rooted in the processual archaeology of the 1970s (e.g., Alcock and Cherry 2004; Shanks 1996: 142) and resulting in major advances in knowledge, there remains a need to discard overgeneral assumptions – for example, that settlement location was always mainly determined by subsistence priorities or natural landscape parameters (Bintliff 1977a: 114) or that individual settlements always represented discrete community units (Yaeger 2000). Such assumptions have helped to confuse interpretation of the remarkable changes in settlement pattern in LBA-Archaic Crete, as I show in Parts Two and Four. On the other hand, highly detailed analysis of settlement patterning in isolation from the rest of the contemporary material culture context can lead to overformalised treatments, with sometimes skewed and confusing results (a tendency recently identified by Watrous: see discussion in Karageorghis and Morris 2001: 246). Recent settlement-centred studies of EIA to Classical Crete have tended to be focused either on single small regions (e.g., Kavousi), on one dramatic type of settlement (e.g., defensible sites); on one subperiod only (e.g., the twelfth century; the Geometric to Archaic period), or on one large but unrepresentative settlement, such as Knossos (Coldstream 2000b; Haggis 1993; Nowicki 2000; Sjögren 2004; Whitley 1991a, 1991b). There is also a chronological imbalance regarding in-depth analysis of settlement for this period. While Crete's twelfth-century settlement pattern has attracted particular attention thanks to its dramatic nature, developments in the tenth century and later have so far been discussed mainly with reference to the mortuary record, which becomes much more elaborate from this date, when mortuary deposition becomes more elaborate and more visible in the record.

Methods of data acquisition are an important issue in assessing settlement evidence. In this study I have taken great account of evidence in the form of surface pottery scatters, stressing the important insight this gives us into EIA history when analysed in conjunction with a good base of excavated data, and the clear inferential patterns that emerge when it is possible – as here – to look at a very high number of surface-documented sites belonging to a single broad period. Indeed, the very *lack* of detail inherent in survey evidence actively promotes the building of bold islandwide interpretative pictures, which can then be tested by reference to the excavated data currently available. However, when comparing survey data within or between regions it is important to remember that it has been acquired using a variety of different methods, leading to uneven levels of detail in the data (Alcock and Cherry 2004: 1–13). This applies even to very recent intensive surveys in Crete, such as the Pediada, Kavousi, Mesara, and Vrokastro projects (Haggis 2005; Hayden et al. 2004, 2005; Panayiotakis 2004, 2005; Watrous et al. 2004). Nowicki's extensive surveys, targeted on particular site types, have recorded huge amounts of information on Cretan EIA settlement but cannot be used in quite the same way as the results of these intensive projects (Nowicki 2000). Unfortunately, few mainland surveys have yet prioritised the EIA-Classical period, and thanks to the limited number of excavated and published EIA sites there, the dating of survey pottery is often much rougher than in Crete (Snodgrass 1971: 24).

In attempting a broad-based, consistent, and diachronic theorisation of settlement pattern and form in Crete, I hope to build interpretations which are able to inform and drive settlement analysis elsewhere in the Aegean in the future. There is great scope for revisiting survey data from the Greek mainland in this perspective. Existing analyses of central Greek society in the EIA have focused heavily on mortuary data – partly because the mortuary record is better preserved and documented, but also because scholars have become locked into this path (Antonaccio 1995, Lemos 2003, where the weight of attention to burial practices and grave ceramics and other goods is huge compared to that given to settlement and landscape; Morris 1987, 1997b: 100, stating, 'Most evidence [for the Dark Age] is funerary'). They could be much improved on, especially at a regional level, by greater attention to settlement, including the framing of new research questions about settlement pattern.

IV) CULTURAL HISTORY AND IDENTITY CONSTRUCTION

'History' concerns the work in a number of other senses besides the encompassing framework of cultural history (Giddens 1984: 244–5). The development of a contemporary historical consciousness, strongly linked into concepts of group identity, seems a very important feature of EIA-Classical society in Crete, as in the rest of Greece. It created social tensions and helped to resolve them in ways that deeply affected the way the state emerged and developed (Morris 2000: 195–227; Whitley 1993: 225). By demonstrating the ways in which history and ancestry were mobilised to construct complex cultural identities at this period, the book also challenges the simplistic identification of ethnic groups and their activities on the basis of the origin and style of artefacts, linguistic forms, or textual/mythic accounts – a tendency of some past scholarship on the Bronze Age to Classical Aegean, which has held back the production of coherent and convincing synthetic interpretation. Understanding of the high, but malleable political and economic salience of ethnicity in the Aegean at this period has been recently moved forward (e.g., by Hall 1997a; Malkin 1998; Morgan 2003). Crete repays closer study in this regard, given that the notion of significant immigration from outside the island, or emigration from it, has been frequently co-opted to explain aspects of its Early Iron Age to Archaic record: Snodgrass (1991b: 64) and Whitley (1998b, 2002) note the problems with such approaches. This book makes no preassumptions about the likelihood of ethnic movements into or out of the island in the period addressed. Instead, areas of the data where facile or partial applications of such explanations have been made in the past, or might seem possible to make on the basis of the rest of the evidence considered here, are given close attention. When applied to EIA-Archaic Greece these types of model have often tended to overgeneralise from a highly restricted selection of archaeological data, and to take textual traditions too much at face value. The case for examining the data in a more open-minded, broad-based perspective is made stronger by the fact that in the post-collapse period itself a number of traditions and accounts developed using ethnicity, ethnic qualities, and population movement to explain perceived social and political realities or changes over time, often in contradictory ways.

3 TEXT PERSPECTIVES

A glance forward: images of the Archaic to Classical Cretan state from texts

It is important at the start of this book to highlight the inadequacy of the text record as a main lens through which to study Cretan polis development. Offering a brief general picture of the character and development of the Cretan Classical state as known from text sources achieves this, highlighting the gaps in understanding that exist and helping identify the most fruitful questions for research.

By the Archaic period many Aegean societies shared some form of consensual or 'citizen' ideology (the notion that a relatively large group of a society's members holding broadly equal social and political status should participate to some degree in its governance). This was a central foundation for the democratic systems emerging by the fifth century (Morris 1991, 1996, 1997d, 2000: 109–95; Morris and Raaflaub 1997; Raaflaub 1993, 1988). Yet the way in which consensualism was interpreted and incorporated in day-to-day politics altered over time and was different in each state. Archaeological evidence supports early texts in suggesting we can identify the rise of a 'middling', 'equality-based' or 'citizen' ideal/principle governing social and political relations across the central and south Aegean from the late eighth century. This seems to have grown partly out of insuperable social tensions between competing small groups in a rapidly changing economic environment. By the seventh century, a consensualist ideology was clearly integral to the structure of the small, unitary states concentrated in the central and southern Aegean, as well as influencing the structure of the rather looser regional political groupings (often referred to as *ethne*) mostly located in the north central Aegean, including the regions of Phokis, Thessaly, and Achaia (Morgan 2003). I shall have cause to compare these *ethnos* state structures in more detail to the structures of Cretan states, but the latter are placed here in the 'polis' category, since each was tied to and embodied in a particular, individual settlement rather than encompassing a number of population centres.

Governance systems based on the notion of citizen equality were supported by developing institutions of state authority, and by laws, which began to be written down as early as the late seventh century (Osborne 1997). A variety of formally defined power groups existed within the citizen unit, including regional-scale tribes (*phylai*), extended kin/affinal groupings (*phratriai)*, the formal assembly of citizens, an elected governing council, and/or a set of elected or appointed senior ruling officials. The council prepared and proposed the laws, while the citizen assembly voted on the passing of laws, on court judgements, and on referenda covering a variety of other issues. The relative size of the council and power of the assembly varied substantially according to the constitution of each polity.

Though the underlying concept of the 'community of equals' was strong and long-lived, it was variously manipulated or adapted at different points in time. Tyrannies arose in many central Greek states through the seventh and sixth centuries – even while the size and role of the citizen council and assembly formally grew in importance – as individuals from powerful competing families manipulated the ideology of the public good to boost their personal status (Salmon 1997). Tyrants were often violently deposed, however, and long-term dynastic inheritance of tyrant status was very rare, though powerful clans regularly saw their members appointed to positions in the senior ruling council, and tribal membership played a formal role in determining representation in the larger council.

By the fifth century, a move towards democracy – the direct participation of all citizens in an assembly with strong decision-making powers – became the dominant tendency in some polis constitutions but was by no means universally popular or stable. Much of our knowledge of ancient Greek democracy has been Athens-based, because the texts available tell us more about Athens than anywhere else, and because Athens seems to have been home to one of the most extreme forms of democracy (Morris and Raaflaub 1997). By the fourth century Aristotle (*Politics* 1279b 20–1280a 6) defined democracy as fundamentally the (didactic) 'rule of the poor' (*Politics* 1298a 30–3) and as such, a deviation from his ideal political structure (*politeia*). He attributed the rise of the most extreme forms of democracy to the swelling size of Greek states and their expanded wealth, permitting, as in the Athenian case, the subsidy of direct citizen involvement in governance (*Politics* 1291b 21–1293a 10). However, study of the history of Athens using a range of text sources shows that many other factors played a part in pushing forward democratic systems at just this place and time. These included revolt against tyranny, but also the machinations of powerful 'prototyrant' players seeking routes to power in popular support, as well as broader geopolitics. The conflict that put Cleisthenes in power and allowed him to pursue an agenda of radical democratic reforms in Athens in 508/7 BC arose partly from Spartan intervention in Athenian politics in support of Cleisthenes' political rival, Isagoras, and a violent reaction to this by the Athenian masses. The take-up of democratic systems in many small Aegean island states during the fifth century was strongly tied into their subjugation to, or alliance with, an increasingly powerful Athens (Davies 1993: 82–3).

Cretan difference

Ronald Willetts's thoughtful work on the Cretan polis, mostly based on ancient texts, included a large number of assumptions and elisions, arising from a desire to present a smooth, uniform encapsulation of the phenomenon and its history (Willetts 1955, 1965, 1969, 1977, 1982). No other major synthetic perspective has yet been put forward. Rather, a number of specific textually documented aspects of the Cretan poleis have been studied in detail, with scholars often extending such unitary studies from the Archaic through into the Hellenistic period (323–67 BC), for which preserved inscriptions are much more frequent, even though further major changes in political power balance and structure occurred in the island through this period (Guizzi 1999; Perlman 1993, 1996, 2000, 2002).

An unusually tight kind of oligarchic system seems to have characterised Cretan states by the late seventh century (or earlier) and to have remained so stable that neither the rise of tyrannies *nor* the promotion of very broad participation in governance had the chance to develop. The nature of Cretan state structures is best documented in the fifth-century Gortyn Law Code, some terms of which are prefigured in other inscriptions from as early as the late seventh century (Perlman 2000, 2002; Willetts 1967, 1977: 216–23). This text suggests a much more consistently limited political role for the citizen body than was the case in many mainland states. By the fifth century, laws were framed by a small council of *kosmoi*, elected from a few specific clans (*startoi*) only. This contrasts radically with the role of the main council at Athens, which numbered five hundred by the time of Cleisthenes' reforms (Andrewes 1982a, 1982b; Ostwald 1988). The contrast is not only due to the fact that the Cretan states were smaller: their political structure can be seen to be intrinsically different. In Athens, by the late Archaic period the power of the individual clan was being dispersed by the Cleisthenic reforms, which formalized tribal membership and representation on a geographical basis, restricting opportunities for the extreme concentration of political power. In Crete, by contrast, a few consistently defined, small and tightly knit clans shared exclusive access to power in each polity over a very long period. Though a consensualist element in lawmaking was established early in Crete, as we know from an inscription from Dreros in the late seventh century referring to a council of *kosmoi*, the authority of the law seems to have remained located in the person of a mythical lawgiver, or in the divine sphere, with the *kosmoi* as its select channel, for a very long time (Meiggs and Lewis 1989: 2–3). An early version of the Gortyn Law Code was engraved on the walls of the Temple of Apollo Pythios, built in the second half of the seventh century and inscribed somewhere in the early sixth (Morgan 2003: 80; Perlman 2000: 60–1). The Dreros inscription is also from the walls of a temple in the main civic area.

The Gortyn code indicates that clan cohesion, power, and wealth in Crete were maintained under tight inheritance laws, which seem to have stayed intact for many centuries: a partible system of land inheritance helped ensure sustainability of the family line (Di Lello-Finuoli 1991; Willetts 1967: 20–2). A particularly complex and subtle kind of social stratification existed by the fifth century, contrasting somewhat with the simpler, stronger social divisions between the citizen group and 'the rest' in central Greek poleis (Morris 1997b: 99–100). Alongside a slave population, a serf (*woikeus*) class, probably subdivided into several subclasses, clearly stayed important in Crete long after slavery had come to dominate the bound labour sector in central Greek states. Serfs had some inheritance rights on the death of their masters, but they (and their children) were their masters' property in many respects, and they took only a limited role in political activity, though they were allowed to attend the *syssition*, or common meal (Willetts 1955: 3–51, 1977: 182–5). This political institution was regularly referred to in the ancient literature as particularly characteristic of Cretan states. Funded partly through the produce of public land, it seems to have embodied the consensual/participative ideal in a very literal sense.

Limits of the data

The written sources available for Archaic to Classical Crete include references in the Homeric epics, legal inscriptions, and works of philosophy, history, and geography. All these sources are limited in accuracy and detail. The literary mentions of Crete are never more than minimal accounts, often presented as hearsay or recopied fragments of lost histories: their authors are rarely Cretans. Legal inscriptions are from a limited number of sites, considering the number of sizeable and probably independent polities we know to have existed in Crete between the

Archaic and Classical periods on the basis of both archaeological and textual data (Perlman 2004a). Most inscriptions are fragmentary. Whitley has argued that public legal inscriptions on stone actually represent the main form of written document produced on the island in Archaic times, suggesting that Cretan political elites limited access to literacy by ordinary citizens in order to enhance the power of written law in their own interest. He has used this to explain the low number of 'personal' inscriptions – particularly graffiti on pots, which are common in other parts of the Greek world – and the fact that where these do exist, they are often written in alphabet variations typical of other Aegean regions (Whitley 1997: 649–52, 1998c). However, we should take into account the lack of systematic excavations of stratified Archaic to Classical town sites in Crete, in which such finds are most likely to be recovered regularly. In contrast, stone inscriptions are often recovered as surface or redeposited finds totally divorced from any primary context. By their very nature, graffito inscriptions (even if more were found) are likely to offer relatively limited information on political and social structure. Even if Whitley is right, we can hardly expect legal inscriptions, as representing elite or public concerns, to tell us much about life across society as a whole. In all, then, the picture of the Cretan state that we are able to build up through texts poses more questions than it answers about how and why Cretan state forms emerged and developed along one particular path, and how the different facets of state culture related to each other. The brief textually based overview of Crete by the fifth century presented above clearly misses out a huge amount of what we might want to know about social and political structures and their origins.

It is these vast gaps in the textual data that the archaeology of the EIA-Archaic periods can help to fill, pending more field research on the Classical archaeology of the island. One of my main purposes in this respect is to find out when, why, and how participatory rights in governance came to be so limited in Crete, even though citizen rights and status and governance by council *did* form an accepted tenet of state systems. Did clan-controlled political structures represent a constriction, or an enlargement, of the systems of power relations in existence before the collapse of Bronze Age states, and how did the process of change in these systems occur? How much of a 'social revolution' (the phrase used by Morris to characterise a major set of readjustments on the mainland in the late eighth century BC, out of which the polis state seems to have emerged) ever occurred in Crete? The answers to these questions, I suggest, have a significant bearing on how Cretan societies reacted to the advent of democratic systems in other Aegean areas during the fifth century – and more generally on the question of how the particular characteristics of the Cretan state, and its formative conditions, affected the island's geopolitical role – causing external communities to view and interact with it in particular ways – throughout the EIA to Classical periods.

4 CHRONOLOGY, TERMINOLOGY, AND DATING METHODS

Defining the Early Iron Age

The starting date for this study, and for the Cretan 'Early Iron Age' as defined in it, is 1200 BC. I avoid the term 'Dark Age', because of its overtones of regression, though the terms have often been used interchangeably (cf. Coulson 1990a; Dickinson 2006: 10–23; Mook 1993: 244–50; Nowicki 2000: 15–18). A still-common view of twelfth-century Aegean material culture as falling within the Late Bronze Age is based on the fact that the fine pottery styles of this period, usually termed 'Late Minoan/Late Helladic IIIC', still show strong connections to those of the thirteenth century (Late Helladic/Late Minoan IIIB) (though see Mountjoy 1986: 134–200; Sherratt 1981). By the late twelfth or early eleventh century, some fine ceramics start to incorporate distinctive new 'Submycenaean/Subminoan' characteristics, usually seen as precursors to the Protogeometric (PG) style and thus often linked with the inception of the 'Iron Age', though their nomenclature still stresses correlations with the Bronze Age sequence. The appearance of PG pottery is traditionally dated in central Greece to 1050–900 BC, but new radiocarbon dates from Assiros in north Greece suggest it may actually appear up to one hundred years earlier. This would not only push back the whole date range for the Early Iron Age as a whole, but potentially shorten the estimated duration of the Submycenaean/Subminoan style, and thereby its significance as a chronological indicator (Lemos 2002: 7–8; Newton et al. 2003, 2005).

The use of iron is almost completely lacking in many areas through much of the twelfth century and is nowhere widespread. This, too, has encouraged many scholars to define the Iron Age using a fairly arbitrary starting date of circa 1100 BC, often citing the rise of the Subminoan/Submycenaean pottery style along with other scattered features of the cultural record as well as the rise of iron (Morris 1987: 1–2; Whitley 1991a: 8–10, 1993: 226–7). For example, Lemos (2003: 10) uses what she calls a 'new emergence' of weapons burials in Attica to mark out Submycenaean-PG as a major historical departure, while Eder (1998: 63–6, 86–8) cites the cutting of graves from the Submycenaean period onwards into some former Bronze Age settlement areas as reflecting the presence of incomers to the Peloponnesian region from this time, and thus marking a new historical horizon.

This book's focus on Crete, and its balanced review and contextualisation of a very wide range of archaeological evidence, suggests circa 1200 BC to be the horizon that best justifies treatment as the Bronze-Iron Age boundary, marking a fundamental change in many different aspects of material culture and social organisation (Haggis 1993: 133; Hallager and Hallager 2000: 173–4; Kanta 1997; Nowicki 2000: 15–17, 267–9; Tsipopoulou 1997b: 247). Though some changes at this period, such as a large-scale relocation of settlement, are concentrated in Crete and the Cyclades, the fact that many others are shared across the wider region, including radical changes in settlement balance and pattern of various kinds, the disappearance of written texts, destructions and/or abandonments at many sites, the first rise of cremation as a burial rite (Desborough 1964: 187–9), and the initial take-up of iron as a prestige good (Sherratt 1994: 91–2), suggests that this horizon should probably be recognised in the wider Aegean, too. Changes in trade orientation closely linked to state collapse are visible in Crete, as in other parts of the Aegean, from this point onward: we see the beginning of a shift of trade interest more exclusively towards the eastern Mediterranean and Cypriot arenas and away from the west Mediterranean, for instance (Sherratt 2001: 234–7). In my view, marginalising or excluding this formative period in any study of the Aegean EIA severely distorts understanding of the reasons for and nature of change in social forms and cultural traditions.

Perspectives have also varied on how to define the *end* of the EIA – Desborough and Snodgrass end the 'Dark Age' with the emergence of the Geometric pottery style circa 900 BC, while more recent scholars have laid emphasis on a late eighth-century 'social revolution' or 'renaissance' foreshadowing the birth of the polis state (de Polignac 1995: 9; Hägg 1983; Morris 1987: 22–3, 1993: 216). The term 'renaissance' seems misleading, in encouraging us to conceptualise the EIA as a neutral or vacuum period between the end of Bronze Age states and a unitary regeneration of the state in the form of the polis, rather than as the generative source of new kinds of complexity in its own right. My grouping here of developments across the Aegean between 1200 and 700 BC (under a single 'EIA' label) does not mean that I think they should be treated as either unified or static at any point (Coulson 1990a: 15). Indeed, the variable rates and types of social and cultural change within this period across the region form a main theme of this book. The period of the late eighth through seventh centuries is certainly a major social and cultural turning point throughout the region, including Crete: the emergence of new levels of social complexity is indicated in the appearance of written texts, the emergence or ongoing expansion of large nucleated settlements, and the appearance of monumental architecture, among other features. As we shall see, however, there is a much less dramatic degree of social change in Crete than in mainland Greece at this time, for reasons connected to Crete's earlier EIA history (Whitley 1993: 225).

'Subminoan'

Regionality, at both island and intra-island level, is a major issue in Cretan pottery dating. Excavations in central Crete – most often of cemeteries, but also of stratified deposits lying above clear LM IIIC material – were the original basis for applying the term 'Subminoan' to ceramic assemblages including features not wholly assignable to either the LM IIIC or the full PG styles (Brock 1957; Catling 1996a; Desborough 1964: 166–95, 1972a: 57–63; Popham 1992; Rocchetti 1970, 1974; see Pendlebury 1939: 308 for an early alternative term, 'Intermediate', covering this period). By direct analogy with Submycenaean on the mainland, Subminoan was articulated as a period of 'transition', dating somewhere in the late twelfth through the eleventh century. Using mainly burial ceramics, Desborough defined a set of positive attributes for the style, including the regular presence of the trefoil-lipped jug and the belly-handled amphora, a generally more ovoid tendency in the body in shapes like jugs and stirrup jars, and a simplification of decoration, with banded and monochrome forms becoming important. Many of these elements were suggested by him to have had a Cypriot origin and to have spread through migratory movements around the Aegean and east Mediterranean during the twelfth century. In a complicated analysis, Desborough thought other features were exported *from* Crete to Cyprus at the end of the twelfth/early eleventh century, again potentially via physical migration (Desborough 1964: 32, 192–4, 231, 1972a: 57–63; Popham 1979).

Desborough explained the patchiness of classic Subminoan elements in east Cretan assemblages, at a date when they were well established in central Crete, by a delay in diffusion from the central region, linked to the physical isolation of the east part of the island (Desborough 1964: 172). Coulson (using a clearly stratified sequence at the east Cretan site of Kavousi Kastro) moved away from this view. He suggested that east Crete never really developed a clear SM style paralleling that seen in central Crete, and that pottery forms and styles there show a more direct transition from Late Minoan IIIC to Protogeometric, with a longer prevalence of the LM IIIC tradition. Coulson argued that the latter lasted as much as 150–200 years here before the advent of PG influences through contacts with the mainland, where PG styles are usually recognised as developing from circa 1050 BC onwards (Coulson 1990b; Mook and Coulson 1997). In this light, he noted for Crete 'the disadvantage of compartmentalising too easily these regional styles and of confining them to chronological boundaries which have no force' (Coulson 1990a: 10). The role of social access or choice, rather than physical access, chronology, or stylistic diffusion, in affecting the production and consumption of pottery at this date has been highlighted by Mook, who suggests the restriction of 'Subminoan' features in east Crete mostly to tomb material indicates that its role was that of a ceremonial or funerary style, restricted to some regions only, rather than an islandwide chronological development (Mook 1993: 245, 2000, 2004). In view of this debate, I consider that the absence of 'Subminoan' pottery cannot reliably be treated as signifying a real chronological gap when it occurs on sites outside the central region (and even possibly within that region), though some scholars still characterise it in this way (Andreadaki-Vlasaki 1991a: 422; Kanta 1980: 326). In this book, when a site is reported as having LM IIIC and Early Protogeometric material, even if Subminoan material is not specifically mentioned by the primary report, I will treat it as having been used between the twelfth and tenth centuries BC ('LM IIIC-SM'). I avoid the use of the term 'Subminoan' on its own as a chronological designation at cross-island level, given the still-flexible dating of the style. For example, the excavators of the Knossos North Cemetery have recently pushed the beginning of the 'Subminoan' phase there back as far as the mid-twelfth century in attempting to demonstrate the cemetery's foundation as something 'foreign' and 'new' in contrast to existing (LM IIIC = 'Late Bronze Age') cultural forms and to tie this event up neatly with a new pottery horizon (Catling 1996c; Coldstream and Catling 1996: 206–7, 715). Tsipopoulou has recently continued the chronological use of the term 'Subminoan' for assemblages from east Crete, notwithstanding the doubts expressed by Coulson and Mook. She suggests the period covers 'the largest part of the eleventh century and the beginning of the tenth' (Tsipopoulou 2005a: 556).

'Protogeometric'

Problems of regionality also occur with the use of the term 'Protogeometric' in Crete. Though diachronic developments in pottery between the eleventh and ninth centuries are notably different from those of the central Greek region, the same basic terminology is used. Allowing for the SM 'transition', pots in the Attic PG style (though already imported to Crete from the mid-eleventh century) have been considered as starting to influence local production fully only in the first quarter of the tenth (for example, Cretan 'Early PG' pottery was found in tombs at Knossos together with Attic 'Middle PG', so that the conventional dating for the start of PG in Crete is circa 970 BC: Brock 1957: 189; Catling 1977: 12–14; Coldstream 1996a, 1996b; Desborough 1952: 233–71). The concept of a PG 'spirit' – canonically defined in Attica and spreading through different Aegean regions over time – has led to the unsychronised doubling up of chronological terminology for Crete and the mainland throughout the EIA (Lemos 2002: 3–4), with the ascribed sequences reflecting the powerful notion of temporally discrete, but ultimately parallel, stylistic sequences in different regions. Thus while in the mainland the advent of the Geometric style is seen as occurring from circa 900 BC, true 'Geometric' pottery is seen in Crete as having started to appear in Crete only after the delaying intrusion into the sequence of a unique local 'Protogeometric B' style (mainly represented at Knossos). Only after 800 are the two pottery sequences (Middle Geometric: to c. 750 BC, Late Geometric: after c. 750 BC) seen to run in parallel (Coldstream 1979a: 385; Desborough 1972a: 153–8). This awkward terminology rests on an assumption that stylistic development is intrinsically and rigidly evolutionary in nature, even while consistently affected by external stimulus. It can be awkward, misleading, and confusing in comparative dating (Coulson 1990a: 10; Whitley 1991a: 84). There are further regional complications within Crete. Tsipopoulou, for example, though recognising a 'Protogeometric B' phase in east Crete ending in the early eighth century, suggests that it was not formally or chronologically equivalent to the same phase at Knossos and represents the borrowing of only a few forms and styles from central Crete, some time after their advent in the latter region (Tsipopoulou 2005a: 556–7). In contrast to the central Cretan sequence, she notes it is not easily possible to subdivide east Cretan 'Geometric' at all and calls it all 'essentially Late Geometric' in character.

Since I am concerned here to compare developments in many different areas of material culture and across regions, I prefer for clarity to speak mostly in terms of numeric dates, with the proviso that all are approximate and are derived anyway from published ceramic datings using the scheme outlined above. So, for example, when I refer to the 'tenth-century' horizon of cultural and social change in Crete, I am dating it (supporting my argument with dated pottery from relevant sites) to the local Early PG, considered here to cover the period between the later eleventh and mid-tenth century. From somewhere within this period generic Protogeometric features become apparent in ceramic assemblages from all over the island. This approach does not solve the root problems of regionality with regard to ceramic terminology, however. The markedly early date and prestigious context of use for imported Attic pottery at Knossos throughout the PG and G periods, for example, suggest selective and regionally uneven contact with and emulation of the PG style as it appeared in central Greece. Cultural influence from the latter region may often have been mediated via producers or traders based at major Cretan gateways like Knossos, causing significant regional variations in the rate and nature of stylistic change. PG settlement ceramics in east Crete show an increasing 'awareness' over time of particularly *Knossian* PG styles, rather than being direct imitations of Attic forms, according to Mook (Mook 1993: 170, 245). As noted above, they appear in the region rather abruptly, rather than via an SM phase, as at Knossos, suggesting that central Crete led the uptake of this style. Yet Tsipopoulou (2005a: 554–5) points out that by LG the eastern region had its own independent connections with various other regions of the island and with the Cyclades, as well as being influenced by Knossian styles. The preceding points argue in favour of conducting more regional and self-referent studies of stylistic development in Cretan EIA pottery, rather than making too many assumptions about processes of general cultural evolution or diffusion based on pottery alone.

'Orientalising'/'Archaic'

Use of the designation 'Archaic' in discussing Cretan history circa 700–480 BC offers further problems. The perceived hiatus in the island's history during the sixth century means a coherent historical conceptualisation of the period is lacking. Chronology is especially reliant on art and pottery styles, thanks to a lack of excavated settlements with well-stratified continuous deposits of this period. A set of 'orientalising' features characteristic of Cretan art during the seventh century has given rise to use of the term 'Orientalising' as a general chronological designation for the island in the early to mid-seventh century, though its use sometimes extends down to 600 BC (Burkert 1998). This can have undesirable effects on analytical thinking, encouraging the setting of Crete aside from the mainland a priori, rather than the use of broad, contextualised studies of material culture to characterise and compare phases of social and historical development in each region. It is additionally problematic that in pottery from some important areas of the island, such as west Crete, no distinct 'Orientalising' horizon is clearly identifiable in stratified contexts (Andreadaki-Vlasaki 2004: 32). As in the case of the Subminoan and PGB styles, easternising cultural features may have functioned more as a regional or prestige marker than anything else (Kotsonas in press; Whitley 2005, in press); Whitley notes that the use of broadly 'orientalising' pottery styles in Crete anyway goes back much earlier than this (being seen in both the SM and PGB styles) so the term is lacking in any real descriptive or historical meaning. For these reasons I refer here to the 'Archaic' period in Crete as covering the whole span between 700 BC and the traditional textual date for the start of the Classical period across the Aegean, at 480 BC. An exception is made in Part Four when discussing mortuary data. Here it is sometimes necessary to reproduce excavators' dating of individual tombs, in which the terms 'Orientalising' and 'Archaic' are often used with distinct chronological meanings.

From the time inscriptions on stone come into use, by the late seventh century, developments in the archaeological record can often be linked to historical dates at the decade level. However, because I continue to use a broad, and not always evenly or accurately datable, selection of archaeological evidence to discuss long-term historical processes, I will mostly refer to centuries and half-centuries in the same way in discussing the Archaic and post-Archaic periods as when discussing the EIA.

Pottery types used in dating

A wide range of pottery types has been used as a basis for site dating in this book, according to the nature of the site in question, the type of research carried out there, and the quantity of information available. This has inevitably led to variability in levels of chronological precision. Many chronological and regional developments in the coarse pottery, which forms the majority of material retrieved from surface surveys and the dominant component of most excavated settlement assemblages (Figure 1) remain to be studied. Systematic study of coarse-ware fabrics at stratified LM IIIC-G sites in the Kavousi area has already proved immensely valuable in delineating chronological relationships between surveyed and excavated sites in the region, including cemeteries. A number of other recent surveys have also devoted considerable attention to coarse fabric analysis as a dating aid (Haggis 2005: 43–59; Haggis and Mook 1993; Hayden 2005: 13; Moody et al. 2000a; Mook 2005; Nowicki 2000: 17, 267–9; Whitley et al. 1999: 244–9). It should be borne in mind that such dating is still often rough or provisional, especially for the later EIA/Archaic

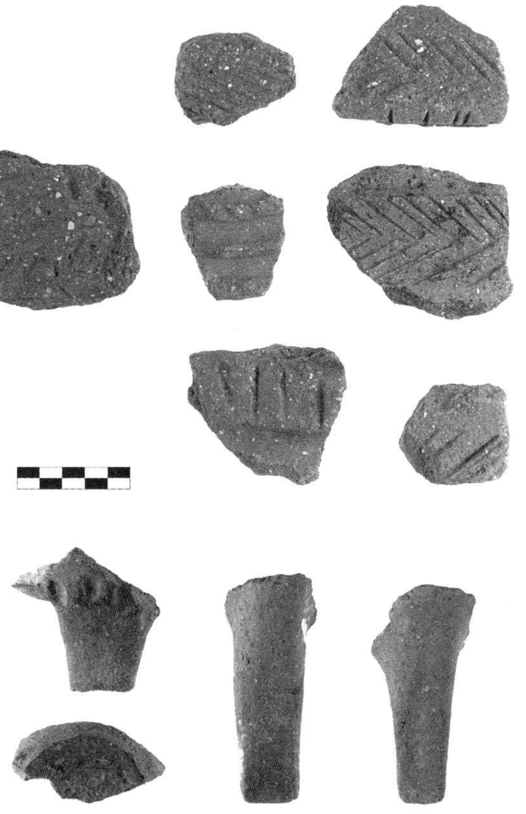

1. Diagnostic coarse ware of EIA date (pithos and cooking pot sherds) typical of the material used for dating in surface surveys. Image by the author.

periods, where there are few stratified settlement contexts for comparison. Additionally, different projects have used different levels of dating resolution: the Kavousi and Praisos surveys made a special point of defining individual EIA phases (LM IIIC, PG, G, O/A) in the surface material, while only the generic term 'EIA' was used in the Vrokastro and Ayios Vasilios Valley surveys to distinguish surface material of LM IIIC-G date from that belonging to the (Late) Bronze Age. Ambitiously, Nowicki has attempted to match datable ceramics from surveyed sites to a typology of EIA defensible settlements, and from this to use settlement types themselves to aid in pottery dating (Nowicki 2000: 224–47). While this framework may help to produce a higher-resolution picture of changing criteria in settlement location over time, it risks circularity.

Accuracy in the dating of fine pottery from the EIA to Archaic periods also varies according to the subperiod in question. Progress has recently been made in the refining of ceramic subphases from latest LM IIIB through LM IIIC, using both newly excavated pottery and restudied old material from sites such as Phaistos, Kavousi Kastro and Vronda, Chania Kastelli, Thronos Kefala, the Knossos Stratigraphical Museum and North Cemetery sites, and Monastiraki Katalimata and Chalasmeno (Borgna 1997, 2003b; Coulson 1997; Coulson and Tsipopoulou 1994; Hallager and Hallager 2000, 2003; Kanta 1997; Mook 2004; Mook and Coulson 1997; Prokopiou 1991, 1994, 1997; Rethimiotakis 1997a; Tsipopoulou 2004b, 2005b; Warren 1997). However, dating for the later EIA periods still suffers from the lack of stratified settlement assemblages so far published, and from an overfocus on fine tomb pottery – though a useful recent overview of selected Geometric ceramics from east Cretan sites appears in

TABLE 1. *Chronological table*

Period	Approximate date BC
Late Minoan I	1675–1490
Late Minoan II	1490–1425
Late Minoan IIIA-B	1425–1300
Late Minoan IIIC	1200–1100
Subminoan	1100–970
Protogeometric	970–810
'Protogeometric B' (not used here as a chronological period)	835–810
Early Geometric	810–790
Middle Geometric	790–745
Late Geometric	745–710
'Transitional' (not used here)	710–700
'Orientalising' (not generally used here)	700–600
Archaic	700–480
Classical	480–323

Tsipopoulou (2005a). Throughout this work I reproduce excavators' or surveyors' terminology for ceramic material, with commentary where necessary, or else equate the ceramic dates to absolute dates using the rough equivalences summarised in Table 1.

Absolute dates

New radiocarbon dates for stratified PG pottery from Assiros in northern Greece (dating the site to the late twelfth century) alongside other recently acquired dates like those from Lefkandi and Megiddo for LH IIIC, together with the revised chronology of the Thera eruption (necessitating a higher dating for the LBA period as a whole), are helping us start to fix the Aegean EIA chronology more directly (Dickinson 2006: 20–1; Newton et al. 2003, 2005). The general inference from all these dates seems to be that the collapse horizon traditionally dated circa 1200 BC may well have to be pushed back into the end of the thirteenth century. I accept this, doubting Dickinson's recent argument that the PG pottery style at Assiros might be a totally independent (earlier) phenomenon than the central Aegean PG style (notwithstanding the fact the regions were demonstrably in contact before, and through the beginning of, the EIA, and that by far the strongest concentration of PG ceramics appears in south central Greece, suggesting an origin there). However, given the fact that the new Assiros dates have yet to be fully evaluated and considered in the literature on chronology, and that questions now arising about the whole reliability of Egyptian-based sequences in the light of the radiocarbon advances will require complex resolution, I will continue to use the standard nominal date for the start of the EIA, at circa 1200 BC.

There is a lack of direct links into the Near Eastern absolute chronologies for Cretan pottery at the LBA/EIA transition in any case (Lemos 2002: 24–5). One long-used general tie-in is the very late LH IIIB imported pottery found at Deir Alla, Jordan, in a context dated to circa 1190 BC or later by an Egyptian find in the same context (Warren and Hankey 1989: 158–62). An Egyptian scarab found in an LM IIIB deposit at Poros near Iraklion in Crete certainly dates to the mid-thirteenth century, potentially allowing an end for this ceramic phase well within the century (Kanta 1980: 4). From the tenth century on, we are able to use more frequent Near Eastern imports to put Cretan developments into a solid chronological framework, though, as always, pottery dates remain relatively loose and flexible (Coldstream 1979a: 385). Table 1 gives the absolute dates for the Cretan EIA used here, which follow those suggested by Coldstream (with the provisos discussed above). The Bronze Age dates follow the scheme proposed by Manning (1999: 335–41) – accepting its still partly controversial character. This fits better with the other new evidence supporting a raised chronology for the start of the EIA.

5 THE LATE BRONZE AGE CRETAN LANDSCAPE AND ITS USE

It is important at this stage to set the scene for the discussion of archaeological evidence to follow with an outline discussion of Crete's natural and cultural landscape by around 1200 BC. An understanding of the long-term climate and vegetation history of the island, and the types of subsistence strategy they favoured, is needed in order to assess the parameters of size, distribution, and growth affecting Cretan communities in the EIA-Classical periods. An awareness of how people had viewed and interacted with their physical surroundings within the political and economic frameworks of the LBA is crucial to understanding how social structures and relationships were conditioned by changes in the spatial setting of daily life during and after collapse.

Below I focus mostly on Crete's LBA environment, land use, and settlement distribution. In the course of Parts Two and Three, I will return to discuss LBA frameworks for trade and mortuary practices, and how these, too, were affected by collapse.

Geology and drainage

Crete's mountainous zones are formed by Mesozoic limestones, overlying Palaeozoic platy limestones and metamorphic rocks (Fassoulas 2000). The highest are located in the west central area of the island (Psiloritis range, up to 2,456m above sea level [asl]), the east central part (Lasithi range, 2,148m asl), and the far west (White mountains, 2,454m asl; Figure 2). Smaller ranges lie in the eastern peninsula (Siteia mountains, 1,476m asl) and along the south coast of central Crete (Asterousia, 1,230m asl). All have many craggy, steep peaks and within the Holocene period seem always to have incorporated large expanses of bare rock, cliff, and scree. The lower-lying areas of the island are mostly formed by Tertiary marls, clays, and conglomerates, deposited in marine transgressions covering inland valleys and lower hilltops (reaching up to c. 800–1000m asl in places; Bonnefont 1972: 115–46). The plains, valleys, and isthmuses that these deposits cover comprise the island's most easily cultivable land, in the sense of being the most easily workable – though interestingly, not always in having the most chemically fertile or moisture-retaining soils (Bintliff 1977b; Morris 2003: 72–6; Wallace 2002: 91–9). As such, these areas were the main focus of settlement and agriculture in most periods from the Neolithic onwards. As we shall see, the EIA period represents an important exception to this rule – perhaps the most striking in all the island's history. Even so, the biggest arable areas – the Amari and Ayios Vasilios valleys in west Crete, Chania plain, Iraklion basin, Mesara plain, Ierapetra isthmus, Lasithi plain, and valleys and plateaus of the Siteia mountains – all housed considerable concentrations of population during this period.

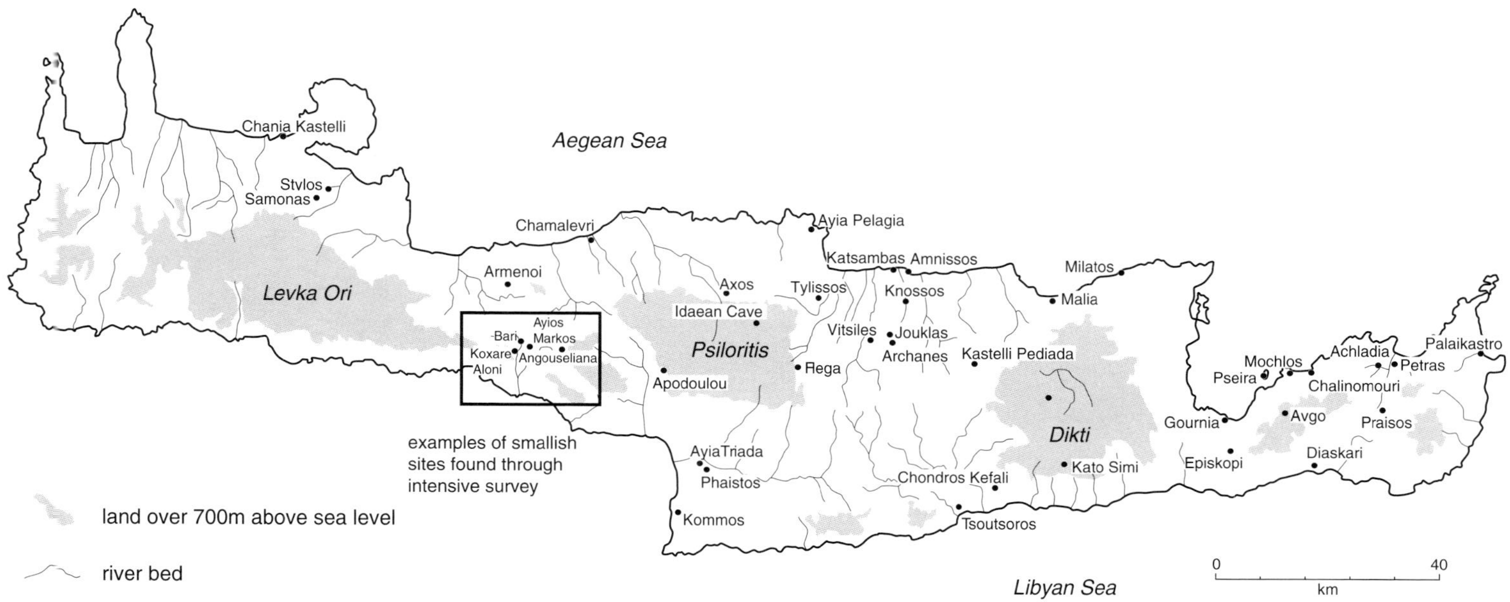

2. Map showing selected LM IIIA-B sites. Image by the author.

Karst processes have continuously affected the limestone ranges, producing *poljes* (raised plains surrounded by steep hills, the largest being the Lasithi plain in the centre of the Lasithi range), numerous caves (some sizeable), and subterranean drainage systems. Groundwater drains through the permeable limestone to emerge on springlines when it meets metamorphic rock. Surface drainage volume has fluctuated considerably over time. For example, during the 'Little Ice Age' of the sixteenth to seventeenth centuries AD, more rivers flowed year-round than was the case in the nineteenth century, and there were also presumably greater volumes of water in the springs (Grove 1992; Rackham and Moody 1996: 20–2, 40–1). This might have applied during the EIA, too: soil evidence suggests a generally slightly moister climate at this time, as I discuss later. Most of the river beds indicated on Figure 2 are now dry year-round. Springs are mostly too small to have been used in ancient times for anything other than domestic needs and livestock maintenance. Traditional agriculture in Crete was mainly rain-fed, with two sowing seasons per year possible. Garden agriculture, recently developed on a market scale, has required the use of deep geological wells, and olive cultivation, now dominating much of the agricultural zone, has also been boosted by intensive irrigation reliant on these wells.

Crete's position near the junction of two continental plates means that it has periodically been affected by tectonic movements. The west end has risen by about eight metres since the Hellenistic period (Rackham and Moody 1996: 195). Studies at Bronze Age coastal sites such as Kommos (south Crete), Mochlos, and Petras (northeast Crete), have produced conflicting models of relative sea level change at regional level. These differences may arise from localised geomorphological changes in conjunction with sea level fluctuation (Davaras 1974; Soles and Davaras 1992: 417; Tsipopoulou 1997b: 235; Watrous et al. 1993: 204). They suggest that few meaningful generalisations can be made about LBA-EIA coastlines in Crete as a whole, but that major changes (more than a few metres) are not likely to have taken place between the Bronze Age and the present day.

Geomorphology

Thanks to the island's long history of dense human occupation, in looking at Crete's geomorphology and vegetation it is often impossible to divorce natural from cultural influences on the landscape (see, e.g., Grove et al. 1992; Rackham and Grove 2001: 37–45; Rackham and Moody 1996). However, several recent studies have been concerned with dating geomorphological events in the framework of archaeological survey projects (Bintliff 1977a: 605–77, 1977b; Pope 1993, 2004). Very detailed studies of geomorphology and soils in two regions, which were overtly tied into archaeological research on the LBA-EIA transition, have also recently been carried out (Morris 1994, 2003; Morris et al. 2005). All these studies agree in reconstructing a major post-Roman colluviation phase in the island, but views have varied on how uniform or singular this was. Bintliff concluded that the geomorphology of the Ayiofarango valley in south Crete conformed fairly well to Vita-Finzi's (1969) model of the 'Older' and 'Younger' Fills, with one major phase of colluvial deposition taking place in the late Pleistocene and another in the post-Roman period (Bintliff 1977a: 35–59; see also Butzer 1974; Davidson 1980; Roberts 1979; 1981: 5, for the Knossos valley; Rackham 1982, 1996; van Andel et al. 1986, 1990; Wagstaff 1981). He attributed a very limited role to anthropogenic soil erosion before Roman times. In contrast, Pope's studies in the nearby Mesara showed a small, but significant, Late Neolithic deposition phase, and other small peaks through the Bronze Age and later, in addition to post-Roman deposition. This picture corresponds more closely to mainland Greek profiles. Pope suggested anthropogenic causes for many of these events.

Morris noted 0.88 metre of colluvium on the north Ierapetra isthmus in east Crete near the Kavousi sites, representing post–Iron Age (not necessarily post-Roman) deposition: a soil buried under it was dated to 3,000 years BP (Morris 2003: 64–76). In the Lasithi range, Morris found another buried soil – formed prior to the LBA-EIA period – in a sinkhole on the Nissimo plain (Morris 2003: 23–44). A disturbed Roman land surface lay some way above it, again indicating significant amounts of deposition *between* the LBA/EIA and Roman periods. On the basis of studies in the Ayios Vasilios valley in west Crete and the Meseleros valley in the Ierapetra isthmus, Moody suggests that significant downward movement of material onto valley floors has taken place periodically since the Bronze Age – sometimes during large single events like flash floods – and fails to isolate any specific major deposition phase (Moody 2005: 465; Moody et al. 2000b: 361–3). Overall, then, a model of the 'Younger Fill' as a regional and recurrent phenomenon, rather than a unitary one, seems the most appropriate for Crete. Relative soil stability over the course of the Bronze Age as a whole may be partly attributable to the fact that soil management measures such as terraces and check-dams first came into use during the period (Bintliff 1977a: 613; Clark 1990), though a phase of Neolithic/EBA deposition, associated with the first widespread take-up of agriculture, may have helped build up soils in areas like the Iraklion basin and Mesara, Chania, and Malia plains to a significant extent. The presence of large and important settlements in the latter areas from at least the EBA suggests they already provided large stretches of fertile, deep, and stable soils and were widely cultivated by this period. Later deposition events have covered the remains of these settlements to varying depths (more than 2m in many areas). They have also affected shorelines, with the silting up of some of the wide sandy bays along the north coast of Crete that were the island's main harbours throughout its Bronze Age. The south coast, where steep mountain ranges run right down to the sea, has fewer of the latter, but the south Rethymnon isthmus and western Mesara, particularly the area around Kommos, did have important harbours.

In reconstructing the LBA-EIA Cretan landscape, then, we can generalise that there is likely to have been greater depth of soil on the hillslopes, and rather less in the coastal plains and valleys, than there is today (Hamilakis 1996: 85). Undoubtedly, though, the distribution of the best land in terms of attractiveness for agriculture (i.e., possessing good workability and depth of soil) was already concentrated on the coasts and in the major plains and valleys, as reflected in the settlement pattern. One of Morris's Lasithi soil studies supports this assertion in negative fashion (Morris 2003: 23–44; Wallace 2006b). Citing the truncation in the LBA-EIA period of long-established buried soils in the vicinity of the mountainous Karfi site, it suggests that agricultural activity here only began during the site's EIA occupation, with minimal soil disturbance at any other period. Deposits of post-EIA colluvium found at various locations on the eastern slopes below Karfi seem likely to relate to the abandonment of cultivation after the site went out of use, provoking increased volumes of soil erosion over a short period. Substantial post-EIA colluvial deposits noted by Morris on the Ierapetra isthmus could similarly relate to reduced cultivation on the higher hillslopes after the later EIA, when a number of small sites lasting into that period were abandoned (Morris 2003: 61–76).

Vegetation and climate

Crete's vegetation history is linked to soil character, geomorphological change, and climate, but also to changes in human activity over time. Notions of extensive deforestation since antiquity, causing catastrophic, irreversible erosion and thereby degradation of vegetation cover which has resulted in the bare-looking mountain ranges of the island today, are now largely exploded. It has become clear that Cretan soils are remarkably resilient, with cultivation able to advance and retreat repeatedly over time (Rackham 1973, 1982, 1992, 1996; Rackham and Grove 2001: 8–24). The character of natural regeneration can be seen to vary greatly according to microclimatic variations, soil composition, and the nature of land use preceding abandonment. Very rapid woodland/maquis regeneration has been shown to occur after the abandonment of cultivation and in the absence of grazing, as in a number of other Mediterranean regions (Blitzer 1993b; Blumler 1993; Koutsidou and Margaris 1992; Margaris 1990; Moody 1997; Shay and Shay 2004). Thus, though humans have had a significant role in affecting plant cover over time, identifying and dating their impact is not always straightforward (Bintliff 1977a: 614).

The range of ancient wild and cultivated plant species able to be reconstructed from pollen coring and archaeological excavation indicates a broadly Mediterranean climate for Crete from at least the Early Bronze Age until the present day. More subtle climatic variations are difficult to reconstruct without detailed evidence, though study of the medieval Little Ice Age has shown the significant effects on the island's vegetation patterns which have arisen from even fairly short-term climate change in the past (Grove 1992; Rackham and Grove 2001: 130–41). Some recent research suggests that significant short-term changes in the east Mediterranean climate occurred within the LBA/EIA transition, circa 1174–1162 BC, though precise characterisation of these and contextualised evaluation of their impact are still lacking. It is suggested that drought and/or increasingly cold temperatures might have helped destabilise complex subsistence systems to some extent (Buckland et al. 1997: 588; Kuniholm 1990: 653–4; Moody 2005).

Fossil pollen from the island is rare, and the few cores obtained have not helped greatly in land cover reconstruction for the EIA-Classical periods specifically, though they do offer a long-term picture (Bottema 1980; Hall et al. 1992; Moody et al. 1996; Rackham and Moody 1996: 123–6). A core from Ayia Galini, in southwest Crete, shows that pine forest was gradually replaced by deciduous oak, with patches of open grassland, during the early Holocene (starting c. 10,000 years BP). This development was probably linked to an increasingly moist, cool climate, but one with relatively few Mediterranean elements (Bottema 1980). A variety of microenvironments must have existed within this natural 'mosaic' of vegetation (Turland et al. 1993: 4). The finding that blanket forest cover did not characterise the early Holocene may well apply to much of the rest of Crete, further falsifying the notion that anthropogenic factors are mainly or consistently responsible for today's patchy tree cover (Rackham 1992: 35). Climate after the 'oak event' at Ayia Galini seems to have become progressively drier. A core from Tersana in northwest Crete shows a rise in olive, though not in other moisture-favouring species, from as early as the Neolithic period. It also shows an increase by the same period in species favouring open areas. Both facts support the idea that fairly large-scale clearance for cultivation (though not necessarily olive cultivation) was already taking place by this period (Moody 1987: 81–93; Moody et al. 1996).

'Phrygana' – a heavily grazed garigue composed of predominantly thorny or spiny evergreen plants resistant to grazing, interspersed with herbs and grasses – is currently common outside the intensively cultivated areas (Polunin and Huxley 1987: 9–14; Rackham and Moody 1996: 53–73; Sfikas 2000; Turland et al. 1993). This low vegetation, dry and brown in summer, can give an impression of 'barrenness' in the often rocky, hilly areas it now covers. Yet because grain cultivation was historically much more extensive in Crete than it is at present (in the eighteenth and nineteenth centuries, particularly, it covered very large parts of the island) phrygana is often now found in areas with a history of past clearance and cultivation, followed by extensive grazing up to the present day (Triandaphyllidou-Baladié 1988: 168–72). The fact that so many upland or hilly areas now have phrygana cover as a result of these changing agriculture patterns, allowing high sherd visibility, offers especially good results in archaeological survey – especially in relation to the EIA period, during which many settlements were located in hilly zones.

Where no recent clearance or grazing has taken place, a maquis or low forest cover is often found, its composition depending on soils, grazing, water, and altitude. Stretches of cypress, oak, and pine forest, of varying density, extend over large areas, particularly the upper parts of the mountain ranges. In the cultivated zones, vines and (since the 1970s) hothouse crops are the main cash species besides olive. Thus the most densely populated areas of the Bronze Age island – when not under modern settlement – are often inaccessible to survey work. Cereals and legumes now cover a very small area of the cultivated land but from the eighteenth through the first half of the twentieth century were extremely widespread, forming the main subsistence crop. Irrigated olive trees (of various ages) are now by far the dominant cultivar in many low-lying agricultural areas. Under current climatic conditions the olive rarely grows above circa 700 metres asl in Crete. Through most of its early human history the island has had the inherent potential to feed its population but is affected, like most other Aegean regions, by a significant year-to-year risk of crop failure, particularly exacerbated by the frequent use of marginal soils; the high-relief landscape, which creates microclimates to some degree; and the scarcity of surface water (Halstead and Jones 1989; Halstead and O'Shea 1982; Moody 1992: 53).

Palaeoenvironmental/palaeoeconomic data for the LBA-EIA

1) PLANTS

The archaeological record allows us to look in some detail at the species cultivated in the period of interest, though diachronic resolution and balanced regional coverage are generally poor. There are broad similarities with the main range of historical and modern crop species, despite probably very different proportions, yields, and uses of the crops. The information provided by archaeobotanical and archaeofaunal assemblages has recently been supplemented by organic residue analysis on ceramics (Tzedakis and Martlew 1999).

Cereals (predominantly barley, emmer, and einkorn) appear at a number of LBA sites, indicating common use in the diet. Bread wheat (*Triticum aestivum*), despite its long history in Crete, appears more rarely – including in a pure deposit from LM II Knossos – suggesting it was a specialised crop for which particular zones of land were set apart (Halstead 1992: 108). It would have demanded more nutrients from the soil than some of the other cereals in use: the practice of crop rotation might have helped to get the best out of land supporting it (Hansen 1988: 43; Jones 1994). Cultivated lentil, pea, chickpea, field bean, and bitter vetch appear in the Aegean from the Late Neolithic and were widely used in LBA Crete, where they are found in varying proportions in the record (Sarpaki 1992; Sarpaki and Jones 1990).

The importance of grape and olive in the LBA diet, and their scale of production, are difficult to gauge exactly. Oil appears as a residue in both domestic cooking and industrial vessels by the MBA (Hansen 1988: 46; Runnels and Hansen 1986; Sarpaki 1999; Tzedakis and Martlew 1999; 115–16, 170). Blitzer has pointed convincingly to cultural evidence for olive processing on a significant scale by the LBA (Blitzer 1993a), and Cretan transport jars travelling around the Aegean in the thirteenth century BC surely contained large quantities of oil (Haskell 2005). While there was certainly nothing like today's monoculture of irrigated olives, these observations, along with the Linear B administrative texts which record considerable quantities of olive oil in everyday circulation, indicate an extensive exploitation of the olive by this period at the latest. Wine is shown by residue analysis to have been a very common beverage in LM III Crete, and archaeobotanical evidence confirms vine as a significant cultivar (Jones 1994; Tzedakis and Martlew 1999: 170). By the Classical period, both texts and archaeology show that wine, oil, and cereal production operated at a large scale in much of central and south Greece. These facts suggest a broadly similar crop base in use throughout the EIA-Archaic period (Amouretti 1986, 1992; Foxhall and Forbes 1982; Hanson 1992; Isager and Skydsgaard 1992: 11).

Turning specifically to that period, although few archaebotanical data have yet been published from Crete, enough is known to confirm that EIA communities relied on the same broad range of crops. The continued use of the main known LBA species is clear – emmer, einkorn, olive, grape, fig, and various legumes have been found at Kavousi Kastro in east Crete, a site dating between the twelfth and seventh centuries, and nearby Kavousi Vronda and Monastiraki Chalasmeno, dating in the twelfth to tenth centuries only: a complete publication by stratified context is awaited (Flint-Hamilton pers comm). Thronos Kefala in west Crete (with twelfth- to eighth-century occupation) has produced a similar profile (Hallager and Hallager 2003: 193; Mylona pers comm). People living at Pobia Vigla in central south Crete, occupied in the twelfth to tenth centuries, consumed figs, olives, and grapes (Vasilakis 2004). Almond is also known from twelfth- to tenth-century assemblages (Flint-Hamilton pers comm for Chalasmeno and Kavousi material; Shay and Shay 2000: 654–6 for the cult site of Kommos in south Crete, where the charcoal assemblage also includes carob; olive, grape, barley, cereal, and almond are also found). Though there have been few systematic excavations at sites used through the Archaic period those at the sixth- to fifth-century site of Azoria have produced olives, grapes, figs, legumes, and cereal remains (Haggis et al. 2004: 373–8, 383–6).

II) ANIMALS

We are rather better informed about animal resources from the EIA record, though published LBA bone assemblages from Crete have hitherto been lacking for comparison (Bedwin 1994; Walker 1996; Wallace 2003a: 607; Wilkens 1996; see, however, Soles 2003a: 129; Soles et al. 2003; Table 2). It seems that sheep and goat remained the most important form of livestock, as they had been through the LBA, after the events of circa 1200 BC. The assemblage from Kavousi Kastro as published to date spans the whole period circa 1200–600 BC, though a detailed breakdown by period and context will eventually be published (Klippel and Snyder 1991; Snyder and Klippel 1994, 1996, 1999). Material from the nearby site of Vronda (c. 1200–1000 BC) has been quantified separately, providing a useful record for the early period on its own: again, a final summary of statistics (Day et al. 2009) remains to be published. At both Kavousi sites, and at Monastiraki Chalasmeno, Chania Kastelli, Kommos, and Chamalevri, all dating in the twelfth through eleventh centuries, ovicaprids were by far the dominant species (Day et al. 2009: Tables 1–40; Hallager and Hallager 2000: 193; Klippel and Snyder 1991; Mylona 1999, pers comm; Reese et al. 2000: 451; Snyder and Klippel 1994, 1999; Tsoukala 1996; Tsoukala and Hatzi-Vallianou 2000). At Kavousi and Chamalevri, the age and sex structure among ovicaprids suggests exploitation for meat and milk, rather than the targeted wool cropping indicated by the Linear B tablets to have been a major feature of the LM III economy (Klippel and Snyder 1991: 184–5; Mylona pers comm).

Pigs are the second most common species in all published assemblages except that from Kavousi Kastro. Cattle were a significant stock animal, particularly well represented at the large Bronze Age settlement of Chania, which continued in use through the twelfth century – a fact that the

TABLE 2. *Faunal remains from twelfth- to eleventh-century Cretan sites*

Site/date	*Ovis/capra* (%)	*Sus* (%)	*Bos* (%)	Others (percentages included where known)
Kavousi Kastro (mostly LM IIIC-PG)[a]	82.2	7.7	8.6	Horse (*Equus*) (<1%), fallow deer (*Dama dama*) (<1%), agrimi (*Caprus aegagrus*) (<0.1%), dog (*Canis familiaris*), small quantities of hare (*Lepus sp.*), badger (*Meles meles*), and other small wild species; shellfish
Kavousi Vronda LM IIIC[b]	70	15.9	5	*Equus* (1%), *Caprus aegagrus, Canis, Lepus*
Monastiraki Chalasmeno LM IIIC[c]	72.9	16.7	5.2	*Equus* (2.1%), *Canis*
Chamalevri LM IIIC (Mylona 1999)	41.3	15	7.4	Indeterminate medium mammals (15.7%), indeterminate large mammals (3.6%), *Equus (1.3%), Dama* (1.4%), *Cervus elaphus* (red deer) (1.3%), indeterminate deer (9.1%), wild *Sus scrofa, Bos primigenius, Canis, Lepus, Melas*
Chania Kastelli LM IIIC (Hallager and Hallager 2000)	56	26	9	*Equus, Dama, Cervus* (all percentages unspecified)
Kommos Temple A (SM-PG) (Reese et al. 2000)	55	10	35	*Lepus, Cervus, Canis,* marine shellfish (all individually quantified)
Other SM-PG in Kommos Sanctuary area	55.6	0	44	*Lepus*, marine shellfish (all individually quantified)
Other EIA assemblages *(not properly quantified)*				
Gortyn (from a Geometric house: Wilkens 1996)	67.2	17.24	rare	*Canis* (about 1%), equid (about 1%)
Smari Profitis Elias[d]	Up to 80% of all bone (2000 data)	c. 19 (of identified fragments, based on 1996 data)	c. 13 (of identified fragments, based on 1996 data)	*Lepus* (12%), *Capra aegagrus* (4%), *Equus* (0.3%), small carnivorous mammals including *Canis, Melas, Felix sylvestris* (1%), marine shellfish (of identified fragments, all based on 1996 data)

[a] Details of the Kavousi Kastro faunal assemblage so far published span the whole period LM IIIC-C: a more detailed breakdown by period remains to be published.

[b] Data for Vronda cited here come from preliminary publications (Klippel and Snyder 1991; Snyder and Klippel 1999). The data published very recently in the first volume of the excavation series (Day et al. 2009) are not taken into account.

[c] Statistics from a very small sample of identified bone: 83% of bone fragments found were unidentified. The site awaits full publication. See Snyder and Klippel 1994.

[d] Identified bone is only 24% of the total assemblage. The site is predominantly LM IIIC-A, but some MM assemblages are included in the preliminary published data (Tsoukala 1996; Tsoukala and Chatzi-Vallianou 2000).

flat fertile landscape around this settlement helps explain. Cattle remains were also frequent at Kavousi Kastro, though the mountainous topography here does not seem the most obviously suited to this species. They may still have been used in ploughing (attested earlier in the Linear B texts; Palaima 1989, 1992) as well as for meat – butchering marks are widely seen on cattle bones (Klippel and Snyder 1991: 181–3, 1999). The dominance of sheep and goat seems to continue at Cretan sites into the Archaic period and most probably beyond (e.g., Haggis et al. 2004: 384).

Equids are evidenced in nearly all published Cretan assemblages of EIA date. The agility of donkeys and mules would have made them suitable as both pack and plough animals in a hilly environment. They must also have been important for wheeled transport: even though the steep topography of many settlements in this period made this of limited use in the immediate vicinity, it would still be needed in the wider agricultural hinterland. Red deer is found in most EIA assemblages and is particularly important at the twelfth-century site of Chamalevri in west Crete (where it is almost equivalent in proportion to pig), suggesting that hunting formed part of subsistence activity and that extensive wooded habitats must have existed in this low-lying coastal region (Mylona 1999). Find contexts need to be taken into special account here, however: many of the reported faunal remains from Thronos and Chamalevri, and all of those from Kommos, are from what are apparently ritually related, rather than ordinary domestic contexts. Other small game species, including badger, hare, and partridge, are frequently present on EIA-Archaic sites, along with with fish and seafood – again best documented at Kavousi and Kommos (Reese et al. 2000: 511–13; Snyder and Klippel 1999: 67).

Older excavations at EIA sites produced unquantified bone assemblages that can only be used to confirm the use of the main species listed earlier: cattle bones appear in tombs at Vrokastro in east Crete, for example (Hall 1914: 140). The settlement at Karfi produced bones of ovicaprid, cattle, pig, and red deer, together with other wild species (Pendlebury et al. 1938). Although the scale and context of exploitation, particularly of sheep and goat, may have changed substantially between the LBA and early EIA – a question dealt with in Part Two – the environmental and infrastructural conditions necessary to support all these animals within a broad-based stock-raising regime clearly applied throughout the period.

6 THE BROADER FRAMEWORK: STRATEGIES OF LANDSCAPE USE BY THE LBA-EIA TRANSITION

Economic organisation

An appreciation of the context of land use in LBA Crete is essential to understanding the implications of the major changes occurring around 1200 BC. Useful information is provided by the Linear B administrative records at Knossos. Considered in conjunction with the settlement record, discussed below, these texts offer insight into how macrolevel sociopolitical and economic systems shaped the cultural landscape. The tablets as a whole can be taken to refer generally to the period circa 1400 to circa 1200, taking into account continued uncertainties about the exact dating of the different tablet deposits found and the fact that political disturbances, upsetting some aspects of the administrative system, may have occurred at Knossos some time before 1200 (Driessen 1997, 2005: 218–19; Hallager 1977; Palmer 1963). A redistributive model for the Cretan economy of the Linear B period, strongly resembling the palatial economies of the Mycenaean mainland, is now established, though there are numerous gaps in information resulting from the highly specialised character of the Linear B records, and significant contrasts exist between the content of the Knossos archive and that of the best-preserved mainland archive, from Pylos (Halstead 1992, 1999a, 1999b, 1999c).

The centralised bodies responsible for creating the archives controlled, or at least invested substantially in, the large-scale production of cereals, wool, and olives. Their main exploited territories were probably the prime arable areas in which the major settlements were located (Figures 3 and 4). Specialisation in the above products seems likely, given that they are the main focus of the records. Despite archaeobotanical evidence for the consumption of additional crops, including pulses and fruits, these are not mentioned in the texts (Halstead 1992: 115). They may have arrived as tradable commodities, taxes, or tribute from smaller producers (whose lands were more limited in extent and/or located in marginal zones) or simply not have been mentioned in official records because of their relatively minor role in the political economy Another way in which the centre seems to have interacted with smaller-scale producers was in the restocking of palatial sheep flocks, a significant number of which were apparently reared for wool production (though meat and milk/cheese production are also monitored) using animals selectively drawn from smaller herds with a different ownership structure (Halstead 1999a, 1999b). The Knossos tablets show these transactions, and the reciprocal movement of younger animals, less useful for wool production, into the smaller herds.

The administrative system at Knossos was concerned with at least 100,000 sheep in central Crete, and a total of 500,000 sheep has been estimated for the island as a whole in the period of

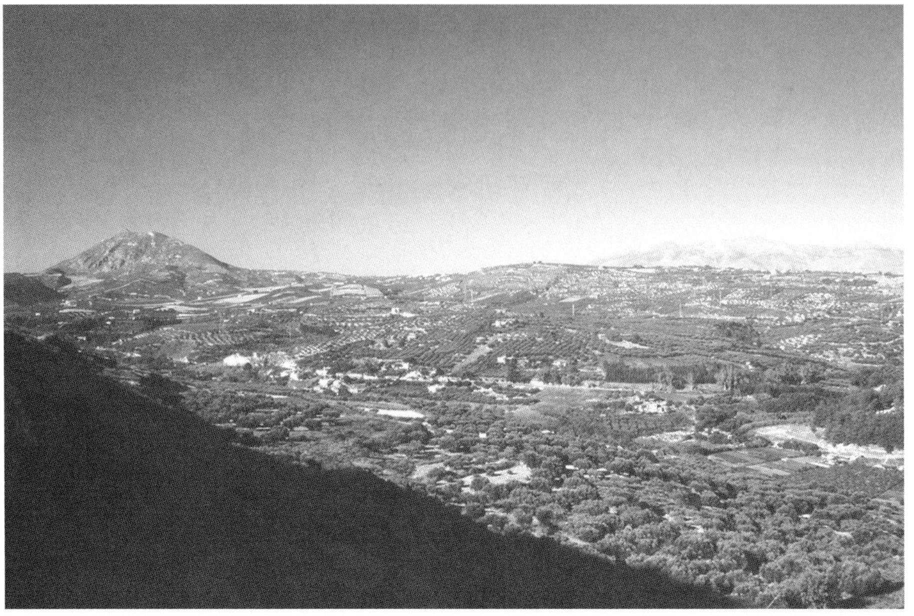

3. The fertile north Cretan landscape around Knossos, showing the mountain of Jouktas to the south. From northeast. Photo courtesy K. Nowicki.

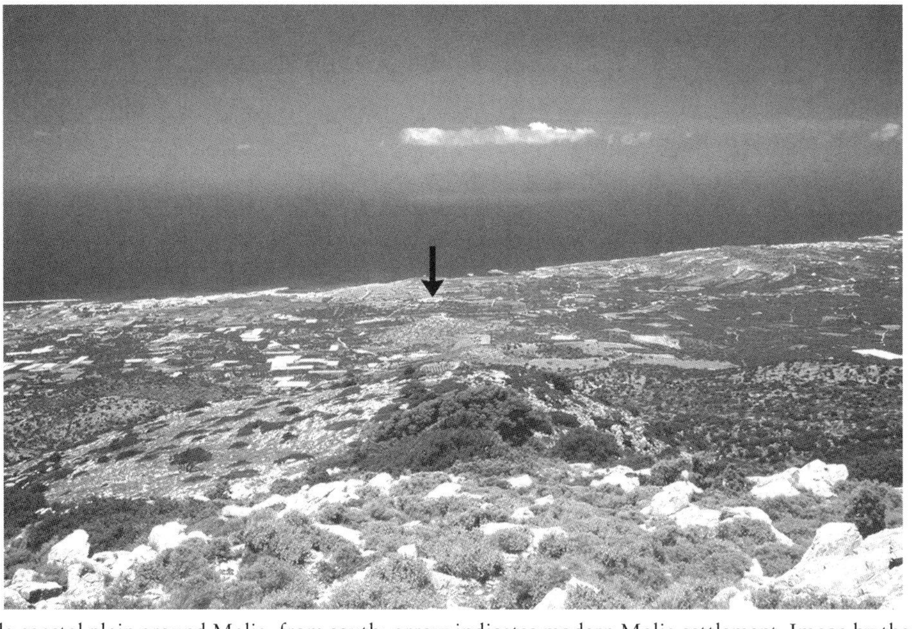

4. Fertile coastal plain around Malia, from south: arrow indicates modern Malia settlement. Image by the author.

the tablets, on analogy with the average number of animals in Crete in the nineteenth to early twentieth century (Halstead 1996: 32; Killen 1964: 5, 1985: 283). A medium- to large-sized herd in traditional/present-day Greece is 200–400 animals, so 500,000 animals might represent up to 5,000 herds, with an average of two full-time shepherds per herd possible to assume on the basis of traditional practices. With a population of around 200,000 (the average historical figure; see

Rackham and Moody 1996: 97–9) and with a maximum 5,000 herds, only about 5 percent of Crete's inhabitants could ever have been fully supported by herding for meat and milk in the LBA (see Halstead 1996: 34, who suggests c. 50+ animals per year would be needed to support one person on a specialised pastoralist regime). This puts the potential subsistence role of herding in the LBA into perspective. It is likely, nonetheless, that wool and textile processing involved a significant number of people, and there are further indications that these groups had considerable autonomy, while still being tied into a centralised system. The so-called collector references in the tablets are personal names in the genitive, associated with a quantified entity and a topographical name in a particular sequence (Bennet 1985, 1992; Carlier 1992; Driessen 1992; Godart 1992; Olivier 2001; Rougemont 2001). Sometimes another personal name, referred to by Bennet as a 'shepherd' name, also occurs in these sequences. The references are nearly always associated with flock records, or with records concerning woolprocessing and cloth manufacture, rather than other kinds of production. A single 'collector' name (CN) sometimes has several flock holdings listed against it, sometimes apparently related to different regions of the island. Around 100 such names are recorded in the surviving tablet sample, suggesting the wielding of significant economic power by this group of people, and a wide spatial range for their activities.

On the basis of the tablet evidence it seems likely that 'sharecropping' systems (in the sense of cultivators receiving shares of a harvest in return for gathering the whole crop on behalf of an owning body or individual, the latter also providing high-investment equipment) were used to organise at least part of the grain harvest on the extensive palatial territories, perhaps in return for loans of palace-owned plough oxen to small farmers (Halstead 1999b, 1999c, 2001; Palaima 1989, 1992). The centres used their capital-invested bulk production of wool and oil to produce high-quality manufactured items for export: it is clear that they also redistributed massive quantities of grain within the territories they controlled, helping to support specialised craftsmen (Catling et al. 1980; Killen 1964, 1985; Olivier 1992; Palmer 1992). Many of the goods the latter produced were exported into the complex trans-Mediterranean trade system of the period. By this means the centres could accumulate other precious raw materials, such as metals, which could be either reexported or consumed locally as prestige items. I will return to Crete's Late Bronze Age trade connections in Part Three.

Alongside artisans, the resources collected by the central administration supported a bureaucracy and a religious sector, including priests at shrines in the countryside as well as at the centres themselves. Large-scale agricultural production was thus integrally bound up with political control over large areas of the landscape, though a significant element of decentralised authority and initiative was also important – even inevitable, given the dissected nature of Crete's topography, which limited easy communication and heightened risk. For the Greek mainland, David Small has recently suggested that outside the palace-owned territories, a large proportion of agricultural activity was controlled by independent lineages at the level of landed estates (Small 1998, 1999). Elements of this model are worth bearing in mind when considering the way in which Cretan and mainland societies were restructured in the post-collapse period, as I shall discuss. Using analogies with traditional farming in Greece, Halstead has suggested extensive areas of arable under crops and large-scale herding of sheep and goats, involving movement over considerable distances, in the late LBA (Halstead 1987, 1992, 1999b; Palmer 1992). This pattern would need large continuous areas of cleared land, and is likely to have relied on a large seasonal labour supply and the production of enough surplus to feed a large number of work animals with high-quality fodder year-round. Political stability – allowing control of, and continuous investment in, large areas of territory by the central authorities – would have been crucial in maintaining this kind of economy (Cherry 1988: 25–8; Halstead 1996: 21). Physical complementarity in land use may have operated within palace-controlled lands, or between palatial and nonpalatial territories – involving bulk production of cereals/olives (perhaps with intergrazing or stubble grazing) on the best land, and other forms of land use, such as extensive grazing, beekeeping, and small-scale mixed agriculture, in peripheral areas not so amenable to extensive plough agriculture (Halstead 1987: 81–2, 1996: 32; Sarpaki 1992).

Site patterning and social/economic interaction

I will conclude this introductory section by briefly examining site distribution on Crete in relation to the political and economic structures existing there by the LBA. Though I focus here on the LM IIIA-B period, throughout the book I shall have cause to refer to earlier developments in Crete's rich prehistoric landscape. The LBA cultural landscape alone deserves its own monograph, and there is no easy way to encapsulate it here. What is most important to note for our purpose is that by the LM III period a complex and hierarchical settlement network was tied into a social system displaying high levels of inequality and the regional centralisation of power.

1) MIDDLE MINOAN–LATE MINOAN I–II PERIODS

Even before the emergence of palatial complexes in the MM IB period (c. 1900–1850 BC) Crete's economic and political centres had been located in the most fertile plains and valleys and the coastal zones. Good communications and high agricultural productivity were clearly important factors in these choices, and a complex infrastructure of roads, defensive settlements and border posts, sanctuaries (including 'open-air' sanctuaries on peaks and in caves as well as built shrines), cleared agricultural lands, and smaller sites developed in and around the same areas (Nowicki 1994c, 1999a; Peatfield 1990; Watrous 1996: 57–100, 1999). By the LM I period (c. 1700–1450 BC) the island had developed several layers of settlement hierarchy, tied into complex political and economic structures, though the exact relationship of settlements within the general pattern is far from clear (Bennet 1990: 194–200). A number of palatial and subpalatial regional centres existed alongside larger centres at Knossos and Phaistos – including important regional towns like Gournia and Tylissos, which seem to have had high concentrations of commodity wealth and their own administrative systems. A sublevel of 'villa' sites – smaller settlements incorporating monumental architecture, some wealth concentration, and evidence of texts and administration – developed alongside them (Hägg 1997). There was also a level below this, of small settlements that lacked their own administrative systems, although the distinction between these and 'villas' is not always easy to make in terms of economic/political function (Schoep 1998). Scattered through the countryside must also have been many individual households or hamlets whose inhabitants were directly involved in farming and/or herding, and had limited access to the resources held by elites at the centres or villas. The wide distribution of administrative texts among higher-order settlements, including villas, points to a devolved, rather than single-centred, type of political and economic organisation.

In this landscape, cult places (many established as far back as the end of the EBA) acted as venues for social interaction and power display at a number of levels, but by the LBA were probably dominated by the palatial centres (Rutkowski 1986: 47–99; Watrous 1996). Some, such as the peak sanctuaries of Jouktas and Tylissos (which continued in use into LM I) and cult caves like the Psychro and the Ideaean caves, were associated with unusual features of the natural landscape (Figure 2). Flourishing port settlements like Chania, Malia, Poros, Kommos, Palaikastro, and Zakros channelled Crete's trade with Egypt, Cyprus, and the Levantine coasts, and its more intensive relations with the Cyclades and the southern Greek mainland (Cline 1999; Shaw and Shaw 1997; Shaw et al. 2006b; Watrous 1992).

II) LATE MINOAN IIIA AND IIIB PERIODS

By the LM III period, changes in the cultural landscape appeared together with adjustments in political and economic systems: many of the latter were related to new kinds of links with mainland Greek polities, after a series of disturbances across the island at the end of LM I. An increased centralisation of political and economic power probably occurred – though in terms of site use, the underlying LM I pattern was often simply adapted, at settlements as well as at sanctuaries. Villas mostly went out of use, and new small and simple agricultural settlements extended into the landscape: both developments seem likely to be a result of increased centralisation. A new spread and visibility of cemeteries is notable, each cemetery probably attached to a sizeable settlement. The advent of the chamber tomb form in these cemeteries is part of a whole set of changes at this time which are rooted in increasingly close interactions with mainland culture (Preston 1999).

Settlement distribution seems to have remained strongly tied into an extensive farming system – still concentrated in the most accessible and productive areas of arable land like the Knossos, Chania, Mesara, and Malia plains (Bennet 1990; Driessen 2001; Halstead 1992, 2001; Rehak and Younger 1999: 442–4). A major change in the distribution of text archives, however, suggests a much more centralised kind of administration: Knossos and Chania are the only sites that seem to have retained their own administrative systems. Even so, many former regional centres surely continued to house people concerned with gathering, recording, and redistributing produce at a regional level, like the 'collectors' mentioned in the texts (Olivier 1997). Archaeology leaves huge gaps in our knowledge with regard to the individual character and function of settlements at this time: for example, there are few detailed whole-site plans available for the period. The apparently scattered or ephemeral character of LM IIIA-B pottery deposits at many large LM I sites (e.g., Gournia, Petras, Palaikastro) partly reflects the fact that this was their last period of large-scale occupation before abandonment (destruction may have been involved in this process in a minority of cases: at Malia, for example, there are LM IIIB destruction deposits in some parts of the site). These uppermost levels are the most disturbed ones, making their close dating or characterisation very difficult (Cunningham in press; Fotou 1993: 21–101; MacGillivray 1997; Tsipopoulou 1997b). Notwithstanding this fact, their character may also reflect a kind of internal organisation at these settlements different from that of the preceding LM I–II period. Such deposits have generally been too little studied, often in the interests of accessing the LM I remains beneath them. At sites like Chania, Kommos, and Malia (Quartier Nu), excavation has produced good LM IIIA-B evidence covering a sizeable contiguous area, with occupation continuing from LM I (Driessen and Farnoux 1994; Farnoux 1997a, 1997b; Hallager and Hallager 2003; Shaw 2006; Shaw and Shaw 1997; Shaw et al. 2006a). In some cases individual buildings seem to retain a very similar, though adapted, plan between the LM I and LM III periods – as at Chania, Palaikastro, and Plati. However, major new building projects also take place at sizeable LM III settlements – as seen at Quartier Nu and in the construction of Gournia buildings Eh and He (Dawkins 1914; Fotou 1993: 82, 95–6). Although the exact sizes of such settlements during the LM IIIA-B period are unclear, much of the island's population must still have been concentrated there.

The exact political role of Knossos following a destruction at the end of the first part of LM IIIA is still much debated. Given the topography of Crete and the value of the LM III settlement distribution, it seems unlikely that the Knossos polity, despite its well-established preeminence in size and wealth, exercised direct control over all regions of the island, though it had strong cultural and exchange links with many, especially the south central zone and parts of the east (Banou and Rethemiotakis 1997; Smith 2005). The character of political relations between Knossos and the other regional population centres of the period is still little understood: the existence of tax/tribute collection by Knossos, well evidenced in the tablets, and possibly of reciprocal agreements on security financed in this way need not imply direct political control (Bennet 1990; Driessen 2001). In Bennet's view, 'for at least part of the time [from LM II–IIIB], the monumental building at Knossos continued to function as the center of an organization run by an elite for the exploitation and possible reciprocal benefit of a hierarchy of lesser sites and individuals: in Aegean terms, a "palace"' (Bennet 1985: 231). Bennet goes on to characterise the status of many other regional nucleations in this period as follows: 'These had probably stood at the head of their own territories ... and were incorporated as pre-existing organizational units by Knossos within its larger, inter-regional area of influence' (Bennet 1990: 209). But many uncertainties remain. The presence of Linear B texts at Chania and the west-Crete–originating fabrics of the inscribed LM III stirrup jars found on the Greek mainland have led some scholars to suggest that Chania, at least, also had a first-order status, especially well-marked or -defined in the period following the destruction at Knossos (Godart and Tzedakis 1997; Hallager 1988, 1999). Bennet once suggested that east Crete, where it is difficult to link any known LM II–III site directly with toponyms listed in the Knossos tablets, may have been under an entirely separate, autonomous system of political control at this time. Some other grounds for this assertion, such as the absence of the LM II pottery style in the eastern region, have now been removed; though there is no exact parallelism between central and eastern pottery sequences at this period, there are certainly strong connections (see Barnard et al. 2003: 99–113; Bennet 1985: 243–4, 1987a; MacGillivray 1997; Manning 1999: 208–9). More recent viewpoints (still based predominantly on the tablet evidence) are that although Knossos directly controlled or exploited very sizeable territories in central Crete, along with a few other zones of particular productive interest, it never established a hold over the whole island (Driessen 2001). The harbours of Knossos (Poros-Katsambas), Chania, and Phaistos (Kommos) clearly functioned as major gateways, intensively involved in interregional exchange activity that helped support Knossos as well as other major settlement units (Alexiou 1955; Catling et al. 1980: 92–3; Cline 1999; Evans 1928: 229–53; Hallager 1988; Shaw et al. 2006b; Watrous 1992, 1993: 87–8).

Looking beyond the ports, the largest centres, and the sizeable regional towns, a picture is gradually emerging, especially from recent surveys, of a fairly developed range of small settlements (a sample group in west Crete is shown on Figure 2). A major problem here is the differentiation of LM I from LM III surface material, and in fact many such sites may have continued in use between the two periods (Hayden et al. 1992: 334; Watrous et al. 1993: 228). Sites of this type include small complexes at Chalinomouri, Chrysokamino, and several locations within the west Siteia mountains (Betancourt 2003; Hayden 1997; Soles 2003a; Soles et al. 2003). The very broad chronological designation 'LM III-EIA' used in the Vrokastro survey record suggests a number of small sites in the valleys south of Vrokastro through this period (Hayden 1997: 201, 2004: 123–37). One such site, at Kavousanidas, is identified as a probable farmstead (Hayden 2004: 144, 156). A similar pattern of sites appears around Kavousi, apparently serving agriculture in the low-lying plain of the north Ierapetra isthmus (Haggis 2005: 81), though a lighter settlement scatter is visible in the LM III than in the MM III-LM IB period). Near Praisos, a single building at Ayios Konstandinos used between LM IIIB and IIIC may well have had a farmstead function (Whitley et al. 1999: 235). In the Archanes area in central Crete, the fairly large LM IIIA-B sites at Vitsiles (c. 18,000sqm) and Archanes itself are surrounded by dispersed LM III individual buildings or hamlets in the landscape; dispersed burial patterns in the region may also point to dispersed settlement at this period (Sapouna-Sakellarakis 1990; Wallace 2002: 80–3). In the Mesara, a spread of small settlement outside the major settlements at Phaistos, Ayia Triada, and Kommos takes place from LM IIIA:2 onwards (Watrous et al. 1993: 228–9, 2004: 300–4). Medium-sized (village) settlements for this period are also known from survey and excavation, for example, at Chondros Kefali and Arvi Kamini in south central Crete (c. 3,000–5,000 sq m) and there are larger ones (c. 30,000 sq m+) at Diaskari on the south coast, and Ayios Antonios in the Kavousi area (Davaras 1973; Haggis 2005; Hood et al. 1964: 91–2; Platon 1997). In the Ayios Vasilios valley survey area in west Crete, the largest LM IIIA-B settlement appears to be a village-type site at Koxare Aloni (c. 20,000sqm), which coexisted with contemporary farmsteads and smaller settlement groupings nearby (Moody pers comm; Moody et al. 1998b, 2000b).

Farming at such locations may have been linked into the wider economic system directly, through contacts with the largest, wealthiest centres, or indirectly – through attachments or obligations to people at regional centres. While groups at these dispersed villages and hamlets might have had their own strong local identities, the sites' distribution and character suggest they also made regular reference to supravening structures of authority and identity based at the largest settlements. The impression of the LM IIIA-B island, then, is one of complex settlement ranking and generally high levels of settlement interdependence. The system of landownership, if any, and the degree of control held by any individual group over land or produce are not clear either from archaeological evidence or from the text records. Elite families and individuals almost certainly moved between the major centres and the wider hinterland as a result of marriage and other kin links, and/or in connection with duties or privileges given to them as part of their role in the centralised economic system. Small-scale producers of the type characterised by Halstead as share-croppers (Halstead 1999a, 1999c, 2001) were probably quite mobile, having shared grazing or harvesting rights to fairly widely separated plots of land within the extensive agricultural system, and even changing residence seasonally in some cases. No across-the-board residential equation can thus be made between large regional settlements and elites, on one hand, and small producers and farmhouses/villages, on the other. It is important to bear this point in mind when considering the social implications of changing settlement patterns in the post-collapse period.

Each village or larger settlement seems to have had its own cemetery, with differential use of chamber and round tholos tombs apparently reflecting distinction in status, both out in the landscape and within cemeteries (Hallager and McGeorge 1992; Kallitsaki 1997; Kanta 1980; Papadopoulou 1997; Sakellarakis and Sakellarakis 1997: 152–268; Tsipopoulou and Vagnetti 1995). Burial groups at all levels seem focused around the small family or couple. Many cult activities remained based at extra-settlement locations, including the Psychro, Idaean, Liliano, and Skoteino caves; Jouktas; and Kato Simi. Watrous argues that the extra-settlement sanctuaries were attached to individual major polities through much of the Bronze Age: this seems especially likely by LM III, in such a centralised political and economic environment (Hiller 1982, 1997; Watrous 1996: 108–11). Throughout the Bronze Age there are traces of intra-settlement cult activities, in private houses and palatial buildings, and this pattern continues into the LBA. Specialised cult areas existed by LM IIIB within large settlements like Knossos (Shrine of the Double Axes), Gournia, and possibly Palaikastro by LM III (Cunningham 2005; Evans 1928: 123–40; Gesell 1985: 41–57), but their character and control structure are not clear. It seems there was considerable variability in practice, depending at least partly on the size, rank, and organisational complexity of the settlement.

PART TWO

'Positive' collapse and its effects, circa 1200–1000 BC: the restructuring of space and place

7 APPROACHES TO STUDYING COLLAPSE: EXPLANATION AND CHARACTERISATION

My aim in this section is to examine the nature of the Cretan collapse of circa 1200 BC in detail, while also bringing a comparative perspective to bear. In-depth regional study can develop our understanding of the real variability of collapse impacts where more superficial attempts to construct universal models of collapse processes fail (Cowgill 1988: 189). Archaeologists and historians are regularly attracted to the study of state collapse and its aftermath, partly because such periods represent potential 'fresh starts', in which radically new kinds of cultural and social relations may be formed: the relative abruptness of collapse offers a focused period in which to pinpoint the origins of social phenomena. Archaeologists working in a broadly processualist framework have been fascinated by how far the process of collapse is regular and predictable; whether it is 'hot-wired' into every human civilization; what features of a society may make its collapse likely or inevitable; and what factors may determine the rate and nature of post-collapse social regeneration (Cowgill 1988; Tainter 1990; Yoffee and Cowgill 1988). The Aegean LBA collapse offers considerable insights in this generalising perspective. At the same time, studying the local circumstances of collapse and the divergent trajectories of post-collapse social development within the Aegean region illuminates the subtle particularities in social structure that cause collapse to occur differently at different times and places.

Breakdown of the top levels of economic and social hierarchy during collapse may leave the social substructure intact or even raise it to new prominence. On the other hand, tensions and changes in this substructure can themselves be major contributors to collapse (Adams 1988; Cowgill 1988: 263–4; Flannery 1972; Small 1998; Tainter 1990: 198). Since much of the existing scholarship on the Aegean Late Bronze and Early Iron Ages has focused on elites and their activities, investigating the nature of collapse offers a valuable opportunity to redress the balance, by assessing the roles and motivations of other social actors in a period when elites suffered a radical, permanent loss of control and stability. In using the term 'collapse' (or rather 'collapses', since each region went through its own collapse process) when discussing this case, it is important to note that the political fragmentation, major cultural and spatial shifts, and economic breakdown that affected all levels of society did not represent a wholesale *civilisational* collapse (that is, the disappearance of the entire material culture package associated with complex societies (Adams 1988; Cowgill 1988: 256). Language, and many other aspects of knowledge and skill, remained firmly rooted in their precollapse predecessors. Apart from writing – which had had only a shallow foothold in Aegean LBA society – few technologies per se seem to have been completely lost. Rather, the elites controlling the centralised economies and political systems with their associated/supporting material culture frameworks (palaces, scripts, monumental tombs) disappeared, altered, or were reconstituted. During the post-collapse period, I shall show, certain elements of earlier elite culture rapidly became mythologised and reified, 'remembered' and celebrated as distinct from contemporary (EIA) social environments. This fact confirms the recognition by EIA societies of the very radical nature of the break. The 'event horizon' of collapse is marked in the archaeological record by destruction levels at major sites across the Aegean and east Mediterranean world, but the phenomenon is just as much about the radically changed nature of social and cultural life as about this physical destruction. The postdestruction communities never returned to what they had been and this fact seems to have been recognised by EIA communities.

Many other scholars have already tried to characterise and explain the Aegean collapse, in both regionalist and generalist perspectives. A rise in political and economic instability across the region circa 1200 BC is widely accepted: its causes and effects are variously argued to have included disruption or reorientation of trade, massive population shifts (connected to invasion, conflict, and refugeeism), and natural disasters, like earthquakes and floods (Deger-Jalkotzy 1994; Dickinson 2006: 24–55; Gitin et al. 1998; Lemos 2002: 191–3; Ward and Joukowsky 1992). Systems failure due to overextension in the trade sphere and/or a cycle of ever-declining returns on investment in bureaucracy and administration is another explanatory model. Tainter (1990: 193–217) encapsulates this well in his generalising treatment of collapse in ancient societies, though there are problems with his view of Aegean collapse as wholly embodied by and contained within events on the Greek mainland alone. Cause and effect are difficult to separate in any study of societal collapse, and especially when the evidence is mainly archaeological, making chronological resolution poor. The fact that the Aegean collapse seems to have stretched over a considerable period, from the last quarter of the thirteenth century through the first half of the twelfth, exacerbates this problem. Comparison of post-collapse cultural developments over the longer term and in various different parts of the east Mediterranean region helps throw more light on causes by showing that some areas made much smoother and earlier adjustments than others to the changed conditions: indeed, that they collapsed in a rather different way.

My view is that the most important factors behind the pattern of site abandonments/destructions and the folding of state structures at this period were human ones: natural events will never provide a simple causal 'key' to these complex developments. Even if we wish to see earthquakes, environmental change, mass migration, or disease as factors, it was the transformation of social and political systems that directed collapse in the immediate sense and that determined the precise course of collapse (Dickinson 2006; Moody 2005). State collapse contributed to a climate of both increased opportunity *and* increased insecurity in the Aegean. The rise of such a climate itself probably helped to promote and extend collapse, heightening its effects. The destabilisation of state systems seems partly to have derived from the actions of small private groups whose activities had previously been limited by state control, particularly in regard to production and exchange. The increased socioeconomic and physical mobility of these groups, as they built on and adapted the formerly broad-ranging contact and market networks of the Mycenaean world, promoted the rise of smaller-scale, more opportunistic trade; intense competition for new routes and contacts; growth in local and long-distance raiding; and some interest in resettlement overseas in connection with all these (Sherratt 1994, 1998). Together, these factors made coastal regions, in particular, insecure, yet often highly profitable, places to be in the immediate post-collapse period, with some groups adjusting to or benefiting from the changed circumstances more than others.

I will suggest below that it is possible to identify a spectrum of collapse patterns in the cultural record of this period, ranging between 'successful' adaptations – where societies in some regions averted the potentially most violent and destructive outcomes of collapsing systems through early and decisive cultural responses – and 'unsuccessful' ones – where attempts to hold on to formerly used systems (or alter them only slightly) failed to prevent such outcomes. 'Success', of course, is a highly relative term. Many regional communities that experienced particularly dramatic kinds of collapse circa 1200 BC (e.g., those of the Argolid, where several major destructions occurred in a small geographical area) often had relatively prosperous subsequent histories in the longer term, as discussed later in this chapter and in Part Four. On the other hand, *all* Aegean areas experienced significant social and cultural change in this period, and no single preexisting system can have remained totally intact, however smooth and successful its pattern of collapse. A recurring theme in my analysis of Crete will be the markedly well-planned and structured nature of collapse in the island. Tainter suggests that in regions like the LBA Aegean, containing many similar small states with parallel resource bases and power spheres, collapse may be a deliberate and planned strategy when complex systems fail, since peers will all be affected in the same way (Tainter 1990: 202–3). It is much less likely, he argues, to be favoured as a strategy among very large territorial states, when another major player can step into the great power vacuum left behind. I will show, however, that Crete's highly successful, planned type of collapse was unusual even in the Aegean context of relatively small states. Collapses in many other Aegean regions seem to have been less easy to structure to advantage: the impression is of inadequate compromise with, or even resistance to, collapse until the last moment.

8 SETTLEMENT PATTERN IN CRETE

The changing use of space: introduction

Since radical change in settlement is one of the most obvious and important correlates of social change circa 1200 BC in Crete and distinguishes the island markedly from mainland Greece and the Cyclades at the same period, I will start by discussing it in detail, before moving on to address other features of the record. After discussion of settlement pattern, I analyse changes in intra-settlement space (diachronically and regionally) to show how societies were literally 're-constructed' during and after collapse. For example, a strong reduction of emphasis on architectural differentiation after 1200 BC suggests some loss of social stratification. Crete is in the forefront of discussion, but again parallels and contrasts with other regions are highlighted. For example, I argue that the existence of some shared intra-settlement features (public temples, secular feasting buildings/spaces) between a number of Cretan sites founded circa 1200 BC indicates that stable community cores with parallel or linked social systems developed quickly across large regions of the island. In central Greece, the record suggests more fragmented, loosely structured social units after 1200 BC.

I then tie the analysis of settlement into a discussion of the wider cultural landscape, including open-air cult sites. In Crete, the combination of ritual reuse of existing noncult sites and the deliberate continuity of ritual practice in situ at established cult locations suggests that selective, self-aware perpetuation and adaptation of earlier cultural traditions was an important element in 'successful' collapse. The phenomenon is only partly paralleled on the mainland, again suggesting less cohesive community structures there.

Lastly, I examine changes in social systems through the analysis of mortuary space. Burial practice in Crete retained strong legacies from LBA social systems (a focus on the role of the small family group). Yet a new 'democratisation' of burial forms is also seen, particularly in the rise of a new type of small built tomb. While a partly similar phenomenon appears in central Greece, in the rise of standardized single burials for the majority of the burying population, family linkages are much less strongly represented there, combining with other aspects of mainland material culture to suggest that communities were increasingly concerned with representing and mobilising individual status, following a particularly deep-rooted kind of social breakdown.

Theorising settlement

Very long-term generalising/processual models of settlement have proved crude tools for the study of ancient Crete, with its rich and complex settlement record. They often give too little consideration to the complexity of relationships between social structure and settlement, or to variability in settlement type, at any one period (Cherry et al. 1991: 49). For example, some scholars have identified a tendency towards nucleation and primate settlement patterns in Crete at times when either external dominance or the internal hegemony of a single authority has been strong (LM III, Roman, Venetian). In an essentially bipolar model, this is contrasted with a favouring of, or 'reversion' to, dispersal in conditions of autonomy, such as in MM-LM IA (Bennet 1990: 207; Moody 1992). Moody (1992) has additionally linked nucleated and primate settlement patterns to intra-island conflict, and settlement dispersal to peaceful conditions. Overall, however, most scholars also accept dispersal as having always been the most efficient mode of settlement for agricultural subsistence in the island's dissected landscape, noting the lack of any special natural resources encouraging the concentration of settlement in any particular region (Haggis 1993: 138–43; Moody 1992: 53). Such generalising models frequently gloss long periods, such as the LM III-EIA and Archaic-Hellenistic periods, as single settlement phases. In reality, as I shall show, there seem to have been a number of different imperatives operating at different points within these periods, reflected in multiple horizons of settlement change. Another common problem with such approaches is a failure to address the role of subtly different circumstances and reactions in producing the same broad 'type' of settlement pattern at various different periods. For example, Moody's attempt to model Cretan defensible settlements in terms of a similar reaction to seaborne threat occurring in several different periods (EIA, Byzantine, Venetian) has some convincing elements. But closer examination suggests that the superficially similar patterns had very different political and economic roots in each period, giving rise to different specific characteristics of settlement pattern, and very different courses of longer-term settlement development.

Some studies of prehistoric Crete still assume the priority of subsistence/economic factors in determining settlement location (e.g., Banou and Rethimiotakis 1997; Bintliff 1977a: 114; Godart 1972: 422; Godart and Tzedakis 1997: 155). There is no doubt that ancient Aegean settlement patterns *were* often closely tied into subsistence. But the fact that settlement in Crete moved around so much throughout the prehistoric and historical periods generally argues against the idea of any naturally demarcated or 'optimum' political or subsistence territories in the long term. Natural topography has often clearly helped to define territorial boundaries, yet LM palatial state units, Classical-Hellenistic city-states, Venetian administrative regions, and modern district boundaries have all varied significantly in their average size and their type of topographic definition (Bennet 1990: 200–11). The twelfth- to tenth-century settlement evidence suggests the absence of very large, formalised, and coherent political and economic territories in Crete, but I will put forward strong evidence to suggest that the inhabitants of individual settlements did identify with broader regional/topographical units in the course of their economic and political interactions. Following from this, I will show that the territories of the Classical Cretan poleis were as much, or more, connected with new political dynamics first starting to operate in the EIA as with adaptations to topography, subsistence constraints, or macroeconomic/political factors. At no time during the whole EIA-Classical period can Cretan settlement *ever* be seen simply to 'revert' to a decentralised template, as Bennet suggests occurred after the decline of external (Mycenaean) 'control' of the island at the end of LM IIIB (Bennet 1990: 202). Yet neither was there a 'blank canvas' for settlement or territory at any time during the EIA: all changes during and after the collapse horizon were strongly tied into relationships between community groupings and the landscape formed at that time.

The impressive body of research now available on EIA settlement in Crete offers opportunities for a more realistic, informative, and historically grounded theorisation of settlement than any of the above kinds of generalising model can provide. When Desborough wrote his synthesis on Dark Age Greece (1972a), about twenty Cretan settlements in total were known to have EIA occupation (Desborough 1964: 191). Five of these, all of them established in the changes of 1200 BC (Karfi, Kavousi Kastro and Vronda, Vrokastro, and Palaikastro Kastri), had substantial deposits of this period excavated – though most of these excavations, unfortunately, involved a low level of accuracy in recording. In the last twenty years, four additional settlements founded in the early EIA have been excavated, producing substantial deposits of the period (Thronos Kefala, Monastiraki Chalasmeno and Katalimata, Smari Profitis Elias) and two have been reexcavated at much higher standards (Kavousi Kastro and Vronda). Several other settlements with EIA deposits have been reexcavated or studied in more detail (Chania, Knossos, Phaistos, Vrokastro, Chamalevri, and Azoria among them). In addition, survey information is now available on the location, date, and approximate size of more than 120 settlements first used in the twelfth century and occupied for various spans of time within the EIA (Nowicki 2000).

The dominant strand of analysis so far has been a focus on the defensible qualities of many of these sites, with insecurity seen as a simple main mover behind settlement change. Another strand has comprised subsistence related perspectives on/explanations of the change. There remains, I think, a need to recognise that settlement represents the endpoint of complex foregoing processes of sociopolitical development, as well as reaction to immediate events, while the behaviour that settlement constrains and creates *itself* feeds back into and changes social structure and experience. Throughout this book I will argue that settlement was an important *creative* factor in long-term social and political change in EIA through Classical Crete, rather than simply reflecting or adapting to it (Barrett 1999: 255–7; Bintliff 1991: 1–3, 10–13; Hodder 1982b: 151; Knapp 1992: 8–13; Lane 1987; Shanks and Tilley 1987: 8–12, 72, 79–117).

The new settlement pattern from circa 1200 BC: the history of research

The concepts of 'inaccessibility', 'remoteness', and 'defensibility', regularly referred to in the literature as characterising sites established circa 1200 BC in Crete, require definition and historical contextualisation if we are properly to understand their role in influencing settlement choices, and recognise the experiential effects of the new pattern (Nowicki 2000: 14–15; see discussion between Mook and Warren in Hallager and Hallager 1997: 369). Study of the sites in their *current* social environment is revealing in this regard. Ethnographic research shows that people currently working and living in the vicinity of the sites have very different perceptions of them from people living in cities, including many archaeologists (Wallace 2005a: 67–8). The first group often treat the sites as part of their work environment, and thus as familiar territory rather than remote and isolated zones. Even so, due to the nature of modern farming and herding practice, even locals perceive many sites as arduous to reach on foot. Agriculture and shepherding do not currently involve regular long journeys on foot to steep hillslopes and high summits: where this is necessary, bulldozed roads now mostly provide access. The positioning of small chapels (infrequently visited) on many of the inaccessible peaks where LM IIIC settlements are located emphasises the way the latter are viewed as viewpoints and landmarks, rather than an intimate part of the working landscape. The above factors have encouraged some archaeologists to view the sites as 'extreme' residence locations. It is important to note, however, that contrasts between these sites and the settlement locations of the LM IIIA-B, traditional, and modern periods – in terms both of straight-line distance and of ecological setting – are often only marginal (Wallace 2002). Relative inaccessibility *from the immediately surrounding areas of landscape* is the main factor differentiating the new sites from their LM IIIA-B predecessors.

The general perception of the new sites as 'extreme' goes back a long way in the literature and has heavily affected historical interpretation. Sites of this type and date were already being observed and discussed by scholars in the early twentieth century, while the Minoan palaces were first being excavated. The early characterisation of the latter as centres of 'civilisation' undoubtedly heightened the perceived remoteness and drama of the EIA sites. Two important early excavations were carried out by Harriet Boyd, at a cluster of Iron Age sites and tombs around Kavousi, and by Edith Hall, at Vrokastro in the Ierapetra isthmus of east Crete (Boyd 1901; Hall 1914; Figures 5 and 6). Both sides were remarked on for their defensible and inaccessible characteristics and recognised to postdate the latest 'Minoan' period. Kastro (c. 700m asl) is a steep-sided rocky peak at the edge of the west Siteia mountains; Vrokastro is a cliff-surrounded hilltop (c. 313m asl) above a coastal promontory on the deep, sheltered Gulf of Mirabello, the most important bay in northeastern Crete. The Venetian borrowing, 'kastro', in both toponyms indicates long recognition by local inhabitants of the sites' defensible character, and the variants 'kastro', 'kastello', and 'kastri' have proven to be shared by many other settlements of the same type and date. Kavousi Kastro was interpreted by Boyd (1901: 130) using an early version of what I shall call the 'refuge model': '[given the fact that] the people of the Bronze Age preferred to dwell in the lowlands, while their ruder successors at the opening of the Iron Age retired to the mountains for security, we may expect to find Mycenaean and pre-Mycenaean remains in the Kavousi plain, and Geometric settlements on the heights above' ('Geometric' was used by Boyd to refer generically to EIA sites).

At around the same time, David Hogarth explored a defensible site at Zakros Ellinika, a rocky knoll located circa 160 metres above sea level in the Zakros Gorge, and Richard Bosanquet and colleagues the area around Palaikastro Kastri – a low coastal promontory with steep seaward cliffs in the far east of Crete (Figure 7). Both scholars gave their findings the same interpretative slant. Hogarth observed of Ellinika that 'hot, beset with flies and remote from the arable lands, [it] must have been chosen under pressure of great danger' (Hogarth 1901: 145). Bosanquet interpreted the desertion of the large low-lying coastal LBA site of Roussolakkos, just as short-term occupation on the nearby Kastri began, as follows: 'unwalled towns and villages on the coast were forsaken and the population withdrew to the hills, a handful of the old inhabitants lingered on the safer hill top. ... Palaikastro, like many other cities on the coast, was abandoned when Crete lost her control of the sea' (Bosanquet et al. 1903: 289).

These models were next built on in the 1930s by John Pendlebury, who investigated what is still the largest excavated site established in LM IIIC, Karfi, 1,100 metres above sea level in the Lasithi mountains (Pendlebury et al. 1938; Figure 8), and also undertook much wider-ranging explorations of the Cretan archaeological landscape. He noted: 'The map shows an extraordinary change after LM III. Most coastal sites, particularly in the South, have been abandoned. Few of the inland towns have survived. Their inhabitants have fled to mountain eyries' (Pendlebury 1939: 303). He referred to the new sites as 'castles of robber barons', where 'The one concern is inaccessibility' (Pendlebury 1939: 16). This interpretation slightly adapted earlier views of the reasons behind the settlement shift – piracy or other threat from outside the island – in positioning the sites' inhabitants themselves as aggressors. Pendlebury also used an ethnic model to explain the foundation of the Karfi site and its architecture, which I examine in more detail later. Ethnically centred explanations of settlement change at this period, often involving the notion of

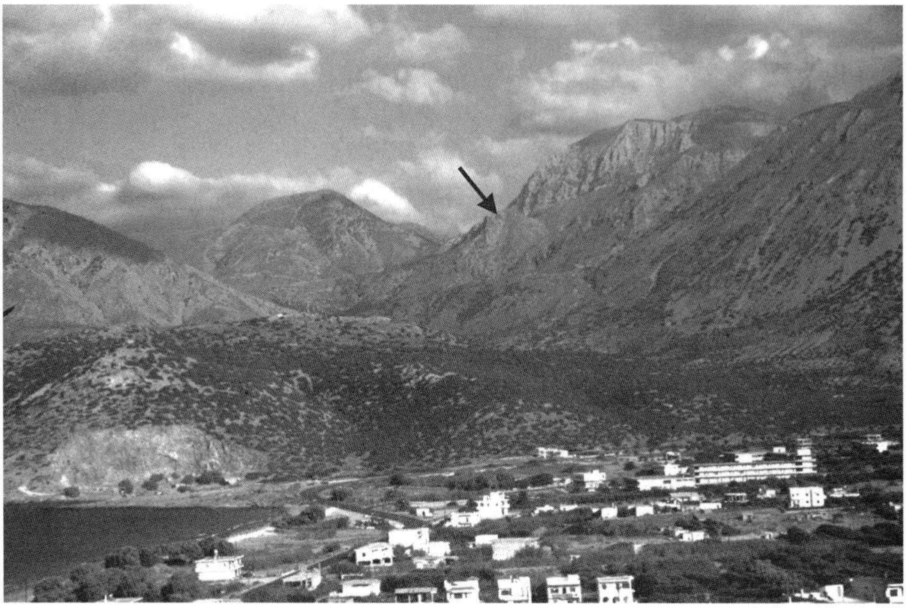

5. Kavousi Kastro from southwest: arrow indicates settlement area on summit. Image by the author.

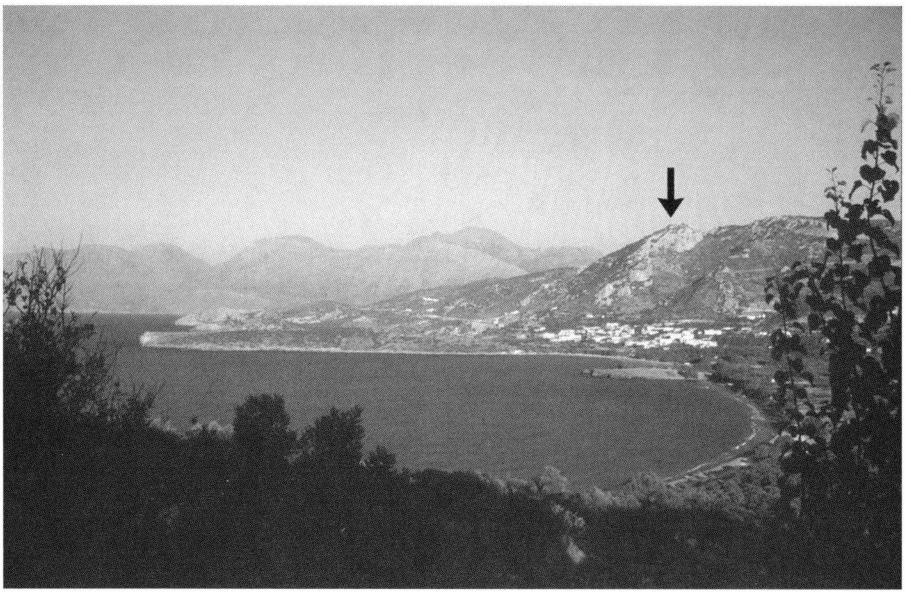

6. Vrokastro from west: arrow indicates settlement area on summit. Image by the author.

a 'Dorian' incursion into Crete during the Bronze to Iron Age transition, were hinted at in other interpretations of Crete's archaeological record produced during the postwar years (Demargne 1947; Willetts 1955; 1965: 16–36, 1977: 143–215; Desborough 1964: 192–4).

This general interpretative context was little challenged in the years before 1980. Though twelfth-century material was excavated at EIA sites of various different types (e.g., Hallager and Hallager 2000; Platakis 1970; Sackett et al. 1965; Warren 1983; Willetts 1969: 87), few scholars seemed interested in defining the settlement shift in more detail, framing new research questions

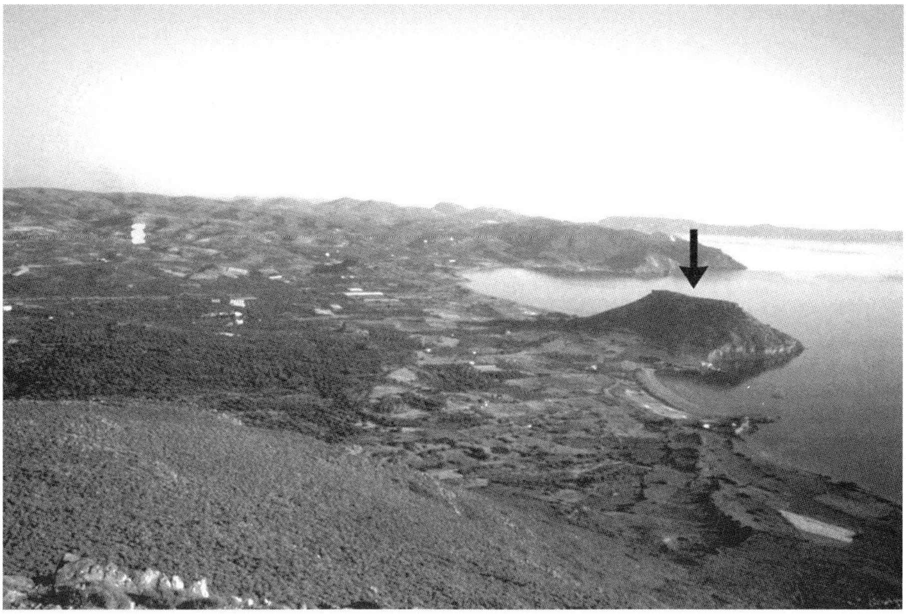

7. Palaikastro Kastri from southwest: arrow indicates settlement area on summit. Image by the author.

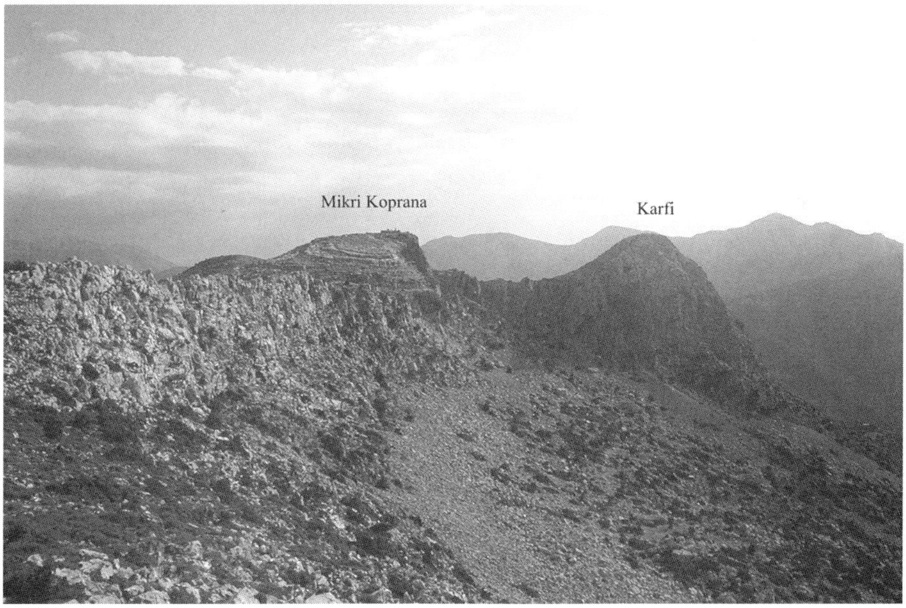

8. Karfi from north: excavated settlement remains occupy the saddle between the two summits of Karfi and Mikri Koprana. Photo courtesy K. Nowicki.

around it, or exploring its meaning in social and economic context (Desborough 1972a: 128; Kanta 1980: 325–6). From the 1980s, however, new stimuli to research arose from general changes in scholarly orientation, including the advent of intensive survey projects, a growing interest in how settlement pattern reflected Crete's political and economic organisation during the LM III period as known from the Linear B tablets, and a renewed concentration of American fieldwork interest in the Mirabello area (Day et al. 1986; Driessen and Farnoux 1997; Gesell et al. 1983, 1985, 1988, 1991, 1995; Haggis 2005; Hallager and Hallager, eds 1997a; Hayden et al. 1992; Moody 2004: 255–7; Watrous et al. 1993, 2004; Whitley et al. 1995, 1999). Kanta's gazetteer of the island in the LM III period was mainly based on tomb finds but spurred complementary interest in the analysis of settlement location and type (Kanta 1980). Reexamination of the Kavousi and Vrokastro sites, and survey in their vicinity, improved knowledge of EIA settlement ceramics, especially coarse wares, and thus accuracy in the dating of surface material for this period (Haggis 2005; Haggis and Mook 1993; Hayden 2003, 2004, 2005). New small-scale research excavations at EIA sites of defensible type (Thronos Kefala and Smari Profitis Elias) also took place (D'Agata 2002; Hatzi-Vallianou 1980, 2004; Hatzi-Vallianou and Evthimiou 2000; Hatzi-Vallianou and Parchapidis 1999; Prokopiou 1991, 1994, 1997; Rocchetti et al. 1994, 1995; Rocchetti 2000, 2006). The growth of survey, in particular, meant that information on EIA settlement patterns was better able to be contextualised in terms of the complex interplay of subsistence, macroeconomic, and sociopolitical factors at regional level. Nowicki's fieldwalking, started in the mid-1980s, has to date retrieved the largest amount of new surface data on EIA defensible sites (Nowicki 1987a, 1987b, 1988, 1990, 1991, 1992a, 1992b, 1993, 1994a, 1995a, 1995b, 1996, 2000, 2001, 2004a, 2004b, 2005; Rutkowski and Nowicki 1985, 1986, 1987, 1990). The interpretative viewpoint which Nowicki has adopted – of a single all-embracing political cause (i.e., threat of attack from outside the island) as lying behind a widespread move to defensible sites – is closely linked to his extensive-survey methodology, which is based on seeking out and documenting likely sites of this type, rather than recording them as just one element in a mass of multiperiod settlement data in any one region. His general interpretative scheme has followed and greatly developed the earlier 'refuge model'.

While Nowicki's perspective on the sites echoes and elaborates the refuge model in many respects, the recently increased quantity of data and the new variety of approaches to gathering and interpreting them have also produced new explanations for the causes and consequences of the settlement shift. The Kavousi researchers emphasised economic factors, citing the faunal and archaeobotanical record at their sites, which supported the notion of a broad-based subsistence regime (Day 1997; Haggis 1993). They recognised that, far from being remote and difficult to cultivate, as earlier scholars had suggested, the hinterlands of the new sites often incorporated significant water sources and cultivable land, and had been traditionally exploited for agriculture by small villages in a noncentralised economy. On this basis, it was proposed that collapse of the centralised political and economic structures of the LM IIIB period necessitated fundamental changes in subsistence modes. Haggis, for example, argued that after the decline of complex political and economic frameworks in LM IIIB, irrigation of the Kavousi plain was no longer able to be organised, greatly reducing the cultivation potential of this area. On this basis he explained the relocation of settlement to a zone that it was possible to farm productively with little investment of this type.

Though they did not completely ignore response to threat as a possible factor in settlement change, such explanations tended to play it down: 'The people of Kavousi were obviously reverting to a simpler economy, based on subsistence farming and without much exchange with larger centres, and they thus moved nearer to their resources and farther from the sea, which no longer offered the promise of exchange, but only danger' (Day 1997: 404); 'The sites are up high, but you have to remember that much of the settlement pattern in Crete throughout all periods was up into the mountains. Some of these sites may be seasonal, summer inhabitations. It has long been the practice to go up into the mountains in the summer. So, some sites may be seasonal, some may be defensible, but I am convinced that the primary reason for their existence is water. The good springs are up in the mountains. In the plains you do not have much available water' (Coulson in discussion in Hallager and Hallager, eds 1997a: 397). There are, however, significant differences between the types of 'economic' explanations offered by different scholars. While some have suggested changes in agricultural strategies at this time, others have argued that the new settlements were established as bases for seasonal herding. The mountainous locations of some sites are usually cited in support of this thesis, but the lack of any detailed reconstruction of the subsistence potential of the sites' environments or any in-depth consideration of the kinds of wider economic frameworks within which these communities operated is problematic (Hood and Andreadaki-Vlasaki in discussion in Hallager and Hallager 1997a: 399; Wallace 2003a for a critique; Watrous 1977: 2–3). Climate change has also recently been cited in connection with the shift, though without any full explanation of how this would favour the very specific topographical characteristics shared by the sites (e.g., Andreadaki-Vlasaki 1991a: 421; Moody 2005).

Krzysztof Nowicki – a main player in propagating and refining the refuge model – has consistently argued for insecurity as the main imperative to settlement change by pointing up striking similarities between sites of this type at an islandwide scale and attempting to situate the phenomenon in its broader historical and geographical context. However, he has devoted relatively little space to analysing settlement change in the context of contemporary socioeconomic systems (though see Nowicki 1999b, 2002). He reconstructs the settlement shift along the following lines (Nowicki 2000: 223–47; I gloss his four-part scheme): 1) a partial movement to dramatic 'refuge places' (perhaps used part-time) and to some full-time defensible settlements, in the late thirteenth/early twelfth century, during which some of the main LM IIIA-B settlements were still occupied, but a general depopulation of the island took place; 2) the widespread establishment of full, sizeable settlements of defensible character, and the final abandonment of most LM IIIA-B settlements, during the early to mid-twelfth century; 3) a slackening of threat, and possibly an influx of people from mainland Greece, by the late eleventh/early tenth century, linked to a widespread move down or away from defensible sites. Nowicki cites economic developments, along with the rise of conflict within the island, as subsidiary movers in the change. In the latter model, the view of settlement pattern is as predominantly determined either by degree of threat or by immigration from outside the island. The focus on defensible sites alone means that Nowicki's analysis, notwithstanding the significant volume and complexity of the data he has gathered, offers only a starting point in understanding settlement's relationship to society at this period.

To date, Donald Haggis has gone furthest in exploring the social and economic relations of the settlement shift and its long-term consequences (Haggis 1993, 1999, 2001). However, his analysis has mostly been restricted to the Kavousi area, often emphasising special local features of settlement pattern at the expense of those shared more generally across the island, and/or in the wider Aegean region. This has led to interpretative problems concerning, for example, changes in population levels around 1200 BC – a topic of keen interest to those who want to see this period as one of significant immigration to Crete. Haggis suggested increased population in the Kavousi area after 1200 BC. However, since his survey zone did not include any major LM IIIA-B settlement (though such settlements do exist in the wider region), the appearance of a number of village settlements in the area from the LM IIIC period, as opposed to the scattered farmhouses of LM IIIA-B, may simply mean that some specific land areas covered by the survey became more desirable to live in, for reasons including secure topography combined with adequate agricultural potential (Haggis 2005: 59–89). A very useful contribution by Haggis has been the characterisation of these new settlements as linked within stable cluster systems, the component parts of which spanned the whole EIA period (Haggis 1993: 159–60, 164–5). Haggis argued that clusters of settlements and tombs at Kavousi, Avgo, and Monastiraki represented extended kin groups living in a close cooperative association and drew parallels between these and other clusters in the West Siteia mountains. Perhaps because he has aimed to qualify the hitherto dominant 'refuge model', Haggis's work has barely discussed the significance of defensibility in EIA site patterning. Although his study region includes highly defensible sites, he has not considered these attributes at any length in relation to the motivations or consequences of the settlement shift. As recently as 2004, he summarised the new pattern as: 'discrete groups of sites centered on upland water supplies, arable land, and pasturage' (Haggis et al. 2004: 341).

The socioeconomic context of the defensible settlement phenomenon is increasingly coming under consideration from other scholars. Recent approaches include the evaluation of the new site locations as parts of a symbolic landscape, though it is not clear that symbolic considerations were a major driver behind the settlement shift (Haggis 1999; Vavouranakis 2000; Wallace 2003b, 2007; Whitley et al. 1999: 251). Other recent studies, attracted by the dramatic character of the settlement change, fail to properly address the complexity and breadth of the data, producing superficial and oversimplified accounts that add little to the debate. For example, Borgna has tried to challenge the role of defence in the new pattern by reference to a very small, unrepresentative sample of sites (Borgna 2003a). The arguments she presents include a reinterpretation of fortified settlements (unexcavated, but with sizes, buildings, and ceramics closely paralleling those of excavated sites) as 'enclosures' for farming. Borgna also suggests that coastal sites (though protected from access from the sea by steep cliffs, marked out as the most defensible spots in their whole surrounding landscapes, and possessing a typical range of settlement material) were salt-panning installations. There is no clear evidence to support either suggestion. Perna (2004) has recently made an argument for the site of Karfi as having a mainly cultic function, perhaps continuing from, or referring to, a cult established on the site in the Middle Bronze Age period. Unfortunately, her argument is entirely based on 'reassessing' the old excavation reports, which do not offer a full, quantified stratigraphic record for any single building at the site. Perna never systematically defines how we should categorise a cult find or building at this period or relates Karfi to its wider settlement context.

Some ethnically centred interpretations of the new settlement phenomenon also continue to be put forward. These tend to attribute the new sites to incomers to Crete and mostly focus on a few sites or regions, rather than patterns across the island as a whole, often picking out just a few unrepresentative elements for analysis (e.g., fortification walls, apsidal buildings) against a questionable background of assumptions about the ethnic significance of such elements (Karageorghis 2001; Prent 2005b: 110–11; 122–3; Warren 1983: 69–73, 83; Watrous and Hadzi-Vallianou 2004a: 310). My own main basic interpretative observations on the new settlement pattern are offered below (Wallace 2001, 2002, 2003a, 2004, 2007).

General characteristics of the new pattern and their significance

The vast majority of sites shown on Figure 9 are new establishments: of these, most have distinctively defensible topography. This can involve extreme local inaccessibility (with sites perched on top of rocky knolls, surrounded by cliffs; Figure 10) and/or a strategic location (commanding views over approaches from the sea or along major valleys; Hayden 1988: 19; Nowicki 1987a, 2000). There are few sites located over 1,000 metres above sea level, and most lie between 200 and 700 metres, with many of the higher examples located in the Lasithi mountains. Thus, the main zone occupied by new settlement is the foothills, rather than the true uplands. Many sites lie within half an hour's walk of the sea, and some are actually on the coast. There is a strong degree of overall contrast with LM IIIA-B settlement distribution, in terms of reduced proximity to the sea and to Crete's largest areas of prime arable land. Viewed at the island scale, the pattern is one of dispersal, though some regions contain very dense scatters of new settlement. The new

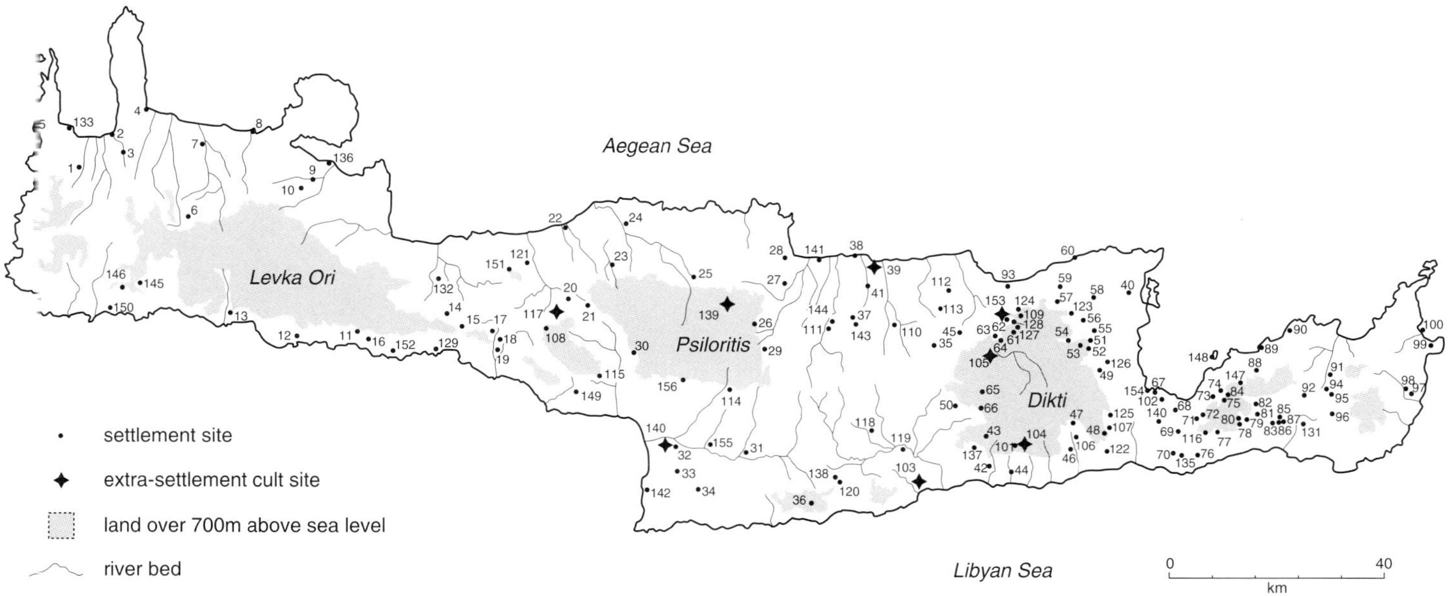

9. Map of twelfth- to eleventh-century sites in Crete, with legend. Very small sites found through intensive survey are not usually shown. Image by the author.

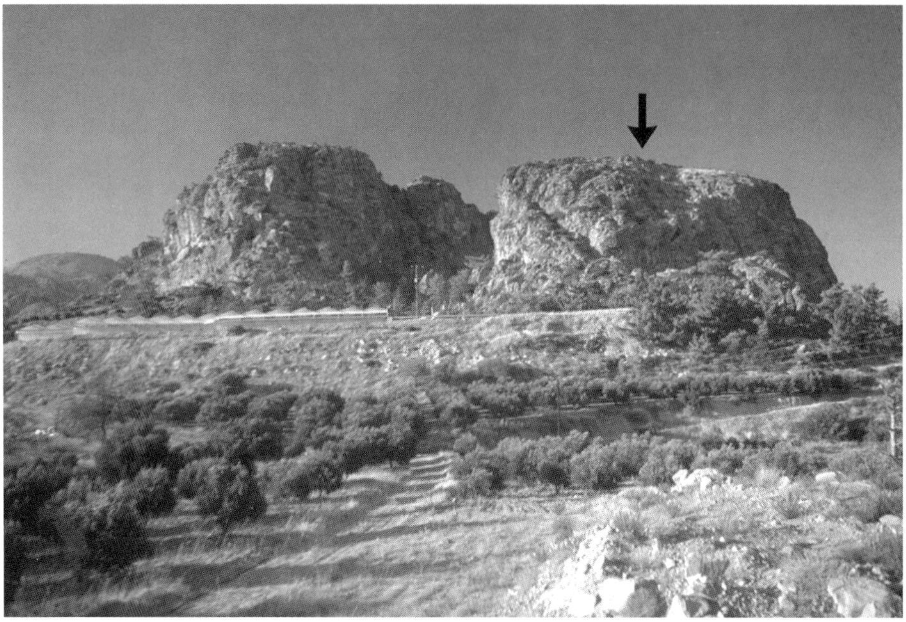

10. Elliniki Korifi, in the southeast Lasithi region, from south. It was necessary to climb the sheer cliff, using toeholds cut in the rock, to reach the settlement on the summit, indicated by an arrow. Photo courtesy K. Nowicki.

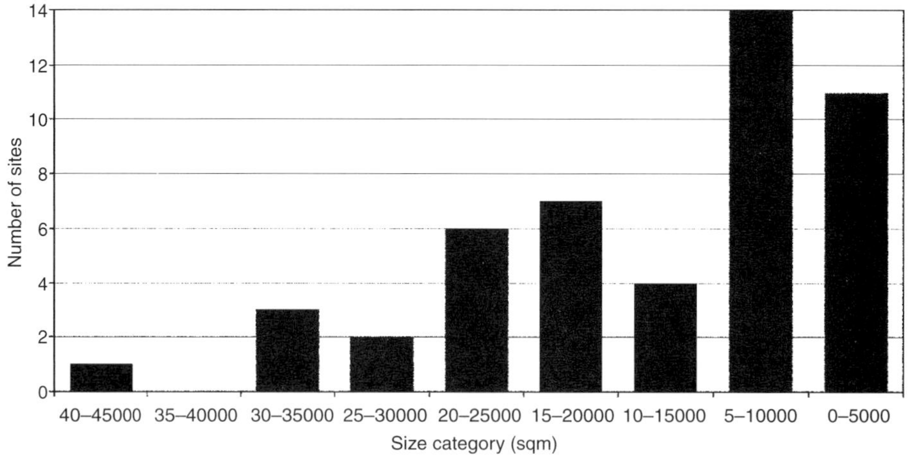

11. Graph of site sizes (for all sites where reliable estimates can be made) in twelfth- to eleventh-century Crete. Image by the author.

sites have a limited size range, with few indicators of the complex size hierarchy and central-place patterning seen in LM IIIA-B (Figure 11). The largest sites whose size can be assessed with any accuracy (i.e., those without later occupation) are three to four hectares in extent (though many of those which have later occupation obscuring their LMIIIC-SM remains may be larger) and the smallest well under 0.5 hectare; there is a full range of sizes between these. Based on the typical architectural layout at excavated sites, a maximum of about 1500 inhabitants seems able to be estimated for those in the larger category (Haggis 1993: 158; Nowicki 1990: 177–8; Wallace 2002: 83–95). Thus, generalisations such as the assertion that Cretan sites outside Knossos had only 'a few hundred people' badly need redressing (Garnsey and Morris 1989: 99).

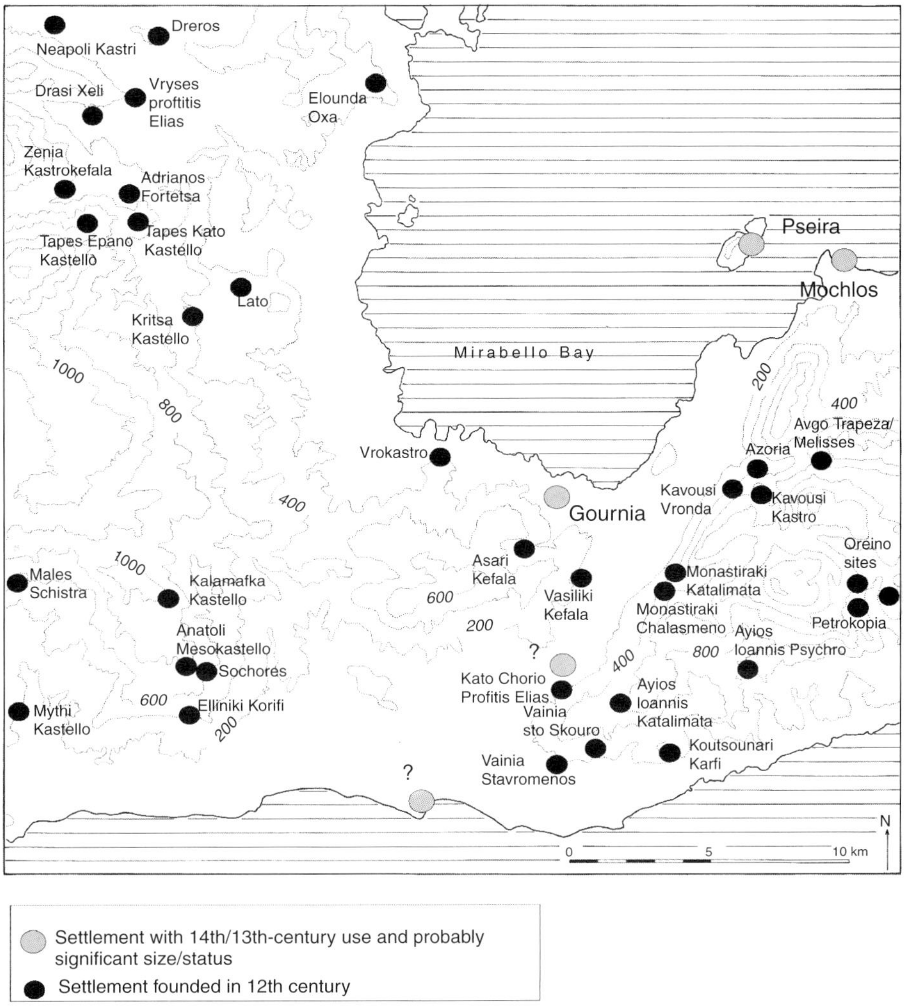

12. Map of Ierapetra isthmus and western Mirabello bay area, showing known settlement sites of twelfth- to eleventh-century date and some major settlements of the LM I-IIIB periods. Image by the author.

Clusters of two to three new sites within a radius of circa one kilometre of each other appear in a number of regions, but particularly the dissected landscapes of east Crete, where rock eminences above protected small valleys offered ideal bases for numerous separate small groups (Haggis 1993: 150–1; Figure 12). Chronological distinctions, and tentative functional ones, can sometimes be made between the components within a cluster. Of three settlements placed strategically above an inland-running valley route near Oreino, for example, one (Petrokopia) is of extremely small size (c. 200sqm) and commands the valley entrance. It may have been a watchpoint serving the two much larger settlements farther up the valley at Ellenika and Kastri (Nowicki 1990: 167–74, 2000: 73–81; Figure 13). A similar arrangement of sites guarding access to a major valley route appears around Orne and Melambes at the southern end of the Amari valley, which links the north coast of Crete with the important Mesara plain, and near Frati at the southern entrance to the Ayios Vasilios valley (Kanta and Stampolidis 2001; Nowicki 2005: 88–90; and see Plate 1 at the beginning of the text). Other sites, like the intrinsically inaccessible Adrianos Fortetsa and a related group in the northeast Lasithi region, are

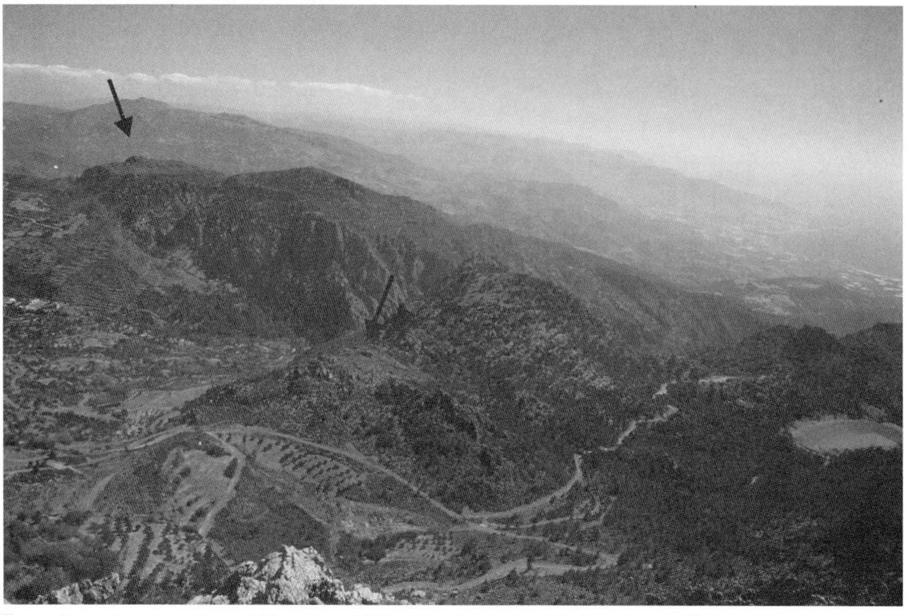

13. Oreino valley, showing sites of Kastri and Ellenika, both founded in the twelfth century. Photo courtesy K. Nowicki.

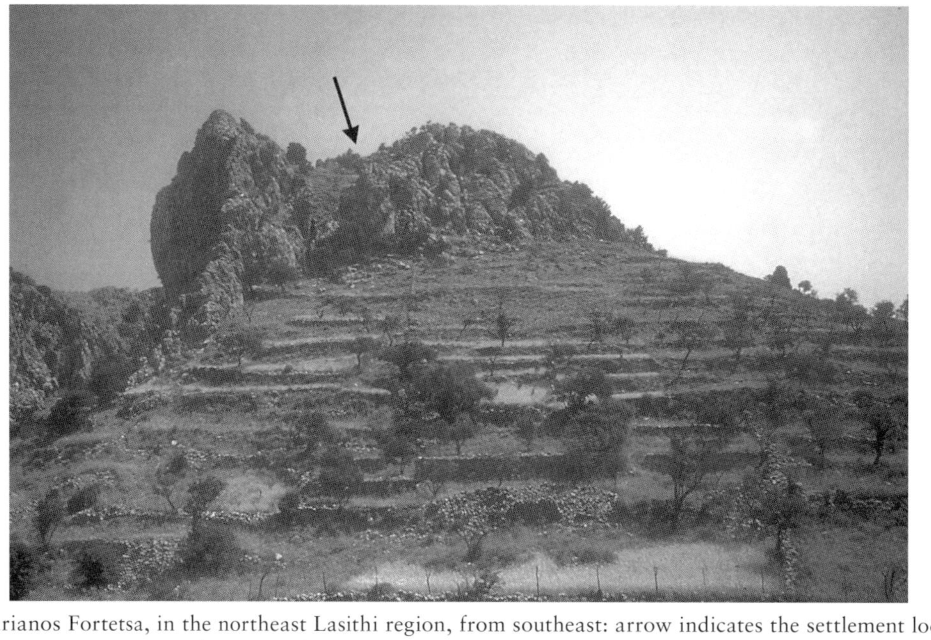

14. Adrianos Fortetsa, in the northeast Lasithi region, from southeast: arrow indicates the settlement location on the summit; occupation also covers the surrounding slopes. Image by the author.

strung out along valley routes in the interior of the island (Figure 14). Nowicki has argued that the regular appearance of such patterns indicates the existence of sophisticated collaborative networks of defence against seaborne attack, incorporating several elements – a few highly defensible coastal sites, settlements strategically positioned to guard valley routes, and a general concentration of settlement inland, with a new focus on naturally defensible areas like the

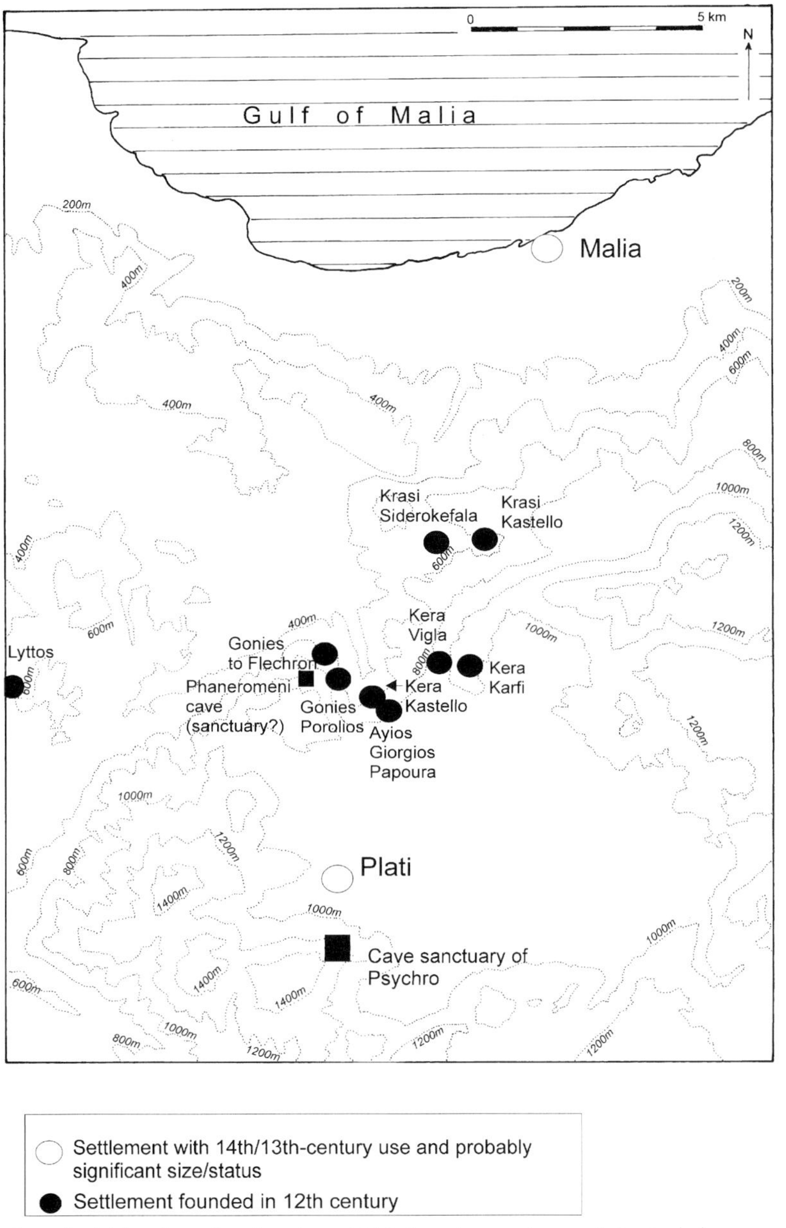

15. Map of northern Lasithi region, showing sites of EIA date clustered around the Ambelos pass, the main route into the Lasithi plain from the north. Image by the author.

Lasithi mountains, which safely enclose a large and fertile upland plain (Nowicki 1990: 178–80; Figure 15). For settlement clusters in highly dissected landscapes, like those at Monastiraki, Pefki, and Tapes, one extremely inaccessible, space-limited site often seems likely to have been used as a refuge place (perhaps on an occasional basis), with a larger, more accessible, full time settlement nearby (Coulson and Tsipopoulou 1994; Haggis and Nowicki 1993: 303, 334–6; Nowicki 1988: 194–5, 1994a, 1994b, 2000: 64–9, 90–7, 123–7, 2008; Tsipopoulou and Nowicki 2003; Wallace 2002: 77–80, 2003a). In more extensive, rolling areas of arable land, like the

Gonies and Potamoi valleys in northern Lasithi and the Ayios Vasilios valley in western Crete, a fairly dense network of small- to medium-sized settlement seems favoured rather than the cluster pattern (Moody et al. 1998b, 2000b; Nowicki 1995b, 2000: 109–17, 147–66).

The new settlements sometimes have fortification walls (Kritsa Kastello, Rogdia Kastrokefala, and Jouktas are good examples), but these are by no means a standard feature (Hayden 1988; Kanta and Stampolidis 2001; Nowicki 1992b). Nor does the presence of walls cross-relate predictably with site size, or cluster in certain regions. Local topography seems to play more of a role in determining it – walls sometimes appear only on the most accessible, vulnerable side of a site whose other characteristics fit the usual criteria of defensibility and access to an adequate subsistence hinterland. This is the case, for example, at the two very different sites of Kritsa Kastello, in the eastern Lasithi foothills, and Elias to Nisi, a small settlement on the coast below Vrokastro (Hayden 2001, 2005: 138–9; Nowicki 2000: 120–3; Wallace 2002: 75–7; Figures 16 and 17).

We see some continued use of large LM IIIA–B settlements located in prime arable and/or coastal hinterlands into the twelfth century, perhaps through reluctance to abandon residence in these highly productive areas, which must have contained significant infrastructure. Tylissos, Kastelli Pediada, Malia, and Chamalevri all fall into this group (Andreadaki-Vlasaki 1991b, 1996; Andreadaki-Vlasaki and Papadopoulou 2005; Driessen and Farnoux 1994: 62; Kanta 1980: 9–13, 50–2; Rethemiotakis 1987, 1988, 1997a). The lack of a full publication means it is not yet possible to draw any good picture of developments at the Archanes settlement after 1200 BC, but some occupation seems to continue there, even while the nearby elite cemetery of Phourni goes out of use for the first time in more than one thousand years, suggesting a major change in the political landscape of the area (Sakellarakis and Sakellarakis 1997: 463–6). Most of the sites *are* finally abandoned, presumably in favour of new defensible sites, by the end of the twelfth century, apparently because they were not sustainable in use under threat. We see a similar delay or abortive attempt at compromise in the case of Tachieri, near Mires in the western Mesara, to a low hill of nondefensible type when occupation established by LM IIIB seems to last only through a short part of the early LM IIIC period before the site is abandoned (Vasilakis 2004: 102). Again, the site is located in an area of very good-quality land likely to have had a highly developed and valuable physical infrastructure. This may explain the residents' desire to avoid drastic settlement change.

Another sign of concern to retain links into existing sociospatial systems during and after relocation is the continued use of some tombs within LM IIIA-B cemeteries well into the twelfth century, as at Kritsa, Milatos, and Mirsini, even after the populations originally using them had relocated to new settlements (Kanta 1980: 125–8, 163–73; Platon 1960a; Tsipopoulou and Little 2001; Xanthoudides 1921). In the above cases, the distance between the new and the old settlement area was small, so that former cemeteries lay in reasonable proximity to the new settlements. Nonetheless, by middle to late LM IIIC we see, all across the island, the establishment of *new* cemeteries adjacent to the newly established sites, suggesting a final breakdown of former local territorial links.

The degree to which relocation on such a vast scale was planned and organised within or between existing communities is a striking feature of the Cretan collapse. The siting of new settlements within clusters or defence networks suggests well-joined-up local decision making. The contemporaneous and broadly similar nature of the change across the whole island indicates a thoroughly well-negotiated, coherent set of actions at an interregional level. Overall, then, the Cretan settlement shift seems to represent an exceptionally controlled and deliberate response to the unstable and threatening circumstances of the late thirteenth-century Aegean. Its success is marked by the adequate time allowed for the adjustment (indicated by the extended timescale of relocation) and by the apparent avoidance of destruction at all but a few existing sites (discussed below).

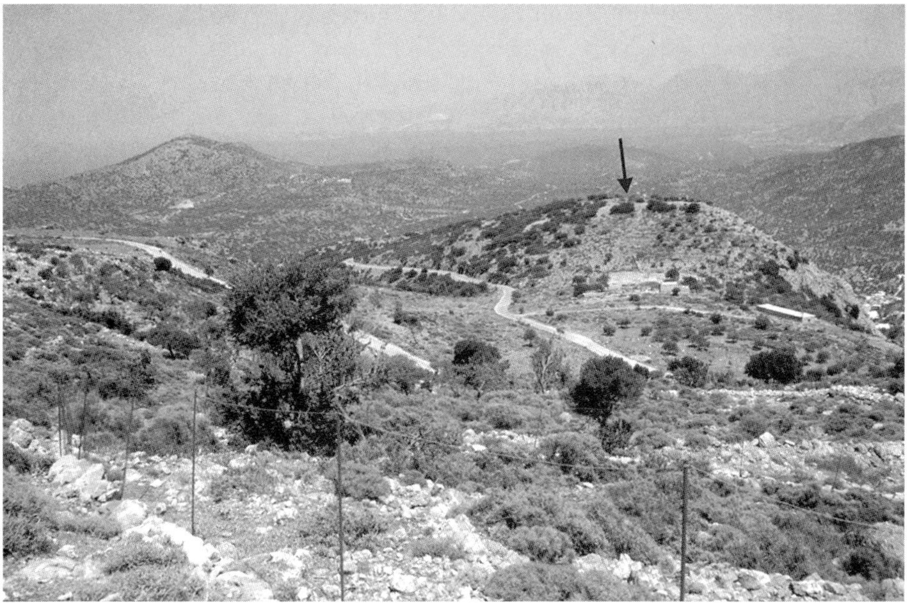

16. Kritsa Kastello from west, showing fortification wall. Image by the author.

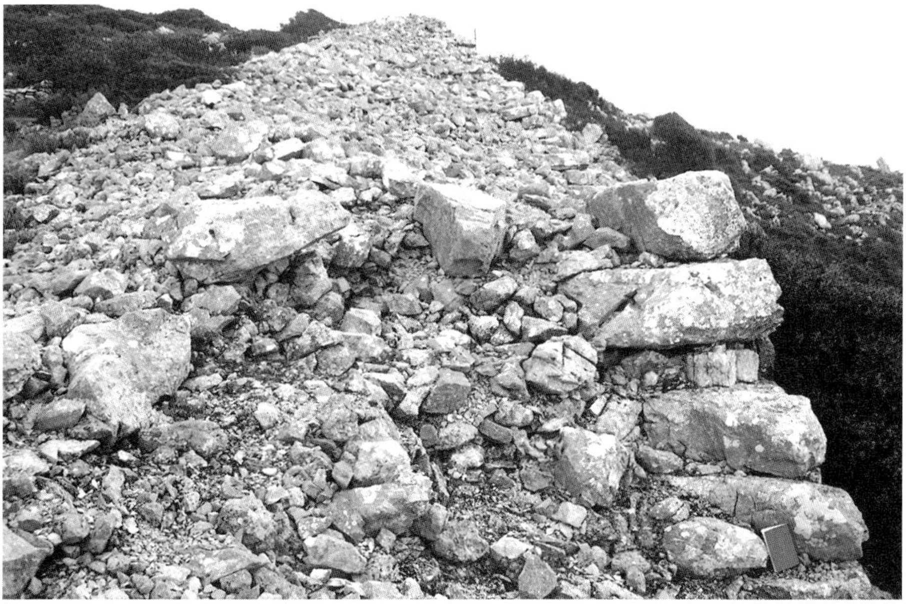

17. Fortification wall at Jouktas, from east. Exercise book at bottom right supplies scale. Image by the author.

The upper size limit for new settlements, at three to four hectares, suggests there were boundaries on the practicability of defending larger groups, and on political and economic expansion, during and after the relocation period. The change from a pattern of large nucleated settlements, each dominating a regional territory containing many smaller villages or farms, to a more equally balanced one of small- to medium-sized villages, with a limited or absent hierarchy of function, must have had a major social impact. Community bonds, structures of political control/ subjugation, and the rights to exploitation of specific territories must have altered substantially

(Kanta 1980: 326). The variation in settlement size within every region, and across the island as a whole, does suggest complexity and possible inequality in intercommunity relationships, but there are no very large new settlements that seem deliberately placed to function as regional centres for a group of surrounding smaller neighbours. Site size and distribution patterns do not obviously relate to resource access or control; nor do they follow predictably from the LM IIIA-B distribution of settlement. Defensibility (whether by virtue of natural topography or artificial fortification) combined with adequate arable territory for self-sufficiency, seems to have been the overwhelming concern in choosing new sites and this must have deeply reoriented the political and economic outlook of their residents.

Continuing large low-lying settlements: short- and long-term developments

In a very few cases, use of major LBA sites continues throughout the LBA-EIA transition and well beyond. These cases include Knossos, Phaistos, and Chania, though the quality of evidence from each varies; the excavators of the Kastelli site at Chania, for example, find it difficult to argue for full continuity through the EIA in any single area of the settlement (Andreadaki-Vlasaki 1991a, 2004; Borgna 2003b: 317–54; Coldstream 2000a; Hallager and Hallager 1997: 48, 229, 2000; Hood and Smyth 1981: 11–13; Kanta 1980: 9–13, 38–43, 2001b: 18; Rocchetti 1970, 1974; Warren 1983; Watrous and Hadzi-Vallianou 2004a). This very restricted pattern of continuing occupation suggests that only the most important former centres (all located close to the coast and in large prime arable areas) were considered worth keeping in use. Their function as trade gateways (for the concept see Hodges 1982) was too valuable to give up, and/or they alone had populations large and prosperous enough to defend and maintain themselves without any long-term recourse to defensible topography.

Even so, the *way* in which these settlements continued in use after circa 1200 BC confirms the idea of a major disjuncture in social and political systems. New cemetery areas were founded at both Knossos and Phaistos in the late twelfth to eleventh centuries (Coldstream and Catling 1996; Rocchetti 1970, 1974; Savignoni 1904; Watrous and Hadzi-Vallianou 2004a: 310). From early in LM IIIC the Knossos settlement appears to have contracted into a relatively compact area to the west of the LBA palace and town (Coldstream 2000a; Coldstream and Hatzaki 2003; Hatzaki 2005; Figure 18) while at Phaistos the settlement area also seems smaller than previously (though given the lack of preserved excavation areas for this period at either site, there is no way of saying how far population size necessarily decreased: Borgna 2003b: 317–54; Cucuzza 1998; Watrous and Hadzi-Vallianou 2004a: 307–11). At Chania Kastelli, no absolute reduction in size between LM IIIB and IIIC seems to occur in the very limited settlement area so far investigated, but the nature of LM IIIC building reuse after a destruction in LM IIIB:2 seems patchy, and the whole excavated area seems to go out of use for some time after LM IIIC (Hallager and Hallager 2000).

Some population from the cluster of rich polities in north central Crete may have moved for only rather short periods to defensible sites nearby, such as the impressively fortified Jouktas and Kastrokefala, the latter located at the western end of the Bay of Iraklion (Kanta 2003a, 2003b; Nowicki 2000: 41–4; Platakis 1970; Figure 19). Kastrokefala is quite a sizeable settlement, apparently not just a refuge place for periodic use. By contrast, the small size of the fortified area at Jouktas and the lack of evidence for domestic architecture here favour the latter description. The presence of substantial fortifications even at sites probably intended for rather short-term use may reflect both the particularly high investment capability of groups originating from the island's former largest centres and the general lack of extremely defensible topography in the central region.

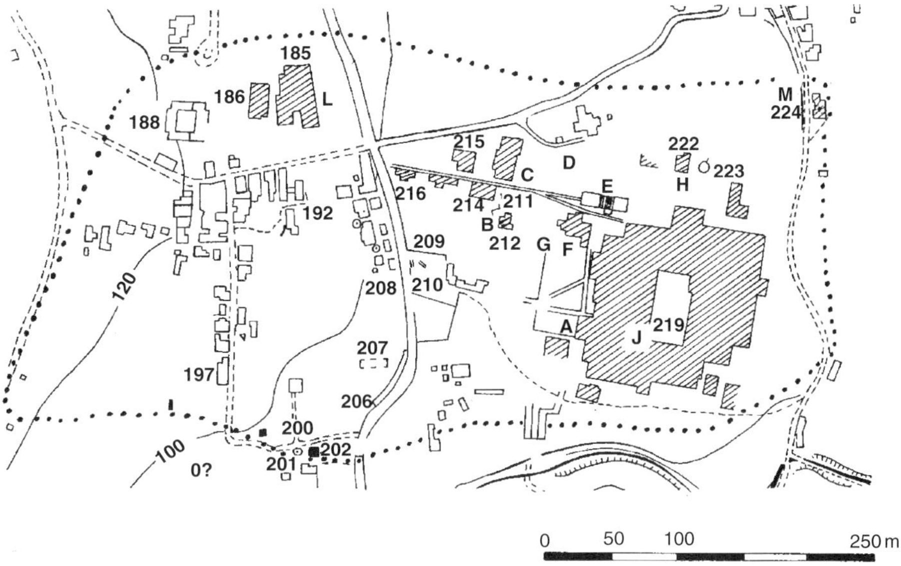

18. Approximate maximal size of Knossos settlement during the EIA (after Coldstream 2000a, Fig. 1). By permission of Nicola Coldstream.

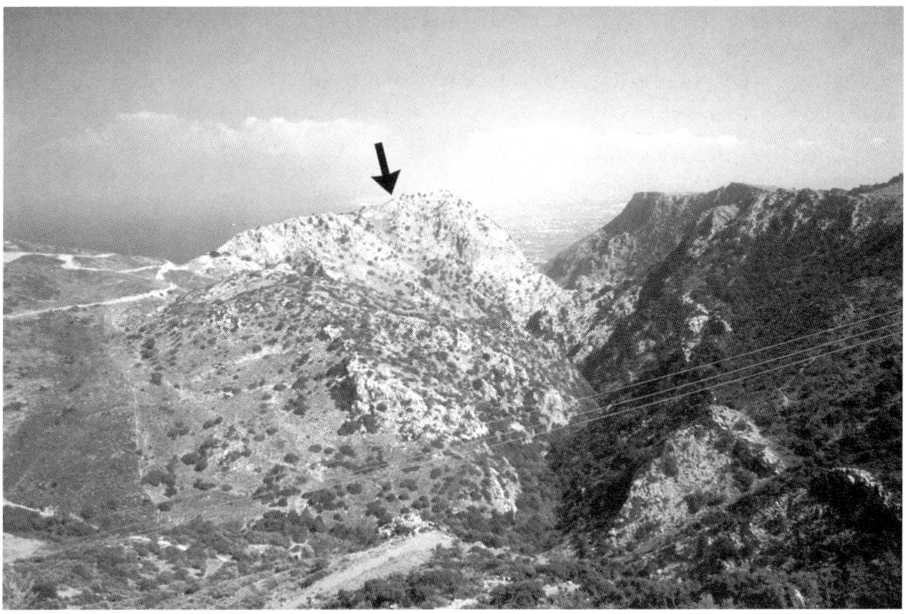

19. Kastrokefala, from west: arrow indicates settlement area on summit. Photo courtesy K. Nowicki.

Since the large continuing sites mentioned earlier occupied particularly poorly defended locations, they would have been vulnerable targets for attack in this difficult period. Apart from the possible periodic use of refuge sites, how did communities based at these settlements weather the storm? Chania Kastelli does show a destruction horizon at the LM IIIB-C transition. Unlike Chania (and most other major sites of the LBA Aegean), Knossos and Phaistos have not produced clear destruction layers dated to the end of LM IIIB. However, the greatly changed character of Knossos occupation soils between late LM IIIB and early IIIC, noted in the recent Little Palace excavations, could also suggest a uniform physical disturbance at this point (Hatzaki 2005: 86; Macdonald and Coldstream 1997: 202). In keeping these largest centres in use, their inhabitants may have been unable to avoid some of the threats affecting their counterparts on the mainland: the settlements surely provided tempting targets for raids and were too large and complex to make (or wish to make) full and effective use of the relocation strategy adopted in other parts of the island. At Phaistos, the most concentrated zone of occupation at this period seems likely to have been the 'Acropoli mediana' (Borgna 2003b: 317–54). Its attraction may well have lain in the fact that it forms the most defensible part of the existing Phaistos settlement area. A massive wall built here in the LM IIIA period may have been adapted for the community's protection in the twelfth century. Other interpretations for the use of the hill at this time – as a ritual or cult place only – exist, but they are not well supported by evidence. No proper stratigraphic or contextual recording has been carried out over any significant area of the summit.

In every case, the disturbance and/or reduction in population numbers at large LM IIIA-B settlements (whether hugely eminent sites like Knossos or smaller regional nuclei like Gournia or Palaikastro) must have affected large zones of political and economic operations around them. Fragmentation or contraction of the largest unit of regional settlement severely disrupted systems in which villages depended on the regional centres, and the latter on the main centres, for security and subsistence guarantees, while the major centres expected both these subsidiary levels to mobilise subsistence produce for them. In no case is there evidence for the direct transplantation of the entire populations of former settlement centres to single new defensible sites nearby, in a way that would have permitted smooth continuity in organisational structure. In some cases movement did apparently take place to sites very close to LM IIIA-B settlements – such as Asari Kefala (from Gournia), Prinias (from Flega), Mirsini Kastello (from the Mirsini tomb area/Chalinomouri), Profitis Elias Rokka/Korifi (from Vitsiles), Karfi (from Tzermiado Ayia Anna), Arvi Fortetsa (from Arvi Kamini), and Palaikastro Kastri (from Palaikastro Roussolakkos) (Nowicki 1996: 259–62, 1998: 43–4, 2000: 103–4, 106–7; Rizza and Rizzo 1984: 238; Soles 2003a; Soles et al. 2003; Wallace 2002: 80–3). However, there are usually major discrepancies between the size and relative regional importance of these pairs of settlements, and the new sites in question often form part of a group of very similar sites scattered through the local region, rather than standing alone.

At a broad regional level, there is continuity in population size in some regions. Central Crete seems to have retained a particularly high concentration of population, with numerous large new sites established there in the twelfth century (Figure 20). This was probably thanks to its large extents of very rich arable land and formerly large population. Because the region is lacking in highly defensible topography, the sheer size of its existing population may have been relied on for defence to a greater extent than elsewhere. By contrast, in other regions the population balance changed dramatically, in line with the new emphasis on defensible topography – as in the case of the Lasithi range, with its dense pattern of large sites from circa 1200 BC.

If we accept Bennet's hypothesis of a decentralised political structure in eastern Crete during LM IIIA-B, contrasting markedly with the central part of the island, we might expect this to affect the way in which collapse occurred in the eastern region, with less radical restructuring perhaps involved (Bennet 1987a). Yet the densely packed pattern of mostly small new settlements seen in LM IIIC east Crete, while indeed showing major differences from the central Cretan pattern, seems more linked to the region's lower overall population, dissected topography, and fragmented carrying capacity than its political structure. In fact, we see a similar or *greater* degree of settlement fragmentation and dispersal occurring here than in central Crete. The region had clearly contained its own set of nucleated regional centres and subcentres (such as Gournia, Mochlos, Petras, and Palaikastro) in LM IIIA-B: Just like their counterparts in the rest of the

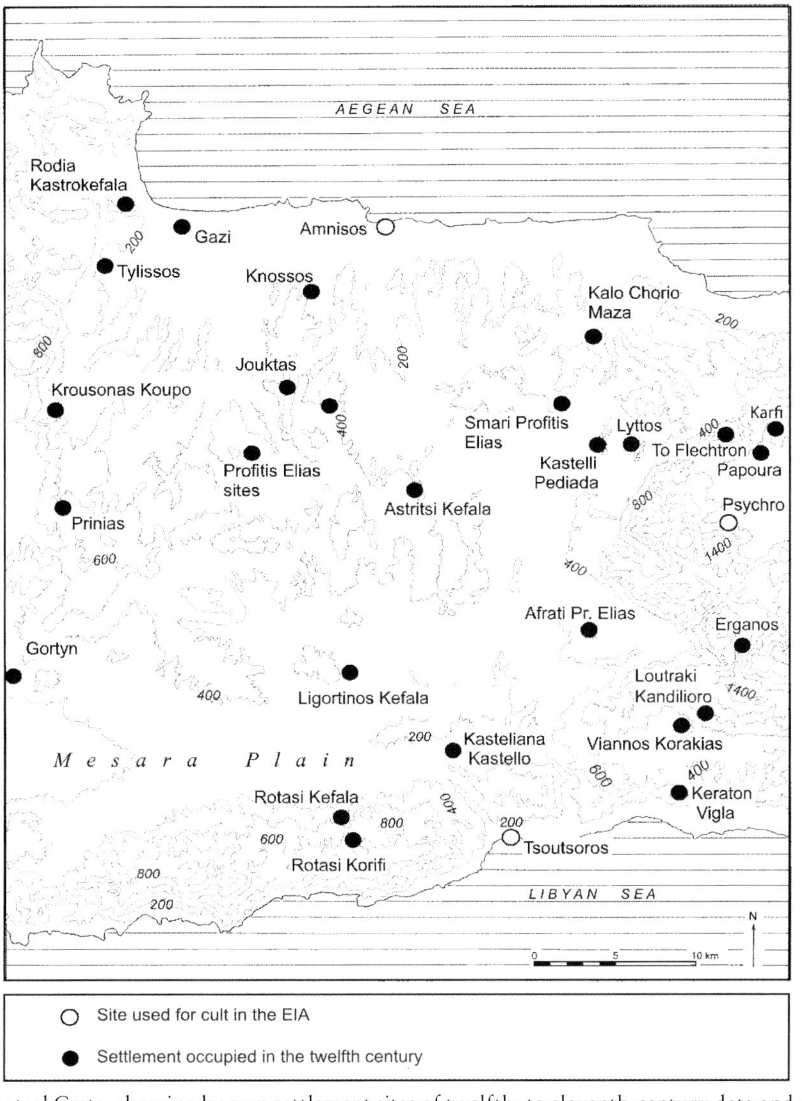

20. Map of central Crete, showing known settlement sites of twelfth- to eleventh-century date and cult sites with EIA use. Image by the author.

island, these were no longer sustainable. There is no sense that these eastern communities were able to adapt more easily to changing circumstances, or keep their boundaries more intact, than their central Cretan counterparts.

Very small rural sites

Another class of site that sometimes continued across the Bronze to Iron Age transition in Crete is that of very small rural 'satellites' – houses, villages, or hamlets, probably connected with farming, that had been scattered through the landscape in LM IIIA-B. Since these were not used as the main bases of settlement in the post-collapse period, it seems that they did not need to be defensible. However, the known examples with continued occupation from LM IIIA-B into the twelfth century do often lie in the vicinity of larger defensible sites, suggesting that some selection operated in the continued use of such sites, and their possible periodic reliance on these larger defensible neighbours as refuges. *New* sites of the same small type are also likely to have been founded at around 1200, as territorial boundaries changed and new infrastructure became needed, notwithstanding the overall tendency to nucleate into small defended communities. Given the inaccessibility of many new sites from the largest areas of easily cultivable land in the vicinity, fieldhouses for short-term intensive/seasonal agricultural use must also have existed. However, both these types of small site are difficult to identify and date accurately even in intensive surveys. In the Ayios Vasilios valley, sites at Angouseliana, Nea Atsipades Bali and perhaps Koxare Ambelos seem to represent a dispersed pattern of very small, nondefensible EIA settlements around the medium-sized villages of Frati Kefala and Atsipades Fonises (Moody pers comm; Moody et al. 1998b, 2000b; Wallace 2002: 67–9). A small site northeast of the main settlement area at Phaistos may have had the same role (Watrous and Hadzi-Vallianou 2004a: 309). A small nondefensible site at Manoulis' Metochi, in the area of Praisos, may have had a function as an agricultural satellite connected to the use of a large new defensible site at Kalamafki Kipia (Whitley et al. 1999: 246).

Moody has additionally noted examples of EIA sites consisting of single buildings or very small pottery scatters in mountainous areas of Crete, where extensive herding may have been an important part of the subsistence regime and required specialised temporary residences. These areas are the Sfakia Madares (historically, and currently, an extensive grazing zone) and the Kouroupas massif, both in west Crete (Moody pers comm).

9 SUBSISTENCE IN THE NEW SETTLEMENT ENVIRONMENT

On the balance of evidence (including the highly selective continuing use of some large LM IIIA-B settlements) it seems unlikely that subsistence concerns formed the main driver of the settlement shift (Wallace 2003a). Yet such an abrupt and widespread change in settlement must have had significant implications for economy, particularly in terms of scale and centralisation. Haggis suggested that the new settlement locations were selected for their 'optimal' economic environments, as part of a broader framework of change in subsistence structures (Haggis 1993). My own research, however, has indicated that far from being optimal, most new site locations actually represent a very tight compromise between defensible topography and access to hinterlands suitable for broad-based self-sufficient subsistence; finding adequate room for building on a hill summit, while still benefiting from its defensibility, was also a central consideration. As noted in Part One, faunal and plant data from the Kavousi sites and others confirm the use of broad-based subsistence regimes (Wallace 2002, 2003a). With the disappearance of settlement hierarchy, existing redistribution and exchange systems are likely to have broken down or at least to have altered substantially, pushing communities to focus more on self-sufficiency. Settlement size almost always fits within the carrying capacity of the immediate (c. one-hour) hinterland when an orientation to self-sufficiency is assumed, but the fit is often very tight (Wallace 2002; see Plates 2–4 at the beginning of the text).

Some scholars have assumed more dramatic changes in economy at this time, on the basis of the sites' present-day environment, but systematic and contextualised study often undermines these conclusions. Halbherr wrote in 1901 of the site of Erganos in south central Crete: 'The whole impression made by the ruins of Erganos and the remains of its necropolis is certainly that of ... a large village of shepherds and hunters; perhaps also the eyry of a bold population of brigands who may have harried the lower settlements around them' (Halbherr 1901a: 280; the view is echoed by Pendlebury 1939: 16). An increased reliance on shepherding as either the cause or the consequence of the settlement shift has also been suggested by more recent scholars (e.g., Watrous 1977; see Wallace 2003a for a full discussion). Many of the new settlements did have large extents of very steeply sloping, rocky land (currently used for herding) in their immediate vicinity. However, in most cases this type of land did not dominate the immediate hinterland; nor would its quality and distribution have prevented cultivation to self-sufficiency levels within a reasonable range (one to two hours) of the settlement. As in the nineteenth and early twentieth centuries, much of it may have been terraced (Triandaphyllidou-Baladié 1988: 172, 1992; Wallace 2002: 68–9). In the immediate post-collapse context, strategies of extreme economic specialisation, such as very large-scale herding, seem most unlikely to have been adopted, given the high risks and the degree of large-scale investment and coordination involved (Cherry 1988).

Bearing in mind the comments on herding capacity I made for LBA Crete in Part One, specialised herding could not have been relied on by a majority of the new settlements – yet as we have seen, *most* of Crete's population relocated. Factors including the broader historical context of collapse, clear concerns with defensibility at the majority of sites founded in the period, the comprehensive character of the settlement shift, and the nature of the palaeoeconomic record, all argue against the idea that settlement pattern became suddenly driven by a seasonal herding economy. The new settlements' relative distribution makes little sense with regard to any kind of herding-focused transhumant models: there is no even balance of the settlement pattern between low-lying and elevated, or prime arable and marginal, locations. This lack of a clearly dualised pattern also argues against new levels of subsistence reliance on piracy or brigandage, with 'robber barons', resident at the defensible sites, preying on prosperous low-lying agricultural settlements. Areas with very high concentrations of new settlement often relate to 'blocks' of naturally defensible topography, in an uneven pattern not suited to this kind of economic model (Nowicki 1987a: 217–19, 1990).

Assertions in previous scholarship that the altitude of some sites made them impossible to inhabit year-round, and that they must therefore have had a specialised, seasonal use, are misleading on several counts (Coldstream 2000b: 162; Watrous 1977). Only a small minority of the new sites are at altitudes high enough (above c. 1,000m) to give them something like their own microclimate, and these (such as Karfi at 1,100m asl) still had immediate hinterlands capable of sustaining broad-based subsistence regimes, as patterns of historical land use around them show. Heavy snowfall in winter at such altitudes, cited in some of these arguments, cannot be seen as a barrier to year-round residence, given the size and complexity of the Karfi settlement and its cemeteries (paralleled at other high-altitude sites such as Erganos Kefali and Tapes Kato Kastello): these suggest a level of social and economic investment not typical of seasonal or special-function sites.

Notwithstanding these points, the substantial herding sector of the LM IIIB economy does seem likely to have left some legacies to twelfth-century economics: animals were among the easiest kinds of asset to take to the new sites. However, in the environment of densely scattered small settlements that characterised many regions, and in a period when new territorial claims were still being fixed, control of the large land areas needed for extensive herding would be difficult to assure. Though we have evidence suggesting that significant levels of contact and collaboration developed quickly between the new settlements, it may often have been agreed during the period of their establishment, while totally new community groupings were adjusting to their new neighbours, to use fairly restricted areas close to each settlement for herding while old and new grazing rights were being reconciled. Individuals like the 'collectors' of the Linear B tablets (whom we may assume to have had their claims protected and supported by the palatial authorities) formerly seem to have had links to several different, scattered zones of grazing land. Maintaining these links after relocation would be difficult, as new residential groups with their own disparate herds and cultivation needs moved into some of these landscapes, significantly changing the balance of their exploitation. As population densities and spread changed, such individuals may often have had to compete more to retain their former spread of access to land or to concentrate their resources on fewer areas firmly under their control.

Though perhaps lessened by many aspects of the settlement upheaval and its associated social changes, economic inequalities must have persisted into life at the new sites. People recombining into the new residential groups must have arrived with unequal quantities of material assets. The differing character of the new hinterlands (some of which already possessed substantial subsistence infrastructure, others not) must also have affected the relative wealth of each community. Preexisting family or affinal connections between people now resident at separate settlements within a region are likely to have boosted prosperity in some settlements more than in others. At the same time, such a radical, large-scale, and deliberate reorganisation of space must de facto have created new sets of links within and between new residence groups. Subsistence and exchange were two important areas in which these links are likely to have been built – whether couched in terms of actual or fictive kinship, dual community membership, some exchange of subsistence products, joint participation in cult at extra-settlement sanctuaries, or (over time) the growth of economic and social obligations on the part of some groups or individuals to others. In many regions, the proximity of a number of new settlements possessing contrasting types of hinterland – for example, in the north Lasithi area, where some very high-altitude and steep sites, such as those at Tapes and Karfi, coexist with sites much closer to a better, more accessible arable hinterland – suggests that complementary exchanges, like those of cereals for olive oil, might have come to operate (Nowicki 1999b: 160–7; Wallace 2002: 77–80, 2006c: 162–3). A developing conception of proximal settlements as bound by some kind of regional community identity may have strengthened these links, and thereby promoted economic security. However, the limited maximum size and distinction of any settlement founded within the period 1200–1000 BC suggests limits on the potential to consolidate or expand specialised subsistence or surplus building.

Lastly, seaborne piracy is unlikely to have been a significant subsistence resource for the majority of the island's population, though Nowicki (1987a: 234, 1990: 179, 2001: 30) has used the term 'pirates' for the inhabitants of some IIIC sites. Dependence on piracy requires regular and large-scale shipping, tied in either to a established, secure convertible exchange system for large volumes of value goods or to a regular bulk trade in subsistence items. Neither seems clearly to apply to Crete in this period, as I shall show in Part Three. The relatively small number of new defensible sites located on the coasts, in conjunction with the large number of sites guarding inland routes or clustered in natural inland 'strongholds' like the Lasithi mountains, suggests a need to guard the coasts against attack by sea much more than an economy mainly geared toward piracy, though members of the new communities surely did take advantage of new opportunities for small-scale trading and raiding in some coastal zones of their own island and of the Aegean generally. The fact that small coastal sites seem *only* to have been able to survive between the twelfth and tenth centuries if attention was paid to their defensibility confirms the notion of generally dangerous seas – for example, Palaikastro Kastri went out of use by the mid-twelfth century probably because it was not secure enough, while the more defensible Vrokastro and Mirsini Kastello on the north coast of east Crete continued longer (Nowicki 2000: 103–4). Coastal attack and raiding were clearly regular occurrences across the Aegean in this disturbed period, and Cretans might well have been involved in it, but settlement pattern within the island, as well as other cultural evidence, suggests it cannot have had a dominant subsistence role for the population of the island as a whole. The few nondefensible sites located close to the coasts in this period, such as Chania, were probably kept in use because of their large size – giving their inhabitants a greater ability to defend themselves – and because of their very well-established, widely known role as exchange gateways (discussed in Part Three). As such, they must have been periodically exposed to raiding by Cretan groups, as well as those from other regions, in an environment of economic opportunism and in the absence of large-scale political authority.

10 SETTLEMENT CHANGE OUTSIDE CRETE: ISLANDS AND PENINSULAS

The earlier history of island settlement

As understanding of the scale and character of the defensible site phenomenon on Crete has grown, analogies have been drawn with similar sites established at roughly the same time in the coastal and insular Aegean and on Cyprus (Figure 21; Nowicki 2000: 249–50). A recent conference, with papers covering a number of different insular/coastal settlements at this period, concluded overwhelmingly that it was a prevalent need for defence that led to the establishment of so many such sites (Karageorghis and Morris 2001). The contemporaneity of the phenomenon over such a wide area, in a period known from other sources to have been characterised by serious political disturbance, is a strong supporting argument. Yet there are subtle differences in response between regions, and comparing the chronology and character of the sites in some detail illustrates the partly divergent nature of collapse processes.

The LBA settlement pattern on the Cycladic, Dodecanesian, and Saronic islands had its roots much earlier in the Bronze Age. It was characterised by large nucleated sites, almost always coastal – Grotta on Naxos, Paroikia on Paros, Phylakopi on Melos, Ayia Irini on Keos, Emborio on Chios, Ialysos on Rhodes, Xilokeratidi (Katapola) on Amorgos (Barber 1981: 12–13, 17, 1987: 224–46; Cherry et al. 1991: 217–35; Hood 1952: 579–623; Marangou 2002: 20–2; Mee 1982: 81–9; Renfrew 1982: 39–41). Their coastal orientation paralleled that of many important LBA settlements on Crete, reflecting island communities' high level of integration with large-scale maritime trade systems. Together with the small scale of the islands, and their limited fertile hinterlands, this factor explains why large settlements in inland plains and valleys were much rarer than in LBA Crete and the mainland, though small settlements were present in these zones.

For the early EIA, known settlements usually number only a few per island. This is partly due to the islands' small geographical scale but also reflects the fact that archaeological exploration has often been more limited here than on Crete. As in Crete, the movement to defensible sites during LH IIIB-C is not universal and in some ways is much more compromised than in Crete. Most new sites are coastal, and relatively few formerly large coastal settlements were completely abandoned, despite the fact that they usually lacked naturally defensible characteristics. Some of the largest former centres, such as Grotta, appear to stay in permanent use right through the period, notwithstanding a destruction event (Lambrinoudakis and Philaniotou-Hadjianastasiou 2001; Vlachopoulos 2003; Figure 22). The site acquired a fortification wall at precisely this time – a compromise solution perhaps best paralleled on Crete by the continuing occupation of

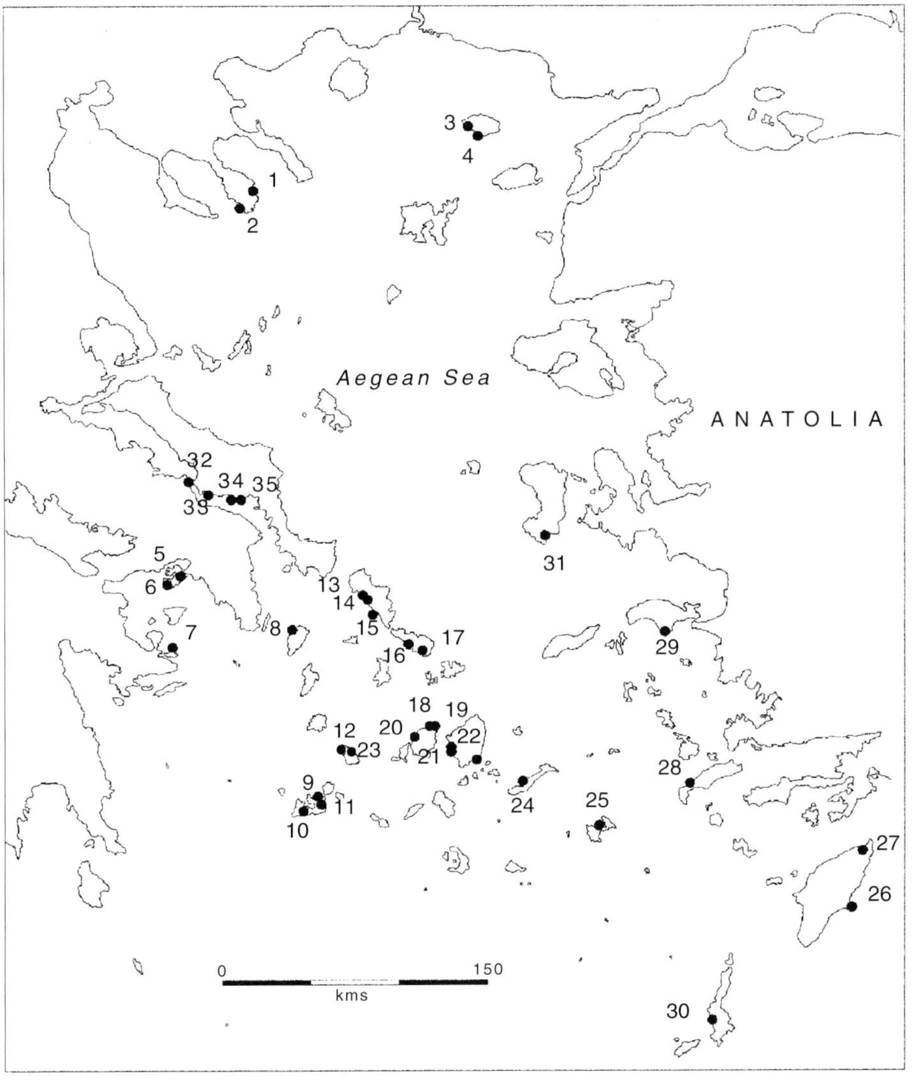

21. Map of Aegean island/peninsula sites of the EIA mentioned in the text. Legend: 1. Koukos Sykia, 2. Torone, 3. Vrychos, 4. Gla Krimniotissa, 5. Salamis, 6. Ginani Kastro, 7. Modi, 8. Ayia Irini, 9. Phylakopi, 10. Ayios Elias, 11. Ayios Spiridonas, 12. Ayios Andreas, 13. Ypsili, 14. Palaiopolis, 15. Zagora, 16. Xobourgo, 17. Vriokastro, 18. Oikonomos, 19. Donoussa, 20. Koukounaries, 21. Grotta, 22. Rizovigla, 23. Froudi tou Kalamitsiou, 24. Minoa, 25. Ayios Ioannis Kastri, 26. Lindos, 27. Ialysos, 28. Iraklio, 29. Samian Heraion, 30. Moulas, 31. Emborio sites, 32. Chalkis, 33. Lefkandi, 34. Eretria, 35. Amarynthos. Image by the author.

the walled Acropoli Mediana at the formerly large settlement of Phaistos. Walls were not enough to stave off destruction, or to ensure continued occupation, however: Phylakopi was soon abandoned, despite its wall.

New island sites of this period all belong to the inaccessible or fortified class, and many have coastal positions. They include Xobourgo on Tinos, Koukounaries on Paros, Ginani Kastro and Aspri Rachi on Salamis, Ayios Andreas and possibly Froudi tou Kalamitsiou on Sifnos, Rizokastelia on Naxos, Ayios Elias and Ayios Spiridonas on Melos, Moulas and Arkasa on Karpathos, Ayios Ioannis Kastri on Astypalea, Palaiopolis and Ypsili on Andros

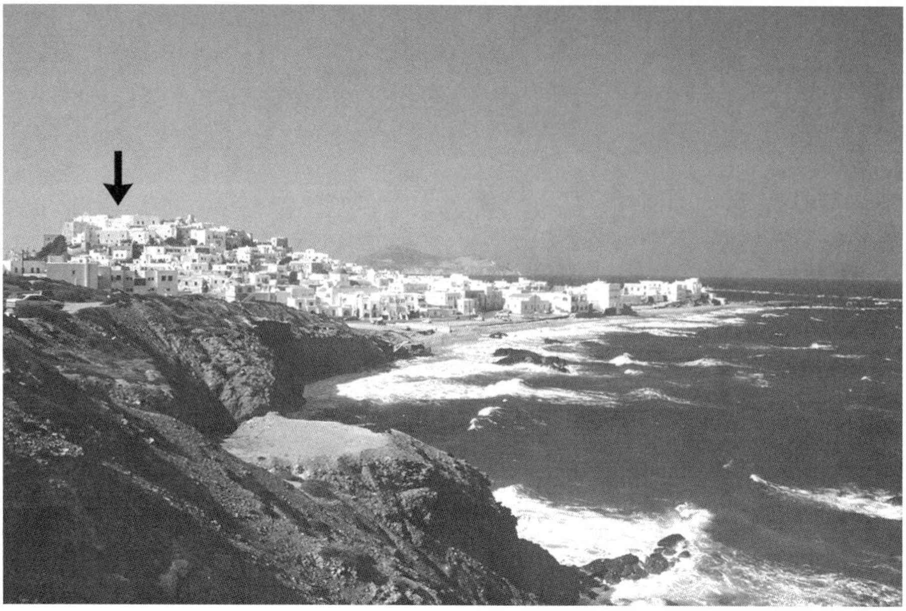

22. Grotta on Naxos, from north: arrow shows the main known location of LH IIIC settlement. Image by the author.

(Barber 1981: 17–20; Cherry 1982: 293; Kourou 2001, 2004; Marangou 2002; Nowicki 2004b: 97–100; Schilardi 1975, 1976, 1984, 1986, 1988; Televantou 2001, 2004: 421–3; Zapheiropoulou 2004; Figures 22–27). The pattern stretches up to the northern Aegean, with two deeply contrasting types of defensive site recently found on Samothraki at Vrychos and Gla Krimniotissa (Figures 28–32), and one on the island-like Chalkidiki peninsula at Koukos Sykia (Carington-Smith 2003; Carington-Smith and βοκοτοπουλου 1988, 1989, 1990, 1992; Cultraro 2004; Matsas 2004; Vokotopoulou 1987; Figures 33, 34). All these sites seem to have been founded in the early twelfth or the late thirteenth century, though the north Aegean sites are more difficult to date precisely. As in Crete, the lower-lying settlement zones from which population moved are often fairly easy to identify at a regional level. However, just as in Crete, there is rarely a clear one-to-one correspondence between old and new settlement zones on the islands, and there are sometimes substantial distances between the new locations and the old, as for example between Phylakopi and any known new defensible site on Melos. The small scale of the islands, however, meant there was rarely more than an hour's distance between any new inland site and the sea.

Reasons for the greater degree of continuity in settlement location on the small Aegean islands than on Crete include the fact that in the case of the islands proportionately greater benefits were attached to residence at former coastal centres. The lack of suitable topography on which to establish new sites that combined efficient defence and a maritime-centred resource base was another factor. This limited scale of adaptation had a high price. As the mainland-based political and economic systems into which they were tied were disrupted or destroyed, island societies seem to have been tipped more damagingly into the subsequent chaos than their Cretan counterparts. As on the mainland, a number of major thirteenth-century settlements in the islands have destruction levels dating in the twelfth century: some of the newly founded sites also experienced destruction (Deger-Jalkotzy 1998). Both internal unrest and attack by newly entrepreneurial groups – whether local or from farther afield – may have contributed to the disturbances.

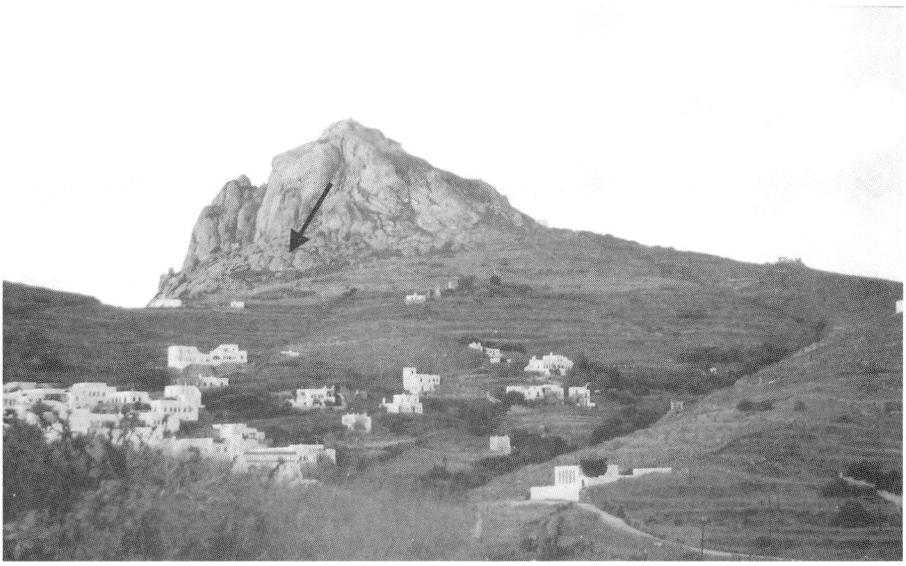

23. Summit of Xobourgo on Tinos, from southeast. LH IIIC settlement evidence has been excavated on the upper slopes immediately below the base of the cliff. Image by the author.

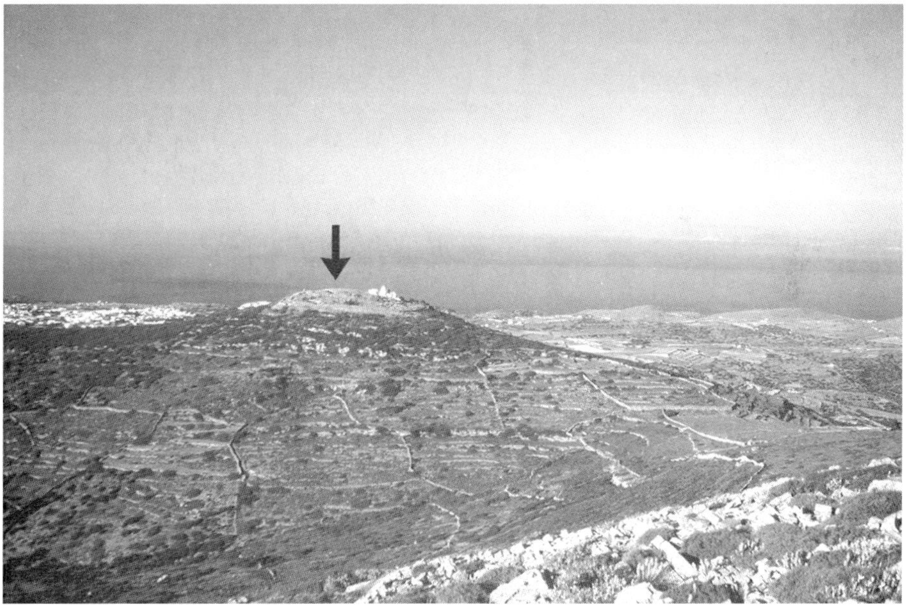

24. Ayios Andreas, Sifnos, from south: arrow indicates settlement area on summit. Image by the author.

Reactive movements to defensible sites, though they did occur, were not widespread, early, or organised enough to prevent catastrophe. Even so, the use of settlement relocation still seems more widespread on the islands than the mainland at this time. The strongly maritime economy and small geographical scale, in conjunction with small populations, produced especially high degrees of risk on the islands but also allowed more scope for a relatively large-scale defensive settlement shift there.

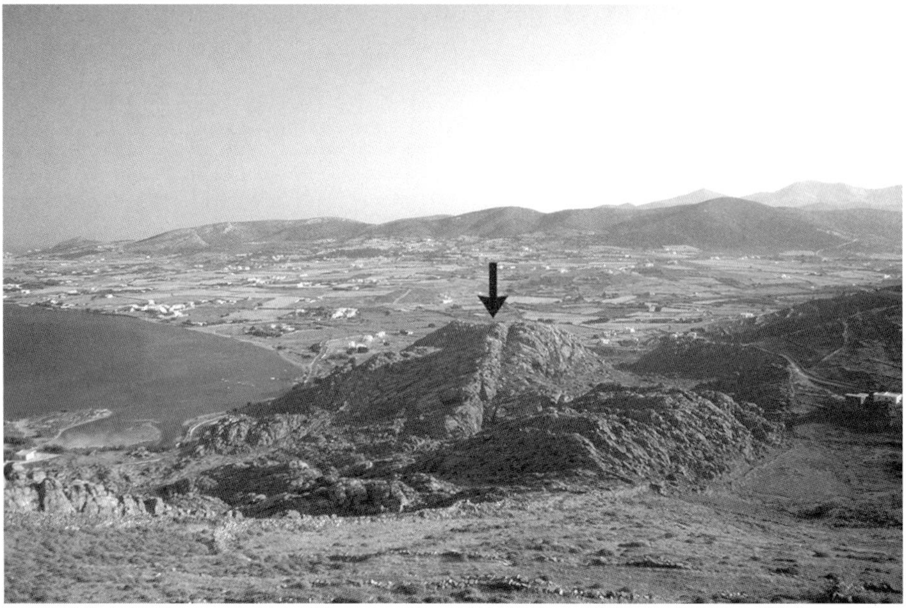

25. Koukounaries and the Panormos bay on Paros, from west: arrow indicates settlement area on hill summit. Image by the author.

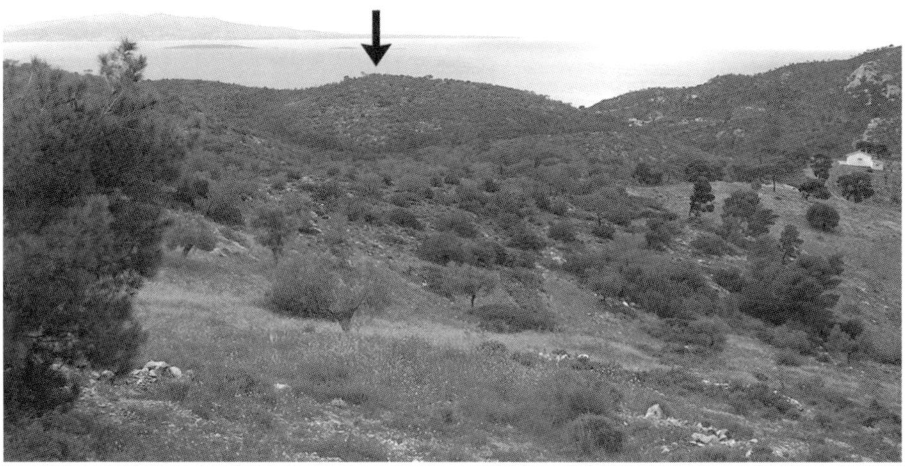

26. Ginani Kastro site, Salamis, from northeast: arrow indicates settlement area on summit. Image by the author.

Use of fortifications at island sites, and their significance

Many mainland polities strengthened their settlement centres through fortification during the latest LH IIIB period, and island groups were clearly making the same sorts of effort by the same date (Deger-Jalkotzy 1998; Iakovidis 1962, 1983). These measures, like their mainland counterparts, were only partially successful, as the number of site destructions shows. A high

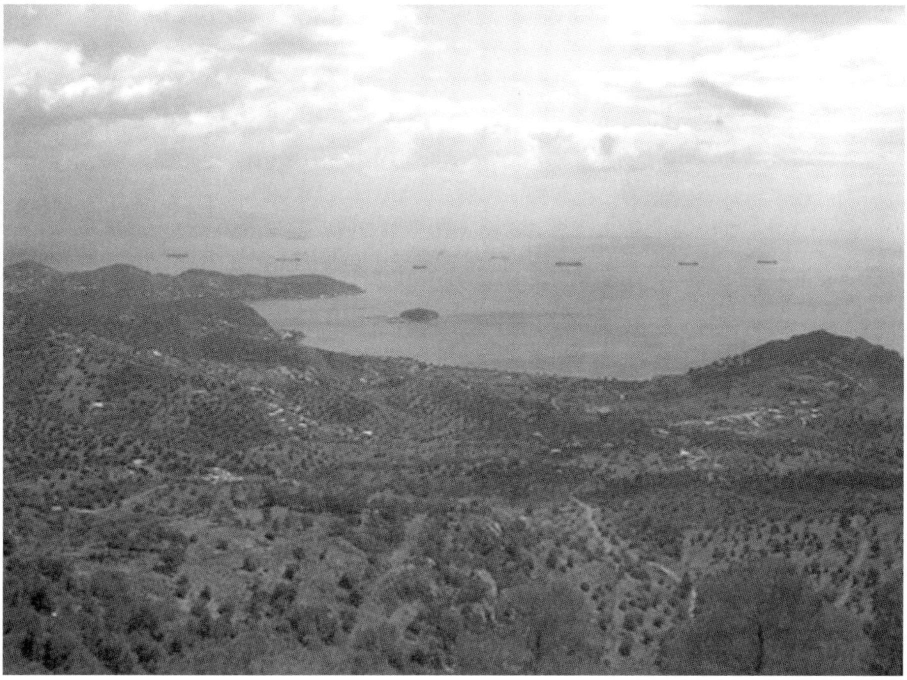

27. View north to the Greek mainland (from the Ginani Asprorachi site on Salamis) across an always-strategic shipping channel. Image by the author.

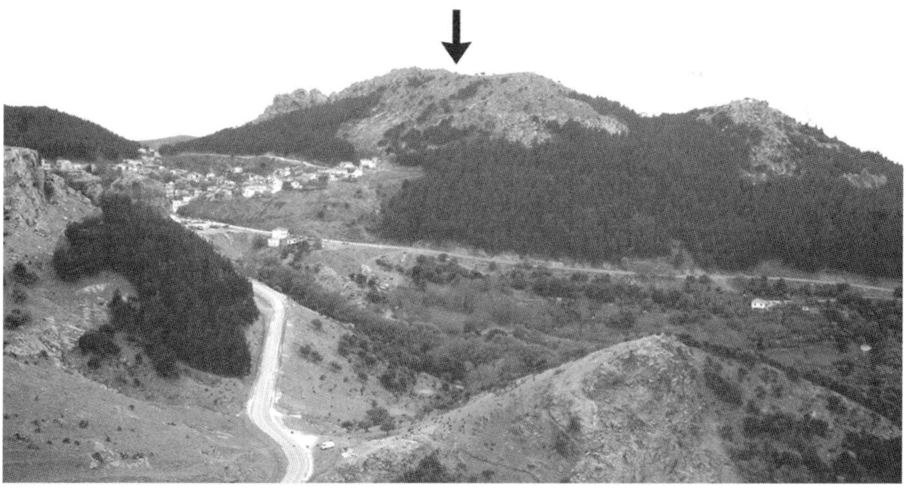

28. Vrychos site, Samothraki: arrow indicates settlement area on summit. Image by the author.

proportion of the *new* island sites of the twelfth century were also fortified – the Ginani sites on Salamis, Vrychos and Gla Krimniotissa on Samothraki, Koukounaries, and Ayios Andreas, for example. Observing this general pattern, some scholars have taken up the idea that fortified (as opposed to simply defensible) sites here represent emigré groups from the Mycenaean mainland, fleeing after destructions or disturbances in that area to settle in formerly 'peripheral' regions.

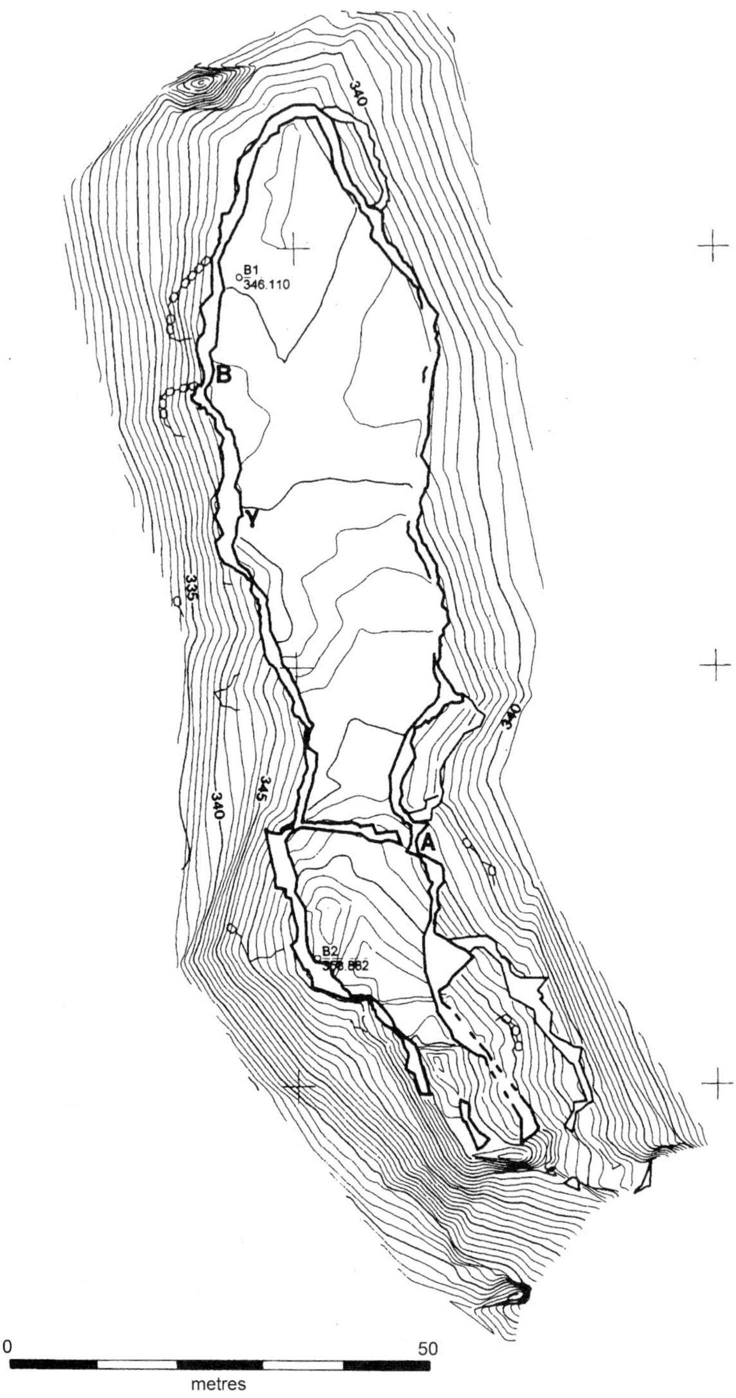

29. Plan of fortifications at Vrychos (after Matsas 2004, Fig. 9, p. 241). By permission of D. Matsas.

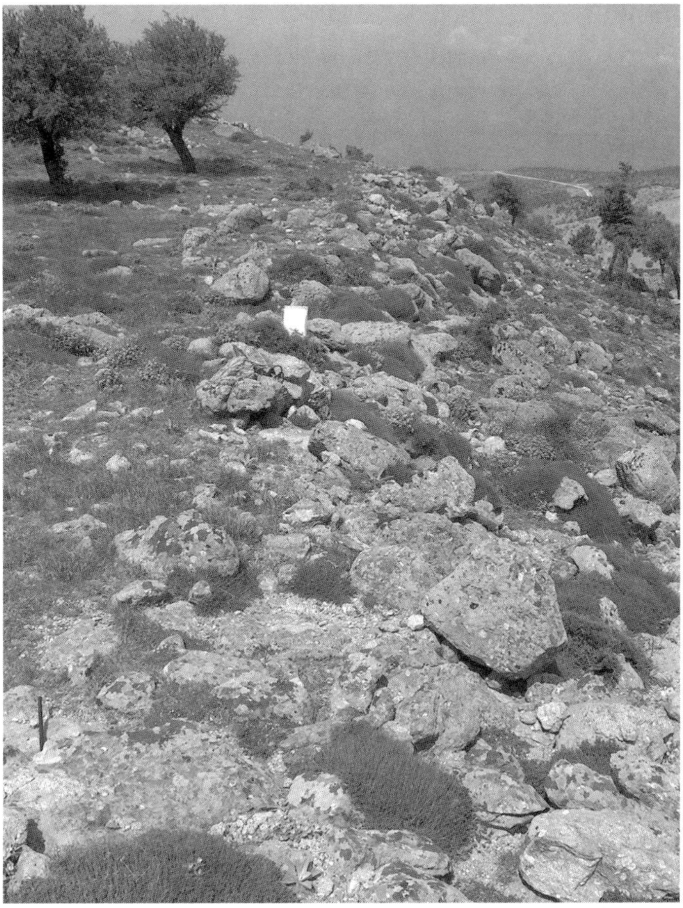

30. Fortification wall at Vrychos, south side, from west. An exercise book in the central part of the wall supplies the scale. Image by the author.

This blanket theory has been applied to fortified sites over a wide area, including Kastrokefala in Crete, Koukounaries on Paros, and Maa Palaiokastro and Pyla Kokkinokremos on Cyprus (Kanta 2001b; Karageorghis 1990b, 1998, 2001).

The basis of this idea seems to be that fortification technology needed mainland-based expertise. This is unconvincing, especially in the Cyclades, where there was an already established practice of fortifying major sites in LH IIIB (as in the case of Phylakopi). Since most of the islands were already strongly linked into the mainland cultural, social, and political sphere in the LH IIIA-B period, there seems little reason to regard the practice as newly intrusive there in the twelfth century. The regional history and context of settlement also need to be taken into account in investigating how far the appearance of fortifications is ethnically diagnostic: Crete's case highlights this. The very widespread phenomenon of movement to naturally defensible sites at this period in the island cannot be disregarded in paying attention to the few fortified examples of the same date – many of which, in any case, use fortification in a very limited and basic way to enhance natural defensibility: the same applies to cases like Koukos Sykia and Gla Krimniotissa. Such fortified sites show little similarity to the former Mycenaean citadels, with their very extensive, complex, and bulky defensive systems. Like their naturally defensible peers, the new fortified sites in Crete and the islands are of widely varying size

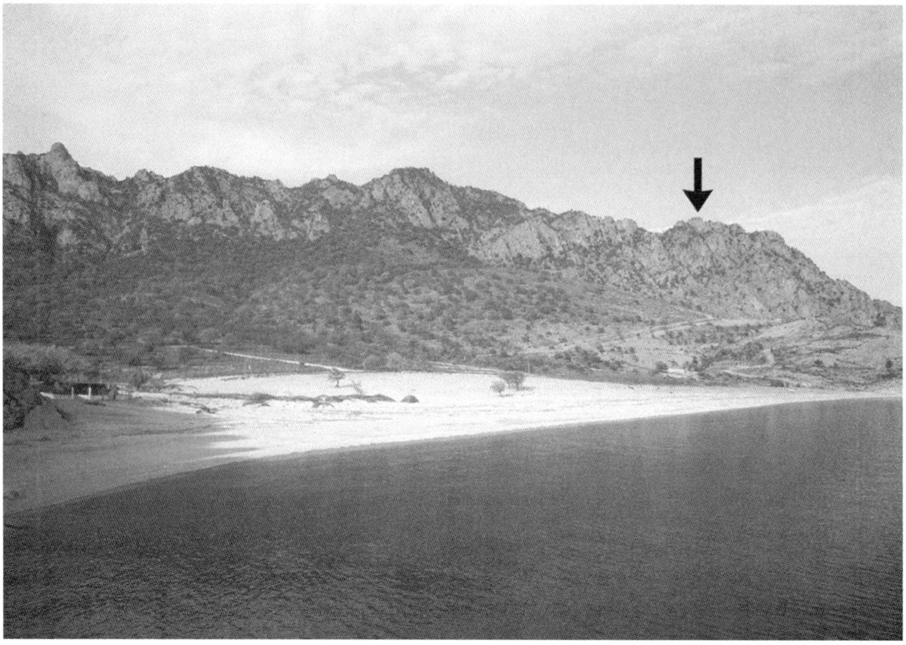

31. Gla Krimniotissa, Samothraki, from the Pacheia Ammos bay to its southwest: arrow indicates settlement area on summit. Image by the author.

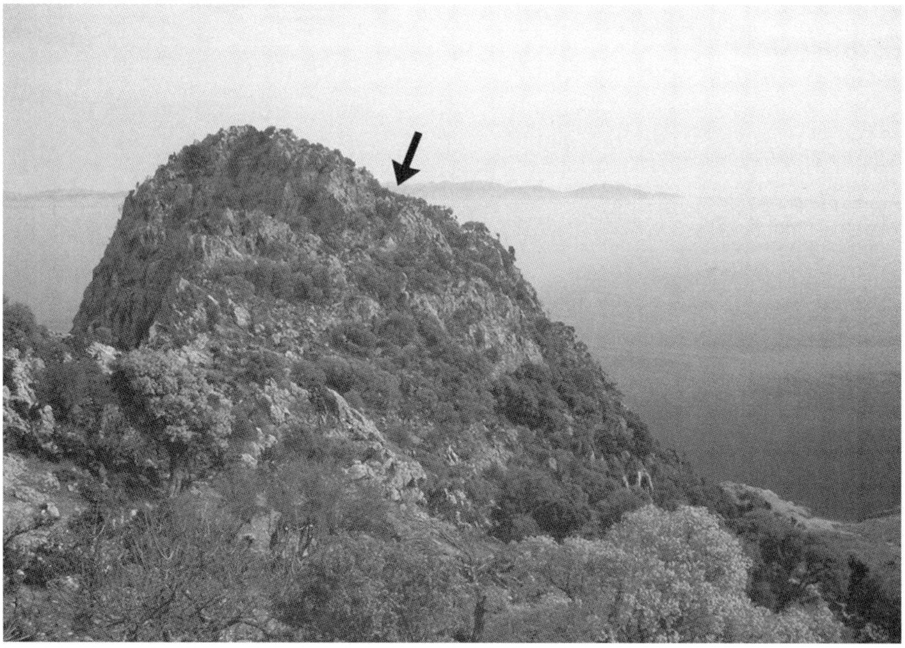

32. Gla Krimniotissa summit from slopes to its southwest (Imbros is visible in background). Image by the author.

and often lie in close proximity to formerly significant population areas, as at Koukounaries, Vrychos, Kastrokefala, Kritsa Kastello, and Zakros Kato Kastello (burial continues in the Zakro gorge throughout LM III, notwithstanding disuse of the palace site). Considering all these elements together, their foundations are more likely to have been local initiatives than

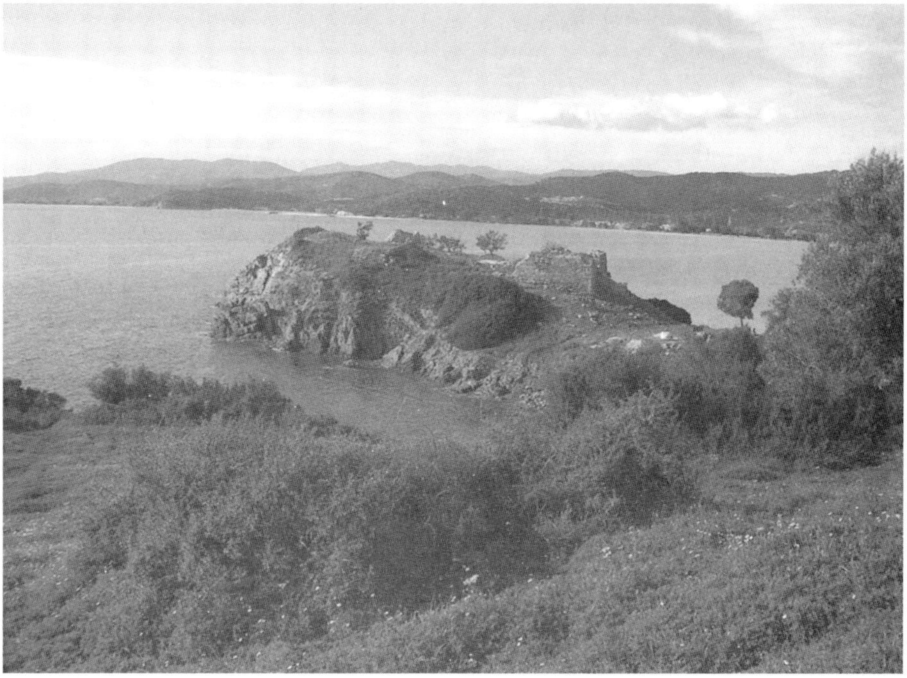

33. Torone: Lekythos peninsula from southwest. Image by the author.

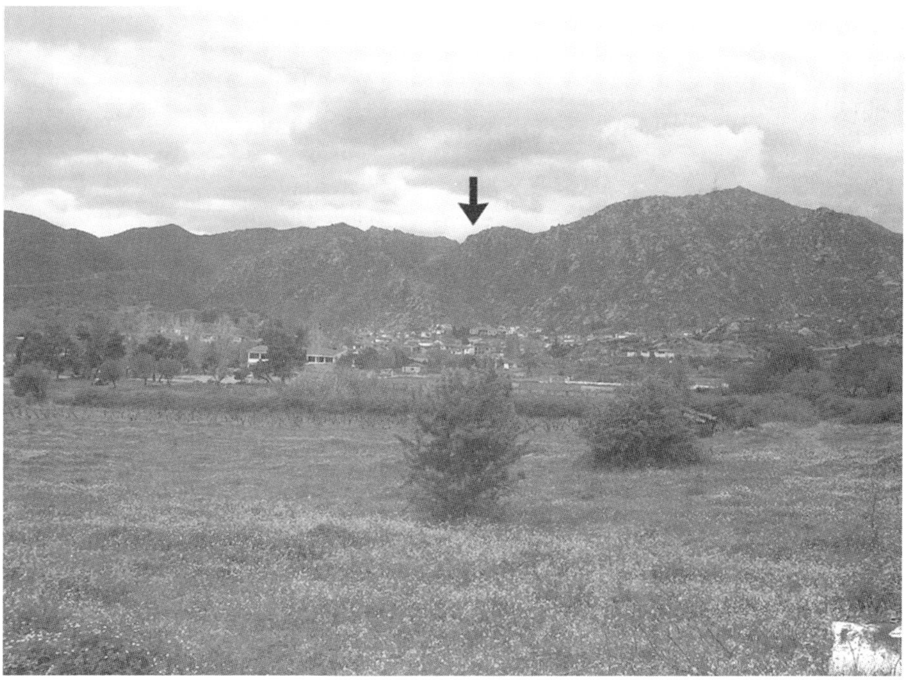

34. Koukos Sykia, from coast to east: arrow indicates settlement area on summit. Image by the author.

anything else (Nowicki 2000: 46–9, 120–3; Wallace 2002: 75–7). In Crete, they have inland, as well as coastal, locations – contrasting with the mostly coastal distribution of fortified sites in the islands at this period, for the reasons noted previously, and making these sites more unlikely to represent incomer strongholds. Thus, neither coastal position nor fortification individually, nor the two features in combination, can be taken clearly to indicate the presence of mainland incomers in island regions. Where a new site (or a continuing one) was desirable in terms of space for building and hinterland but lacked strong natural defences, it might be fortified to improve its defensibility (though this must also have depended on whether the community was large enough to command a good labour force), otherwise (and in the majority of cases) reliance was on natural defensibility. The more regular use of fortification at island sites than Cretan ones seems mainly to reflect greater problems in finding defensible topography in combination with good coastal access.

It is worth noting that the vast majority of LBA mainland settlements outside the major state centres (apart from the concentration in the Argolid) seem to have been unfortified or protected only by perimeter-type walls. Thus, models based on the direct equation 'walls at new sites = people from earlier walled settlements' in the twelfth-century Aegean would suggest either that a large new population on the islands originated in a very limited number of former major centres on the mainland or that people originating from these centres managed to gain a level of direct control over island populations *greater* than that which had operated in the LBA, when all other evidence suggests the opposite to be the case. It is anyway difficult to say why relocation to the islands, rather than within their own wider regions, would be uniformly attractive to displaced mainland groups, given the apparently very widespread nature of disturbances and danger in the Aegean at this time. While generally increased mobility was encouraged by the new economic and political circumstances, this is unlikely to have taken the form of a massive one-way movement.

Comparing settlement in the Aegean islands with patterns on the mainland and Crete shows that while common considerations and reactions did prevail across the region at this time of crisis, many elements of response differed in relation to local history and culture; like Cretan patterns, island ones cannot be seen as wholly representative of the Aegean at this time but must be viewed in their own historical and geographical context (Morgan 2003: 50).

The east: Cyprus and the coastal Levant

As a postscript to this discussion of the islands, and a prelude to the following brief consideration of the Greek mainland, Cyprus and the adjacent Levantine coast should be mentioned. It seems right to link the fortified sites of Maa Palaiokastro and Pyla Kokkinokremos on Cyprus, both dated to the BA-EIA transition, to the similar naturally defensible, coastal, and fortified sites appearing in the Aegean at the same period, since they seem to reflect the same changing historical circumstances (Karageorghis 1998, 2001). On present evidence, however, this type of site seems too infrequent on Cyprus to indicate a widespread adjustment in settlement of the type seen on the Aegean islands and peninsulas. Most of the thirteenth-century coastal centres on Cyprus were rapidly rebuilt and flourished after destructions around 1200 BC, apparently thanks to the new mobility and entrepeneurship opportunities available to their residents. Cypriot metals resources and skills, in particular, continued to be a solid and increasingly profitable asset, able to be traded more directly, and at a greater range, after the collapse of the Mycenaean polities (Karageorghis 1990a, 1992; Sherratt 1994).

The appearance of defensible settlements in Cyprus at this time has been tempting to explain using Aegean incomers partly because it does *not* seem widespread. Certainly, it is possible that those living at the Maa and Pyla sites may have been politically separate from – even at odds with – the large settlements housing most of the island's population. The sites clearly did not defend the nearest large coastal settlements in any organised network, and the size of the latter in any case allowed them to be defended in other ways. But it is impossible to determine clearly the ethnicity of the new sites' inhabitants, on the basis of either the presence of fortifications there or the Aegean and Aegeanising pottery found there. Cyprus already had a material culture closely integrated with that of the Aegean in the thirteenth century, when it imported large amounts of Aegean fine pottery: in the twelfth century it started to make a great deal of Aegean-style pottery locally (Steel 2004: 187–213). The range of Aegeanising pottery and other goods at the new settlements is broadly paralleled at contemporary Cypriot sites of nondefensible type, though concentrations do vary between sites. The best way to read the Cypriot sites seems to be as indicating that destabilisation of the former political and economic power base offered some new opportunities for small-group restructuring and aggrandisement in this region, as in others, causing insecurity (particularly around the coastal zones) and encouraging the creation of some new settlement bases for communities with new kinds of outlook and strategy vis-à-vis the outside world. The sites may be so few in number here because the very rapid recovery and success of the large Cypriot port sites meant that most people's best interests lay in joining activities there, rather than splintering off. As with many of the new Aegean defensible sites, the Cypriot examples had a short lifespan, going out of use in the eleventh century.

Like those in Cyprus (with which they clearly remained linked through trade systems after 1200 BC), many large LBA settlements on the Levantine coast experienced continuous use right through the crisis period (even while suffering destructions) and a rapid recovery of prosperity. Here too, though, some political and economic fragmentation and regrouping did occur. A pattern of 'village' dispersal appears in some inland regions of the southern Levant in the early twelfth century, though there is a return to the large urban type of site by the late eleventh century (Dever 1992). One of the most important trade centres of the thirteenth century, Ugarit/Ras Shamra, never recovered, though parts of its wider territory saw limited reoccupation. Farther south, Tyre, Sidon, and Byblos remained important cities, like their Cypriot neighbours (Bikai 1992; Caubet 1992; Yon 1992). The cities of Ashdod, Ashkelon, and Dor all suffered destruction circa 1200 BC, but saw early reoccupation: some new cultural elements in this phase, including large amounts of Aegeanising local pottery, have been used by some scholars to adduce major Aegean migrations into the region at this period (Dothan 1982, 1992). Tell Miqne avoided destruction altogether and saw expansive building, including fortification, in the twelfth century.

The long tradition of large fortified settlements on the Levantine mainland, the very large and complex scale of social and economic organisation there before and after collapse, and the lack of extensive naturally defensible topography on or very near the coasts, all help explain the lack of any major shift in the settlement record from large undefended settlements to the kind of small defended ones seen in the insular Aegean. Widespread fragmentation into small, secure communities was apparently neither a workable nor a necessary option. Given the history of large fortified sites in the region, there is little reason to connect the simple presence of fortification walls here in the twelfth century to large numbers of permanent settlers from the Aegean. Yet there is clear evidence for continuing – and in some aspects, more intense – contact and cultural borrowing between this region and the Aegean/Cypriot world during the twelfth century. This needs consideration in the wider context of changing contacts and movements in the region at this period, which I undertake in Part Three.

11 MAINLAND CENTRAL GREECE: SETTLEMENT PRIORITIES DURING AND AFTER COLLAPSE

Quality of evidence

We still lack adequately complex models of change, based on a representative spread of evidence, for twelfth-century settlement in central Greece, though useful attempts at synthesis have been made (Dickinson 2006: 79–114; Foxhall 1995). Greater variation and complexity may be expected, and seem indicated, in this large geographical area than in Crete, the Aegean islands, or Cyprus. This fact, and the ephemeral nature of the record at many sites, makes comprehensive interpretation challenging: much more extensive research is still needed. Here, I will simply pick out some features of contrast and similarity between settlements on the mainland, on Crete, and on the islands that cast light on the character of collapse in the different areas.

In contrast to the pattern seen on Crete and the islands, only a small number of *new* sites seem to have been founded on the mainland at or after 1200 BC. On the other hand, settlement continuity was restricted to a very limited number of existing sites. Together, these features have led some scholars to suggest large-scale depopulation (Desborough 1972a: 18; Snodgrass 1971: 89, 131, 379). However, the evidence must be considered in the light of the generally poor representation and limited study of EIA material on the mainland, especially at large LBA and Classical sites (Eder 1998: 195–208). Many major LBA sites continuing in use into the EIA had experienced destructions in the late thirteenth or early twelfth century. In the wake of such events, partial rebuilding often seems to have left only scattered and insubstantial deposits behind. At sites where occupation continued directly into the Classical period, involving the erection of heavy monumental architecture with deep foundations in the longest-established civic areas, EIA levels must often have been severely disturbed, and material of this date is often represented on the surface by only a very small quantity of sherds. These can be easily missed or misdated, making regional settlement patterns and site sizes difficult to reconstruct through either intensive survey or excavation (Jameson et al. 1994: 372–3; Lemos 2002: 6; 135).

Another problem is that many survey publications offer no drawings or other details of the sherd material used to date their sites. The reader must trust in pottery experts working across a broad chronological range (those working on post–Bronze Age sherds are often specialists in the study of Classical fine pottery styles and forms) to identify and correctly date EIA material (e.g., Callaghan et al. 2000; Johnston 2005; Langdon 1995). The latter is likely often to be in the form of coarse ware, for which few excavated comparisons are available (McDonald and Rapp 1972: 126; Snodgrass 1971: 24). The result is usually either a very general or an overprecise dating, based on fine ware shapes only. Matters are made more difficult by the usual conception of LH IIIC pottery as belonging firmly in the 'Mycenaean' period, its potential confusion with some LH IIIB forms when in a fragmentary state, and the treatment of Submycenaean pottery styles as representing a defined chronological period, when making large-scale analyses of settlement change. Thus, when the most recognisable EIA fine ware forms (those of the Geometric period) are identified in survey alongside clear LH III material, the tendency is often to talk of a site's abandonment after the 'Mycenaean' period, then its 'reoccupation' from Late Geometric onward, rather than consider its possible continuity through the whole period after 1200 BC.

As a result of all this, it is almost impossible accurately to evaluate the number and character of mainland sites used in the early EIA, or the extent of the occupied area at each. Thus, we cannot take claims of extreme depopulation in EIA central Greece at face value (Dickinson 2006: 93–4). The field seems open for the use of comparison with better-documented regions to help improve models of settlement change, and I undertake this later (Figure 35). As a result of the very gaps in evidence outlined above, however, it is difficult to verify some of my arguments, particularly that of a likely rise in population at formerly large mainland sites continuing in use through the EIA (though not necessarily a major expansion in size, given the difficulties of the period). I consider this, when viewed against the full range of data for the period, as a more convincing and likely model than that of massive depopulation.

Features of LBA settlement

Already in LH IIIA-B, mainland Greece shows significant contrasts with Crete in terms of settlement topography and form. Many major settlements were on low hills overlooking strategic routes and large flattish arable areas: most were located inland. The favouring of such 'acropolis' locations, and the fact that many had been fortified by the LH IIIB period, seems related to the large-scale topographic divisions of mainland Greece, which created very extensive arable plains and foothill zones, and to the large scale and wealth of these polities, facilitating the investment in infrastructure needed to cultivate these landscapes at optimal level. The elaborate fortifications also suggest a consistently high degree of rivalry or conflict between Mycenaean states: the Argolid provides the best example of a region densely packed with fortified acropoleis by the thirteenth century. Many of these sites had a degree of natural defensibility, with low cliffs on most sides: examples include Mycenae, Asine, the Larisa acropolis at Argos, and the acropolis of Athens. On the other hand, sites like Tiryns, Thebes, and Pylos (Ano Englianos) are hardly defensible at all and badly needed artificial protection (Gauss and Ruppenstein 1998; Glowacki 1998; Iakovidis 1962, 1983; Papadimitriou 2002: 137–8; Piteros 2003; Shelmerdine 1999: 337–8).

The impressive scale of the fortifications, especially at the richest settlements, alongside their concentration at major sites (irrespective of their local topography) suggests they had important prestige/display functions, as well as practical ones, forming a significant part of elite culture. There is clear evidence for the existence of complex regional hierarchies of settlement, tied into complex political systems, during LH IIIA-B, though the degree of centralisation of power is still debated (e.g., Bennet 2001; De Fidio 2001; Jameson et al. 1994: 253, 547; Small 1999; Voutsaki 2001). The distribution of fortifications suggests that conflicts occurred, symbolically and practically, at the highest political level – the biggest centres, rather than the second-order sites, represented the main targets for attack. They also probably acted to some extent as refuges for residents of the wider territory in times of stress.

A variety of topographic choices appear elsewhere in the settlement hierarchy, too. Some second-order sites known through survey that lack fortifications nonetheless seem to have been

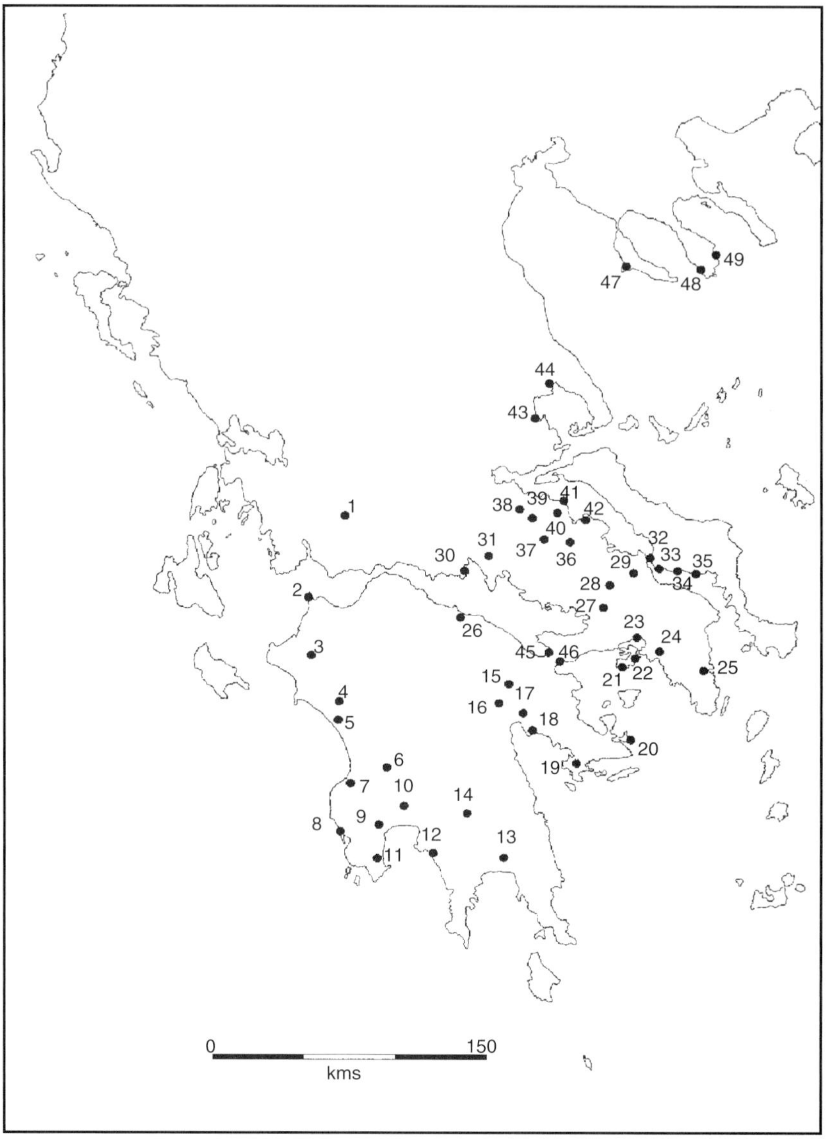

35. Central Greece: map of EIA sites mentioned in the text. Legend: 1. Thermon, 2. Teichos Dymaion, 3. Elis, 4. Olympia, 5. Samikon, 6. Krebeni Kato Melphia, 7. Kyparissia Kastro, 8. Palaiokastro/Osmanaga, 9. Nichoria, 10. Aithaia Ellinika, 11. Kaphirio, 12. Kardamili Kastro, 13. Asteri, 14. Sparta, 15. Mycenae, 16. Argos, 17. Tiryns, 18. Asine, 19. Kranidi Profitis Elias, 20. Modi, 21. Ginani sites, 22. Salamis, 23. Eleusis, 24. Athens, 25. Perati, 26. Aigeira, 27. Thebes, 28. Plataia, 29. Tanagra, 30. Galaxidi sites, 31. Delphi, 32. Chalkis, 33. Lefkandi, 34. Eretria, 35. Amarynthos, 36. Gla, 37. Orchomenos, 38. Elateia, 39. Kalapodi, 40. Atalanti, 41. Kynos, 42. Mitrou, 43. Alos, 44. Volos, 45. Corinth, 46. Isthmia, 47. Mende, 48. Koukos Sykia, 49. Torone. Image by the author.

chosen with an eye to self-defence, as well as to their rich agricultural hinterlands and coastal position: Aithaia Ellenika, Nichoria, and Kardamili Kastro, in south Messenia; and Kyparissia Kastro, in north Messenia – all surrounded by low cliffs and deep gullies – are examples, though the character and extent of the LBA settlement are not at all well understood in the last two cases (McDonald and Rapp 1972: 264, 276, 282, 288, 290; Figure 36). On the other hand, some major settlements were neither strongly fortified nor intrinsically very defensible, such as the large and

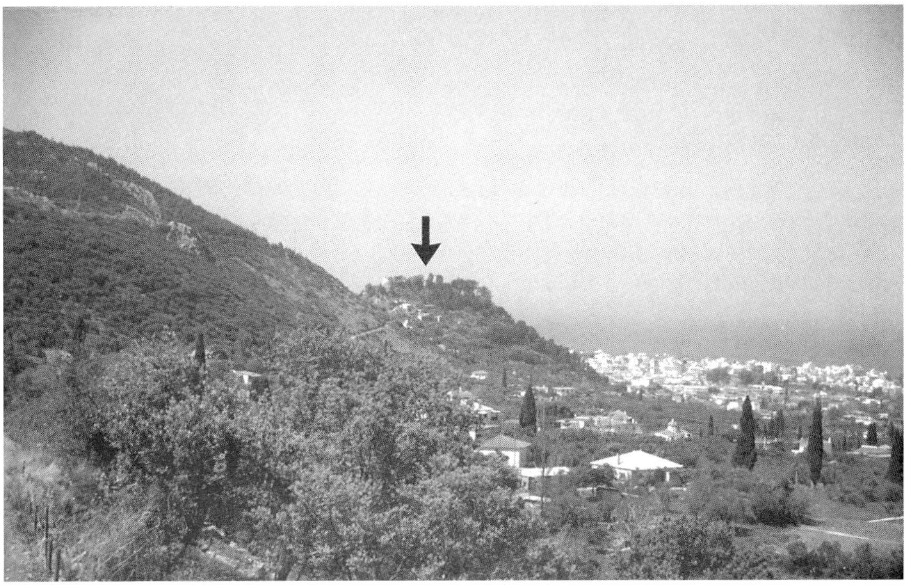

36. Kyparissia Kastro, from north: arrow indicates probable settlement area on hill summit. Image by the author.

clearly important Palaiopyrgi site in Laconia (Waterhouse and Hope Simpson 1960: 76–8). The artificial protective features accorded to any settlement in LH IIIA-B, then, depended partly on the local topography, partly on the settlement's security of position within a hierarchy, and partly on the resources it had to invest.

During the late LH IIIB period, many important sites either were newly fortified or had their fortifications strengthened or extended. In one extraordinary case at Gla an elaborate new site, strategically located in the middle of a lake or marshy plain and heavily fortified, seems to have been especially designed to protect and support a regional elite (Dickinson 2006: 40–2; Iakovidis 1989, 2001). The pattern seems to reflect similar conditions of insecurity – rooted in the fragmentation of existing power bases and the emergence of newly aggressive aggrandising groups – to those that encouraged new defensive settlement foundation in Crete and the islands at around the same time. However, this response, in which 'normal' elite security provisions were simply extended, while attempting to retain all other aspects of physical and social systems intact, was inadequate to prevent a violent and damaging collapse, in which destructions occurred at most major sites in the region – fortified or not – with Gla a notable example.

Second- or third-order settlements seem more often to have been abandoned than destroyed at this time (though some, like Zygouries and Korakou, were destroyed: Rutter 1974; Shelmerdine 1999: 372–7). The inhabitants often never returned to these smaller abandoned sites. However, a number of the destroyed former centres *did* retain residents and even appear to have attracted new ones, in a pattern of regional concentration following the collapse period. Some medium-sized settlements, formerly probably of second-order status, such as Nichoria and Lefkandi, also continued to be used after burnt destructions (Evely et al. 1996; McDonald et al. 1983; Popham and Milburn 1971). In a short paper, Lin Foxhall once tried to explain the pattern of mainland settlement post 1200 BC in terms of the power positions vacated by the main centres being taken up by former second-order settlements (Foxhall 1995). In fact, there is no clear indication that this simple kind of 'promotion' was a generalised process. The patterns of continuing settlement do not clearly correspond to those of settlement rank or size in the old hierarchy (Foxhall's analysis selected only a few examples out of many). Part of the problem lies in the varying quantity and quality of the evidence – identifying LBA settlement ranking is problematic in large and little-researched regions like Boeotia, for example – and on how we evaluate 'continuity' of use on sites where the whole character of Early Iron Age occupation is poorly understood, as noted above. Without considering changes in the size or character of settlements, or in the regional *balance* of settlement pattern, after 1200 BC, attempts to identify simple or predictable patterns of continuity are unlikely to be successful. Many and complex elements of selection were clearly involved in these changes. By considering the post–1200 BC settlement distribution in more detail, and at the level of the region, it seems possible to identify some major factors influencing this selection.

Favoured topography after circa 1200 BC: selective continued use of existing sites

Factors favouring continued site use on the mainland after the collapse horizon were clearly the rich agricultural environments in which the former centres lay and the valuable infrastructure that had been built up in these hinterlands. Another seems to have been the physically secure locations of some former major sites in topographic terms, and/or the presence of fortifications there that could be reused. At continuing sites like Tiryns, for example, the remains of the LH IIIA-B fortifications may have encouraged continued residence, though these walls could not have been properly defended without large numbers of people under some degree of centralised control (Maran 2006; Papadimitriou 1998; Pierart 1991). Concerns with security were often better served by the continued use of LBA acropolis sites possessing high *natural* defensibility (sometimes enhanced by existing walls) such as Athens, Argos, and Asine in the Argolid, and Kardamili Kastro, Nichoria, and Aithaia Ellinika in Messenia though the latter was difficult to defend because of its large size (Eder 1998: 25–86; Gauss and Ruppenstein 1998; Glowacki 1998; Lemos 2002: 136–8, 2006; McDonald 1983; McDonald and Rapp 1972: 288; McDonald and Wilkie 1992; Papadimitriou 2006; Rapp 1978: 27–9). However, staying at and enlarging these former centres often seem to have invited further attack and destruction, notwithstanding any defensive features the sites possessed. This echoes the pattern in the Cyclades, where settlement adjustments were also not early, deep, or radical enough to prevent destructions. In both cases, however, the stakes of continued occupation were clearly considered worth the risk.

The new priorities in settlement necessitated major rebalancing of site distribution across and between regions, with many political and economic implications (Morgan 1986: 68). Tiryns, for example, continued to support some occupation through most of the EIA but ultimately seems to have lacked the size, power, and longevity of the community at the naturally well-defended Argos, which, along with Asine on the coast, became the focus of population in the region after PG (Eder 1998: 25–72; Maran 2006; Papadimitriou 1998). In the Corinthia, a number of sizeable sites on low hills (Aetopetra, Zygouries, Korakou) were abandoned in the twelfth century, with new concentration of occupation developing at the existing site of Corinth (Lemos 2002: 161; Morgan 1999: 347–67, 2003: 55; Rutter 1974: 536–48). Again, the presence of naturally defensible topography may have favoured a concentration of population here: people seem to have moved (perhaps in the time of most extreme need) up from the Corinth site on the plain to the lower slopes of Acrocorinth, where LH IIIC and later settlement remains underlie the later sanctuary of Demeter and Kore, probably founded in LG: tomb use in the same area suggests a stable occupation (Bookidis and Stroud 1997: 1–19; Morgan 1999: 245; Pfaff 1999). The upper slopes and large summit of this massive single mountain would provide a substantial refuge place to be accessed from the lower settlement. The long-term regional focus of population on the Corinth site may have been a gradual process: the nondefensible site of Isthmia, nearby, continued to be used as a settlement into the LH IIIC period, and burials at other sites show use into LH IIIC at least (Morgan 1998: 77–8, 1999: 295–369).

In Messenia, many small- to medium-sized LH IIIA-B settlements located on low hills around the former centre at Pylos were abandoned, circa 1200 BC, with subsequent concentration of occupation at a few widely scattered sites formerly of second-order status, such as Nichoria and Aithaia Ellinika (Harrison and Spencer 1998: 149; McDonald and Rapp 1972: 280). At Nichoria, significant rebuilding at this time potentially suggests a new organisation and role for the settlement (Aschenbrenner et al. 1983; Coulson 1983). In Laconia, medium- to large-sized LBA sites on low hills all down the Eurotas valley seem to be abandoned in favour of an early EIA nucleation at the nondefensible site of Sparta: the origins of habitation at the site are unclear, but there is definite Mycenaean material on the acropolis, as well as use of the site in PG, suggesting continuous use (Coulson 1985, 1988; Eder 1998: 109–13; Hall 2000: 86; Raftopoulou 1997; Waterhouse and Hope Simpson 1961: 170–3). In the Helos plain of south Laconia, Asteri Karousi may have become the main centre of occupation (Waterhouse and Hope Simpson 1960: 90–2).

In Elis, though few settlement sites have so far been identified or excavated, a pattern of focus on much fewer, large settlements also appears from around 1200 BC. Cemeteries at Ayia Triada and Agrapidohori, which may be assumed to represent sizeable LH IIIA-B settlements in inland river valleys, remained partly in use into LH IIIC, before being finally abandoned just as a major settlement started to grow at Ancient Elis, a low hill with a history of occupation earlier in the Bronze Age (Arapoyianni 1996, 1997; Eder 1999a, 1999b, 2001a; Eder and Mitsopoleos-Leon 1999; Parlama 1974; Schoinas 1995: 113–19; Figure 37). As in some Cretan cases, the first residents at the new Elis site may have continued to bury at their old cemeteries. Looking at the region in its wider context, there is every reason to suppose that this settlement actually began in LH IIIC rather than in the Submycenaean period, as the dates of several excavated tombs there have been suggested to indicate. The hilltop site at Samikon, used as a settlement until LH IIIB and with a possible BA fortification wall on its highest summit, has PG burial evidence in its vicinity and had expanded into a very substantial walled settlement by Classical times. The peak, at least, seems likely to have continued in use as a settlement throughout the EIA (McDonald and Hope Simpson 1961: 230; Sperling 1942: 85–7; Figure 38). Like most other EIA sites in the northwest Peloponnesian region, Elis and Samikon are not markedly defensible in the wider Aegean context. In their own environment, however, they are by far the most defensible locations possible for settlement and seem deliberately selected for this purpose. It is vital to appreciate this landscape setting in understanding why EIA settlement concentrated at the sites. Both give outstanding views over the flat coastline for many kilometres to north and south and command the huge cultivable plains that characterise the area, with very few visual breaks (Figure 39).

In Boeotia, a pattern of population concentration at fewer, larger sites in the early EIA is *not* visible, perhaps because LBA settlement here had never developed the full hierarchical extension into scattered small villages seen in other regions (though this impression may be a result of inadequate study of the area). In this rolling landscape, there are few more obviously defensible sites to which movement could usefully take place. Large, basically nondefensible sites like Thebes, Orchomenos, Plataia, and Tanagra all seem to continue in use through the whole period between LH and G (and later), each probably drawing population from smaller settlements in their regions, though there is discontinuity, patchiness, and variability in the quantity of EIA material found on all these sites (Aravantinos et al. 2001: 15; Bintliff 2007; Bintliff

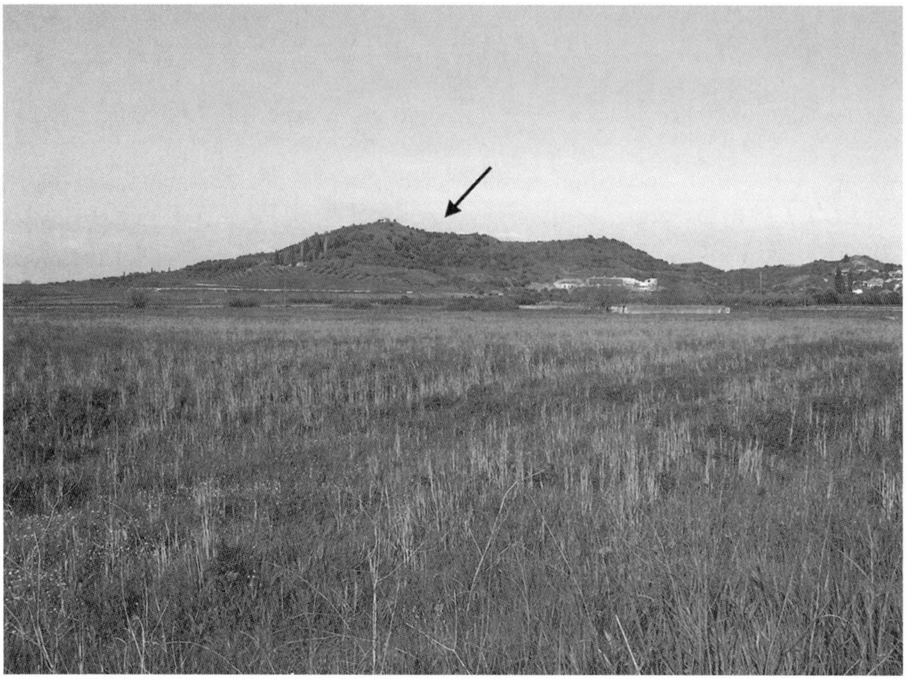

37. Ancient Elis from south: the multiperiod site spreads over the whole hill summit. Image by the author.

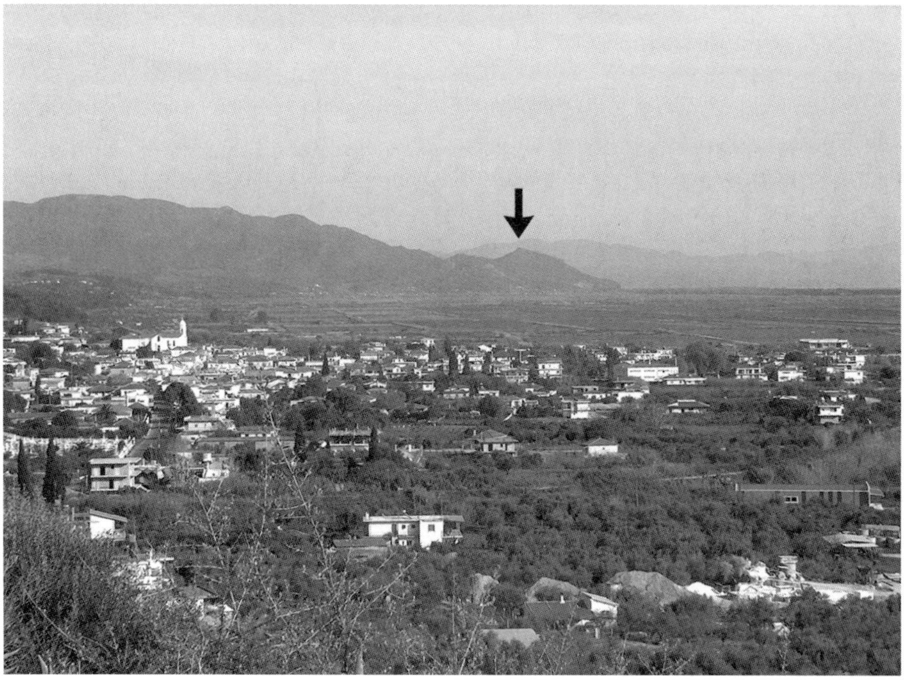

38. View of Samikon, from north; the likely LBA-EIA settlement area is on the summit. Image by the author.

et al. 2002: 51–2; Blackman 2002: 51; Fossey 1988: 43–101, 351–67, 199–251). In Euboea, too, we see the continued use of multiple large coastal settlements of nondefensible type at Chalkis, Lefkandi, and Amarynthos, which all probably suffered destruction episodes (Andriomenou 1972, 1990; Boardman 1957). Again, more defensible topography is lacking on this coast.

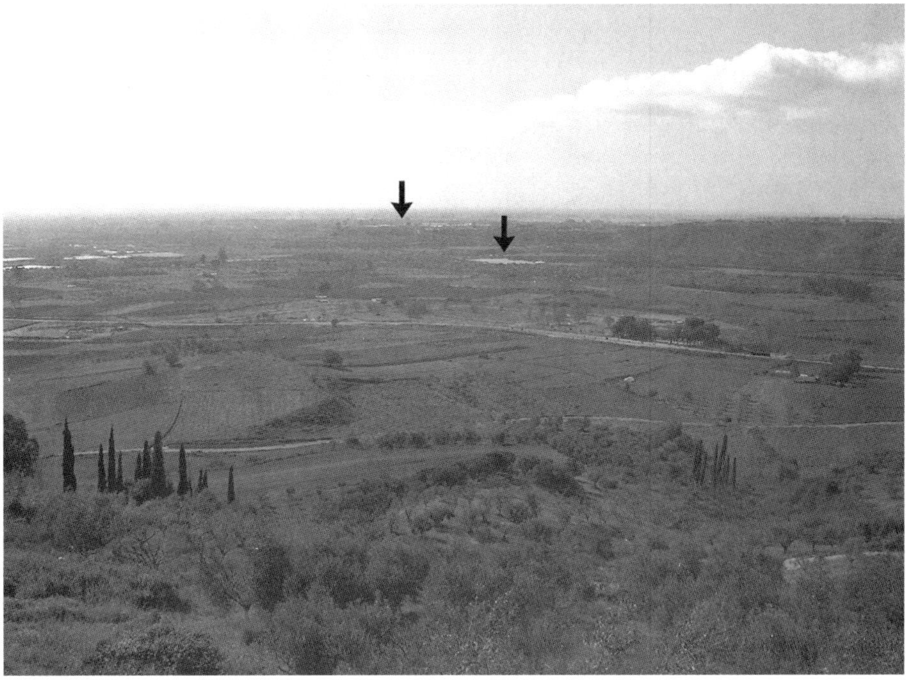

39. View from Ancient Elis, looking west to Peneios river (indicated by arrow) and the coast. Image by the author.

New defensible sites at the LBA-EIA transition

The impression that defensibility was a strong consideration in site selection through this difficult period is supported by the foundation of some new sites of notably defensible character at the LH IIIB-C transition. However, the proportionally much lower representation of these sites on the mainland than in the islands, their small size, and their often apparently short-term occupation suggest a less pronounced, or concerted, response to insecurity by this means; the topography and population size/history of mainland Greece simply did not allow such drastic rebalancing. The short-term use of these sites may go a long way towards explaining why it is often just the LM IIIC-Submycenaean period that is not represented in the material at many mainland sites with indications of both LH and PG-A occupation and encourages caution in talking about regional depopulation at any point during this period.

In a pattern paralleled on the islands and Crete, occupation sometimes moved to a more defensible part of an existing settlement area, or over a very short range, at the crisis period. The use of Acrocorinth was such a case, and the pattern also occurred at Aigeira, where the settlement moved up from the coast to an 'acropolis' location above, with outstanding strategic views over the whole coastal strip and the long approaches east and west along the Corinthian gulf (Blackman 2002: 36–7; Deger-Jalkotzy 1991; Kolonas 1997: 488). Such locations were rarely defensible in the extreme style of some island sites (often needing fortifications to protect them) but offered greatly improved vantage points against attack, especially from the sea. In the Pylos area, the clearest evidence for LH IIIC-PG settlement is from the slopes of the steep-sided Palaiokastro hill, located right above the coast and commanding the well-protected Navarino bay (Figure 40). This is sited directly above, yet is significantly more defensible than, the small LBA settlement immediately below on the Koryphasion promontory and is much more intrinsically defensible (though

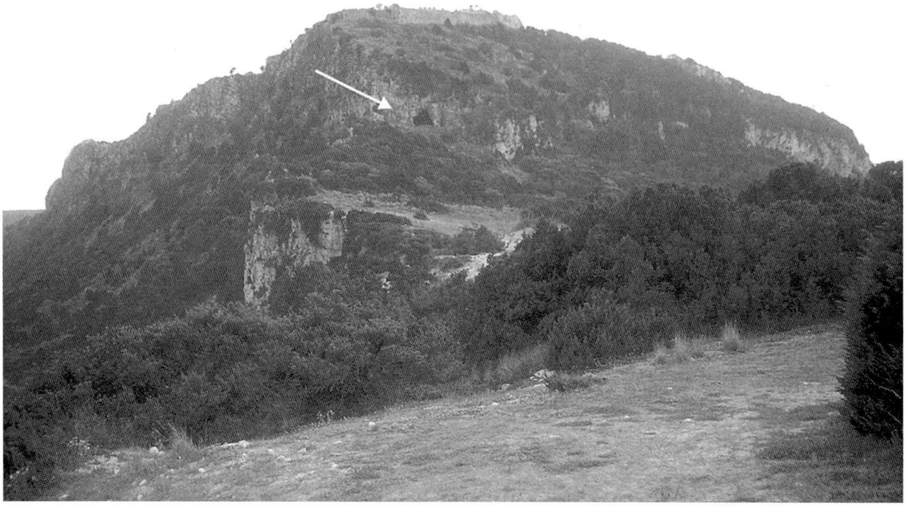

40. Palaiokastro hill and the 'Cave of Nestor', Messenia, from the Koryphasion peninsula to their north: arrow indicates cave. Image by the author.

also more exposed in its position) than the former palatial site at Ano Englianos. The presence of LH IIIC material in the 'Cave of Nestor' on the upper north slopes, PG tombs on the south slopes, and LH IIIB and PG sherds at Petrochori, in the Osmanaga lagoon area to the northeast, as well as a number of tombs in the wider area with use continuing through LH IIIC, strongly suggest some EIA occupation in this coastal region (Chatzi 1982; Eder 1998: 141–79; McDonald and Rapp 1972: 264). The possible use of the Palaiokastro hill as a temporary defensible settlement should be considered. The fact that many of these newly founded sites are coastal, or overlook the coasts, echoes elements of patterns we have already seen in Crete and the Cyclades. A defensible settlement on the islet of Modi, just off Poros, and other new sites on Salamis, another island closely adjacent to the mainland, indicate that mainland residents are likely to have been very familiar with the types of settlement strategy being used by island communities (Konsolaki 2003; Lolos 2001).

At the northwest corner of the Peloponnese, the rocky peninsula of Teichos Dymaion, currently surrounded on two sides by marsh and steep cliffs, which had had earlier occupation in various periods of the Bronze Age, saw new settlement activity from LH IIIC onwards, probably including the building of new fortifications (Kolonas 1991; Mastrokostas 1962a, 1962b, 1963, 1964a, 1964b, 1965; Papagiannopoulos and Zachos 1991; Figure 41). The fortified area is of quite substantial size – circa 25,000 square metres – and use of the site is continuous into the eleventh century but does not seem to continue throughout the Iron Age. Two fortified sites at Galaxidi in Phokis were also established at this time, immediately overlooking the Corinthian Gulf coast and another very important harbour (Baziotopoulou and Valvanis 1993; Figures 42–4). One, Ayios Athanasios, is simply the fortified corner of a large upland plateau and is very small and short-lived. It suggests the emergency establishment of a watchpoint or refuge – perhaps an attempt at avoiding full-scale relocation early in the crisis period. It overlaps in date with a neighbouring site at Ayios Vlassis, a much larger and longer-lived, fully fortified site occupying a whole hill summit, but commanding slightly less strategic views. This settlement seems to represent a more permanent refuge solution, though

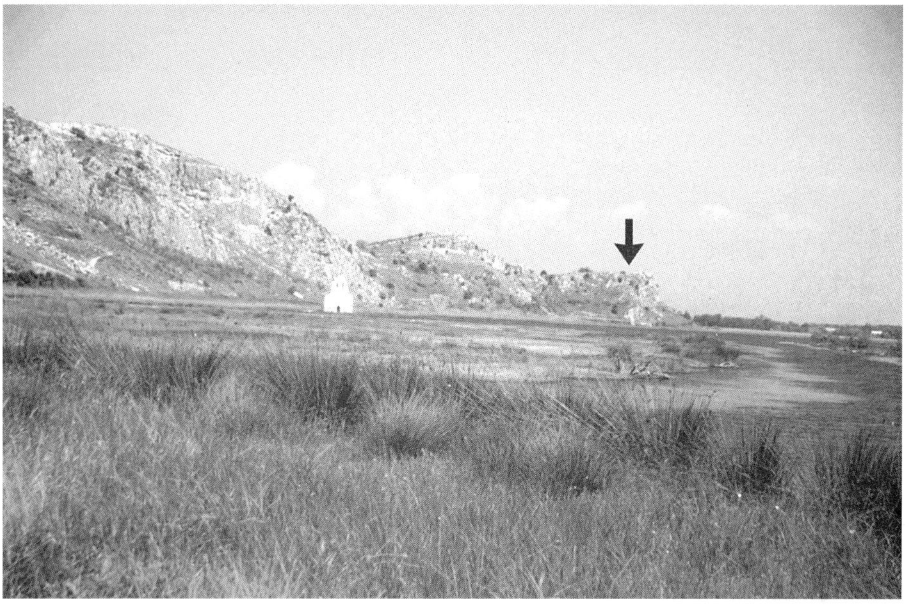

41. Teichos Dymaion from southeast: arrow indicates settlement area on summit. Image by the author.

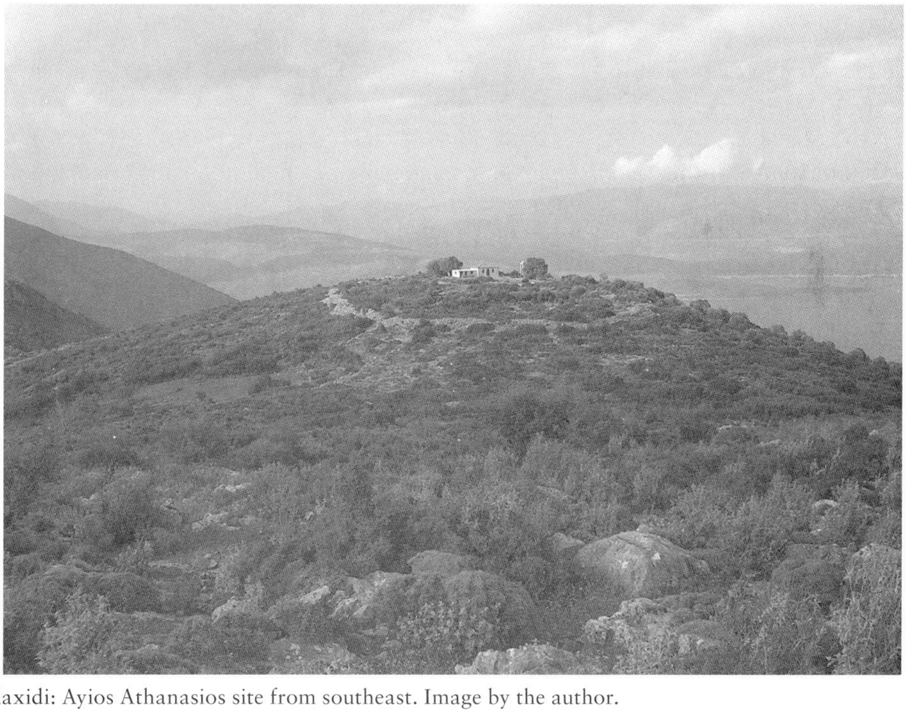

42. Galaxidi: Ayios Athanasios site from southeast. Image by the author.

it still seems too small to have permanently housed the surely sizeable Bronze Age population of the coastal region below. In the southern Argolid, a fortified site at Kranidi Profitis Elias seems to have been established at the end of LH IIIB and occupied a short way into LM IIIC (Jameson et al. 1994: 444–5; Figures 45 and 46). Its small size and position in the centre of the southern Argolid peninsula, roughly equidistant from the latter's three coasts, suggest a collaborative effort

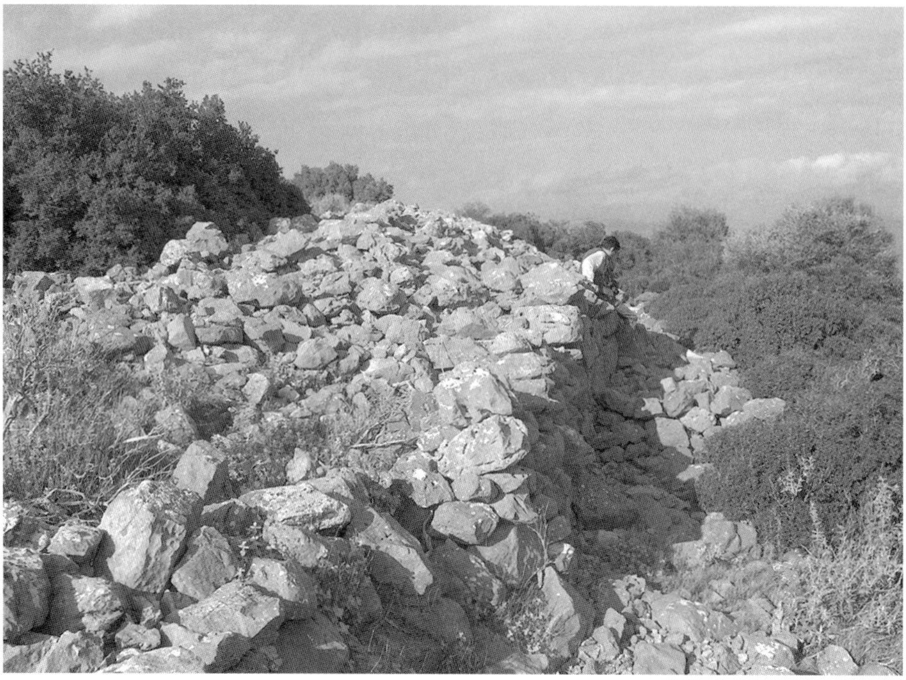

43. Remains of fortification wall around the summit of the Galaxidi Ayios Athanasios site, from northwest. Image by the author.

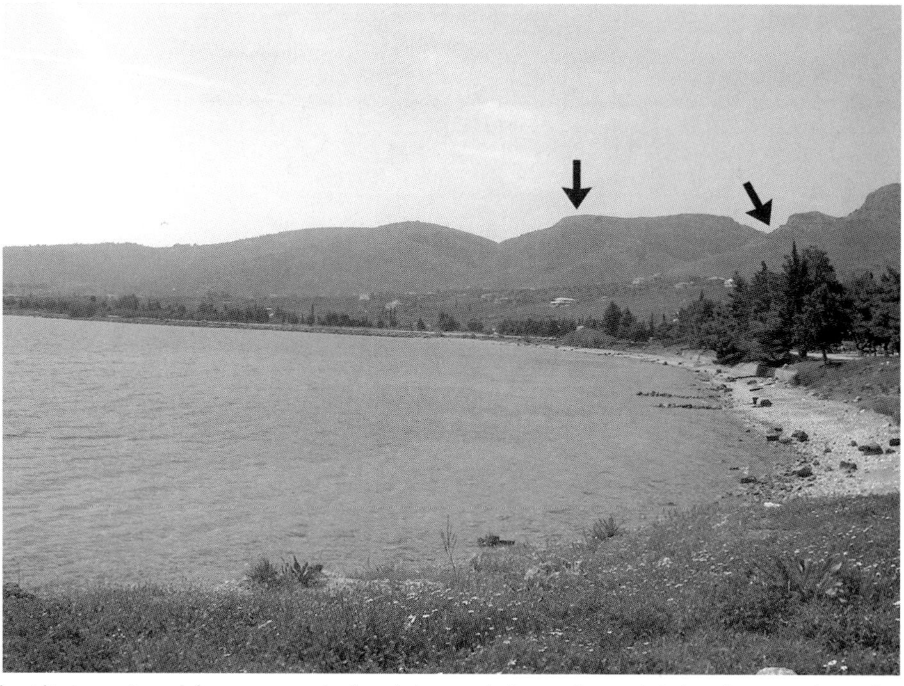

44. Galaxidi sites, viewed from across the bay lying to their northeast: left-hand arrow shows location of the Ayios Vlasis site; right-hand arrow indicates the Ayios Athanasios summit, not visible. Image by the author.

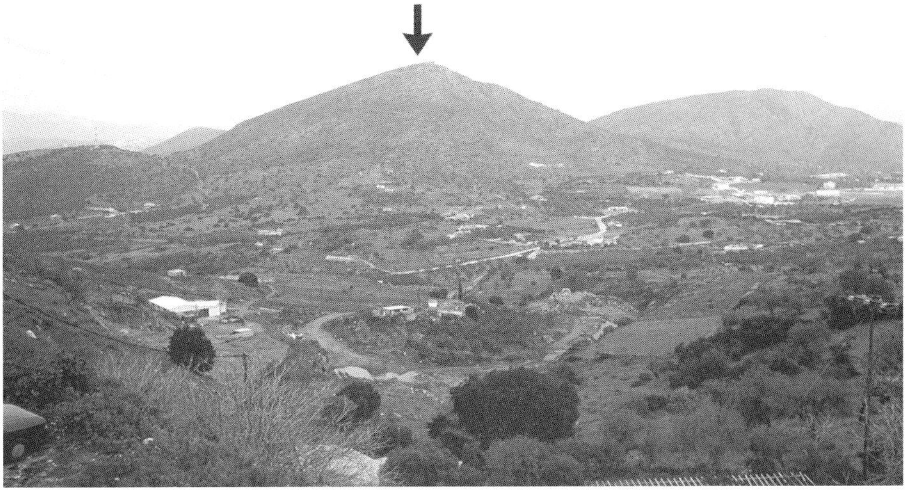

45. Kranidi Profitis Elias, from south: arrow indicates settlement area on summit. Image by the author.

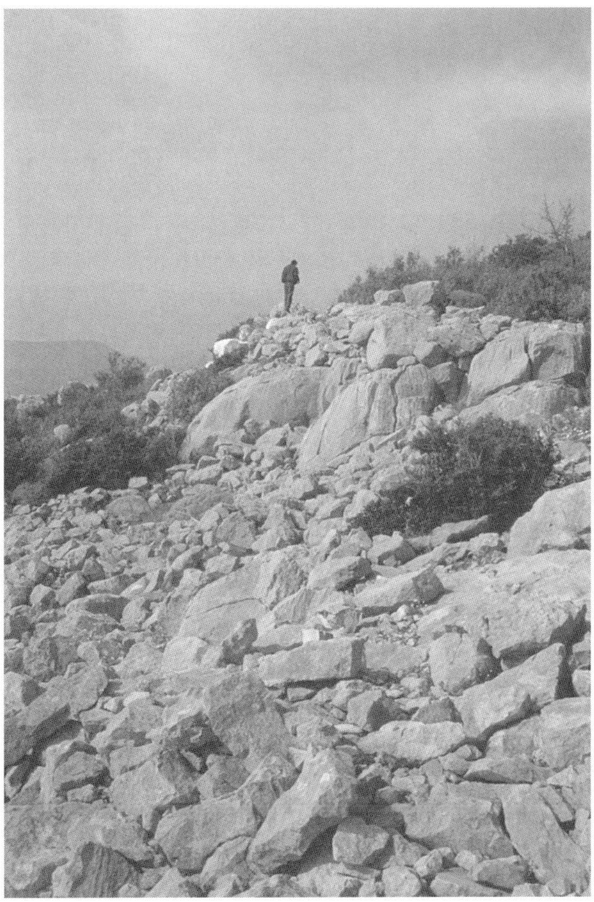

46. Fortification wall at Kranidi Profitis Elias, from east. Image by the author.

to provide a small-scale, temporary security refuge for the main LBA polities of the region (located at Ermioni Magoula/Hermion, Halieis, Sambariza, and possibly Dhroukoulina). The latter sites' locations on the coastal plains made their populations vulnerable at this time, yet they were probably never completely abandoned during the EIA (Jameson et al. 1994: 372–4, 437; Runnels et al. 1995: 372–3; van Andel and Runnels 1987: 101–2). The same pattern of basically continuous occupation at or around some large stable coastal settlements, probably assisted by the use of temporary refuge sites at the most dangerous period, is seen in the Methana peninsula. It is often difficult to prove absolute continuity from the LBA right through to Archaic period at these coastal sites, and settlement may have moved inland within a small radius during part of the earliest EIA (Gill and Foxhall 1997). The Velika cave in Messenia, from which some LH IIIC sherds are reported, may have been a temporary refuge for some of the Nichoria population. It is located deep in a river gorge, so that access for at least half the year currently has to be by boat or swimming (McDonald and Hope Simpson 1969: 234; McDonald and Rapp 1972: 282).

Some other defensible sites founded at this period look more permanent, though we still need to learn much more about them. The history of the site at Krebena Kato Melpia, in the inland Peloponnese, which has LH IIIC-Archaic surface pottery, is unclear: an LH IIIB settlement exists not far away, at Agrilovouno (McDonald and Hope Simpson 1969: 143; McDonald and Rapp 1972: 294; Figure 47). With its lack of fortifications, limited space for building, and high natural defensibility, Kato Melpia bears a strong resemblance to some of the new defensible sites on Crete and the islands. Perhaps long-term, stable relocation to this type of site was an option most suited to small rural LH IIIB communities, but less practicable or desirable for the large populations at former centres.

The importance of communications access

On the mainland, coastal or near-coastal location was clearly an important criterion in the selection of sites after 1200 BC for *either* continuing *or* new occupation – indeed, one that apparently

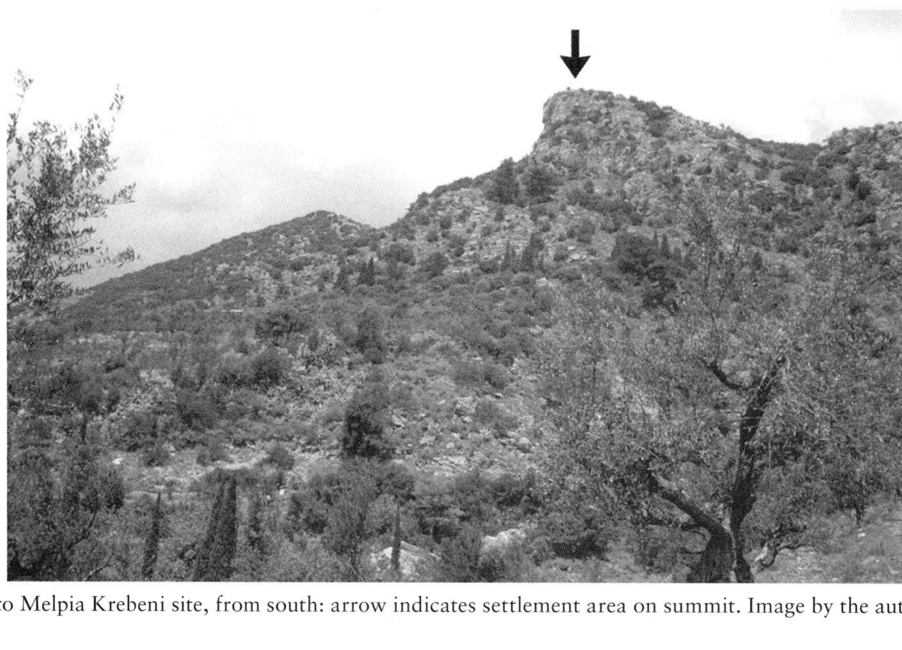

47. Kato Melpia Krebeni site, from south: arrow indicates settlement area on summit. Image by the author.

overrode the quality of defensibility in many cases. This fact seems to have had a great deal to do with trade. The scale of the mainland landscape meant that access to the coast offered proportionately much greater wealth-building opportunities than applied in the insular Aegean, even in this disturbed period. Along the eastern Greek and Euboean seaboards, new nondefended sites such as Oropos, Mitrou, and Kynos were established, while existing sites like Lefkandi, Amarynthos, and Chalkis also flourished (following destructions) during the twelfth century (Figures 48 and 49). Either the wealth to be gained from trade, or the existing size of the population here, or both, encouraged concerns with defensibility to be sacrificed or compromised (Dakoronia 1993a; Lemos 2002: 171–2; Mazarakis Ainian 1998; van de Moortel and Zachou 2006). The continuation of occupation at Asine during the EIA seems to owe as much to the site's coastal location as to its defensible characteristics. In Messenia, the use of Kardamili Kastro, the Palaiokastro hill, and the Aigeira acropolis reflects the same kind of interest (McDonald and Rapp 1972: 290). At Volos, as the major palatial centre at Dimini and the port at Pefkakia-Kastro declined, it was the coastal unit, at Kastro, that remained in use, though in a contracted form (Adrimi-Sismani 2006; Batziou-Efstathiou 1992, 1994, 2003; Feuer 1983, 1994; Kalligas 1992; Lemos 2002: 146–7; Morgan 2003: 96–102).

Strategic positioning on major communication routes also applies to many inland sites selected for continuing occupation from LM IIIC onwards. In east central Greece, the wealth and growth of the Atalante and Elateia cemeteries during LH IIIC point to important settlements nearby: though not on the coast, these sites are on major routes from the coast inland, and the flourishing coastal sites of the east Greek region undoubtedly contributed to building the wealth of residents there (Dakoronia 1991, 1992, 1993a, 1993b, 2006; Deger-Jalkotzy and Dakoronia 1990; Eder 2003). Elis lies on a strategic river valley, halfway between the sea and a rich inner hinterland. Thebes and Orchomenos in Boeotia are located on the main valley routes through

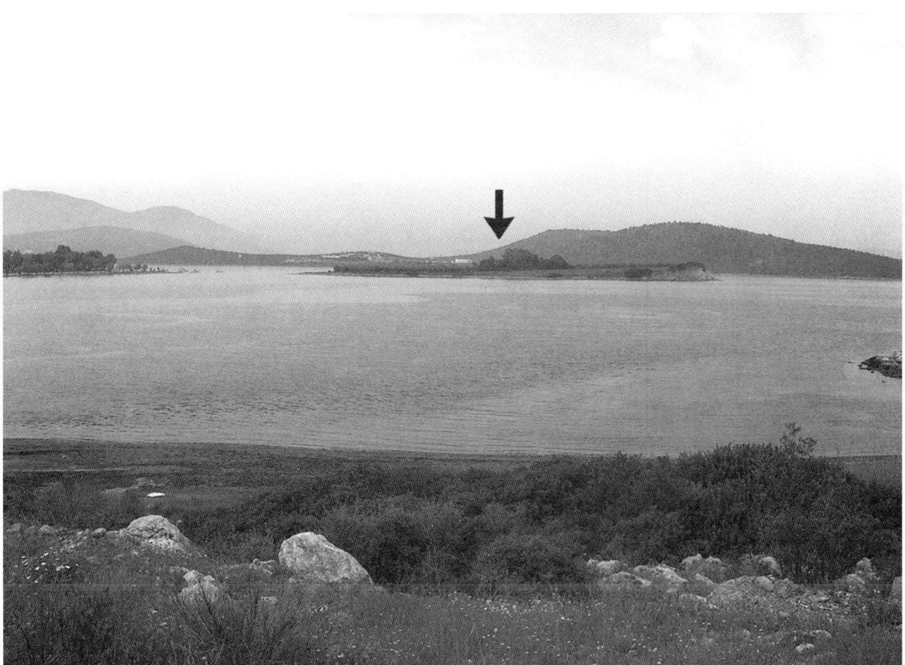

48. Mitrou, from west: arrow indicates settlement area. Image by the author.

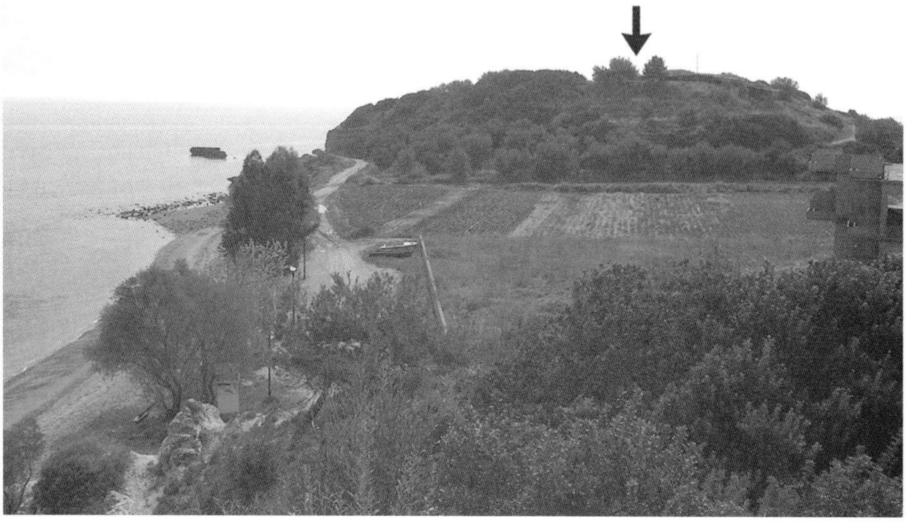

49. Kynos (Pyrgos Livenatou) from north: arrow indicates settlement area on summit. Image by the author.

the region, and Argos and Tiryns are located midway between the sea and the hinterland of the Argolid plain (Eder 1998: 25–72; Tomlinson 1972; Touchais and Divari-Valakou 1998: 11–18).

In northeast Greece, strong patterns of continuity and/or expansion of both coastal and inland settlements appear at this time – Akanthos, Torone, Thessaloniki Toumba, and Assiros are just a few examples (Cambitoglou et al. 2001: 280–94; Moschonisioti 2004; Papadopoulos 2005; Savvopoulou 2004; Souaref 2004; Tiverios 2004; Traxasopoulou-Salakidou 2004; Wardle 1980, 1989). This occurred even though destructions affected many settlements, and even though the region had become tied into the south Aegean economy by end of the LBA and clearly shared in its disruptions. The area also sees the new establishment of long-lived and important coastal settlements, such as Mende and Poseidi, at this time (Vokotopoulou 1988, 1989, 1990, 1991). Neither class of site was particularly defensible (though there was a tradition of fortification): as in east Greece, there was clearly enough to gain from staying at old settlements, or in establishing new coastal ones, to make the risk worthwhile, especially when the population was large enough to defend an exposed site effectively. We do see some naturally defensible sites being founded at about this period, such as Koukos Sykia, but these were of limited size and tend to be in exposed island or peninsula locations, as discussed. The high level of successful settlement continuity in this region parallels developments in Cyprus better than those in the central Greek mainland (see discussion below). But while Cypriot societies of the twelfth century consolidated and built on their existing economic status, Macedonia really came into its own, as both trade node and producer region, at just this time. The effects of collapse in the southern Aegean were very advantageous in this respect – the importance of the northern region as a channel for the movement of metals, amber, and other goods to southern destinations was directly boosted. Wheelmade fine pottery flowed back in return, in a trade which surely used coastal zones including the Chalkidiki as important interfaces (Cambitoglou et al. 2001: 64–5; Harding 1984: 213–29; Papadopoulos 2005: 578, 589–92; Sherratt 2001: 234–7).

Overall, then, the notion of an insecure east Mediterranean, with people heavily occupied in raiding and looting by sea, must be reconciled with a picture of people being actively and regularly involved in long-range maritime exchange activity. In many cases, these two groups must have overlapped heavily. Particularly on the mainland, where a significant number of former centres continued in use, some of the people most directly affected by the collapse of state economies were well positioned in terms of location, skills, and experience to build profitable new contact and trade networks on the ruins of the great long-distance systems of the LBA. At the same time, the presence of a good agricultural hinterland, as well as defensibility, always had to be carefully considered in choosing settlement location.

Conclusions on settlement patterns

The preceding discussion provides only an impressionistic view of mainland settlement, and one likely to be challenged by further detailed research. My main aim has been to show how the spatial correlates of collapse in the central and insular Aegean differed from those of the Cretan collapse. This contrast is partly connected to the fact that the mainland states had been particularly large and powerful nodes in the region as a whole during the LBA. Their populations seem to have been especially unwilling – or simply unable, as a result of their size – to abandon the core of their power (that is, control over large prime arable areas and coastal resources) and fragment into neat, small, easily self-sufficient units for the purposes of improved security.

We have also seen that though Crete, the islands, and the mainland differ substantially in their settlement patterns after 1200 BC, we cannot view these patterns in terms of simple dichotomies – continuous/noncontinuous, coastal/inland-orientated; defensible/nondefensible – and must consider how these features were selected and combined differently in each region. What is clear is that radical settlement disturbance occurred across the Aegean in this period: *all* except a few Cretan settlements were abandoned, and the *majority* of mainland and island settlements suffered either destruction or abandonment. The important differences lie in the mode of response to crisis. On the mainland, existing large LBA settlements, sited for optimal access to prime arable land and seaborne trade, continued as main population cores much more frequently than was the case on Crete. The moderately defensible topography of many mainland LBA settlements, and the large size of regional populations, enabled the continued secure use of these sites after 1200 BC in a way not so often possible at sites on Crete, or on the Aegean islands and peninsulas. At the same time, large populations and limited availability of defensible topography made physical fragmentation and dispersal difficult and impractical for defence purposes on the mainland. I will argue that a high price was paid for this continuity, in terms of long-term social tensions in large, noncohesive mainland communities during the EIA. Ironically, a greater degree of settlement continuity *did not* produce greater social stability. The contraction of large populations to a much smaller number of sites meant that formerly coherent structures of regional political identity, linked to complex settlement hierarchies within well-defined territories, are likely to have fallen apart. People came together in large new groups, with no easy way to build new frameworks of identity or status. In contrast, the high level of settlement dispersal seen on Crete, in conjunction with the proactive, deliberate, and coherent structure of the shift and relatively small community sizes, may have allowed cohesive identities and institutions to emerge more quickly and to have been better maintained over time. Below, I look at how other aspects of Cretan material culture in this period support this idea.

12 CONSTRUCTING POST-COLLAPSE SOCIETY: INSIDE CRETAN SETTLEMENTS, CIRCA 1200–1000 BC

Evidence quality and comparisons between sites

As large numbers of new settlements were established and continuing settlements contracted, we would expect changing social and economic relations within communities to be reflected in architecture. At the same time, deliberate maintenance of earlier architectural traditions could help build social coherence in the new community units by embodying the sense of a common heritage. In fact, we see both features in the twelfth- to eleventh-century record, but the overall picture is of pressure to create a fundamentally *new* framework for everyday interactions. Considerable planning and design went into this, supporting the notion of a 'successful' collapse that I have outlined. Once established, the new spatial frameworks themselves helped to structure and reinforce new social relations (Wallace 2005b).

Many excavations at Cretan sites established in the early EIA took place in the early twentieth century, and in keeping with the standards of that time produced only limited documentation of developments in architecture. Several excavated sites have occupation extending into the Geometric period, so that this material dominates the record, and data on building context and function for the earliest part of the EIA are anyway restricted. Notwithstanding, available data on settlement planning in Crete are much more densely concentrated than for the mainland, and the Cretan record is more often extensively preserved at site level, not least because of the large number of settlement abandonments occurring in the tenth century BC. As such, the Cretan record has probably been over-cited in discussions on the social relations of EIA architecture in general. This can produce misleading generalisations, since the very specific character of the new Cretan settlement pattern, as well as the particular social responses of the island's communities during collapse, heavily conditioned the type and layout of architecture in the post-collapse period, as I shall show.

Recent excavations at Monastiraki Chalasmeno and Katalimata and Kavousi Vronda, all in east Crete, throw light on life at the smaller type of new settlement (Coulson and Tsipopoulou 1994; Day 1997; Day et al. 1986; Day and Snyder 2004; Gesell et al. 1983, 1985, 1988, 1991, 1995; Tsipopoulou 2001, 2004a, 2004b, 2005b; Tsipopoulou and Nowicki 2003; Figures 50–52). For larger and more complex sites established at this period, Karfi, in the Lasithi range (where much of the settlement remains unexcavated), still provides the most information (Pendlebury et al. 1938; Wallace 2005b; Figures 50–56). I will consider all these sites in some detail. At the continuing sites of Knossos, Phaistos, and Chania, only relatively small areas of architecture dating

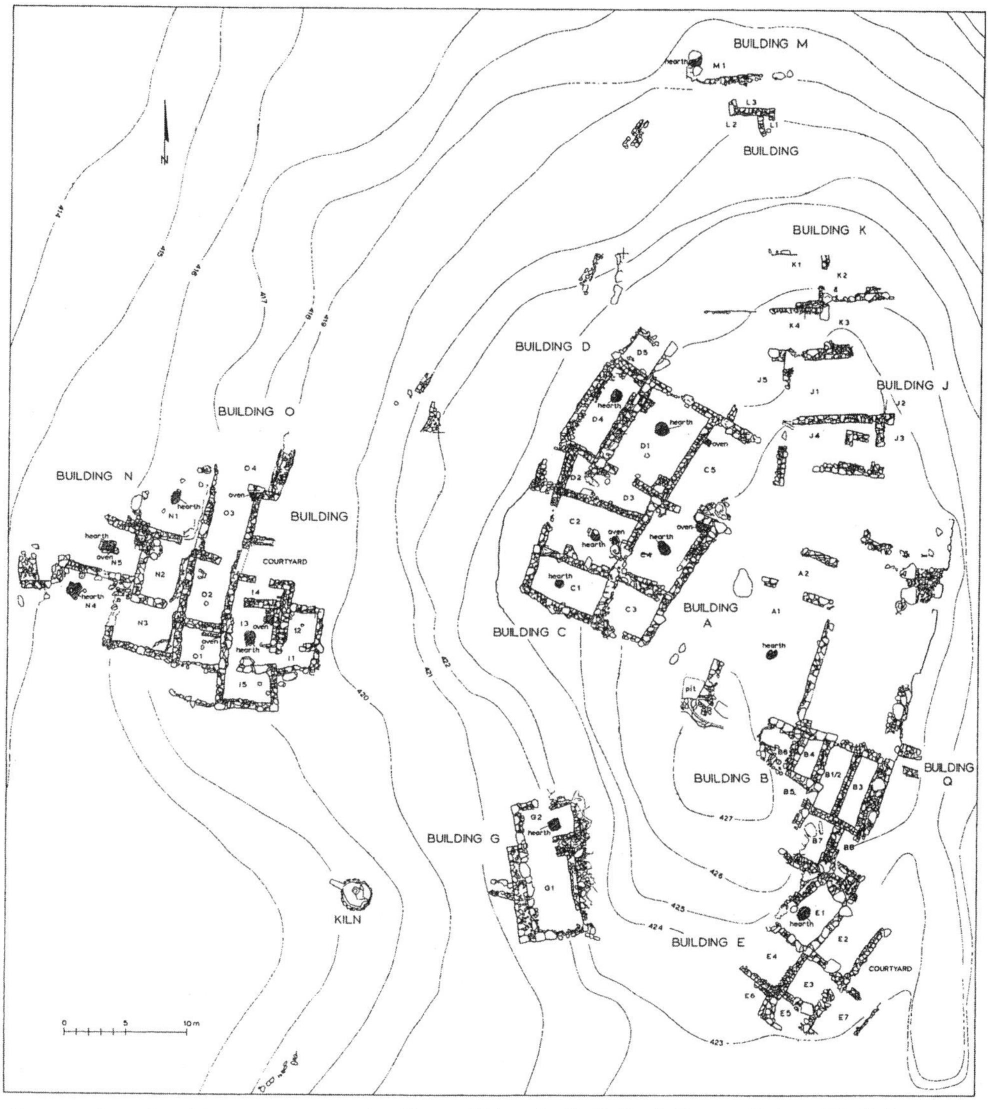

50. Current plan of architecture excavated at Kavousi Vronda (L. P. Day). By permission of L. P. Day.

to this period have been exposed, thanks in part to heavy later occupation, with associated levelling and filling activities. No good overall picture of the early EIA settlement is available in any of these cases, though I will highlight particular elements of interest.

Architecture: general features of the record and issues for discussion

Although functional, symbolic, and wealth-related differentiation in building construction, size, and form appears at the new sites, this is notably subtle and modest, in what is generally a non-elaborate built environment. The move to a much less highly differentiated kind of intra-settlement landscape is a core feature of Cretan post-collapse culture, with a number of social implications.

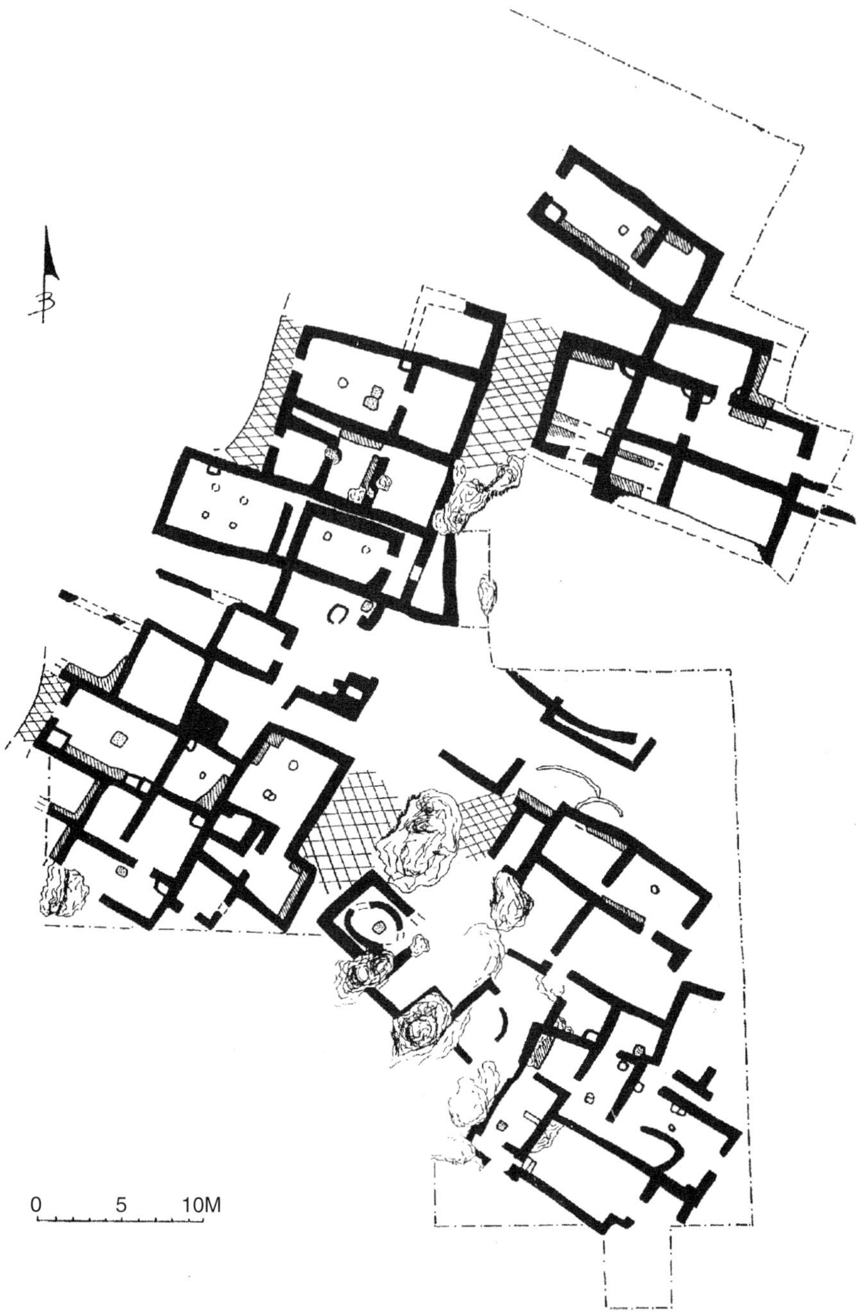

51. Current plan of architecture excavated at Monastiraki Chalasmeno (after Tsipopoulou 2004a, Fig. 2, p. 129). By permission of M. Tsipopoulou.

The standard construction technique was worked rubble, used either throughout the building or as a foundation for mudbrick walls (Coulson and Tsipopoulou 1994: 80; Day et al. 1986: 366, 385). The technique adopted usually applied across a whole site, and how far mudbrick was used may have depended partly on the local environment: Karfi, for example, with its many stone outcrops and large screes nearby, had exceptionally good access to building stone, a fact reflected in the stone walls preserved to seven or eight courses. Evidence for second storeys is not common

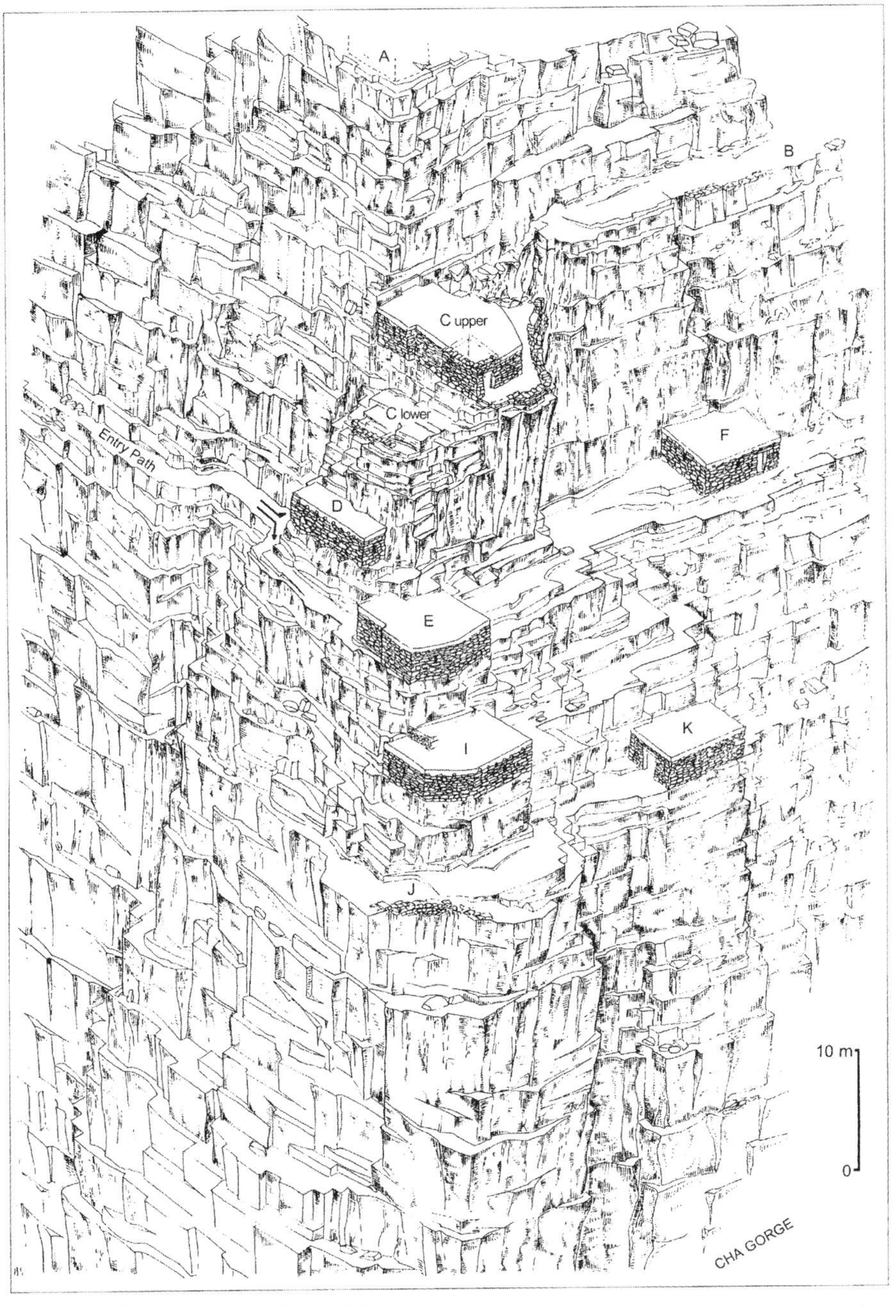

52. Reconstruction drawing of LM IIIC buildings at Monastiraki Katalimata, showing entry path to the site. The excavated area is Terrace C (after Nowicki 2008).

anywhere, though some may have existed at Vronda: mudbrick construction would have made them easier to build (Day et al. 2009: 61–2).

The steep, rocky topography of the new sites encouraged terracing of buildings into slopes, the use of extra-thick rear walls, and narrow, linear plans running along natural rock ledges or artificial terraces. Sometimes rooms in the same house were built on different levels, linked by

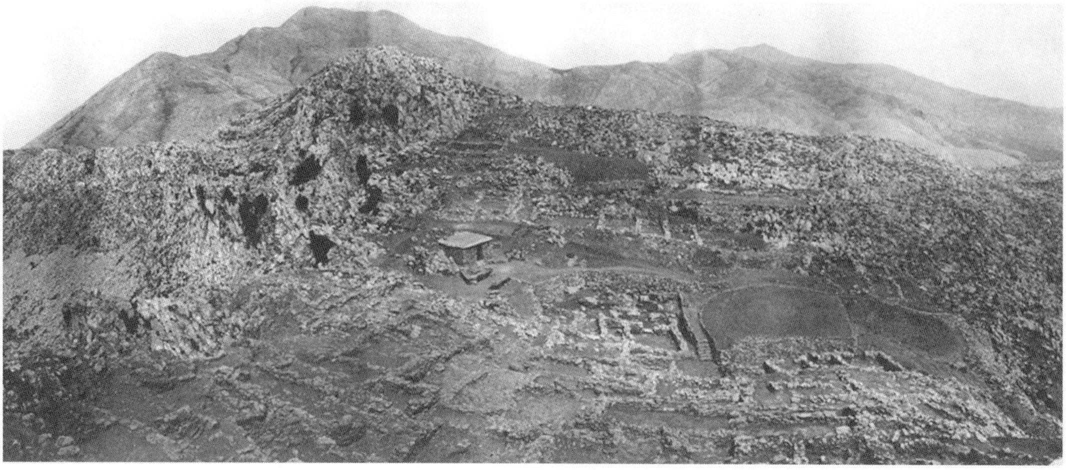

53. Karfi settlement site immediately after excavation, from Karfi peak looking east (after Pendlebury et al. 1938, Plate XV (2)).

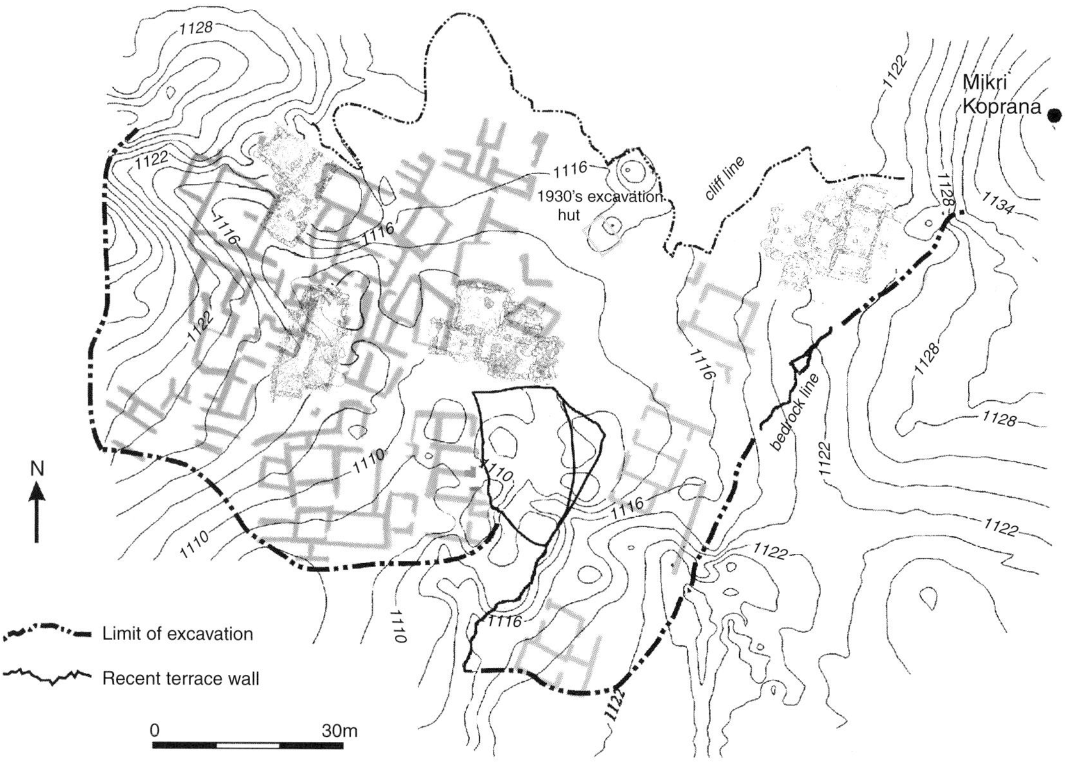

54. Full topographic plan of the excavated area at Karfi, 2002. Buildings studied and recorded in detail by the author in the period to 2006 are shown in their correct positions, with a 'best fit' positioning of the 1938 site plan. Image by the author.

steps, as at Karfi. The irregular bedrock of the hill summits and slopes was often incorporated into the architecture, highlighting the fact that the new sites were certainly not chosen for ease of building – many flatter-topped, but less defensible, summits went unused (Gesell et al. 1985: 353; Hatzi-Vallianou 2004: 114; Hayden 1983: 374; Wallace 2005b). Restricted space for building

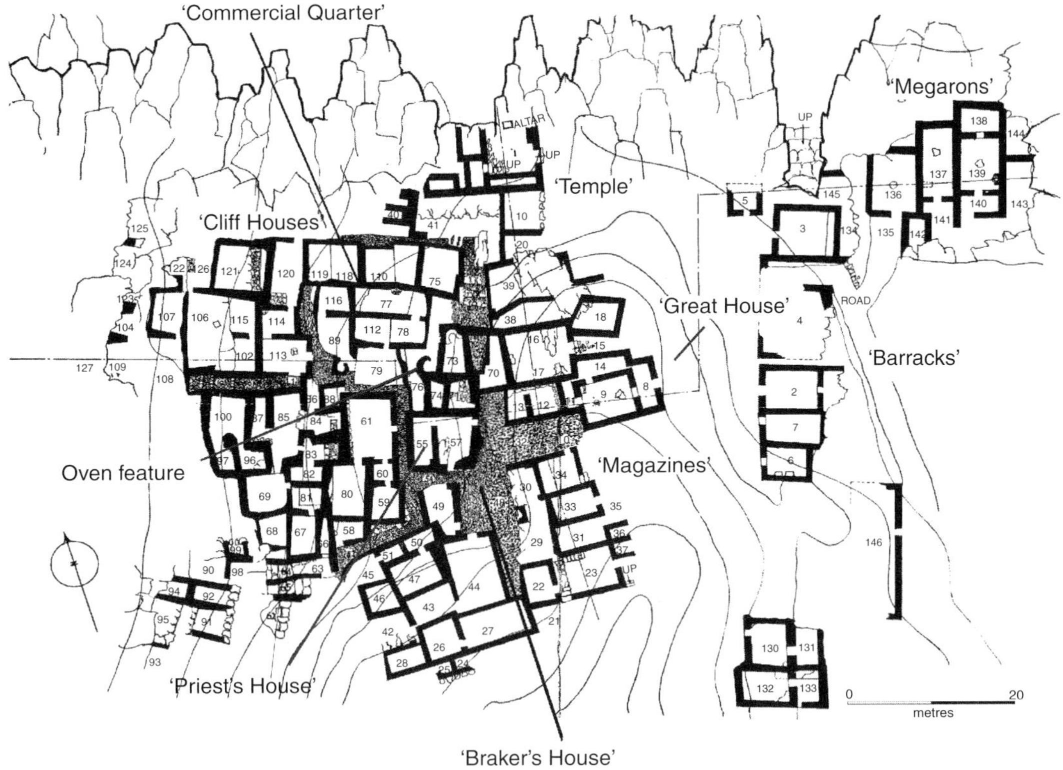

55. Annotated original plan of excavated area at Karfi, with building sectors/features labelled according to their original designations (after Pendlebury et al. 1938, Plate IX).

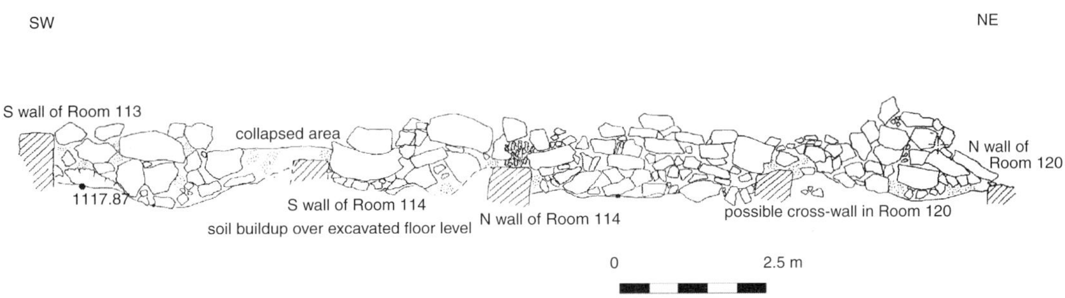

56. Elevation of west wall of a building in the western saddle of Karfi (rooms 113–20) showing shaped rubble construction. Image by the author.

at these locations also encouraged agglutinative construction, with additions being made over time onto an initial plan of relatively small buildings with spaces between them. Karfi, Vronda, and Chalasmeno all illustrate this well (Figure 57; Glowacki 2004). Agglutinative growth had already been a feature of space-constricted sites like the hilltop village of Chondros Kefali in the LM IIIA-B period (Hayden 1987; Platon 1997; Figure 58). The level and rate of agglutination varied according to the topography of each new site, as well as its degree of growth over time: it seems to have been a standard method of expansion, planned for in the use of exceptionally thick external walls as 'spines' in many early building cores (Day et al. 1986: 375–6; Wallace

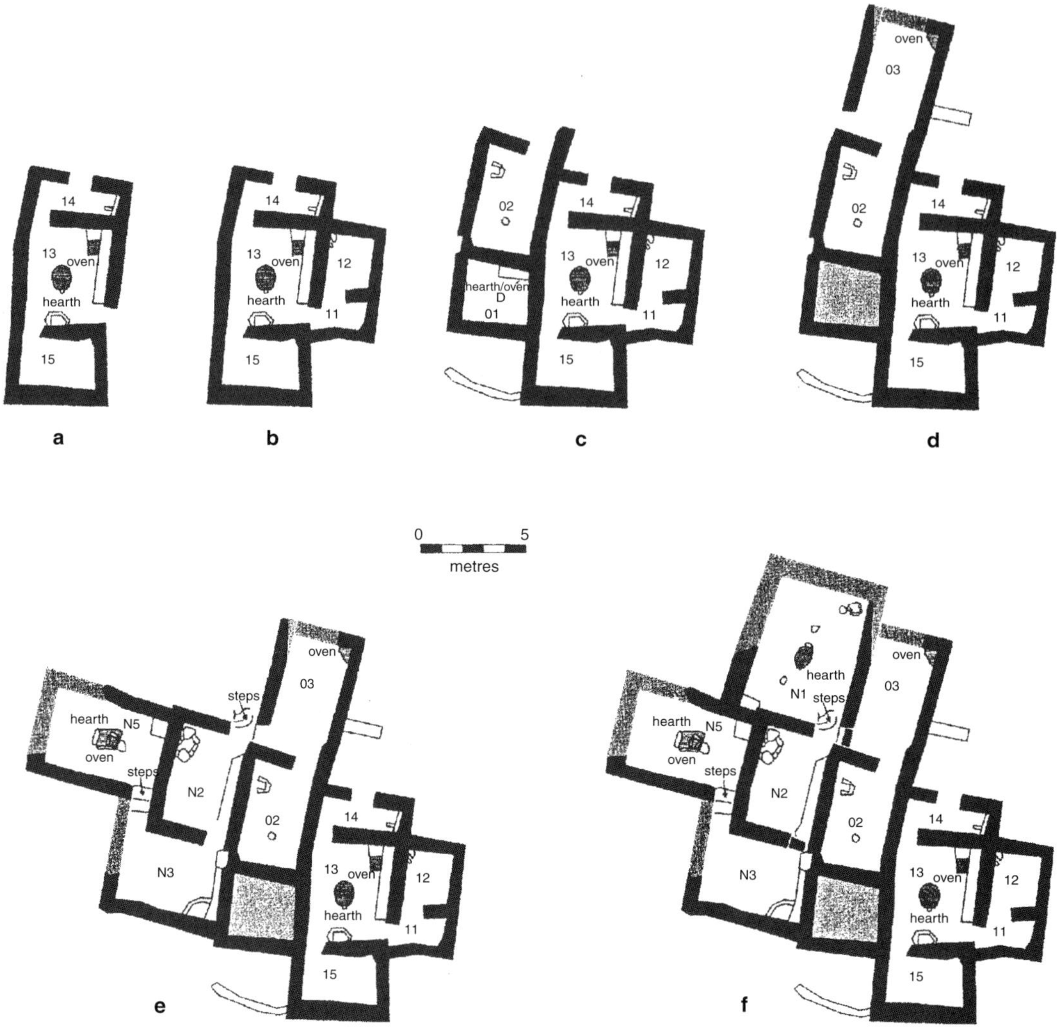

57. Growth over time of building complex I-O-N at Kavousi Vronda (after Glowacki 2004, Fig. 14.4, p. 133). By permission of K. T. Glowacki.

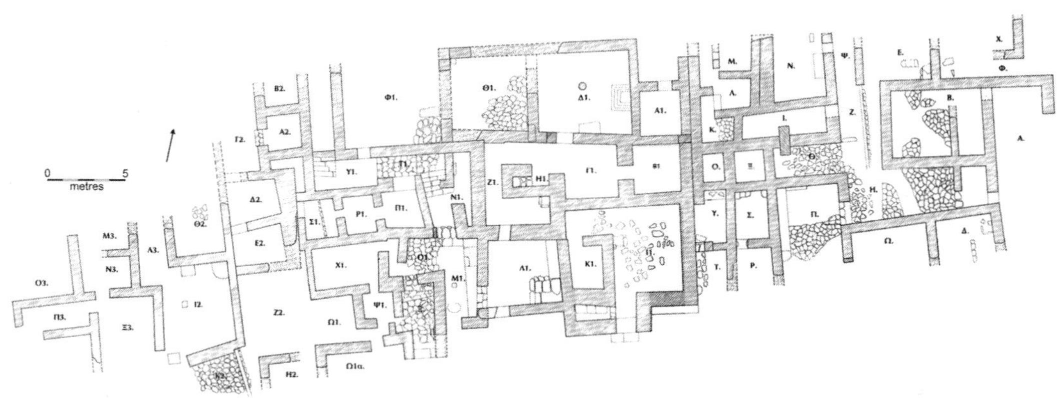

58. Plan of excavated settlement area at Chondros Kefali (after Platon 1997, Fig. 4, Plate 363). By permission of L. Platon.

2005b: 248). Agglutination was also a form of social interaction and power building, important in constructing relationships, whether at the level of the kin group's everyday needs, or beyond these, in the public arena (Glowacki 2002, 2004; Haggis 1993: 151; Jameson 1990a: 108). For example, in the so-called Great House complex at Karfi, which eventually became one of the largest and richest in the excavated settlement, the main room 16–17 had its impressive entrance, incorporating an exceptionally large threshold slab, drastically reduced in size when a storage extension was added to the neighbouring house or room, 9, with which it did not ever communicate (Pendlebury et al. 1938: 77–9; Wallace 2005b: 238–42, in press a; Figure 59). This change may have marked either a newly close collaboration between two originally separate groups or the annexation of one group's space by the other, and may well be connected with a developing public remit for the complex. The 'Priest's House' at Karfi is distinguished by two large main rooms, 61 and 80 (most houses have only one main room). These eventually came into communication (Pendlebury et al. 1938: 84–6; Wallace 2005b: 242–4; Figure 60). Room 80, which eventually assumed a specialised storage function, may have been added onto room 61, or had its use changed into that of an exceptionally large storeroom, as the building's owners/users grew in prosperity or acquired more of a public role (discussed below). The late addition to this complex of an unusual small extension (room 58), containing cult material of the type found in contemporary public shrines, may represent an attempt to appropriate some elements of public cult practice into the private sphere, in the interest of prestige and power building on the part of the group living here.

Despite the 'messy' appearance of many final site plans as a result of agglutinative spread in an awkward and constricted topography, a considerable degree of planning is clear in the early stages of the new settlements' development. Karfi, for example, has paved courts/squares and

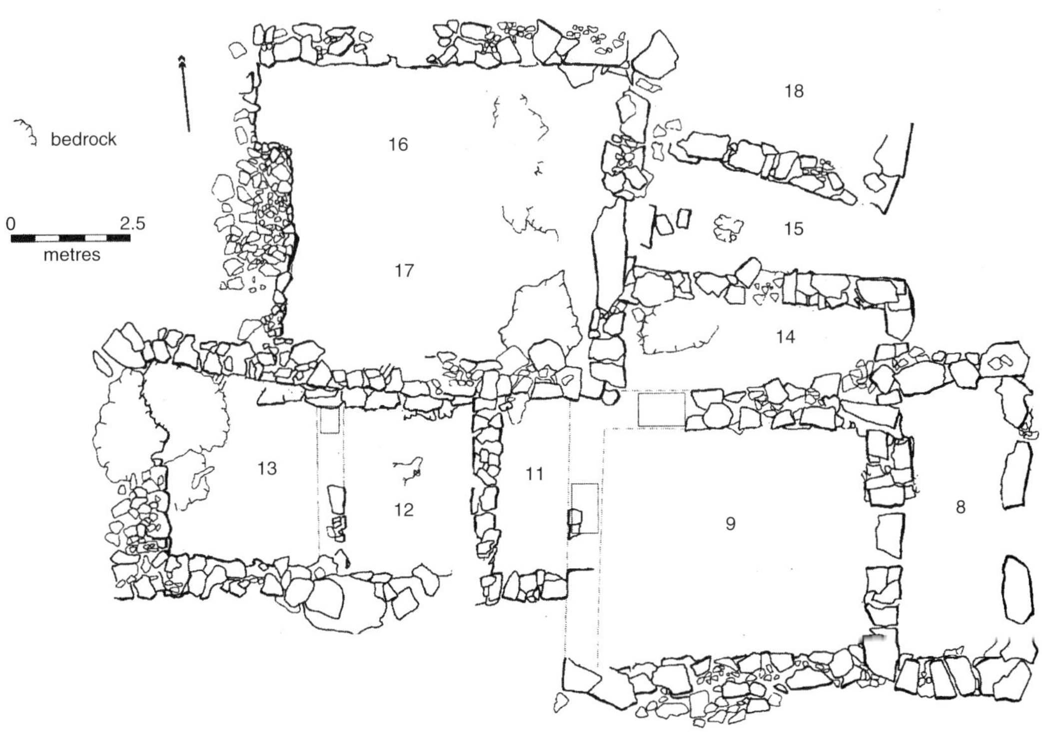

59. State plan of Karfi 'Great House' (rooms 8–17), 2002. Image by the author.

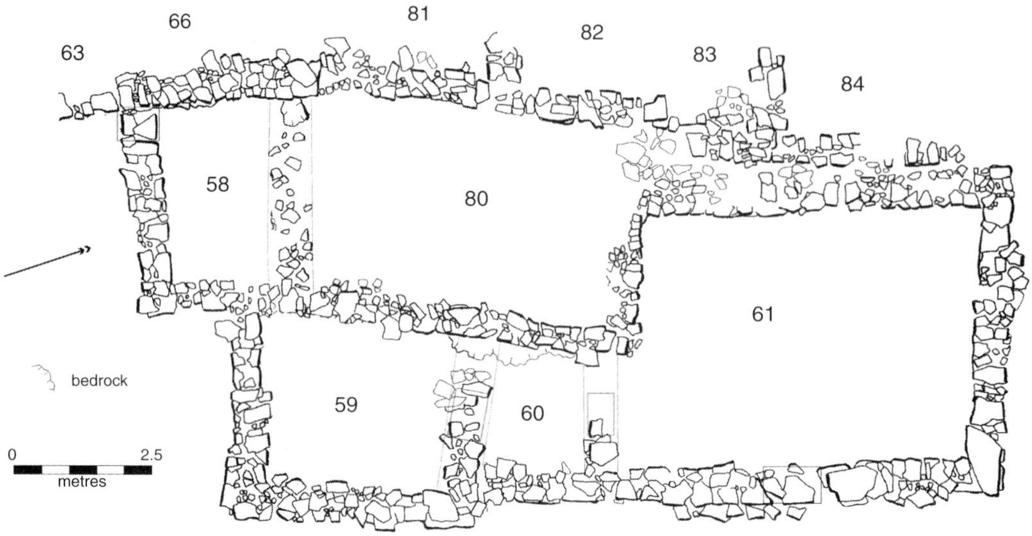

60. State plan of Karfi 'Priest's House' (rooms 58–80), 2002. Image by the author.

streets, paralleled at Vronda (Day et al. 1986: 360; Pendlebury et al. 1938: 79, 93; Tsipopoulou 2004a: 127; Wallace 2005b: 252; Figure 61). However, the many building alterations that occurred over the lifespans of all sites, including blocking of and infringement onto these established open spaces, suggest regularly changing dynamics of space control, rather than the permanent, uncontested recognition of civic space from an early stage. Like the special kinds of building extension mentioned, this ties in with a social model for the period recently put forward by Day and Snyder (2004), suggesting that power in some of the new communities (especially the larger ones) was spread among numerous different small groups, who regularly renegotiated their standing using various facets of material culture, including domestic architecture – expanding and altering the latter for functions including ceremonial feasting or cult practice at a level beyond that of the household, but still distinct from that of a public institution.

The fact that new public institutions *were* becoming established at the new Cretan sites from soon after their foundation is also reflected in the architectural environment. In the context of other patterns in architecture at this period, it is unsurprising that the buildings associated with these institutions were only subtly and quietly differentiated from domestic houses and shared many morphological features with them. It seems that these ties, and this simplicity, were crucial in helping give the institutions a firm, grounded role in the potentially volatile new community groupings and in enabling a broad cross section of residents to access and participate in the associated activities. There is little sense that this modesty of design was a top-down strategy. Rather, given the new political and economic circumstances affecting the new communities, it may have been difficult for any one group to establish an elite position from which to engage in the exclusive or dominant support of elaborate institutions and their related culture. One well-defined institution was public cult practice at settlement level, in specialised shrine buildings. The specialised connection of some buildings to feasting at a public level is also hinted at not only by features of plan but by especially high concentrations and particular combinations of fine drinking pottery, cooking facilities, food storage, and food remains. This applies to cases like Vronda Building A/B, the complex on the summit of Smari Profitis Elias (dating LM IIIC through LG), and the Karfi Megarons (Day and Snyder 2004; Hatzi-Vallianou 2004; Hatzi-Vallianou and Evthimiou 2000).

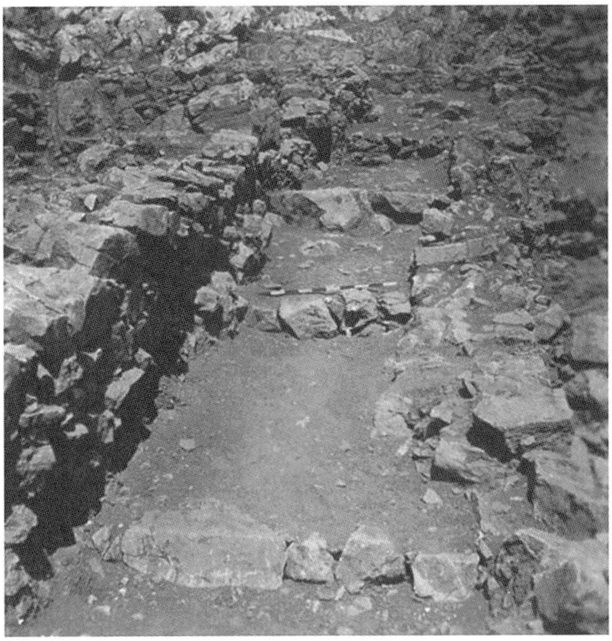

61. Stepped street (units 101, 103, 105, 111) between buildings in Karfi's western sector, from east (after Pendlebury et al. 1938, Plate XXII).

Interpretations of these buildings' use that have been proposed by other scholars to date stimulate further discussion and analysis. For example, Day and Snyder (2004, 2009: 61–3) suggest Vronda A/B was a chief's dwelling within a stably ruled small community – yet use of the building as a public feasting venue could stand as an additional or alternative interpretation. The work of Mazarakis Ainian has focused very closely on the idea of single preeminent rulers in EIA communities (1997: 375–81). He suggested that on the EIA mainland, the house of the most important family or 'ruler' – assuming a permanent chief – had the main role in the hosting of public feasts, and that public cult activity took place in the same houses, and under chiefly control. This idea is used by him to explain the absence of defined temple buildings in mainland settlements of the early EIA, but the evidence supporting this model in Crete is limited, as the author himself acknowledges.

Despite the interpretative difficulties caused by the subtle nature of architectural differentiation at this period, it does seem possible, using contextualised studies, to identify locales of formal collective feasting and cult separate both from each other *and* from the dwellings of powerful families at a number of new settlements. I shall return to these issues below.

Building differentiation: size and construction

The move towards buildings of modest size and limited elaboration after about 1200 BC in Crete is striking. Buildings at LM IIIC sites are generally smaller than many of those at LM IIIA-B settlements – though the greater variety in LM IIIA-B site types and topographies, explored earlier, must be borne in mind in this regard. I have already suggested that the architectural changes in LM IIIC were related to the economic and social disruption of the period: the level of resources and status required for certain groups or individuals to invest in very large or elaborate buildings was lacking in most of the new communities. However, in cases where site topography stayed similarly restrictive between the two periods, as in the case of the LM IIIA-B hilltop village of Chondros Kefali (Platon 1997), there is sometimes little direct contrast in building plans. In the space-limited cores of urban sites like Chania and Katsambas that continued in use into LM IIIC, house forms and sizes also changed little (Alexiou 1955; Hallager and Hallager 2000).

Overall, buildings were much more similarly sized *between* different settlements in LM IIIC than they had been in LM IIIA-B (Figure 62; Wallace 2005b: 255–7, in press a). This fact clearly relates both to the flattening of settlement hierarchy and to the special topography, contemporary origins, and roughly parallel developmental circumstances of the new settlements. The sizes of LM IIIA-B buildings had varied according to the former history of each site, as well as its place in the hierarchy and internal social organisation.

Few plans of LM IIIA-B settlements are well enough preserved over an extensive area to give a good picture of *intra*-settlement differentiation. Significantly, though, even in a small and fairly simple settlement like Chondros Kefali, one centrally positioned building (H1-G1) stands out in terms of size, elaboration, and assemblage profile (Platon 1997). This occurs on a much grander scale at Malia, where the large and elaborate Quartier Nu complex clearly forms a single discrete unit – though since we do not have a good picture of the organisation of LM IIIA-B Malia as a whole, it is difficult to ascertain the building's exact role or status (Driessen and Farnoux 1994; Farnoux 1997a; Figure 63). In LM IIIC, the new physical factors keeping building size generally small and similar between sites (as well as the changed social environment) generally also reduced the scale of intrasite building size differentiation. In this context, larger structures, even if only modestly differentiated from others in the settlement, may not only have been *built* by the largest or most powerful families, but have promoted special social roles for their occupants from the beginning (Barrett 1999: 257; Donley-Reid 1990; Lane 1987: 57).

Some examples clearly stand out. At Karfi, the large room 16–17, in the Great House complex, is marked out by its exceptionally long threshold block (more than 2m, where all others on the site are below or barely clear 1m); another large building, the Priest's House, also has a large single-block threshold. These buildings have other special features – traces of wall plaster

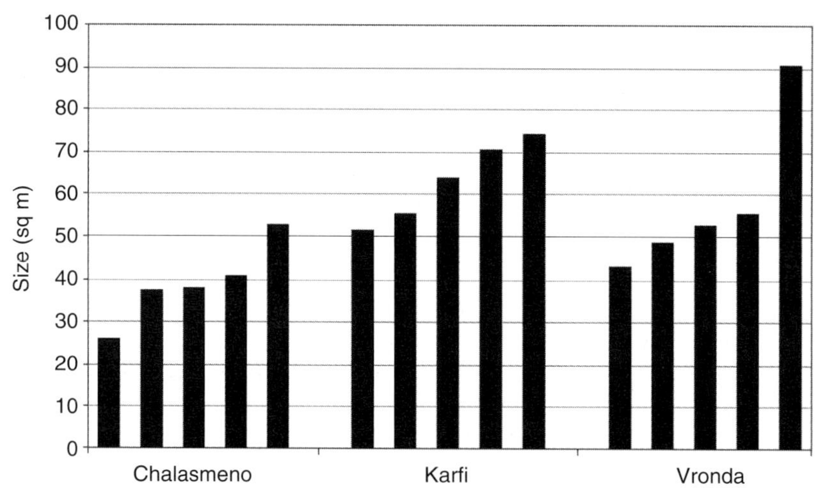

62. Graph comparing largest building sizes (sets of rooms with preserved or assumed communicating doors) in the three most extensively excavated LM IIIC-SM settlements. Image by the author.

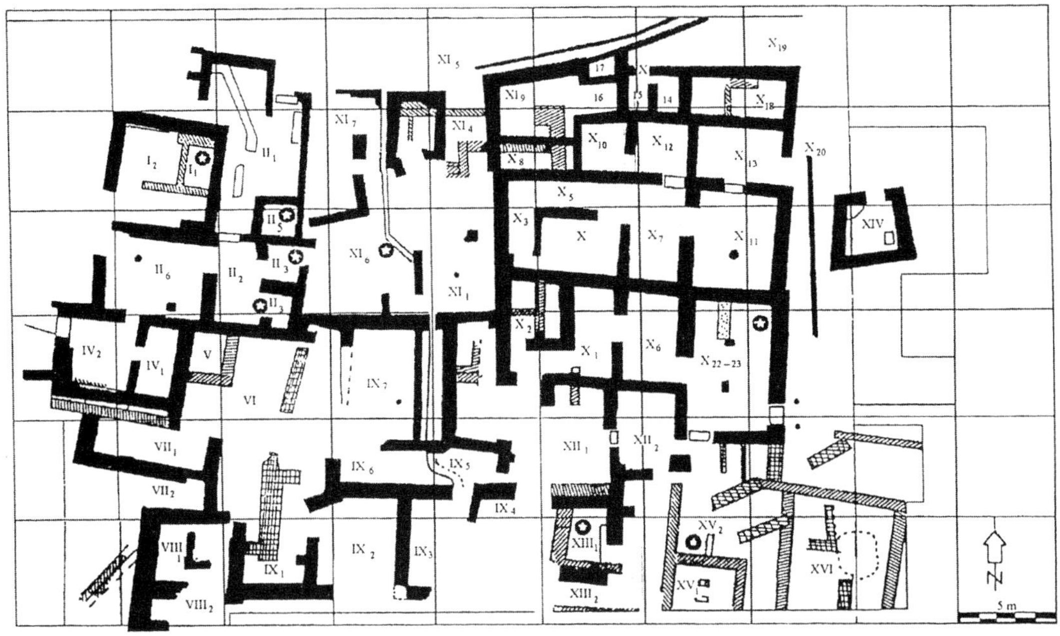

63. Plan of the Quartier Nu complex, Malia (after Driessen and Farnoux 1994, Fig. 2, p. 57). By permission of J. Driessen.

and a unique long bench in the Priest's House, unusually massive wall construction in the Great House. The 'Megarons' complex, in the eastern part of the Karfi site (Rooms 135–40), has a unique concentration of hearths and an unusually static plan, not appearing to be altered over time in the way seen at many other buildings on the site. It incorporates distinctive architectural features similar to those of the Great House (Figure 64; Pendlebury et al. 1938: 70–2; Wallace 2005b: 238–42; see discussion below). Thus several buildings are subtly distinguished in size and form from others in the settlement. This supports the notion (if we assume, on the basis of their plans and basic artefact assemblages, that they had a residential use) that those owning/using them had competing social roles, and that one group never assumed a unique public prominence. Artefact evidence supports this idea, though the differentiating factors vary in each case. The Great House has an unusual concentration of large fine drinking cups (*kylikes*), cult material of a type normally associated with public shrine buildings (goddess figurines with upraised hands), and a concentration of metals. The Priest's House has an unusual deposit of animal horns (potentially connected with ritual) and some cult items in the special room, 58, referred to above, as well as an exceptionally large storage area. The 'Megarons' also have an exceptional concentration of storage space. Unusually, a significant amount of it is located in what seem to be unroofed areas.

Smaller settlements show a more concentrated and singular type of architectural differentiation. At Vronda, Building A/B not only is far larger than any other on the site, but includes a set of special features in both its architecture and its finds assemblage, suggesting a long-term, fixed distinction from any other dwelling in the settlement. These are an ornamental window-frame, so far unique not only for Vronda but for any LM IIIC site; a large courtyard in front of the building; particular concentrations of fine ceramics, including unusually large *kylikes*; a unique set of modified animal skulls which the excavators think hung on the interior walls and had a special symbolic significance; large-scale storage vessels, and a specialised storage (Day and

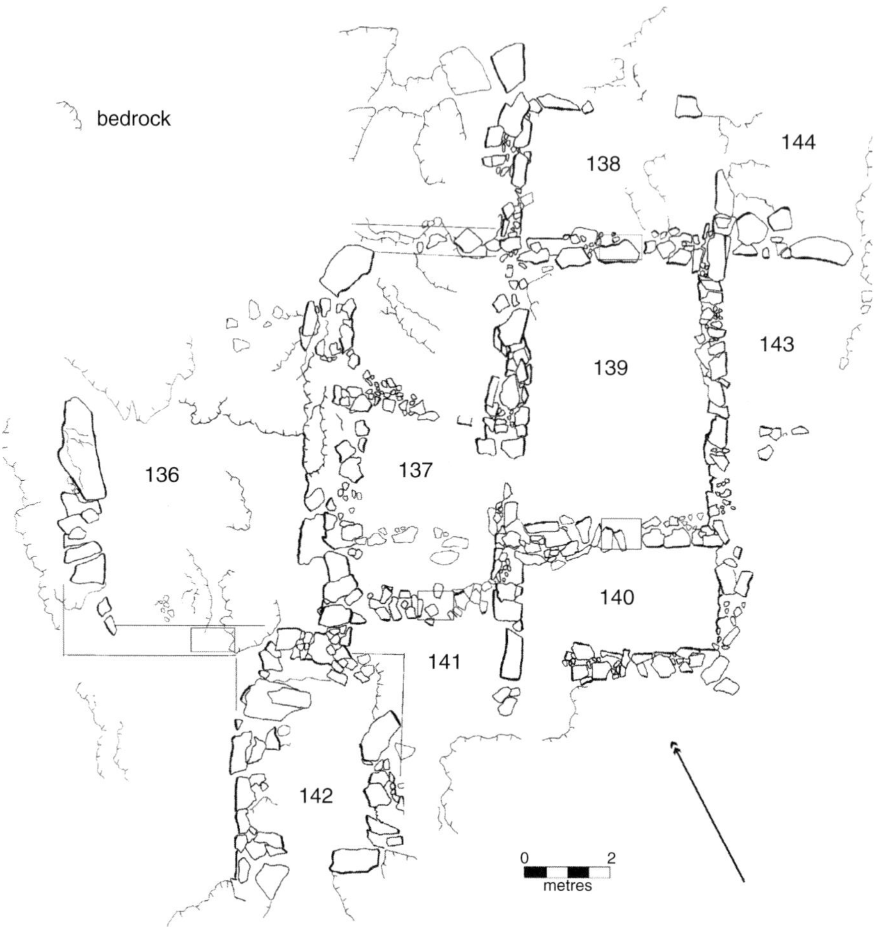

64. State plan of 'Megarons' complex (rooms 136–44), Karfi, 2002. Image by the author.

Snyder 2004). At Chalasmeno, too, a block of axially planned buildings (the 'Megarons') in the centre of the settlement, adjacent to a large open space, stands out architecturally from any other block on the site in terms of layout and orientation, though its finds record is limited (Paschalidis 2006; Tsipopoulou 2004a, 2005b).

Identifying building/room functions from finds assemblages and features: general comments

Turning to finds assemblages for insight on room function, we are again hampered by incomplete recording at Karfi, while benefitting from the results of new, high-quality excavations at the smaller east Cretan sites. At most sites, assemblages tend to be broadly similar for all types of building and suggest that the majority of units functioned mainly as houses. Only a few, subtle differences in finds point to buildings operating beyond the household level, as I have already noted above. Just as distinctions in building form were kept subtle and limited in the new social context, specialised/ceremonial activities did not tend to involve large concentrations of exclusive, exotic, or showy items. Even temple buildings (see below) often include cooking and storage pottery and spindle-whorls and spools, alongside concentrations of cult objects (Gesell et al. 1988: 289–90, 1991: 162; Pendlebury et al. 1938: 75–7; Tsipopoulou 2001). Within houses of various types and scales, we can see that cooking and dining, storage, craft production, and cult activity (where present) all overlapped closely in the areas of space they used (Glowacki 2002, 2004). The layout of these activities was never repeated exactly from house to house, again suggesting considerable flexibility in space use, with no rigid format for particular activities. Ongoing agglutination as the main means of settlement growth must have encouraged this flexible approach.

The single large rectangular room is the focus for most buildings in LM IIIC Crete, just as on the contemporary mainland at sites such as Nichoria and Lefkandi (Walsh and McDonald 1983). It sometimes comprised the entire residence: assemblages from Vronda rooms N4 and C4 parallel those of the individual Karfi units 2, 3, 7, and 23 (Glowacki 2004: 130–2; Pendlebury et al. 1938: 72–5, 80–1; Wallace 2005b: 255–61). One-room houses are also known from LM IIIA-B sites, where they represent a minority building form (Hayden 1987: 201–2, 223–4). In the main rooms of most Karfi buildings, and of those at Vronda, Chalasmeno, and Smari Profitis Elias (where the only building so far published outside the summit complex looks like a domestic house in both form and contents), a mixed assemblage is typically found, comprising storage vessels, cooking wares, dining and drinking pottery, loomweights, stone tools, and food remains. If read as the material construction/representation of the basic family unit, the limited size of these rooms and their regular distribution through expanding blocks suggests that adult children usually relocated out of the parental home (Glowacki 2004). Yet, the clustering over time of a number of these main-room units within large blocks suggests strong attachment to the extended kin group and close collaboration between its members. Plans incorporating a multiple-use main room combined with small subsidiary rooms had existed in modest LM IIIB structures such as an excavated house at Katsambas (part of the port settlement for Knossos) and most buildings at the village of Chondros Kefali (Alexiou 1955; Platon 1997). In larger houses at LM IIIA-B regional centres, like Gournia, there seems to have been greater differentiation in room function, with a larger number of sizeable subsidiary spaces for storage and perhaps for sleeping.

Though *building* size in LM IIIA-B varied greatly within settlements and between different site types, the largest *room* sizes (even in very large buildings) are often roughly comparable with those of LM IIIC – maximal room size was probably limited by roofing technology. The size of the main room in Gournia Building Eh is 34.3 square metres, and in Building He, 30.2 square metres (Figure 65). The main room in Plati Building A is 29.5 square metres, and the large eastern hall of Malia Quartier Nu (X 11), 26.5 square metres. Sizes of the largest main rooms are similar across new and continuing sites post 1200 BC (Karfi c. 29.9 to 56sqm; Vronda c. 24–38.9sqm), with the exception of Vronda Building A's unique main room, which may in fact be two rooms (74.2sqm; Smari c. 31.2–32.5sqm); Chalasmeno sizes are up to 28 square metres (Figure 66). The slightly higher upper room size limit at Karfi may be representative of larger and more complex settlements, but could also relate to technical considerations – mostly stone-built walls could more easily support wide roofs. Overall, then, elaboration in terms of numbers, uses, or forms of rooms is more restricted and less variable at LM IIIC sites than at many LM IIIA-B settlements. Again, we have the impression of much less marked social inequalities in the new communities and more room for negotiation of power than had previously existed.

In the next two sections, I consider the distribution, role, and organisation of some common activities at both household and settlement level, as far as they can be identified securely from the archaeological record, and compare these features between sites. I then focus particularly on spaces for public ceremonial within settlements, building on all the preceding discussion.

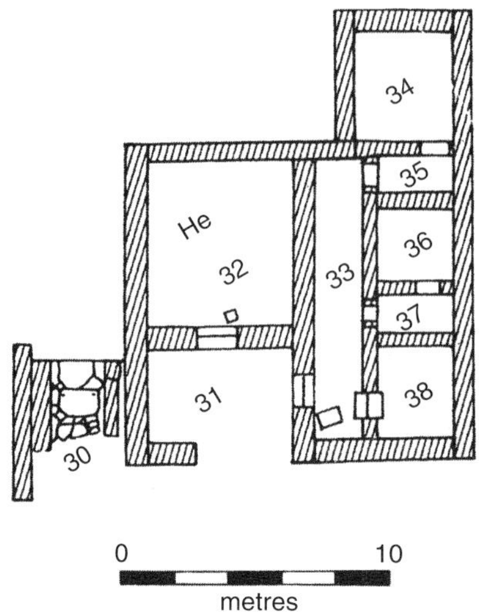

65. Plan of building He, Gournia (after Fotou 1993, Fold-out plan B). By permission of V. Fotou.

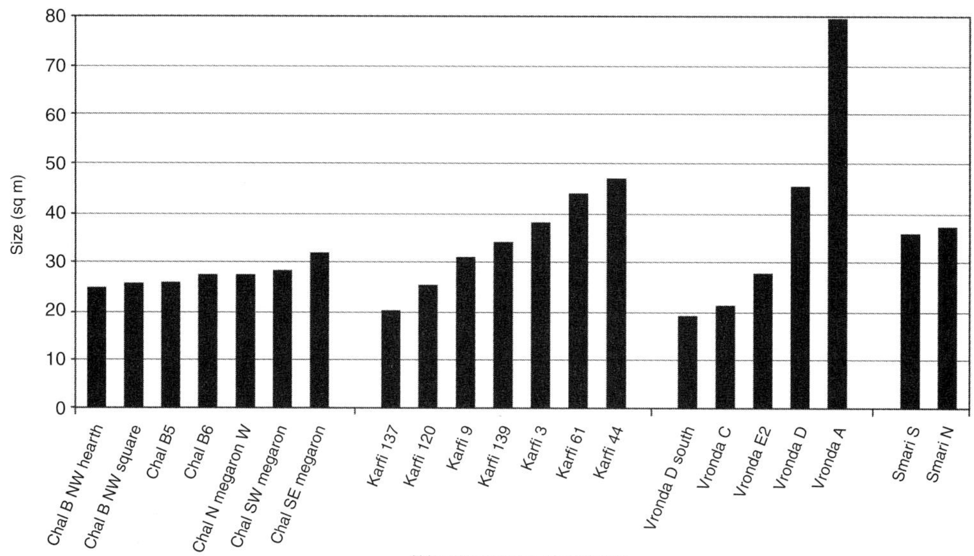

66. Sizes of largest rooms (excluding cult buildings) in the three most extensively excavated LM IIIC-SM settlements. Image by the author.

Cooking, dining, and storage

Centrally positioned hearths of burnt soil/clay appear at the few LM IIIB sites that continue into LM IIIC, and at many of the new defensible settlements (Coulson 1997: 64, 71; Coulson and Tsipopoulou 1994: 71, 76–7; Day 1997; Day et al. 1986; Glowacki 2002: 42; Hallager and Hallager 2000: 30–4, 49–51, 2003: 30–1; Wallace 2005b: 249–50). These had already appeared in LM I-IIIB domestic contexts – weakening any argument that they represent new 'mainland'-type features directly linked to incomers entering Crete after 1200 BC (Nowicki 1999b: 148). They are not present at *all* sites in either the LM IIIA-B or the LM IIIC period;

nor is their distribution standardised at any site. Examples of stone- and clay-built ovens are also found at all extensively excavated IIIC sites, but like that of central hearths, their frequency varies widely between sites and buildings. At Vronda, particularly, they appear along with central hearths in many houses – usually being located in the main room (Glowacki 2002: 42, 2004: 129–30).

The importance of ceremonial or ritualized dining as a mode of social bonding and power assertion is clear from the archaeological and Linear B evidence for the LBA Aegean. It had a significant, multilevel political role in the Archaic and Classical polis (Bendall 2004; Mazarakis Ainian 1997: 375–96; Murray, ed, 1990c; Nevett 1999: 154–75; Tsipopoulou 2004a: 136–8; Whitley 2001: 296–300, 309–10, 341–65, 361–2; Wright 2005); thus we might well expect it to have a significant (though changing) social role during the EIA. Observed patterns of cooking and food consumption at twelfth-century Cretan sites back this up, suggesting that formal feasting was less exclusively controlled by single centralised elite groups (whether at regional or settlement level) than it had been in the LBA. Notably unequal distributions of cooking facilities had appeared at some large LM IIIA-B sites. At Kommos, hearths were sometimes found clustered in separate 'kitchens' attached to major complexes where feasts might have been hosted (e.g., rooms 019, 012, Building P; the latter situation is paralleled at Malia Quartier Nu; Driessen and Farnoux 1994: 60; Shaw 1990: 238–9). Some form of communal dining hosted by a single established elite is also hinted at even in small settlements like Chondros Kefali, where the uniquely large and complex building in the centre of the settlement included a special storeroom for fine drinking wares. It appears that even very small-scale local elites engaged in ceremonial feasting at a beyond-household scale, perhaps as a way of maintaining cohesion and loyalty in the rural producer communities they dominated and developing their own prestige and standing. These feasting activities often seem to have taken place within structures that were large and complex enough also to be used as residences.

Turning to the LM IIIC record, Karfi, a concentration of hearths (generally very rarely recorded on this site during its 1930s excavation) in the 'Megarons' block, in conjunction with the concentration of storage facilities in the same building, is striking. A unique large oven containing cooking vessels appears at the centre of the site (room 73), also suggesting centralised organisation of food preparation, though of a different type (Pendlebury et al. 1938: 86–7; Wallace 2005b: 257–8). The settlement at Chalasmeno also shows differential concentration of cooking activity: Sector B has a special concentration of hearths and cooking pots (Tsipopoulou 2004b; Yasur-Landau 2006a, 2006b). At Vronda, Building A/B stands out for its cluster of storerooms, hearths, and cooking pots. At both the latter sites, these possibly specialised facilities existed alongside quite numerous domestic cooking facilities elsewhere in the settlement. At Karfi, however, while widespread cooking at household level is hinted at by the spread of cooking pots and trays through the settlement, and it seems likely that hearths were often missed during the original recording process, the more irregular appearance of domestic cooking installations might suggest a proportionately greater role for public facilities. The settlement at Smari Profitis Elias has been only partially excavated, but the central summit area houses an isolated complex of buildings with high concentrations of animal bone remains, and also distinguished by specific architectural features including central hearths. This may have been a specialised cooking and dining complex at some point between LM IIIC and Geometric (Hatzi-Vallianou 2004; Hatzi-Vallianou and Evthimiou 2000; Hatzi-Vallianou and Parchapidi 1999; Figures 67 and 68). At both Chamalevri and Thronos Kefala in the LM IIIC period, a set-apart zone of pits, each containing broken drinking ceramics, cooking pots, and animal bones, also suggests some kind of ritualized, collective food preparation and consumption activity (Andreadaki-Vlasaki and Papadopoulou 2005; D'Agata 2002).

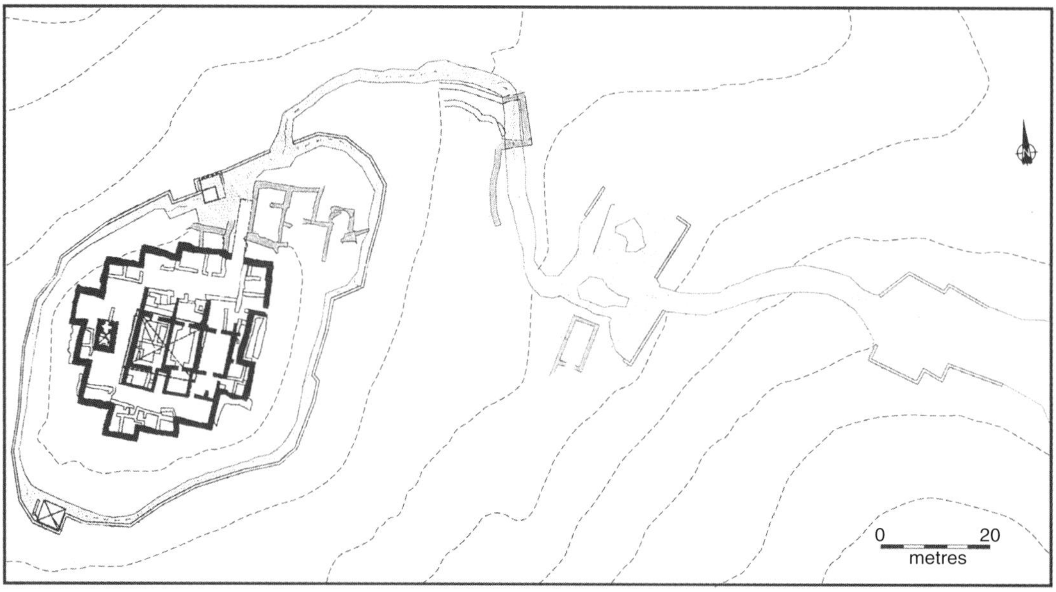

67. Smari Profitis Elias: general topography (after Hatzi-Vallianou 2004, Fig. 2, p. 107) By permission of D. Hatzi-Vallianou.

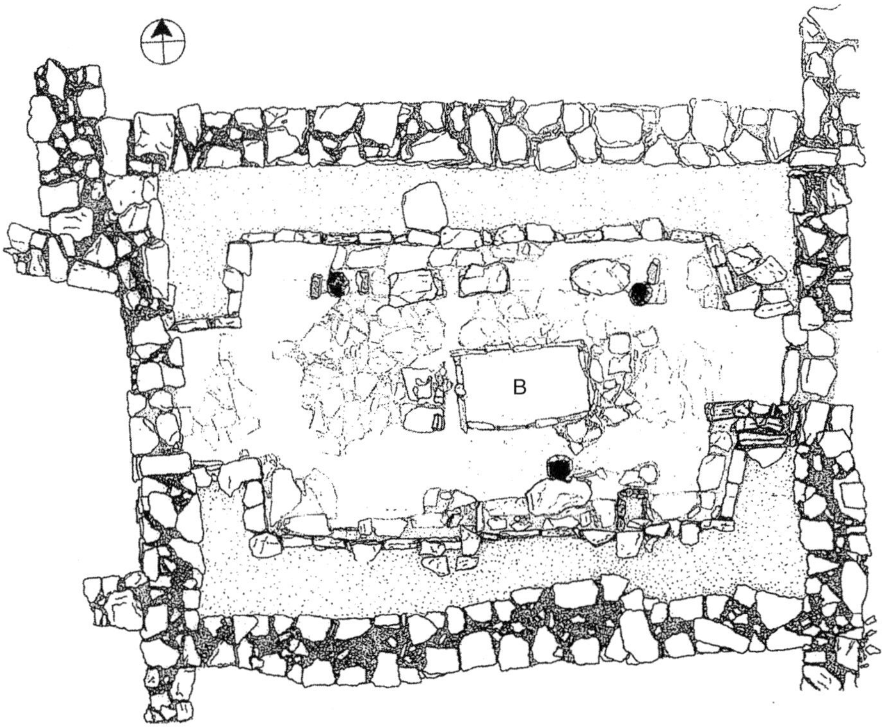

68. Smari Profitis Elias: detailed plan of main room in the central part of the Megarons complex (after Hatzi-Vallianou 2004, Fig. 12, p. 119). By permission of D. Hatzi-Vallianou.

Cooking and feasting with an element of public participation could play an important role in bonding new residential groups and developing their identities as communities. It could also act as an important arena for rivalrous private display and competition (Clark and Blake 1996; Dietler and Hayden 2001). Given the typically limited size and complexity of houses at the new sites, some central coordination of cooking would help small private groups to take on a public hosting role when required. By the same token, however, it would hold back the full or permanent appropriation of public feasting by any single small emergent-elite group, limiting the potential for power building by this means. This may help explain why it acquired a new importance as an institution in the relatively volatile social environment of the twelfth century. As with many other aspects of cultural life, it seems at the same time to have become more standardised and 'democratised', stripped of any very elaborate architectural setting, and dissociated from the absolute control of any one group, in a way that facilitated the building of stable, strong, and low-key social bonds.

Another factor that may help identify spaces used for public ceremonial dining with a public dimension is exceptional storage capacity. Most LM IIIC houses included a separate storage area containing food jars (*pithoi*), though part of the main room was also often used for this purpose. Overall we see a generally more standardised, modest scale of storage provision in LM IIIC buildings than in those of LM IIIA-B. Groups of small storerooms, similar to those found in large, high-status LM IIIA-B buildings, are suggested by the small units 81–84 and 102–105 at Karfi, and by the complex of small rooms in Building A/B at Vronda (Day et al. 1986: 357; Pendlebury et al. 1938: 89–92), but these do not always correlate with especially large or impressive buildings; nor do they offer anything like the same total storage volume as the LM IIIA-B storeroom groupings. Single storerooms are much more common in LM IIIC, varying widely (both between and within sites) in their capacity and in the numbers of pithoi they actually contained. This variation probably relates to the size of the residence group, but also to the level of hosting/feasting activities engaged in within the building, any additional uses of the storeroom (there is evidence for storage of fine ceramics and craftworking/metal tools in some examples), and the storage space available in the main room of the building (Wallace 2005b: 258–9).

Cult within settlements

During LM IIIA-B, centralised political authorities clearly had a strong interest in public cult practice – but so, apparently, did some powerful individuals and groups at local level, tied only indirectly to those authorities. At village level, 'ownership' of some aspects of cult by powerful local groups is suggested by the case of Chondros Kefali, where the largest house (H1-G1) seems to have incorporated a cult area, perhaps on a second storey (Platon 1997). There are also indications of a cult focus in Building E, a medium- to large-sized private house at LM IIIB Palaikastro (Cunningham 2005). Malia Quartier Nu, a large and wealthy complex with a quasi-public function, may have contained its own small shrine in room VII:1 (Driessen and Farnoux 1994: 63). Significantly, however, no separate cult building is known from any of these settlements. One did exist at the LM III regional centre of Gournia, though the control and operational arrangements relating to it are not clear (Boyd 1905: 41–2). The Knossos settlement contained a public shrine, the Shrine of the Double Axes, in the thirteenth century. Located within the palatial complex, this seems very likely to have been controlled by the central authority (Evans 1928: 335–44; Gesell 1985: 41–57; Prent 2005b: 514–15). In LM IIIA-B, then, cult practice (though separately defined in spatial terms at the largest sites) seems to have had no clear formal or regular status separate from elite control, and to have derived its political weight from the level at which that elite operated. Large regional cult sites in the wider landscape, like the Psychro Cave, Jouktas, and Kato Simi, also seem likely to have been under the sway of individual centres (Hiller 1997; Kanta 1991; Lebessi 1985; Watrous 1996: 57–70, 98–100).

In the light of Prent's recent comprehensive overview of the archaeology of cult in EIA Crete (Prent 2005b) there is no need here for an extensive characterization. Instead, I will present only a brief summary of the main cult-related features of the archaeological record for the early EIA, then focus, in the separately dedicated section that follows, on examining how cult fits into the model of social and political transformation from circa 1200 BC that I propose here for Crete.

One of the most striking features of the new settlements is the frequent appearance, in most of the examples so far excavated, of a single specialized cult building with a loosely standardised form. This is a stand-alone structure, sometimes with subsidiary rooms, set apart from block-type developments in the rest of the settlement. Internally, the plan often centres around one main room with a built ledge or bench on one or more sides on which the cult equipment appears to have been arranged. The size of the room (which may contain a hearth) varies little from that of domestic main rooms in contemporary settlements. As already noted, the assemblages from these buildings bear many resemblances to those found in houses. In most cases, construction technique is not notably different from that of domestic architecture. In general, then, the forms and features of temples echo those of contemporary houses as discussed earlier, except that in some cases the bench seems more solid or elaborate than typical benches within houses (Gesell 1985: 41–57; Prent 2005b: 188–200; Rutkowski 1987; Wallace 2005b: 250). Chalasmeno, Vronda, Karfi, and Vasiliki Kefala all have well-preserved examples of LM IIIC shrines matching this broad description (D'Agata 2001, 2006; Eliopoulos 1998, 2004; Gesell et al. 1988: 289–90; Klein 2004; Pendlebury et al. 1938: 75–6; Prent 2005b: 126–54, 188–200; Rutkowski 1987; Tsipopoulou 2001; Wallace 2005b: 253–72).

Even where sites continued directly in use from the LBA, as at Knossos, there is a significant readjustment in cult practice, in terms of its location and spatial format. The Knossos Spring Chamber shrine, incorporating many of the features of other LM IIIC shrine buildings listed above, was newly established at a spot outside, while still close to, the former palace area, and contained cult equipment similar to that of shrine buildings at the new defensible settlements (D'Agata 2006: 405–7; Evans 1928: 123–40; Prent 2005a, 2005b: 134–6, 198–9, 515–16).

These shrines seem to develop (though on an entirely new social plane) a set of practices and an architectural tradition already established in the LM IIIB period. Though they vary considerably in the details of their plans, they are linked by the basic features outlined above and by their distinctive artefact assemblages. The latter also have LM IIIB antecedents but now develop into a new and more elaborate package – one of the most important elements of which are the large wheelmade goddess figurines with upraised arms. At sites where later occupation obscures LM IIIC levels, indications that specialised shrine buildings existed appear in the form of deposits containing this distinctive artefact package. At Prinias, the badly preserved 'SM/EPG' building under the Geometric-Archaic Temple B shows a typical assemblage for a settlement shrine of the twelfth to eleventh centuries. A building of this type was clearly located on the Gortyn acropolis, within the twelfth- to eleventh-century settlement there (Mazarakis Ainian 1997: 224–6; Pernier 1914, 1934; Rizza and Scrinari 1968: 206–8). Most recently, traces of a typical LM IIIC shrine assemblage have been uncovered under the sixth-century remains at Azoria (Haggis and Mook pers comm). The range of diagnostic finds for such shrines includes, alongside the large hollow wheelmade goddess figurines with upraised arms, snake tubes, stands, plaques, and *kalathoi* in marked concentrations (Day et al. 2006; Eliopoulos 1998, 2004; Gesell 1985: 47–53; Prent 2005b: 174–84; Figures 69–71). Although many of these elements occasionally appear

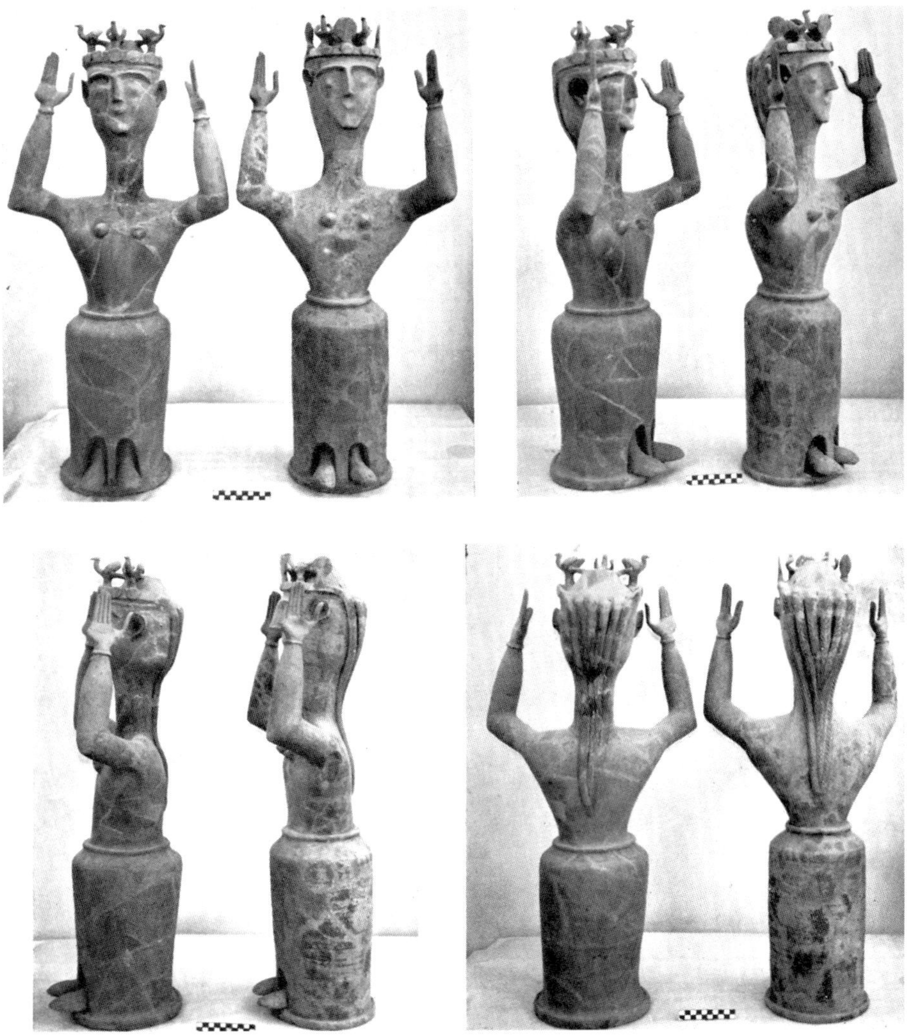

69. Large figurines of goddesses with upraised arms from the Temple at Karfi (after Pendlebury et al. 1938, Plate XXXI).

individually or in small groupings elsewhere on a site, they are uniquely concentrated, and represented in their full range, in these buildings.

At Karfi, besides the main concentration in the Temple, cult material of various types was spread in small amounts around other parts of the main excavated area, covering about 6,000 square metres in the saddle between Karfi and Mikri Koprana (Gesell 1985: 45–6; Pendlebury et al. 1938: 77–9, 81–7, 91–2, 95–6; Rutkowski 1987). This could suggest fairly broad social access to participation in cult via domestic shrines or (potentially) an increased concentration and specialisation of public cult activities in part of the site only – the central saddle – by the end of the occupation period, perhaps adapting or reusing domestic structures. The lack of stratigraphic recording in the original excavations permits limited insight. Domestic shrines are indicated at Chalasmeno and Vronda, where some cult-related items are found in buildings otherwise suggesting ordinary houses. These include animal and human figurines at both Chalasmeno and Vronda (Gesell et al. 1995: 70–1; Tsipopoulou 2004b). A domestic shrine with use extending into LM IIIC is also suggested within the excavated house at Katsambas (Alexiou 1955). For the

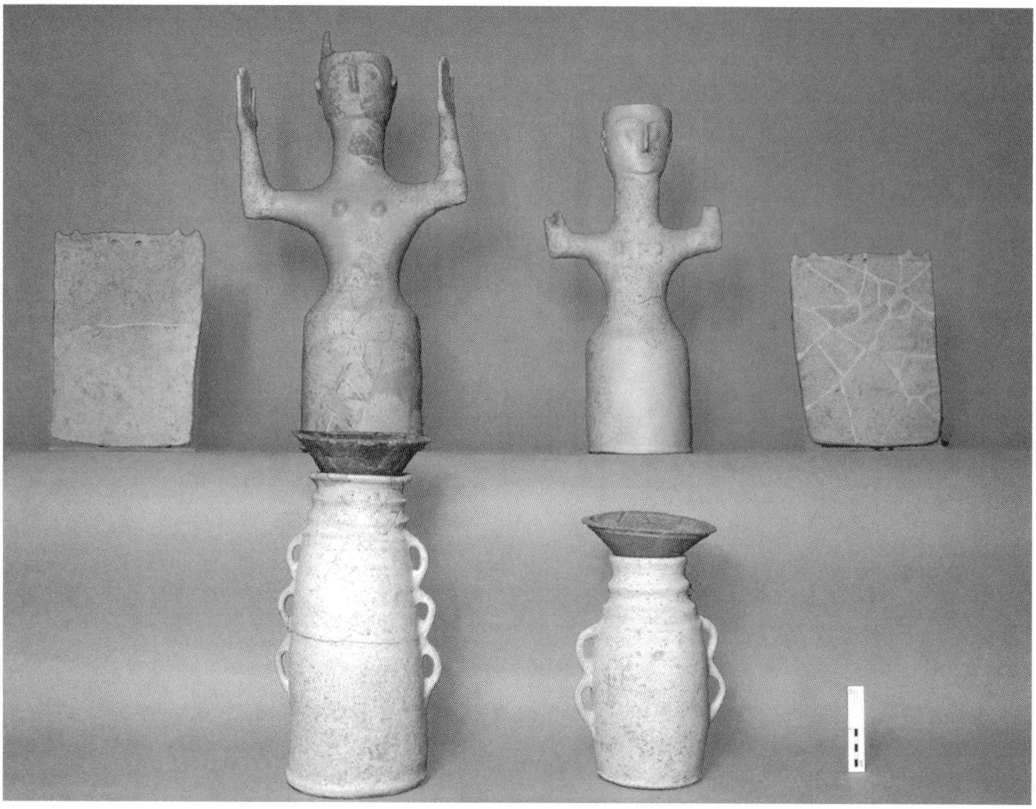

70. Cult equipment from Kavousi Vronda (G. Gesell). Unpublished image. By permission of G. Gesell.

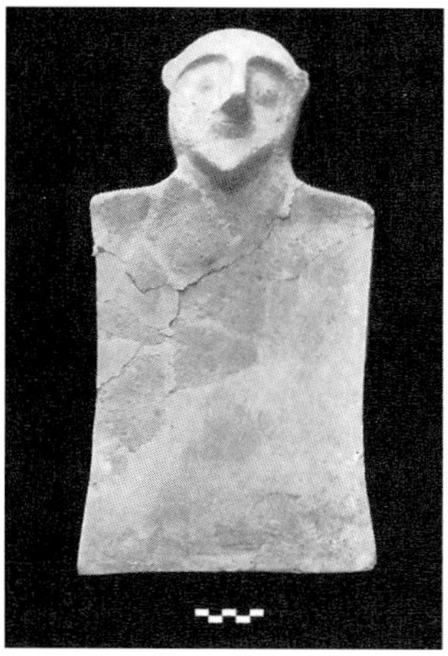

71. Plaque with human head from Karfi (after Pendlebury et al. 1938, Plate XXXV (1)).

Karfi material, contrasts in the type of 'cult' items found in different buildings (leaving aside the shrine complex itself) may be significant. Goddess figurines, snake tubes, and concentrations of kalathoi were found in rooms 58, 16–17, 70, 27, 57, and 116, while jewellery, other small metal items, and an anthropomorphic rhyton came from rooms 16–17, 85, 106, and 27. The latter most resemble the types of material deposited at contemporary extra-settlement sanctuaries, which I discuss below. When looking at cult practice within LM IIIC settlements as a whole, then, we sense once again that the boundaries of building and room function, and the categories of ritual activity engaged in within any particular space, were to some degree flexible or negotiated, *even while* dedicated spaces for ritual activities at a public level did exist.

Production areas

Few specialised areas for metalworking or ceramic manufacture have yet been identified at the new sites established in the twelfth century, and generally there seems to have been tight integration between craft production activity and domestic life. The similarity of Karfi's ceramic fabrics to those of surrounding smaller settlements like Kera Vigla, Krasi Siderokefala, and Kera Papoura suggests, given its size, that the site and/or its large neighbour at Papoura (which holds a similarly strategic position) might have acted in some ways as a regional production centre. However, on analogy with sites elsewhere in the island, some types of production almost certainly occurred at the smaller neighbouring sites as well (Nowicki 1995b, 2000: 147–70). The small Vronda site had its own kiln less than 30 metres from the settlement, and a potter's wheel was found in an otherwise ordinary-looking house (B2) at Chalasmeno (Coulson and Tsipopoulou 1994: 77; Day et al. 1989; Gesell et al. 1988: 290–3; Figure 72). The wide distribution of clay spools, spindle-whorls, and loomweights at Karfi and other sites of the period suggests textile-working was also spread out, in both spatial and social terms, seemingly taking place in most households (Day

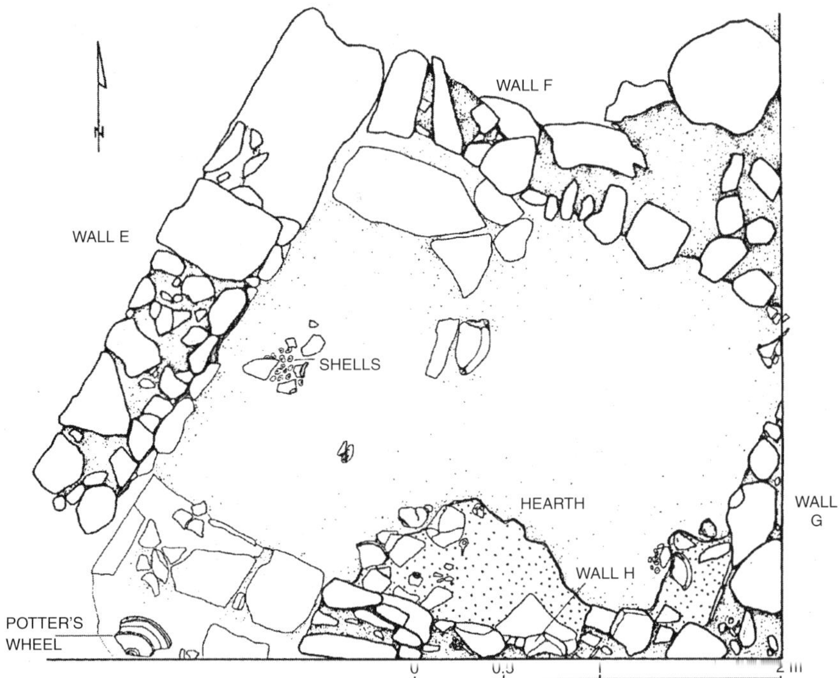

72. Plan of room with potter's wheel find from Monastiraki Chalasmeno (after Coulson and Tsipopoulou 1994, Fig. 12, p. 77). By permission of M. Tsipopoulou.

et al. 1986; Glowacki 2004). The clay spool, a newly common feature in twelfth-century Aegean assemblages and widely found at Karfi, may be in some way connected with newly decentralized forms of cloth production (Pendlebury et al. 1938: 131; Rahmstorf 2003).

The Karfi settlement has remarkably large quantities of bronze objects in comparison to much smaller sites like Vronda and Chalasmeno, suggesting that the most sizeable of the new sites might have acted as regional manufacturing or distribution centres for metals. It is noteworthy in this regard that Karfi burials are not exceptionally wealthy in the context of the island as a whole; nor do they otherwise stand out in this context. Thus, the concentration of metal at the site does not necessarily suggest a greater average wealth for individual inhabitants there. Metal items seem concentrated in the central part of the excavated saddle area. Room 26 contained exceptional quantities of bronze tools together with numerous pithoi, possibly suggesting a combined workshop/store; use of the room for cult activity has been put forward as an alternative interpretation (Pendlebury et al. 1938: 81–3; Prent 2005b: 193–4). The cluster of bronze tools and jewellery in Room 12 suggests it might have been a workshop or craft-related storeroom attached to the large and wealthy Great House: the latter, as we have seen, seems to have moved further and further away from a purely domestic role over its lifetime (Pendlebury et al. 1938: 77–9). Both cases could indicate the concentration of some production activities in the central saddle.

The general lack of evidence for very large-scale craft specialization, even at sizeable sites, contrasts notably with an apparently complex hierarchy of production in Crete during the LM IIIA-B period, represented archaeologically and in the Linear B tablets (Olivier 1997). This is discussed further in Part Three.

13 FOCUS ON CEREMONIAL AND RITUAL PRACTICE WITHIN SETTLEMENTS

In the following sections I focus closely on public feasting and public cult – aspects of specialised activity tied to two important institutions of the post-collapse period. My aim is to examine the broader context and structure of their development in the early post-collapse period.

Feasting places: houses or public spaces?

Since LM IIIC communities clearly planned and separated off spaces for public ritual, we could well expect collective, ceremonial cooking and dining to be organised in separate, specialised, public venues, as well as within the private residences of powerful families. In a social environment where an entrenched, highly distinguished elite was missing, the hosting of such feasts was surely a very valuable power-building tool at a number of levels. In view of the evidence considered earlier, I think the notion of in-residence feast hosting has been overrelied on for the early part of the EIA, with scholars suggesting that collective/ritualised feasting was *totally* controlled and contained at the level of the dwelling by a single community leader or a number of eminent persons/groups (Mazarakis Ainian 1997: 375–81). Mazarakis Ainian's study does, however, acknowledge that explaining the Cretan record necessitates at least some divergence from this model. For example, at Karfi the presence of more than one large and elaborate building with evidence for feasting argues strongly against the control of such ceremonies by any single group.

Histories like those of the Great House and Priest's House at Karfi, described above, suggest that successful hosting of public feasts could only be easily reconciled with domestic functions in relatively spacious buildings. Ambitious families may have expanded their houses with this kind of activity in mind, within the normal framework of agglutination current at the new settlements. The existence of social, as well as practical, restrictions on the ultimate expansive capacity of any single building at the new sites may help explain the emergence of a *number* of buildings with this role in large settlements, each differing only slightly from its peers in size or degree of elaboration. The use of shared public cooking facilities elsewhere on the site would help them to take on this role. Still, however, only about thirty people could be accommodated for communal dining activities in the main room of any building at Karfi, even assuming that storage, everyday food preparation, and sleeping were located elsewhere in the building. In general, given the estimated population sizes at the new sites and the typically modest scale of buildings at all of them, any such structures would still probably have to be used on a rotating basis by small affinal or kin groups, rather than the whole community being able to eat together (Nowicki 1990: 177–8). The Karfi Megarons block seems a good candidate for an 'official' feasting venue, both by comparison with other buildings in the excavated part of settlement and when considered in a cross-island context. Its uniquely well-recorded concentration of hearths (suggesting these were particularly large and noticeable features for the 1930s excavators) are laid out in exactly the same way in each of the three very similar large rooms that dominate the complex. This fact, and the unchanging plan of the building over time, may indicate that even though the component units had separate entrances, the block operated as a single building. If so, it had a significant capacity for formal feasting (and the storage to support it) but a much *lower* potential than other large buildings in the excavated part of the site to support combined domestic life and feasting (Wallace 2005b: 238–42, 264). For example, there are no subsidiary rooms except those clearly used for storage, and a large proportion of the total storage space was, unusually, located outside the main set of rooms, in and around a lean-to against the bedrock cliff to the east.

At Vronda, Building A/B never had serious competition from any other building in terms of size, architectural elaboration, or evidence for concentrated feasting. With its exceptional size, at 70 square metres, it could theoretically combine domestic and feasting roles more easily than any Karfi structure. However, arguing for this kind of combined function assumes there was no social imperative to restrict access to the domestic quarters during public activities or to hide domestic trappings or family members from visitors' eyes: sleeping, everyday storage, and work activities would all have had to take place in the single large main room. In view of this fact, and of the broader context of evidence from other sites, there is at least some possibility that this building developed a specialised 'official' use for dining, even though the excavators have read it as the residence of a single ruler of the settlement, used by him personally to host large feasts. In either case, the small size of the Vronda community (unlike that of Karfi) would have restricted scope for competition in the hosting of public feasts from an early date, and the building seems to have remained the single main venue for this activity throughout the settlement's lifespan.

The contrast between the patterns of feasting practice observed at Karfi and Vronda need not indicate fundamentally different social systems or structures, as Day and Snyder have argued (Day and Snyder 2004). Instead, it may mainly reflect differences in scale between the two communities, with competition more difficult to control in a large group, and thus greater prevailing scope for competition in hosting feasting events and a more difficult path towards institutionalisation of the feast.

The evidence pattern at Chalasmeno looks at first sight similar to that of Vronda: one single complex, the 'Megarons', stands out because of its static plan, its concentration of Mycenaeanising architectural features, and the open space in front of it (Tsipopulou 2004a, 2004b, 2005b). The finds record is too limited to tell us much about this building's use, though specialised reuse of part of the block for feasting practices in the Late Geometric period might possibly reflect earlier associations of this type. At Smari, the visual dominance and the size of the summit building compared to the rest of the settlement (both replicated in the Vronda A/B building) and its long use, as well as its exceptional built features, static plan, and finds assemblage, all strongly suggest a specialised feasting use: there is very little separate space in the building available for, or evidence suggesting, other activities.

It is particularly interesting that the inhabitants of Chamalevri and Thronos in west Crete seem to have dispensed with any kind of formal architecture in their specialised feasting space, perhaps referring to different traditions (such as those of an open-air cult) to legitimise and promote the role of 'secular' feasting (Andreadaki-Vlasaki and Papadopoulou 2005; D'Agata 2002).

Yet the role of the open-air pits at these sites seem does closely linked with that of the other venues I have suggested, as clearly set apart for feasting in a public sense. The character of these zones greatly strengthens my previous arguments, that such spaces often may have neverbeen residential and were planned as set-apart public areas.

Possible specialised feasting buildings: distinguishing architectural features

At Karfi, the several large and distinctive buildings that seem to have had a feasting-related use are marked out by certain architectural features, as well as by their finds assemblages. The 'Megarons' block, as well as possessing the hearth concentration and exceptional storage facilities mentioned above, was additionally distinguished by a plan that altered minimally between construction and abandonment, unlike the plans of the other two complexes at the site possibly used for public ritualised feasting (Nowicki 1987b, 1999b, 2002; Pendlebury et al. 1938: 70–2). The Chalasmeno and Smari Megarons and Vronda Building A/B share this feature of a plan that changed little over time (Wallace 2005b: 261–3). In the case of the Karfi Megarons, located in the eastern half of the excavated area, the static plan has previously been suggested simply to reflect the longest-term concentration of settlement on the most defensible area of the site (around the peak of Karfi on the west). The eastern buildings are argued simply to represent a late afterthought, with no time available for the usual agglutinative additions to be made before the site's abandonment (Nowicki 1999b: 158–61). However, at Vronda, though the topography is much more regular than at Karfi, and agglutination took place in a more balanced fashion across the site, space was always left around Building A/B, which has a notably simple and static plan. Chalasmeno, like Karfi, does have distinct zones of more 'static' and more 'agglutinative' planning, yet here the more agglutinated sector lacks any special defensible topography differentiating it from the other zone. These observations suggest the use of static building plans was often a deliberate, targeted, and symbolic action. In all these cases, and in that of Smari, the blocks with static plans often share *other* distinctive architectural characteristics in various combinations (axial plans with short-side entrances; central hearths; short anterooms spanning the building's width; open areas in front of the entrance; the Smari complex also contains benches on all its walls). Though none of these features is individually unique at any of the sites in question, their high clustering in these buildings is notable (Wallace 2005b: 50–8). When they are analysed in historical and site context and considered in conjunction with the buildings' other special features and finds, it seems possible that they were incorporated, in the context of a static, unchanging plan, in order to invest the buildings with a particular symbolic resonance. These combinations of features echo the architectural styles of central mainland Greece, which had spread to Crete in the fifteenth century BC and been taken up at first mainly in elite, monumental structures. Scholars have often encapsulated them in the term 'megaron' – a term retrojected from Homeric accounts onto the Mycenaean past and laden with ethnic overtones (Darcque 1991; Wallace 2005b: 224–5). By the end of the LBA in Crete these traits had become more widespread in settlement architecture (e.g., at Malia Quartier Nu and Chondros Kefali). Like some other characteristic elements of LM IIIA-B architecture, they were incorporated, in various combinations, within many LM IIIC buildings.

Because they possess concentrations of these features, the Karfi and Chalasmeno Megarons have in the past been explained as associated with separate 'Mycenaean' or 'mainland' ethnic groups living within LM IIIC communities (Mazarakis Ainian 1997: 219–20; Paschalidis 2006;

Tsipopoulou 2005b). Yet the features are too long-established and widespread in Cretan architecture by the twelfth century, and these buildings too unusual in their site contexts in other ways (their finds assemblages and their static plans), to make this very convincing. Concerning the static plans, it is difficult to believe that only one ethnic or power group in a newly established community would not have needed to expand or adapt its buildings over time. It could be argued that one such group controlled large areas of building space, allowing more spaced-out construction, while others were forced to develop agglutinatively in a constricted area. However, this does not work well with the evidence – at most sites the static building zone seems much more limited in size than the agglutinative one.

Preucel's (2000) study of seventeenth-century AD refuge villages in New Mexico, founded by the former residents of various Pueblo settlements during Spanish attacks on the region, is useful in assessing arguments for ethnically driven settlement planning at this period in Crete. These New Mexican villages often had bizonal plans – one zone formal and regular in character, the other roughly built and apparently unplanned. Building plans in the 'formal' sectors show a strong regard to established cosmological tenets, which is not the case in the informally planned sectors. These differences are known to relate to the different ethnic origins and traditions of the settling groups. Growth in size over time occurred in *both* zones – regular, formal expansion within the formal sector, and looser, messier agglutinative growth in the other. This contrasts with the Cretan case, but there are some meaningful parallels to the Cretan pattern. In New Mexico, elements of traditional building templates were deliberately adapted at the new locations to invest communities there, or groups within them, with a legitimacy and solid identity under pressure from invading colonists. In a politically disturbed period, Cretan communities may also have developed new sets of design rules about buildings or zones used for special activities. The static-plan structures mentioned above seem to draw on earlier prestige traditions in their architecture, perhaps as a means of grounding and bonding the new communities with reference to a common past. Discussing the 'formal' sector of one of the New Mexico villages, Preucel notes, 'The form and layout ... can be interpreted as an architectural assertion of tradition. In this sense, it is an archetype village, the outcome of the broader pan-Pueblo discourse on shared origins and the local invention of tradition by the Chichiti people' (Preucel 2000: 70). In EIA Crete, we might well talk about the emergence of 'archetype' blocks of formalised plan, which drew on a recognised and prestigious pan-Aegean heritage to consolidate bonding institutions in the new communities. Static plans, and new concentrations and combinations of 'Mycenaeanising' architectural features, may have combined to mark out a template for buildings with a public or quasi-public role, in the subtle kind of way typical of this period.

Public feasting as post-collapse institution: a summary

During LM IIIA-B, the existence of strong regional settlement hierarchies may have obviated any need to maintain separate gathering/feasting venues at small sites, or may have allowed single powerful families at these sites to control these types of gatherings within their dwellings. In the twelfth century, in a pattern of mainly small- to medium-sized settlements lacking strong hierarchical relationships, such venues seem to have come to act as more important foci for societal self-conception and interaction at local level, and to become less tightly controllable with individual private groups regularly attempting to emulate, or even appropriate, their function and appearance. For example, the addition of an entrance anteroom to the Karfi Great House during its lifetime may mimic the archaising plan of the Megarons, designed as a single unit.

With the large axial room as the focus *both* of the typical household *and* of specialised cult- and feasting-linked buildings, the conceptual line between household-level, affinal, and cult-related feasting practice (see below) seems to have been easy to cross in the generally modest built environment of this period. Buildings specifically dedicated to cult are discussed separately below, but it seems that while they were distinctive in their space and equipment at some levels, the sphere of cult activity should not in this period be treated as one entirely separate and bounded from that of collective feasting or other 'secular' types of ritual. Several of the buildings with possible public feasting use discussed here contain evidence for some kind of cult activity of the type seen in contemporary temples, as well as their other special features.

The sharing of a rough template for possible specialised feasting-related buildings between a number of sites in east central and east Crete suggests that similar social structures and norms operated across large areas of the island in the immediate post-collapse period. This conclusion is greatly strengthened when we consider the shared characteristics of public cult buildings at this time. Both imply very regular contact between the new communities and the development of new cultural norms beyond the level of the small community. This is a remarkable finding, considering the scale of the social and cultural disruptions occurring around 1200 BC.

Feasting venues: comparisons between Crete and other regions

Evidence from the mainland suggests that gathering places (of either built or open-air type) where feasting activity occurred were a feature of post-collapse social life. They often seem to have been located well outside or at the fringes of settlements and contrast with the Cretan cases I have mentioned in these and other striking respects. The fact that known cases inside settlements are so rare may partly reflect the generally low evidence quality at mainland settlements, earlier, but could also be related to a lower level of community cohesion in large mainland groups in the immediate post-collapse period.

There is even less reason on the mainland than in Crete to assume personalised ownership of the specialised feasting spaces we *can* identify. As well as having predominantly extra-settlement locations, these show exaggerated contrasts with ordinary houses. Examples of special buildings dating as early as the twelfth century seem to include Megaron B at Thermon, which overlies the remains of what seems to be an LBA settlement site. The building had feasting or other specialised use in the early EIA signified by dense deposits of animal bone, ash, and fine pottery (Mazarakis Ainian 1997: 123–35; Morris 2000: 227–8; Papapostolou 2003; Wardle and Wardle 2003). There are contemporary graves nearby. This echoes in part the case of the tenth-century building at Lefkandi Toumba – another exceptionally large structure dated in early PG and surely visited for ceremonial activities, perhaps including feasting, before or after the elite burials made under its floor and before its filling in to create a tumulus, which was then surrounded by later graves (Popham et al. 1993; Popham and Lemos 1996). Architecture at PG-G Asine (the Kapsorachis plot, with remains dating to LG, at the foot of the Barbouna hill, and the area of the long building C in the Karmaniola plot east of the acropolis, dating PG) shows the same pattern of possible feasting/cult buildings associated with graves (Mazarakis Ainian 1997: 68–72 usefully summarises). This association of collective consumption rituals with the funerary sphere differs from anything seen in Crete and strongly indicates that the relevant structures were not used as residences. The facts that the Thermon building stands in the midst of LBA settlement remains, the Asine buildings very near to abandoned LBA settlement remains, and the Lefkandi building close to, but separate from, a contemporary settlement at Xeropolis suggest that feasts were hosted in relatively neutral spaces, well outside settlement centres and accessible to a range of nearby residents (potentially including those from quite a wide catchment region), yet could still be powerfully imbued with historically rooted identity associations. In the large and volatile post-collapse communities, the possibility of conflict or aggrandisement in the use of these buildings might have been a permanent and uncontrollable threat if they had been placed within a settlement context.

Some buildings located within EIA settlements have been claimed as having a cult/feasting use and/or role as chiefs' residences, such as Nichoria Building IV-1 or the large apsidal PG building A on the summit at Koukounaries. Contextual information at settlement level is crucial in judging this (Mazarakis Ainian 1997: 78–9, 82–3) but is unfortunately often unsatisfactory in quality or quantity. Perhaps the best-evidenced case of a probable feasting-related building with short-term use located within a settlement is that of Tiryns building T, which overlies and adapts the central architectural focus of the LBA town, the palace. There are possibly similar, less well-documented developments at Mycenae and Midea. Neither of the latter settlements, however, survived far into the EIA as a substantial entity (Maran 1999, 2006). It may have been the stable continuance of Tiryns as a large settlement that allowed the rapid and direct adaptation of an existing public remit for the summit space, notwithstanding the collapse of the LBA elite's authority and support structure. The choice of location for the building and its direct reference to the prestige architecture of the preceding period are strong indicators of a special function, but there is very little indication that its use was ever a residential one. Maran (2006: 142) refers to the building as a 'communal hall', its use possibly orchestrated and maintained by ambitious families within the EIA settlement.

As in Crete, a deliberately archaising template may have guided the design of such structures, which included certain combinations of features rooted in prestige traditions from the Mycenaean past. Though they were concentrated and enlarged in these special buildings, the features were shared (as in the Cretan case) with many 'ordinary' houses of the early EIA, which often possessed a central rectangular room, sometimes with benches; often contained hearths; and frequently seem to have incorporated a porch (Mazarakis Ainian 1997: 292–3, 259–69). Deliberate references to earlier architectural traditions are thus even more difficult to characterise and quantify on the mainland than on Crete, where the 'megaron' template probably retained more strongly exotic and prestigious associations. For this reason, and because of the different scale of mainland communities, size may have been particularly emphasised as a distinguishing feature in 'special' buildings on the mainland. Apsidalism is another new and distinctive architectural feature often (though not exclusively) associated with these buildings.

The use of such buildings (and, as I shall note below, of regional cult places) suggests that post-collapse communities in central Greece did incorporate some kinds of social institution from an early date, though there is no need to associate the practice of formal feasting with chiefly control (Mazarakis Ainian 1997: 111–13). The large size of the new residence groups and the severe nature of the disturbances that had created them apparently made such institutions looser, more divergent in form, and less strongly grounded than those emerging in the new Cretan communities.

Cult as settlement-level institution

After the major settlement relocation and deep social restructuring in Crete circa 1200 BC, cult seems to have become a much more important, formalised, and independent focus of community identity, investment, and bonding at local level. Its housing in a unique and separate building, its newly consolidated equipment set, and its broadly standardised and developed format between settlements, all suggest it was less socially alienable by elites than it had been in LM IIIA-B. On the other hand, with a recognisable 'package' of public cult practice and equipment now firmly in place at most settlements, some subsidiary/parallel private appropriation of it by powerful groups or individuals may have become easier and more effective. The impression is of a carefully balanced and insulated social environment, in which private aggrandisement through engagement in beyond-household ceremonial activity was allowed, but never permitted to usurp the public institutions of cult and feasting. There are indications that each of these institutions strengthened the other through overlaps in space use, imagery, and practice. The deposit of horn cores in the Karfi Priest's House, and the horned skulls in Vronda Building A/B and the Smari summit complex, have a cultic resonance echoing back to the Bronze Age but were found in buildings with what I have suggested were public-feasting-related deposits/plans (Figure 73). Like the eventual addition of room 58 to the Priest's House and the presence of typical temple-type figurines in the Great House room 16–17, they suggest a place for the sophisticated manipulation of religious symbolism in the 'secular' feasting arena, whether public or private, *alongside* a strong role for public cult in single fixed locations and yet another, different role for household cult (Hatzi-Vallianou and Evthimiou 2000; Pendlebury et al. 1938: 84–6). The likely existence of a symbolic and pragmatic crossover between the cult and feasting spheres at a public, institutionalised level is illustrated by Building E at Vasiliki Kefala. This seems to combine elements of a typical shrine building with those of a dining complex bearing strong similarities to the template for public feasting buildings that I have argued for previously (Eliopoulos 1998, 2004; Wallace 2005b: 270–2; Figure 74). It proves how much more we have to learn about the way the public cult institution functioned and developed over the period 1200–1000 BC, particularly in the larger and more complex settlements.

The early strength of a separate public cult sector in Crete supports the notion of leadership within the new communities as transient or only weakly enshrined, with cult needed to act as

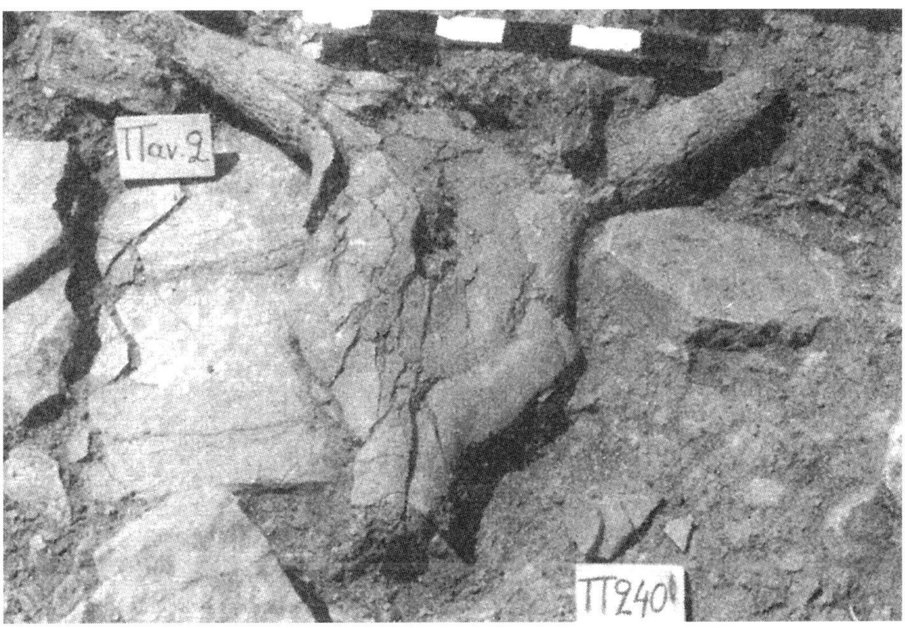

73. Bovid cranium with horns from floor of Smari Megarons, suggesting that ritual activities took place in this structure (after Hatzi-Vallianou and Evthimiou 2000, Plate 3, p. 418). By permission of D. Hatzi-Vallianou.

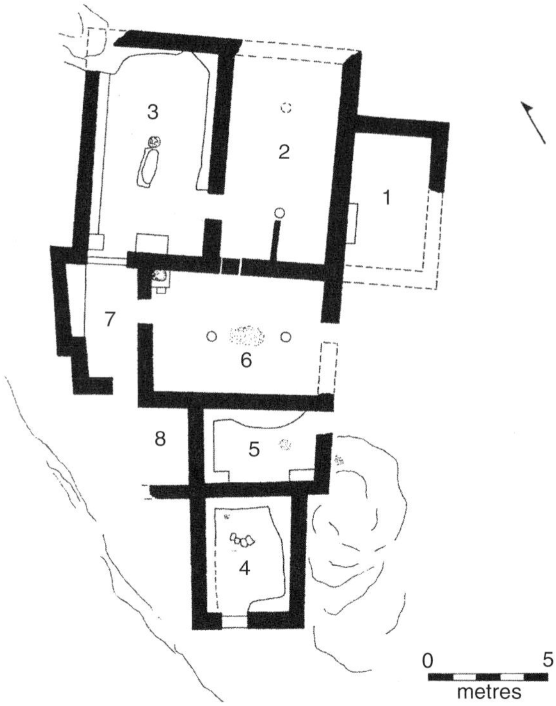

74. Vasiliki Kefala: plan of 'shrine' building (after Eliopoulos 2004, Fig 6.5, p. 85).

a buffer between groups and individuals who were regularly competing for status (Clark and Blake 1996). If this was the case, however, it does *not* follow that these societies were generally 'unstable', as Whitley (1991b) has argued. On the contrary, the solid public institutionalisation of cult, as well as feasting, at settlement level suggests relatively stable systems of communal authority and cohesion. Whether or not single leading individuals or groups were able to achieve permanent, heritable high rank, social power always seems to have had a strong lineage- or affinally rooted dimension (as the mortuary record illustrates). The separate institutionalisation of public cult prevented any group from overconcentrating power through this means and thus limited the emergence of extreme inequality. An example of just such a combined social base, incorporating elements of lineage-based as well as achieved rank, is discussed by Allen (1984). Cult is also likely to have helped regulate extreme or destabilising social competition via formalised public feasting (the other important public institution of this period) by offering an alternative arena for collective interaction and display. Each institution balanced the other in providing a different kind of insulation against extreme social competition in the new communities.

Cult within settlements: comparisons with other regions

Major LH IIIA-B population centres on the mainland like Mycenae and Tiryns had already incorporated central cult complexes located very close to the palaces that formed their cores: the Linear B texts show that cult dedications were a prominent concern of the palatial administrations, as was the case in Crete (Bendall 2001; Shelmerdine 1999: 362–72). But a significant difference in social structure between Crete and central Greece after 1200 BC seems reflected in the lack of any clearly identifiable settlement-level public cult buildings in the central Aegean. Few clear examples are known on the islands, either, at an early date (though see Skerlou 2004 for the cult-type deposit at Iraklio on Kos). It should be noted here once again that the lack of extensively preserved settlement plans for EIA central Greece means such blanket assertions are still open to revision.

As noted earlier, Mazarakis Ainian has suggested that public ritual, including cult, in EIA Greece was centred in the house of the local chieftain and largely under his command. In fact, however, little clearly identifiable cult material (as opposed to evidence for feasting) has been found in many of the structures proposed as 'rulers' houses'. A further problem is how to define and separate cult material in the first place in the central Greek context, given the partial cross-over between the two spheres, both in conceptual terms and in terms of material correlates, in most regions through much of the EIA. What does seem clear is that the cult 'package' of distinctive temple buildings associated with distinctive equipment, as found in Crete, is missing from mainland settlements generally before the eighth century – though see Morgan's comments on unit IV-I at Nichoria (Morgan 1999: 377); Building T at Tiryns may possibly have had a cult remit, since an LBA altar outside was apparently reused (Coulson 1983; Mazarakis-Ainian 1988: 113–5, 1997: 159–62, 160–2). This formerly important aspect of social and political life seems unable to have been widely recreated in permanent public form at settlement level after collapse. This suggests, once again, that a much less tight, coherent organisation of the social body applied in mainland communities than in Crete. I suggest this is likely to have been linked to a less controlled, more uneven, and more problematic collapse in many mainland regions circa 1200 BC.

Nonetheless, public cult places are not totally absent on the EIA mainland. *Extra-settlement* cult locations with use starting in the twelfth century are a feature of central Greece from early in the EIA, appearing in a number of regions. These have some parallel features with extra-settlement sanctuaries in Crete, which I discuss below, but also have marked contrasts. Cult *was* being actively and consciously restructured in most Aegean regions following state collapse, but often in very different ways than applied in Crete.

14 BEYOND SETTLEMENTS: THE CHANGING CULTURAL LANDSCAPE

Open-air sanctuaries in Crete

Some large and impressive caves, often remote from contemporary settlements, were used as 'open-air' (i.e., mainly architectureless) sanctuaries though much of Crete's Bronze Age: these include the Psychro, Idaean, Tsoutsouros, and Amnisos caves (Alexiou 1963a; Rutkowski 1986: 47–99; Rutkowski and Nowicki 1996; Watrous 1996: 47–98). Another kind of 'open-air' cult site with similarly long use was Kato Simi, an isolated architectural complex associated with extensive outdoor cult areas, located in a valley in the south Lasithi foothills (Kanta 1991; Lebessi 1975, 1985). In view of the Linear B evidence for significant and regular dedications to a range of cults at different locations by the ruling authorities, it seems likely that worship at these sanctuaries was under centralised control or influence at either regional or supraregional level. The votives dedicated there were often of high value, many undoubtedly made at or traded from workshops at urban centres.

Given the deep-rooted social and spatial change occurring at this period, it is remarkable that most of these major sanctuaries were continued and adapted in use by the newly constituted communities of the twelfth century. The Psychro, Idaean, and Tsoutsouros caves and Kato Simi all saw continued dedications through the EIA; at Amnisos, the long-used cave site was paralleled, or temporarily replaced, by a coastal open-air sanctuary circa 900 metres beyond it on the coast to the north (Marinatos 1929; N. Marinatos 1996; Prent 2005b: 154–74, 200–11; Schäfer 1991; Schäfer et al. 1992: 182–3; Watrous 1996: 100–2). The relocation of the settlement bases from which these sites had been accessed – the most dramatic and comprehensive settlement shift in Crete's long prehistory – appears *not* to have destroyed or diminished their perceived value and status as places of worship and their regular intensive use, even though it probably transformed the way that use was structured. Indeed, the disruptions may even have enhanced the status of these sanctuaries, as secure points of social reference in a changing world. In some cases, an influx of population into a sanctuary's neighbourhood, driven by the new settlement choices, may have changed the whole traffic and profile of that sanctuary. This probably occurred in the case of the Psychro Cave in the Lasithi region, which became a major 'refuge zone' from circa 1200 BC. The danger and insecurity around the coasts at this period seem, counterintuitively, not to have caused the decline of coastal sanctuaries, but actually to have encouraged their development as secure and buffered interaction points at beyond-settlement level, especially for the purposes of trade – a role that was to grow hugely over the course of the EIA.

The physical, social, and political reorientations of 1200 BC also seem to have promoted the establishment of *new*, relatively small open-air cult sites, which maintained the nature sanctuary tradition but also adapted it. These seem deliberately sited close to new settlement locations, while still using natural landscape features. For example, we see significant cult depositions starting in the twelfth century at a cave in the Patsos gorge in the Amari region of west Crete, and at the Phaneromeni cave in the northern Lasithi mountains (Kourou and Karetsou 1994; Rutkowski and Nowicki 1996: 34–6, 42–5). Such establishments helped fix and ground the new communities in space, by investing their local landscapes with new resonance. Another type of new sanctuary used selected aspects of the LBA cultural landscape as its reference point. This was the case with the abandoned LBA settlement sites of Ayia Triada, where an open-air shrine was established in the twelfth century, and Kommos, where a coastal sanctuary was established by the late eleventh (D'Agata 1997, 1998; Shaw and Shaw 2000: 8–14). The fact that these were stable and known points, each with an important past, must have lent huge resonance to the cults based there. We see in these actions a sophisticated, self-conscious, and deliberate adaptation of existing traditions to serve new social needs and new conceptions of political identity. At the same time, it seems that cultural history – in the form of the old sanctuaries, with their existing territorial/ownership associations – partly *conditioned* ways of thinking about identity structures and regional interactions in the new political environment.

Not only the settings of the old cults, but many aspects of their practice, seem to have been selectively perpetuated in the post-collapse era. In contrast to the new settlement cults, which seem strongly focused on a goddess figure, open-air cults seem more tied into celebration of the natural world and used animal figurines as votives, as they had in the Bronze Age. Human adorant figurines (often in bronze) were also deposited, and small personal value items like jewellery and weapons (similar practices had occurred at Bronze Age cave sanctuaries: Boardman 1961; Hogarth 1903; Prent 2005b: 174–82; Rutkowski 1986: 47–73; Figures 75 and 76). Clearly a different kind of power base remained invested in these sanctuaries, even as they changed. Animal sacrifice and sacred feasting, for which there is some, but rather limited, evidence in intra-settlement shrines (the early deposits in Prinias Temple B, for example), may have become a particular focus of extra-settlement cult. The Kato Simi sanctuary incorporated an ash altar and extensive animal bone remains from an early stage in the EIA; so did the coastal sanctuaries at Amnisos and Kommos, and the Ayia Triada sanctuary. There are also some regional variations in practice, including an apparent focus on the use of large painted wheelmade bull figurines at shrines in the southwestern bay of Crete. The latter phenomenon was perhaps originally inspired by forms of cult practice and equipment current on the LH IIIB mainland, as well as by earlier practices in Crete itself, but was redeveloped to meet changing social needs in the EIA, in the same way as the use of small goddess figurines in the LM IIIB period was adapted and fitted into the new context of settlement-level cult (D'Agata 1997, 1999; Gesell 1985: 53–4; Kourou and Karetsou 1994; Shaw and Shaw 2000: 142–4). It was almost certainly through Cretan interactions abroad, perhaps from the Kommos region itself, that cult practices using wheelmade bull figurines of a very similar type were extended to parts of the Dodecanese in the twelfth century (Skerlou 2004).

Though the special nature of these cult locations in themselves and their long traditions of use (rather than convenient access to them from settlement centres) had been the main force behind their use in the late LBA, the far-reaching networks of territorial control in the latter period had allowed regular supervision of and access to the sanctuaries by ruling elites based at regional centres. In making choices about continuing and new sanctuary use in the EIA, in a much more fragmented, ahierarchical political and spatial environment, it may have been much more of a struggle for any one group to assure direct access to and control of a sanctuary. This explains the

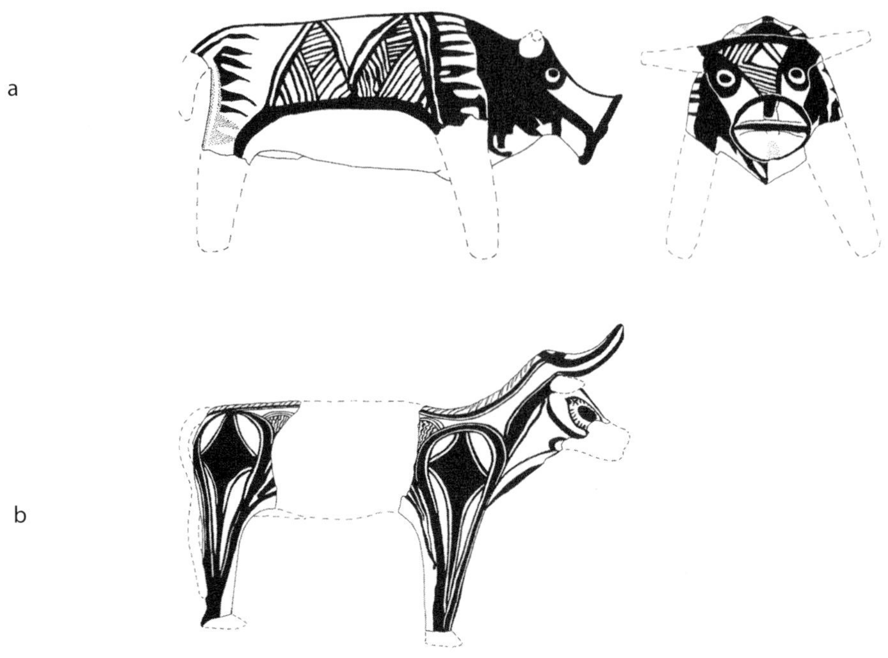

75. Wheelmade bull figurines from Patsos shrine (after Kourou and Karetsou 1994: a, Fig. 10, p. 92; b, Fig. 11, p. 92). By permission of N. Kourou.

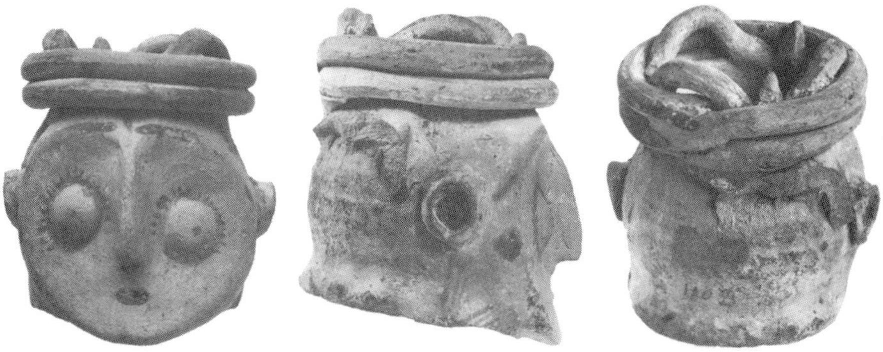

76. Clay human figurine with snake headdress from Patsos shrine, dating LM IIIC-PG (after Kourou and Karetsou 1994, Plate 76). By permission of N. Kourou.

fact that, alongside the use of old sanctuaries, an interest arose in establishing new sanctuaries more closely physically aligned to one settlement or regional group. It also suggests that the older sanctuaries often found themselves the focus of competition or even conflict between groups within a region. In view of their inflexible locations and the generally small size and dispersal of the new settlements, few of the older open-air sanctuaries could have been annexed or isolated easily by a single community. Thus, these probably had a slightly different role from the new cult sites within the changing hierarchy of cult places – perhaps being less regularly visited than the new and more accessible sanctuaries, and acting as the site of special and rare cults: both the Idaean and Psychro caves were associated in later tradition with the cult of Zeus.

In a changing society, major extra-settlement sanctuaries also surely acted in new ways as sources of political and economic inequality – places for exchange and other types of advantageous interaction between developing communities, or groups within them (Watrous 1996: 100–2). Though we might expect them to retain quite a broad 'ownership' structure, whether this structure was collaborative, negotiated, or openly conflict-ridden probably varied in each case. Certainly, the traditional political symbolism formerly attached to those sanctuaries with Bronze Age roots is likely to have been transformed, becoming less concretely or overtly connected to the history of any previously recognised group. Even if the affiliated group remained nominally the same, the real social profile of the group is likely to have been totally transformed as a result of the collapse process and its related spatial and social shifts. In the course of all these adjustments, participation in ritual surely became more socially and economically diversified, helping to consolidate new class relationships within post-collapse societies.

By contrast, at the newly established open-air sanctuaries it is likely that ownership of the cult *was* claimed from the outset by single regional or settlement-level communities, in early attempts at power aggrandisement or consolidation. The Kommos and Ayia Triada sanctuaries were almost certainly of special interest to the Phaistos polity, and this link seems to have become stronger and more formal through the course of the EIA. The Patsos cult was surely established for the benefit of the important groups of settlements to its east in the Amari valley, and to its west in the Ayios Vasilios region: the sanctuary is easily accessed from the main valley route between these areas. The Phaneromeni cave seems likely to have been closely attached to a new group of north Lasithian communities, particularly To Flechtron and Porolios (Nowicki 2000: 147–50). Claims to ownership of these sanctuaries by individual communities were surely often based on notions of community heritage, sometimes directly embodied in the physical remains of old settlements reused for cult. The latter practice seems to have been especially appealing because although the old settlements in question were not visually impressive in character, they were established as important interaction points. Re-use harnessed the power of collective memory of these locations in a wider population (outside as well as inside the island) to swell recognition of the founding group's legitimacy. This pattern of using social memory to add resonance to emerging cult sites seems even stronger on the contemporary mainland, as I shall discuss below. In Crete, partly thanks to the existing strong tradition of open-air cult places, many of which continued in use – but also thanks, surely, to the strength of new social institutions in the island, including settlement cult – there was less impetus to develop new extra-settlement cult places and thus to appropriate the material past in cult practice in the same way.

Comparisons outside Crete

On the mainland, we see the establishment of a high number of *new* shared cult places out in the landscape from soon after the collapse. Though many were placed on the sites of recently abandoned settlements, and thus fixed firmly into established 'mental maps', this move represents a very pronounced, deliberate new choice about cult practice and structure. As noted above, there seems not to have been much of a role for intra-settlement temples in the large noncohesive community groups of the early EIA mainland. The expansion of extra-settlement cult seems to have operated as an alternative structure of social cohesion, but at a much looser, regional level. This reinforces the impression gained from other aspects of the mainland record, of a lack of solid institutions at the small community scale.

LBA settlement locations reused for cult as early as the twelfth century include Olympia and Amyklai, with Isthmia and Delphi established as sanctuaries by at least the ninth century and probably much earlier (Desborough 1952: 199–200; Demakopoulou 1982; Eder 2001a, 2001b, 2006b; Kyrieleis 2002: 627–8; McDonald and Rapp 1972: 317; Morgan 1990, 1999: 379–80, 382–4). This emphasis on the past may relate to a need to bind and regulate mainland communities at regional level through reference to a common heritage, in the absence of many other strong binding institutions in large loose post-collapse communities. As in Crete, however, there is no exclusive or rigid adherence to either historic locations or distinctive natural locations in the placing of new sanctuaries: convenience of use for settlements in particular regions, and/or strategic placement to mark the extent of political or economic territory, were also considerations. All of these seem to apply in the case of Isthmia, a former settlement site located on a strategic harbour and land crossing, and almost certainly linked to Corinth from an early point in its life as a sanctuary. In general, the use of highly visible locations seems not to be favoured for such sites: some, like Olympia and Kalapodi, are hidden in gentle valleys. Kalapodi is a new sanctuary founded on a probable settlement site of the MBA-early LBA, in a nonobtrusive and unremarkable inland valley location offering excellent accessibility for a number of the burgeoning new settlements in east Greece. The choice of the site deliberately privileged ease of access from these settlements, relying on the deep local territorial knowledge of the users to bind them together in use of the sanctuary. The same applies in the Olympia case (Felsch 1981, 1999; Felsch et al. 1996; Morgan 1997: 187, 1999: 382, 2003: 114, 133–5; Niemeier in press; Figure 77), and the sanctuary at Tegea in Arkadia, perhaps in use for cult as early as the PG period, is similarly distinguished by its central positioning, prioritising accessibility rather than any kind of dramatic topography: its later use by a number of different poleis emphasises this quality (Lemos 2002: 146; Østby 1997; Østby et al. 1994).

Other scholars have stressed the role of these mainland sanctuaries as gathering and trading places for interregional elites, creating 'communities of cult' beyond any single settlement's/

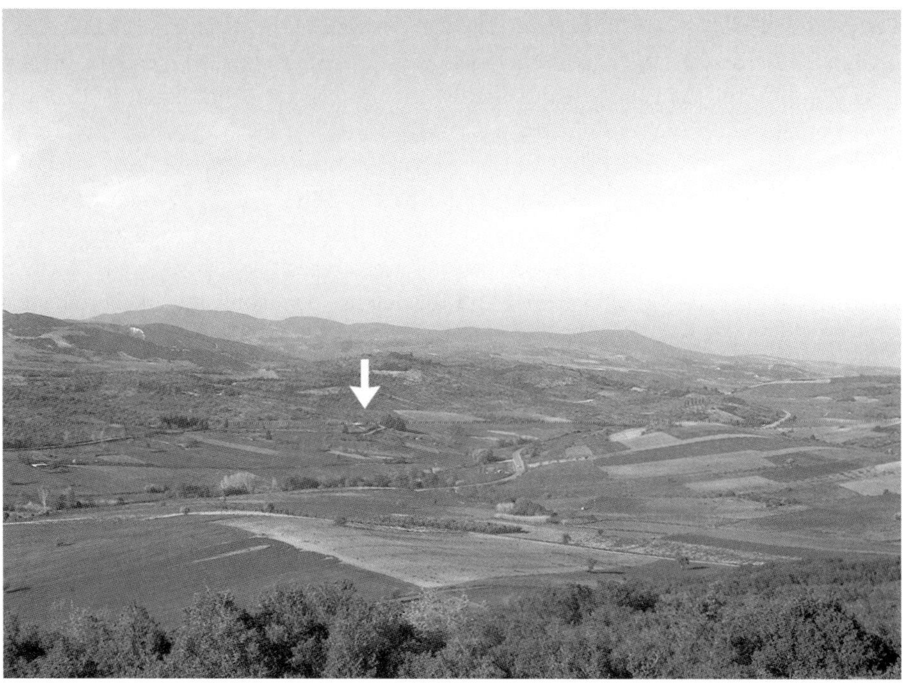

77. Kalapodi sanctuary location, from east: arrow indicates site location. Image by the author.

polity's control, which were strongly influential on how polis states later emerged and defined themselves (Morgan 2003: 107–64). In Crete, too, the 'landscape' dimension of cult, with its appeal to broad regional populations and conscious forefronting of history, gives us important insight into how regional identities were conceived and developed. In each case, extra-settlement cult developed in ways directly linked to the type of social breakdown and adjustment that a region had experienced circa 1200 BC. The question is emphatically not one of straightforward 'continuity' versus 'change', in cult places or practices, as scholarly discussion has so often framed it, but of *types* of change made during and immediately after collapse (Dickinson 2006: 219–38; Morgan 2003: 107; Prent 2005b: 1–37). In each case, what is striking are the *deliberate* nature of the new choices made about cult and the powerful and conscious way the past was used in establishing new political relationships and identities through this means: such choices seem sensitively rooted in local knowledge and history, rather than representing any kind of imposition by newcomers. This pattern also strongly supports the notion that groups across the Aegean were in contact through and right after the collapse period in ways that allowed them to share ideas about heritage and its significance.

Despite their insecurity, the coasts, as in Crete, were an important part of the new sacred landscape in central Greece, enabling interaction between deeply fragmented and often potentially hostile communities. Isthmia is one example. At Phylakopi, too, after a destruction circa 1200 BC, the temple alone stayed in use. At Ayia Irini, after a short gap, the old town sanctuary also came back into use between LC IIIC and PG (Mazarakis Ainian 1997: 170–1; Renfrew 1985: 361–93).

Changing worldviews and the new cultural landscape

The physical fact of settlement relocation in Crete, and the social changes accompanying it, must have stimulated change in ways of looking at the landscape. In LM IIIA-B, the conceptualisation of an individual community seems likely to have been tied strongly to its rank in the centralised hierarchy: it was probably engaged with by others mostly via fixed and controlled channels of communication. The twelfth-century changes in physical locations and in political structures must have permanently disturbed the use of these channels and the mental maps of the island associated with them that had been established though most of the Bronze Age.

The visual perspective from many new settlements is very different from that obtained at most LM IIIA-B sites (Wallace 2007). The difference lies in the sheer amount of land commanded by the eye from the new sites – very large panoramas are often able to be viewed. While this fact mainly arose from the strategic selection of sites for defensive reasons, it is likely to have affected residents' definitions of themselves in a number of different ways. The prominent topography of many new settlements meant they could often be clearly picked out in the landscape from one another, with views from some settlements encompassing three or four of their peers in the wider region. From Dreros, Lato, and Kritsa Kastello, for example, much of the hinterland of the bay of Mirabello can be seen, including the sites of Elounda Oxa, Vrokastro, Kavousi Kastro, and the area of the Cha Gorge, with the sites of Chalasmeno and Katalimata. The sites comprising high, rocky, and dramatic peaks (e.g., Karfi, Kavousi Kastro) and some of the more massive 'acropolis' sites – for example, Veni in the Amari valley, or Profitis Elias Rokka (Kanli Kastelli) in central Crete – act as landmarks, recognisable for many kilometres around (Nowicki 2000: 197–99; Wallace 2002: 80–3, 2005a: 67–8, 2007). The inhabitants of Lyttos, ten kilometres away to its west, could clearly see the characteristic peak of To Flechtron in the north Lasithi mountains (Nowicki 2000: 147–8).

Wide-ranging communications and exchange possibilities and the potential of extending subsistence and political territories (whether or not this was possible in reality) would surely be regularly brought to mind by prolonged exposure to these kinds of panorama (Figure 78–81). Prominent viewpoints/landmarks must occasionally have been visited during the LM IIIA-B period in the course of subsistence activity. But living on them permanently, and the process of creating an infrastructure in and around them – work almost certainly involving close relationships with a variety of new neighbours – must have helped promote new kinds of understanding and awareness of the landscape, and of how one could move through it. The residents of Karfi (unlike their predecessors at sites down in the Lasithi plain or in the coastal zone around Malia) were able to cover both these areas with the sweep of an eye, as well as a whole new set of neighbours to the north and west – with whom, given the differences in altitude, they could productively build collaborative relationships regarding the production and exchange of subsistence items.

Intersite distances (as between Karfi and To Flechtron, very close as the crow flies but separated by a deep valley and three hours' walk) must have looked much smaller from up at the new sites. In east Crete, even the relatively low-lying Chalasmeno site offers views north and south across nearly the whole length of the Ierapetra isthmus, while from the large settlement of Ayios Ioannis Katalimata, both coasts are clearly visible, as well as other settlements including Vasiliki Kefala and Kalo Chorio Profitis Elias (Nowicki 2004a). Despite the lack of very dramatic relief contrasts, impressive and wide-ranging vistas were also obtained from sites in central Crete, an open and rolling landscape. Horizons and worldviews expanded, even while populations experienced the more restrictive political and economic parameters of a world of small-sized, inaccessible, and dispersed settlements.

Not all the new sites commanded such views, however. Coastal sites mostly looked out to sea and were backed by hills that blocked perspectives inland. From many sites in the west Siteia mountains and the southern Lasithi range, only the immediately adjacent valley routes could be seen in some directions, with wider perspectives being blocked out by surrounding hills (Nowicki

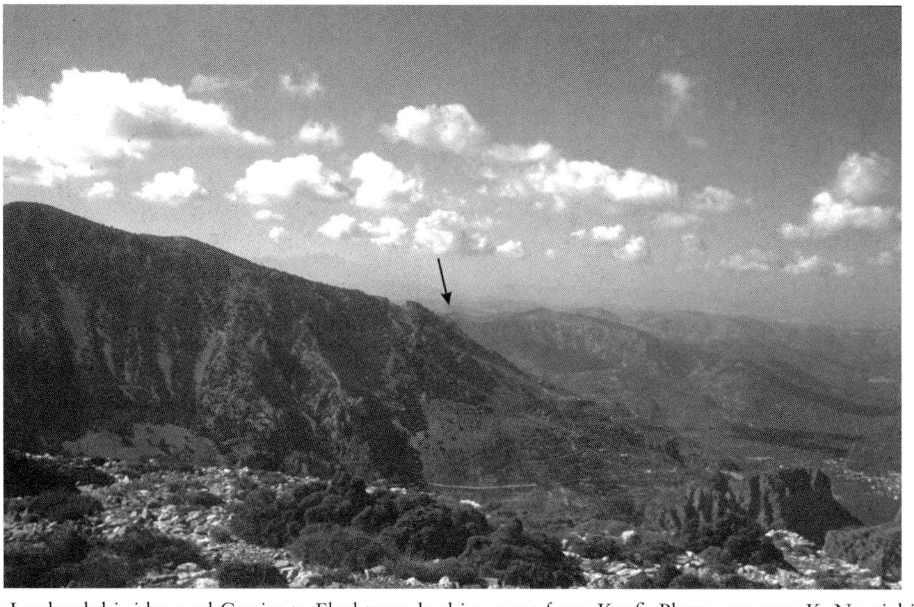

78. The Louloudaki ridge and Gonies to Flechtron, looking west from Karfi. Photo courtesy K. Nowicki.

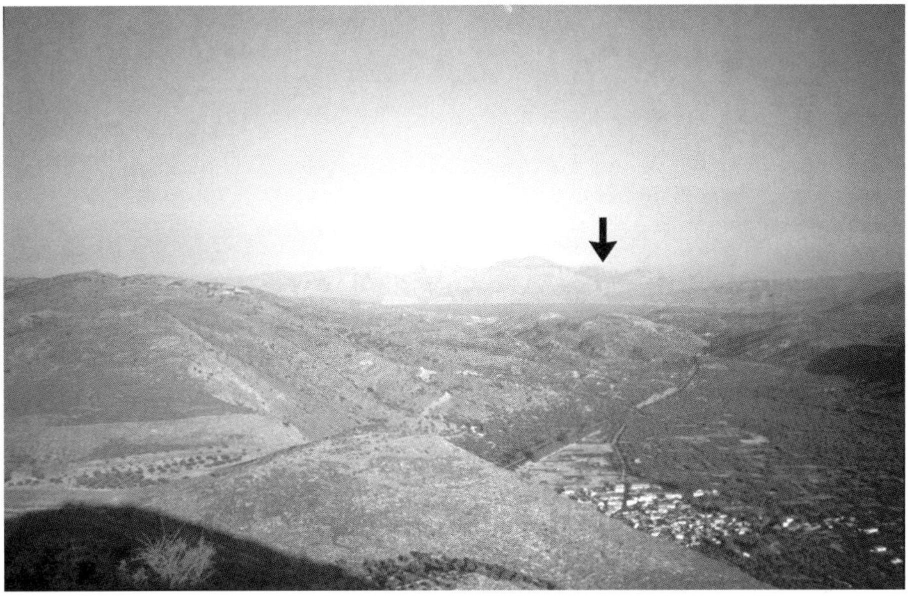

79. View from Dreros east across the Mirabello bay: arrow indicates Cha gorge in the distance. Image by the author.

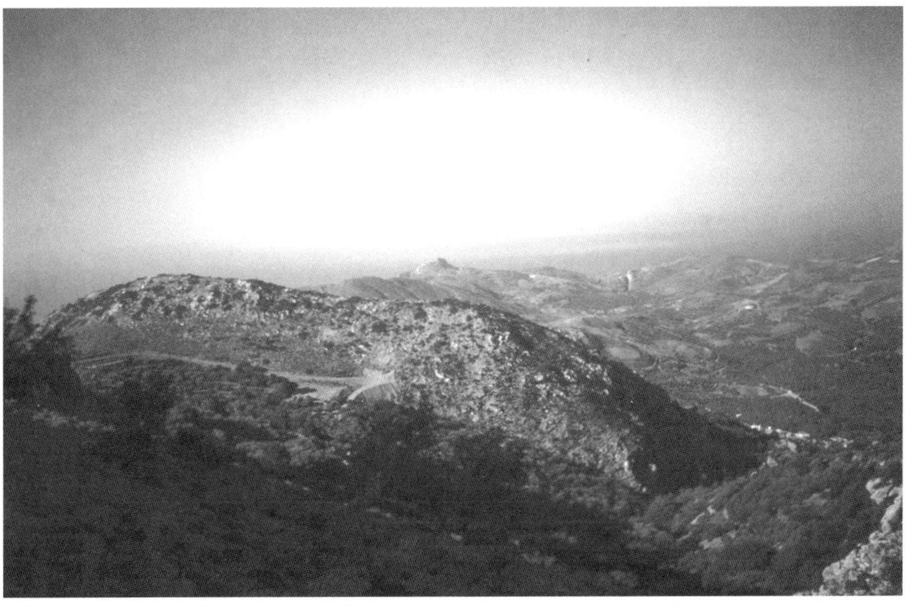

80. View from above Loutraki Kandilioro, showing the site's strategic positioning, with outstanding views over approaches from the coast far to its south. Image by the author.

1990, 1995a; Figure 82). As herding contracted to the closer vicinity of the new sites, an increased growth of shrub and tree vegetation on now-ungrazed areas may have obscured extensive views over the surrounding topography from some sites and lengthened actual travel distances through these landscapes. In these cases, community self-conceptions may have been tied more to very general regional identity groupings, grounded in Bronze Age traditions: new contacts and collaborations may have been restricted. This practical isolation may have helped encourage subsistence

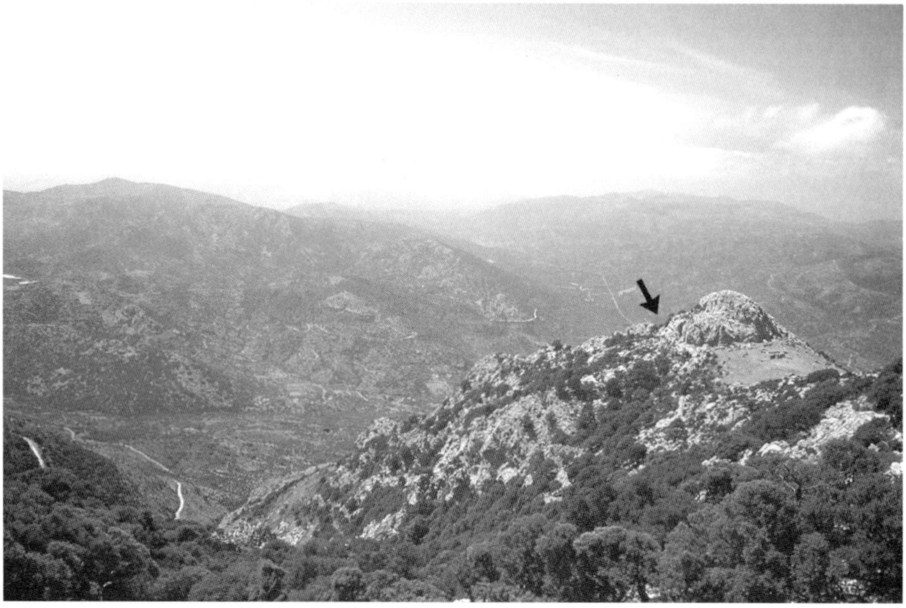

81. View north from the Louloudaki ridge above Gonies to Flechtron (the hill summit in the foreground) along the main approach valleys. Image by the author.

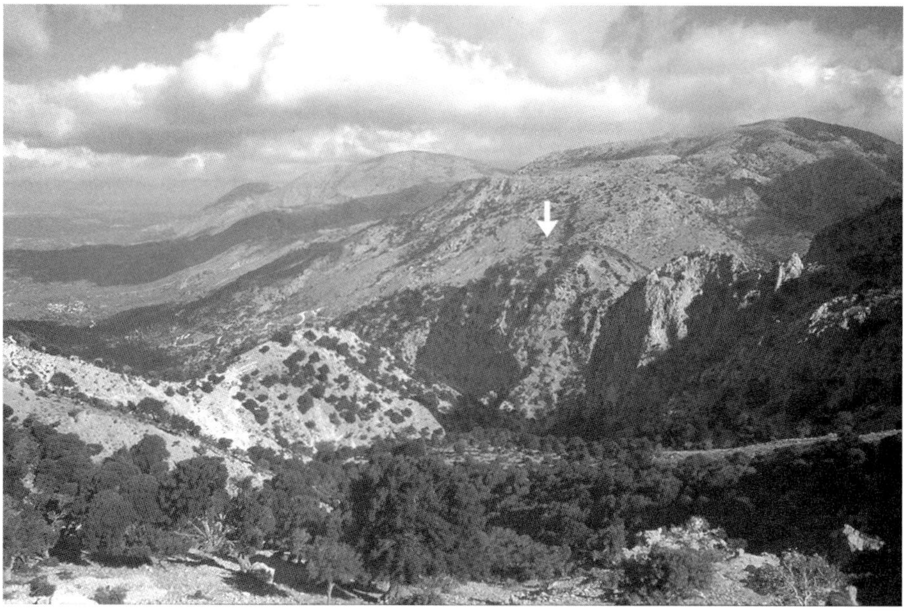

82. Looking west to Erganos Kefali and the main valley route into the Lasithi plain from the south. Views from the site are open to the south but blocked by narrowing valley sides to the north. Photo courtesy K. Nowicki.

self-sufficiency, as well as helping to rapidly break down the fabric of complex society. Even so, the small scale of Crete and its relatively dense population meant it was hard to avoid contact with neighbours, especially in the agricultural hinterlands of the new sites.

All over the island, route networks must have altered after the settlement shift, with further implications for how communities conceptualised themselves and interacted with others. While most main natural routes were directly controlled and defended by new settlements located close to them (such as Axos, Eleutherna, Kalamafki Kipia, Vrokastro, Frati, Thronos, and Karfi) the priority in doing so now seems to have been the collaborative defence of access to the island's interior by outsiders, rather than the special benefit of certain large polities, as had been the case through much of the Middle to Late Bronze Age (Evans 1928: 61–92; Kanta 1994; Pendlebury 1939: 7–16; Sakellarakis and Sakellarakis 1997: 72–3; Tzedakis et al. 1989, 1990). Nonetheless, the fact that major arteries stayed in use, along with some of the former main settlement centres and cult places, must have given some sense of grounding and orientation to people moving around the changing landscape. Once again, the changes of 1200 BC, drastic as they were, did not cleanly sever links to past mindsets but built on and transformed them. Some formerly little-used tracks and pathways must now have been turned into main routes as new sites were established, while some formerly important routes became less relevant and thus abandoned and overgrown. Areas of likely new infrastructure development include, for example, the valley-bottom routes linking the densely scattered sites in the northeastern Lasithi foothills and west Siteia mountains (Hayden et al. 1992: 328). Changes in route emphasis are also likely to have affected the use of extra-settlement sanctuaries. In LM IIIA-B, access to these sanctuaries, at that time controlled by the major polities, must often have been through pilgrimages along standard, well-known, and monitored routes from the main centres and subcentres. The twelfth-century settlement changes freed up physical, as well as conceptual, access to these sites, helping to stimulate new processes of self-definition through new and varied scales of contact, both at small group and at community level.

It is interesting to consider the symbolic role of the most dramatic and highly visible new settlement locations themselves, as viewed from the immediately surrounding landscape and its routes for hours each day by people working in the fields for many kilometres around, and as seen by visitors approaching along adjacent routes. A highly resonant symbolic role for them seems likely, during a period in which existing power systems focused on large centres had collapsed and a large part of the population was dispersed to relatively unfamiliar territory. Though dramatic appearance was not a driving factor behind the selection of new settlement locations in the twelfth century, it did often go hand in hand with the criterion of defensibility. Some of the new sites (e.g., Kavousi Kastro, Tapes Epano Kastello, Karfi, Elliniki Korifi, Frangkokastello Kastri) have highly dramatic visual characteristics, with very steep approach slopes; high, sharp cliffs; and large expanses of bare rock (Nowicki 2000: 99–100, 129–30, 210–13; Wallace 2002: 77–80, 2003a: 608–14). It seems likely that people gradually learned to think of some communities in the 'shorthand' terms of their distinctive topography – with the mental image of, say, the Cha gorge or Vrokastro peak in their minds when referring to the groups living at settlements on or near these features (Figures 83 and 84). From the sea, too, during a period characterised by new levels and types of mobility, prominent peaks may have formed particularly important landmarks for the identification of specific regions and visual targets to aim for when journeying inland in unfamiliar territory (Figure 85).

In the Karfi area, the largest settlement in the local landscape was also the most visually distinctive, surely giving the community there an extra standing and recognisability. A similar case of a settlement cluster in which one site stood out as a major landmark is that of Tapes in the northeast Lasithi mountains, though here the landmark site is a very small one (Epano Kastello). It is possible that a whole cluster of small settlements, as in the case of the Kastro-Vronda-Azoria-Avgo or Tapes-Zenia-Adrianos-Drasi-Vryses sites, might (consciously or not) be represented to the wider populace of the island, and to visitors from other regions, by means of the single most visually dominant site in each group – Kavousi Kastro and Tapes Epano Kastello, respectively.

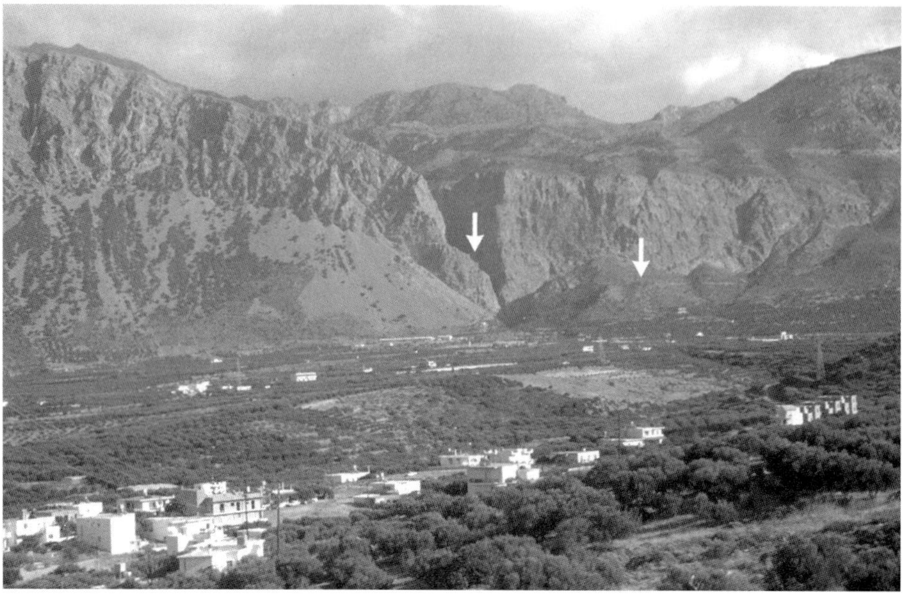

83. Monastiraki Katalimata (indicated by left arrow) and Chalasmeno from west; the Cha gorge surely functioned as a major natural landmark identifying these sites. Image by the author.

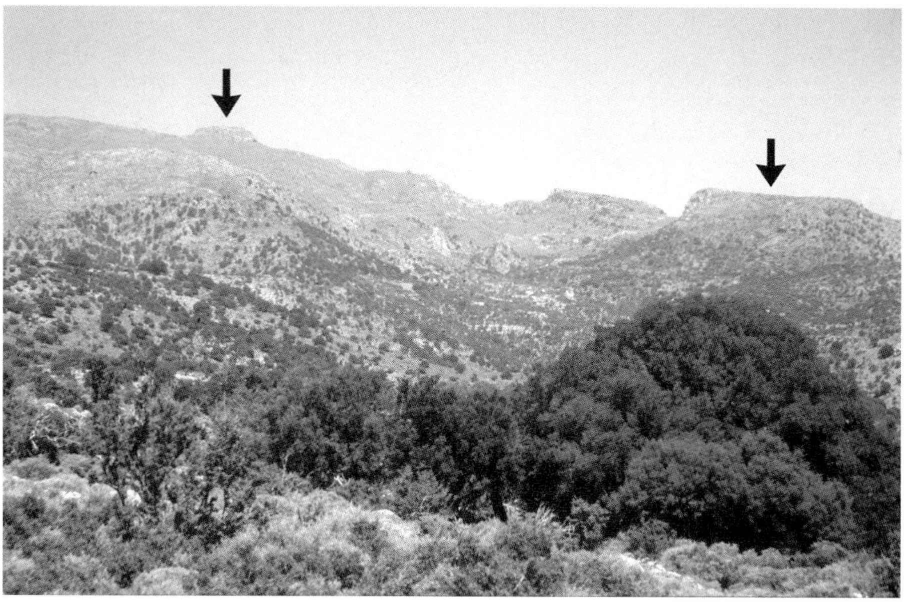

84. Tapes Epano and Kato Kastello sites from south, showing their relationship and their status as prominent landmarks from the surrounding countryside. Image by the author.

Exploring the full range of conceptual and experiential changes potentially involved in the new cultural landscapes of central Greece and the islands would require a far longer analysis, based on much more regionally targeted field research involving long periods spent walking the landscape: I make only a few suggestions here (Wallace 2007, in press d). In the island case, where relocation to defensible new sites was signficant, we might expect some of the same impacts as in Crete, though less strongly marked, since the rebalancing of population was less

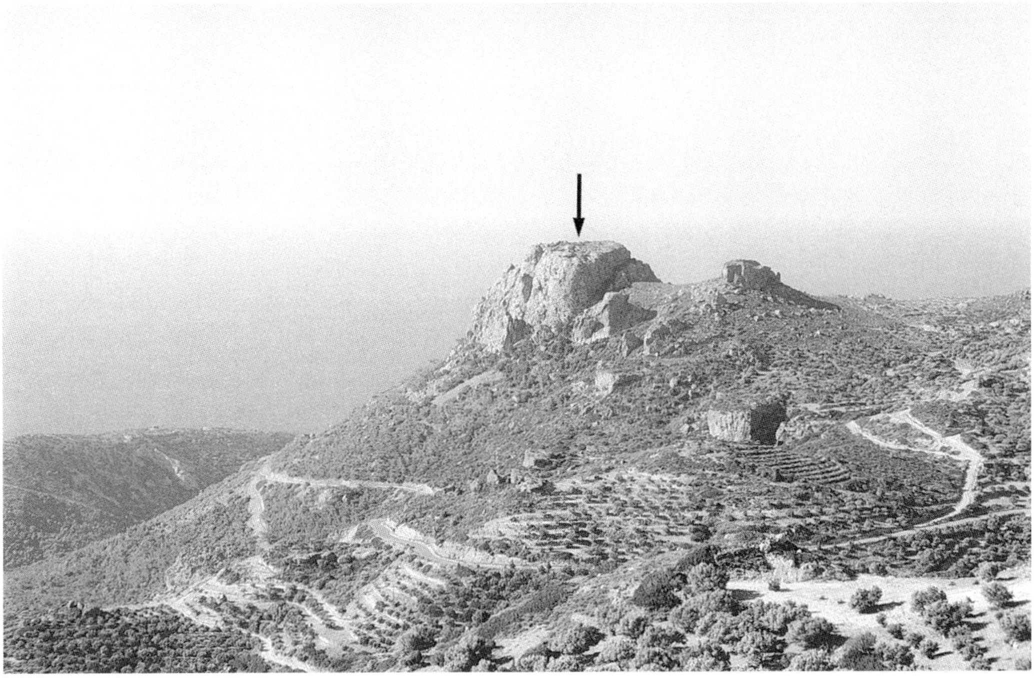

85. Koutsounari Karfi from southeast. The site was a clearly visible landmark from the south coast and inshore waters. Photo courtesy K. Nowicki.

pronounced and covered much shorter distances, and the topographic contrasts are generally less extreme.

One obvious difference between the mainland and Crete is that most EIA mainland sites are not dramatic in appearance; nor is there any very large-scale shift to new sites at this time – surely producing a much lower-calibre experiential impact. In the later part of the EIA, since mainland communities had no visually symbolic reference at landscape level for this major horizon of change in their history, they may have relied more on abstract tradition and myth to recall it. This may help to explain the tendency of mainland communities throughout the EIA, when using history to structure their identity at a number of different levels, to develop generic traditions of 'the past' focused on the material remains of the LBA, rather than of the crisis period itself. In Crete, as I have argued elsewhere, we see a much greater diversity of reference to the past through cult and other ritual practice, and also a deliberate singling out of the twelfth-century change horizon in this respect (Wallace 2003b).

The lack of any distinct or comprehensive change in the visual or experiential landscape in central Greece must have had other, related long-term effects on social and political outlook. In large, loose community groupings, which apparently lacked strongly enshrined rulership structures (highly differentiated houses and tombs, for example, are missing) and were often isolated visually by long distances from other communities, self-conceptualisation of new community units after 1200 BC is likely to have been less rapid, dynamic, or coherent than in Crete. Strong collective identity concepts, rooted in place, were central to the state structures emerging across the Aegean by circa 700 BC. We already see them well established in Crete by the tenth century, but they may have taken longer to crystallise in parts of central Greece, and remained loose in some regions, partly for these reasons.

Contact with the past

Closer visual and physical contact with older elements of the cultural landscape was a side effect of settlement relocation that is likely to have been instrumental to a significant degree in the development of new identity structures in Crete. Twelfth-century settlements were placed on the dramatic peaks of Jouktas and Kofinas in central Crete, which had been important peak sanctuaries until the early LM I period. Both have fortification walls probably dating to the twelfth century, and limited EIA surface pottery on or near the summits suggests they were possibly used as refuges (Alexiou 1963b: 384; Karetsou and Rethimiotakis 1990: 429–30; Platon and Davaras 1962: 287–8). New residents there, however temporary, must have come across and wondered about the cult material on the surface, which paralleled many of the artefacts seen at BA cult sites continuing in use at this period, including animal figurines. The same applied with even more force at Karfi, which had also been an MBA peak sanctuary: now the area immediately below the peak to its east formed a major settlement core.

Other new settlements (e.g., Katalimata, Vronda, and Azoria) had settlement remains dating from the Final Neolithic and/or Middle Minoan II periods, when defensive settlement topography was also extensively used (Day pers comm; Haggis et al. 2004; Nowicki 1994b, 1999a, 2000: 29–37, 2006, 2008; Tsipopoulou and Nowicki 2003). These remains must also have been 'discovered' in the LM IIIC relocation (or rediscovered, since traditions almost certainly existed about them, and a few local people during any part of the Bronze Age must always have had first-hand experience of the sites). Such discoveries offered the new communities access to a rich symbolic resource, which they must have referred to and valued in ways only hinted at in the record (for example, MM-LM I stone vessels, LM I seals, and Neolithic stone axes, apparently collected at the site or in the vicinity, were found within LM IIIC houses at Karfi (Pendlebury et al. 1938: 89–92, 96; Figure 86); at Katalimata, LM IIIC settlers reused Final Neolithic and Middle Bronze Age walls.

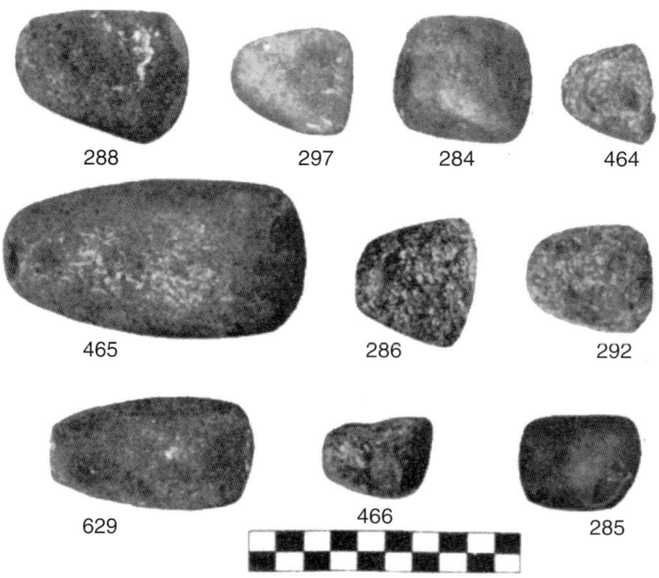

86. Stone axes found in the Karfi settlement (after Pendlebury et al. 1938, Plate XXX [2]).

That such largely accidental or incidental contacts with the remote past did have a major impact on the new communities' self-conception is suggested by the *deliberate* symbolic reuse of *other* types of old site from soon after collapse and through the course of the EIA – showing that communities were defining and rooting themselves with reference to a closer, more recent history. Alongside the cases related to cult, which I have looked at earlier, this practice appears in the funerary sphere at an early date. As the Knossos polity underwent contraction and rearrangement in LM IIIC, some older, mostly monumental tombs in the immediate environs of the site were reused for some kind of ritual practice, possibly including burial, as if to maintain claims of belonging to the urban core by several interested groups. These might have been groups that had been powerful in the LM IIIB polity, but possibly also included newly emerging power groups staking their own claims (Cadogan 1967; Evans 1906: 140–1; Hood and Coldstream 1968; Hutchinson 1956; Preston 2005; Wallace 2003b: 269–79).

15 MORTUARY SPACE AND PRACTICE IN CRETE AND OTHER AREAS

General changes in emphasis, 1200–1000 BC

Though a number of elements in mortuary practice are perpetuated from the thirteenth century into the twelfth, certain changes confirm radical and permanent social restructuring in Crete at this time. Various types of evidence, including sealing distribution and the contents of the Linear B tablets, suggest that social stratification had existed at the regional settlement nodes, as well as the main centres, of LM IIIA-B Crete (Carlier 1992). The differential use of tomb types at sites like Armeni, Achladia, and Archanes is revealing in this regard (Godart and Tzedakis 1994; Papadopoulou 1997; Sakellarakis and Sakellarakis 1997; Tsipopoulou and Vagnetti 1996; Tzedakis 1978c, 1980). Chamber tombs had become the standard form of burial across the island by LM IIIA, yet circular vaulted tombs (*tholoi*) were used in a distinctive way within the chamber-tomb cemetery of Armenoi, set out alone in the landscape near Achladia, and clustered in an exceptional and long-established elite cemetery at Archanes Phourni. In each of these cases, tholoi seem to mark out the standing of powerful individuals or family groups within the burial community. The nuclear family seems most usually to have formed the basic unit of burial at all social levels. Most chamber-tomb cemeteries consist of small mixed burial groups of adults and children, partly differentiated in wealth, age, and gender terms by grave goods (Hallager and McGeorge 1992). We see the continuing (even enhanced) social importance of the small kin group represented in the mortuary practice of the twelfth and eleventh centuries. Burials of most types and wealth levels retain a family-type structure: group size ranges up to about six adults in some cases, with tombs probably used over several generations (such as the well-preserved example excavated at Chalasmenos: Coulson and Tsipopoulou 1994; Figure 87). The practice of feasting at the grave, evidenced already in the LM IIIA-B period, clearly continues, indicated by the inclusion of drinking vessels in graves and finds of animal bones and teeth (e.g., in Karfi Ta Mnimata tomb 11), though evidence for this practicc is not very widespread (Pendlebury et al. 1938: 105–6).

In much of central Greece, particularly the south central zone, twelfth- to eleventh-century communities started to favour single burial in modest cist graves, replacing the elaborate hierarchy of LBA burial monuments. Like the change in Cretan practices, this shift must in some part reflect the new importance of competitively acquired, rather than inherited or otherwise insitutionalised status, for the individual in society (Dickinson 2006: 174–96; Iakovidis 1969; Lemos 2002: 151–84, 135–49, 184–90, 188–9; Vanschoonwinkel 1991: 55–171). Nonetheless, the new graves often seem to be grouped within family plots. David Small has argued that

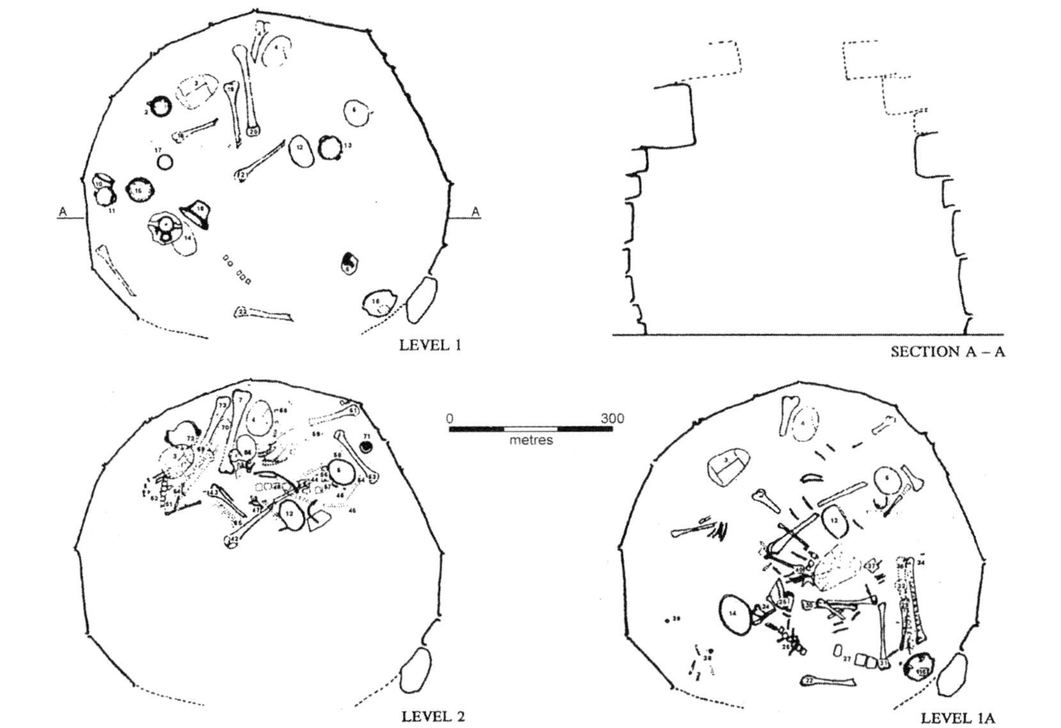

87. Plan of LM IIIC tholos tomb with contents at Chalasmeno (after Coulson and Tsipopoulou 1994, Fig. 17, p. 83). By permission of M. Tsipopoulou.

family-/clan-based power (tied to rural estates) was actively enhanced in the post–1200 BC period being automatically 'promoted' to fill the vacuum left by mainland state collapse (Small 1998, 1999; for the idea of promotion, see Flannery 1972). My view is that a straightforward peeling away of the elite layer to reveal an intact substratum was not a very likely outcome of the disturbances occurring in Aegean societies at this time. The deep social and cultural dislocation evidenced in the settlement and cult records, discussed earlier, suggests that small clans would find it difficult to appropriate or maintain very secure power bases after relocation into large mixed communities (which included multiple former-elite groups) after the collapse of centralised systems. The burial record, with its primary emphasis on the status of the individual, tends to support this view.

In Crete, though the greater focus on the nuclear family unit in burial does support other evidence for core social stability and the emergence of strong new social institutions from soon after the collapse, mortuary representations also reflect the generally fragmenting and levelling effects of events circa 1200 BC. A marked 'democratisation' of burial monuments appears, seen in the start of widespread use in many regions of small rectangular-based built tombs usually termed 'tholoi', though they are markedly different from the round LM IIIA-B tholoi. A variation on this, a half-vaulted structure, has also been noted and termed a 'pseudo-tholos': Kanta and Davaras 2004. These tombs are fairly standard in their form over cemeteries across Crete, for example, at Afrati, Karfi, Kourtes, Erganos, Krya, Veni, and Kavousi Vronda (Figures 88–90; Gesell et al. 1983; Halbherr 1901a: 271–9, 283; Kanta 1980: 75; Kanta and Davaras 2004; Kanta and Karetsou 1998; Pendlebury et al. 1938: 107–9; Rocchetti 1989, 1990; Tegou 2001). Importantly, they are usually the dominant or single form in the cemeteries in which they occur,

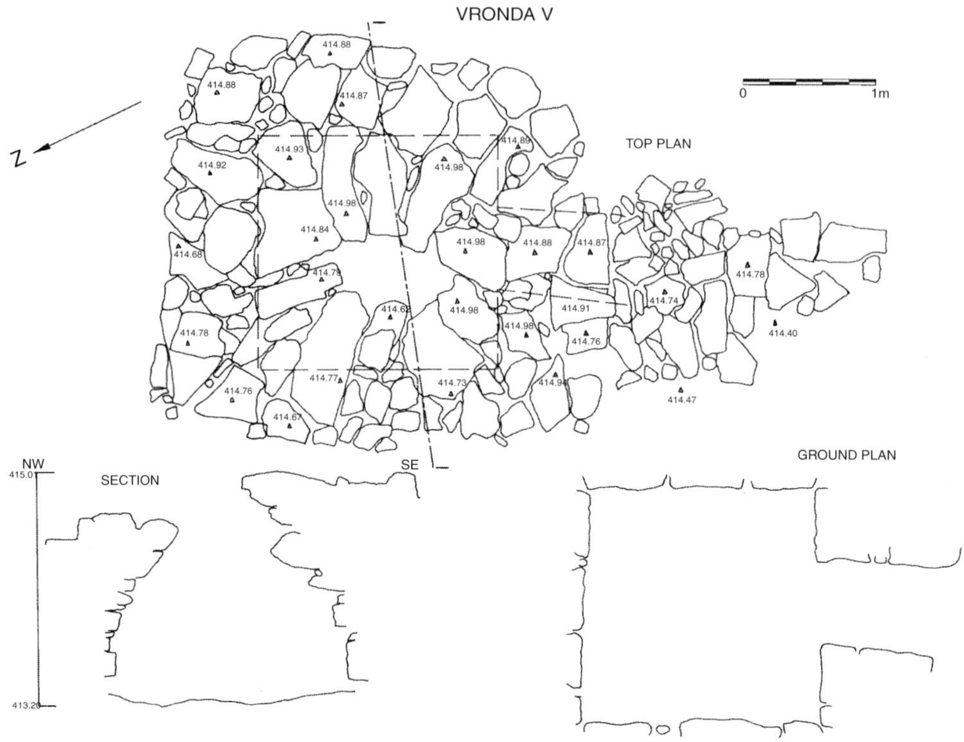

88. Plan and section of a typical small built tomb (Tomb V) at Kavousi Vronda (after Gesell et al. 1983, Fig. 5). By permission of L. P. Day.

rather than being used as an exceptional, distinctive feature. In other cemeteries, most notably Knossos, chamber tombs remain the standard form, alongside occasional use of various types of pit or shaft grave.

This pattern contrasts with the sharply distinctive use of the larger circular tholos in the preceding period, when the form still seems likely to have had prestige connections with the truly monumental mainland tholoi. The fact that the very last vestiges of prestige and monumentality attached to the tholos seem to have disappeared early in the twelfth century suggests a new lack of relevance in this kind of status marking – perhaps a tacit or overt agreement in the new communities to discourage extremes of private competition in this aspect of the architectural arena, as in others. The new pattern in tomb construction parallels the very limited and subtle differentiation in settlement architecture at IIIC sites discussed previously, and, like it, may represent a deliberate, conscious attempt to promote social cohesion. At the same time, differentiation in grave *goods* remains and flourishes, as I discuss below – indeed, the range of grave goods in tholos tomb cemeteries supports the idea that they represent a substantial sector of the burying population, rather than any exclusive group. The sizes of built tombs do vary slightly within cemeteries, as at Vronda – perhaps simply according to the number of interments planned in each tomb (with a larger family building a bigger tomb). Inhumation in clay coffins, or larnakes, a strong feature of the LBA in Crete, diminishes starkly through the twelfth and eleventh centuries, also seeming to suggest a deliberate move away from any marked differentiation in mode of burial. In some cases it survives into early LM IIIC, but is already used alongside the new practice of cremation, as in the case of the larnax burial found alongside a cremation in a jar and a pithos inhumation in a group tomb at Lakkoi, Kritsa, dating to LM IIIC (Tsipopoulou and

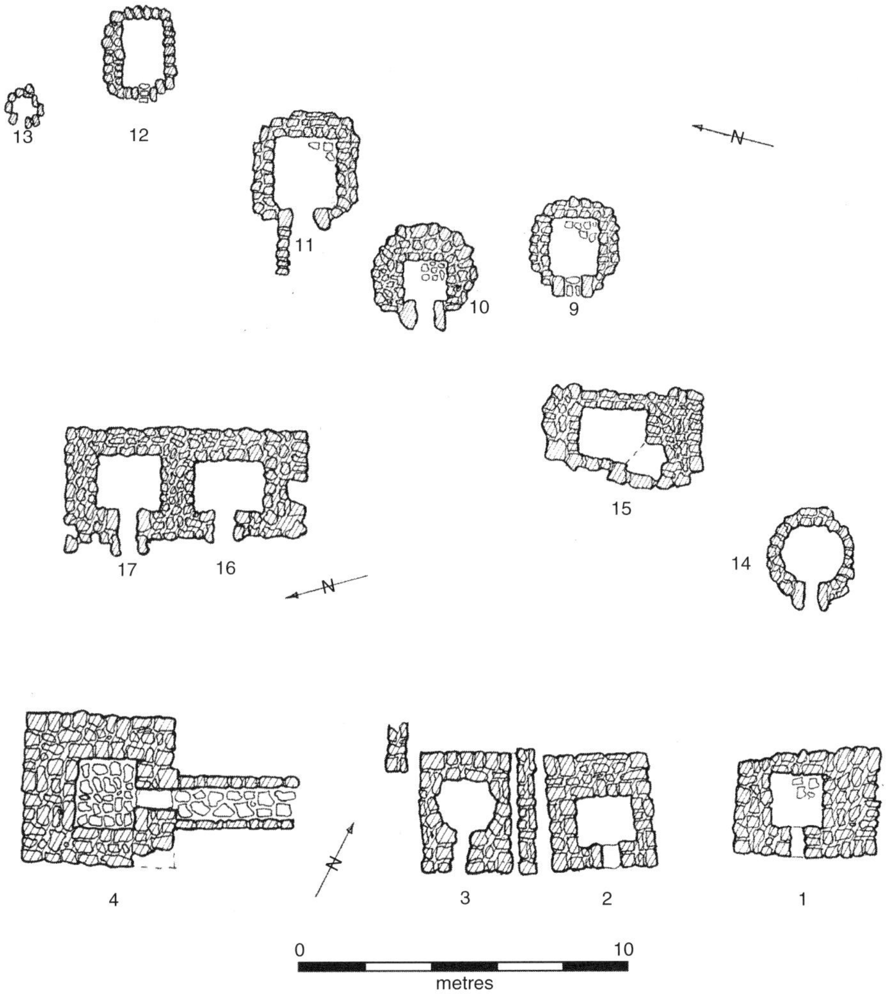

89. Cemetery of small built tombs at the Karfi ta Mnimata location (after Pendlebury et al. 1938, Plate XIII).

Vagnetti 2006). As on mainland Greece from this period, cremation gradually rises in use: its rarity at first suggests a prestigious or otherwise distinctive association in some cases, but it becomes widely used by the tenth century.

Broad distribution patterns of cemeteries and tomb clusters

The spatial relationship of twelfth- to eleventh-century settlements to their cemeteries was typically much as it had been in the LM III-B period – fairly close proximity was standard. Burials often continued to be made for a short period in some old family graves, mostly in cases where settlements had moved only a relatively short distance away: perhaps a full sense of belonging at the new settlements was not really established until a second generation had been born there. Nevertheless, as we have seen, concerns with developing and representing new communities as

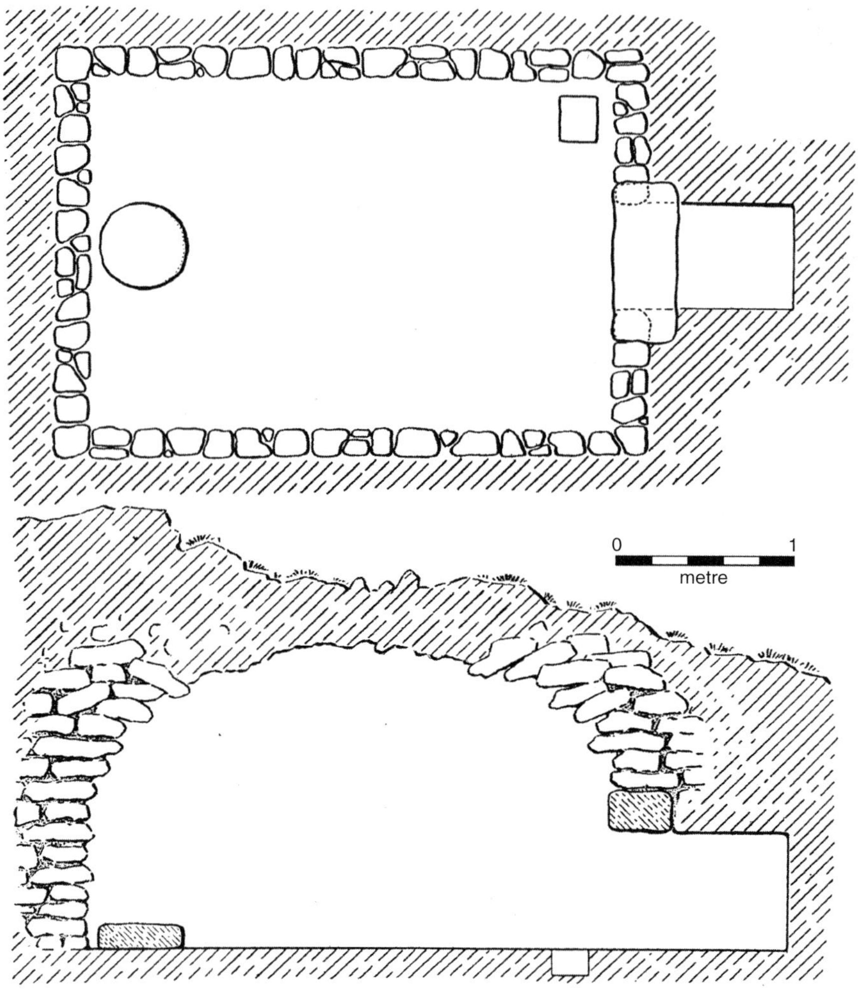

90. Plan and section of 'Chamber Tomb' I at Vrokastro (after Hall 1914, Fig. 74, p. 124).

cohesive units, including through burial in new forms and within new cemeteries, seem to have arisen quite soon after relocation. Despite some elements of continuation or readaptation of old traditions, a fundamental restructuring of communities and their internal relationships was clearly occurring, in large part via the medium of material culture.

The positioning of cemeteries and tombs in the landscape throws additional light on the structuring of the new communities. Especially in large communities, scattered groups of tombs around the settlement usually coexisted with a unitary cemetery core. Within this core, disparate tomb groupings are also sometimes visible, perhaps reflecting clan units. The central zone of the Knossos North Cemetery held the richest graves – there is a whole cluster of early burials here in large and well-made chamber tombs. Some of these were suggested by the excavators to be of Bronze Age date, reused (Coldstream and Catling 1996: 718–19). If this is indeed the case, reuse would link in clearly to the pattern of tomb reuses elsewhere at the site in the earliest EIA period discussed above, which look like a kind of new claim-staking to the site and its heritage by certain powerful or aspirant families during a disturbed time. Whatever the case, by the end of the century the wider Knossian community had struck out into a number of new and long-lived cemetery groupings. We see separate clusters of tombs, probably linked to clan groupings, scattered around the core settlement area (some of these locations, such as Gypsades and Ayios Ioannis, had already been used for burial in the LBA), as well as several different nodes of burial within the North Cemetery. I discuss these in more detail in Part Four.

At Karfi, there are at least three distinct tomb groupings, separated by stretches of up to 300 metres of empty space – large groupings at Ta Mnimata and Astvidero and a probably smaller one at the bottom of the cliff to the north of the site (Apostolakou and Kanta pers comm; Nowicki pers comm; Pendlebury et al. 1938: 100–12). Within these broad groupings there are other sets of spatial associations, with tight clusters of two or three tombs perhaps reflecting extended family ties. At LM IIIC-SM Phaistos, tombs also seem scattered in various locations around the town site. Given the markedly modest and fairly uniform character of the large Tombe delle Plebe cluster at Liliana, it is possible that the divisions between some of these clusters may have been more class- than clan-based, though these two categories may, of course, have been correlated (Savignoni 1904). The distribution of two different types of grave, each with markedly different wealth levels, at the separate Chavga and Karakovilia locations near Vrokastro also suggests an element of class division, rather than/as well as clan division. A pattern that may deliberately mirror the LM IIIA-B pattern of isolated wealthy tombs (like the Achladia tholos) is that of single examples or small groups of large, notably rich tombs dating in LM IIIC and apparently separate from any wider cemetery context, as found at Praisos Fotoula, Vasiliki, and Mouliana. The local context is, however, still poorly known in each of these cases, and there may yet prove to be other tombs nearby (Kanta 1980: 175, 179–80; Platon and Davaras 1960; Xanthoudides 1904; Tsipopoulou et al. 2003).

Any notion that the spacing of clusters *within* cemeteries at this time was correlated with wealth status alone is not well substantiated. For example, within the North Cemetery of Knossos, though clustering is apparent and sometimes seems to correspond broadly with wealth, poor graves are quite often found closely adjacent to much richer ones.

Differentiation in tomb form and burial rite: patterns within and between cemeteries

By the later twelfth century, when the North Cemetery was established at Knossos, we see a large community, with particularly good access to a range of exotic value goods, engaged in a more pronounced and complex differentiation of status through burial practice than was the case at most small new sites. This was partly done through tomb form, with a contrast between the very simple shaft-grave burials of some individuals with few or no grave goods (Tombs 153 and 160), and the use of 'pit-cave' tombs (shallow excavated hollows), as well as traditional chamber tombs, by some wealthier burial groups in the same cemetery (such as Tombs 2, 186, and 200–201). Though the pit-cave form is also very simple, its form seems deliberately distinguished from that of the shaft graves (Coldstream and Catling 1996: 58, 181–3, 190–5; Figure 91). At the Phaistos Tombe delle Plebe cemetery, by contrast, the tomb forms, like the assemblages, link a whole swathe of the community in a fairly uniform and low-key manner. This could theoretically represent a 'block' differentiation of one group in a large and complex community, with a richer spread of tombs at LM IIIC Phaistos remaining to be discovered. Yet the few other tombs with LM IIIC-SM material so far found closer to the settlement do not have a markedly different form.

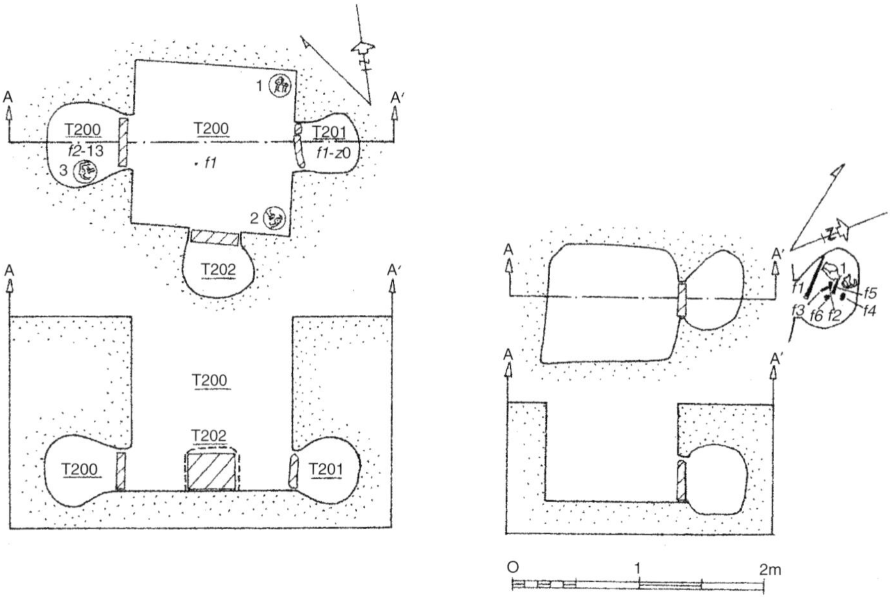

91. Examples of tomb forms at Knossos North Cemetery: *left*: Tombs 200, 201, 202, *right*: Tomb 186 (after Coldstream and Catling 1996, D. Smyth del., Fig. 43). By permission of H. W. Catling.

At the newly established settlements, some differentiation in tomb form within cemeteries is also noticeable, even though the chronology of tomb construction and use is often poorly documented. At Vrokastro, for example, there is a clear contrast between the large and well-built chamber tombs at Karakovilia and the contemporary burials in small pit graves in the nearby Chavga area (Desborough 1952: 262–8; Hall 1914: 173–5; Hayden 2005: 156). Echoing the patterns we have seen in some settlement architecture, the large built tombs on the prominent ridge of Karakovilia may suggest a number of equivalently powerful families at the site already setting themselves apart spatially, as well as in terms of burial form, from less powerful groups burying on the Chavga slopes.

The fact that burial practices varied quite widely between different sites and regions during LM IIIC, contrasting with the more standardised situation in LM IIIA-B, suggests the development of strongly regionalised cultural traditions. However, most practices built on aspects of former burial customs, providing no strong indicators of major immigration to the island at this time. Communities used burial in new ways to define themselves against each other or build internal coherence or ranking. At the same time, general patterns of mortuary practice exhibited strong supraregional features covering large parts of the island (e.g., in the changing use of the tholos) indicating the early emergence of pervasive new social and cultural norms. We also see strong ties into the conventions of the changing wider Aegean world, showing close contacts and shared social concepts. In particular, cremation and the burial of the ashes in jars, which was spreading through the Aegean region from the twelfth century onward – probably as a result of contacts with the central European or east Mediterranean areas – became sporadically used across Crete from early in the twelfth century, though some isolated examples are known prior to this date (Kanta 2001a). It increased in popularity here at about the same rate as on the mainland and may at first be associated with rather wealthy burials, a pattern paralleled in Athenian cemeteries through the earlier part of the EIA; it notably characterises the rich Tombs 200 and 201 at Knossos (Dickinson 2006: 188–92). This is not a simple or absolute rule, however, and specific local traditions may have developed regarding the use of cremation from its earliest introduction. A group of rather modest twelfth- to eleventh-century burials at Atsipades Pezoules in west Crete, for example (perhaps associated with the nearby settlement at Fonises), were nearly all cremations (Agelarakis et al. 2001; Kanta 1980: 209; Petroulakis 1915).

Detailed status mapping through grave goods and skeletal material: evidence quality

As I stress in Part Three, the forms of Cretan grave goods and the nature of their deposition in this period suggest not only regular trade contacts with regions outside the island, but awareness of consumption practices applying across most of the contemporary east Mediterranean: they cannot therefore be looked at in isolation (Crielaard 1998). This particularly applies when assessing the role and meaning of exotica in grave assemblages. A particular problem in assessing the relative wealth and prestige of burials from their goods is the rapid change in physical access to some kinds of value items, and in the social rules governing their use in burial, over the course of the EIA. For example, iron (at first a rare and highly prestigious material) changed its value status rapidly over time and in different regions and cannot be used on its own to assess status differentials when dealing with burial groups or cemeteries spanning a considerable period (Sherratt 1994; Snodgrass 1971: 213–96, 1980b, 1982a, 1989). Since the quantities of pottery deposited in tombs of this period appear to correlate strongly with the simple number of individuals in a tomb, the overall types and quantities of value items deposited in graves (including bronze, iron, gold, ivory, faience, rock crystal, and some specialised ceramic types) seem the most sensitive indicators of inequality between burial groups. Below, I outline the insight into ranking systems offered by grave goods and skeletal evidence at the best-documented cemeteries, first analysing the data at an islandwide level, then an intra-cemetery one.

In each case my observations are necessarily broad and general. There are many problems with data consistency and quality, and pottery chronology for the LM IIIC-SM period is still much debated, as discussed in Part One. In what follows, I include all tombs datable wholly or mainly within the period 1200–1000 BC. Tombs are often used over several generations, but it is rarely possible to separate each burial neatly by date, and ongoing reuse often damaged or mixed bones and grave goods. The data available from any individual cemetery are too limited to produce many useful statistics for the twelfth to tenth centuries on their own. I am cautious throughout in assuming a direct relationship between categories of burial practice and general categories of status differentiation, and burial data are ultimately considered alongside many other types of evidence in drawing conclusions about social ranking (Barrett 1996; Binford 1972; Hodder 1982b; Morris 1987: 110–18; Parker Pearson 1982; Saxe 1970, 1971; Shanks and Tilley 1987: 42–5; Wason 1994: 87–102; Whitley 1991a: 23–34). A feature persisting across the Aegean between the thirteenth and eleventh centuries is the so-called warrior burial – characterised by an assemblage dominated by metal weapons (and by its very nature usually congruent with generally wealthy graves, nearly always of males). However, talking about 'continuity' of this phenomenon is not very meaningful, as the category is so broad and the general context and character of burial changed in so many ways through this period. The newly modest character and greater ubiquity of central Greek weapons burials in the twelfth century have already been noted in the scholarship (Dickinson 2006: 73–4). The frequency of extremely rich and elaborate cases seems to decline after the end of the LBA, along with monumental tombs and other appurtenances of a very well-established elite. However, even in the highly stratified societies of the LBA, people of a variety of wealth levels had access to this form of interment, and given the new economic opportunities arising after collapse, it is not surprising that a significant range of users continues to exist, and even to expand, after 1200 BC. Twelfth-century Cretan examples of this type of burial appear from Mouliana and Knossos, in Knossos Tombs 186, 2, and 200 (the latter particularly wealthy, with its gold items and heirloom boar's tusk helmet: Coldstream and Catling 1996: 58, 190–5; Figures 92 and 93). A recently excavated tomb at Pandanassa Veni in western Crete is another, slightly more modest, example (Kanta 1980: 175; Tegou 2001; Xanthoudides 1904). The direct identification of weapons assemblages like those in the Knossos tombs with real 'warriors' is questionable, especially for the most generally wealthy graves subsumed under the 'warrior grave' heading (Catling 1995, 1996c: 646; Deger-Jalkotzy 1999; Driessen and Schoep 1999: 395; Whitley 1998b, 2002; Figure 94). The literal role of the male as warrior may indeed have gained in importance in this politically disturbed world, and we have noted that in some respects LM IIIC communities were particularly concerned with defence. But the continued use of the warrior trope to confer or represent wealth standing in burial primarily suggests that some widespread LBA conceptions of status and ranking retained meaning, despite marked changes in lifestyles and power structures. In making these kinds of burials, Cretan societies were actively linking themselves into existing trans-Aegean traditions and ongoing cultural discourses of wealth and status across the whole east Mediterranean region.

Notwithstanding the obstacles to meaningful comparison listed, I strive here for a cross-island perspective. The Knossos data, thanks to their large quantity and up-to-date, detailed publication,

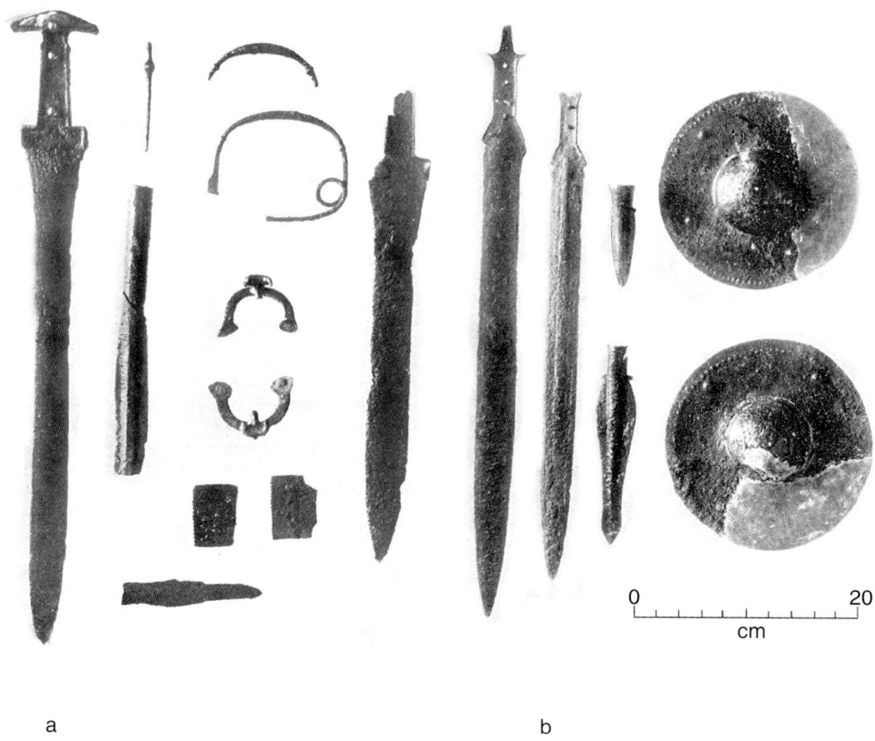

92. Assemblages from Mouliana Tombs A and B (after Xanthoudides 1904: *a*, Fig. 7, p. 30; *b*, Fig. 11, p. 46).

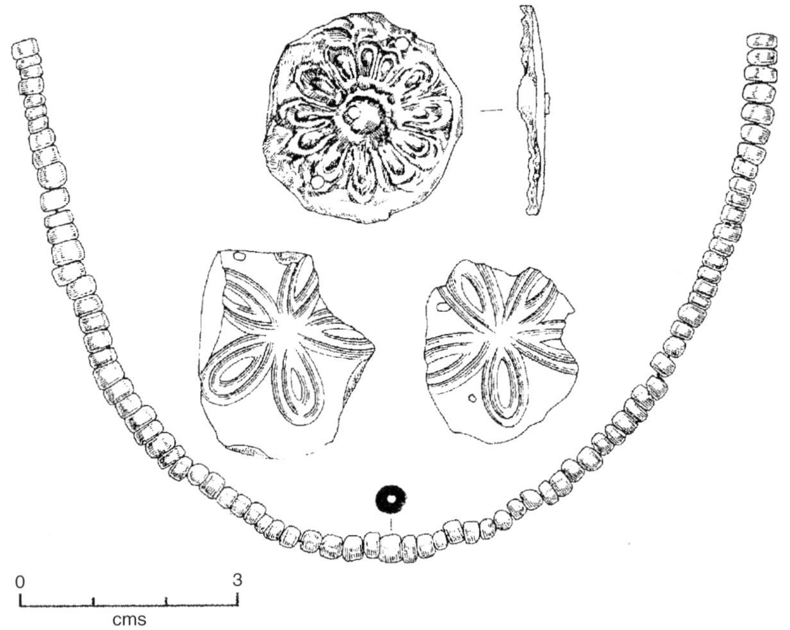

93. Gold jewellery from Knossos North Cemetery Tombs 40 and 200 (after Coldstream and Catling 1996, E. A. Catling del., Fig. 153 [40.f2; 200.f3; 200.f8]). By permission of H. W. Catling.

have till now been the main source for social analysis of Cretan EIA cemeteries (Coldstream and Catling 1996; Whitley 1986, 1991a: 184–91). But since, as we have seen, Knossos is something of an exception in terms of Cretan settlement at this time, it seems vital to look at other sites, despite the limitations of data quality. Karfi is in many respects a more representative and useful case to examine for the early EIA, given the site's short occupation span, its typically defensible character, and its relatively large number of excavated tombs dating entirely in this period. The record is further boosted by data from Kavousi Vronda, Vrokastro, Phaistos Liliana, Erganos, and Fatsi/Droggara (Davaras 1972; Gesell et al. 1983; Halbherr 1901a: 271–9; Hall 1914: 123–75; Kanta 1980: 176; Pendlebury et al. 1938: 100–12; Savignoni 1904; Tsipopoulou 1997a). Apart from these, we are dealing with scattered tombs, whose contents can only be useful in the analysis of social representation if analysed in the context of the island as a whole.

Observations on ranking: general patterns across the island

Overall, the very variable quantities and combinations of rites, burial numbers, and grave goods in Cretan cemeteries of this period suggest that wealth, while clearly cross-relating with social status and (because most easily analysed), giving us the most detailed insight into status representation, was only one factor in that status – age, sex, and lineage all played roles (Saxe 1970: 19, 1971; Wason 1994: 90–2, 98; Whitley 1986; 288–90, 1991a: 186–7). The repeated emphasis on family groupings, the presence of rich female burials, and the clear linking of children into the wealth display – a richly furnished child burial accompanies the wealthy couple in Knossos Tomb 201, for example (Coldstream and Catling 1996: 191–5) – all argue for the inheritance of wealth and status within close family units. The size of the family unit represented

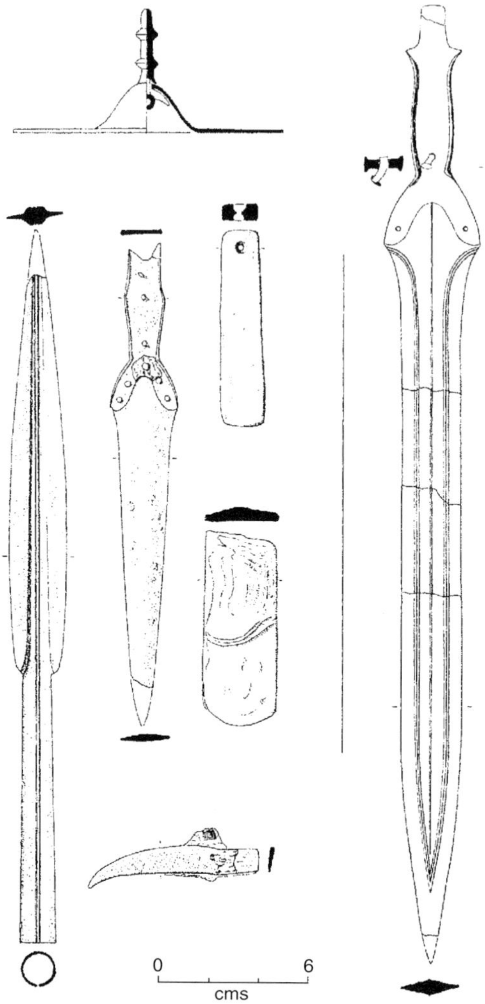

94. Weapons assemblage from Tomb 186, Knossos North Cemetery (after Coldstream and Catling 1996, E. A. Catling del., Fig. 163 [f1–f7]). By permission of H. W. Catling.

in burial seems linked to the wealth and status of the group involved: some of the richest tombs have single or couple burials only. But in overall contrast to central Greek patterns, kinship seems to have constituted a deliberately perpetuated and prominent framework of social power – a consistently important supplement (or alternative) to rank achieved through the competitive accumulation and display of wealth.

Looking at the island as a whole, the richest tombs are an order of magnitude above the rest. Some Knossos North Cemetery examples (200/201, 186, 40, and 2), Mouliana tombs A and B, and the Praisos Fotoula tomb, all combine relatively few burials with a large assemblage of value items. These are mostly in intrinsically valuable, convertible materials, especially gold and bronze (Coldstream and Catling 1996: 58, 86–9, 191–5; Kanta 1980: 175, 179–80; Platon 1960b: 302; Platon and Davaras 1960; Xanthoudides 1904). Notably, the burial rite used here is often cremation (see Crielaard 1998: 188–9). Most tombs of this level have a few iron objects – extremely rare at this time – though some early examples, such as Mouliana A, are without iron altogether. The metal items found with males in these graves are often very large and expensive pieces of fighting equipment (such as the Mouliana shield bosses and sword, and the sword and dagger from Knossos Tomb 186) adapting and continuing the 'warrior grave' trope.

Another, subsidiary, level of wealth/status seems represented in a larger number of tombs spread throughout the island, typically characterised by an assemblage of several pots, a small amount of bronze, and sometimes one or more objects of iron, clay beads, a spindle-whorl, or a piece of rock crystal. These seem to represent people who had social and physical access to some of the prestige-good types in circulation but were not able either to amass or to deposit a large quantity of them. In male burials of this kind weapons are often present, but often of small types – knives and daggers. It is possible that this group had no physical/social access at all to goods at the highest end of the value range, such as gold. Tombs of this type are not usually set apart spatially and often involve a larger group (though still about the size of an extended family) than the one or two individuals found in the richest category of tombs. At Knossos, Gypsades Tombs VIa and VII (both representing the latest phase of use of existing LBA tombs) and Ayios Ioannis IV, as well as North Cemetery Tombs 121 and 208, fall into this category and are closely paralleled by most of the Karfi tombs, such as Ta Mnimata 4, 7, 9, 10, 16, and 17 (Boardman 1960; Coldstream and Catling 1996: 164–5, 199–200; Hood et al. 1959: 205–8; Pendlebury et al. 1938: 103–7). Vronda tholoi 4, 7, and 8, used over the LM IIIC/SM through PG period, seem to be of the same 'medium' wealth level, as do the single tholos excavated at Chalasmenos and a roadside tomb at Phaistos, which includes several small pieces of bronze jewellery (Boyd 1901: 132; Coulson and Tsipopoulou 1994: 86–91; Gesell et al. 1983: 398–9, 401–3).

There are also examples of really poor tombs. Some apparently intact examples at Knossos North Cemetery contain one or two pots only, and no other grave goods (Tombs 112, 160, and probably 153; Coldstream and Catling 1996: 162–3, 181–3). Their single burials indicate that small numbers of individuals per tomb were not just characteristic of wealthy interments. At Erganos, two unlooted LM IIIC tombs had only a few pots or value items as grave goods, despite the probably large size of the burial groups (one has six individuals; Halbherr 1901a: 271–7). The assemblages of the 'Tombe delle Plebe' at Phaistos Liliana, with a few burials each, are similarly poor, though a higher level of wealth/status certainly exists among the burying population in the wider vicinity – as indicated, for example, by the single moderately rich tomb found during a roadside excavation in another part of the area (Desborough 1964: 183–4; Kanta 1980: 100; Levi 1955: 159; Rocchetti 1970: 46–54; Savignoni 1904: 637).

Evidence for ranking within cemeteries

Intra-cemetery analyses tell us only a small amount more about social relations, though they help to refine the analysis presented previously. The level of variability in wealth assemblages is clearly different at different types of site (negligible at Phaistos Tombe delle Plebe; moderate at Karfi; considerable at Knossos), but the incomplete publication of many cemetery data often fails to allow more detailed interpretation. Overall, this pattern of variability within and between cemeteries does *not* suggest restriction of access to burial to elites only, of the kind argued to have operated in eleventh- to eighth-century Athens (Morris 1989).

There are traces of subtle and complex differentiations in status even within broad wealth/gender groups at single sites, which we are not yet able to understand. At Knossos, for example, several wealthy male burials, two single and one in a family group, have very similar sets of the typical warrior equipment (Tombs 2, 186, and 201; Coldstream and Catling 1996: 58, 190–5). In Tomb 40, however, which includes at least one male, there are no weapons, despite the richness of the assemblage, which contains iron, bronze, and gold. This suggests that a status other than warrior was recognised for this grave's male occupant, wealthy though he was (Coldstream and Catling 1996: 86–9).

Rite also seems to be used in complex and subtle ways to represent a variety of different status categories within cemeteries. The very richest burials at Knossos are usually cremations (though children are usually inhumed), while some of the poorest tombs are inhumations (18, 16, 98). Interestingly, though, the generally poor North Cemetery Tomb 112 contains one cremation and one inhumation (Coldstream and Catling 1996: 66–70, 130–2, 162–3). In this regard, there seem once again to be strong differences in practice at a local regional level. At Phaistos Liliana, the only cremation seems to be that of a child (and not a wealthy one), and there is also a child cremation at Erganos in a grave of only moderate wealth (Halbherr 1901a; Savignoni 1904). It is notable that there is no restriction of children's access to burial, as once argued for EIA Athens by Morris – though the latter is also now convincingly queried by Liston (Liston pers comm; see Lemos 2002: 186; Morris 1987: 72–110). Nor, conversely, is there any special focus on burying children.

At the Karfi cemeteries, the lack of very pronounced differentiation in either grave goods or rite by comparison with Knossos may relate to the smaller size and comparatively limited wealth of this community, offering fewer opportunities for the consolidation or display of status. Since nearly all tombs were looted or damaged and no detailed skeletal studies were carried out, we know little about the use of rite in differentiating groups or individuals: most burials appear to be inhumations. The size and relative wealth of the assemblage in Ta Mnimata Tomb 11 do mark it out (though not dramatically) from many of the others in the cemetery. It has only two burials but contains a relatively large amount of metal, including several items of iron and some special ceramic types. Ta Mnimata Tomb 8 parallels it in several respects (Pendlebury et al. 1938: 104–6).

The generally modest 'Tombe delle Plebe' at Phaistos Liliana are only slightly differentiated by type, number of burials, or quantities of grave goods – and the individual pit burials F, G, and H have no grave goods preserved at all. The richest tomb (with the most numerous pots, alongside two bronze items) is D, but this has four burials, supporting the suggestion that ceramic grave goods, at least, simply increase quantitatively with the number of burials in a tomb (Kanta 1980: 100; Savignoni 1904: 637). At Vrokastro, in the set of tombs at Kopranes spanning the LM IIIC-EPG periods, Tomb V is distinguished from Tomb VI in terms of the number of pots it contains. Tomb VII is rather poorer than both the others, though all three tombs contain approximately the same number of individuals. In their form as well as their contents, all seem clearly set apart in status from the cluster of large built tombs on the ridge above (Hall 1914: 149–54).

In general, then, the cemetery evidence backs up what we had learned from the settlement record: in most communities, no single very preeminent wealth or power group existed (or was acknowledged). Instead, especially in the larger settlements, there are a high number of competing small, relatively prosperous family units. If rank *had* been very well established and fully heritable, we would expect more polarised, consolidated inequalities in wealth/status display in the mortuary sphere. At Knossos, which forms our most extensive sample of mortuary practice and was an exceptionally large and rich site of the period, status is clearly tied to wealth and lineage, but also to other attributes, including age and sex. However, the extreme concentrations of wealth in a particularly large number of tombs here may indicate the existence of a more substantial, better-resourced, and more entrenched elite class than at Karfi or others of the new sites.

In discussing EIA Knossian cemeteries, Whitley has suggested that a marked lack of clear social restrictions on wealth good deposition, the high overall quantities of wealth goods deposited, and the diversity of style and provenance in these goods reflect a kind of free-for-all in acquisition and display, where 'eclecticism is the only rule' (Whitley 1991a: 186–8, 1991b: 355–6). I have shown here that social rules and institutions *did* govern the use of mortuary forms and practices in the island, as with other areas of cultural life. We are simply as yet unable to analyse the way this worked in detail. However, I would agree with Whitley's important point that the sphere of prestige good/exotica acquisition and deposition in graves was one in which social control was relatively difficult or undesirable to exert in Crete, especially among populations at the major import gateways, of which Knossos was one. I suggest that the early emergence of strong social institutions within the new communities may have helped make such types of control unnecessary, while the geographical position of the island, close to the east Mediterranean export 'core', anyway made them difficult if not impossible to achieve. The sheer numbers of prestige goods an individual could accumulate and deposit in burial probably depended more on his tradable wealth resources and physical access to such goods than on strict social rules. Still, however, the types of goods deposited, the rite, and the tomb form *were* strongly bounded by new norms and institutions in Cretan society. I will argue in later parts of this book that it was the very strength of early post-collapse social institutions in Crete that permitted the relative freedom of wealth acquisition – yet the mode of consumption and display of that wealth was by no means unregulated.

16 THE STRUCTURE OF COLLAPSE IN CRETE

The impression that Cretan communities of the late LM IIIB period collapsed in a particularly 'successful' way emerges not only from the pattern of their physical relocation, but from the strength and variety of new social institutions they developed very soon afterwards. A solid framework of institutions, including kin-group membership, public cult at settlement level, and formalised gathering/feasting, seems to have held them together in a relatively stable way. These institutions were all rooted in existing traditions but also reflected a significant degree of social innovation. As well as promoting internal bonds, they supported the building of complex inter-community networks of subsistence, defence, and cult, covering large regions. These, in turn, encouraged the development of important new structures of collective identity from very soon after 1200 BC, which fed back into and transformed social institutions over time.

The evidence presented here suggests there was no straightforward promotion of existing sub-groups within Cretan society to positions of prominence after collapse. The settlement evidence is particularly meaningful: from a pattern of highly ranked settlement at regional level emerged one with a much smaller range of settlement sizes and very little discernible hierarchy. There are completely new regional concentrations of settlement – suggesting the widespread mixing and transformative regrouping of preexisting community units. Even though many of the same subsistence resources were used as in the LM IIIA-B period, this was done from new settlement bases: though many small farms clearly continued in use, they do not form any 'default' pattern of post-collapse settlement. Groups that had held low- or middle-ranking status in LM IIIB seem to have needed to adjust their lifestyles and build a new social position just as much as former elites did. Systems of social differentiation were radically restructured, with a notionally more 'equalised' cultural environment nonetheless providing considerable scope for status negotiation and mobility within a stable framework.

Any notion that Crete's successful response to crisis indicates that the island was simply 'less affected' by collapse than other parts of the Aegean is unconvincing. The point could potentially be argued within a perspective viewing the island as a 'peripheral' area of the Mycenaean world, with a less complex economic and social structure than mainland central Greece. Yet the deep-rooted and widespread nature of cultural readjustment on Crete proves that it *was* profoundly affected and transformed by the crisis. The real difference is that its collapse had a remarkably positive structure: Cretan communities responded in an early, planned, and successful way to conditions of increased insecurity and new opportunities. The nature of these reactions was closely connected both to the physical scale and positioning of the island and to its history of relations with the wider Mediterranean world, but not in any straightforward or predictable way. Local cultural and social history and the form and history of the natural and cultural landscape also played very important roles in determining the response.

Despite the positive and 'successful' nature of this response, Cretan communities show few signs of expansion – either politically, economically, or physically – during the course of the twelfth to tenth centuries. This fact seems to reflect the very considerable levels of social and cultural adjustment during and after the collapse. High settlement density, a new focus on subsistence self-sufficiency in these insecure times, and the presence of strong institutions countering social volatility in the newly formed communities, all combined to restrict growth. On the other hand, there is little sign of any extreme kind of social instability of a type likely to inhibit growth permanently – such as the dominance of achieved-rank social systems (contra Whitley 1991b). Whitley's characterisation of much of early EIA Cretan society along these lines, based on an uneven comparison of settlement and cemetery data, views the relatively short-term use of some new sites as reflecting constantly shifting power structures at this time. However, it relies heavily on a nonbalanced analysis of the mortuary evidence (failing to compare the unrepresentative site of Knossos consistently with the new defensible settlements). This gives a misleading impression. In fact, very few sites founded by the mid-twelfth century, see abandonment before the tenth. Those cases of abandonment that do occur usually represent transitional stages in relocation from low-lying settlements of the thirteenth century, or relate to short-term highly defensible refuge places, never used for full-time occupation. The archaeological analogy Whitley chooses to illustrate unstable communities is of swidden cultivators in highland Burma, whose whole subsistence regime is based on regular shifts in settlement base – a model totally inappropriate for the economic conditions of ancient Greece (Foxhall 2002; Friedman 1975; Leach 1954; see Part Four).

The family-based structures of wealth inheritance indicated by mortuary practices, the evidence for well-enshrined institutions of public cult and feasting at excavated settlements, and hints from the architectural and mortuary records that while powerful families did compete with each other, inequality tended to become consolidated over time within certain fixed limits, all argue against the dominance of achieved-rank social structures. Certain families or individuals were able to establish reasonably stable roles of social prominence, though this seems to have been more easily achieved on an exclusive basis in smaller than in larger communities. Boundaries existed on extreme and overt private power building through wealth display in some forms, such as domestic architecture, from very soon after collapse. The burial sphere provided greater leeway for display in grave goods, yet many aspects of mortuary practice reflect a tendency to formal egalitarianism. These limits on the consolidation of either individual or group power are likely to have been crucial to maintaining social cohesion in the early post-collapse period. In summary, early EIA Cretan communities were neither simple achieved-rank societies nor stable hereditary chiefdoms. Rank at this time could be enhanced through competition and aggrandisement but was also connected to personal and collective lineage, and any kind of extreme social mobility was bounded by a set of strong institutions.

An important feature emerging from the evidence is the role of *groups*, from the extended family to the village community, as conscious agents in structuring social life through the manipulation of culture – drawing on history and tradition to develop coherent social identities. Some changes could only effectively be undertaken at this kind of collective level – the comprehensive, interdependent, and planned relocation process; the early establishment of settlement-level public cult; the continued large-scale use of old sanctuaries within a totally new settlement map. Those responsible for taking the initiative in relocation and reconstruction can have done so only by developing a very broad-ranging base of social support. Again, this discourages adoption of a model of social revolution, cast in terms of simple promotion of an existing subclass. Good intracommunity links during and after the crisis period were crucial to the survival and security of the new community units and the consolidation of the new cultural landscape.

At the same time, the culturally constructed and culturally reinforced levelling tendency in everyday life seen after 1200 BC does point to a 'quiet revolution' in class relations at an island-wide level. Elements of actual or potential contest, as well as cooperation, must have been part of the collapse process and its outcome. Factional rivalry and competition within communities are suggested by the evidence pertaining to ceremonial feasting and may well have been involved in the use of extra-settlement sanctuaries. This type of tension, repressed in the highly stratified LBA social systems, may now have burgeoned, helping to hold back smooth or rapid growth in economic and social complexity during the post-collapse period. The dismantling or decline of the control systems in place during the LM IIIA-B period almost certainly caused various resentments, losses, debts, and obligations among those who had formerly held power and resources but now saw them reduced, and among those who had depended on those groups to protect them economically. The splitting up of old territorial power bases by the reality of the new settlements' distribution, and the new subsistence territories associated with the latter, must have left some feeling disenfranchised, even cheated, while others saw new opportunities for personal aggrandisement. The egalitarianism of everyday life at the new sites might sit badly with some formerly high-ranking groups (though others must have accepted and even promoted it in the interest of community stability). Such groups or individuals may have tried to grab back what they felt they were owed in terms of status at the expense of other community members, in terms of land rights, political weight, marriage rights, or prerogatives in the circulation and consumption of value items. Overall, however, the need for security of various kinds following the disintegration of a highly complex, centralised, and interdependent political structure seems to have produced a critical mass of willingness to frame cultural and social compromises among the majority of the island's population. While many of these may have been rationalised at the time as temporary changes, this chapter has shown the cultural and social shifts of the period to have been so deep-rooted that there could be no going back. Cretan society was drastically and permanently reshaped by the adjustments (not least the material ones) made at circa 1200 BC. More pronounced social inequalities were to emerge again in the Protogeometric period and to become consolidated in ways that eventually led to the rise of polis states. But these developments were, as we shall see, themselves heavily influenced by the twelfth- to tenth-century history of the island, rather than representing any kind of return to a Late Bronze Age social 'norm' after a period of disruption.

Much energy has been expended in previous scholarship in assessing the degree of cultural 'continuity' versus 'change' in EIA Crete. I have shown here that a huge horizon of change circa 1200 BC did deeply affect social and cultural life: where elements of cultural continuity are seen, they are often highly selective and deliberate and situated in a symbolic or ritual dimension. I suggest that the common scholarly perception of particularly high levels of 'cultural continuity' in Crete compared to other Aegean areas in this period ultimately reflects the relatively smooth and sophisticated *adaptation* of Cretan societies to change, not a lack of change. It also reflects a strong and continuing interest among communities of this period in the past (real or invented) and its relevance in building new social identities. Ironically, as we have seen here, it was through radical cultural and structural change in many areas that Cretan communities preserved their ability to invest selectively in the *appearance* or *tradition* of continuity in highly symbolic ways.

PART THREE

After the fall: Crete's interactions with other Mediterranean regions in the twelfth to eighth centuries BC

17 INTRODUCTION

I now turn to look at the evidence for Crete's overseas interactions between the twelfth and eighth centuries, comparing them to those of the Aegean mainland and islands, and to those of Cyprus, Italy, and coastal western Anatolia, which all had strong contacts with the Aegean by the end of the eighth century. In this regard it makes sense to cover the whole period up to and beyond the rise of the polis state within a single discussion. Long-distance interactions possessed dynamics that are most clearly recognised over the long term and were strongly influential on the nature and chronology of state emergence in the period 1000–700 BC. One of the most important themes of the discussion will be Crete's singular and long-term lack of an export trade in nonperishable luxury goods. This seems to have heavily influenced social and economic developments in the island throughout the EIA, particularly from the tenth century onward. I argue that the ultimate reasons for it lie in the drastic and formative cultural break of the twelfth century. Thus, I start my narrative again at around 1200 BC, prefacing the discussion with an overview of Crete's external contacts in the fourteenth and thirteenth centuries.

As well as studying what entered the island from outside, I use the distribution of imported goods and raw materials, local imitations of exotica, and production-site evidence to identify how exchange networks operated *within* EIA Crete. Such networks seem to have been efficient in linking the island's interior to the coasts from an early point in the EIA, and there is plenty of evidence to suggest that many Cretans, while forced to move their residence from the dangers of the coasts, had no intention of abandoning the useful and profitable contacts to be found there or of ceasing to travel abroad. Whether operating in the island or outside it, Cretans seem to have been active participants in interregional trade throughout the EIA: ports like Kommos, Chania, and the harbours north of Knossos, at Poros-Katsambas and Amnisos, had an important role as provisioning stops and meeting points on major routes into the Aegean and between the central and east Mediterranean (Alexiou 1955; Andreadaki-Vlasaki 2004; Schäfer et al. 1992: 182–3, Figures 73–80; Shaw 1989, 1998; Shaw and Shaw 2000). The island kept a strong orientation towards the east Mediterranean exchange sphere even as other Aegean regions were experiencing breaks in this connection and/or seeking connections with other supply cores, including the metal-rich south Balkans. This placed Crete consistently in leading-edge contact with the trends towards technological innovation and trade growth in the complex east Mediterranean societies of the period.

The small size, dense scattering, local inaccessibility, lack of economic specialization, and non-optimal subsistence context of many twelfth- to tenth-century communities in the island meant that the Cretan goods exchange economy had a generally limited potential for growth in the early part of the EIA. These conditions changed from the tenth century onward, with external trade relations growing during a marked Aegean-wide boom. Unusually, however, Crete's economic focus remained on developing commodity production to supply the needs of increasingly complex societies *within* the island, rather than engaging in export production. I suggest that the combination of strongly embedded social institutions developing in the early post-collapse period and an early and sustained 'connectedness' with the outside world, especially the east Mediterranean trade core, in the same period made Cretan societies less open than their central Greek counterparts to either extreme disruption *or* extreme stimulation by the eastern import trade. This helps explain both the lack of social restrictions on the consumption of eastern value goods in Crete throughout the EIA (already highlighted by Whitley 1991a: 186–9, 1991b: 360–1) and the distinct lack of impetus to develop specialised exports. In this light, I will argue that models of state formation for EIA Greece that stress increased eastern contacts by the eighth century as a driving force in polis state development need reconsideration: more flexible paradigms, and a much longer timescale, are needed to explain the Cretan response (Morris 1987: 1).

Any discussion on the above themes must engage with questions of ethnicity and the social context of cultural transfer and consumption (Crielaard et al. 1999; Sherratt 1998; van Wijngaarden 1999). Throughout my analysis, I will show how deeply Crete was tied into a Levantine cultural framework and economic outlook, a fact that helped maintain the island's profitable role as a trade channel for eastern goods reaching the Aegean but also gave it an ambiguous identity status in the Aegean world, where 'oriental' culture had a strong political resonance and was being heavily appropriated and manipulated in local power relations up to and through the period of state emergence (Morris 2000: 195–257). From at least the ninth century, a spread of Aegean products, culture, and people to the central Mediterranean and northwestern Anatolia was also occurring that was vitally important in building Aegean state identities and linking them within a pan-Hellenic framework (Coldstream 1994b; Cook 1959; Holloway 2000: 43–86; Osborne 1998; Ridgway 1992). Crete seems to have had only a limited role in this development, and I will suggest that the particular nature of its links to the eastern trade may have helped create this situation.

'Levantine' and 'Greek' ethnic identities in this period are notoriously difficult to separate, given the complex, closely knit, and rapidly changing nature of cultural interactions and the new kinds of ethnic weight consciously attached to cultural forms. We can rarely, if ever, move directly from any cultural form to a single clear ethnic definition of the agent depositing or consuming it: to try to do so is to misunderstand the nature of how the whole world of EIA interregional contacts operated and grew. We need, instead, to look at broad regional and historical patterns of cultural identity creation. It is especially important, if we really want to understand how society was changing in the period, to move beyond the study of elites' behaviour and look at the representation of other groups in consumption practice: I try to do this in much of the following discussion.

18 LONG-DISTANCE CONTACTS BEFORE AND AFTER THE COLLAPSE HORIZON, CIRCA 1300–1000 BC

Overview: the impact of changes in the Aegean circa 1200 BC

Susan and Andrew Sherratt have admirably encapsulated the Bronze to Iron Age transition in the Mediterranean in economic terms: 'During this period of fundamental social transformation, the command economies of the second millennium gave way to less centralized forms of economic organisation which were to characterise a period of accelerating growth that lasted for the whole of the first millennium BC.... Fundamental to this new pattern was the dissociation of trading activity in high-value materials from the control of the state... . New forms of political power gradually emerged in response to the erosion of direct control of mercantile activity' (Sherratt and Sherratt 1993: 362). As the tight control of routes and materials by large Aegean and Levantine states operating in a multiple-core system broke down around 1200 BC, opportunities for alternative forms of interregional articulation arose. The coastal Levant, Egypt, and Cyprus had been source areas for a number of high-value commodities and materials and seem to have possessed a socially diversified exchange infrastructure during the thirteenth century (Catling 1994; Cline 1999: 124–5; Heltzer 1988; Karageorghis 1994; Knapp 1986: 85–115; Liverani 1987, 1990: 205–85; Steel 2004: 150–215; Zaccagnini 1977). These factors gave them an economic head start in the subsequent period. As we have seen, the Cypriot/coastal Levantine area 'bounced back' especially quickly from the destructions and disturbances of the early twelfth century, with rapid rebuilding of major port centres and a notable level of prosperity. Though further major readjustments occurred in this region in the eleventh century, the export sector did not suffer: indeed, it boomed as post-collapse markets, including those of the Aegean, started to develop.

The Aegean had been a major trade player in the east Mediterranean region during the latest LBA – supplying, in particular, high-value decorated ceramics and perfumed olive oil to the east. After circa 1200 BC, however, it seems for at least two centuries to have become primarily a consuming periphery to the eastern core, operating at a relatively small scale. The region continued to offer useful transshipment zones and provisioning points for goods crossing to the west Mediterranean, where Cypriot and Phoenician economies already had strong trading interests, apparently connected to metals, from early in the EIA (Bartoloni and Campanella 2000; Crielaard 1998: 187; Deger-Jalkotzy 1998: 115; Lo Schiavo 1982, 1995; Lo Schiavo et al. 1985). Even more importantly, people from the Aegean seem to have continued moving into and around the core zone, perhaps in larger numbers than before and in different ways, as shown by new types and/or concentrations of Aegeanising cultural features in the coastal Levant, northern

Aegean, and Cyprus. In some cases this suggests that regular trade connections were built up, while in others, permanent relocation of small groups or individuals occurred. This possible increase in movement/new direction of movement is most likely to have been linked to the large-scale breakdown in control systems over Mediterranean seaways from circa 1200 BC, offering new opportunities for small-scale travel and trade. Though such movements might involve friction and conflict with other travelling groups, as well as with locals, in the visited areas, they clearly paid off on a consistent basis.

In contrast, evidence seems *lacking* for any kind of *organised* mass migration from or to the Aegean at this period (whether of aggressive or defensive character), for any neat transfers of Aegean palatial elites intact to a happier exile in the east, or for the foundation of sizeable settlements operating as Aegean cultural enclaves on east Mediterranean coasts. The overwhelming amount of evidence for social breakdown in the Aegean at the deepest level, discussed earlier, argues against such models. Rather, some elements of Aegean culture, many already possessing prestige connotations in the east during the thirteenth century, seem to have been taken up selectively to mark new kinds of social distinction in the changed economic and social conditions of the post-collapse east, in a process having as much to do with changing social conditions there as with new numbers and types of Aegean visitors. This uptake occurred at a variety of levels – from the use of central hearths in temples or public buildings at some 'Philistine' sites on the south Levantine coast (a feature often said to recall Aegean practice, though we have seen how varied the distribution of such hearths was within the Aegean) to the Aegeanising drinking wares widely used in twelfth-century Cyprus – now locally made there, though they had previously been imported (Dothan 1982, 1992; Karageorghis 1990b: 27–30; Steel 2004: 192–3). The latter change must be at least partly due to the collapse of Aegean manufacturing and export structures, which must have weakened import procurement systems for Cypriot consumers. Some increased presence in Cyprus, or contact with Cypriots, by people of actual Aegean origin was also surely involved, especially in the introduction of the fast wheel to Cypriot ceramic traditions at around the same time. But the long preceding period of close contact and the huge disturbance in marketing and production systems around 1200 BC play important roles in explaining this as a shift in production strategy in order to meet an already well-established demand. Difficulty in maintaining mass import routes surely encouraged new, local production of this pottery, which was able to be supported and invested in on a large scale thanks to the concentration of wealth being acquired by Cypriots in other spheres. Trading of this pottery into the Levant also relied on a certain level of economic capacity and organisation in Cyprus post 1200 BC: it replaced trade in Aegean imports and their imitations from Cyprus into the same region in the thirteenth century, rather than representing a radically new phenomenon.

Crete's trade interactions before and after circa 1200 BC

Crete's south coast lay on a well-established sailing route from the east to the west Mediterranean, while its north coast was linked into trans-Aegean routes (Shaw 1989: 182). Both these networks continued in use after 1200 BC, though in altered ways, and it is impossible to see the island as isolated from external contacts at any point after 1200 BC. Indeed, in the early post-collapse period it seems to have had some of the most intense contacts of all Aegean regions with the burgeoning Cypro-Levantine core, even though the scale of these contacts was certainly much reduced from that applying in the LBA (Coldstream and Catling 1996: 721; Hoffman 1997: 7, 147, 255–6). The idea of a gap in imports to the island between circa 1050 and 950 BC, once suggested by Morris, is not sustainable (Morris 1997a: 42): Knossos North Cemetery tombs of SM-EPG date include imported goods originating from the east Mediterranean and from the central Aegean, which was itself articulating with the east at the same period. The relatively substantial and smoothly growing volume of iron in Crete between the twelfth and tenth centuries also suggests continuous eastern contacts (Dickinson 2006: 148; Sherratt 1994: 91–2; see most recently Tsipopoulou et al. 2003: 107–8). So do the amount of eastern-originating or inspired bronzework in the island (including a large bronze krater from an eleventh-century tomb at Veni, accompanied by a Cypriot ceramic juglet or close local imitation) and the well-developed local production of large easternising bronzes by the ninth century (Hoffman 1997: 109–36; Matthäus 1998: 127; Tegou 2001). The appearance of Phoenician transport amphorae in rapidly increasing bulk at Kommos from at least the early tenth century onward is further evidence for continuous (though quantity-limited) trade contact throughout this period (Bikai 2000; Shaw and Shaw 2006: xi–xii).

The LM IIIA:2-IIIB period had already seen some reduction in the island's exchange contacts with the east Mediterranean. This development was probably related to the expansion of the Mycenaean states and their increasingly direct trade with Egypt and the Levant, and latterly perhaps to the early phases of disruption in social and economic systems within the Aegean itself (Cline 1994: 10, 35, 1999: 121–2). Still, however, Cypriot and Levantine imports continued to arrive at Kommos and Chania within LM IIIB:2 (Cline 1994: 61; Karageorghis 1967, 1979; Watrous 1992: 159–60, 161–3, 181–2). Crete's trade with the Aegean world remained significant, though it too was undergoing changes by the period around 1200 BC. Cretan oil in large coarse stirrup jars was exported from west Crete (partly via Knossos) to the Aegean and Cyprus in LM IIIB. Some such exports stretch right into the early twelfth century (Catling et al. 1980; Godart and Tzedakis 1997; Haskell 2005; Kanta 2005; Maran 2005). In turn, like many other areas of the insular Aegean, LM IIIB Crete consumed quantities of fine drinking ceramics from the Peloponnese, which had significant influence on local pottery styles (Borgna 1997, 1999, 2003b: 74–308; Figures 95 and 96). Crete produced at least some of the Aegean ceramic material transported to gateways in coastal Apulia, Sardinia, and Sicily, though this may well have travelled in mainland ships (Ferrarese Cerruti et al. 1987; Hallager 1985; Kanta 1980: 294–313; Sherratt 1981: 187–8; Vagnetti 1998; Watrous 1992: 179). The use of western and southern Cretan ports by those engaged in direct return trade from Italy – whether Aegeans or Cypriots – is documented by the appearance of pots bearing strong relationships to Italian forms and fabrics (imported at Kommos, but locally made at Chania) in LM IIIB. These have open shapes, and their find contexts are usually dumps/occupation debris, suggesting casual use on board ship or within the port (perhaps by settlers or returned sailors) and relatively low value (Hallager 2003: 253–4; Watrous 1992: 168–9). Central Mediterranean contacts seem to have continued into early LM IIIC, allowing a few western value imports to be acquired and deposited in high-status Cretan ritual contexts. Italian-type metal items, clearly treated as prestige goods, appear in LM IIIB–early IIIC contexts at the Psychro Cave and the Knossos Zapher Papoura cemetery, and in deposits at early LM IIIC Knossos and Phaistos (Hallager 1985: 295–6).

Over the course of the twelfth century, trade emphasis changed, but not in a stark or abrupt way. As mainland economies collapsed, specialised Peloponnesian pottery manufacture saw a general decline and simplification, and its former target export markets, including Crete, stopped receiving the pottery in large quantities (Sherratt 1981: 186–7). Similarly, by the mid-twelfth century Crete gradually seems to have stopped sending bulk oil shipments to its Aegean neighbours. However, some ceramic imports, together with stylistic influences on locally produced ceramics, show that Crete remained in regular contact with the mainland and the Dodecanese, the latter area perhaps acting as the channel for some eastern metal items reaching the island in this period

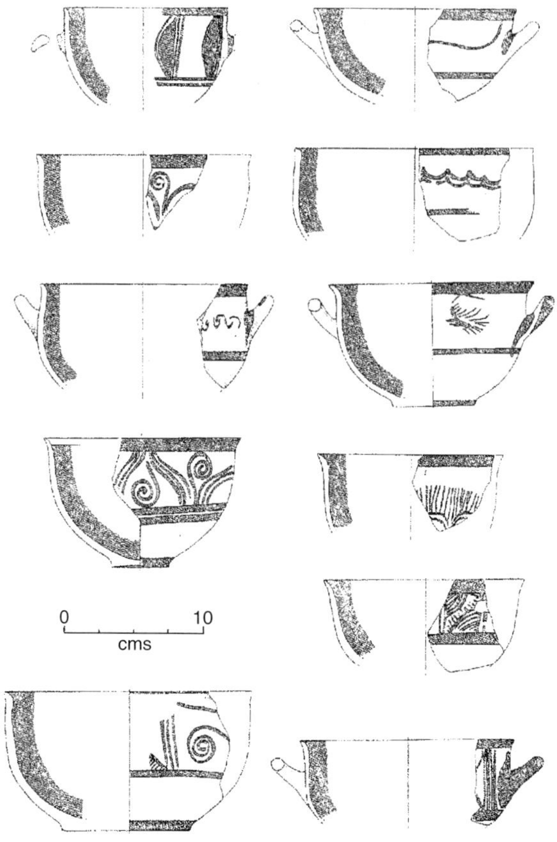

95. Deep bowls dating to the LM IIIB-C transition at Phaistos (after Borgna 1997, Fig. 6, p. 278). By permission of E. Borgna.

(Hallager and Hallager 2000: 172–3; Macdonald 1986: 140–1; Sherratt 1981: 187; Warren 1983: 79). During the early twelfth century Cretan and Cretan-type ceramics were appearing in significant numbers in Rhodes and the Dodecanese, perhaps filling a gap left by contracting export production on the mainland: at Ialysos, for example, Cretan imports or imitative pieces in the tomb assemblages start to outnumber those of mainland inspiration or origin in the LH IIIC period (Jones 2000: 47; Karantzali 2005; Macdonald 1986: 138–9; Sherratt 1981: 187). In the same region, finds of cult material with strong similarities to that of Crete (as the case of the latest finds under the Artemision at Ephesos and at Iraklio on Kos: Kerschner 1997; Skerlou 2004) may indicate the new settled presence of Cretans, or newly intensive contact with them, on the southwestern Anatolian coasts and neighbouring islands after 1200 BC.

Evidence for direct south Italian contacts dies away in Crete through the course of the LM IIIC period, as in most other parts of the contemporary Aegean – though in western Greece it continues through much of the twelfth century (Eder 2006a; Sgouritsa 2005). Direct Cretan trade with the Levant continued, appearing now to have become very much an eastern-led and -financed initiative, focused mostly on high-value goods or materials such as copper/bronze, gold, ivory, and iron, though the contacts also influenced pottery manufacture, as noted in Part One. The fact that Cypriot imports become particularly well represented in Crete and some other Aegean regions in the twelfth to tenth centuries is unsurprising, in view of Cyprus's rapid economic recovery, formerly close contacts with the Aegean, and exceptional copper resources, together

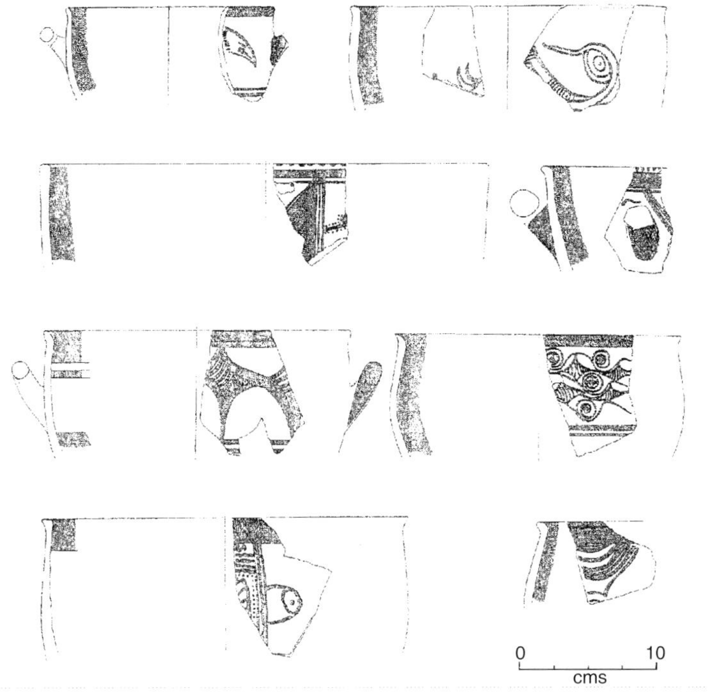

96. Kraters dating to the IIIB-C transition at Phaistos (after Borgna 1997, Fig. 20, p. 288). By permission of E. Borgna.

with the advanced metalworking skills developed in the island in the latter connection (Catling 1964; Knapp 1986: 85–115; Muhly 1982; Steel 2004: 166–9, 196). In the twelfth century Cypriot communities were increasingly engaged in extending their trade initiatives west, building connections with the neighbouring Phoenician area and its traders in a process that took their products as far as Sardinia and Spain (Bartoloni and Campanella 2000; Lo Schiavo 1982, 1995). Crete's proximity to this eastern core region, position on major trade routes, long coastline, and large size must have made it an important market, refuelling and transhipment point for traders from the east in the early EIA, just as they had done in the LBA.

Geography, however, is not the only explanation for Crete's relatively strong continuing connections to the east, and especially Cyprus, after 1200 BC. The successful character of the Cretan collapse, discussed in the last chapter, seems to have offered a positive stimulus to trade. The types of social and cultural adaptations seen in the island made it easier to maintain existing eastern links, and/or to rebuild them quickly, in adapted forms. This was clearly less easy in other Aegean regions, some of which turned their trade connections in new directions, including northern Greece and central Europe for amber and metals, after 1200 BC (Harding 1984: 82–3; Sherratt 2001: 234–7). The selective continuity in occupation of the most important low-lying port settlements in Crete, notwithstanding the overwhelming emphasis on planned relocation for most communities in the island, points strongly to a positive, structured interest in trade throughout the collapse period. Eastern-type goods deposited in graves at sites as distant and diverse as Knossos and Karfi show that internal distribution networks for long-distance trade products were quickly reorientated to serve the new communities. However, such networks surely took a very different form than they had in LM IIIA-B, when the existence of a settlement and political hierarchy promoted the movement of high volumes of goods via central points (e.g., in the case of woollen textiles, which the Linear B texts suggest were gathered at and distributed from the main centres).

The evened-out economic structure and strong social institutions of twelfth- to tenth-century Cretan communities surely helped to broaden participation in the acquisition of value goods, while providing a fairly risk-limited base for this activity. That is, because social status in Crete was *not* totally dependent on wealth competition and display, social stability was not vulnerable to fluctuations in the available quantities of luxury imports, allowing consumption of the latter to stay socially unrestricted (Hoffman 1997: 14; Morris 1997a: 42; Whitley 1991a: 186–9, 1991b: 360–1). This contrasts with conditions in the central Greek mainland, where social restrictions on the mortuary deposition (and probably also of other forms of consumption) of value goods, particularly bronze, may already have been in place by the eleventh century, in an attempt to regulate social mobility through consumption (Lemos 2002: 157, 190; Morris 1989: 507; Sherratt 1994: 76–7). Notwithstanding, some practical limits on the volume of investment in import activity are likely to have applied in the initially slow-growing EIA Cretan economy, where most communities were apparently orientated towards subsistence self-sufficiency. Smaller quantities of imports made their way into the island, probably through a larger number of traders, and at more widely scattered points, than had been the case in the LM IIIA-B period.

19 THE SOCIAL ROLE OF EXOTICA

Identifying prestige goods

Across the Aegean, changes in the circulation of value goods in this period clearly affected, and were affected by, regional social structures. Understanding how this dialectical relationship developed over time involves looking closely at how social relations in any one region were constructed and represented through the consumption of these goods. Patterns of consumption practice throw most light on social structure when they are considered within complex models of social systems, based on a range of evidence types, of the kind developed in Part Two. Unfortunately, however, much recent work on exotica in EIA Crete has been concerned with using the provenance or style of exotic goods to identify imports, immigrant presence, or 'influence', rather than studying consumption context (Hoffman 1997; Jones 1999, 2000). Such studies largely fail to theorise the construction of social identity through material culture, or to put their conclusions in context via a broader-based evaluation of the evidence for population movements. Thanks to its very wide-ranging geographical coverage, even some of the best synthetic work on trade in this period pays relatively little attention to the social context of consumption in individual regions (Crielaard 1999; van Wijngaarden 1999). By bringing the latter to the fore, we can build a much better, deeper understanding of the changing world system.

In many cases, the prestige value of an artefact type is suggested by its appearance predominantly in tomb contexts. There is, of course, a circularity inherent in then using the numbers of these items per burial to assess social ranking (as I did in Part Two) without further evaluation. Objective consideration of other attributes, such as exotic status of the good in the consuming area, high intrinsic/convertible value, general rarity in the consuming area, aesthetic or technologically desirable/innovative qualities, and antiquity, is also necessary when identifying and exploring its prestige status (Davenport 1986; Douglas and Isherwood 1980: 6–10; Gell 1986: 112–13; Kopytoff 1986: 80–3; Renfrew 1986: 159, 162; Wason 1994: 95–8, 103–4). In the Late Bronze Age Aegean a prestige role had clearly been held by goods and materials of highly convertible and/or naturally rare character, such as gold, silver, bronze, and ivory, as well as value-added products including faience and some fine pottery types. This pattern seems to have been perpetuated right through the collapse horizon. At the same time, new additions to the range of prestige items appear in Cretan and mainland graves from the twelfth century onwards. Nearly all are of eastern origin or easternising form. They include small iron objects, new types and forms of large bronze item (such as stands), smaller ones (such as new forms of dress pin), and special ceramic types probably associated with luxury unguents – lentoid

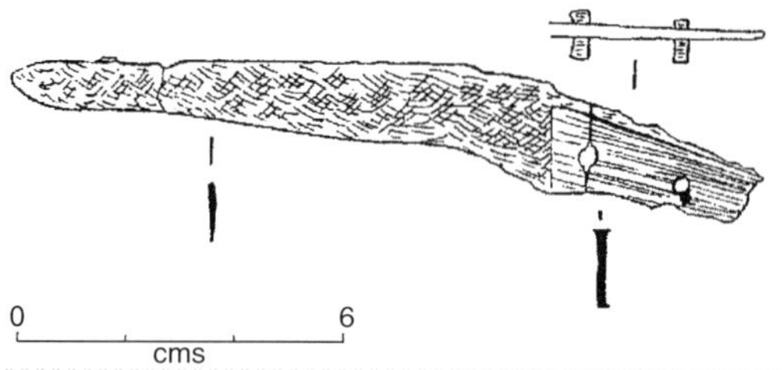

97. Early type of curved iron knife with bronze rivets from Gypsades grave VII (after Hood et al. 1959, Fig. 32 [VII 12]). By permission of S. Hood and the British School at Athens.

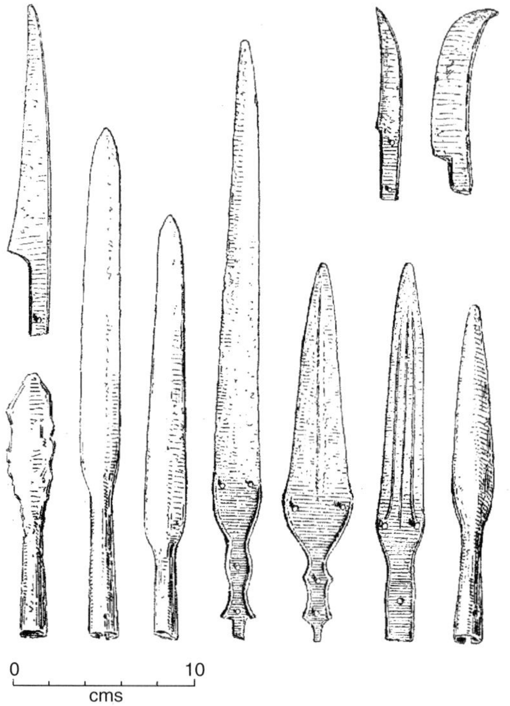

98. Iron weapons and tools from Vrokastro tombs. Early type of curved iron knife from Chamber Tomb 1 is at top right (after Hall 1914, Plate XXI).

flasks and bird askoi – as well as new versions of the ceramic drinking sets popular in the thirteenth century (Amiran 1982: 166–7, 266–72; Catling 1996a: 310; Deger-Jalktozy 1994: 19; Desborough 1972a; Dickinson 2006: 114–74; Hall 1914: 126–7, 133, 152; Hayden 2003: Figures 21–22; Iakovidis 1969: Plates 81, 93; Lemos 1994; Matthäus 1988; Popham 1994a: 14; Tegou 2001; Figures 97–102). Though the unguent vessels are of low intrinsic value and mostly locally made, the fact that they are much more numerous and widespread in the Levant and Cyprus than the Aegean (where they are nearly always found in tomb contexts) in the twelfth and eleventh centuries suggests that there was an added value associated with eastern provenance and that Aegean-made examples copied imported prototypes. The introduction of several new prestige types at this time suggests self-aware economic and cultural readjustment, not only in the supply zone, but also in the consuming region: people had a new outlook on what was desirable to trade and consume, as well as changing access to goods and materials.

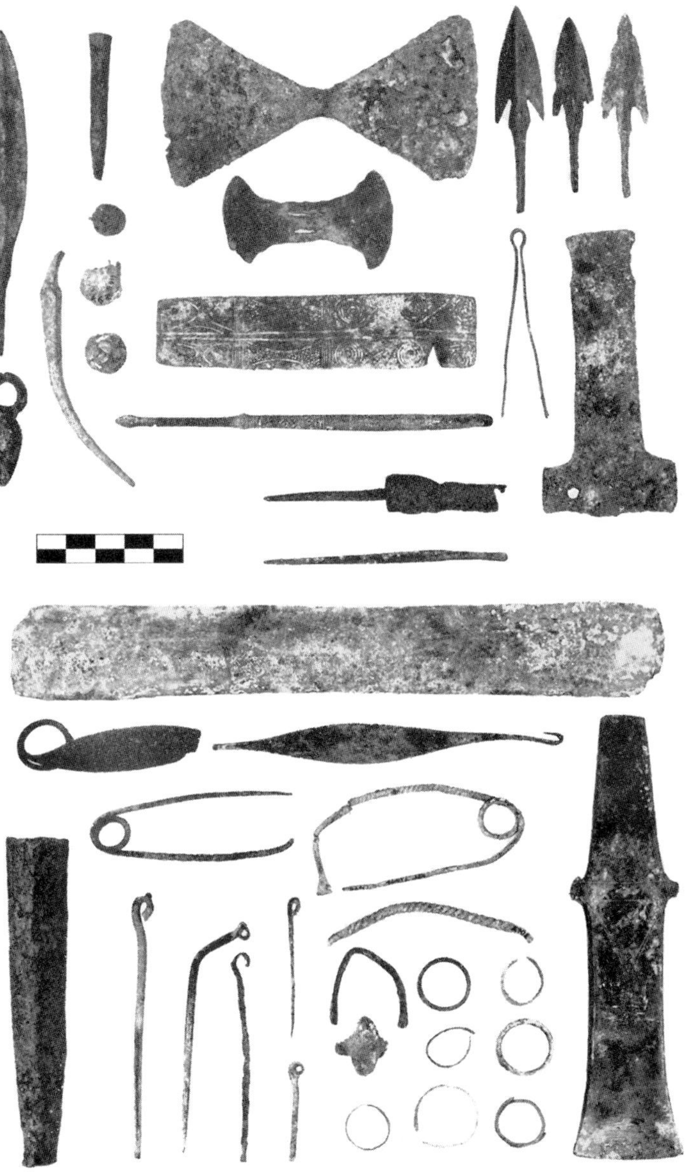

99. Bronze objects including 'violin-bow' fibulae, rings, blades, axes and arrrowheads from Karfi (after Pendlebury et al. 1938, Plate XXIX [1.2]).

Understanding consumers

In Crete, as we have seen, the pattern in which value objects were deposited in tombs suggests that a relatively large proportion of society was able to access small-value items in metal, as well as value-added types like the ceramic unguent containers. Large and/or high-intrinsic-value items like bronze stands and gold jewellery were often concentrated together in a smaller number of graves, suggesting that access to them was restricted to wealthier consumers. There were clearly several levels of consumption in place. Some scholars, however, have argued for the growth after 1200 BC of an 'international elite' in the east Mediterranean and suggested that the

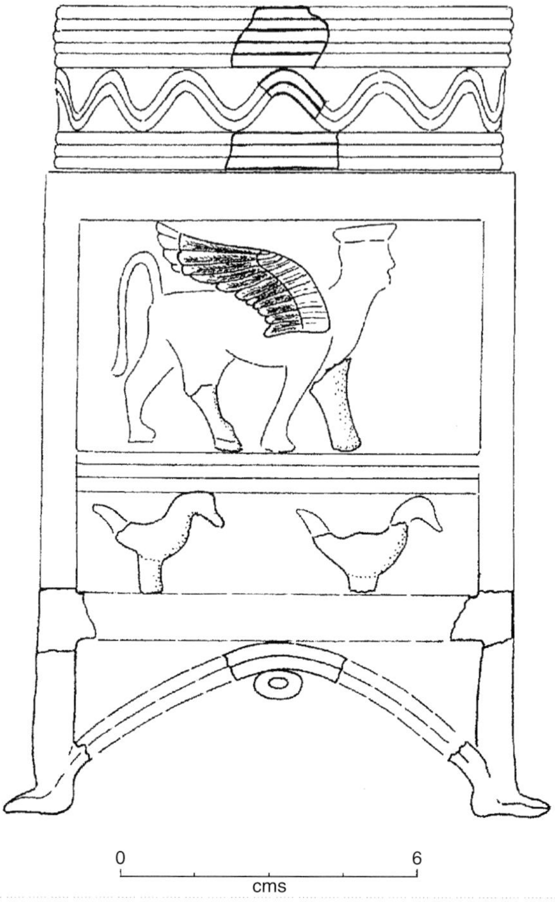

100. Bronze stand from Knossos North Cemetery Tomb 201 (after Coldstream and Catling 1996, E. A. Catling del., Fig. 166). By permission of H. W. Catling.

exchange of exotic value items /materials occurred mainly within these social circles. This model has been used to explain the close similarities in the *forms* of value goods deposited across the region during the EIA (Coldstream 1983; Crielaard 1998; Desborough 1964: 228; Qviller 1981). For example, despite the clearly dominant role of Cyprus as an exporter of luxury 'easternising' items to the Aegean in this period, some Cypriot-made luxury goods of the twelfth and eleventh centuries seem based on Aegean models of the thirteenth – the bird askos, the ceramic drinking sets and bronze kraters, and bronze weapon types (Desborough 1972b; Steel 2004: 197–8). At this time, then, similar types of item seem to have simultaneously possessed 'exotic' (and therefore prestigious) characteristics for people in different east Mediterranean regions.

The socially fragmented, opportunism-friendly environment of the post-collapse east Mediterranean actually seems an unlikely framework for very strong cross-regional elite class coherence, *even while* it might favour relative standardisation in prestige culture. The notion seems more pertinent to the late LBA period (although here, too, huge and consciously maintained differences in status between elites in different regions are evident from sources like the Amarna Letters; Moran 1992; Zaccagnini 1987). On their own, the similar forms and partly similar deposition contexts of prestige items do not indicate that 'comparable socioeconomic conditions' prevailed at a general level between Cyprus and Crete, for example, after 1200 BC (Crielaard 1998: 190–1). Significant regional variations in the types and quantities of goods

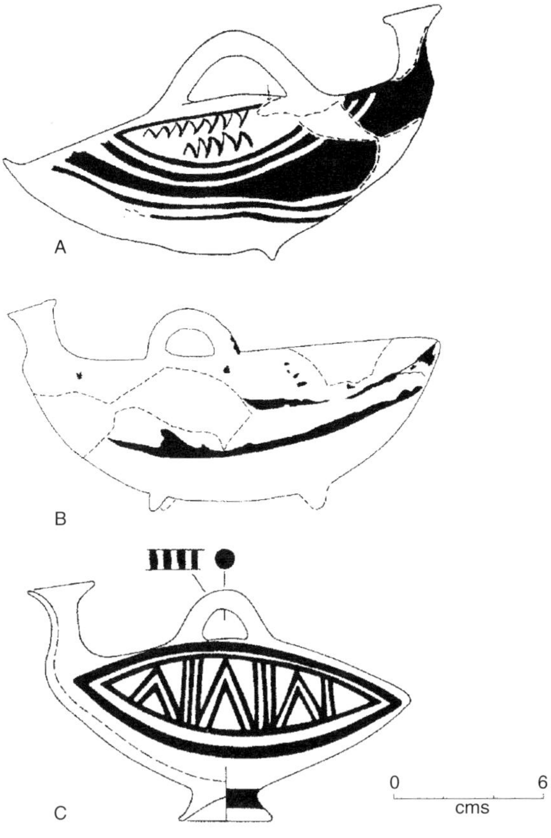

101. Bird askoi from tombs at Vrokastro (A–B, after Hayden 2003, Fig. 21 [96; 97]) and Kavousi Vronda (C, after Gesell et al. 1983, Fig. 4 [5]). By permission of B. J. Hayden and L. P. Day.

deposited in graves in different regions actually suggest subtly different contexts for value good consumption in Aegean and Cypro-Levantine contexts, even within shared broad tropes such as the 'warrior grave'. The availability of and/or consumption preference for a range of value goods of Cypro-Levantine origin was clearly much stronger in the Aegean than vice versa in the twelfth through tenth centuries. Assemblages from rich twelfth- to eleventh-century Cypriot tombs include Canaanite and Egyptian alabaster jars, never found in the Aegean at this time. Much higher concentrations of gold and iron and of large metal vessels appear in some of these tombs than in any Aegean counterpart of this period (Benson 1973; Catling 1996b: 522–4; Karageorghis 1983, 1990a; McFadden 1954; Steel 1996, 2004: 200–1). These facts are unsurprising, given the highly developed procurement systems, rich metal sources, and advanced metalworking technologies that existed on Cyprus and the neighbouring Levantine mainland right through the period of collapse. These factors contributed to producing generally much wealthier and more complexly ranked societies than those of the contemporary Aegean. Economic power was embodied here in a broader variety of resources and contacts and channelled and displayed in different ways. Opportunities existed to amass really large amounts of wealth and consolidate extreme power – for example, through the type of hoarding that becomes apparent during this period in Cyprus (Steel 2004: 208–10).

In the Aegean, by contrast, the deposition of eastern value objects often suggests a down-the-line pattern of trade movement, as well as reflecting a generally different level of social access

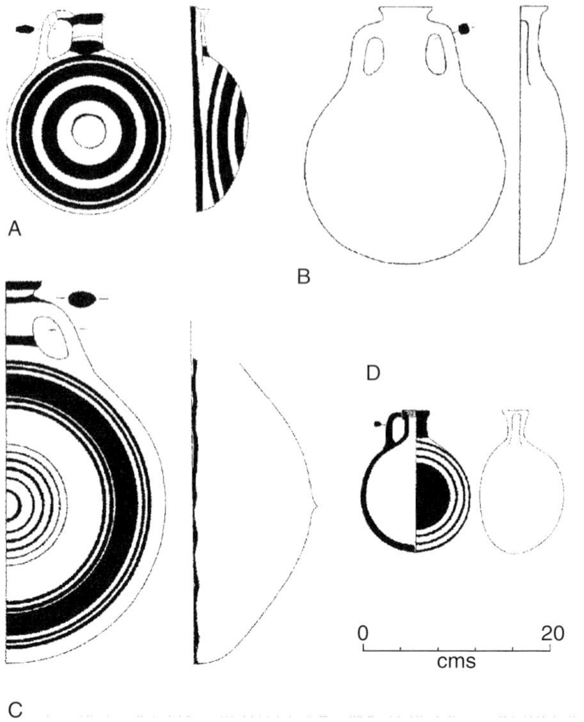

102. Lentoid flasks from tombs at Kavousi Vronda (A, after Hayden 2003, Fig. 99 [99; 101]) and Vrokastro (B–D, after Gesell et al. 1983, Fig. 4 [2]). By permission of B. J. Hayden and L. P. Day.

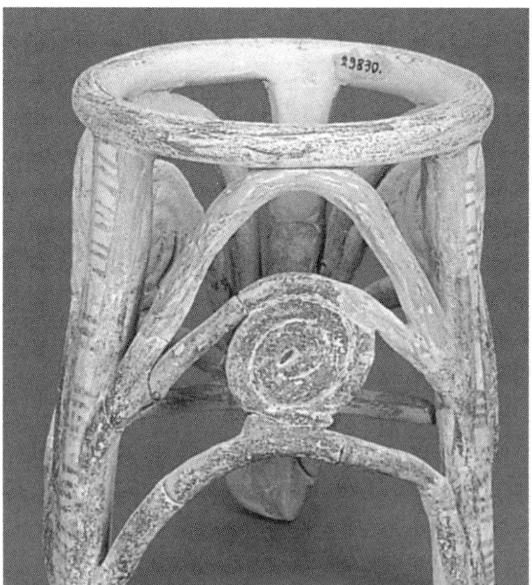

103. Clay tripod stand from Afrati (after Stampolidis et al. 1998, Fig. 36, p. 73). By permission of N. Stampolidis.

to prestige goods in this region. The coastal or near-coastal island distribution of the highest concentrations of imports and their imitations stands out in many areas. The relatively high volumes of imports in places like Crete may indicate particularly close contacts with easterners and/or their goods, offering special opportunities for the social and economic aggrandisement of local elites, rather than parity with eastern social structures. In arguing that iron was actively 'marketed' to the Aegean by eastern traders at this period, Sherratt has drawn a distinct contrast between consumers in the eastern core and those in the Aegean: 'We may be dealing primarily with the fostering of an elite or aspiring-elite market for rare and exotic luxuries, rather than the active creation of a sub-elite or substitute-elite market, as may have been the case in Cyprus and in parts at least of the Levant' (Sherratt 1994: 70–1). This model seems applicable to trade in other value goods, too. In the Aegean part of the world system, even the wealthiest consumers may only have been able to aspire to the wealth and status of the subelite in the eastern core. If so, these differences must surely have been recognised, whether overtly or not, by the players involved. One sign of limited physical or economic access to ownership of imported eastern luxuries, despite significant contact with them in the context of trade circulation and/or social display, is the imitation of original eastern items with high intrinsic value in a lower-value material. Clay tripods in tombs at Arkades and a four-sided clay stand at Karfi (another was recently found in a shrine context at Monastiraki Chalasmeno) imitate large imported bronze types already present in Crete, but much more numerous in Cyprus at the same period (Catling 1964: 190–224; Hoffman 1997: 118; Kanta and Karetsou 1998: 163; Pendlebury et al. 1938: 34; Stampolidis et al. 1998: 119–20; Tsipopoulou pers comm; Figure 103). This kind of imitation shows early local initiative in developing local substitutes for the limited import flow and thus undermines the idea of the Aegean periphery as either a passive receiving entity *or* a full economic peer to Cypriot societies.

Hector Catling has argued for a long delay in the Aegean manufacture of large easternising bronzework items like stands and kraters. He labels most large bronzes found in twelfth- to tenth-century Aegean contexts as either imports or heirlooms of pre–1200 BC date, and suggests the earliest local production only started in the tenth century (Catling 1964: 216–23, 1984, 1993, 1996b: 517–18). This model tends to minimise the role of an active, developing, and diverse aspirant elite in Crete and characterise the island's inhabitants as passive consumers. It is partly undermined by the identification of possible mould fragments for a large moulded bronze item, possibly a tripod stand, from LM IIIB/C Palaikastro (though the dating of the deposit, and whether the mould was really for a stand or not, are in doubt; Hemingway 1996; Catling 1997; Figure 104). The fragments of a bronze tripod from Karfi, the recent find of a bronze amphoroid krater from an eleventh-century tomb at Veni, and the significant number and broad spread of bronze stands found in Crete by the tenth century also weaken it (Hoffman 1997: 117–20; Matthäus 1998: 127–8, 139; Pendlebury et al. 1938: 117–18; Tegou 2001; Figures 105 and 106). On balance, there now simply seem to be too many large bronze objects in the earliest EIA of Crete for them *all* to represent imports. Provenance analyses of bronzes from LM IIIC Chania show that raw material was being obtained from a variety of sources, including Aegean ones, at this time, suggesting independent sourcing of metal by Cretan craftsmen, whether the metal in question was from remelted items or new raw material imports (Stos-Gale et al. 2000). These acquisition networks seem much too diverse and complex to suggest that a single solid, uniform, or bounded trading elite controlled them.

In sum, then, the pattern of value good circulation in the EIA east Mediterranean seems to have both geographical and social determinants, which intersected each other in different ways. We should not lump Aegean regions together as having a single type of social context for value good exchange and consumption, nor treat their societies as structurally identical

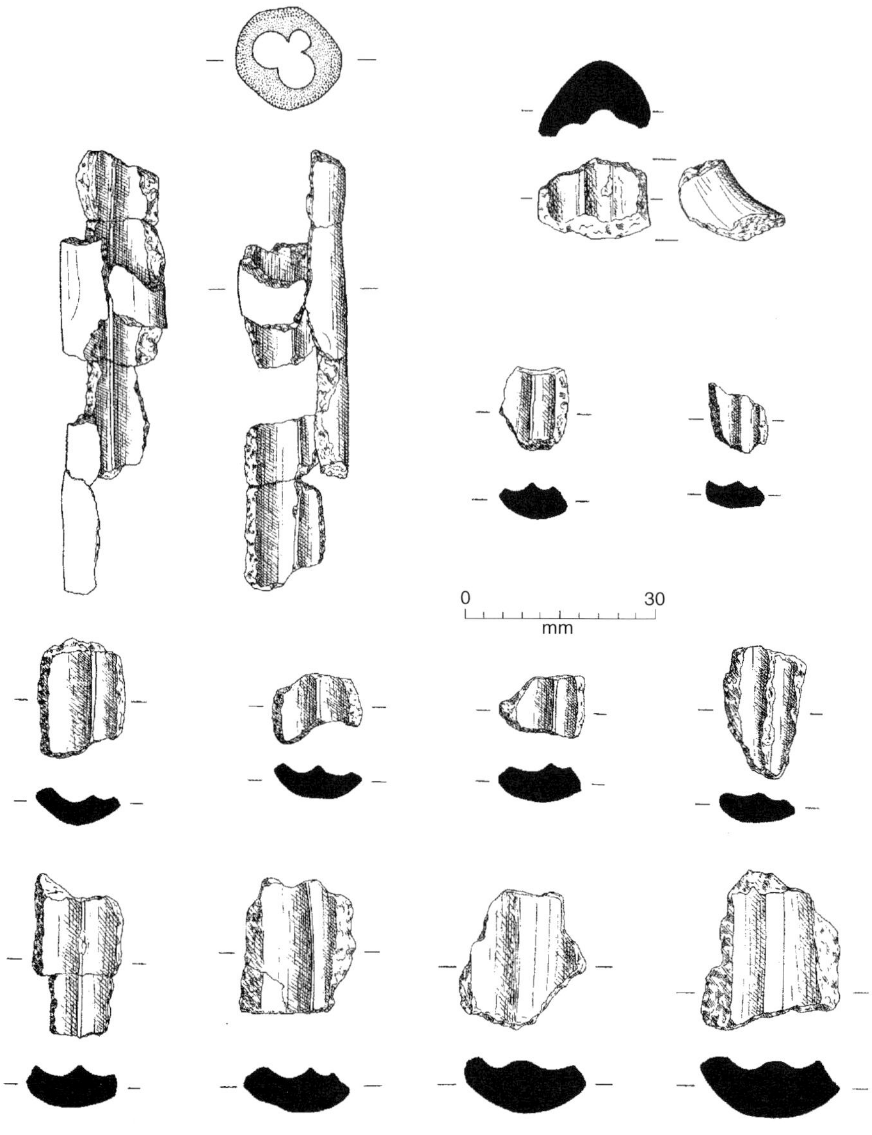

104. Possible fragments of mould for a tripod stand from Palaikastro (after Hemingway 1996, Fig. 7, p. 231).

to those of their eastern trade partners, if we really want to understand their development in this period. The model of gift exchange within a single coherent interregional elite class as the main mode of circulation for prestige goods (largely derived from Homeric studies) is of limited use in furthering our understanding of EIA society and is not fully supported by the evidence (Coldstream 1983, 1994a: 159; Finley 1979; Foxhall 1998; Jones 2000: 34–5, 59–66, 301; Morris 1986; Qviller 1981; Sherratt 2003; van Wees 1992: 222–37). Notwithstanding, recognition of the 'international' prestige status of a number of goods at this time is crucial to understanding their consumption. *Underrecognition* of it can lead to simplistic interpretations in ethnic terms of grave assemblages rich in exotica – as in the case of Tomb 186 at Knossos (suggested by its excavators possibly to belong to a Cypriot on the basis of the bronze stand and other objects found in it; Catling 1996c: 644–9, 1995: 128; Whitley 1998b: 613). In a similar vein, eastern

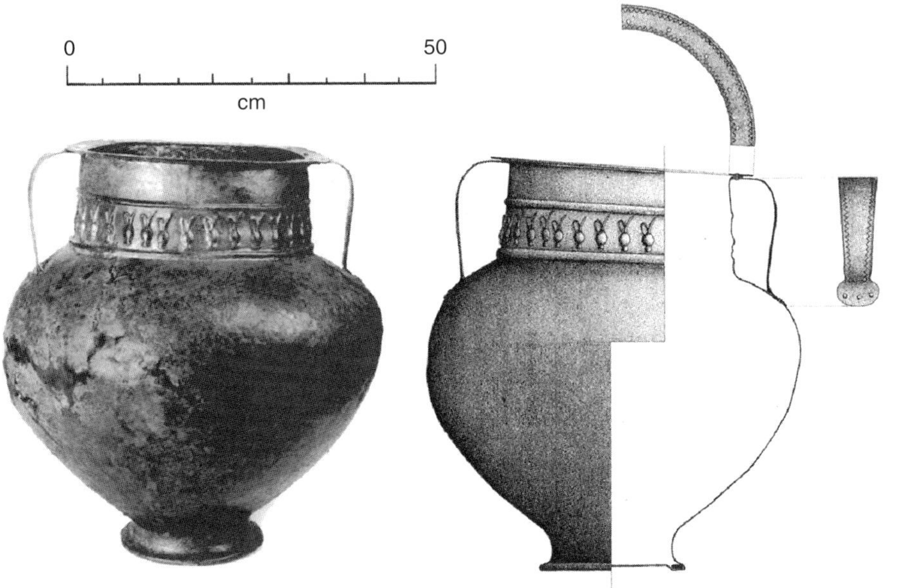

105. Bronze krater from tomb at Pandanassa Veni (after Stampolidis et al. 1998, Fig. 55, p. 84). By permission of E. Tegou.

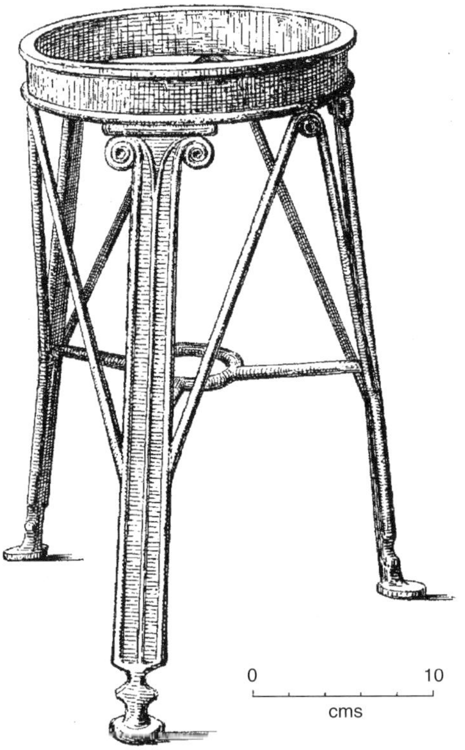

106. Bronze tripod stand from Chamber Tomb 1, Vrokastro cemetery (after Hall 1914, Fig. 80, p. 133).

immigrants are suggested to have been present at PG Lefkandi mainly on the basis of the easternising types of artefact found in the Toumba cemetery (Popham 1994a: 22). Recent suggestions of an ethnically mixed population of Aegeans and foreigners at the site of Afrati/Arkades in south central Crete are based mainly on the exotica in the EIA tomb material (Kanta and Karetsou 1998: 170). For reinforcement, such arguments sometimes cite poorly grounded models (themselves linked tenuously to ancient traditions) of settlement and cemetery distribution in twelfth- to eleventh-century Crete as representing large-scale immigration at the end of the Bronze Age (Catling 1995: 128, 1996a: 295–7; Coldstream and Catling 1996: 715; Warren 2005; Watrous and Hadzi-Vallianou 2004a: 310).

To further our understanding of economy and society in post-collapse Crete, it seems essential to distinguish between the different kinds of identities potentially being constructed through the consumption of value goods, including their deposition in graves. The widely shared recognition of status-linked attributes in goods sourced through interregional exchange and with exotic characteristics seems best to explain why we often see the strongest 'exotic' associations in the assemblages from rich burials, for example. Such items might not only mark out general wealth/status ranking and 'well-travelledness', itself potentially a prestigious attribute (Helms 1998), but be deliberately used to claim *particular* fashionable or politically salient 'ethnic' links. The economic role and construction of ethnicity in the EIA have only recently been brought to the fore. The Sherratts, especially, have emphasised the growth of various scales of ethnic consciousness as important in creating and maintaining new long-distance exchange relationships and markets from soon after the collapse (Morris 2000: 228–38; Sherratt and Sherratt 1993: 366, 1998: 335).

20 EXCHANGE STRUCTURES INSIDE POST-COLLAPSE CRETE

Trade sites and networks

I now want to turn to look at how value goods were moving around within Crete during the early EIA period. Harbours and large sites near the coast surely remained crucial nodes for the local distribution of exotic goods and raw materials. The overall dip in the volume of external trade with the Aegean in the earliest part of the EIA has been used to explain the contraction or abandonment of many former port/gateway settlements (Hallager and Hallager 2000: 193). Yet as I discussed earlier, the Knossos North Cemetery finds dating in the late twelfth to eleventh centuries, and those from Kommos dating from the later eleventh century onward, show that some of the highest concentrations of early post-collapse imports were still acquired/consumed around such sites, which either never lost or quickly resumed a gateway role – however intensified or restricted this role now was. The main reason for the short-term contraction or decline in port sites is likely to have been prevalent insecurity, as I explained in Part Two. Trade contacts were in fact the main – if not the only – reason to maintain the use of selected coastal or near-coastal settlements in circumstances of considerable risk.

Alongside these few continuing gateways, a scattering of smaller trade nodes is likely to have developed in other parts of the island quite soon after the collapse of the old settlement system. Though new sites like Vrokastro, Chamaizi Liopetra, Mirsini Kastello, and Palaikastro Kastri had coastal defence as their primary function, their positioning close to broad bays and beaches that offered excellent stopping points for coastal shipping must have allowed (and encouraged) their residents to participate in direct economic interactions with the outside world, assuming they could build the necessary contacts (or adapt existing ones) in the changed circumstances. Coastal sites in east Crete would have especially good access to the Cypriot trade that dominated Aegean prestige good consumption in the earliest EIA. This could help explain the use of some rather ineffective and short-term sites, like Palaikastro Kastri, around 1200 BC – the latter perhaps a last-ditch attempt to avoid abandoning the prosperous LBA port of Roussolakkos and the valuable exchange systems centred around it. The Vrokastro cemetery includes examples of Cypriot-inspired or imported lentoid flasks and at least some iron dating to the twelfth or eleventh centuries: some of these goods may have reached the site directly by sea (Hall 1914: 132–9, 152–3, Plate XXI). A rich tomb at Vasiliki, located at the midpoint of the Ierapetra isthmus with good access to both coasts, contained a great deal of gold jewellery, perhaps imported directly to the region at this time (Desborough 1964: 176–7; Seager 1906: 126–32). Yet some inland sites show the same range and spread of imports as these coastal examples: assemblages from the

Karfi tombs echo those at Vrokastro, and the gold in the Praisos Fotoula assemblage outstrips the deposit at Vasiliki (Platon 1960b; Platon and Davaras 1960). This suggests that circulation systems for luxury and exotic items stretched to cover large areas of the island's interior.

We need to examine different types of commodity separately, as I do below, in investigating how internal production and exchange systems operated. In general, the physical spread and relatively broad social distribution of value good consumption in post-collapse Crete argue against highly controlled exchange systems. The insecure environment and dispersed settlement pattern would allow many flexible, short-term, and opportunistic exchange transactions. It may be that only very high-value materials like gold and ivory, found in the fewest graves, were in any way restricted in circulation, moving mainly via specialised commissioning and procurement – either directly from eastern traders or via intermediaries in rare transactions carried out at major gateway sites. We can learn more about the internal circulation of some higher-end luxuries by looking at the distribution of more broadly circulated, often locally made value items in ceramics and metal. Exchange of these goods is likely to have helped keep open demand and circulation channels for more costly imported goods of the same type. For example, imported Cypriot unguent flasks might circulate alongside local imitations of the same items, as well as other high-quality or 'exotic' ceramics of local or imported production (Hayden 2003: 47 notes a nonlocal clay in a flask from the Vrokastro cemetery, found alongside locally made examples of the same vessel type).

Production scale and context at island level

I) CERAMICS

In LM IIIA-B Crete, value goods like fine pottery, carved ivory objects, seals, stone vases, and bronze weapons had already been produced in a fairly decentralised framework, but production was still concentrated at regional settlement nodes (Doxey 1987: 310–14; Haskell 1997; Poursat 1997). Large regional-scale ceramic workshops/traditions were attached strongly to the major polities. Chaniot and Knossian pottery products, in particular, circulated in significant amounts to many outlying regions – though some of the latter, particularly east Crete, had their own strong independent traditions (Banou and Rethemiotakis 1997; Hallager 2003; Kanta 1980: 289; Popham 1994b: 90–1; Smith 2005; Tzedakis 1969). Around 1200 BC, settlement relocation, involving drastic social and economic reorganisation, must have limited the availability of investment capital (in terms of subsistence resources) at large settlements, and, together with disturbances in existing exchange systems for fine ceramics across the east Mediterranean, reduced and dispersed the scale of production activity. The standardised regional traditions of the precollapse period seem likely to have crumbled as craftworkers came to serve more circumscribed local constituencies. Many of these workers must have been the very same skilled individuals who had operated in the precollapse system (or their apprentices), now adapting their production in response to the changing types and scales of demand for value goods.

This notion of a greater spatial spread of producers, working at a more modest scale, in the post-collapse period is supported by the record. At LM IIIC Chania, for example, the manufacture of fine pottery seems to diversify, contrasting with the dominance of the distinctive regional 'workshop' of LM IIIA-B (Hallager and Hallager 2000: 171–2, 203–4). Interestingly, however, some broad stylistic *homogeneity* in fine ceramics at cross-island level also appears in the twelfth century. This may reflect the disappearance of the LBA pattern of multiple large polities concerned to represent themselves through highly distinctive pottery manufacturing traditions, even while the regular exchange of fine ceramics between different parts of the island, as well as acquisition and stylistic borrowing through external contacts, continued (Hallager and Hallager 2000: 163–4, 173, 194; Sherratt 1981: 187). Rutter (1992: 65–7) refers to a condition of 'stasis' in innovative pottery production lines across the Aegean in the post-collapse period. But some scholars attribute this new level of standardisation to the sudden presence of large numbers of immigrants in the island, accompanied by a standardised new ceramic 'package' of mainland origin (Warren 2005). This is hard to accept, given that many of these ceramics have extremely close antecedents in the LM IIIB period, that Crete-mainland relations had been so very close and frequent before 1200 BC and were ongoing, and that the notion of large-scale immigration is not very well supported by other aspects of material culture in the island at this time. Rather, as the innovative, regionally distinctive, and heavily export-driven mainland pottery industries disappeared, Cretan fine pottery styles, while staying within the same broad established tradition and maintaining contacts with mainland styles, tended to become more generic, lacking specific, well-defined regional direction. Counterintuitively, we *cannot* equate the collapse of mass production and subsequent smaller-scale diversification of production with stylistic diversity. Indeed, the converse may be the case, with older generalised prestige traditions reverted to as security in a doubtful and disturbed market.

There seems little reason to assume a general regression in ceramic production skills in Crete at any point in this period. Highly-skilled potters, regularly in touch with changing fashions and forms outside and inside the island, must have been responsible for large elaborately decorated ceramic products like the wheelmade animal figurines from Ayia Triada and Patsos, the 'chest-shaped vessel' from Kastelli Pediada, and the large and elaborate painted kraters found in some tombs (D'Agata 1999; Kanta 1980: 175; Kourou and Karetsou 1994; Rethemiotakis 1997a, 1997b; Figures 107 and 108). The Mouliana assemblage shows that painted clay larnakes continued to be made throughout the LBA-EIA transition, though their numbers decreased sharply in the twelfth century: it seems that many larnax workshops did not survive the collapse, as changes in burial practice, linked to new social frameworks, took root. The quality of the large ceramic pieces described suggests potters often worked 'to order' when investing time in highly elaborate products that could be consumed only in special contexts and at special times. This indicates the ability of at least some new communities to support highly skilled (though often probably part-time) specialists from an early date.

Turning to coarse wares, it is important to note once again that the interregional comparison and technological study of these wares with the aim of throwing light on production are in their infancy. Here I simply work with the available published data and the result of my own primary studies, acknowledging that these resources are not substantial enough at this stage to support complex generalising models. On the basis of extensive surface studies at EIA sites, coarse fabrics often look rather similar between sites within the new regional settlement clusters/networks, but notably different between regions. For example, there are very strong similarities between most sites in the north Lasithi and Kavousi regions, respectively, in terms of their cooking pot and pithos fabrics. This might suggest some centralisation of production at the larger sites in a particular cluster or region, though this has not yet been investigated by systematic studies of pottery technology. Decorative forms show similarities across larger, cross-regional zones – matching the indications we have seen in the fine ware patterns of a broadly homogenised (though distinctively Cretan) ceramic culture and indicating strong, regular contacts across large areas of the island (Haggis and Mook 1993; Haggis 2005: 43–59; Moody pers comm; Moody et al. 2000a; Mook 2005; Nowicki 2000: 267–9; Wallace in press b, in press c). However, broad stylistic differences also appear (for example, between western and central/east Cretan styles of pithos decoration) showing the limits of contact zones and a

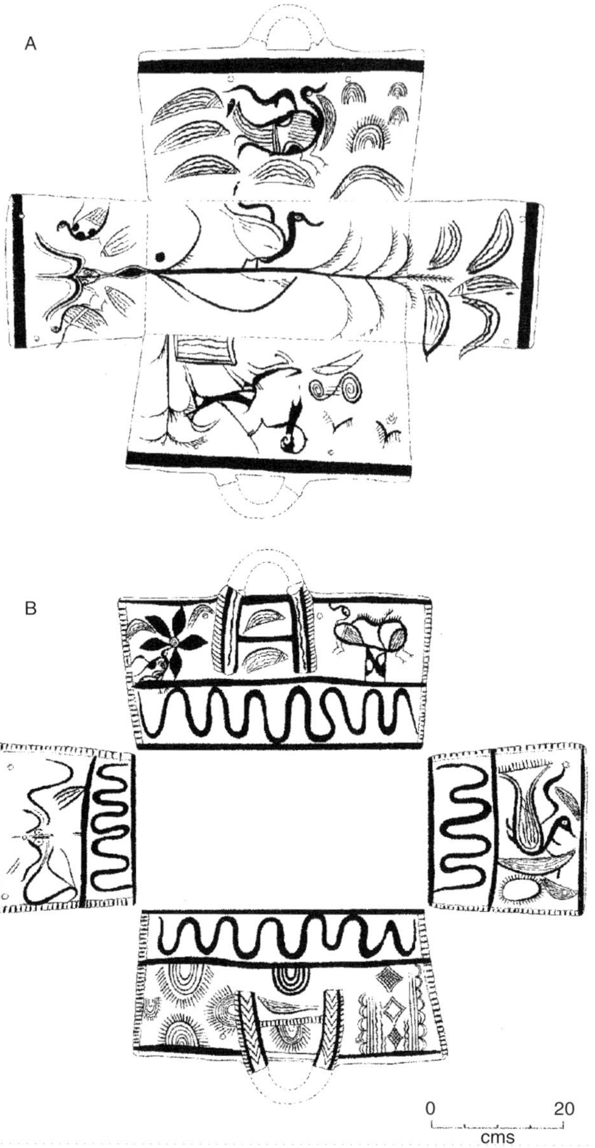

107. Chest-shaped vessel from Kastelli Pediada: A) exterior; B) interior (after Rethimiotakis 1997b: A, Figs. 10–11, p. 412; B, Figs. 12–13, p. 413).

lack of very long-distance trade in these bulky and utilitarian vessels (Hallager and Hallager 2000: Figure 84a; Figures 109 and 110).

Moody et al. (2000a) note links between EIA coarse ware fabrics in the adjacent Ayios Vasilios valley and Sfakia regions of west Crete, supporting the notion that new regional-scale production and exchange networks were developing alongside the new settlement patterns. Interestingly, though, the nature and strength of the links vary according to the precise type of pottery in question. One fabric type ('Greasy Blue Phyllite ware') links sites in both regions; another, the 'Coconut Chunk' fabric, seems most highly concentrated in the Sfakia area, suggesting a mostly local production and distribution. Such differences suggest fairly complex and sophisticated

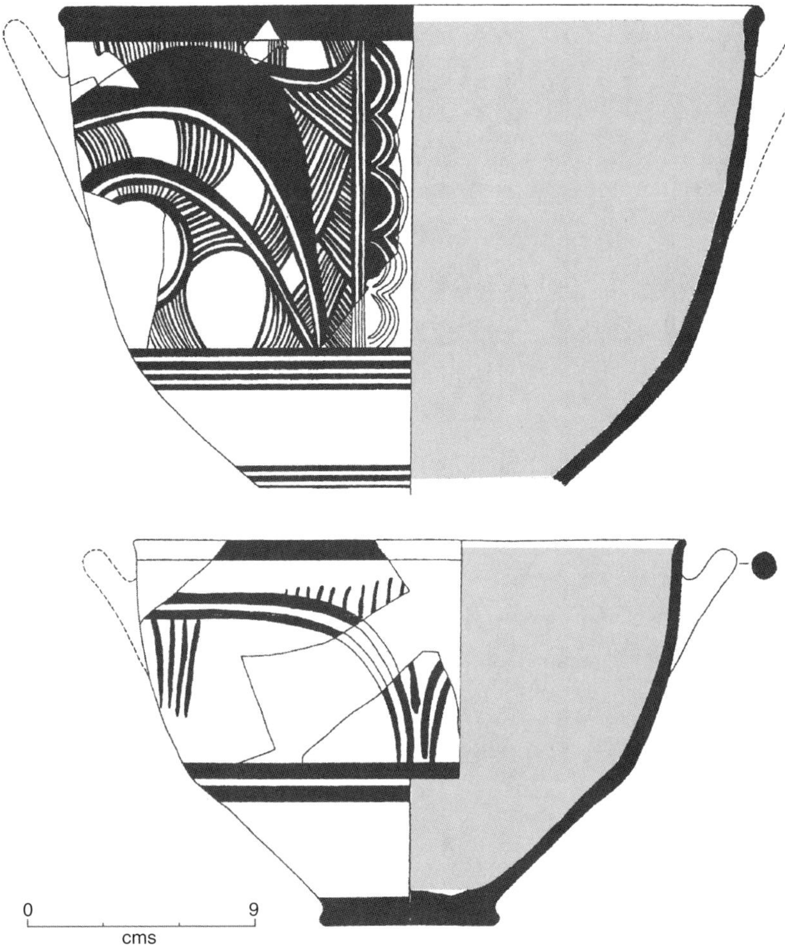

108. Kraters from the LM IIIB-C transition at Chania (after Hallager and Hallager 2000, Plate 39). By permission of E. Hallager.

relationships between producers and demand sectors emerging quickly across large regions after the relocation of 1200 BC, with strong elements of selectivity and targeting able to operate even in the acquisition and distribution of everyday 'working' ceramics.

II) METALS

The number of bronze items found in twelfth- to tenth-century Crete, in settlements as well as tombs (the Karfi material is particularly striking in this respect), suggests relatively wide circulation of this metal, and thus fairly numerous points for its working and/or trade in the island. However, we have seen that there is no clear evidence for specialised metalworking areas at any new settlement so far excavated; nor do we know of any extra-settlement metalworking sites. No ingots, slags, or scrap bronze hoards of this date have yet been found, suggesting either that much metalworking took place near the metals' entry points to the island and/or that remelting was very common, perhaps because access to imports of raw metal had become less predictable. The regular appearance of clay imitations of some special bronze types indicates some restriction of access to the imported original items themselves, or to adequate quantities of metal, rather

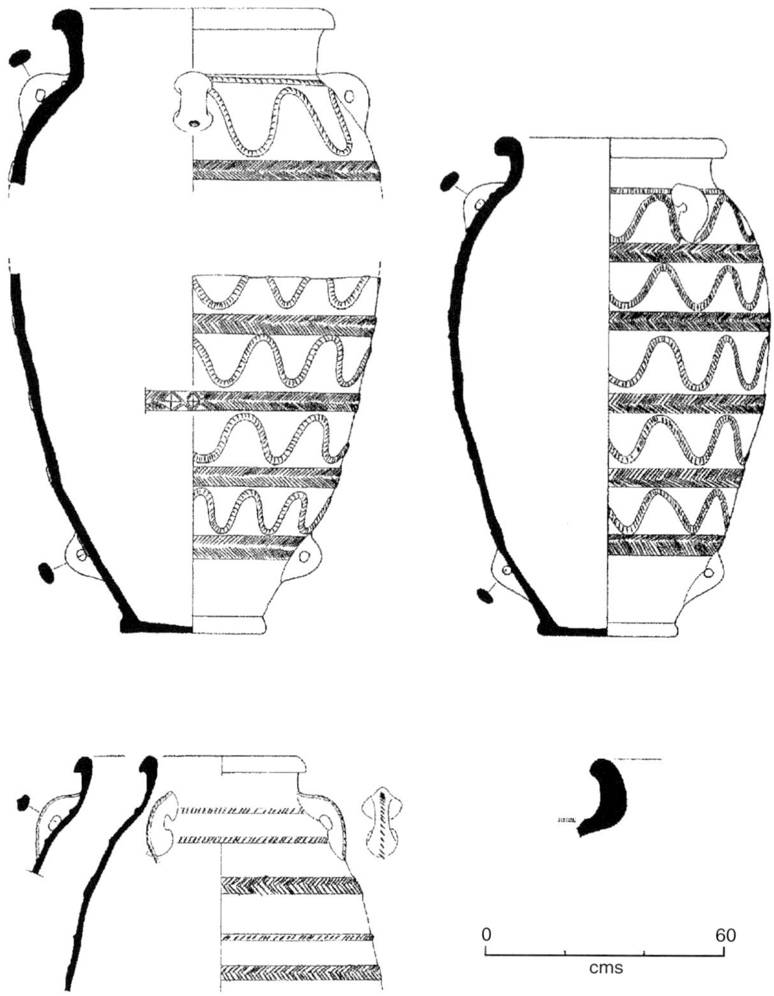

109. LM IIIC pithoi from Kavousi Vronda settlement (L. P. Day). By permission of L. P. Day.

than lack of skills, since the sheer numbers of large bronze items in twelfth- to tenth-century Crete – from the Mouliana weapons to the Veni krater – suggest that sophisticated bronzeworking skills existed throughout the island.

In contrast, the comparative rarity of iron in Crete in the early post-collapse period – whether in the form of finished objects or scrap – suggests, given the novelty of ironworking in the east Mediterranean generally, that knowledge of this new technology was limited to a fairly small number of producers, and that many items were imported (Hoffman 1997: 139–47; Sherratt 1994: 91–2). Any local producers seem to have borrowed heavily in stylistic terms from iron goods produced in the east Mediterranean, and surely learned their skills from contact with people originating in, or having lived in, that region – whether this learning process took place in Crete or outside its borders. There is no clear evidence that early Cretan ironsmiths were also workers in bronze, but this seems likely often to have been the case: a similar hypothesis has been used to explain the early sophistication and uptake of iron in Cyprus, with its highly

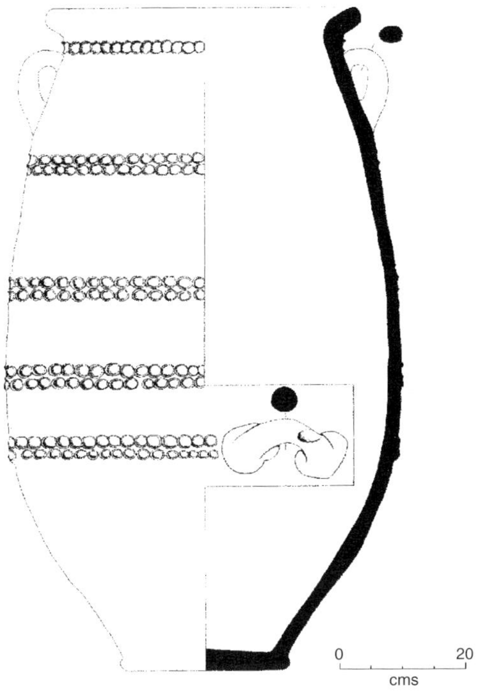

110. LM IIIC pithos from Chania settlement (after Hallager and Hallager 2000, Plate 41). By permission of E. Hallager.

developed LBA bronze industry (Maddin 1982; Peltenburg and Pickles 1998: 84–91; Sherratt 1994: 66).

I have already noted strong evidence to suggest that the new communities were in regular and well-maintained contact with each other across sizeable regions from soon after their establishment. This would support the notion of a fairly smooth physical flow of metals through the island according to consumer wealth. Nonetheless, movement of metals must have been affected in the earliest post-collapse period by the development of new routes and new concentrations of settlement, and by the disappearance of many former settlement gateways and centres. Both foreign metals traders and local intermediaries in trade had to learn a whole new 'demand map'. It is perhaps hardly surprising that in some sense a down-the-line effect seems to have operated, with the highest concentrations of metals being found at a few obvious gateway sites like Knossos, which probably functioned as nodes for new internal exchange systems. Ironically, then, given the newly freed-up trade environment, channels for high-value import trade may in some respects initially have become *narrower* in Crete.

One way in which metal products may have reached some of the smaller and remoter communities is through travelling smiths. In some unstratified societies, transient workers are commissioned to produce 'one-off' value objects by prominent groups or individuals who possess limited power to accumulate wealth, and thus to support permanent specialists (Davenport 1986: 95). This description may well apply to the smaller and more isolated new communities of this period, especially with regard to iron. At the Kommos coastal sanctuary in the later EIA, there is evidence for smelting of iron, as well as the dedication of iron objects, strongly suggesting a role for highly specialised transient ironworkers, whether originating inside or outside the island (Rehder 2000).

Summary

The reorganisation of regional trade networks, and a limited capacity to produce large subsistence surpluses, seem to have discouraged very high-scale investment in craft production in early EIA Crete. The absence of centralised political/economic systems able to organise large-volume materials procurement, finance, and distribution; the relative physical dispersal of craft specialists in the new settlement pattern; and Crete's geographical proximity to unregulated supply sources of finished value items/raw materials, must all have promoted considerable variability in access to luxury goods (and fluctuation in their value). This had potentially destabilising effects on social systems in which interpersonal competition played an important role in building political power bases.

Thanks to its 'successful' mode of collapse, involving extreme dispersal of population in many areas, as well as its geographical position, Crete experienced this challenging volatility in the supply of value goods earlier, and to a greater extent, than other Aegean regions. Rather than being pressured to respond with increased levels of social control over access to luxury goods, I suggest Cretan societies were buffered against instability through the early entrenchment of alternative forms of status, authority, and identity construction (as outlined in Part Two) which became consolidated further through the tenth to seventh centuries. These ultimately bounded the social significance attached to the accumulation of personal wealth, thereby allowing socially diverse consumption to continue and flourish in an insulated environment. The contrast with central Greece in this respect, discussed below, highlights the different social contexts in which commodity circulation and consumption were embedded at this time, and the complex, indirect ways in which physical and social environment, as well as earlier histories of consumption and long-distance exchange, could affect the social 'valency' of luxuries. Controls over mortuary deposition of metals in central Greece seem to have disappeared by the eighth century as overall metal availability rose in the Aegean as a whole, and new social institutions developed that sidelined the political role of personal consumption.

21 LIFT-OFF: EAST MEDITERRANEAN TRADE AND THE CENTRAL AEGEAN FROM THE TENTH CENTURY

Trade as a stimulus to the rise of complexity

From the late tenth through the ninth century, the central Aegean region saw two important new features in trade: much higher levels of eastern imports and the beginnings of a return trade with the east Mediterranean in fine drinking ceramics, with an extension of the trade to the west Mediterranean also becoming well established by the end of the eighth century (Crielaard 1999; Popham 1994a; Ridgway 1992: 11–45). Crete was partly involved in the same developments: indeed, the island saw a significant boost in eastern value imports from an early stage in this period, as I explore later (Hoffman 1997: 257).

Like their Aegean peers, Cretan societies developed significantly in economic and social complexity from this period onward – I discuss other types of evidence to support this in Part Four. The growth in complexity was clearly connected to growth in the goods exchange economy. In the classic secondary state formation model, the inhabitants of peripheral consuming regions are stimulated by contact with markets and trade systems in more complex 'core' areas to develop their own manufacturing and trade roles and thereby greater economic complexity; competitive emulation of consumption practices prevalent in the core region also drives emergent social stratification in the periphery. Though there is clearly value in the application of such models at a very general level to the EIA Aegean, they seem inadequate in predicting or describing the economic reactions of *individual* Aegean societies of this period, or the rate at which transformation occurred. There are striking contrasts in the way complexity emerged and developed in each region: different patterns of response to, and integration with, the value goods economy were connected to local social and cultural conditions.

Responses in the central Aegean

I have noted a heavy concentration of settlement along the eastern Greek seaboard in the twelfth century, suggesting this reflected a strong interest in exploiting the opportunities offered by eastern trade. By the late tenth century, these communities were accessing a greatly increased quantity and range of eastern value products (Popham 1994a). Imports, and local imitations of them, in the Lefkandi cemeteries between the late tenth and eighth centuries include many of the established types of prestige object – now in increased volumes – but also some new

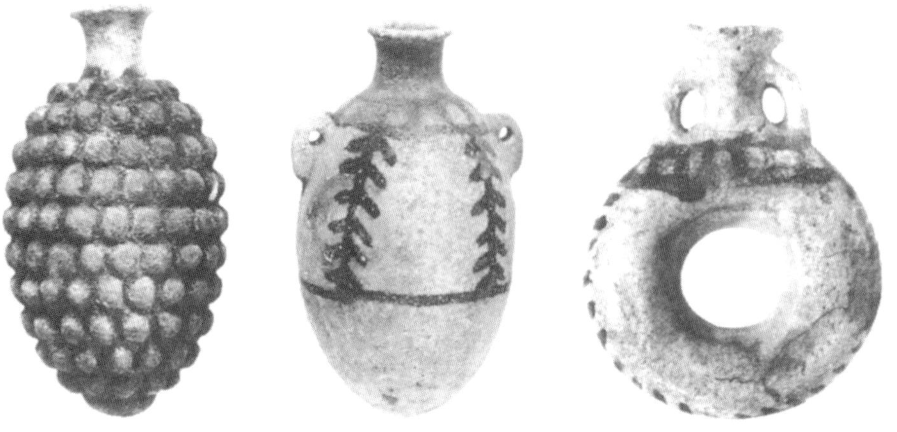

111. Easternising artefacts from the Lefkandi Toumba cemetery – faience flasks from Tomb 39 (after Popham and Lemos 1996, Plate 141 [b, c, f]). By permission of I. S. Lemos.

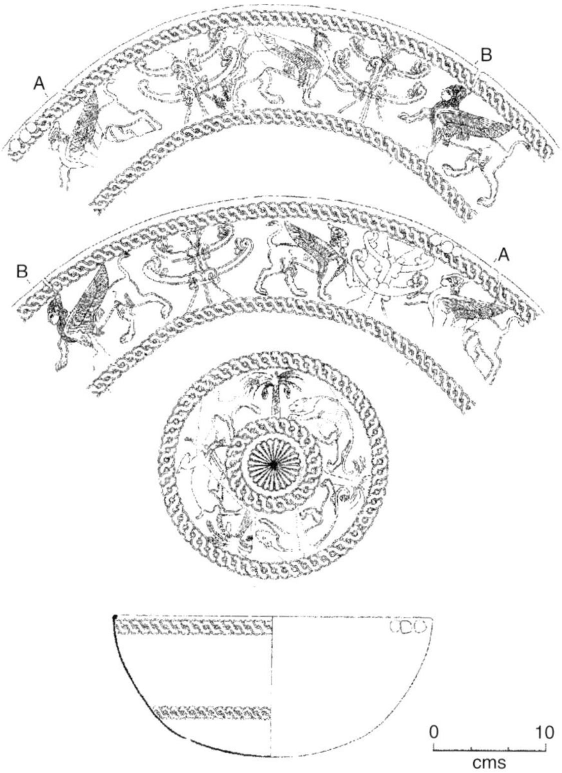

112. Eastern-type artefacts from Lefkandi Toumba cemetery – engraved bronze bowl of Levantine type from Tomb 55 (after Popham and Lemos 1996, Plate 133). By permission of I. S. Lemos.

ones (Figures 111–13). Faience becomes much more common, appearing both as jewellery and as small vessels. Greater volumes of bronze are deposited – in more elaborate forms of stand, in characteristic Levantine/Cypriot types of shallow bronze bowl, and in bronze maceheads of clear eastern provenance. Unguent vessels increase in quantity and diversify in form, now

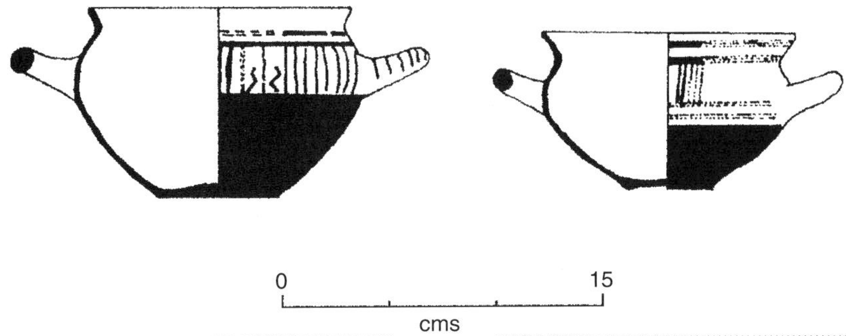

113. Eighth-century imported Euboean skyphoi from Finocchito, Sicily (after Leighton 1999, Fig. 129, p. 243). By permission of R. Leighton.

including faience flasks as well as derivatives of the ceramic lentoid flask and bird askos forms, both imported and locally made. Gold becomes more plentiful, and the jewellery made in it uses techniques developed in the east but new to the Aegean in this period.

The competitive acquisition and display of exotic goods were clearly becoming more important for Aegean communities, which seem increasingly to have placed these activities at the very heart of social life (Morris 2000: 195–257). But there is also a clear empirical increase in the *availability* of value goods across the whole Aegean, and in the eastern core itself, suggesting that the booming Levantine production sphere had a dynamic role in building this demand, and thus in indirectly conditioning intra-Aegean social relations. The flow of value imports that had prevailed in the twelfth to tenth centuries looks in some ways like a kind of market-building exercise by easterners, which only now started to pay off in full. In response to the trade stimulus, central Aegean societies started to build and serve a newly developing eastern market for the fine drinking pottery of central Greece, with its distinctive Protogeometric style of decoration. At first, exports appear only in small quantities, most likely representing novelty prestige acquisitions by easterners on a small scale. They seem often to have travelled in small quantities and have ended up in very high-status contexts, as in the case of the Euboean drinking vessels found in tombs on Cyprus – at Amathus in the tenth century and at Salamis in the ninth (Coldstream 1986, 1988: 92–3). By the late ninth century, much larger quantities of Aegean drinking wares were also arriving at gateway sites like Al Mina on the north Syrian coast, from which they were clearly traded on to the Levantine interior. From the late eighth century, their popularity was such that they were being replaced by mass-produced Cypriot imitations in the Levant and travelling in small quantities to growing markets in south Italy, Sicily, and even Spain (Figure 114). In the north Aegean and west Anatolia, the development of deep links with central Greek pottery traditions had been established at a much earlier date. In each of the above cases, rather different networks of trading contacts and intermediaries were involved (Boardman 1990: 23–102, 225–64; Harrison 1988: 69–73; Ridgway 1992: 11–145; Tsetskhladze and de Angelis 1994). This developing pottery export trade had huge implications for the scale of exchange in the Aegean, becoming the means for communities here to acquire larger volumes of eastern exotica on a more regular basis, and thus to develop significant economic power in the wider region. By the eighth century the quantities in circulation suggest a well-organised and large-volume production of export ceramics in central Greece.

The popularity of these products, in both the east and west/central Mediterranean, was almost certainly first built up by trade initiatives in which easterners (Phoenicians and/or Cypriots) had a strong, if not a dominant, role (Coldstream 1988, 1994b; Kopcke 1990; Muhly 1999; Popham

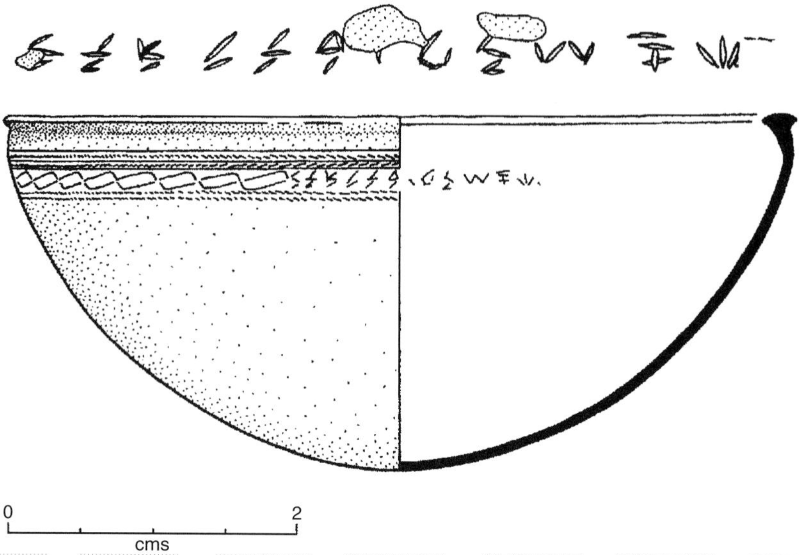

114. Phoenician bronze bowl from Knossos North Cemetery (after Coldstream and Catling 1996, Fig. 157 [Jfl]). By permission of H. W. Catling.

1994a). Much of the appeal of Aegean ceramics, whether for easterners or others, apparently lay in their association with the wine-drinking ritual. This association, as well as the exotic origin of the equipment, seems to have connoted high status for external consumers. Western and central Mediterranean communities may have first taken up this pottery as part of a generalised 'eastern' luxury package arriving in the area with traders and travellers from the east. Over time, however, a broader cultural package of distinctively Aegean type was promoted and 'bought into' abroad, particularly in the central Mediterranean. In developing and exporting this package, people in the central Aegean not only gained access to increased volumes of Levantine goods, but created new channels for metals acquisition from the central Mediterranean region. They formed increasingly close and complex relationships with trade partners in both areas, and by the late ninth/eighth century a growing number of Aegeans had clearly settled abroad in this connection, at trade-based settlements that later developed within a distinctively 'Greek' cultural and political framework and were termed *apoikia*, 'colonies' (Boardman 1990: 161–216; Holloway 2000: 43–86; Leighton 1999: 219–61; Osborne 1998).

Ceramic styles and cultural identity

Decorative style, with its particular regional, historical, and ethnic connotations, was inseparable from form and function in selling the new Aegean export ceramics, which were continuously and variously adapted in this regard to fit demand. The Protogeometric style, closely associated with Attica, was novel and distinctive in the Aegean context, as well as overseas. Attica was one of the earliest proactive exporters of drinking ceramics, and these products seem to have been as desirable in the Aegean world as in the east. The Euboean region, too, had long connections with eastern trade that served it well in developing and promoting its own attractive ceramic exports, distinct from Attic styles and with their own wide spread of influence, though still within the

PG tradition (Lemos 2002: 212–17). The Corinthia was another major exporting area by the eighth century. Here potters/traders deliberately adopted a strongly eastern-influenced iconography on their ceramics, apparently designed to build the appeal of the products both in the east (as 'Greek' and therefore exotic, but still with links into a local iconographic tradition) and in the west (as part of a generally desirable and marketable easternising package: Rasmussen 1991). Within the Aegean market, Protocorinthian pottery joined other elite-associated easternising products as a desirable item in itself but could also be traded onward for real Levantine imports. The east Aegean islands formed a dynamic part of this enterprising network by the eighth century. Having consumed central Aegean ceramics in quantity since at least the tenth century, they developed their own successful export styles by the late eighth, which mixed Aegean and eastern characteristics in a distinctive way and as a result were consumed widely in the Mediterranean (Boardman 1998: 141–77; Cook and Dupont 1998).

The various and fine-tuned adaptations in ceramic form and style between the late EIA and Archaic periods emphasise the extent of planning and marketing behind the ceramic export trade. They also indicate the huge political and economic relevance of regional cultural identity, as symbolised by exports, in this crucial formative period for trade 'territories'. The ceramic trade, first entered into by small groups on a locally competitive basis, must, as it grew, have involved the increasing coordination of production and a larger scale of investment in export missions. Since marketing depended so strongly on the regional distinctiveness of ceramic forms, the circulation of ceramics in an ever-wider geographical arena must have fed back into, and strengthened, ethnic self-conceptions. This is likely to have helped boost political and economic coherence at regional level – which in turn further supported the organisation of large-scale production and marketing. By the eighth century, the prestige and distinctiveness of physical exports were also enhanced by their association with a range of elements defining 'Hellenic' culture, including epic tradition and its associated references. Knowledge of the latter spread partly through early inscriptions on pottery (as on the 'Nestor cup' from Pithekoussai), as well as through imagery on pottery and other materials, and orally. Within this general cultural framework, specific regionally linked features could be picked out and emphasised as required by particular supplier or consumer groups (de Polignac 1995: 89–128; Hall 1997a: 34–65; Malkin 1998; Osborne 1998; Ridgway 1992: 55–7).

Internal change in central Greek societies was promoted by the trade boom in other ways, too. In communities where personal status was heavily linked to the acquisition and display of wealth goods, and cohesive social institutions were lacking, the boom meant that fluctuations in price and availability became especially powerful in their effects, potentially threatening to destabilise social and economic relationships. At Lefkandi, the elaborate Toumba 'heroon' building, latterly turned into a tumulus, suggests that conventions governing the representation of social rank in burial were altering, perhaps in response to this volatility, by the tenth century – with rank becoming more consolidated and formalised, using new means. The elite couple and horses buried in the building had as their grave goods exceptional pieces of antique eastern jewellery, as well as other high-value eastern or easternising items, including large bronze vessels (Popham et al. 1993). A number of other rich tombs around the mound, of tenth- to ninth-century date, indicate the existence of a sizeable group of wealth-consuming individuals, all at about the same high level of prosperity, within a relatively large community. Differentiation in status between these people and the couple earlier interred in the heroon is marked not only by the exceptional wealth of grave goods in the latter, but by the form of grave monument. This striking innovation suggests a new consolidation of rank, perhaps with an inherited aspect. It is important to note that the Toumba building is so far unique as a burial monument and may reflect special local circumstances more than a sustained pattern of change in central Greece at such an early date.

Changes in the representation of status in the burial sphere also emerged at Athens from at least the ninth century. The visual symbolism of decorated cremation urns, rather than sheer quantity of wealth goods in a grave, started to play a more consistently important role in signifying rank and gender (Whitley 1991a: 87–162). Though wealth never stopped being deposited in graves, more care now seems to have been invested in representing other dimensions of status in the mortuary sphere, and these modes of representation seem to have become formalised across large communities. Again, the change may represent an attempt to buffer the destabilising effects of extreme competitive consumption in the luxury goods sphere. Nonetheless, the latter continued right through to the end of the eighth century, suggesting that these measures had a limited effect.

22 NOTHING TO DECLARE? CRETE IN THE TENTH THROUGH EIGHTH CENTURIES

Evidence for change

In Crete, as formerly, it is the coastal or near-coastal locations that show the largest concentrations of imports – and of value goods generally – from the tenth through the eighth centuries (Hoffman 1997: 248–60). These goods are predominantly found in graves, but extra-settlement sanctuaries form another important context of their deposition and exchange, a pattern paralleled elsewhere in the Aegean and the colonial Mediterranean by the end of the eighth century (de Polignac 1995: 11–32; Morgan 1986: 61–89, 137–46, 1999: 295–347, 369–41).

The number of large bronzework pieces of clear eastern provenance or inspiration now found in the island illustrates the higher-volume circulation of eastern value imports from this period onward. The provenance of these imports seems to be mainly within the Cypriot-Syrian-Phoenician area. A bowl of late tenth-century date with Phoenician inscription appears in Tekke Tomb J at Knossos (Coldstream and Catling 1996: 30; see Figure 114 in Chapter 22). Bronze bowls and jugs of Cypriot/Phoenician and Syrian origin or inspiration appear in consistently increasing quantity at the Eleutherna cemetery, at the Kommos sanctuary, and at the Idaean cave, from the early ninth through the eighth centuries (Catling 1996d; Sakellarakis 1983, 1987, 1988; Shaw and Shaw 2000: 395–8; Stampolidis 1998; Stampolidis et al. 1998: 121–6; Figures 115 and 116). Unique items like a late ninth-century engraved bronze quiver from Knossos Fortetsa tomb P, with iconography incorporating strong north Syrian elements combined with local styles, support the impression of significantly increased local skill and investment in the production of very high-value goods (Brock 1957: 134–5; Figure 117).

Considerable amounts of carved ivory, with strongly orientalising forms, were deposited in locations such as the Idaean Cave and the Knossian cemeteries during the same period (Evely 1996: 629–33; Hoffman 1997: 53–66, 109–36, 147–8, 153–89; Sakellarakis 1992, 1993; Figure 118). Quantities of faience increase substantially by the ninth century, and objects in this material often have strong eastern stylistic connections, though at least some seem to be made in Crete (Webb 1996). Some rich tombs at Knossos, most notably the 'Tekke tomb', now contain much higher average quantities of gold jewellery than anything seen in the twelfth to tenth centuries – often of markedly oriental design or technology. The Tekke tomb also contained a hoard of scrap gold, suggesting strongly that goldworking in these same techniques was taking place within the island (Boardman 1967a; Hoffman 1997: 191–247; Figure 119).

The amount of iron in circulation grew substantially from the tenth century onward, as in other parts of the Aegean (Snodgrass 1971: 213–96, 1980b, 1982a, 1989, 1996; Waldbaum 1978, 1982). Though its days as a prestige good were not yet over, iron became socially devalued

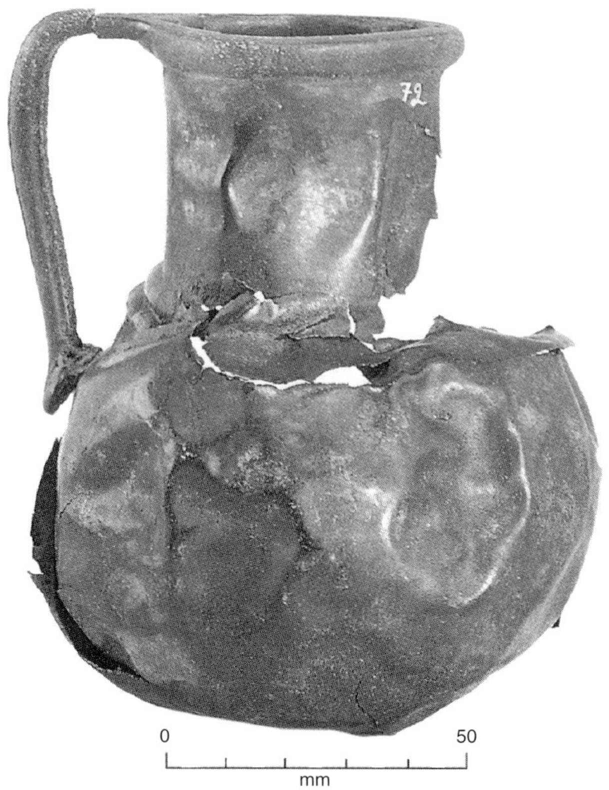

115. Bronze jug from Idaean Cave (after Stampolidis et al. 1998, Fig. 271, p. 229). By permission of N. Stampolidis.

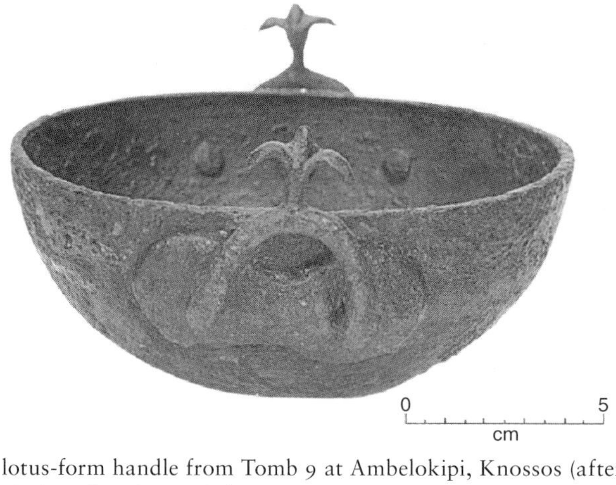

116. Bronze bowl with lotus-form handle from Tomb 9 at Ambelokipi, Knossos (after Stampolidis et al. 1998, Fig. 281, p. 235). By permission of N. Stampolidis.

as contacts with the east increased in quantity and intensity, a development promoting better sharing of technological information within the Aegean, and between the Aegean and eastern Mediterranean (Morris 1989: 511–12). Large iron types which retained clear prestige associations (probably linked to funerary feasting) were the spits (*obeloi*) found in tombs at Knossos

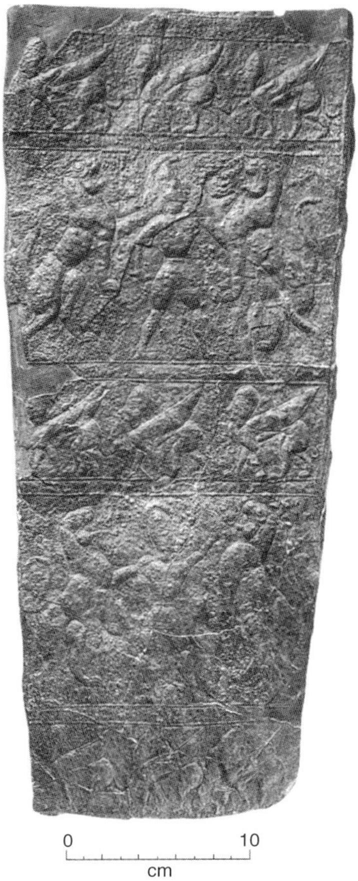

117. Bronze quiver from Fortetsa cemetery, Knossos (after Brock 1957, Plate 169 [1569]).

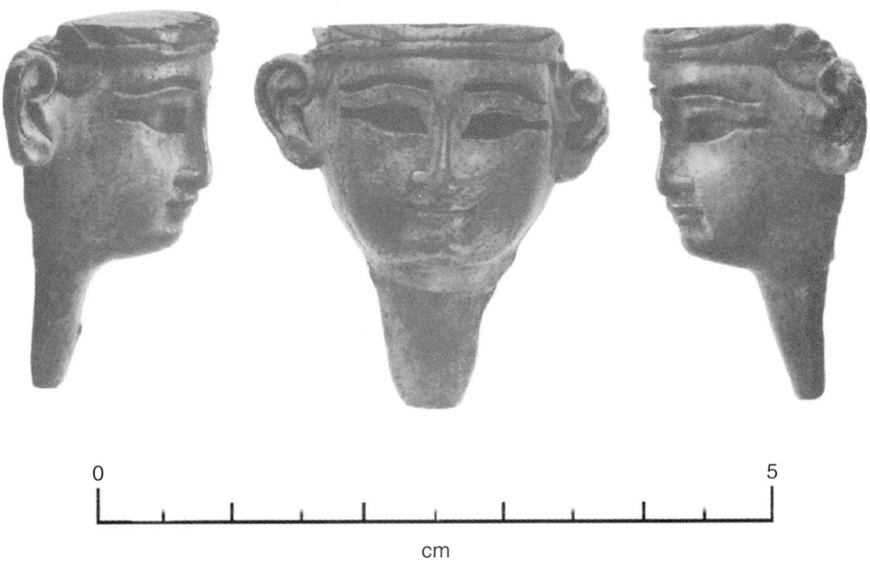

118. Fragments of a Phoenician ivory figurine from the Idaean Cave (after Sakellerakis 1992, Plate 13 [a–f], p. 132). By permission of Y. Sakellerakis.

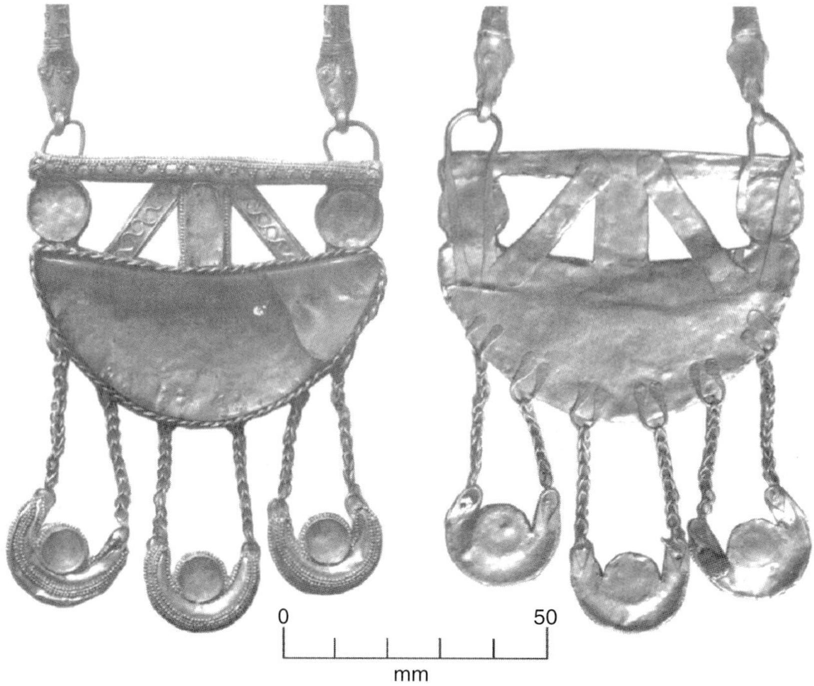

119. Gold pendant from the Tekke tomb, Knossos (after Boardman 1967a, Plate 7). By permission of J. Boardman.

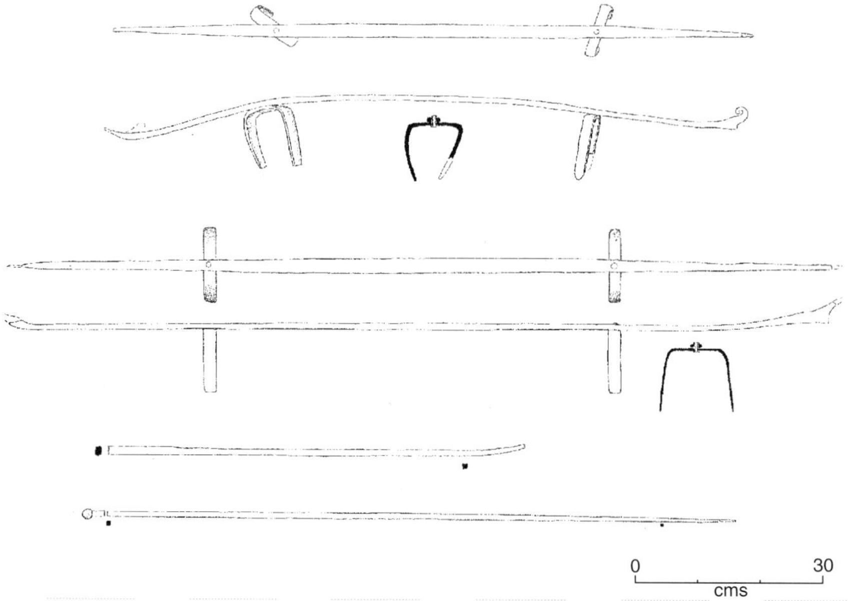

120. Iron obeloi from Knossos North Cemetery (after Coldstream and Catling 1996, E. A. Catling del., Fig. 179). By permission of H. W. Catling.

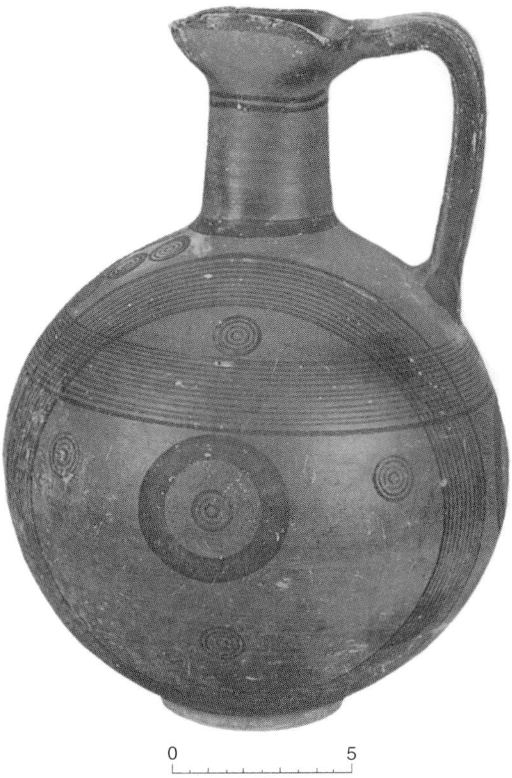

121. Globular juglet of Cypro-Phoenician type (imported) from Eleutherna, Orthe Petra cemetery (after Stampolidis 2003, Fig. 4; Stampolidis et al. 1998, Fig. 100, p. 148). By permission of N. Stampolidis.

and Gortyn and at the Kommos sanctuary in the tenth and ninth centuries, which had strong parallels with Cypro-Levantine types. Such items may often still have been imports or directly inspired by imports (Coldstream 1979a: 48–9; Hoffman 1997: 141–6; Shaw 1980: 231; Snodgrass 1996: 590–1; Figure 120).

Growth in the quantity and diversity of imported eastern or easternising ceramics is also seen by the ninth century, particularly in the strong circulation of small globular unguent juglets or *lekythoi* of Cyro-Phoenician manufacture (Coldstream 1979b, 1984a, 1996b: 408–9; Stampolidis 1998: 177–8; Figures 121 and 122). As in the twelfth to tenth centuries, most of the value goods listed, along with smaller exotic items of added-value type, such as steatite, faience, and glass seals, scarabs, rings, and figured beads, are found in graves ranging across a number of social levels, and in very variable quantities. Social access to eastern imports and to imitations of them seemingly remained relatively uncircumscribed, but the expanding range of goods means that new kinds of rules are likely to have applied to their consumption: in Part Four I try to elucidate these by examining changing forms of burial deposition during this period.

The export gap

The increasing volume of items of advanced technical quality, made in distinctively local styles or local materials, but incorporating strongly orientalising elements of style and technology, reflects

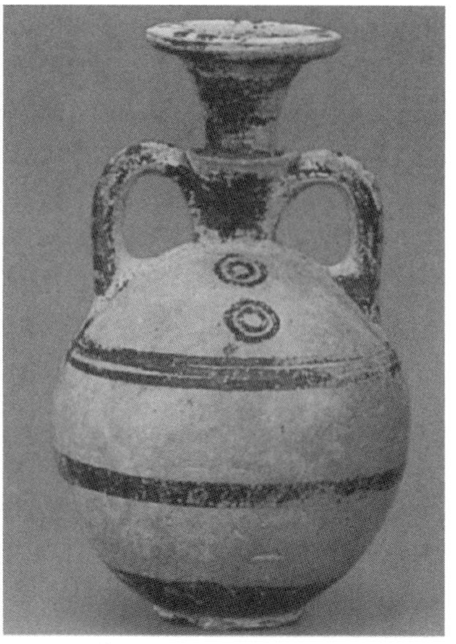

122. Globular juglet of Cypro-Phoenician type from Eleutherna, Orthe Petra cemetery (after Stampolidis et al. 1998, Fig. 152, p. 170). By permission of N. Stampolidis.

the growth of a highly specialised and skilled local production sector in Crete, in close touch with both international developments and local demand profiles (Hoffman 1997: 116–26, 149–51, 161–5, 248–9). However, while other areas of the Aegean were developing the production of specialised exports, Crete seems to have articulated in a very different, more restricted way with the expanding world system, focusing most of its production and procurement resources on goods for *local* consumption. There is very little evidence for the large-scale export of Crete's own manufactured products, notably in the ceramic sector, where we have seen that other Aegean regions were pushing ahead (Coldstream 1979b: 261; Hoffman 1997: 247–60; Matthäus 1998: 127–9). Textiles, oil, wool, or other perishables that do not survive in the record might theoretically have been significant exports (as in the LBA and the Classical periods). Yet it is surprising that no identifiably Cretan transport vessels are found abroad, if the oil trade was sizeable. After the collapse of the large centralised investment and administrative units of the LBA, the coordination of mass textile manufacture and trade would be difficult, at least at first, though there is no reason why cloth could not have formed a major export by the late eighth century as larger and more complex economic systems became established in the developing states. There are hints in Archaic tradition that Cretan ports or merchants were involved in the purple-dye trade (for example, the presence of a purple-fisher named Korobios at Itanos is mentioned in Herodotus 4.151). But even if these commodities were major exports, Crete would have remained in an entirely different export class from either the contemporary east Mediterranean or the central Aegean region, which both specialised in mass-produced, easily shipped, and high-added-value export products, bringing in huge and rapid profits. The idea once put forward by Markoe (1998), that Crete provided a major source of iron ore for the Cypro-Phoenician zone, has no evidence to support it. Iron ore is present in most regions of the Aegean and east Mediterranean, and Crete's iron technology, while precocious in an Aegean context, was less developed than that of Cyprus and the east for much of the EIA. This is not likely to have been the case if Crete were a major iron-supplying area, especially given the other indicators of close Cretan contact with eastern crafts and craftsmen. Throughout this period, the island's ports surely filled important reprovisioning and transhipment roles, potentially supplying many kinds of everyday perishable goods for the flourishing eastern export trade. Cretans themselves often probably acted as travelling agents of trade between the east and 'termini' like Athens and Lefkandi, with many value imports entering intra-Cretan circulation in this way (Markoe 1998: 236). Because the local production of orientalising metalwork in Crete develops at such an early date and in relatively high volumes, it has also been suggested that Crete took on a role as bronzework supplier to the central Aegean by the later part of the EIA, perhaps supporting or replacing eastern bronze imports with products of its own (Boardman 1982: 225; Lebessi 1996: 146; Matthäus 1998: 134). If Cretan metalwork was exported in quantities, it might help to explain why specialised pottery export did not 'take off' in the island. Ultimately, however, there is no proof that metalwork export was a significant element in the Cretan economy. Many parts of the Aegean, including Crete itself, were still receiving numerous imports of finished bronze artefacts from the east: on the other hand, there is good evidence for well-developed regional traditions in luxury metalwork on the mainland by the eighth century, seen, for example, in the depositions made at the Olympia and Delphi sanctuaries (Morgan 1990). Any attempt by Crete to enter the metalwork market as a primary producer would involve competition with the Levantine suppliers, in which the latter would have huge advantages of scale and resources: since the eastern Mediterranean zone was constantly innovating, imitations of eastern products might quickly date. It was much more in Cretan interests to allow easterners to do the hard work of marketing and for the island to ride on the back of their success, as a trade intermediary and as a skilled production base for locally consumed metal goods.

Drivers of economic complexity? The nature of relations with 'easterners' and 'the east'

By the ninth century the record reflects the extension and development of Cretan procurement systems in the Aegean, as well as the east. Coldstream notes that the very large Attic amphorae in Early Geometric Knossian tombs were deposited in a completely different, much less regulated way than at Athens, where they were part of a tight symbolic system (Coldstream 1996a: 137; Coldstream and Catling 1996: 716–17). They clearly had an independent role as luxury commodities in this context, yet their size and fragility suggest they were not transported to Crete in a speculative, opportunistic trade framework: they must therefore represent regular commissions by prosperous merchants or buyers. The heyday of mixed, small-scale opportunistic trade in the Aegean may already have been disappearing with regard to many sorts of goods. Exchange seems likely to have been increasingly channelled through large settlement centres and ports, which were perhaps already developing specialised procurement roles. In central Crete, with its accessible and well-placed harbours, for example, Attic ceramics arrive at a specially early date and in notably high volumes (Catling 1977: 12–14; Coldstream 1979a: 88–9, 1996a; Desborough 1952: 233–40); while by the eighth century Chania sees a large number of Peloponnesian ceramic imports, as well as Attic ones (Andreadaki-Vlasaki 2004; Figures 123 and 124).

At the same time, the important role of sanctuaries like Kommos and Amnisos as entry points for imported value goods suggests that highly centralised organisation or control of trade was still lacking, making the regular use of cult as an interface or buffer important (Schäfer et al. 1992: 182–3; Shaw 1980, 1989, 1998; Shaw and Shaw 2000: 210–336). The use of sanctuaries as arenas for long-distance exchange was also developing on the mainland at sites like Delphi

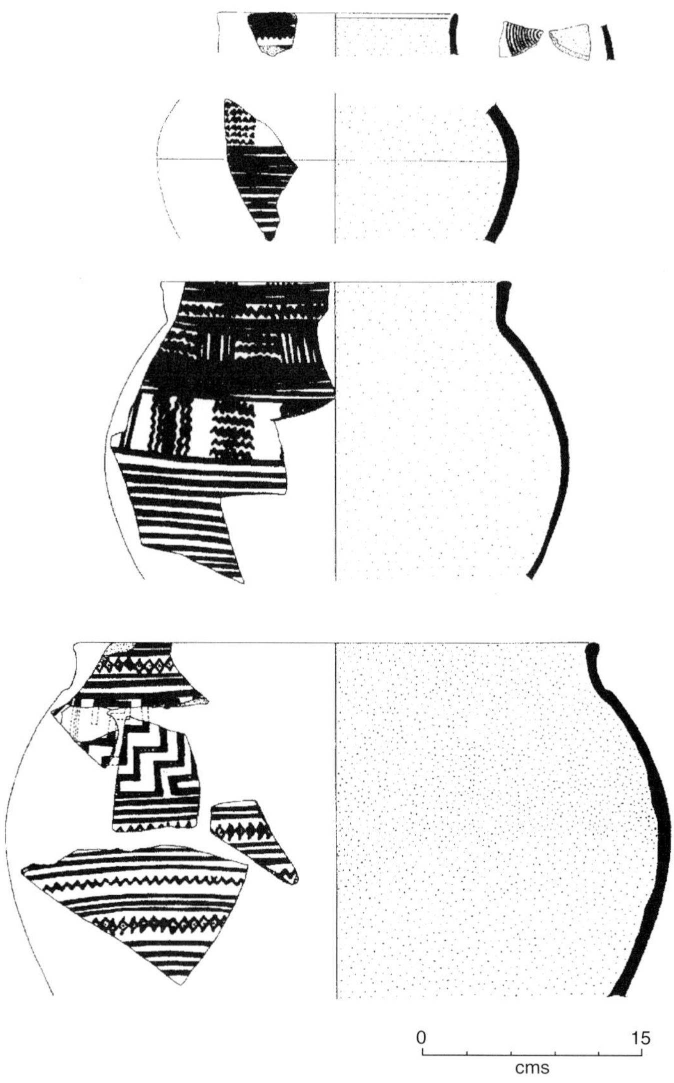

123. Imported Argive pottery from late eighth-century Chania (after Andreadaki-Vlasaki 2004, Fig. 7, p. 26). By permission of M. Andreadaki-Vlasaki.

and Olympia during the same period and was to intensify by the eighth century, with the rise of Greek sanctuaries at important trade points all over the east and south central Mediterranean (Morgan 1990; Sherratt and Sherratt 1993). By the eighth century at Kommos, the adaptation of the sanctuary's design to accommodate interaction with eastern visitors is unique in the Greek world: the famous 'tripillar' construction in Temple A closely resembles Phoenician cult installations of the same period (Shaw and Shaw 2000: 14–21; Figure 125). It suggests that trade visitors from outside the island still often needed to be engaged with in a highly ritualised fashion. The bulk transport jars of Phoenician provenance found at Kommos from the late eleventh through tenth centuries suggest that some of these visitors were involved in large-scale, relatively low-value 'commercial' exchange, not elite gift exchange. That this level of exchange continued through the sanctuary's later life is suggested by the simple drinking cups with graffito inscriptions of various regional types deposited at the site in the late eighth through seventh centuries, by passing traders/worshippers.

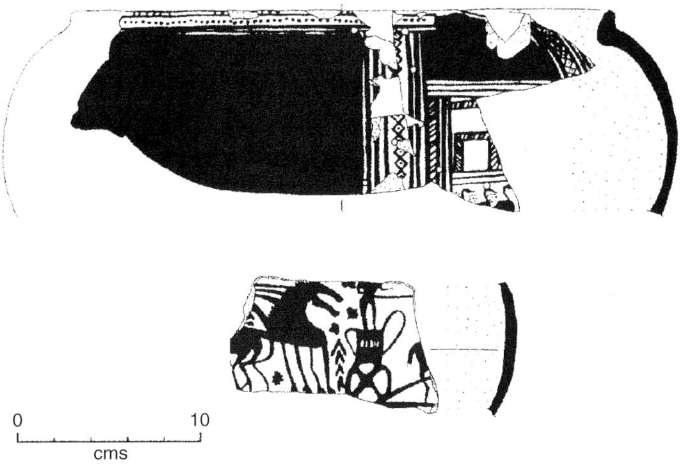

124. Imported Attic pottery from late eighth-century Chania (after Andreadaki-Vlasaki 2004, Fig. 8, p. 27). By permission of M. Andreadaki-Vlasaki.

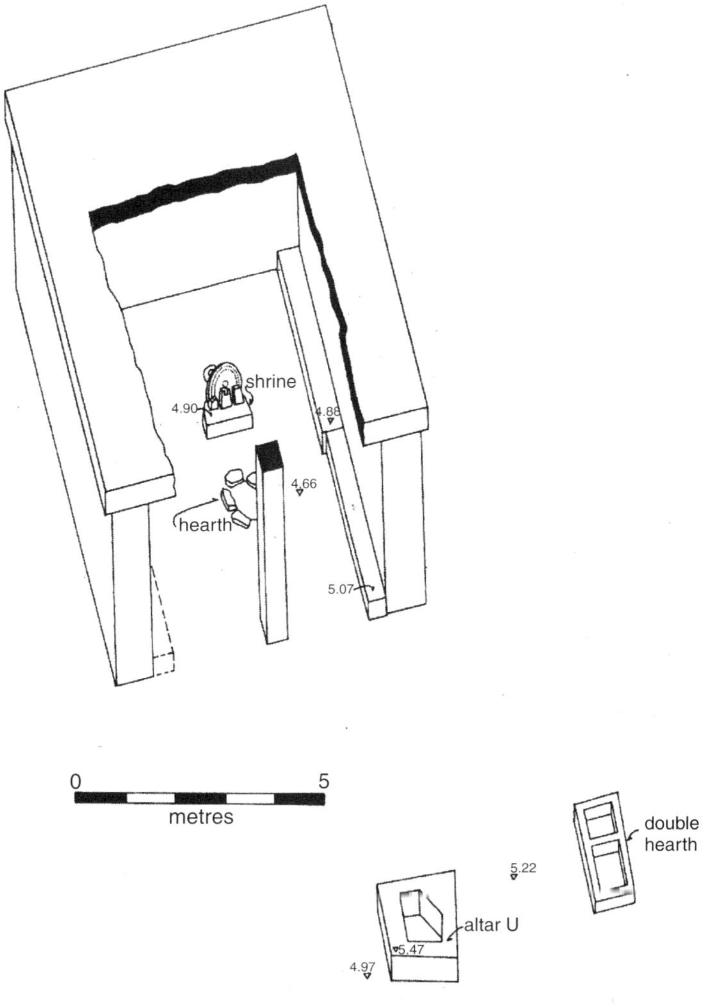

125. Reconstruction of tripillar shrine of Phoenician type, Kommos (after Shaw and Shaw 2000, Plate 1.31). By permission of J. W. Shaw and M. C. Shaw.

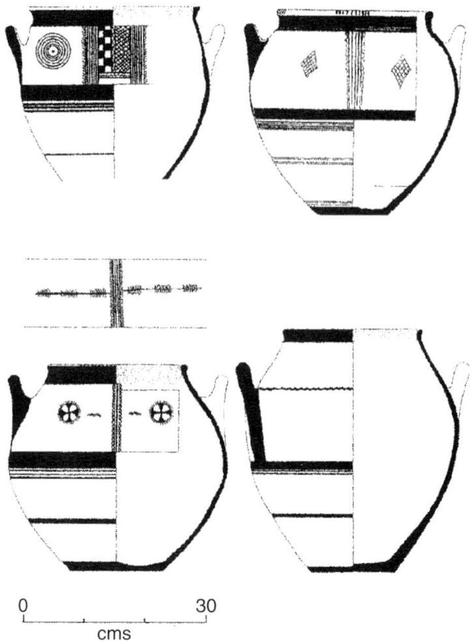

126. PG kraters from Knossos North Cemetery, Tomb 48 (after Coldstream and Catling 1996, Fig. 86). By permission of H. W. Catling.

The generally high level of skills, planning, investment, and technology seen in goods production and procurement in the island suggests that the non-engagement of Cretan traders in specialised pottery export was in part a deliberate and conscious strategy. The fact that a clearly defined pottery 'identity' for the island failed to develop also seems related to the earlier history of the Cretan economy, discussed previously. In the Cretan pattern of multiple scattered small communities it was not easy to develop standardised, large-scale production of fine pottery to suit a rapidly growing export market. The particularly intense and mixed contacts and cultural influences affecting Crete's ceramic production at the same period might also make it difficult and undesirable to develop an export style targeted at one particular regional market: we see these multiple influences reflected at Knossos, for example, in the rise of Attic-influenced PG styles alongside the flourishing of a local orientalising style ('PGB') by the late ninth century (Figures 126 and 127). As noted, cultural identity assertion in this period had long-lasting economic and ethnopolitical implications, and Cretan societies seem to have had a lot to gain, in terms of both economic success and social stability, by keeping their cultural identity, as expressed through commodiy production, open and flexible.

Over the course of time, some interest in specialised ceramic export production did develop in Crete, but in a very unusual way. Cretans consumed eastern unguents at a steeply rising rate between the ninth and eighth centuries, as indicated by the large volumes of Cypro-Phoenician-type lekythoi found at Knossos and other major settlements such as Eleutherna and Gortyn. Their contents seem to have been strongly identified with the form of the container, making the whole package of high added value (Coldstream 1984a, 1996b: 408–9; Stampolidis et al. 1998: 86–91). We see significant local imitative production and long-range internal circulation of these vessels and their contents, with some very possibly being exported on to the wider Aegean from Crete, with its exceptional concentrations, by the eighth century. This is perhaps the closest Crete ever came to marketing its 'own' distinctive ceramics. Still, though, most of the evidence is

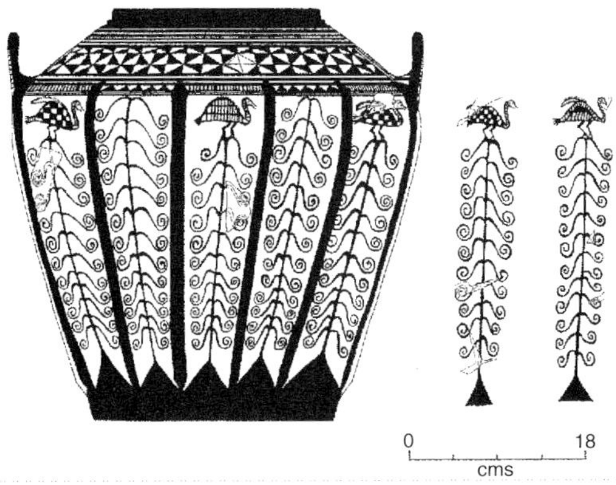

127. PGB Orientalising cremation jar from Knossos North Cemetery (after Coldstream and Catling 1996, Fig. 133 [283.11]). By permission of H. W. Catling.

for local consumption. In contrast to contemporary popular Aegean ceramic 'lines' that deliberately incorporated easternising elements, like the Protocorinthian or Rhodian Wild Goat styles, the producers of these juglets did not transfer an eastern flavour onto an original local form, but directly imitated an eastern product as a whole. Because of this feature, the vessels have sometimes been argued to represent Phoenician- or Cypriot-run 'unguent factories' located in the island under the direction/control of resident easterners. A parallel model is that of expatriate Aegeans (or culturally Aegeanised easterners) rebottling bulk-imported eastern unguents in local wares, whether for onward trade, or local consumption, or both, at Pithekoussai in the central Mediterranean in the late eighth century (Ridgway 1992: 113–14).

Easterners trading in or through Crete might indeed have preferred to use locally produced containers for their 'trademark' unguents, to save resources in shipping these heavy items (the regular favouring of such transshipment practices is suggested by the Phoenician transport jars found in dumps at Kommos earlier in the EIA). If so, they might well have entered into active partnership with Cretan producers to make the juglets (Shaw 1989, 1998; Shaw and Shaw 2000: 302–12). However, there is no reason why the juglets should not have been produced on a purely or mainly Cretan initiative to replace imports in the local market or even farther afield. This is hinted at by the fact that production took place at several different locations in the island, rather than a single control centre: at Gortyn and Eleutherna, as well as Knossos, for example, they were made in local clay (Kotsonas in press; Santaniello in press). Assuming direct management of the project by easterners dubiously equates ceramic characteristics with actual ethnic identity, and I have noted how risky this is in studying trade at this period. It is particularly problematic for Crete, where a coherent ceramic export identity is lacking and take-up of and familiarity with eastern styles across a range of materials are present from an early date. The 'Phoenician unguent factory' model of this period treats Cretan communities as essentially passive – led by eastern initiatives – when in fact they may have been starting to compete directly or, more likely, collaborate proactively with them by this time (a view reflected in Boardman 1961: 128–59, 1967a: 63; Brock 1957: 143). Overall, the fact that the island continued to receive and circulate large quantities of eastern goods for local consumption and onward trade suggests a basically collaborative relationship with eastern merchants. Relationships between Aegeans and easterners combining rivalry with open collaboration in a spirit of enterprise are suggested by cases from the protocolonial world, like that of Pithekoussai – though uneven power balances clearly existed in many cases, ultimately giving rise to separate Greek and Phoenician colonial establishments across the Mediterranean. Cretan communities cannot easily be seen as neutral, passive units exploited, stimulated, taught, or led by eastern entrepreneurs to sell eastern products or substitutes for them. The long-term lack of Cretan export markets abroad would, in fact, discourage the latter strategy. If easterners wanted profit-driven partnerships, they were better off building them with groups in Ionia or in the central Aegean and colonial worlds, with which they were also well connected. On the other hand, it is significant that nowhere on Crete do we have evidence of a Phoenician trade colony of the type found in the contemporary central and west Mediterranean, which we might expect if easterners had really wished to, or been able to, act as direct managers of local value good production for onward trade purposes (Aubet 1990: 185–218; Harrison 1988: 41–51; discussion in Karageorghis and Stampolidis 1998: 253–4). Crete's consistently active (though circumscribed) involvement in international trade right through the Bronze to Iron Age transition, and the relatively complex, institutionalised character of its societies through the collapse period, meant there was no good blank sociocultural 'canvas' for this type of colonial establishment – the social and economic gap between Crete and the eastern core was too small to be exploited in this way.

If we discount eastern directives in their production, should we nonetheless see the enthusiastic production and consumption of these recognisably Levantine-type products (at a time when most other Aegean regions were constructing their political identities through production and export of pottery of a very different type) as a statement of Crete's deliberate or wholesale political alignment with 'the east'? I think not, at least in any sharply exclusive way. 'The east' was itself a complex and multivariate cultural entity that can never have operated as a political or economic bloc, even if its products were lumped in a single 'exotic' category in Aegean minds. Cretan societies exploited the highly prestigious cultural symbolism of the east in their relations with the Aegean world through a number of different levels and types of connections with the Levantine and Cypriot regions. Residents of other Aegean regions must have been aware of the close contacts and links between Cretans and eastern traders/producers and their culture. At the same time, these other regions had their own separate and direct links with eastern traders, plugging them directly into the 'real' east. Familiar Crete, which had been so closely linked to central Greece by language and culture in the precollapse Mycenaean world, could never be confused in this way with a fully integrated part of the eastern core; nor could any of its products, whether metal or ceramic, easily carry the same 'eastern' value as those actually produced in Cyprus or Phoenicia. The island's deep historical, cultural, and social links to central Greece in the EIA were highly visible in its material culture and referred to in spreading traditions like the Homeric epics, discussed further in Part Five.

It seems fair to say, however, that Cretan cultural and economic developments were *differently* linked with the eastern trade than those of central Greece. The island was an especially important and valuable customer for eastern imports – partly thanks to its lack of social restrictions on luxury good consumption – but never the source of really substantial moveable profits for eastern traders. The best interpretative model seems to be of a rather limited number of eastern settlers (permanent and temporary residents) using the island primarily as a customer base and stopping point, alongside trade-active locals. Both groups would profit through serving a high local demand with luxury imports and their high-quality substitutes, and in provisioning onward trade. Both groups benefited from the island's links into multiple external markets as a result of its history and geographical position. This model of shared interests is backed up by a variety of evidence for especially deep, positive acculturation to an eastern presence in the island, *even while* no eastern colony was established there. The Kommos shrine, the Tekke goldwork, a Phoenician inscription on a reused burial pithos at eighth-century Gavalomouri in west Crete, and traces of individual Phoenician or Phoenicianised burial monuments (*cippi*) at Knossos and Eleutherna (Andreadaki-Vlasaki 1987; Boardman 1967a; Hoffman 1997: 67–9, 191–247; Kourou 1991; Kourou and Karetsou 1998; Tzedakis 1976, 1977, 1978a, 1979) are all striking in this respect.

In the later EIA, the concentration of easternising goods and contacts remained consistently strong in central Crete (which had always shown particularly intensive contacts with overseas regions, including early imitative production of eastern exotica) and at the richest sites. These facts, with the other observations above, confirm that eastern interaction with Crete was linked more to the sharing of interests in, and channels for, trade-based prosperity than to the takeover of an empty political and economic niche.

Conclusions

The growth of complexity in Crete from the tenth century through the period of polis emergence is not able to be explained in terms of direct, conscious eastern 'leadership', nor in terms of a classic secondary state formation process. Rather, it relates, among other factors, to a specific, bounded kind of participation in a newly extended world system, in which the circulation and consumption of eastern value goods offered major opportunities for economic development. In this environment, Cretan communities took decisions about production that seem ultimately founded in self-interest, not maximal profit for external parties. Economic benefits for a wide and diverse sector of society (rather than only a small elite) clearly accrued as a result of the increased volume of materials and products in circulation, and of the island's role as a way-station for trade. The existence of exceptionally strong social institutions in Crete (analysed in Part Four), rooted in twelfth-century developments such as the consolidation of community-level cult and feasting and the secure social role of the kin unit, minimised the risk of severe social instability in connection with booming trade. The social impact of wealth-based competition, and thereby the impetus to develop specialised exports, were ultimately restricted in this way. At the same time, local social systems *were* deeply affected by interactions with the changing Mediterranean economy – and at an exceptionally early date. While many other Aegean regions show few clear signs of major social readjustment until the late eighth century (despite the trade changes from the tenth), Crete saw its turning point in complexity much earlier, corresponding broadly to the start of the trade expansion period, as I shall show in Part Four.

Long-distance exchange in the EIA Mediterranean may be best seen as a 'nested' form of world system (Chase-Dunn and Hall 1993). In Crete, the already complex economic systems of the Near East articulated early with developing production areas in Attica and elsewhere, so that at least three individual types of socioeconomic system were involved. Crete's position as a physical 'border' between two zones with very different contexts of production and consumption might well lead us to expect very idiosyncratic social reactions there. Interestingly, we never see the emergence of strong forms of control on access to goods from the east Mediterranean core area. The existence of other forms of social control and cohesion obviated any need for this. In turn, the early lack of need or ability to control import flow limited pressure to develop specialised exports in order to compete with or reciprocate the incoming trade. Rather, these conditions favoured collaboration and integration with the agents of that trade, wherever they originated. The symbolic conflict of 'eastern' and 'Greek' cultural identities in the Aegean by the eighth century (discussed further in Part Five) was one that Cretans had little interest in, or benefit from, entering. In that regard, in fact, we see parallels in outlook and operation, particularly with regard to trade and the external-facing structuring of identity, between Crete and contemporary Levantine polities. Much less emphasis seems placed here than in central Greek societies on building a single distinct, exclusive cultural/trade identity tied into a single ethnic unit, and more on profiting from the trade transactions themselves in a relatively flexible manner.

23 MODES AND ROUTES OF EXCHANGE WITHIN CRETE IN THE LATER EIA

Class relations in trade

In the LBA, the interregional exchange of goods between elites in state systems that differed radically in scale and wealth had often been couched in the highly formalised and symbolic terms of 'gifts' between 'equals'. These exchanges existed in a context of many other sorts of trade (Liverani 1990; 205–85; Sherratt and Sherratt 1991). If gift-exchange models are of limited value in characterising the nature of LBA trade in its entirety, they seem even less useful in describing the freed-up world of twelfth- to tenth-century exchange, and definitely much too simple for the increasingly complex trade environment prevailing from the tenth century on. By this time, so many different types of goods were clearly moving around in such varying quantities and being deposited/consumed in such very different contexts, that it is difficult to see a gifting mode as dominant. This is especially true of the rise in mass-produced Aegean export ceramics by the eighth century, although the earliest traded examples of these do end up in very wealthy contexts, and the market for these ceramics may initially have been built by 'gifts' made to, or between, rich easterners.

The Homeric texts suggest that elite gift exchange did exist, but never that it was the main means of trade in value items in the later EIA. Winter notes that descriptions in the *Iliad* and the *Odyssey* of complex 'genealogies' of exchange for outstanding value objects within the Achaean elite, and between this group and eastern rulers, appear alongside references in the same epics to a very different dimension of interregional trade – eastern merchants engaged in profit-led exchange (Winter 1995). As noted, it is likely that some Aegean counterparts to these merchants, in a broad sense, operated through most, if not all, of the EIA. Trade is likely to have settled down within a more formally defined merchant class as export production grew and states emerged. Prior to this, however, the role of an Aegean 'merchant' may well have been a looser, more often part-time, and perhaps rather higher-status one, dependent on varying access to tradable goods at different times. In the eastern core – where the formal status of merchant had been long established in the Levantine LBA palatial economies and the independent ports of Cyprus, and where such a rapid post-collapse recovery took place – it seems likely to have been a regularised and consistent role from quite early in the EIA, tied into a relatively large-scale production and investment sphere. When people from these two kinds of groups had contact, class differences must have been apparent and felt.

Ian Morris stresses the value of gift exchange frameworks between pretended 'equals' – whatever their real status – in providing a 'front end', or acceptable social framework, for the more commercial, socially inclusive trade that must certainly have existed in many commodities (Matthäus 1998: 141; Morris 1986: 5–6). Thanks to the regional social and economic inequalities noted earlier, Cypriot or Levantine commercial traders may often have been received in the Aegean as high-status individuals. Morris cites in this respect the ambiguous chief/trader identity of the disguised Athena, and her ceremonial reception, in the *Odyssey*. As the trade boom gathered pace, sanctuaries seem to have taken on increasing importance as buffered arenas for interaction between people from widely different areas, who were often unequal in relative status. A contemporary Afghan case, cited by Helms, is of interest here (Chaffetz 1981: 158; Helms 1988: 152). Here, personally competitive community leaders display hospitality and generosity to travellers (including traders) in the same way as they do to their own communities. This contributes to building the leaders' status, and they acquire in return goods of prestige value as 'gifts' that they use in future local gifting or convert through trade. Among the Asante of west Africa in the nineteenth century, Helms notes that it was even more important to gain prestige by entertaining foreign traders/embassies than to acquire valuable items from them (Helms 1988: 156). In the last case, the two societies involved in the trade were clearly unequal in structure and wealth. While their contacts were ceremonialised in friendship terms, onward local exchange of the goods received had a definite commercial character. In a society like EIA Crete, where clan links were very strong, cross-cultural studies like those of the Tiv by Bohannan (1968) suggest that downward convertibility in exchange is likely to have covered most goods and materials, with few social barriers to the process.

The changing spatial context of trade

The variety of social and physical contexts of exchange existing by this period suggests that the geographical circulation of imports within Crete was complex and makes it hard to map. The still-dispersed settlement pattern of the tenth to eighth centuries suggests that alongside trade organised by well-resourced, highly organised enterprises via the main gateway sites, some exchange is likely to have been carried out by other traders (whether Cretan or non-Cretan) moving around the island in a more opportunistic way. Itinerant craftsmen or traders in metals might continue a (now larger-scale) trade between settlements, which had reduced in number and now mostly comprised sizeable regional nucleations, as I explain in Part Four. Goods must also have changed hands in formal prestations, dedications, and gifts – for example, during gatherings at some open-air sanctuaries. The political readjustments of the period (discussed in Part Four) surely helped to swell the volume of such transactions.

In this context, we must avoid oversimplified interpretations of goods' movement on the basis of their find locations alone. One example of the latter is the suggestion, based on eastern imports at the cemetery of Arkades (Afrati Profitis Elias) dating between LM IIIC and Geometric, that a harbour site existed on the south central coast between Keratokampos and Tsoutsouros, with imports going directly to Arkades, as the nearest settlement, after entering the island (Kanta and Karetsou 1998: 171). Others include the suggestion that the ninth-century metal imports at the Idaean Cave were taken there directly by easterners landing at Kommos (Shaw 1989: 182) or that imports ending up at Eleutherna entered the island at a port site between Panormos and Stavromenos on the coast nearest the site (Stampolidis 1990: 388). In fact, it seems probable that the Knossos harbour area and other large near-coastal settlements, including the Kommos/Phaistos zone and Chania, served as gateways for large quantities of imported value goods, and that indirect dispersal of these items took place from them through exchange and conversion, over various distances and at a variety of social levels. The authors of the first hypothesis outlined above themselves note the large amount of Knossian ceramics at Arkades in the Geometric to Archaic period, suggesting that indirect trade channels account for at least some of the imports reaching the site (Kanta and Karetsou 1998: 171). As early as the late twelfth century, the number of exotic items appearing in tombs at the Knossos North Cemetery suggests that Knossos and its surrounding area was an important articulation point in the exchange of both imported and locally produced goods, and this function never seems to have been lost. Kommos and the Mesara region also show high concentrations of imports and maintained an important role as contact points with the outside world, especially for the Amari valley and Psiloritis area (Kanta 1994). The assemblage from a ninth-century tholos tomb at Gortyn in the Mesara includes eastern imports but also has strong Knossian links in its pottery, suggesting that the important route between the Mesara and Knossos had come back into regular use by this time, facilitating the spread of imports from the gateway settlements through the whole central Cretan area (Coldstream 1979a: 48–9, 271; Negbi 1992: 613). The operation of this axis explains the continuing concentration of imported value goods in central Crete generally, and many luxury goods must have made their way to the farther reaches of the island, especially the east Cretan and Lasithi areas, from this 'core' (Desborough 1972a: 237–8). With so much more at stake in the trade sphere, gateway settlements may have begun to specialise in orchestrating particular trade connections. Chania was another important gateway by the eighth century, strongly linked into the Peloponnesian trade zone (Andreadaki-Vlasaki 2004). In general, the imports at Chania show stronger links with the Aegean, including the Dodecanese, than directly with the Levant. There are strong links between Chaniot material and the pottery from Gela, an early Sicilian colony with traditional links to Crete, showing the importance of this western port to participation in the central Mediterranean trade (Andreadaki-Vlasaki 2004: 33).

We shall see in Part Four that central Crete retained a particularly high number of large inland settlements from the tenth century onwards. Though the basic pattern of settlement here, as elsewhere in the island, was ultimately rooted in the twelfth-century settlement shift, this concentration of successful settlement surely relates to the region's intensive involvement in the exchange (and production) of high-value goods. By the eighth century, in this densely packed and increasingly prosperous environment, more formal, structured roles for different settlements in production and exchange had surely emerged – though the continuing lack of a major ceramic export industry, and the sheer density of settlements, meant they never needed, or were able, to develop distinctive, competing styles of ceramic products. The Knossos and Phaistos/Kommos zones probably still retained a different role from that of the inland sites of the region, in terms of especially intense articulation with the outside world, but internal economic relations and circulation patterns must have become increasingly complex during this period. There are numerous Attic and Cycladic imports at both Gortyn and Phaistos, which might have originally made their way there from Kommos but could also have been traded independently between the two inland sites (Santaniello in press). The Cypro-Phoenician-type lekythoi, as we have seen, were produced at a number of central Cretan centres and moved between them. Tombs around the east Cretan site of Kavousi Kastro contain lekythoi of the same type with an actual Cypriot provenance, which are identical to imports found in central Crete, possibly suggesting a redistributive trade role for the latter region in this commodity (Tsipopoulou 2005a: 540, 544–6). Yet given major discrepancies in circulation patterns of other commodities such as Attic ceramics between the central and eastern zones, direct reliance by individual communities on external supply systems may have stayed stronger in the east than in the central Cretan zone of intensive economic development and interaction.

24 CRETE'S MEMBERSHIP IN THE 'ORIENTALISING' AND COLONIAL WORLDS FROM THE SEVENTH CENTURY

Colonies and quasi-colonies

By the seventh century, Mediterranean trade systems were again developing in new ways. Colonial bases with strong, formal political attachments to individual Aegean and Levantine polities were becoming established in Italy, in south Spain, and on the Black Sea coasts. In the same connection, the popular Aegean trade ceramics were now being made and traded onward in quantity in the central Mediterranean, almost certainly by skilled locals as well as Greeks – moving profits from these goods onto a much larger and more complex scale. The developing colonial economy, with the increased flow of resources, complex organisation, and ethnic/territorial self-awareness it involved, was a major factor in the emergence of small-state structures in the Aegean itself, as well as in the colonial regions (de Polignac 1995: 89–128; Malkin 1994, 1998; Osborne 1998; Sherratt and Sherratt 1993: 362). By the early sixth century, coinages had come into use – very largely, it seems, in order to represent and consolidate the position of these developing states in the expanded trade world (Kraay 1976: 41–55; Sherratt and Sherratt 1993: 374).

The east Aegean region now operated as a closely aligned part of the Greek political and cultural sphere, developing polis-type states. It is hard to view this process of acculturation as directly parallel to the longer-range colonisations in the west, since the region lacked the low-complexity background that sparked economic growth and rapid secondary state development in areas like south Italy. Like Crete (and like the north Aegean) it had been closely linked in cultural and historical terms to the central Aegean world in the Late Bronze Age and already had large communities with fairly complex organisation, strong Aegean contacts, and partly Aegeanised culture from early in the EIA (Boardman 1990: 84–102; Cambitoglou et al. 2001; Cook 1959, 1962; Cook and Nicholls 1998; Cultraro 2004; Nicholls 1959; Papadopoulos 2005: 581–8). Unlike those of Crete, Ionian communities developed their own very active and original export ceramic trade over long and short distances, making them significant colonial players in their own right by the later EIA (Cook and Dupont 1998; Roebuck 1959; Sherratt and Sherratt 1993: 370). In sum, though much of the Mediterranean, from the Phoenician states in the west to the coasts of Sicily, and including Crete, was characterised circa 700 BC by small states with a strong ethnic definition and intense interest in trade, the histories of interaction behind this outcome were all very different, and usually very poorly and inaccurately represented by later colony foundation traditions.

Connections with Egypt and the Dodecanese

By the seventh century, in common with (and via) the inhabitants of Ionia and the Dodecanese, Cretans seem to have been building up especially strong cultural connections with Egypt (the latter now emerging as a stronger Levantine power after Assyria's conquest of the Phoenician states) and forming a cultural and trade bloc with the southeast Aegean fringe. Important connections also continued between Crete and the northern Levant, with imports and cultural influences from that region clearly identifiable in Crete. The Egyptian and Dodecanesian connections proved particularly profitable for the island, and had a strong and long-term impact on its value goods consumption sector. For the rest of the Aegean and Mediterranean world, there is little doubt that in this period Crete became especially associated with Egyptianising cultural features and goods, some of which were soon to be taken up strongly in other parts of the Aegean.

The closeness and scale of links between Egypt and the southeast Aegean are seen in graffiti at Abu Simbel, written by Ionian and Rhodian mercenaries fighting for the pharaoh Psammetichos II in campaigns against Nubia in the early sixth century (Boardman 1990: 114–17; Herodotus 2.152 also refers to Carian and Ionian mercenaries of Psammetichos). Given their strong cultural connections with Egypt and Rhodes, and their geographical proximity to the Egyptian delta, it is possible that Cretans were involved in the region in the same way, though we lack direct evidence. Intensive trade between the southeast Aegean region and the Delta certainly played the main role in the foundation of Naukratis as an isolated Greek trading settlement by the end of the century, heavily dominated by activity from the Rhodian and Ionian polities. Again, this is likely to have brought Cretans into regular, even if often indirect, touch with Egyptian fashions and culture (Boardman 1990: 118–33; Bowden 1996; Cook 1937; Coulson 1996; Möller 2001; Petrie 1886). Naukratis shows clearly how Aegean intercourse with Egypt differed from that with other areas of the Mediterranean: the Egyptian state seems to have been concerned to control and limit the extent of Aegean trade activity via a tightly restricted system of controlled colonies and market points bringing together a number of Aegean players, rather than allowing the most powerful Aegean trade states to stake numerous individual colonial claims, as they did in the west. This potentially left more room for nontypical trade players like Crete to develop relationships with the region, aided by the close proximity of the two areas.

The nature of some other evidence for cultural contact seems to suggest regular travel to/residence in Crete by Egyptians, or those having spent extensive time in Egypt. In keeping with its long-standing attitude to export specialisation and its role as waystation/intermediary, Crete seems to have taken in a lot of Egyptian imports without any obvious direct exports in return, making Cretan travel less visible in the archaeological record. Cretan sanctuaries saw exceptional concentrations of Egyptianising and other easternising bronzes being deposited in the seventh century (Boardman 1961, 1990: 113–14). Small figurines of Egyptian deities such as Sekhmet and Nefertum in ivory or faience, popular all over the Levantine world, had an especially high frequency of consumption in Crete at this time – reflecting Crete's continued role as a stopping point and intermediary in the eastern goods trade, but also suggesting a particularly strong or direct connection to the Egypt-related branches of that trade (Shaw and Shaw 2000: 168–70, 189; Stampolidis 1998; Stampolidis et al. 1998: 146–8; Figures 128 and 129). The figurines' appearance in tombs of a range of wealth levels suggests they moved in a relatively accessible exchange sphere. Especially high concentrations at port sites like Kommos suggest that such goods entered the island through visits by traders – whether Cretan, Aegean, Levantine,

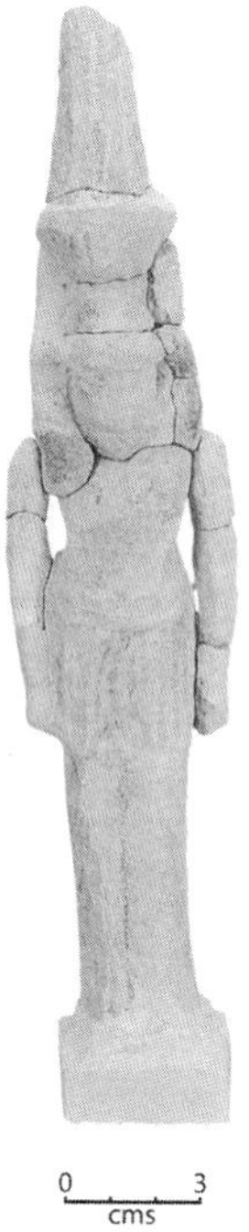

128. Nefertum figurine in faience from Knossos North Cemetery, Tomb 78 (after Stampolidis et al. 1998, Fig. 255, p. 220). By permission of N. Stampolidis.

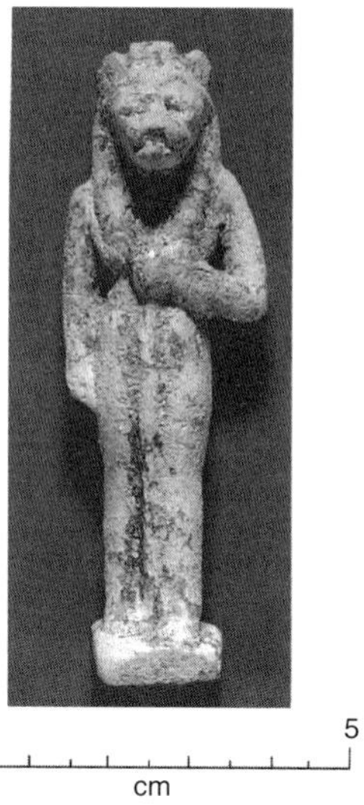

129. Sekhmet figurine in faience from Eleutherna, possibly of Cretan production (after Stampolidis et al. 1998, Fig. 251, p. 219). By permission of N. Stampolidis.

or Egyptian in origin – thence being passed on through local systems. Other popular small Egyptianising items circulating intensively in the southeast Aegean include small faience vessels and scarabs (Hoffman 1997: 86–92; Schwab 2000; Skon-Jedele and Dabney 2000; Stampolidis et al. 1998: 143–8; Webb 1978: 61–136, 1996). Capability in faience production techniques, already on the rise since the Protogeometric period, had now become widespread in the south Aegean, and many such objects were now probably made in Crete or Rhodes themselves. The scale of Rhodian scarab and other faience production of the seventh century, often interpreted as evidence for a so-called scarab factory on the island, seems to represent a very solid and invested-in enterprise, building and exploiting the demand for Egyptianising goods in the Aegean (Boardman 1990: 112; Webb 1978: 9–10). A dedicated scarab workshop also appears at the colony of Naukratis itself in the early sixth century (Boardman 1990: 118–33; Cook 1937: 227). In both cases, Greek craftsmen/traders may have employed, or collaborated very closely with, skilled Egyptian or Levantine workers to boost their skills in the material, but the main demand, initiative, and support for the export industry seem most likely to have been from the Aegean side.

Cretan cult equipment at this time shows especially early and strong links into Egyptian iconography. The dress and hairstyles of humans shown on figurines, plaques, and stone sculpture (whether these represent deities or adorant figures) are all heavily Egyptianising in character, though other aspects of some representations, such as nudity, represent local adaptations of the style (Hatzi-Vallianou 2000; Pernier 1914, 1934; Prent 2005b: 388–92, in press; Rizza and Scrinari 1968: 155–260; Figures 130–2). The fact that Cretans retained their own pantheon, broadly congruent with that of the wider Aegean and tied into their history and identity as part of the Aegean world, suggests that the intensity of cultural links did not lead to the development

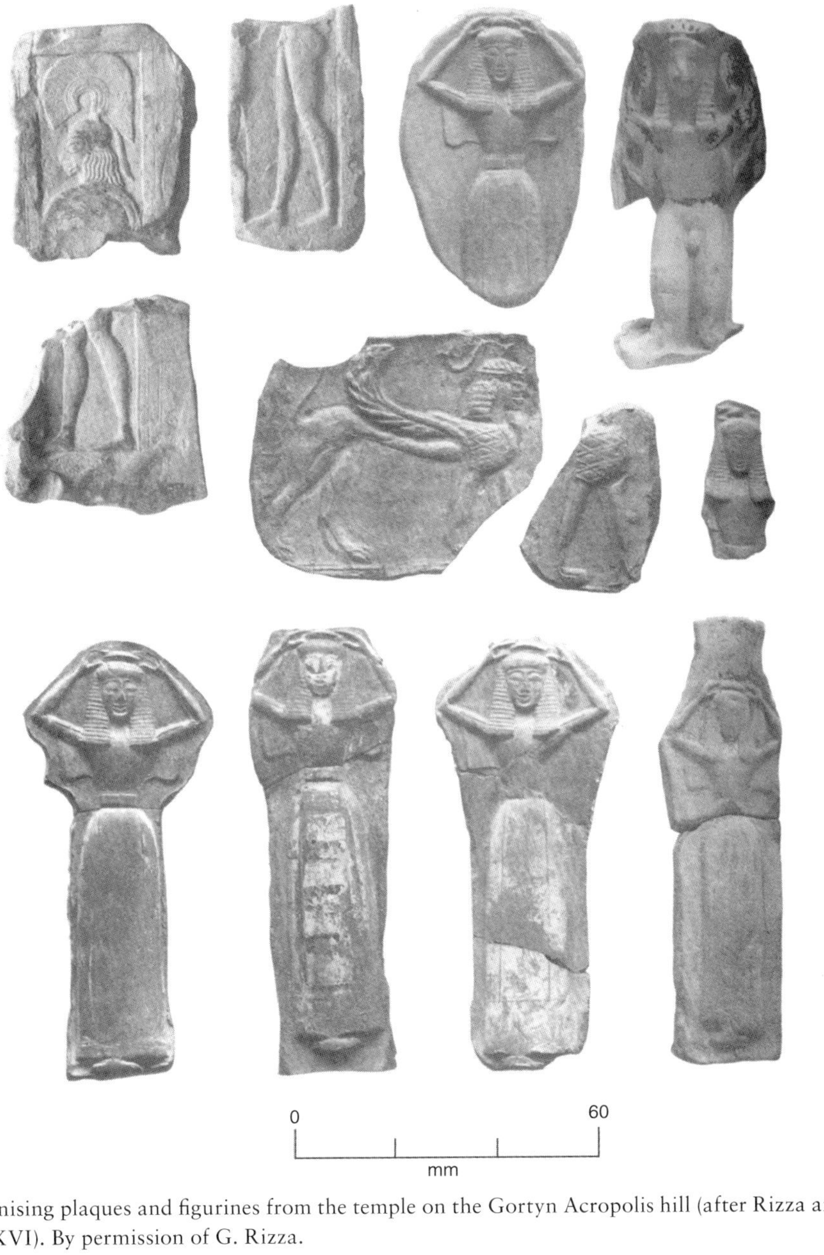

130. Egyptianising plaques and figurines from the temple on the Gortyn Acropolis hill (after Rizza and Scrinari 1968, Tav. XXVI). By permission of G. Rizza.

of any deeply Egyptianised social, political, or religious structures in the island. However, that the links are so early, enthusiastically, and imaginatively exploited in Crete, especially in the emergent sphere of monumental sculpture, does suggest Egyptianising culture was built on to considerable political effect by the developing state authorities. High-investment monumental reliefs and three-dimensional sculpture in a highly Egyptianising ('Daedalic') style are used on the monumental public buildings developing at this period such as Temple A at Prinias (Carter 1997: 87–96; Pernier 1914, 1934; Schäfer et al. 1992: 233; Watrous 1998; Figures 133–5). Similar influences appear from about the same period in mainland Greek stonework, but the particularly early take-up of both stone reliefs and inscriptions in Crete suggests that

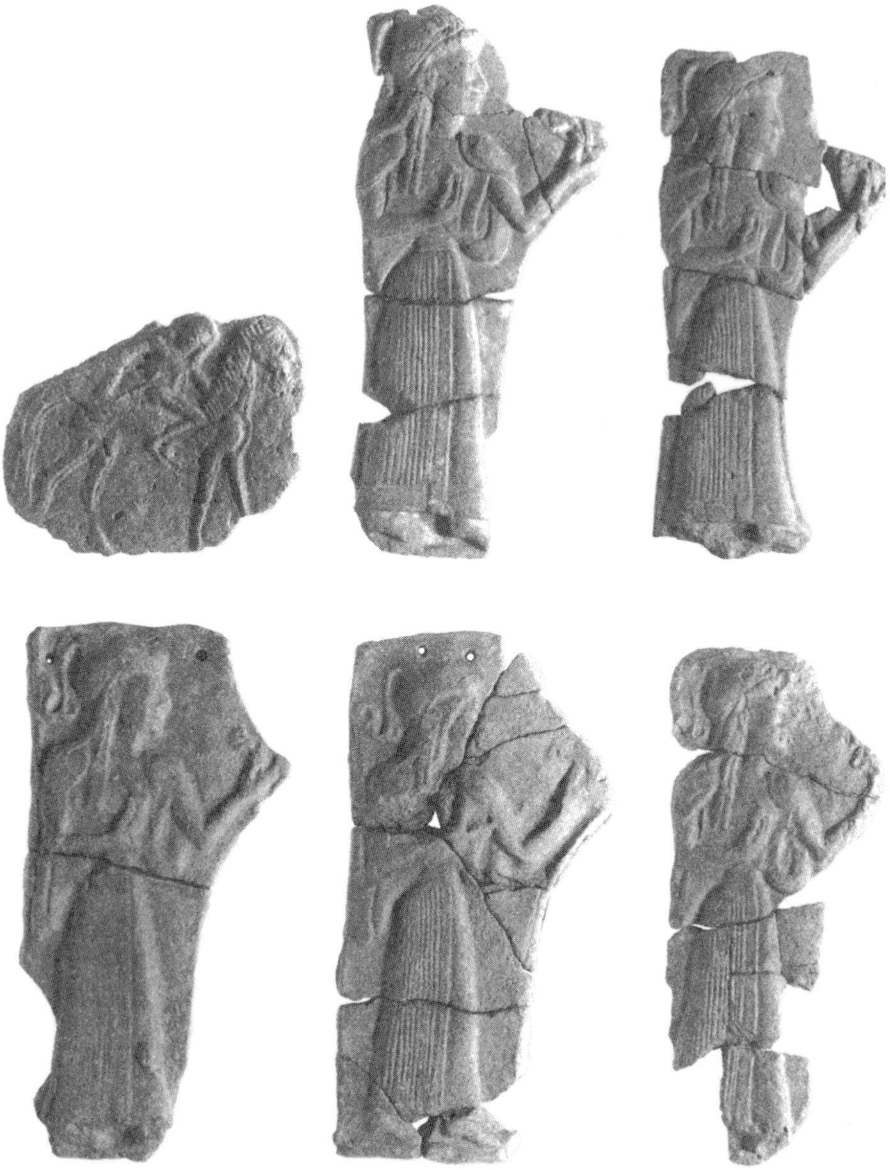

131. Clay plaques from the temple at Smari Profitis Elias (after Hatzi-Vallianou and Evthimiou 2000, Plate 10, p. 535). By permission of D. Hatzi-Vallianou.

the southeast Aegean was a major conduit for this aspect of Archaic culture. The forms seem inspired by Egyptian monumental art in its original contexts, and at least some Aegean masons must have learned the techniques and styles through direct experience in Egypt. Monumental stonework was used in civic temples to symbolise the power and prestige attached to the state; legal inscriptions on stone, again likely to have had an originally oriental inspiration, also appear by the seventh century and belong firmly to the public sphere. It is not surprising to see so many Egyptianising features first being adopted in the cult sphere, given that sanctuaries (of different types) functioned as both major arenas of personal interaction with easterners and statements about the power and legitimacy of early states. Though the Egyptianising trend operated so

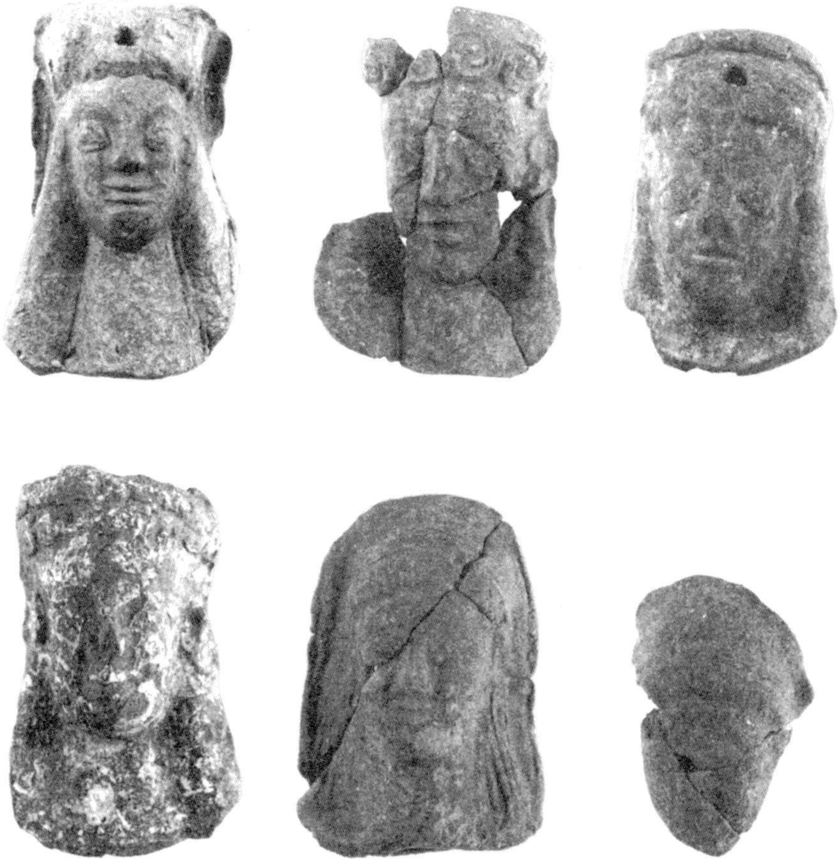

132. Clay protomes from the temple at Smari Profitis Elias (after Hatzi-Vallianou 2000, Plate 8, p. 533). By permission of D. Hatzi-Vallianou.

strongly within the ritual arena, often with public connotations, its spread also into figurative decoration on fine painted pottery and relief pithoi suggests a socially broad interaction and familiarity with Egyptian culture. Evidence for regular *personal* contact, and a more intimate level of cultural interchange and borrowing, between Egypt and the southeast Aegean (though again linked with cult and monumentality, and thus probably occurring at an elite level) is shown by Egyptian statues in basalt and granite transported to Lindos and Kamiros in Rhodes as votive dedications and inscribed in Greek with the names of individual dedicatees, who clearly valued such work highly and accepted at least part of its original symbolism (Blinkenberg 1931: Plate 81; Francis and Vickers 1984; Trölle 1978).

The economic opportunities offered by Cretan links with Rhodes, and by the shared links between both these regions and Egypt, must have been apparent to all sides – Crete was a long-established, centrally positioned intermediary trade hub for the Aegean world (and thus the colonies); Rhodes was a producer of very fashionable and profitable export pottery and had powerful links to the Ionian bloc (Coldstream 1998a). The inhabitants of both islands seem to have participated in the trade economy mostly as intermediaries or small mixed groups of traders, rather than large independent trading and political units. Crete's lack of broad commercial outreach through specialised ceramic exports became less relevant as it built specific connections of this type, allowing growth in its role of intermediary trader. This is seen,

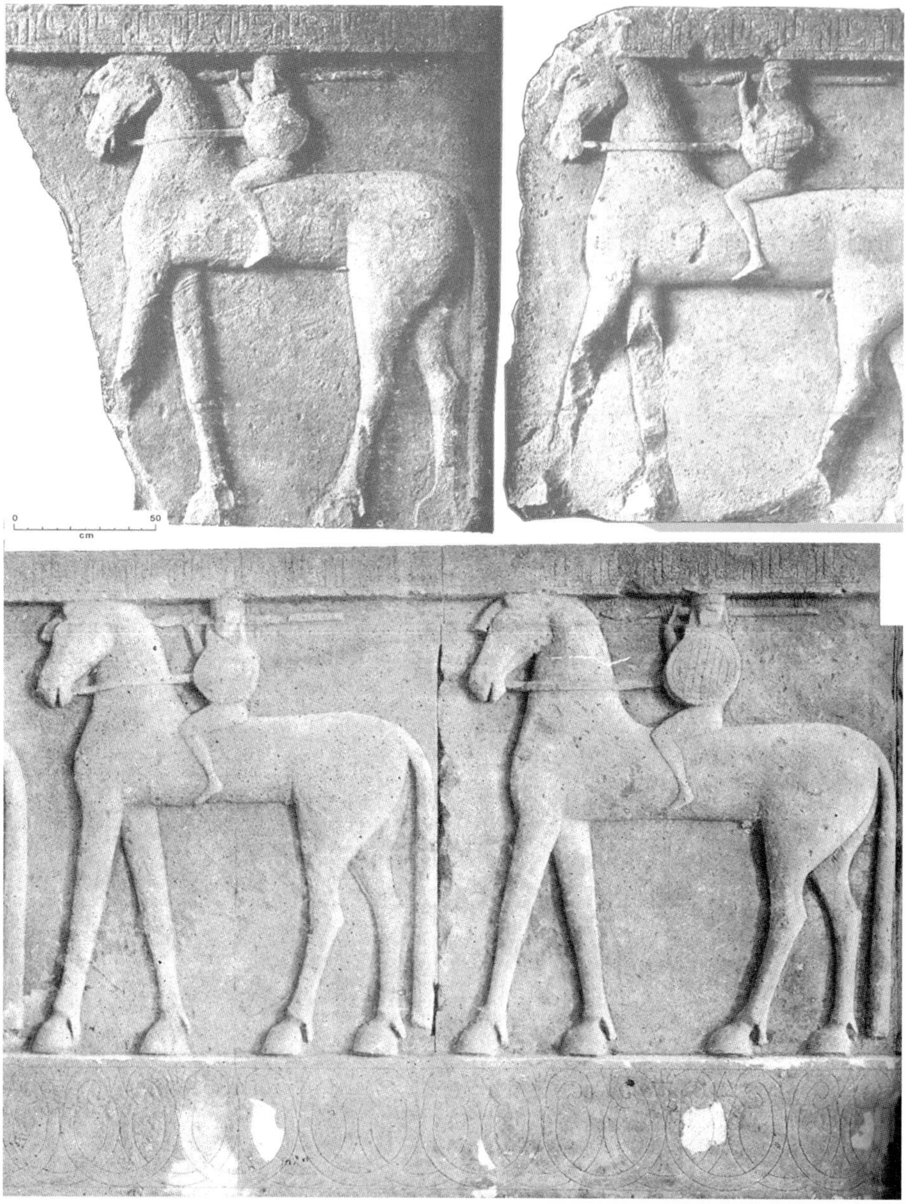

133. Monumental stone reliefs from Prinias Temple A (after Pernier 1914, Plate VIII).

for example, in the colonial arena: the colony of Gela is recorded as having been founded by Cretans and Rhodians together presumably as an outcome of joint trade enterprises. The close physical proximity of Egypt, and the strength of connections there on the part of both Crete and Rhodes, opened up special opportunities for trade along the north African coast. These also had 'compromise' types of colonial outcome: Cretans are seen in trade partnership with Therans, Rhodians, and others in the foundation of a trading base and eventually a colony at Cyrene (Boardman 1982: 224–5, 1990: 153–9; Herodotus 7.171). Other points on this coast, like Tocra, obtained Cretan pottery in a minority among a range of other Aegean wares, including Rhodian and Spartan (Boardman and Hayes 1966: 14, 78–9, 1973: 36–7, 73). Again, it seems likely that Cretans often marketed the popular central and eastern Aegean ceramic

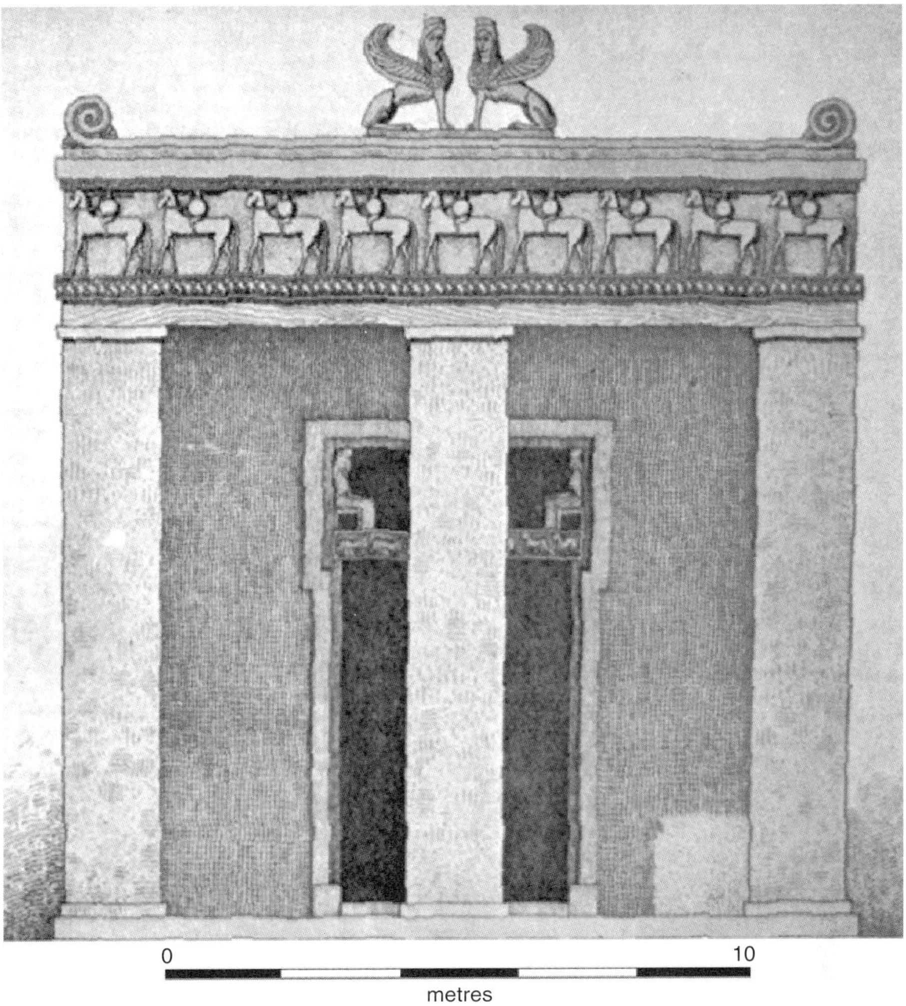

134. Reconstructions of the positioning of the Prinias Temple A stone reliefs (after Pernier 1934, Plate XIX).

exports rather than their own products, and that no substantial foreign trading/colonial settlement was exclusively linked to Crete.

Some comparisons with other Aegean regions

Given the close links noted above, it is interesting to compare Crete at this period with the east Aegean polities in terms of political and economic structure. Both groups were heavily tied into Levantine trade and political interests and had a partly orientalised culture – yet were integrated into, or operated in parallel with, Aegean social and economic systems from a date early in the EIA. Ionian societies used the advantage of their close eastern contacts in a very 'Aegean' way, engaging in a specialised export ceramic trade with the east. When state-level polities emerged in Ionia, they did so at about the same time as in the central Aegean, in association with a set of marked cultural changes similar to those of the latter region. As we shall see in Part Four, complex polities in Crete developed at a different rate and in a different way.

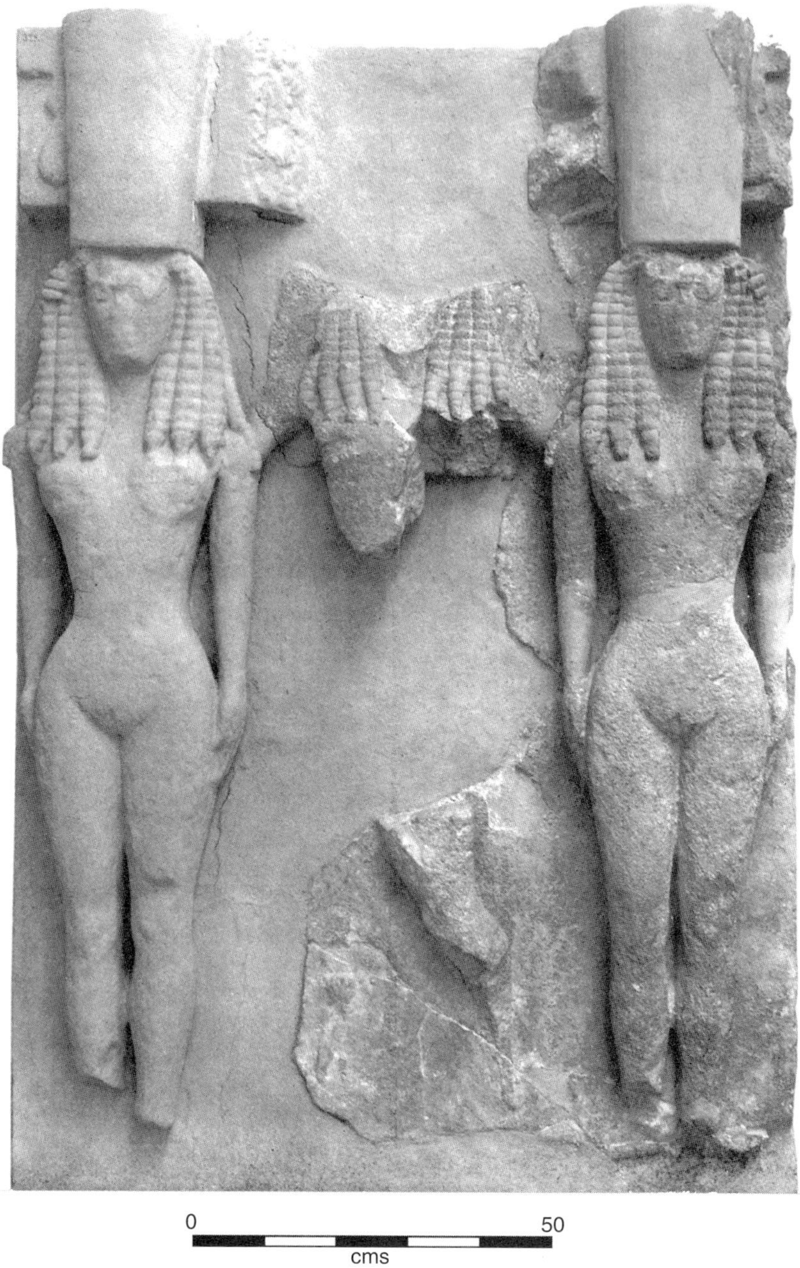

135. Egyptianising stone sculpture from the temple on the Gortyn Acropolis hill (after Rizza and Scrinari 1968, Tav. IV [9]).

These contrasts remind us that simple proximity to the east Mediterranean core and/or high levels of orientalising cultural 'influence' or 'contact' did not solely or predictably direct the course of any area's political and economic development. We have seen that Crete's specific history and culture, from the period of its successful collapse onwards, strongly influenced the way it developed contacts with the east. We should not be misled by the extreme orientalising culture of the island in the seventh century – which is in fact mainly a continuation and expansion, under changing wider conditions, of its established eclecticism and openness with regard to the consumption of eastern luxury goods from a point early in the EIA – to treat the island as more fully part of the 'oriental' than the 'Aegean' world in a political and social sense in the early state period. The polarization is anyway meaningless, since 'the east' was not a static or cohesive political unit. At the same time, Crete did clearly retain a markedly different trajectory of interaction with the world of trade from many of its central Aegean peers (even while interacting closely and regularly with the latter).

As specialised exports from other Aegean regions circulated the Mediterranean at an ever-increasing scale, it is ultimately unsurprising that Cretan societies spent little or no effort in developing this aspect of trade – as latecomers, they would find it hard to make headway. In the sixth and fifth centuries, however, the balance changed again, as a trade in bulk subsistence goods grew up in the Mediterranean (Garnsey and Morris 1989: 100; Sherratt and Sherratt 1993: 371–4). Crete, which had presumably already offered these products to passing trade in a provisioning capacity, now began exporting wine and oil to the Aegean in larger quantities. Its earlier history of trade collaborations may have helped drive this move, in that Rhodes was heavily involved in the same trade (Marangou 1999; Viviers 1999). Cretan coinages appear from the fifth century – later than in Ionia, the central Aegean, or the Italian colonies (Stefanakis 1999). This delay is almost certainly linked to Crete's less-intense involvement than its central and east Aegean neighbours in the specialised ceramic trade, and to the less individually polis-centred nature of Cretan trading activities abroad (further discussed in Part Four). The final emergence of coinage may well have been stimulated by a newly developing trade role in the area of bulk goods.

Despite Crete's differences from other Aegean regions, it was closely bound up with a central cultural development in the Greek world at this period – the emergence of writing. Greek alphabetic script, a feature clearly linked in its earliest appearance to trading contexts, appears as early here as in other areas of the Aegean, and possibly earlier. The site of Kommos, like other coastal sanctuaries of the seventh century, has pots with inscriptions dating in the LG-A period (Csapo et al. 2000; Johnston in press; Figure 136). Many of these inscriptions mainly serve to identify provenance and maker, being inscribed before firing, usually on amphoras. However, inscriptions on cups include personal names of dedicatees; one such inscription on a hydria occurred after firing. The scripts and names used confirm the use of the port by travellers and traders from all over the Aegean but mainly represent central Greek areas – Attica, Boeotia, and Locris among them. Two look more like local Cretan scripts. Kommos, which was distinguished by its heavy volume of Phoenician trade and associated high levels of integration with Phoenician culture, yet was clearly also an important node of intra-Aegean interaction, is likely to have been one of the earliest venues in which the Greek alphabet was developed (probably through adaptation of the recording systems used by Phoenician visitors) and thence spread via deep and continuous links with the wider Greek trade world.

Conclusions

External links and contacts had very varied and subtle effects on Aegean societies in the period prior to and during polis state emergence, with long-term implications. Development of these links fed into societies' self-conception and conditioned their geopolitical standing. Crete's special history of cultural and social development in the early EIA, and its geographical position, both help explain its always-distinctive role with regard to external interactions through the

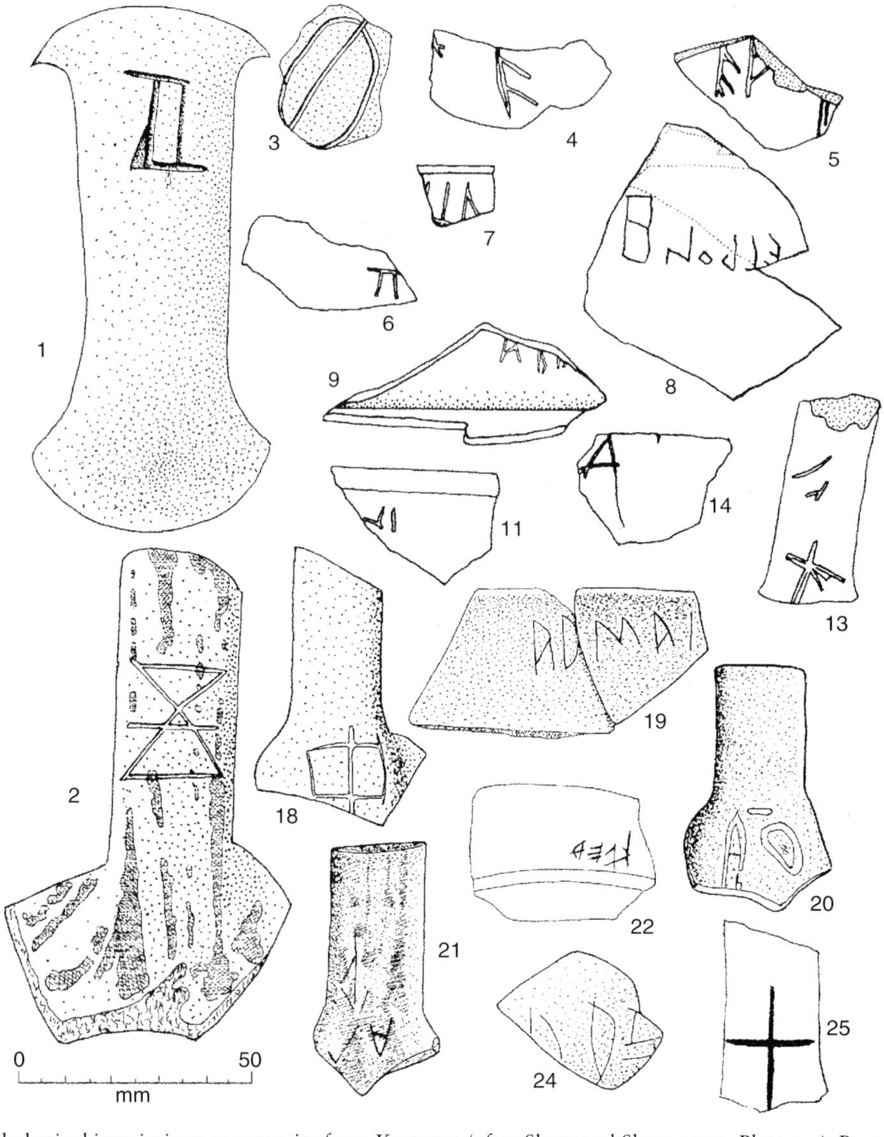

136. Alphabetical inscriptions on ceramics from Kommos (after Shaw and Shaw 2000, Plate 2.1). By permission of J. W. Shaw and M. C. Shaw.

later EIA and into early Archaic times. Special features of this history include the established existence in the island since the early EIA of multiple, small, independent, yet similar community units. This may have held back the emergence of any single marketable 'Cretan' cultural identity in both internal and external perceptions. On the other hand, Crete's sustained divergence from central Greek trends with regard to trade relationships encouraged the growth of certain generalised perceptions about the island among its peers, which themselves affected the nature of its economic interactions. Sherratt has noted that Crete and the Cretans seem to have held a rather ambiguous status with regard to the emerging pan-Hellenic identity reflected in Homer and other texts by the eighth century, and that this was almost certainly linked to Crete's strong eastern connections (Sherratt 1996). I have shown here that it was not only especially close relationships with the east, but a particular set of attitudes to commodity trade in general, that set Crete apart.

PART FOUR

'Proto-poleis'? The growth of social complexity in Crete from the tenth through the seventh centuries

25 MAIN SOURCES OF EVIDENCE DISCUSSED

This chapter investigates a whole set of cultural and social changes occurring from the tenth century onward which constitute a formative horizon in the development of small states in Crete. A qualitative change occurred in the nature of community self-conception at this time that is not paralleled in central Greece – though, as we have seen, there are indicators of social change in the latter area also in this period, including shifts in burial practice and the growth of interregional sanctuaries. Conversely, though all Aegean regions see very significant cultural shifts at around 700 BC, the usually recognised horizon of polis emergence, these were significantly *less* radical in Crete than in central Greece.

The tenth-century cultural 'watershed' in Crete, and its political implications, have not been isolated or discussed in any previous analysis, greatly restricting our understanding of this seminal period in the island's history. The record from this point shows a number of features typically linked to emergent complexity in ancient societies – settlement nucleation, territory expansion and formalisation, subsistence expansion, manufacturing growth, increased import consumption, port and exchange route development, and changed emphases in social systems, indicated by altered mortuary practice. But the growth of complexity in this case is by no means a straightforward or predictable process, and has its own special characteristics. One of these is an important counterpoint pattern to the dominant settlement nucleation phenomenon – the continued existence of small defensible sites, often with a coastal orientation, into the eighth or early seventh century. Echoed in the Cyclades, this pattern may reflect special interests in eastern trade routes and a continued need for secure topography in connection with trade, but also suggests a special role for small-group, place-focused identity structures within the emergent state. Another special feature is the role played by an awareness of recent, as well as more remote, semimythic history in building the emergent Cretan state, by moulding the strong collective self-consciousness that underpinned it. The evidence for this includes various kinds of tomb and settlement reuse, and the nature of choices made about cult locations, in the PG to early Archaic periods. I discuss some parallels in meaning between these practices and central Greek customs like 'tomb cult', much described in the literature and usually seen as reflecting new concerns with asserting small-group identity at the period of state formation.

Other special features are seen in the mortuary data from tenth- to seventh-century Crete, but have not yet been addressed in relation to social systems in any thorough or wide-ranging way. Their detailed analysis and discussion here make an important contribution to my argument for major social changes from the tenth century onward. A pattern of large-group burials in single tombs starting in this period suggests that kin-group identities were being drastically redefined and newly asserted. One effect of this seems to have been to prevent emergent large-scale public institutions from marginalising kin-group power, which had been a core element in the cohesion of Cretan societies in the immediate post-collapse period.

26 SETTLEMENT PATTERNS (1): THE NUCLEATION PHENOMENON

Introduction: what settlement pattern tells us

While the defensible site pattern of the twelfth to eleventh centuries has by now been well researched, the history of Cretan settlement between the PG and early Archaic periods remains poorly investigated and theorised. Until the start of recent large-scale excavations at Azoria, few scholars had systematically tried to explore the roots of the Cretan polis as a settlement entity. A long-term project at Prinias remains unpublished in any detailed way, while work at Thronos and Praisos has been small-scale (Haggis et al. 2004, 2007a, 2007b; Haggis and Mook in press; Nowicki 2000: 245–7; Rizza 1991, 2000, 2006; Rizza and Rizzo 1984; Rocchetti 2000. 2006). This situation has discouraged any attempt at detailed, sophisticated interpretation of the Cretan polis and its roots. Though some brief overviews have been essayed, they leave many questions open. Lack of grounding in the data makes Whitley's model (discussed earlier) of an evolutionary process toward the state through the course of the EIA, predicated on the notion of 'stable' and 'unstable' settlements, unconvincing. Recently, Haggis et al. (2004: 340) have argued for a single main phase of settlement change associated with polis emergence – nucleation in large polities in the late eighth/early seventh century. I shall argue that this is only partially right. While change does occur at this period, it is heavily conditioned by an earlier horizon of nucleation, associated with significant political and economic changes, from the PG period. The model of Haggis et al. is partly based on the date of the last phase of use of a minority type of small site, which I discuss later. Osborne's attempt to discuss Cretan EIA settlement change (simply arguing for 'more settlements' in Crete from the eighth century on, and thereby a parallel of sorts with mainland developments) is based on an extremely small, poorly published, and unrepresentative tranche of data and is so superficial as to be misleading (Osborne 1996: 70–1). In terms of synthetic overviews of settlement, the generalisation put forward by Willetts, which assumes a top-down, managerial, and instrumentalist model of social change and marginalises the relevance of earlier Iron Age history and archaeology, is ironically one of the least controversial: 'The more inaccessible refuge sites were eventually abandoned after about 800 BC. Others, more conveniently situated, were developed into city states' (Willetts 1969: 87–8; see also Boardman 1982: 774; van Effenterre 1991). However, enough data now exist, from survey and excavation combined, to identify diachronic patterns of settlement change in a much more sensitive way, both at regional and at cross-island level, and thereby greatly improve our historical understanding.

As the scale and volume of commodity production developed from the tenth century on, Cretan communities seem likely to have extended their subsistence base to support more craft specialists. This could be done through taking in more territory, using territory more intensively, or specialising in particular crops for local exchange (as I noted earlier, long-distance bulk subsistence exchange is little evidenced before the sixth century). All the above responses would involve increased levels of investment and specialisation, promoting the emergence of more complex and unequal social relations. Together with involvement in the growing trade economy (requiring more intensive off-island and port-centred activity) these changes would lessen the efficiency and relevance of the pattern of small, dispersed, and inaccessible inland settlements established in LM IIIC. Observable patterns of settlement change from PG onward support these general predictions, though they are more complex, and more chronologically and regionally variant, than a simple urbanisation model would predict (Morgan 2003: 105). In contrast, despite its expanding economy during the same period, mainland central Greece saw no very radical settlement changes until the late eighth century, while Cycladic developments more closely parallel some of those in Crete. The rate and nature of settlement change seem strongly connected to the way each region had collapsed around 1200 BC. The particular spatial mould created by Crete's 'successful' collapse seems to have proved restrictive as the new conditions for growth developed. In the mainland, both physical and structural expansion had more room to take place, at large sites already well placed for communications and trade, and in what were probably more loosely institutionalised communities. The scale and orientation of the Cycladic economy constrained settlement options in their own particular ways throughout the period.

Nucleation and expansion: new priorities in settlement

An up-to-date review of evidence from across the island suggests that a strong degree of settlement nucleation took place somewhere in the Early Protogeometric period (Figure 137). Settlement change may have slightly preceded the main growth of import trade discussed in Part Three. The process seems to have been a gradual one, however, with the main shift of population not completed in many regions until the end of the century. It appears that more than 50 percent of all known sites established in LM IIIC went out of use within the PG period. Few or no new sites of any substantial size seem to have been founded at this time, or at any other point until the seventh century, showing how strongly decisions made at the collapse period drove subsequent cultural and social developments. Continued use of and expansion at, the selected sites from 1200 BC all the way through to the Archaic period is indicated by continuous pottery sequences, some of which are illustrated in Figures 138–41. The fact that so few sites of this type are excavated or well published, and that so much of the dating material is from survey, makes detailed reconstruction of the development of occupation there difficult. However, better-quality documentation from some sites allows the more limited data from many others to be put in contex: On balance, where any large site dating in LM IIIC also has substantial PG-early Archaic material, use is very likely, on the overall balance of evidence, to have been continuous.

A significant expansion of settlement size often occurred at these sites between the PG and early Archaic periods. The excavated settlements of Prinias, Azoria, Gortyn, and Thronos demonstrate this well, as does the distribution of surface material in other cases. At Gortyn, the LM IIIC settlement area on the summit of the 'Acropolis' hill continued in use until Late Geometric,

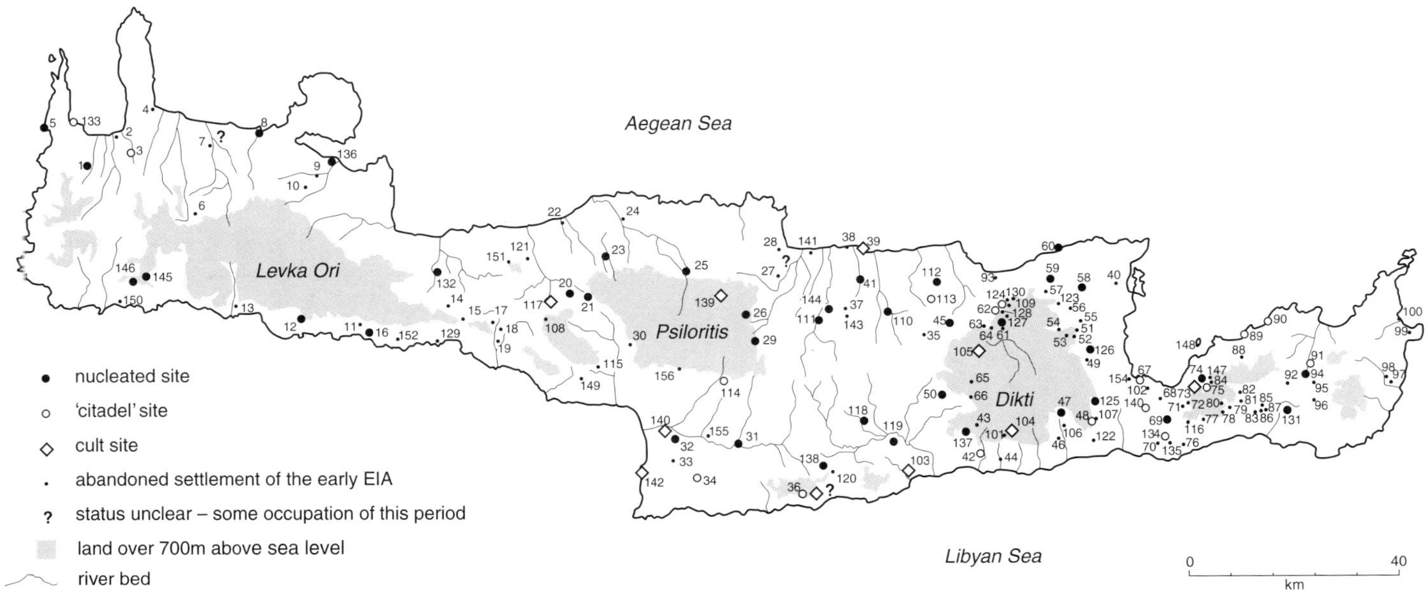

137. Map of Cretan sites occupied in the PG-early Archaic periods. Image by the author.

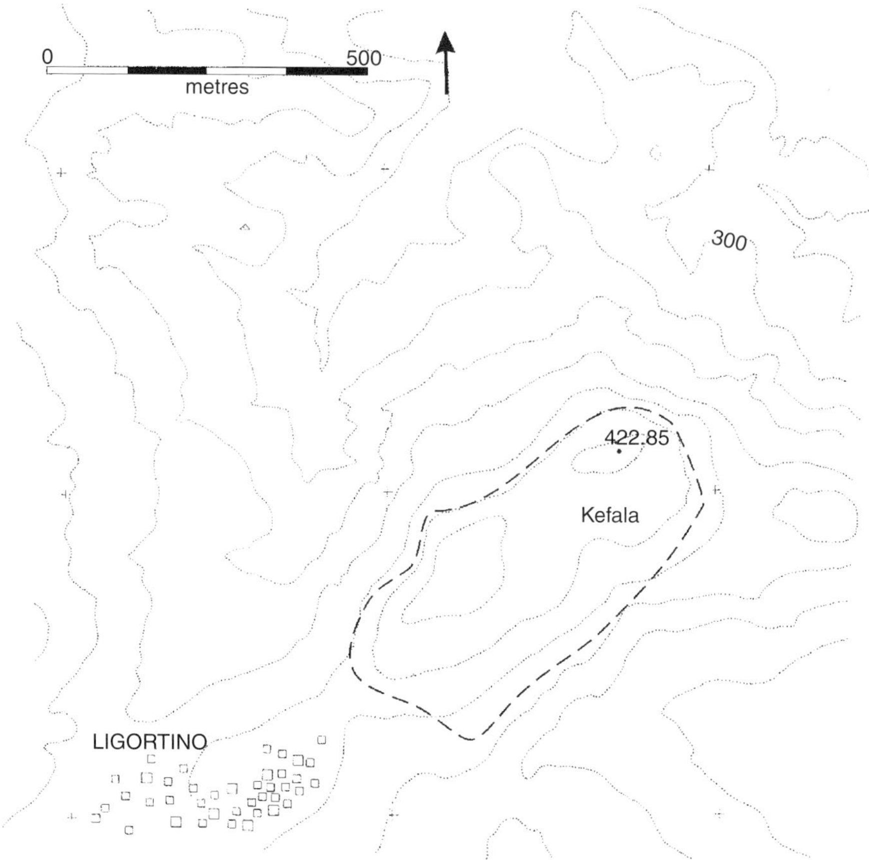

138. Plan of the sherd scatter area at Ligortinos Kefala, showing approximate site size by the latest period of use. Image by the author.

but by the same period the settlement had also spread out over a much wider area, including the summit of Profitis Elias to the east, the Armi ridge, and probably part of the plain to the south, with PG-G material noted around the Odeion, for example (Allegro 1991; Di Vita 1991; Johnannowsky 2002: 108–16; Perlman 2000; Rizza and Scrinari 1968: 4–63; Figure 142). At Prinias, spread of settlement material over much of the top and slopes of the hill occurred by the G-O period: in contrast, stratified LM IIIC-SM material is seen only in some places on the summit (Rizza 1983; Rizza and Rizzo 1984: 143). At Thronos Kefala, excavations under Geometric buildings on some parts of the site, such as the east summit, show they were founded on virgin soil, while other structures overlie LM IIIC-PG predecessors (D'Agata 2002, pers comm; Rocchetti 2000, 2006; Rocchetti et al. 1994, 1995). By the Archaic period a process of expansion was still under way, with settlement spreading over the north and south slopes of the hill (Belgiorno 1994: 205–6). The PG-early Archaic size of Praisos, where only very limited settlement seems to have existed during the twelfth to eleventh centuries (the defensible Kalamafki Kipia being the main site in the vicinity at this period) was circa eighteen hectares (Whitley et al. 1999: 247). At Azoria the final (fifth-century) size of the settlement looks to be at least fifteen hectares, though excavation suggests a much smaller spatial limit for LM IIIC-SM occupation, with EIA occupation in general estimated at six hectares (Haggis 1993: 148–9; Haggis et al. 2004: 341). By PG-G, the size of the Phaistos settlement is estimated at fifty hectares, spreading

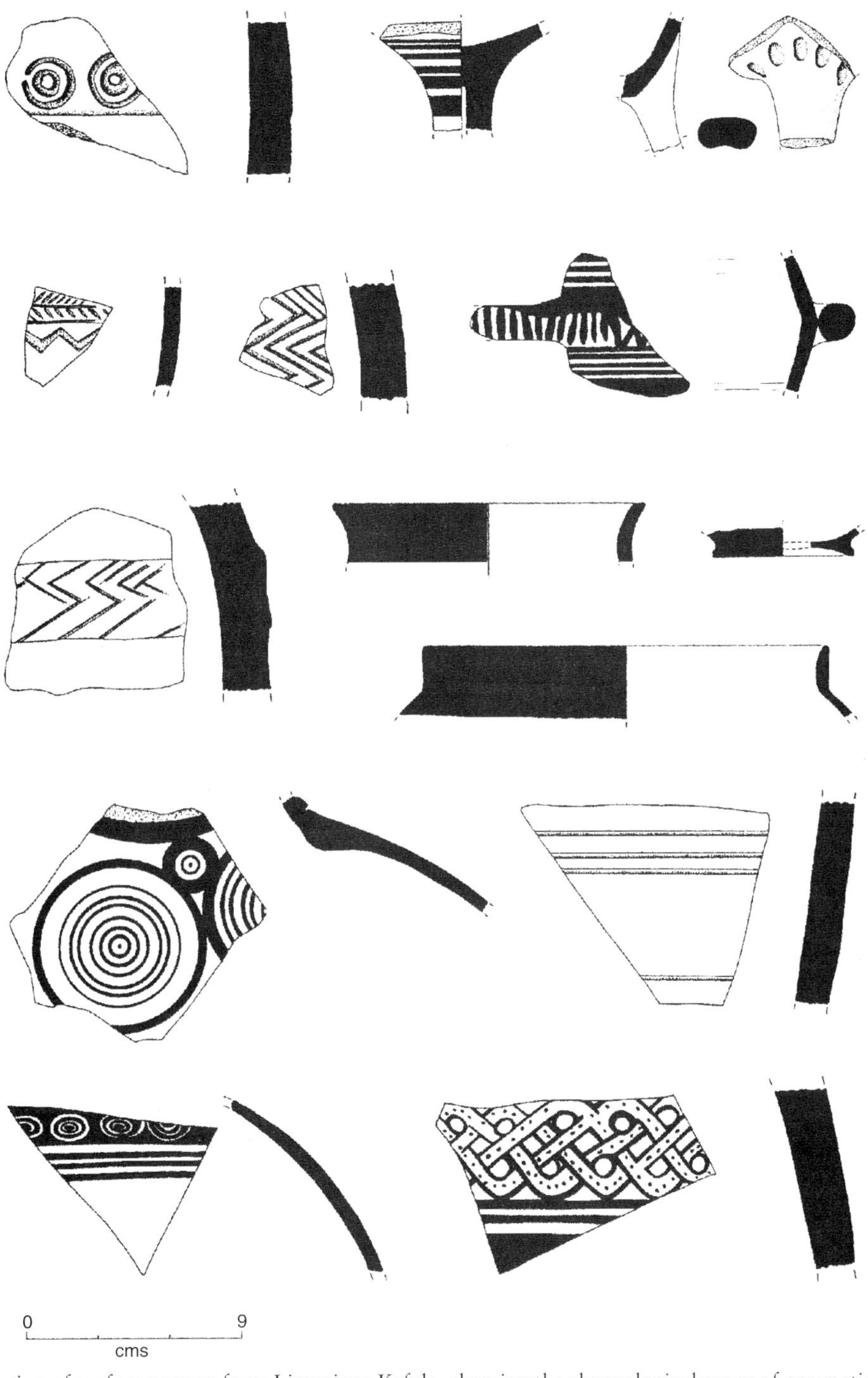

139. Selection of surface pottery from Ligortinos Kefala, showing the chronological range of occupation. Image by the author.

well beyond the Acropoli Mediana area, which seems to have formed the core of the LM IIIC settlement (Watrous and Hadzi-Vallianou 2004b: 342; Figure 143). Assuming the same kind of architectural density observed in LM IIIC settlements (which was not necessarily the case, though excavations do suggest that large sites of this period had densely packed agglomerative

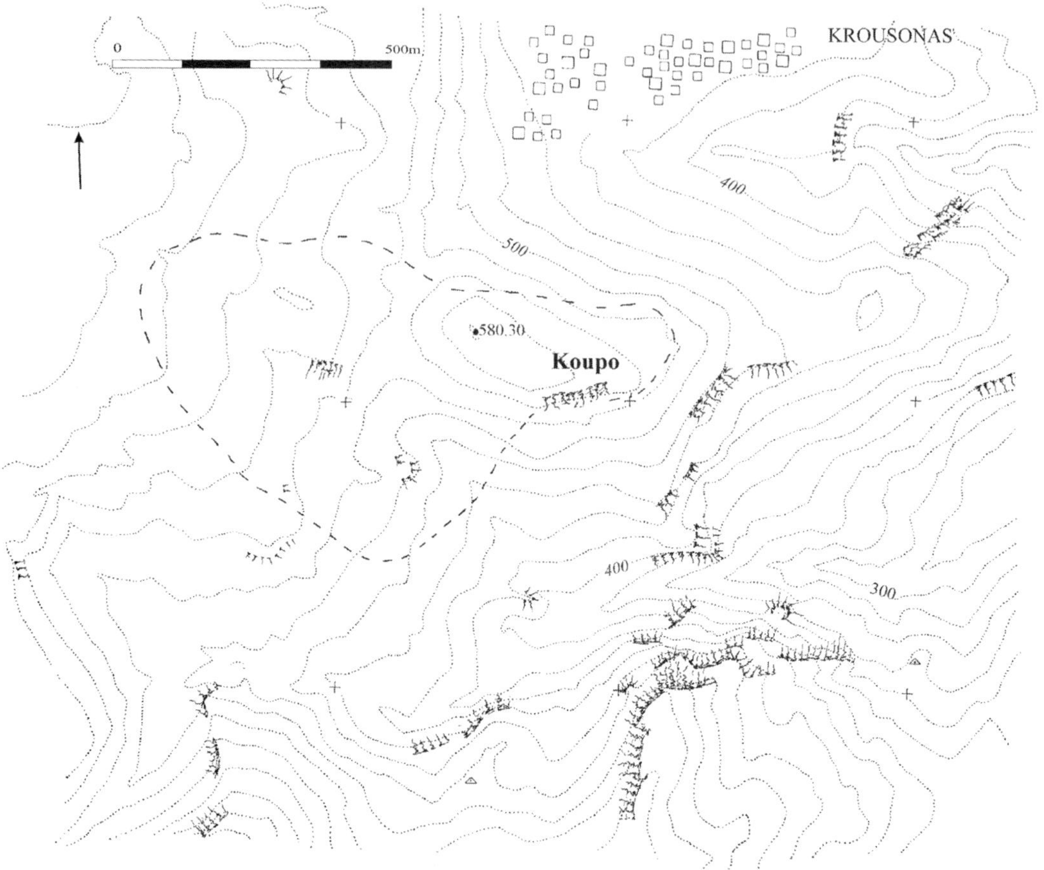

140. Plan of the sherd scatter area at Krousonas Koupo, showing approximate site size by the latest period of use. Image by the author.

architecture), these last two sites could have housed 6,000 and 13,000 people, respectively, by the Archaic period. We have seen that the largest size for sites used in the twelfth to tenth centuries only was about three to four hectares, housing 1,000 to 2,000 people at most. Room for expansion, then, would seem to have been one of the most important factors in selecting sites for continued occupation.

Nucleation seems to have been a deliberate, selective, and broadly contemporaneous, rather than scattered or random, process. It happened in all regions of the island, and the sites chosen had strong linking characteristics. So, too, did the abandoned sites, which were usually those of the most defensible type – rocky knolls or high ridges, inaccessible from the largest areas of arable land in their immediate area. Their hinterlands often contain large areas of steeply sloping land and limited quantities of prime arable. Karfi is a representative example of such a site. Its assemblage barely dates into the PG period, when it seems to have been abandoned for nearby Papoura, a lower, larger, and more accessible flat-topped hill dominating the major natural route into the Lasithi plain along the Ambelos pass. Excavated and surface material here dates between the twelfth and sixth centuries (Nowicki 2000: 167–70; Wallace in press c; Watrous 1980; Figure 144). In contrast, Monastiraki Chalasmeno, which shows no continuation into Protogeometric and was probably abandoned in favour of the nucleated settlement at Azoria, lacks the extreme topography of Karfi – so does the nearby Kavousi Vronda, abandoned

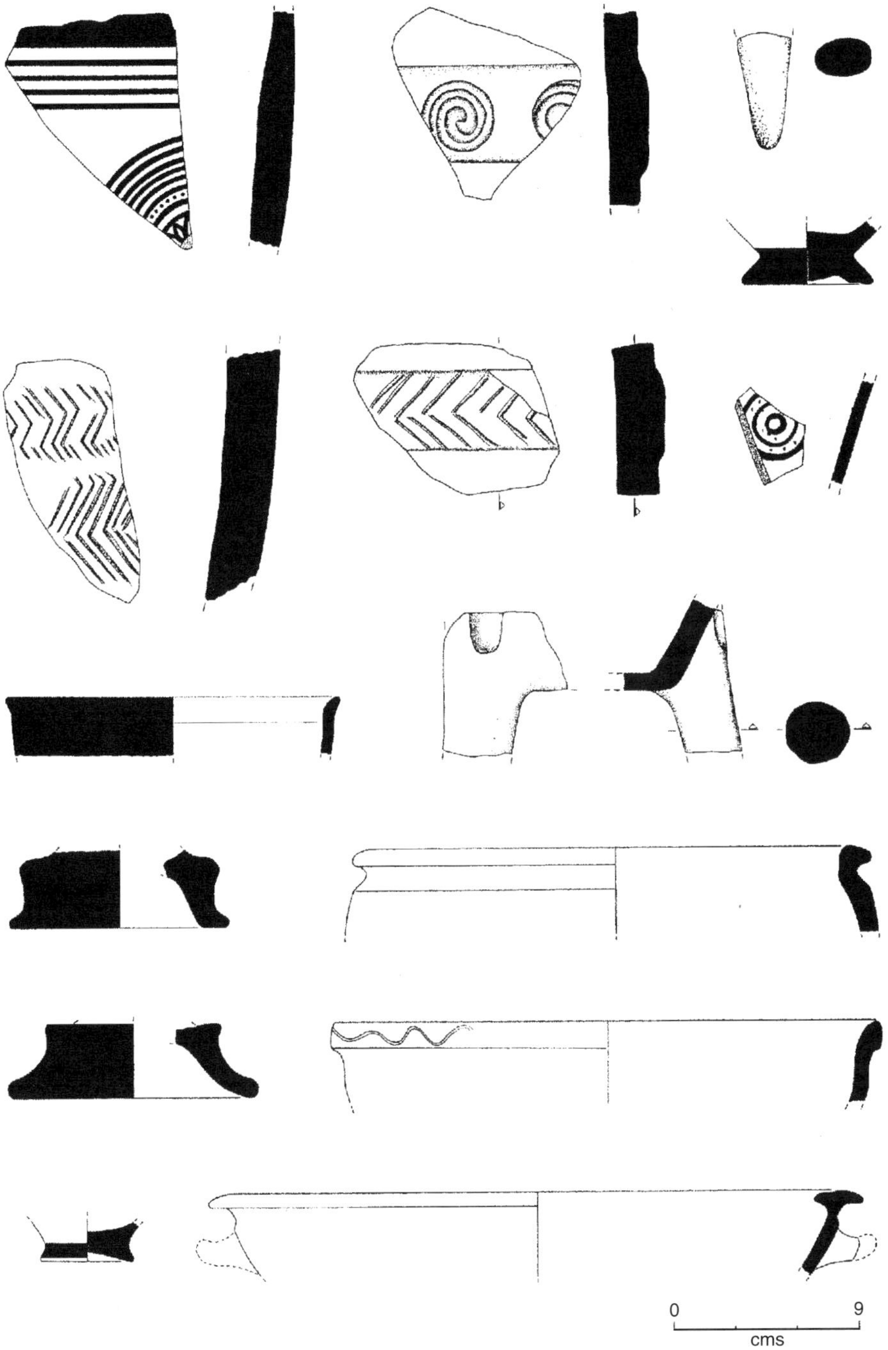

141. Selection of surface pottery from Krousonas Koupo, showing the chronological range of occupation. Image by the author.

at the same time. Yet like Karfi, both sites do lack space for significant settlement expansion beyond the LM IIIC settlement size. In contrast again, the large defensible/fortified LM IIIC sites of Kritsa Kastello and Loutraki Kandilioro were both abandoned by PG, even though they *did* possess fair room for expansion and had easy access to nearby arable zones. A range of other

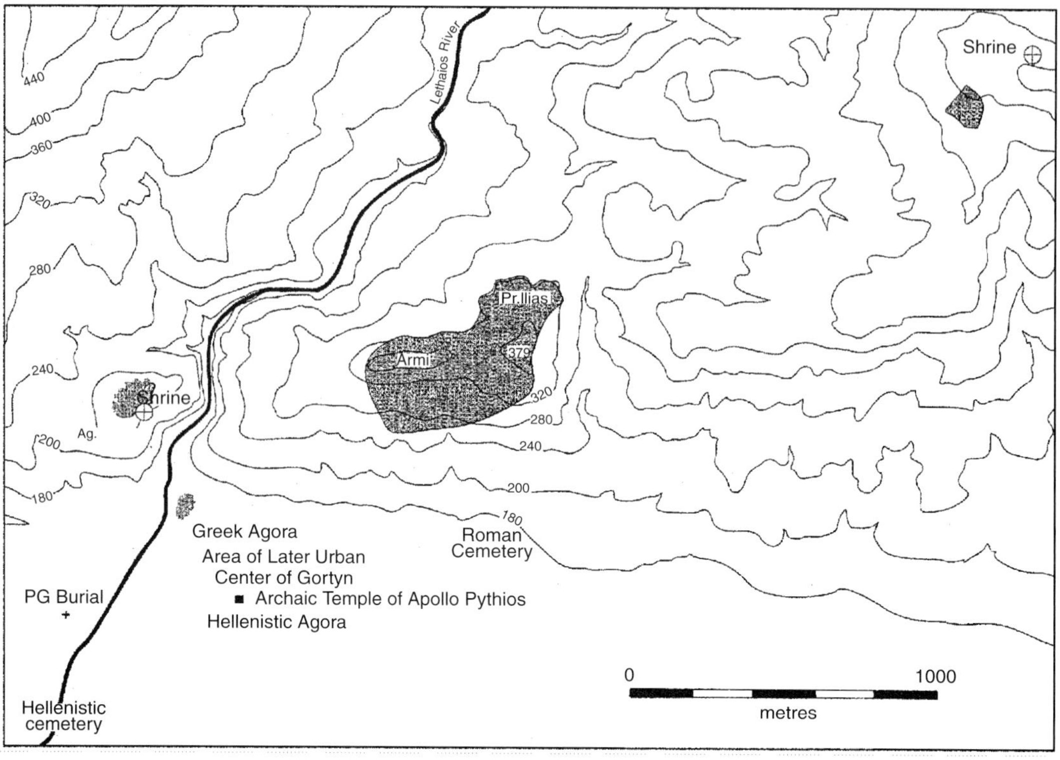

142. Map of the Gortyn area, showing remains dating to different periods and indicating the site's expansion over the course of the EIA (after Allegro 1991, Fig. 2, p. 323).

considerations, alongside the factor of room for expansion, were clearly relevant when selecting locations for continuing settlement (Nowicki 2000: 123–5, 136–8).

One of these was communications. While much of the LM IIIC settlement pattern already had regard to protecting and overseeing communication routes, settlements continuing in the Protogeometric through the Archaic were all directly sited *on* or very easily accessible *from* major routes, commanding easy access to notably large arable and political territories (Belgiorno 1994: 224; Hayden 1995: 93, 2005: 171–6; Kanta 1994). Usually large flattish-topped hills in open or rolling landscapes, they also provided a highly visible and accessible focal point for a potentially extensive territory (Figures 145–52). Exemplifying the increased concern with access to routes and communications generally are the locations of Thronos Kefala in the Amari valley, a major transit route; Praisos, dominating the most direct route between north and south coasts in the east Cretan peninsula; Kato Chorio Profitis Elias, located at the midpoint of the Ierapetra isthmus; and Arkades/Afrati Profitis Elias, standing at an important crossroads in central Crete. Similar locations are shared by Lyttos, Kalo Chorio Maza, and Profitis Elias Rokka/Korifi, alongside many other sites in the central region (Lebessi 1969, 1970; Levi 1929: 15–31; Nowicki 2000: 175–8; Wallace 2002, 2003b, in press b, in press c; Watrous 2001). In west Crete, Axos dominates the important Mylopotamos valley route linking the north central area to the Rethymnon isthmus, and Polirinia controls a major access route inland in the far west (Nowicki 2000: 192–3, 221–2); the latter's history of EIA occupation is very uncertain, and here, as in the case of Lyttos, I rely on Nowicki's dating of surface material. On the western coast, Falasarna, apparently in use from LM IIIC right through PG-EA and beyond, lacks some of the other most characteristic attributes of continuing sites (very extensive prime arable hinterland, space for expansion, accessibility). This suggests that these considerations could sometimes be made up

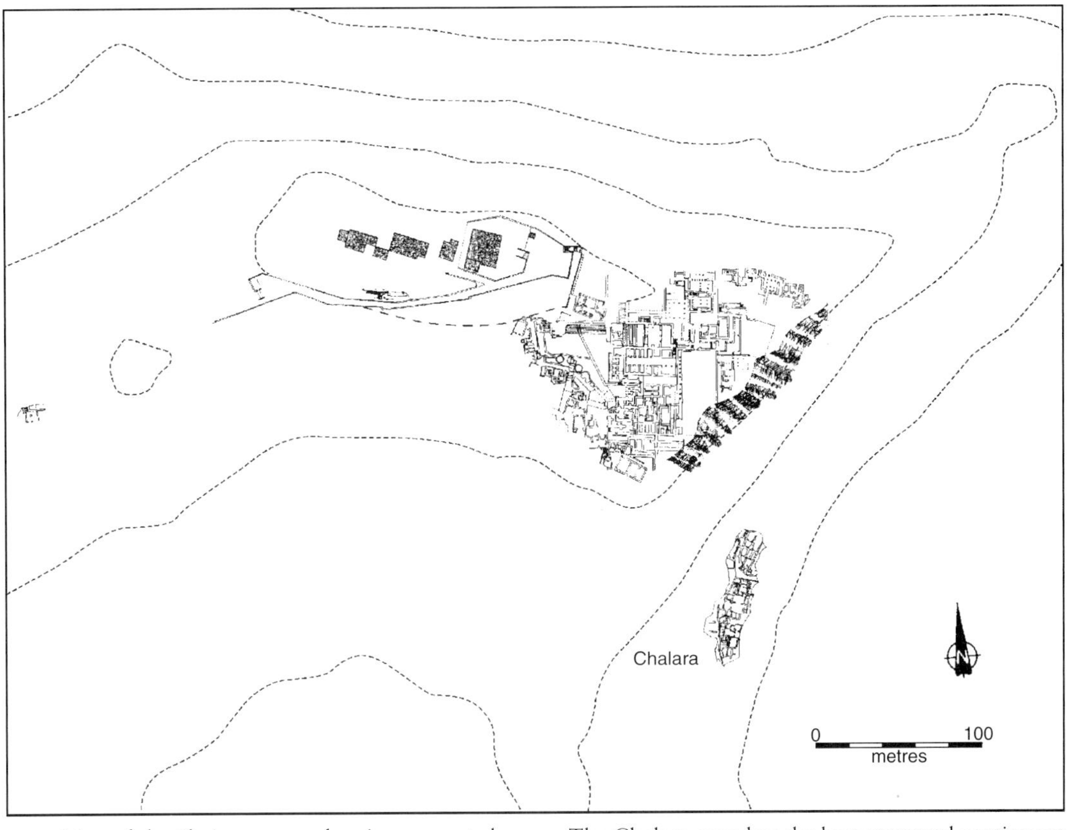

143. Map of the Phaistos area, showing excavated zones. The Chalara area has the best preserved continuous area of EIA settlement (after Cucuzza 1998, Fig. 6.1, p. 63). By permission of N. Cucuzza.

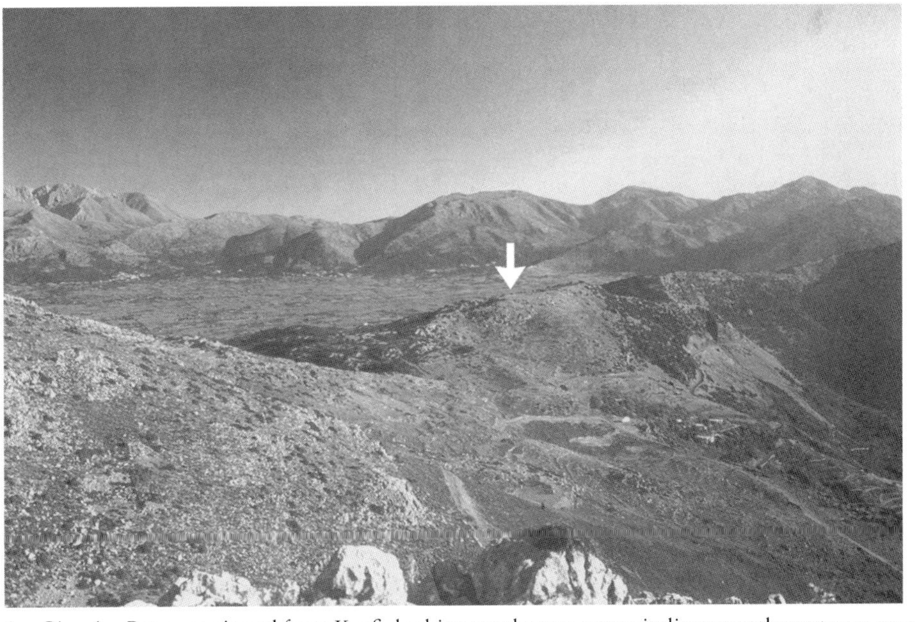

144. Ayios Giorgios Papoura viewed from Karfi, looking southwest: arrow indicates settlement area on summit. Image by the author.

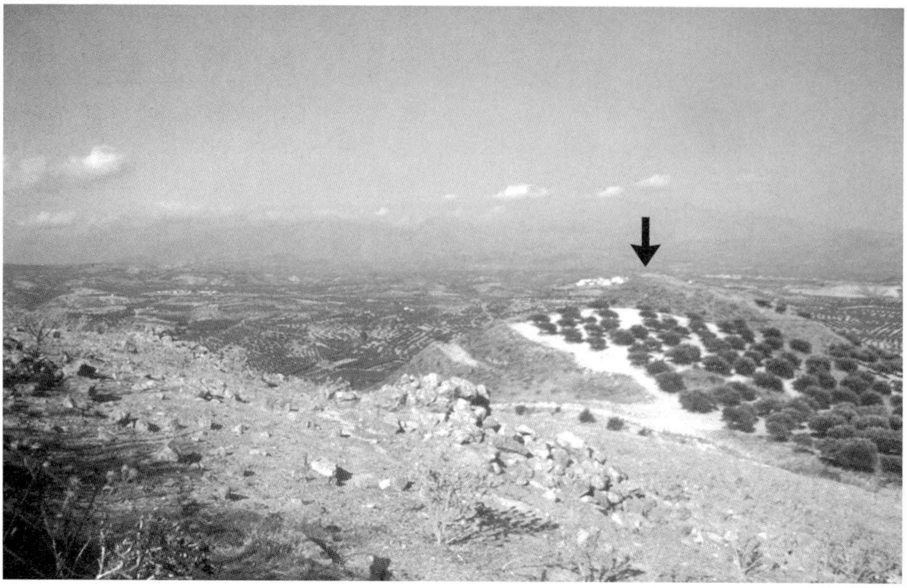

145. Ligortinos Kefala from northwest: arrow indicates settlement area on summit. Image by the author.

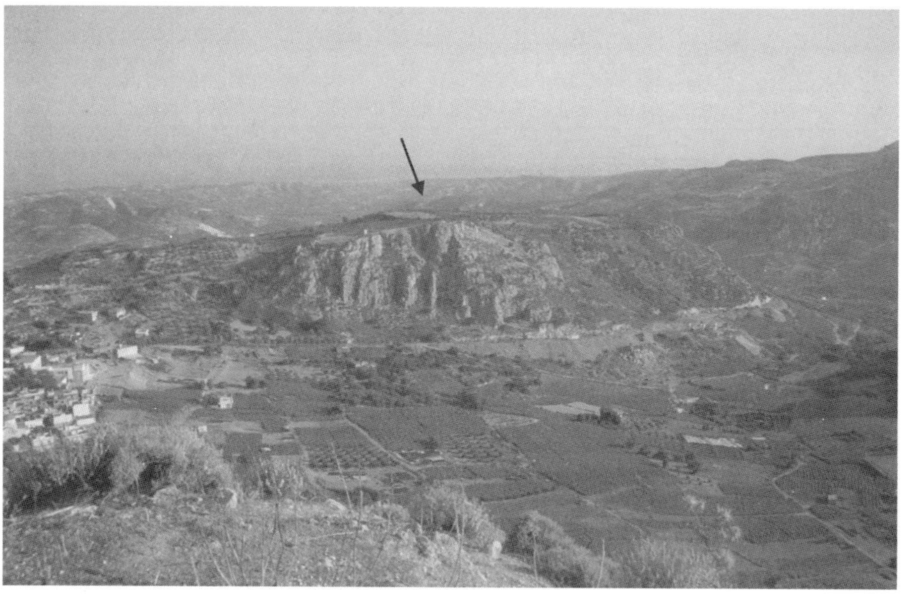

146. Profitis Elias Rokka from east: arrow indicates settlement area on summit. Image by the author.

for by good access to sea, as well as land, routes (Gondicas 1988: 85; Nowicki 2000: 222). Across the island, however, the earlier framework of settlement heavily conditioned the choices being made, meaning the majority of sites were still inland.

In the changing economy, with many more resources invested in the movement of goods and people, control of movement, whether on land or sea, was clearly essential to any successful community. The importance of access to, and through, an extensive arable hinterland in the selection of continuing sites ties into the picture of increasingly structured and invested-in economic growth from this period.

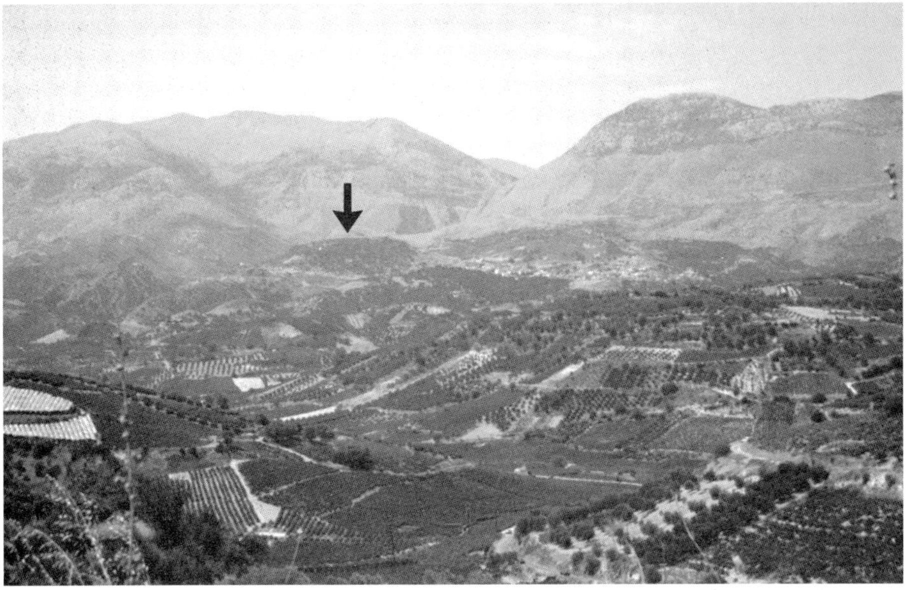

147. Krousonas Koupo from northeast: arrow indicates settlement area on summit. Image by the author.

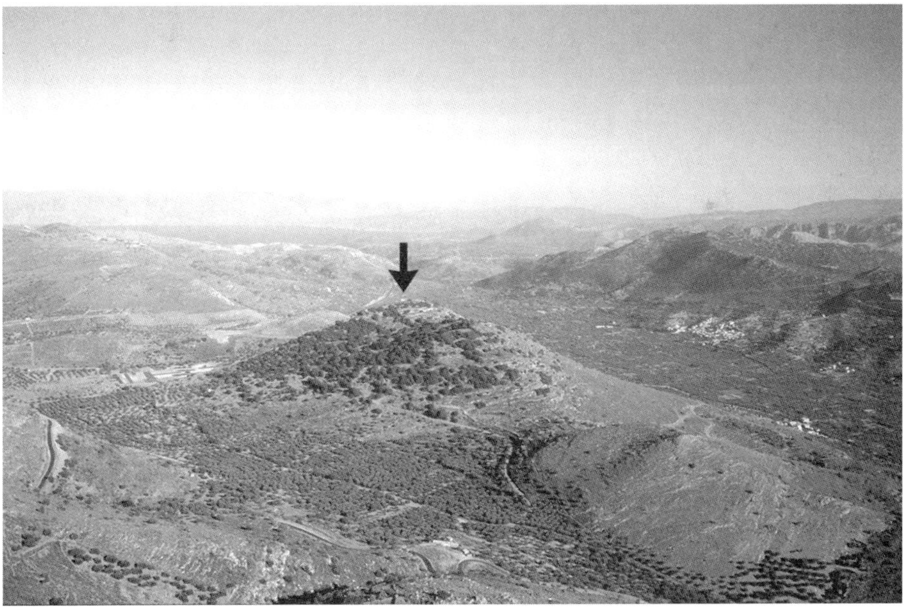

148. Dreros from west, with the Mirabello bay beyond it to the east: arrow indicates settlement area on summit. Photo courtesy: K. Nowicki.

Regional patterns

Nucleation often seems to have occurred over short distances, within the close locality of LM IIIC sites. The general pattern of nucleated sites across the island from PG thus strongly reflects the regional patterning of twelfth-century settlement. Very close spatial relationships between continuing and abandoned settlements are seen all over east Crete and parts of central Crete – in

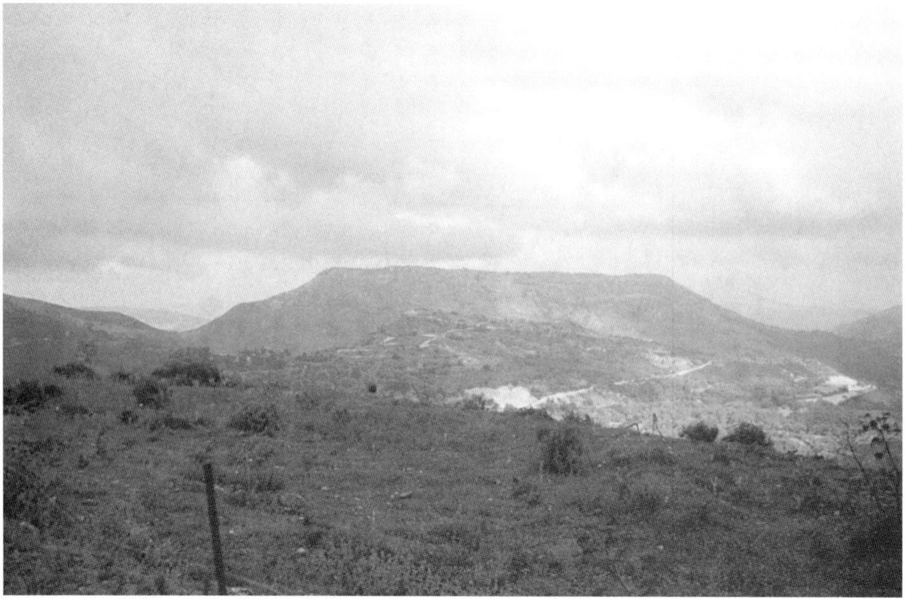

149. Pandanassa Veni from west. Image by the author.

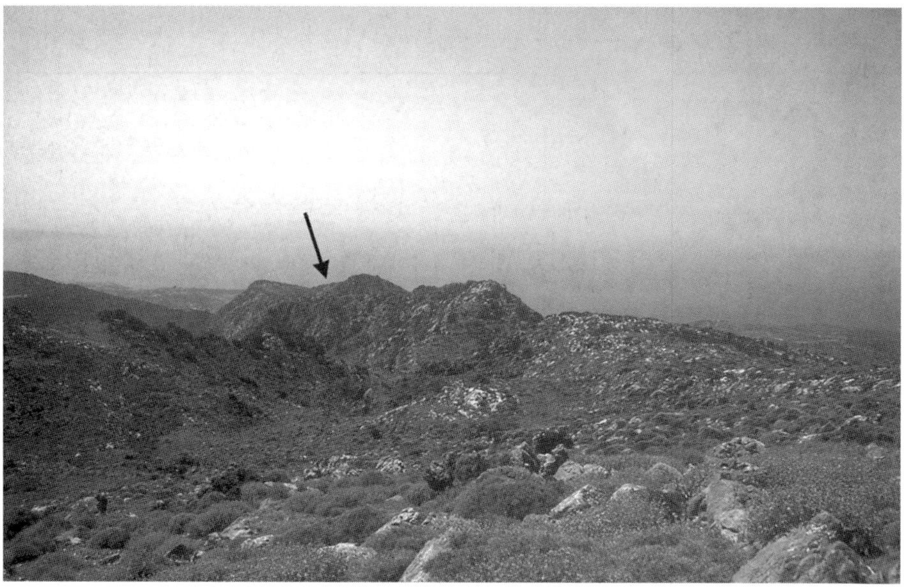

150. Vrachasi Anavlochos from southeast: arrow indicates settlement area on summit. Image by the author.

the Karfi-Papoura case; in the Azoria-Kavousi-Monastiraki region; at Lato, where large LM IIIC communities nearby at Kritsa and Tapes probably nucleated; at Anavlochos (with an abandoned settlement at nearby Neapoli Kastri); at Dreros (likely to have drawn population from Vrises Profitis Elias and other abandoned twelfth- to eleventh-century sites in the Potamoi valley); at Rotasi (with abandonment of the settlement at the high, extremely defensible Korifi site coinciding with growth at the lower, much more accessible Kefala, lying just above the fertile Mesara plain; and at Praisos (following the abandonment of Kalamafki Kipia) among many others (Demargne 1901, 1903, 1931; Farnoux and Driessen 1991; Hadjimichali 1971; Haggis et al.

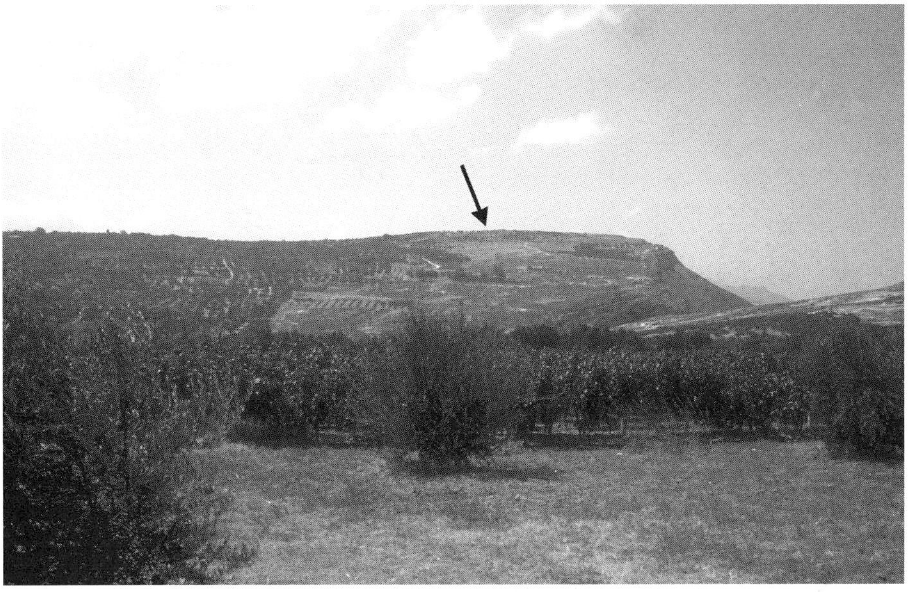

151. Astritsi Kefala from east: arrow indicates settlement area on summit. Image by the author.

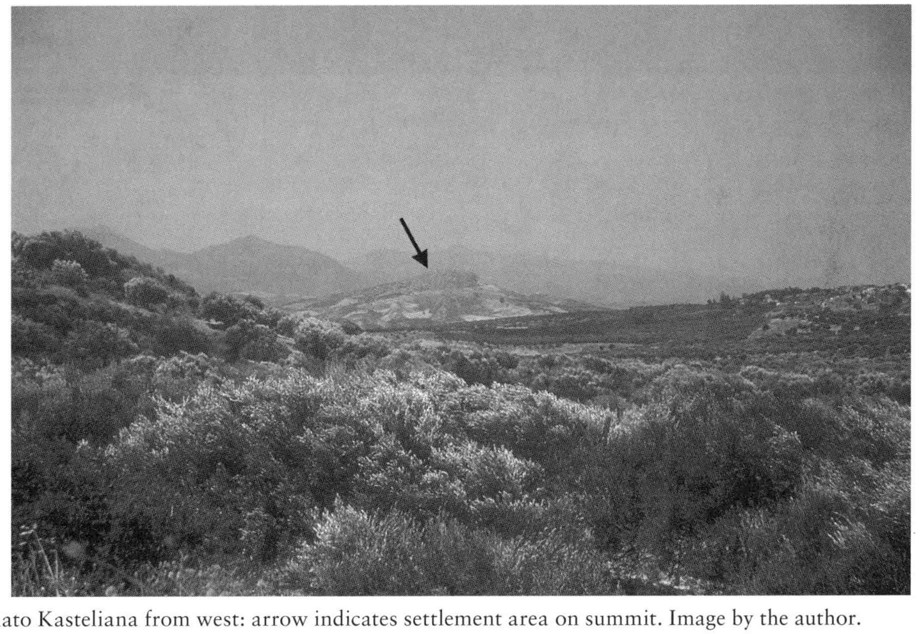

152. Kato Kasteliana from west: arrow indicates settlement area on summit. Image by the author.

2004; Nowicki 2000: 109–19, 119–25, 170–3, 190–1; Wallace 2003b: 256–62, 2008; Watrous 2001; Whitley et al. 1995; Figure 153). In west Crete, patchier retrieval of evidence makes it difficult to identify regional patterns so clearly, but here, too, many large Geometric-Archaic sites have abandoned LM IIIC settlements in their vicinity and probably expanded in size through the course of the EIA in a regionally tied nucleation process. In the Sfakia region, the large LM IIIC community at Kolokasia Kastri may have nucleated at the gentler, lower-lying hill of Patsianos Kefala (Francis et al. 2000: 453; Nowicki 2000: 209–13). Scattered and sizeable LM IIIC-PG

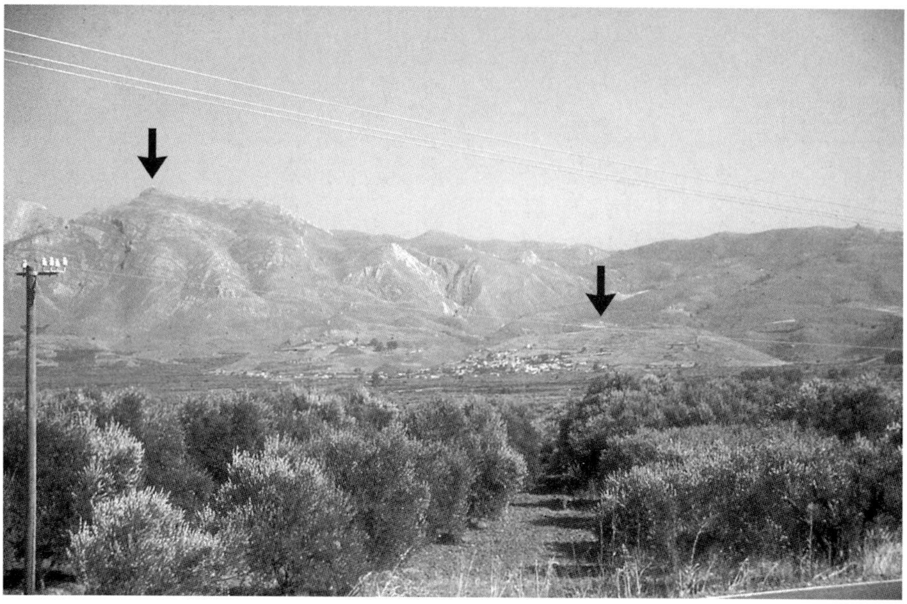

153. Rotasi Korifi and Kefala from north: arrows indicate settlement areas on summits. Image by the author.

sites in the rich Ayios Vasilios valley have no obvious PG-EA nucleation nearby, though several relatively small settlements of PG-Classical date are known from the area, at Koxare Ambelos, Kerame Pyrgos, Kionia, and a site east of Koxare (Hood and Warren 1966: 177–8, 180; Moody et al. 1998b, 2000b; Nowicki 2000: 201–6). Perlman (1996: 247–8) notes the lack of a large, dominant settlement in this region into Classical and Hellenistic times. Thronos Kefala/Sybrita and Panadanassa Veni in the Amari valley may possibly have acted as settlement foci for this entire region from PG onwards. Unusually, they are very close together for two such sizeable sites, with no very obvious division of catchment, perhaps suggesting that special political circumstances applied in this region during the state emergence period (Hood et al. 1964: 70–1; Nowicki 2000: 197–9).

Other regional differences are apparent within the broader pattern. While the Mirabello bay and the area beyond it up to the western border of Lasithi show the 'classic' type of nucleation described, the far east Cretan peninsula has a partly different pattern. We have seen that this area was characterised in the twelfth to eleventh centuries by numerous, dispersed, and comparatively small sites. This distribution seems related to the region's highly dissected topography, encouraging the use of scattered, limited arable pockets from a number of small defensive bases. Although some of these settlements might have already been linked to each other by collaborative and kin-based relationships (Haggis 1993: 150–1), the large number of small groups may have taken a relatively long time to form nucleated units. A divergent path is suggested by the relatively high number of small to medium-sized continuing settlements (many of defensible type) in this region during the PG-EA period, with few large nucleations apart from Praisos: conditions were already changing by Archaic, however, with the development of important coastal settlements like Itanos, a phenomenon discussed later in this chapter.

Central Crete had its own idiosyncrasies. Here, the scale of nucleation is often unclear, because the *majority* of known settlements (such as Astritsi Kefala, Kalo Chorio Maza, Arkades [Afrati Profitis Elias], Gortyn, Prinias, and Ligortino Kefala) seem to continue and stay large in size (though clearly also expanding over time) all the way from LM IIIC through Archaic, with few cases of abandonment (Nowicki 2000: 174–87; Wallace in press b, in press c). In cases where regional nucleation of settlement, rather than just site expansion, seems to have occurred, the question of whence the nucleated sites drew their populations is only partly answered by the few known cases of settlements abandoned by or before PG, at Tachieri near Mires (dated LM IIIB-C) and Grigoria Kartalos (LM IIIC). Kastrokefala Almyrou (LM IIIB-C) also supports the pattern (Kanta 2003a; Nowicki 2000: 188–90, 221; Platakis 1970; Vasilakis 2004: 100–2). Indicators of further nucleation in this region appear towards the very end of the Iron Age, when some continuing small 'citadel' sites like Smari Profitis Elias and Kourtes Kefala are finally abandoned. However, these are a minority phenomenon and their abandonment forms part of a different process, discussed below. A number of different factors (large population, inclusion of a number of trade gateways, a particularly rich arable landscape, lack of defensible topography on which to establish twelfth-century sites, and thus no pressure to relocate when insecurity lessened) seem to have been influential in the longevity and large size of so many settlements in this region. These two features, though, are likely to have made central Crete the first region in which regular inter-settlement conflict, linked to parallel expansion processes by densely packed early states, began. In the Classical to Hellenistic periods Crete was notorious in the Greek world for its numerous and drawn-out interstate conflicts, and within this book's remit we need to consider how this had come about. Central Cretan sites could not for long expand their subsistence hinterlands or concentrate population from neighbours without conflict with nearby peers of similar size and strength. The increasingly intense, yet almost certainly uneven building up of external links by PG-A groups in the region (related to the concentrated circulation of and demand for value goods) must also have contributed to friction. In my view, the early Archaic period, marked by a number of cultural shifts, seems likely to be the point at which regular conflicts started to grow. Their existence, involving disturbances and discontinuities at many sites, may partly explain the problems of obtaining a coherent record for the island through much of the later Archaic to Classical periods – though as I note below, the main problem is the lack of targeted archaeological research, especially settlement excavations, for those periods. Given the difficulty of providing an archaeological narrative for this phase of Crete's history, the shifts of the early Archaic period require close attention for the light they can potentially throw on a number of subsequent developments, including the rise of interstate conflict.

Experience of and attachment to landscape during and after nucleation

The ways in which the new Cretan cultural landscape, dominated by the nucleated sites, was experienced and viewed, and how these experiences fed into the construction of social identities and economic outlooks, will form recurrent themes in the following discussion (Morgan 2003: 17, 45–106). In order for nucleation to take place, the benefits of physical colocation in one large settlement, such as better risk-buffering through the more closely coordinated sharing of labour and rewards (perhaps orchestrated through the development of institutions like the public feast), must have been seen to outweigh the inconvenience of a longer journey time to farming zones. These zones, which had previously been worked from small local settlements and probably attached to or customarily 'owned' by residents there, were probably now more often exploited via the use of fieldhouses. There is also evidence for some small-scale continued use, probably agriculturally related, at some otherwise abandoned LM IIIC-SM sites, perhaps now adapted as field bases – Tapes Kato Kastello, Frati Kefala, Atsipades Fonises, Oreino Kastri, Pefki Stavromenos, and Vrises Profitis Elias are among sites possibly used in this way (Nowicki 1994a, 2000: 64–7, 73–8, 113, 123, 201–6). Though people probably tried to maintain some kind of ownership attachment to the land areas they had formerly worked, a new formalization of these rights surely now became necessary. As large unitary territories came into being, centred on the new settlement units, gaps between the hinterlands of former settlements were probably filled in by new claims, significantly enlarging the total size of the territory. The balance in overall land access and ownership may have changed radically in this new environment, with the potential for significant renegotiation of, or conflict over, existing land rights.

In experiential terms, going back to the main settlement, instead of one's former or ancestral village, after each day's work – while having seen, in that work's course, the often visually prominent location of the old village from a very close range (and perhaps met residents of some still-inhabited small villages within the territory) must regularly have provoked thoughts about the basis of the nucleated settlements' social and economic unity, and the meaning of ownership of, and ancestral links to, land. The concept of a single concentrated body owning, controlling, and defending a region formerly united by a rather loose, generalised regional identity and sense of collective history, but containing a number of similarly sized independent, scattered communities, must have taken a while to adjust to. The permanence and coherence of the concept were surely visually reinforced by the large size and open, prominent (though usually undramatic) positions of the nucleated sites.

Considering the landscape in an experiential perspective, with a view to its potential symbolic loadings, offers valuable insight into how agents and communities 'built themselves into' states (Wallace 2003b, 2007, in press d). It is important to stress, however, that the changes in the landscape are not explainable outside the broader context of historical and archaeological evidence, in which we must ground any phenomenological analysis. Recently, for example, Whitley et al. have used isolated examples of EIA sites to propose that symbolic or associative aspects of landscape could actually have *driven* the character of the settlement change; in particular, that the roughly 'triangular' topography of some LM IIIC sites, formed by the limestone peaks and ridges they incorporate, could somehow explain the choice of sites to nucleate at from PG onwards (Whitley et al 1995: 246). Citing this kind of natural layout at both sites, they suggest that people at the site of Kalamafki Kipia, established circa 1200 BC saw the move to Praisos in terms of 'recreating' their local landscape, and that a certain visual template may have driven new settlement choices here and elsewhere. This argument is largely contextless. The more general topographical setting of several small peaks with valleys between them is in fact extremely common among Cretan hilltop sites, thanks to the limestone geology, making any argument for a deliberate seeking-out of precise topographic similarities questionable. Very few PG nucleation sites present this exact topographical form or replicate the topography of sites established circa 1200 BC in this or any other way. The latter fact is hardly surprising, given the wider economic and political changes occurring from PG, which I suggest strongly conditioned the nucleation movement. Though Whitley et al.'s model is thus something of an interpretative dead end, it does seem right to consider the long visual and experiential familiarity of a region's residents with their nearest emerging nucleation site as crucial in consolidating a new, larger-scale community identity focused on that site. The importance of historical/mythic and symbolic associations with the cultural landscape in tying together the new larger communities is indicated by new kinds of formalized references to the past now being made in the wider landscape. Some abandoned LM IIIC-PG sites were reused for ritual within PG-G, a choice apparently connected to their place in the collective memory of residents at the nearby nucleated polities. Within the newly broadened construct of political identity, a variety of subidentities seem to have been being claimed, often apparently attached to historically resonant places. I discuss this phenomenon in more detail later in this chapter.

Continuity and expansion at gateway sites

Chania, Phaistos, and Knossos all grew substantially by Geometric, almost certainly in conjunction with the boom in trade and its wider economic implications. We know this from a range of different sorts of evidence – limited town excavations at all three sites, extensive cemetery excavations at Knossos, and finds of scattered tombs at Chania and Phaistos (Andreadaki-Vlasaki 2004; Coldstream 2000a; Coldstream and Hatzaki 2003; Coldstream and Huxley 1999: 298; Cucuzza 1998, in press; Hallager and Hallager 1997; Macdonald and Coldstream 1997; Rocchetti 1975; Watrous and Hadzi-Vallianou 2004a: 311–13; Whitley 1986: 265–6). At Knossos, settlement develops in parts of the Minoan town, around the South Houses area, and spreads to the north, in the area of the Villa Dionysos, during PG-G. At Phaistos a new and extensive settlement quarter is well established by Geometric, and at Chania, settlement deposits extend again by the G period after a retraction between late IIIC and PG.

Given the new priorities in settlement I have identified as emerging in PG-EA, continuity and growth at these locations is hardly surprising. They commanded some of the largest continuous prime arable areas in the island, as well as major routes. Their topography was less intrinsically defensible or visually impressive than that of many inland nucleations, but their history of long-term occupation and strategic location vis-á-vis sea and land routes almost certainly counted for more than these factors in maintaining them as settlement cores. The resurgence of the port of Kommos as a sanctuary from the latest eleventh through the tenth centuries, in clear connection with the booming sphere of external trade, reflects growing concerns to facilitate communication with the outside world, and the community at Phaistos was well placed to benefit from the increasing volume of trade here from the ninth century. As we have seen, significant growth in the volume of imported and imitated luxuries at the Knossos North Cemetery from the PG period indicates the increasing importance of the site and its ports in long-distance exchange networks: the same applies to Chania by Geometric times.

Are these large sites candidates for centres in a newly emerging hierarchy, operating at a level above that of other nucleations? There is not enough evidence to identify them as having had unique functions, but their location and history, and the amount of wealth concentrated in and around them, suggest that people travelled long distances to trade there, treating these settlements as communication nodes easily accessible by land or sea from most other parts of the island. Craft skills and the opportunity to learn them, including through contacts with craftsmen trained in other parts of the east Mediterranean who were passing through or resident at these locations, surely became strongly concentrated there. In turn, the standing of any commodities produced or exchanged at these settlements may have been boosted by association with the sites' long (and surely already mythologised) history. Yet the size and complexity of many other nucleated settlements, especially in central Crete, illustrates the rapid emergence of new social and economic cores with their roots in the twelfth century, rather than any kind of reprise of the Bronze Age settlement hierarchy.

Comparisons with other Aegean areas

On the central Greek mainland, the number of settlements abandoned before 700 BC is very limited. The good facilities for development and growth already offered by many sites used through the crisis period circa 1200 BC and beyond must have had a lot to do with this. As we have seen, most of them possessed good access to coasts and communication routes and/or large arable hinterlands. We do, however, see the falling out of use of small and short-term refuge places founded around 1200 BC (like Kranidi Profitis Elias) long before PG – almost certainly because the most severe threat of attack had now reduced. Some small and non-defensible coastal sites established circa 1200, such as Kynos, also decline, perhaps because the increasing scale and complexity of the trade economy promoted the concentration of economic and political power at large sites in this east central Greek region, such as Lefkandi, Chalkis, and Eretria (Andriomenou 1972; Boardman 1957; Kalligas 1992). Notwithstanding, it seems that most mainland settlements – which were already large in the early EIA in comparison to those on the islands – did not undergo significant further nucleation until the LG period, along with a whole set of other cultural and social changes. This is particularly well illustrated in the Argolid, Messenia, and Attica (de Polignac 1995: 81–9; Morris 1987: 156–71; Snodgrass 1971: 416–21, 1983). The contrast with Cretan patterns again highlights how strongly events around 1200 BC conditioned long-term cultural developments, with effects on the construction of political territories and identities right through into the period of polis state emergence.

In the Cyclades, as on Crete, we see existing major coastal sites founded in the BA, such as Grotta and Paroikia, flourishing, and probably expanding, right through the PG-early Archaic periods, a process perhaps involving relocation by residents of the more extreme defensible sites in the islands established around 1200 BC (Morris 1998: 34; Schilardi 1983: 182–3; Zapheiropoulou 2004). These expanding sites emerged as polis states by the late eighth to seventh centuries. At the same time, as I shall discuss-later, the Aegean islands and coasts share with Crete the continued use of a number of small naturally defensible sites founded early in the EIA. These stay in use right up until the end of LG, and sometimes beyond, *without* major expansion.

A common pattern in all Aegean regions in this period is the following type of settlement expansion over the course of the EIA: a defensible knoll (whether first settled in the twelfth century or, as in many mainland cases, continuing from the Bronze Age) sees a spread of settlement down its slopes by the end of the eighth century, and in many cases from as early as the tenth. This confirms the notion that defence was becoming much less of a priority, while also highlighting a newly increased interest in controlling extensive arable areas and more direct coastal access. Settlement on the Palaiokastro hill in Messenia moved down to the Koryphasion peninsula, just above the sea, by Protogeometric; at Argos, settlement seems to have spread from the Larissa acropolis down to the east from at least the same period. The coast below the Aigeira peak was also resettled. Occupation at Athens had spread outward from the Acropolis to the Agora area and beyond by the eighth century, while a similar process seems to have happened around the acropolis of Larissa in Thessaly (Chatzi 1982; Eder 1998: 25–72, 141–79; Glowacki 1998; Lemos 2002: 135–49, 195–7; Petropoulos 1988, 1990). At Xobourgo on Tinos and Ayios Elias on Melos, the same type of spread occurs from Protogeometric on, and a similar pattern is seen at Males, Milatos, and Rokka, among others, on Crete (Kourou 2004; Nowicki 2000: 134–5, 170, 186–7). In the Dodecanese, too, we see a pattern of large LBA/early EIA settlements on relatively defensible acropoleis or promontories continuing and spreading onto the coastal zone immediately below by the Archaic period: Ialysos and Lindos are good examples, although we have no detailed documentation on their character as settlements during the EIA (Farmakidou 2004). At Emborio on Chios, a partly related kind of shift/expansion takes place, with settlement moving a short distance across an important bay. The small rocky peninsula occupied in the twelfth century is deserted in favour of the summit and slopes of a massive coastal acropolis (Boardman 1967b; Hood 1952: 579–623; Figure 154).

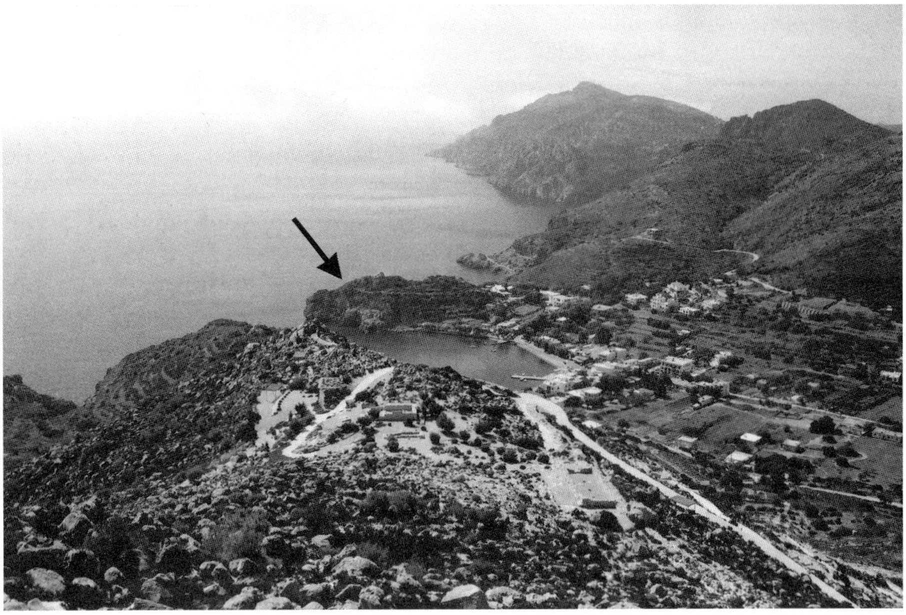

154. Emborio sites, Chios: looking west from the upper site to the lower promontory used in LH IIIC (indicated by arrow). Image by the author.

Nucleation and the state-emergence process

In characterizing the state as a political entity, Aristotle, writing in the fourth century, presented it as an amalgamation of several village-level organizational structures, themselves built up of household units (*Politics* 1252b23–35). Since the context is a metaphorical one – a rationalisation of the state's existence and structure – it seems deeply unwise to read this as an accurate historical analysis (Davies 1997: 26; Hall 1997b: 91). Notwithstanding, many scholars have been tempted to see in this text a clue to the material roots of the polis, and to use it, together with a selection of archaeological data, to model the emergence of the state as a universal process occurring circa 700 BC, involving the nucleation of scattered groups within a territory into a single physical core. The model has been applied in Crete to Knossos and Phaistos, but also elsewhere in EIA Greece, including to the cases of Athens and Lefkandi, often mainly on the basis of cemetery distributions (a fact partly due to the poverty of settlement research: Coldstream 1984b, 1991; Donlan and Thomas 1993; Haggis 1993: 162–5; Lemos 2002: 135). Scattered cemetery locations are often seen as representing EIA residential units which eventually nucleated.

The notion can be usefully reevaluated in the light of the nucleation pattern for PG Crete that I have outlined. The nucleated PG-EA sites, many ofwhich went on to become Classical poleis, were substantial and continuous community 'cores' already established from the beginning of the EIA, *yet also* entities that expanded physically and structurally over time to incorporate, at both a symbolic and aphysical level, several smaller, formerly separate population/identity units. We should note distinctions, nonetheless, between the processes affecting the unrepresentative sites of Phaistos, Chania, and Knossos, which never lost their large 'core' population element at the Bronze to Iron transition and continued to spread out and fill in between the PG and early Archaic periods, and the new settlements established elsewhere in the island in the twelfth century, which saw significant population growth *only* from the tenth, as population relocated there from neighbouring small sites. Since the latter are the majority, using sites of the Knossos type on their own as general models of settlement nucleation is misleading. Using cemetery data to do so is even more problematic. As at Corinth, Athens, and Argos, the spread-out burial plots at PG-G Knossos are better read as reflecting complex social relationships within a large community than the straightforward history of the settlement's spatial development.

How far any Cretan nucleation can be called 'urban' by the early Archaic period is an issue I will address further in discussing architecture and settlement planning. It does seem, though – in the light of evidence like the Dreros inscription of circa 630 BC, which already refers to the *polis* and to the institution of the *kosmoi* – that social organization at these sites was at a formalised, stratified level by the late seventh century, and that they had perhaps developed some centralised functions within a defined regional territory (Meiggs and Lewis 1989: 2–3). Small continuing settlements within or bordering their regions, discussed below, seem likely to have been in some relation of dependence/subjugation to them, and small farming sites were beginning to spread out around them as satellites, by the end of the eighth/early seventh century, as I show later in Part Four.

Conclusions

The fact that the nucleated sites forming the backbone of settlement in PG-EA Crete did *not* cluster in new patterns across the island, but related closely to former local settlement networks, suggests most people already moved within, and identified with, fixed regional-scale political units by this period. This fact, together with the broadly contemporaneous nature of the change across the island, and the fact that the sites at which nucleation took place do not seem to have been preeminent in size or complexity compared to other sites in their close regions during the twelfth to eleventh centuries, also hints that the phenomenon was initially related to new economic priorities (agricultural expansion – in an environment where security from attack was no longer a driving priority in structuring hinterland size and form – and engagement in an increased-volume production and exchange of value goods) and to a general pressure for changes in political systems, rather than the conquest and takeover of sites that were somehow 'unsuccessful' by more 'successful' ones. The same points also argue strongly against evolutionary models like that proposed by Whitley (Whitley 1991b: 345, especially note 20) involving a direct correlation of settlement form with social structure. In this model, the category of 'unstable' settlements is suggested as encompassing sites occupied for any period 'from fifty years to three centuries' within the EIA. Whitley sees these groups as having achieved-rank social systems and reconstructs periodic physical shifts in their location in order to follow changing leaders. He suggests that, by contrast, settlements and/or cemeteries continuously in use through the EIA had intrinsically 'stable' structures, which directly enabled their longevity. The main example of this type cited is Knossos – largely untypical, as we have seen, of EIA settlement patterns across Crete. The functional similarities and contrasts between the continuing settlements and their noncontinuing peers, linked to the special historical circumstances in which they were founded and the role of agents (at community or individual level) in making decisions about the continuation or abandonment of a site based on pertinent factors in the economic, cultural, and political environment, are not identified or addressed in this argument.

In fact, most of the sites abandoned from PG seem to have had rather similar occupation spans, of about 200–250 years. Neither this broadly shared date of abandonment, nor the relatively long period elapsing before it, fits well to the idea of fluctuating leadership status and/or flexible residence patterns based on personal competition at the level of the small community. The tight regional patterns of nucleation from PG make this notion even less convincing: it is simply not credible that groups of closely proximate communities, accessing very similar bases of support and having no obvious hierarchical relationship, would have maintained fundamentally different structures for such a long period. Whitley is right to highlight a connection between the continuation and expansion of settlements from the tenth century onwards and the development of complexity. But we should, I think, see one of the main drivers of settlement change as deliberate and self-conscious choice at a community level, reflecting new conditions and priorities in social and economic life.

I would like to end this discussion with a note of caution. Given the limited information available from surface survey, we still cannot be certain that *all* large sites of PG-EA date in Crete had their roots in the twelfth century. This is particularly true of some very poorly investigated west Cretan sites, but also of places like Lato and Lyttos, where the evidence for LM IIIC use is extremely sketchy. At some large nucleated sites, such as Oleros and Viannos Korakias, it is not demonstrable at all. Thus, we cannot exclude some major new foundations at the PG period. But if these exist, they would seem to be in a very small minority.

27 SETTLEMENT PATTERNS (2): SMALL SITES, SMALL-GROUP IDENTITY, AND TRADE

Defining the 'citadel' site

Accompanying the nucleation phenomenon, we see the continued use of some highly defensible LM IIIC sites, though without significant expansion, through the PG to early Archaic periods. These – which for convenient reference, without implying anything about their role – I shall call 'citadel' sites, include Kavousi Kastro, Vrokastro, Chamaizi Liopetra, and Mirsini Kastello in east Crete; Keraton Vigla, Kourtes Kefala, Pobia Vigla, and Smari Profitis Elias in central Crete; and Trachilos Selli in the west (Halbherr 1901a; Hatzi-Vallianou 2004; Nowicki 2000: 71–2, 103–4, 112–13, 245–6; Rocchetti 1989, 1990; Vasilakis 2004; Wallace in press b; Figures 155–60).

The sites of this type have never previously been considered as an islandwide phenomenon. Because of their defensible topography, some have been argued to represent groups physically resistant to incorporation into the main nucleated communities of the period (Snodgrass 1991a: 7–10). However, they seem to me much more likely to reflect *agreed* autonomy of residence on old territorial bases for specific segments of society (lineages?), who were nonetheless fundamentally well incorporated into the regional-scale community units now becoming centred on the nucleatrons. The fact that all such sites remained restricted in size throughout the EIA is significant, suggesting they were not able to command the political and economic resources needed to develop as large independent centres. In most cases, their topography also discouraged physical expansion. Yet they clearly functioned as full, permanent settlements (usually with their own cemeteries) until the LG-A period, suggesting they were never simply refuge places or forts for the nucleated polities nearby.

It seems unlikely, certainly by Archaic times, that the main nucleations, now well consolidated and in command of sizeable territories, could have been forced to tolerate politically resistant small groups. But a negotiated or *controlled* existence of smaller-scale community units with distinct identities, within newly consolidated regional territorial structures, might constitute a useful pressure release, helping to prevent political fragmentation in the long term. In fact, the typically dramatic, highly visible locations of the 'citadel' sites might have acted in the landscape as identity signifiers and memory prompts vis-à-vis the nearest nucleation – drawing attention back to the shared roots of the whole regional community in the twelfth-century crisis – as sites with similar topography had for regional settlement clusters in the earlier EIA (Wallace 2007, in press d). Thus, for example, Kavousi Kastro, directly above Azoria, could have acted as a reminder of the dramatic history of origin of the Azoria community – giving its inhabitants, as a result, a special role and status in the wider community. The prominent small site at Sfakia

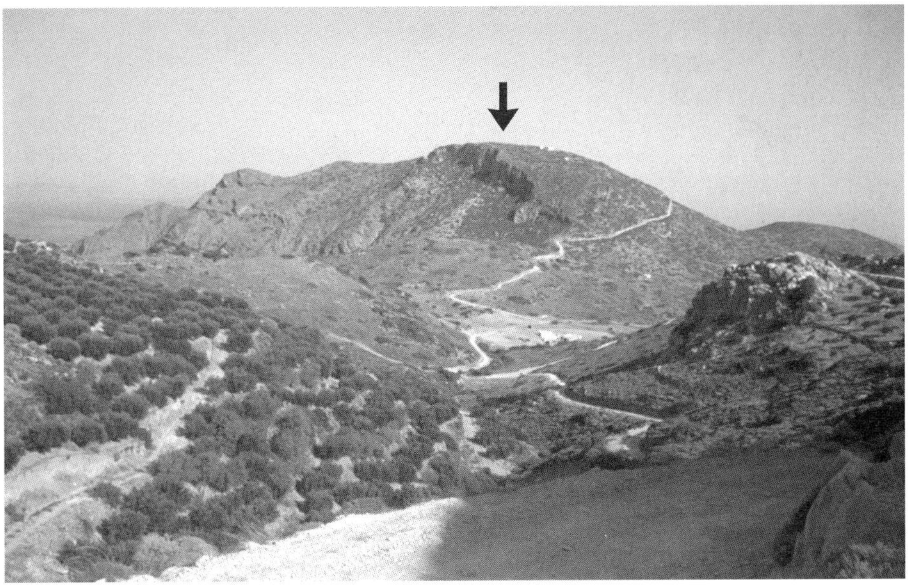

155. Chamaizi Liopetra from south: arrow indicates settlement area on summit. Image by the author.

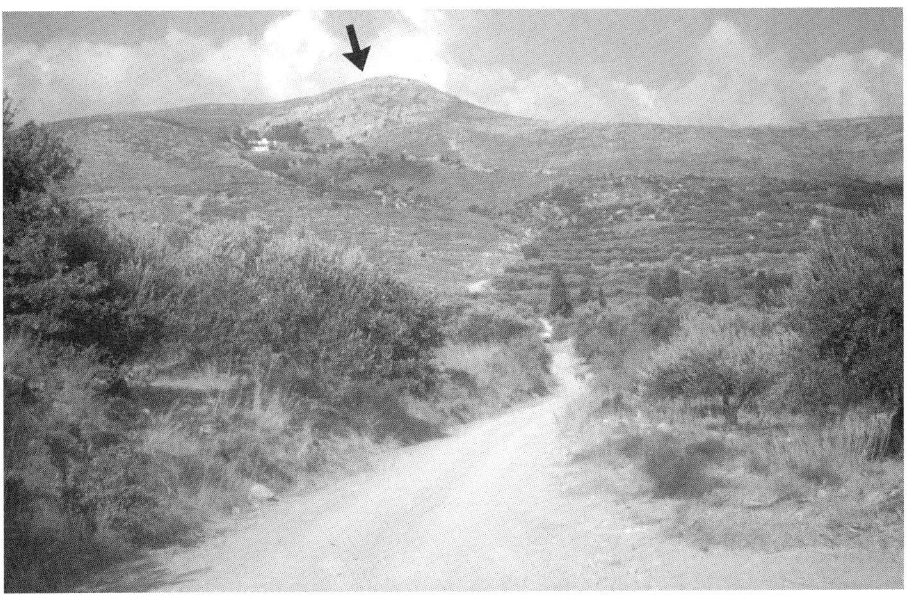

156. Smari Profitis Elias from northwest: arrow indicates settlement area on summit. Image by the author.

Kastri (Nowicki 2000: 54–5), at the north entrance to a major east Cretan valley route, may have functioned in the same way for the large Praisos nucleation lying farther inland along the same valley – reminding both locals and visitors about the identity and history of the area. A similar symbolic role may have applied to Keraton Vigla, towering above Crete's south coast (Nowicki 2000: 138–9; Wallace in press b, in press c; Figures 158–60). Founded in the twelfth century, this small site clearly remained in use until the eighth and must have been firmly linked into the territory of the large nucleated PG-EA settlement at Viannos Korakias, located farther inland in the high, sheltered, and fertile Viannos valley. Keraton's peak may well have marked

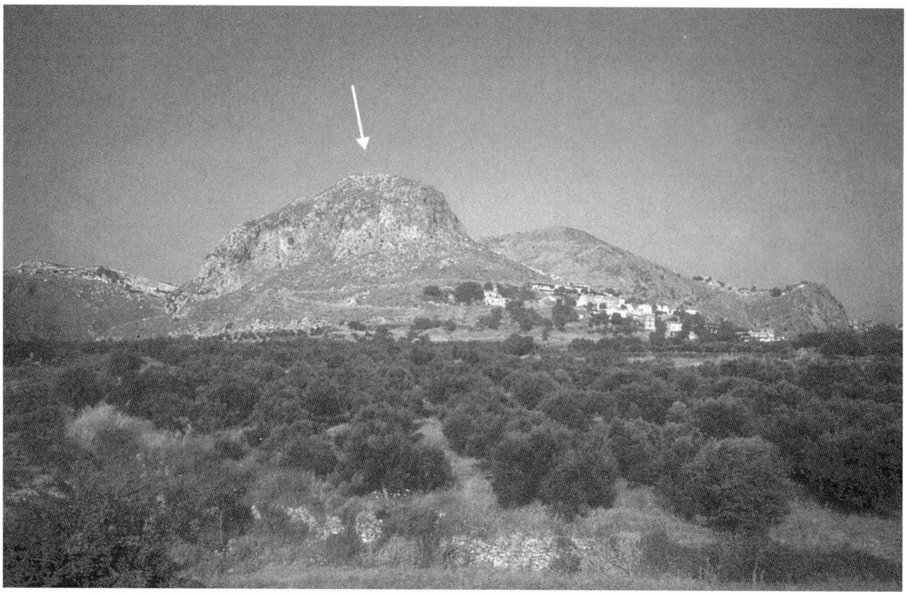

157. Rokka Kissamou from south: arrow indicates probable EIA settlement area on summit. Image by the author.

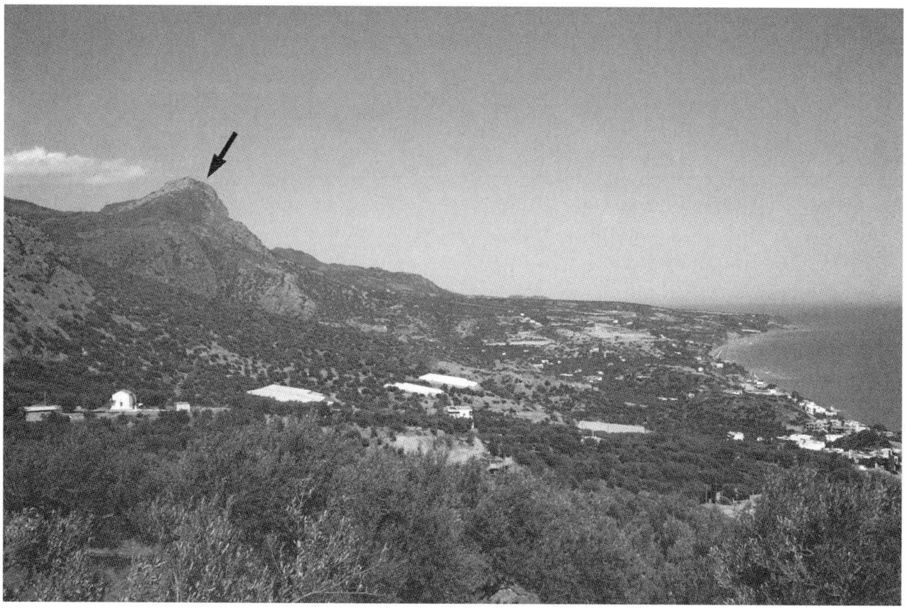

158. Keraton Vigla from west: arrow indicates settlement area on summit. Image by the author.

and symbolised the wider territory and its history for anyone approaching from the coast or surrounding lowlands. While this model fits a fair number of cases, the wider political relations of some citadel sites, such as Vrokastro, are still unclear. The latter never seems to have emerged as a sizeable protostate polity in its own right, yet neither was it ever clearly attached to a major nucleated site.

Overall, a compartmentalisation of social and political roles, rather than extreme social inequality, seems to have prevailed between the citadel sites and their nearest nucleations. The

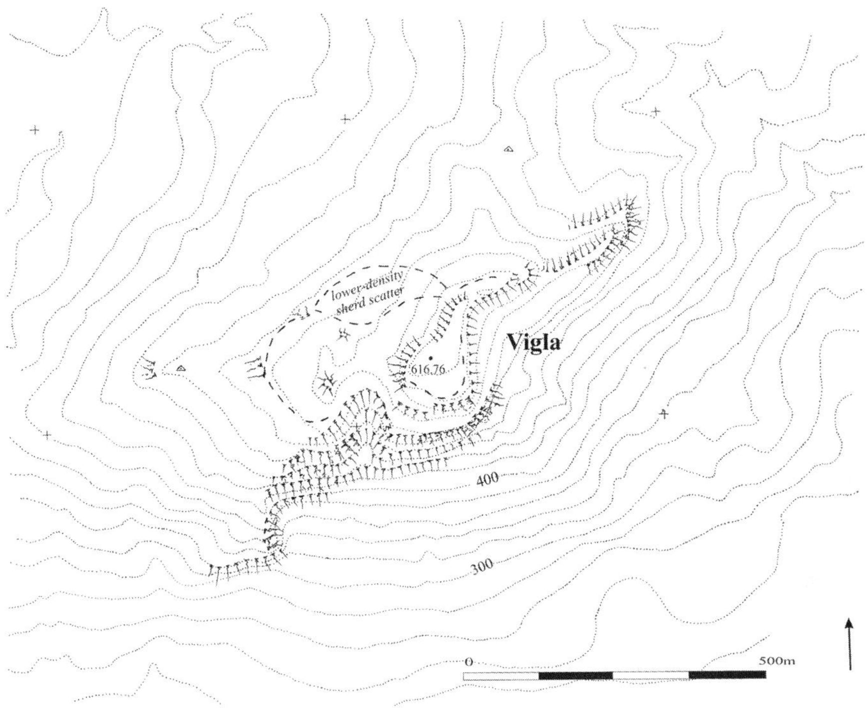

159. Plan of the sherd scatter area at Keraton Vigla, showing approximate site size by the latest period of use. Image by the author.

strong regional patterning of the nucleation movement suggests that groups resident at both types of settlement within a region were likely to view themselves as closely bound with their neighbours, often by extended-kin ties as well as by a shared political identity, and that they probably exploited closely adjoining and intersecting territories. People living at the small citadel sites could not easily build up an exclusive power base in such circumstances. Living at the nucleations must have offered substantial and increasing pragmatic rewards over time, in terms of force and coherence in power bargaining at interregional level. The standing of any group or individual at regional level might be enhanced by the honour and historical resonance of 'belonging' by descent to a distinctive citadel site – but only, surely, to a limited extent. Most citadel settlements had finally gone out of use by the early Archaic period. The seat of political power became much more solidly located in the nucleations, which had by now developed state-level complexity. A new spread of very small nondefensible sites into the wider territory started at around this time, probably in connection with agricultural expansion.

Thus, it would seem that rather than having a primarily defensive function, these sites persisted in use until state structures were consolidated, to the extent that clan/territory links no longer needed (or were able) to be asserted through physical separation from the main regional settlement. As such, they represent a particularly interesting transitional, 'protostate' phase in Crete. Even allowing for area bias in fieldwork, citadel sites seem best represented in the far eastern region. This fact may reflect an especially slow process of political amalgamation into nucleated polities in this region, as already argued. Given the frequently coastal locations of these sites, external trade interests are also likely to have played a role in their support, just as they did for island sites of the same type. In both cases, insecurity around the coasts connected with trade and raiding seemingly encouraged continued use of defensive locations here at a time when

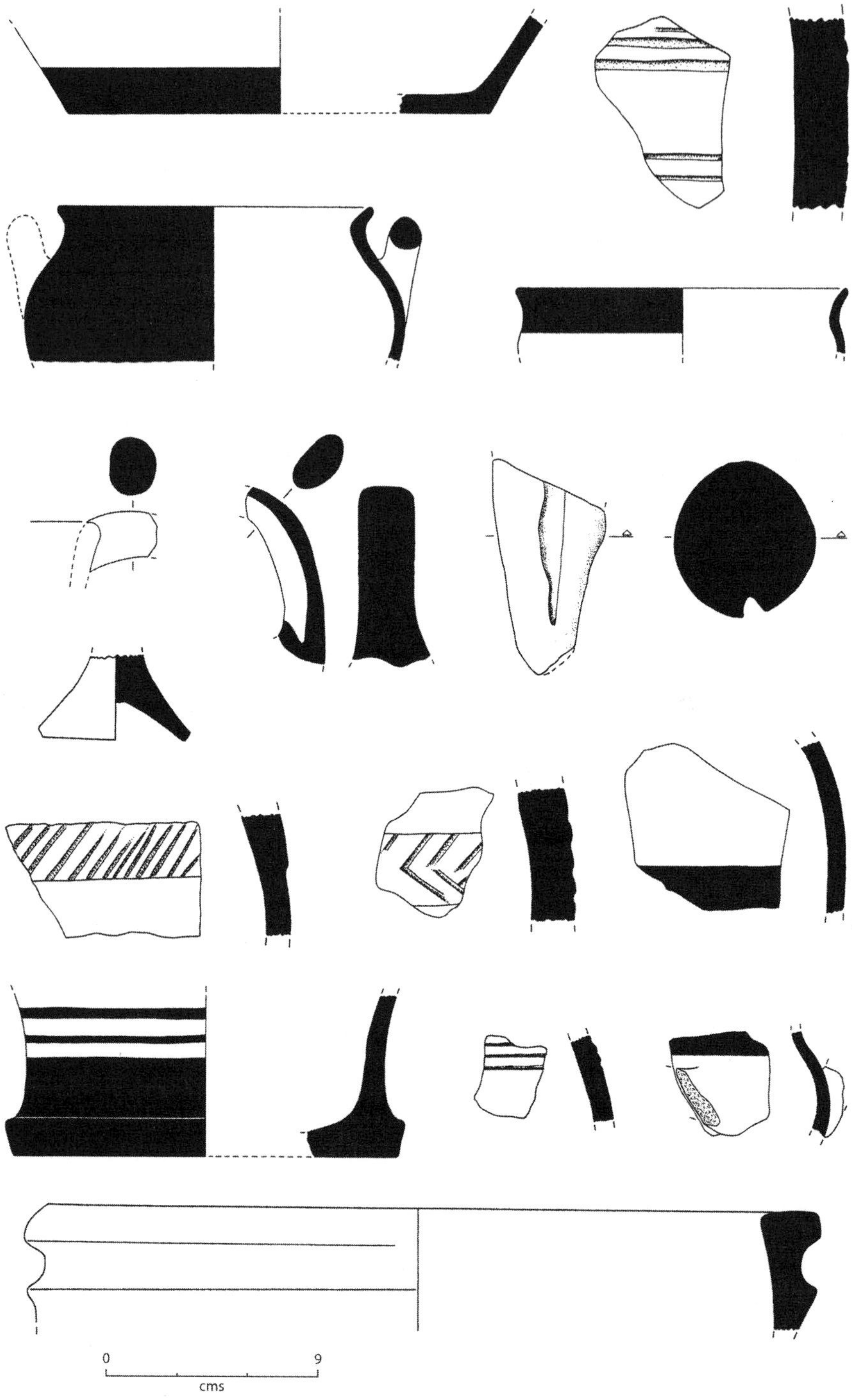

160. Selection of surface pottery from Keraton Vigla, showing the chronological range of occupation. Image by the author.

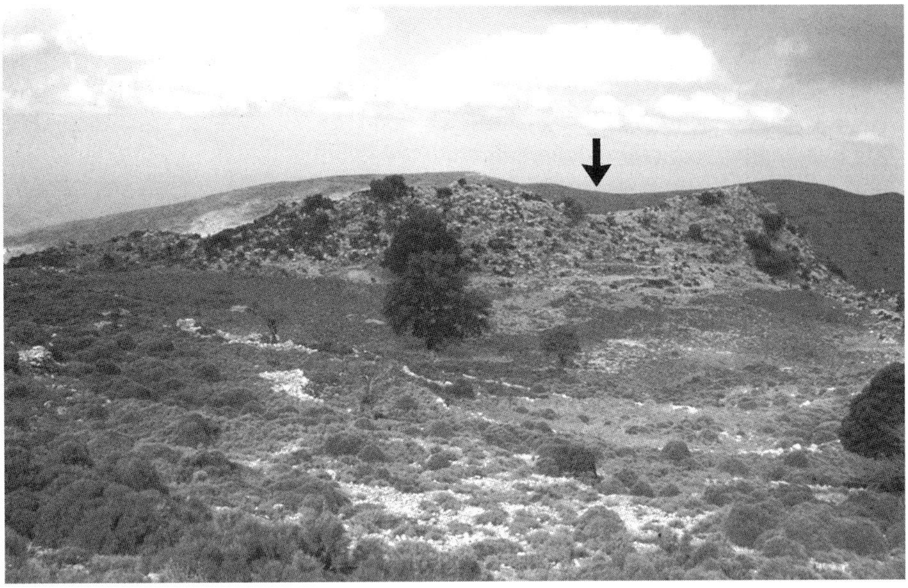

161. Krasi Kastello from south: arrow indicates settlement area on summit. Image by the author.

insecurity was becoming in general less important as a settlement driver (Nowicki 2000: 247). Inland examples of such sites in east Crete are not lacking, however: cases apart from those already listed include Anatoli Mesokastello, Zakros Ellinika, and Stavrochori Skalia, all inland (Nowicki 2000: 54–5, 104–5, 112–13, 128–9, 135–6, 218–19; Vokotopoulos 1998).

Around the Ambelos pass, in the low foothills north of Papoura, a notable inland cluster of citadel sites is seen. Small settlements apparently *founded* in PG and lasting into the LG period appear at Kera Kastello and Krasi Kastello, while another, at Kera Vigla, continues from LM IIIC right through LG (Nowicki 2000: 152–70; Figure 161). These sites are defensible, but not extremely so. Their value seems to lie in the fact that they formed a network protecting and exploiting the major route in the area, somewhat as their LM IIIC predecessors had. Indeed, they are often located close to predecessor sites of very similar type (Krasi Siderokefala, Krasi Armi) and very probably represent more or less the same groups. However, they are significantly larger in size and lie closer to the valley bottoms and the main arable hinterlands. They are also concentrated closer to the pass itself, now dominated by the Papoura nucleation. These choices reflect the changing settlement criteria affecting the rest of the island at this time – concern with routes, trade, and the agricultural base (Nowicki 2000: 152–70, 166–7, 245). But specific local relationships also seem likely to have affected their positioning. Their predecessors seem to have been positioned mainly with regard to strategic defensive collaboration with the Karfi and Papoura sites, but the new sites' locations make more sense in terms of a role as agricultural suppliers for the emerging nucleated settlement at Papoura, which controlled a very sizeable subsistence territory in a landscape of sharp relief contrasts, making for relatively difficult movement. The new choice of locations may also have been linked into increased volumes of trade passing through this important valley from the tenth century. This trade was probably increasingly dominated by Papoura, which directly controlled the pass. Despite their likely very close links to the Papoura polity, these sites could still fit the model I have outlined, of groups perpetuating some kind of independent political standing and territorial claim, perhaps embodied in a clan structure. They fit this description better than that of directly tied farming satellites established by the group at Papoura, not only because of their close proximity to former settlement bases, but because they seem to be full settlements of moderate size, not single houses or complexes. In this well-studied region, we see how carefully the form and location of small settlements, as well as large ones, were adjusted to fit the new conditions affecting Cretan communities from the tenth century on.

Comparisons outside Crete

Similar sites are found on the islands in the PG-EA period, and here we additionally see the apparent foundation of some *new* small sites of defended type from PG or G onwards. As in Crete, twelfth-century settlement patterns and forms strongly moulded those of the later Iron Age. Fortification walls were again used at a relatively high proportion of island sites, again apparently because of the lack of very extreme defensible topography.

Though many of these sites may actually have earlier roots (the amount of systematic research on them is still limited), the prominence of PG and later material there suggests particularly intensive use from this period. Many sites are coastal – a feature related to the already coastally focused patterning of LH IIIC sites in the islands. Examples include the Ginani Kastro and Aspri Rachi sites on Salamis, Ayios Andreas on Sifnos, Koukounaries on Paros, and Xobourgo on Tinos (all with LH IIIC roots); there is also a new intensity of activity on the coast of Tinos by the Geometric period, with a strategic small promontory site at Vriokastro. Zagora and Ypsili on Andros (with activity traced from at least the PG period); Oikonomos and Donoussa in north Paros (both of G date); the Emborio acropolis, discussed earlier; and Minoa on Amorgos (currently supposed to have been established from LPG) were all of highly defensible or fortified character. Most of these sites stayed relatively small up to the end of the G period, though a few developed into large state polities thereafter. Because choices about topography were more restricted than in Crete, and for the historical reasons already mentioned in Part Two, such sites often seem to have concentrated a larger proportion of their islands' total population than was the case with Cretan citadel sites (Boardman 1967b: 3–97, 247–57; Cambitoglou et al. 1971, 1988; Kourou 2001, 2004; Lemos 2002: 147; Lolos 2001; Marangou 1989, 2002; Schilardi 1973, 1988; Televantou 2001, 2004; Figures 162 and 163). This pattern suggests particularly prolonged, significant, and widespread insecurity through the EIA on the islands, as areas that combined high-intensity maritime trade contacts with small vulnerable populations heavily dependent on this trade and thus tied into coastal residence. The type of defensible site use adopted in the LH IIIC period appears in many cases to have remained the best way to deal with this insecurity. At the same time, island settlement emphases did change by the LG-A period in partly similar ways to those on Crete, with a tendency apparent towards nucleation at relatively low-lying coastal locations such as Emborio, Grotta, and Paroikia.

Trade was also a factor in EIA settlement choices on the islands. In the Cyclades, the fact that defended coastal positions for small settlements became even more attractive in the PG-G period, with the foundation of new sites of this type as late as LG, seems connected to the expanding volume of trade between the Aegean and the east. Sites of this type lie along a many-branched corridor that leads from coastal Turkey/Syria and Cyprus past the southern tip of Chios, along the north and west coasts of Paros and Naxos, and up along the coasts of Andros and Tinos to Euboea and eastern Greece with their large undefended trade centres. An alternative route follows the west coast of Amorgos and the north coast of Crete to arrive off eastern Greece. The pottery record confirms the notion that the Cycladic routes were in an important period of development as trade channels linking the east with the emerging big Aegean players.

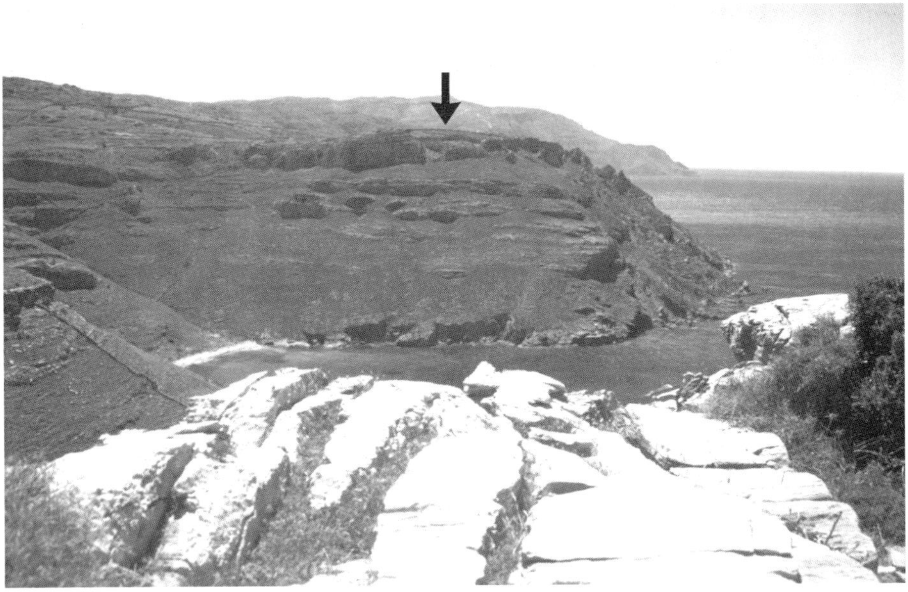

162. Zagora on Andros, from north: arrow indicates settlement area on summit. Image by the author.

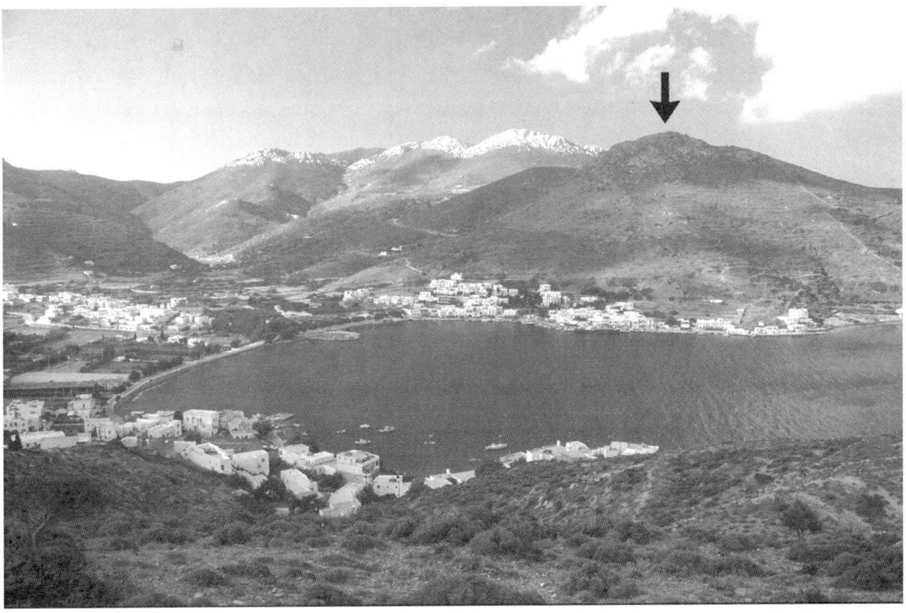

163. Minoa on Amorgos, from north: arrow indicates settlement area on summit. Image by the author.

PG-G cemeteries on Paros, for example, have significant volumes of Dodecanesian imports, while Tinos pottery shows a strong dominance of Euboean styles and imports. Tenth-century pottery from Minoa has links to Attica, Euboea, and the Dodecanese (Kourou 2004: 427–8, 434–6; Marangou 2002: 109; Zapheiropoulou 2004).

On the mainland, a few fortified or defensible sites of limited size founded in the twelfth century also continued in use into the G-A period, especially in coastal areas. The fortified Ayios Athanasios site above Galaxidi continued in use into LG after the smaller defensible site nearby was abandoned (Baziotopoulou and Valvanis 1993). The location of the Galaxidi bay on the increasingly important Corinthian Gulf trade route may have placed too much at stake, and the population have been too small, to defend itself by force of numbers and thus abandon the protection the site offered – though an EIA cemetery on the bay does suggest a return to settlement on the coast by this period, echoing the pattern seen on some Aegean islands (Morgan 1990: 254–6). Koukos Sykia, in the Chalkidiki region, is a similar example of a defended site established in the twelfth century continuing in use to the end of the EIA. However, as already noted, its exposed location on a peninsula makes it much more similar in outlook to an island site. Though small in comparison with the vast majority of mainland EIA sites, such settlements are often more substantial than the Cretan or island examples of citadel sites (for example, the Galaxidi Ayios Athanasios site is 4ha in size). By the LG-A period, just as in other regions, population was finally moving away from such sites down to the lower slopes and coastal zones. The growing port of Torone, for example, may have attracted part of the Koukos Sykia population.

Elsewhere on the mainland, too, immediate proximity to the coast became ever more important, even for small sites. The undefended Euboean sites see a boom in this period, with Eretria in particular seeing extensive new building by Geometric times (Lemos 2002: 233). In the southern Argolid the former coastal centres of Mases, Ermioni, and Halieis regain their role in full. Coastal or near-coastal sites seem to flourish (and some expand) in the southern Lakonian and Messenian peninsulas – at Kaphirio, Kardamili Kastro, Kyparissia Kastro, Koryphasion, Antheia Ellinika, and Nichoria. In the Argolid, coastal Asine remained a sizeable settlement, even while Argos grew in strength (Eder 1998: 25–86; Jameson et al. 1994: 372–4, 437; Lemos 2002: 136–8; McDonald 1983; McDonald and Rapp 1972: 288; Runnels et al. 1995: 372–3; van Andel and Runnels 1987: 101–2). Krebena Kato Melpia, deep in a central Messenian valley and apparently dating between LH IIIC and Archaic, looks more like the Cretan type of small inland citadel site and probably held a separate, long-established political identity within its region, given that its nearest large contemporary settlement was some distance away on the coast at Kyparissia Kastro (McDonald and Hope Simpson 1969: 143; McDonald and Rapp 1972: 294).

28 SUBSISTENCE AND LAND USE IN THE EXPANDING CRETAN POLITIES

Evidence for subsistence expansion

That the original Cretan settlement choices of the twelfth century needed such large-scale adaptation in the tenth is clearly connected to a changing subsistence agenda, along with the other factors I have discussed. I have suggested that there was limited potential for economic growth at many LM IIIC-SM settlements, thanks to their small size, high density, and the fact that their immediate hinterlands contained much land of suboptimal arable quality. The limited circulation of prestige goods in Crete in this period also indicates relatively little opportunity for capital accumulation. In contrast, there are notably larger proportions of accessible, high-quality arable land in the hinterlands of sites selected for continuation and expansion in PG-early Archaic. In a study comparing productivity potential within the one-hour hinterlands of a mixed sample of six EIA sites, the most concentrated evidence for extensive multiperiod agricultural exploitation, easily worked and nutrient-rich soils, and easy accessibility of cultivable areas from the residence area was recorded around the two sites continuing into the Archaic and/or Classical periods – Vrachasi Anavlochos, in the Mirabello bay area, and Profitis Elias/Rokka in central Crete (Wallace 2002; see Plates 5–7 at the beginning of the text). The same kind of correlation is apparent at sites all over the island. Some of the regional contrasts in PG-A Cretan settlement patterns, mentioned previously, support the idea that subsistence expansion was a major concern. For example, the fact that the criterion of an extensive arable territory was already met at most LM IIIC sites in central Crete helps explain why relatively little settlement movement took place in the region from PG. In east Crete, with its highly dissected landscape, rapid and large-scale nucleation might initially have made farming more difficult, helping explain the relatively high numbers of dispersed small settlements remaining there until a relatively late date, and the full transformation of the island's economy.

The expansion of the trade economy occurring at this time must have required an increased volume of subsistence production, both to support goods manufacture and to finance growing procurement systems. Was subsistence expansion able to take place *as a result of* settlement nucleation – the latter being driven by other factors, including the trade boom and pressure for political change – or did it *drive* the nucleation process? The answer is probably both. Nucleation seems to have been a deeply embedded and integral part of the process of complexity development. While itself stimulated by a number of new factors, *living* in large settlements also surely drove change very strongly (Morgan 2003: 55, 71–3, 107).

As a result of the lack of diachronic excavation data from large nucleated sites, we have few insights into the nature or rate of subsistence expansion, such as evidence for extensification or cash cropping. The evidence from the recent Azoria excavations should prove illuminating and already indicates a larger scale of food storage around one complex (the so-called andreion, A800) than anything seen at LM IIIC sites (Haggis et al. 2004: 373–9). The context seems to be that of public feasting: increased surplus production would be needed to finance this kind of developing political institution in large polities. The main foodstuffs in use at Azoria are the same as those found at LM IIIC sites, and in the PG-EA layers at the 'citadel' site of Kavousi Kastro (including different wheat varieties, barley, legumes, olives, vine, and fig). However, one possible indicator of subsistence reorientation does appear in the PG-G faunal record at Kastro. Sheep and goat representation diminishes slightly in favour of pig, perhaps suggesting that the village by this time formed part of an expanded and intensified economic system, using the bottom-land as well as the hillslopes (Snyder and Klippel 1999). This suggests that even where settlement locations retained the nonoptimal characteristics of the IIIC period, *all* settlements within an emerging political territory participated in a changed type of economic system from PG onwards.

The Kommos excavations have produced one of the best published sources of organic remains for this period, but the status of the site as a sanctuary means these cannot be taken as representing the full range, or normal proportions, of food species in regular use (Reese 2000; Shay and Shay 2000). Again, the record shows that olives, pulses, fig, and grape were cultivated. The animals sacrificed reflect the same species being exploited domestically elsewhere, though certain emphases are probably specifically related to the cult. The increasing presence of pig over time echoes the subsistence record from sites like Kavousi and may again reflect higher-investment subsistence strategies at expanding large sites with access to large areas of bottom-land. Fish consumption was also common at Kommos, including exotic species probably brought in (perhaps for dedication) by traders visiting the port. The Kavousi record shows that fish and shellfish were also used in the daily diet, but not to an extent suggesting that fishing was a dominant subsistence activity (Snyder and Klippel 1999: 68). Interesting patterns at Kommos are a rise in the amount of olive charcoal and pollen and a reduction in representation of 'scrub species' by the Classical period. Shay and Shay suggest the gradual extension of olive replanting in the area after a drop during the EIA. Growth in this high-investment activity would fit the pattern of expansion in subsistence systems proposed earlier and is supported by finds of olive pips of relatively large size, suggesting more intensive cultivation (Shay and Shay 2000: 652, 656–7, 663).

Another indication that a wider subsistence hinterland was coming into use, and in a more organised, formalised way, is the appearance of very small scattered fieldhouses or farmsteads in the vicinity of the large nucleated sites, though these are known only from survey and are difficult to date: many may belong only to the Archaic rural expansion (see below). On the lower slopes of Anavlochos, there are traces of at least two small sites dating somewhere between the PG and Archaic periods (see Plate 5B). These have much easier access than the main settlement on the summit of Anavlochos to the large areas of prime soils in the local region, suggesting an increasingly intensive and more invested-in use of the arable territory during this period. I discuss the spread of small sites within the Archaic period more fully below. In the Kera valley, the small PG-G settlements around Papoura, mentioned previously, were located closer to the valley bottom than their LM IIIC predecessors in the region, promoting more efficient, larger-scale subsistence activity. Further examples of probable satellite sites of PG-A date are located around Vrokastro – the latter, of course, itself not a large nucleation, but more of a citadel site (Hayden 2003: 383, 2005: 140, 142, 144–5, 159–67, 169–70). The sites of Kato Arniko, Ayios Phainourios 3, and VK 3 seem to fit the satellite description, and there are more widely scattered and sizeable (though still small) sites in the same broader area.

Likely changes in landholding and the rise of land-based debt: Crete and other regions

I noted previously that the PG nucleation must have produced larger integrated territories. As a result, a more formalised definition of landholding rights almost certainly came about. Potential must have existed during this transition for considerable adjustments in the balance and quality of land worked by any individual. Together, increased labour specialisation in the sphere of commodity production and the generation of larger surpluses as a result of agricultural extensification probably encouraged significant growth in the volume and complexity of borrowing, trading, and sharing arrangements regarding subsistence produce: Hesiod tells us these practices were common in central Greece by the seventh century (*Works and Days* 349–51). Repayment of debts incurred in this way may have continued to be regularised in part through public or private feasting/hospitality events, of the type I discussed in Part Two. But the larger stakes now in play must also have encouraged other types of economic transfer. The growth of labour specialisation and the increased size of economic territories would limit the ability to pay off such debts by the simple periodic transfer of agricultural labour to the creditor's land, or by concentrated labour investment in one's own land in order to raise a short-term surplus. Thus, payment probably increasingly took place in commodities and in 'rights' to quantities of subsistence produce, or their equivalents, from the debtor. The political institutions emerging in the large nucleated settlements would have helped regulate and develop such complex economic arrangements. I have already argued for an extremely strong attachment to place on the part of scattered new, small communities from very soon after the settlement shift circa 1200 BC. The supposition is supported by various elements of the PG-EA record, including the tight regional format of nucleation, the prolonged use of citadel sites, and the symbolic reuse of some abandoned LM IIIC settlement sites, discussed below. During the period of nucleation, with its associated restructuring of territories, such attachments are likely to have become formally consolidated, and to have been valued highly as the basis of claims to membership in the state. Thus, mounting debts to neighbours or peers seem unlikely often to have been financed by the direct exchange of land as an alienable commodity. Instead, they may have been paid in terms of a theoretical percentage of yearly produce from the land of an indebted individual. This arrangement may have over time involved the acquisition by regular creditors of permanent rights to some of the land's produce – the effective foundation of serf systems, which were to have such a long history in Crete (Cowgill 1988: 260–1).

On the mainland, much less secure attachment to agricultural territories, and more open competition for them, may have existed during and after the collapse period, given the nature of the new settlement landscape. New, large, loosely structured communities stayed resident in very large and rich arable territories that had been neatly divided up in controlled packages, and managed through a hierarchical settlement pattern, under palatial economic systems (Small 1998, 1999). At the broadest scale, territories probably stayed attached to the same regional communities – the general pattern of settlement rebalancing around 1200 BC suggests they were unlikely to be claimed by entirely new groups. At the same time, the disruptions of the period were substantial enough to shift the balance of rights to land in many small respects. As economic complexity grew from PG onward, the absence of strong community-level institutions suggests that the welll-controlled types of local territorial adjustment associated with large polity formation in Crete (based in strong attachments to land by individuals and small groups) did not apply. As a result, land-tied debt was probably always more piecemeal and less well embedded socially, with obligations more often repaid in other ways, especially as a complex trade economy emerged.

Though serf systems did exist by the Archaic period or earlier in the mainland, they seem less important in some areas than was the case in Crete: EIA settlement history may help explain why.

Certain features of the Laconian EIA settlement pattern suggest why this region, in contrast to other parts of the mainland, *did* develop a particularly strong serf system, known about from later texts. The topography of the region offers a single main route from the sea inland up the Eurotas valley. The most attractive arable land comprises a large blanket zone in the north, with another large zone of considerably poorer quality to the south, in the Helos plain area. In the LBA these areas had an exceptional spread of large to medium-sized settlements, rather than the extreme hierarchy found elsewhere in mainland Greece (Waterhouse and Hope Simpson 1960, 1961: 170–3). From the end of the Bronze Age, almost all were abandoned, with the probable contraction of population into a very few large settlements, including the Sparta site (Cartledge 2001: 61; Catling 2002: 153–5; Cavanagh and Crouwel 2002; Coulson 1985; 1988; Eder 1998: 109–13; Raftopoulou 1997). This pattern isolated many people far from their formerly worked territories. Yet thanks to the powerful territorial identity structures likely to have existed in the LBA pattern of densely scattered and sizeable settlements, they probably kept particularly strong residual attachments to those lands. These groups must have quickly found themselves in unequal economic relations with the established users of territories closest to Sparta – the new settlement focus of the EIA, located in the region's best arable zone. In combination, these factors might have promoted the rise of land-tied debt here, rather than other kinds of wealth transfer, as the economy became more complex from PG onward.

29 INSIDE SETTLEMENTS

Introduction

I will now turn to look at how architectural developments inside PG-early Archaic Cretan settlements reflect societal change. The small number of PG-EA stratified settlement deposits so far excavated poses an obstacle here, but some interesting observations can still be made. Certain questions are of particular interest. For example, how far did the large nucleated settlements take on centralised functions in relation to smaller sites in their regions? If this occurred, was it under terms of political dominance by the larger units, or of structured collaboration within a single integrated political territory? As noted earlier, settlements of 'citadel' type are few in number in any region and do not appear at all in some regions. There are also relatively few known examples of permanent outlying hamlets in the PG-G period. Where found, the latter usually cluster very closely adjacent to the nucleated sites, rather than having an independent existence in the wider hinterland. Thus, there is little indication from settlement pattern at this stage that the new nucleations acted as full functional centres for a hierarchy of of smaller surrounding settlements. By the seventh century, however, the distribution of rural sites and their relationships with large nucleated settlements were changing, as territories and political institutions both became more firmly consolidated.

Cult spaces

Despite lacking a clear status as functional centres, the nucleated sites may gradually, as they grew, have co-opted some social and ritual functions from the neighbouring citadel sites, in a pattern typical of emergent complex polities in other cultural contexts (Pauketat 2000: 34). At some small citadel sites, spaces for public cult and secular feasting may have become aggregated by the end of the EIA, as the nearest nucleation appropriated formal cult. At Kavousi Kastro, no cult building was found, and Vrokastro, too, lacks a clear PG-EA temple. The Vrokastro LG Building 16–17 (77.1sqm) is larger than others on the site, and some finds there (deposits of small votive figurines and jewellery) suggest a use for cult (Figures 164 and 165; Hall 1914: 108–9; Hayden 1983: 377, 1991: 109–10). It is, however, significantly different in form and content from the kinds of town temples found at nucleated sites by the seventh century. These have a distinctive plan and are often associated with features like monumental stonework and inscriptions, as

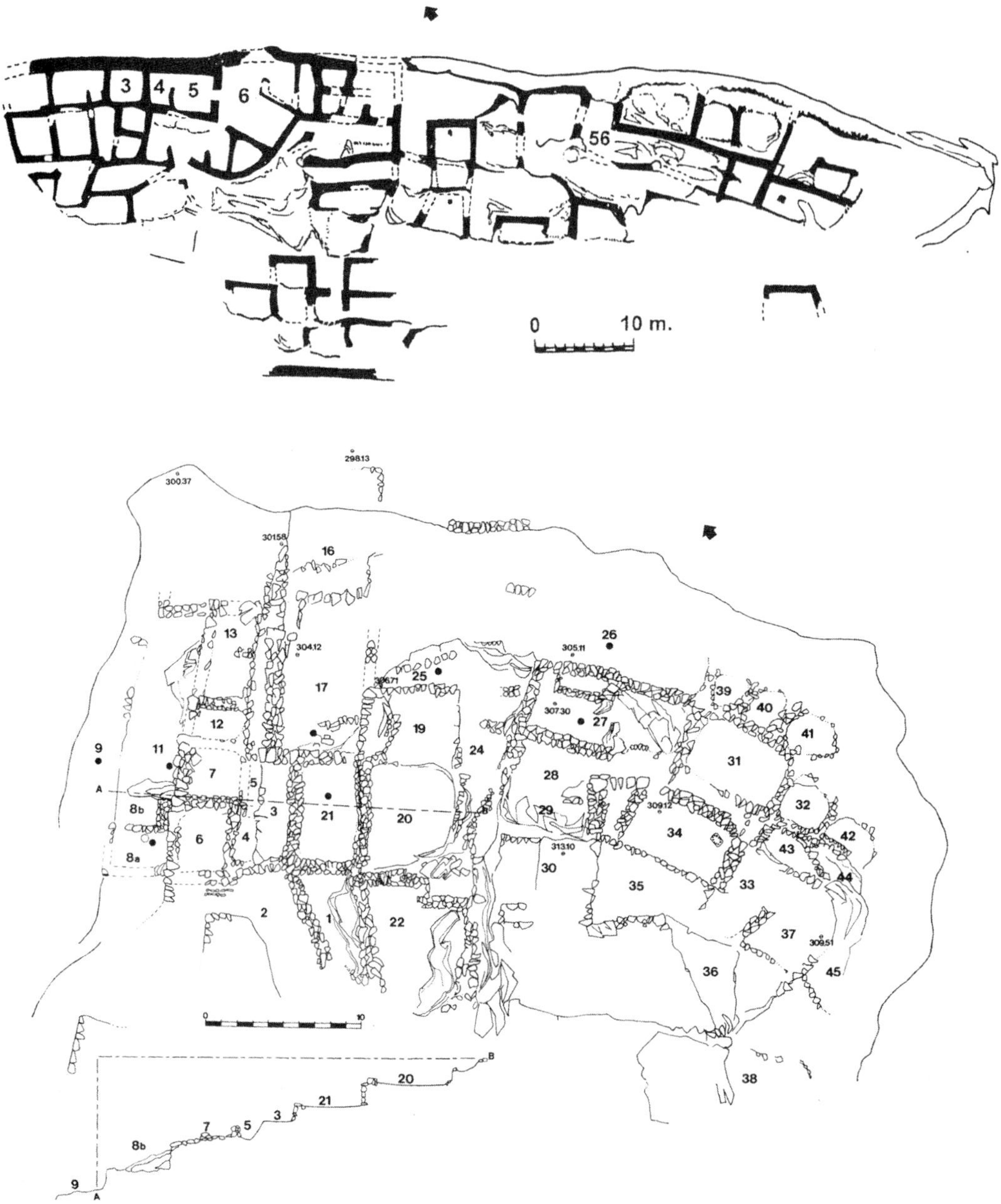

164. Settlement plan of Vrokastro, upper and lower sectors (after Hayden 2003, plans 1 and 2). By permission of B. J. Hayden.

at Prinias (Pernier 1914, 1934). The Vrokastro building perhaps functioned as a combined secular gathering/feasting and cult unit, as the main settlement cult became focused elsewhere (by the early Archaic period Vrokastro's population was leaving it for a large settlement core inland and a port on the coast to the north: Hayden 2004: 167–9).

A partly related phenomenon is the transformation of small settlements into territorial cult places (apparently for use by communities resident at the nucleations) during the last stage of

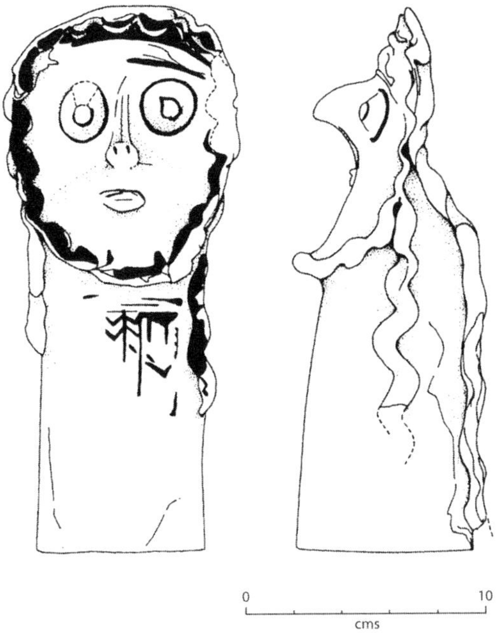

165. Human figurine from Vrokastro Building 16–17 (after Hayden 1991, Fig. 13, p. 136). By permission of B. J. Hayden.

their use or shortly after their abandonment. As the Smari citadel settlement was abandoned in the seventh century, the area of the long-lived public feasting complex on the summit was reused for a temple alone. The site probably now became a territorial cult place for the nearby large polity of Lyttos (Hatzi-Vallianou 2000; Figure 166). On the islands, too, temples at small citadel settlements used into the Geometric period were sometimes often turned into territorial cult places for larger polities after the settlements went out of use – Zagora and Koukounaries provide good examples (Cambitoglou et al. 1988: 167–8; Mazarakis Ainian 1988, 1997: 82–6; Schilardi 1988). Having amalgamated the populations of these small sites, the large nucleated polities on the islands seem to have aimed to tie the sites' history and identity associations firmly and permanently into their own. A similar pattern appears over a much shorter distance (within the same polity) at Gortyn (see below) and at Emborio, where a temple established in the settlement on the summit in the Geometric period stayed in use into Archaic times long after settlement had moved down to the harbour (Boardman 1967b). We see related patterns on the central mainland, too. At Isthmia, a site finally abandoned for settlement in LH IIIC-PG was turned into a sanctuary strongly connected to the polis settlement at Corinth by the eighth century (Morgan 1998, 1999). In the Argolid, temples became firmly established at Mycenae, Tiryns, and Asine (all settlement sites that had had some occupation during the EIA) as Argos extended its territory between the eighth and seventh centuries: the state is likely to have financed or controlled all of these temples to some degree (Hall 1997b; Klein 1997; Lemos 2002: 135–49; Mazarakis Ainian 1997: 164–5).

Inside the few excavated examples of nucleated PG-EA settlements on Crete, cult shows signs of having developed in elaboration and complexity as the settlement expanded, with more than one cult building appearing in each settlement. In LM IIIC I have already suggested the spread of elements of public-type cult practice into private contexts in large settlements such as Karfi, apparently in connection to the interests of competing power groups. However, the public status of the cult institution seems to have been too highly valued at this time, or the political strength

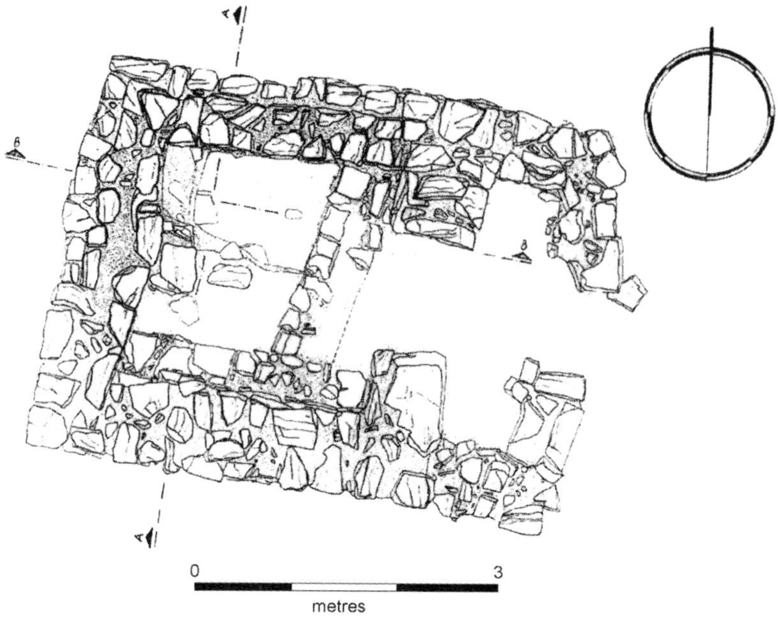

166. Plan of temple at Smari Profitis Elias (after Hatzi-Vallianou and Evthimiou 2000, Fig. 2, p. 527). By permission of D. Hatzi-Vallianou.

of private groups too limited, allow or require the establishment of more than one formal temple per settlement (at least in the cases of small to medium-sized settlements for which we have complete or near-complete plans). In the growing PG-EA polities, attention seems to have been paid to monumentalising cult – removing it further from the personal sphere – but also to diversifying it spatially at a more formal, public level – especially at very large sites. The latter development may have been a controlled response to the consolidation and growth of competing private (clan-based) interests in the expanding communities under the new economic conditions.

There is still a relative simplicity in the temple buildings at nucleated sites of PG-A date, and a marked crossover with the format of domestic space. Strong references are made to recent cultural tradition when marking out these buildings as special. The seventh-century cult buildings at Dreros and Prinias differ little from LM IIIC shrines in many aspects of their plan, being simple rectangular buildings with benches; both almost certainly had predecessor shrines of the early EIA in the same locales (Gesell 1985: 57; Marinatos 1936; Figures 167 and 168). The central rectangular hearth is a new feature, marking out these buildings more clearly from domestic structures as part of an emerging civic apparatus, even while the traditional houselike plan was retained. Monumental reliefs and inscriptions have the same distinguishing role. At Thronos, the open-air cult/feasting location on the summit seems referred to in the siting of a separate cult building nearby as early as the ninth century (D'Agata 2000). At Prinias, there appear to be at least two cult complexes in different parts of the settlement by the time of its abandonment in Archaic – one still on the site of the old LM IIIC temple area (Pernier 1914, 1934; Rizza 2000, 2006; Figure 169). At Gortyn by the sixth century, several temples existed, including one on the early EIA settlement site on the Acropolis hill – perhaps built over the original temple building of that settlement (Johannowsky 2002; Rizza and Scrinari 1968). At Phaistos, a number of cult locales developed between the seventh and sixth centuries, including a temple close to the remains of the palace in the southeast part of the site and another on the main LM IIIC settlement area at the Acropoli Mediana (Cucuzza 1997, 1998; Watrous and Hadzi-Vallianou

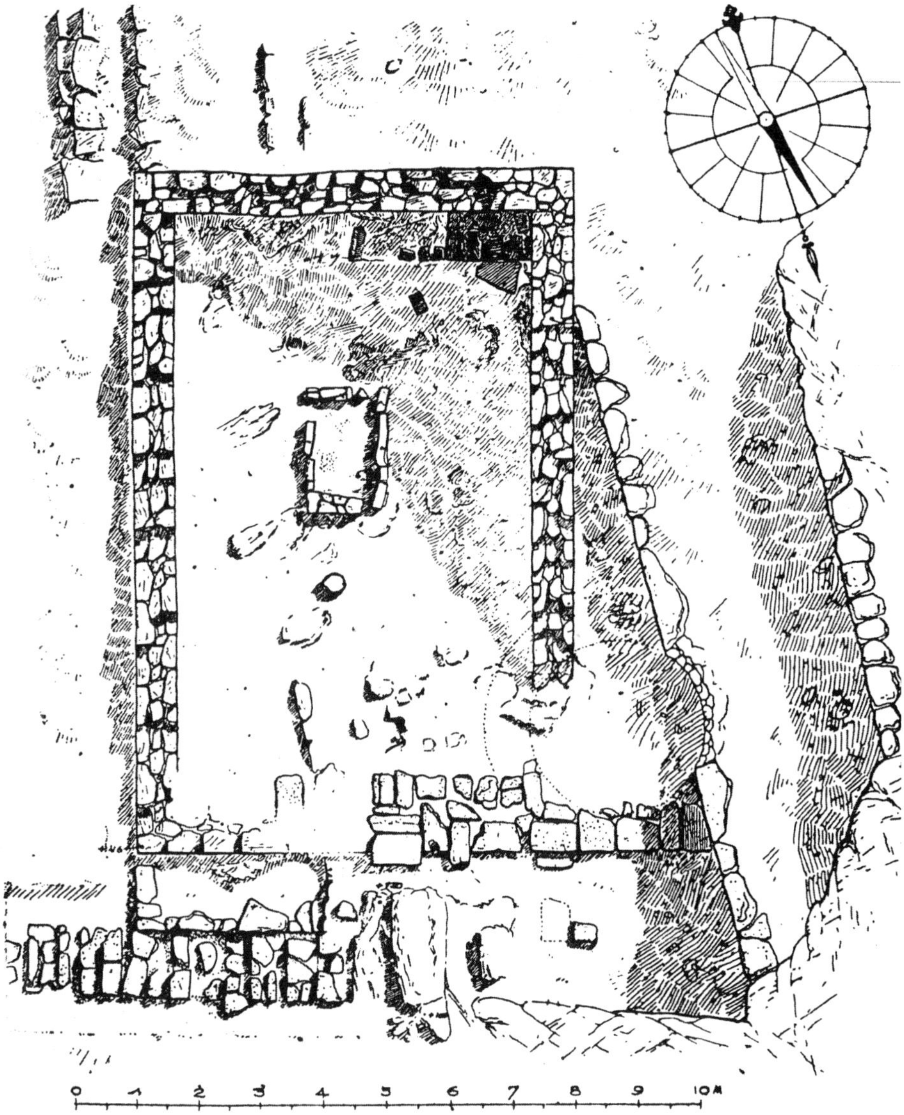

167. Plan of Dreros temple (after Marinatos 1936, Plate XXVII, p. 161).

2004a: 315). At Knossos, too, several cult locales developed by Archaic – including the temple of Demeter, south of the Bronze Age palace, and the smaller 'Sanctuary of Rhea' built in the palace's remains, as well as perhaps the 'Glaukos shrine', west of the palace, a building used in the seventh and rebuilt in the sixth century. It was not definitely used for cult, though its later use encouraged the excavators to think it had a dedicated cult use in its sixth-century incarnation (Callaghan 1976; Coldstream 1973; Prent 2005b: 261, 378).

Domestic space

Inside large settlements, there are few signs of the contesting of space or of the development of distinctive kinds or zones of domestic architecture by new residents anxious to mark themselves

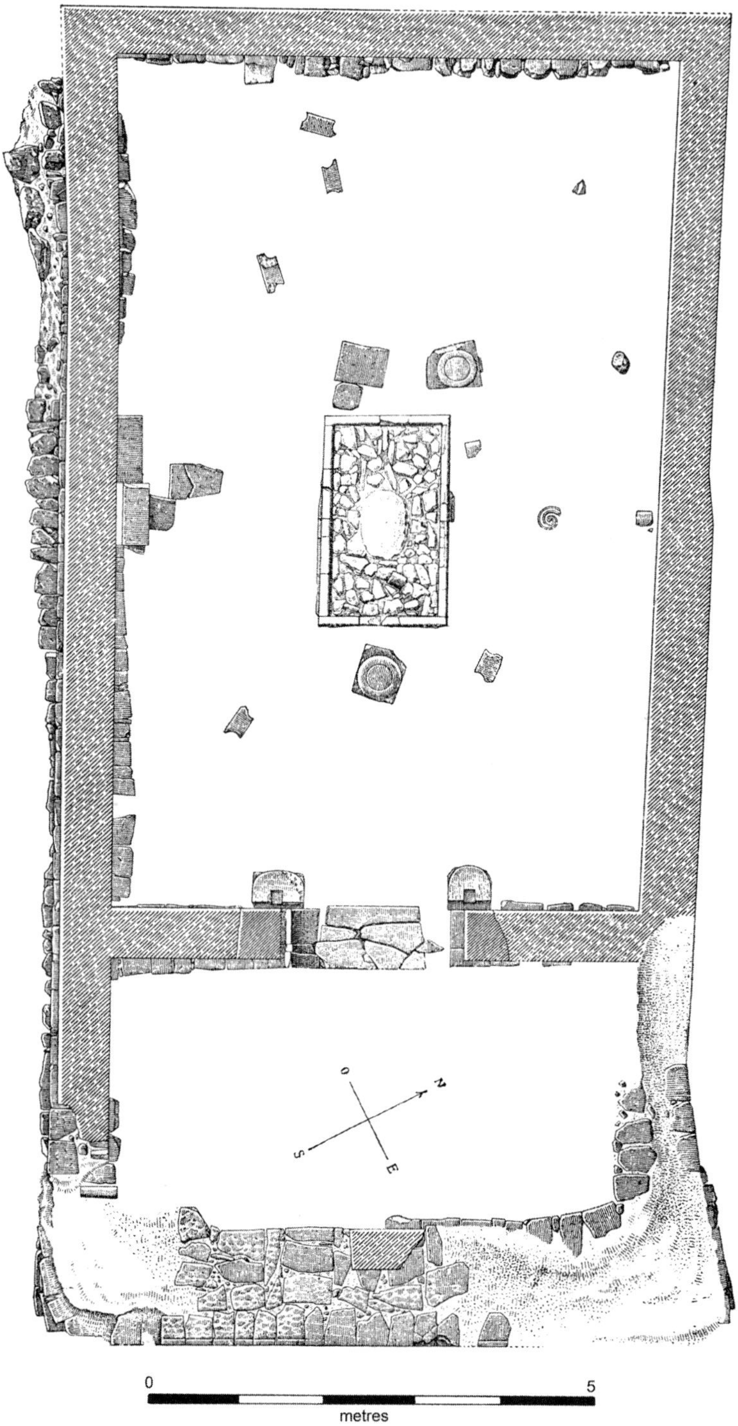

168. Plan of Prinias Temple A (after Pernier 1914, Plate VI).

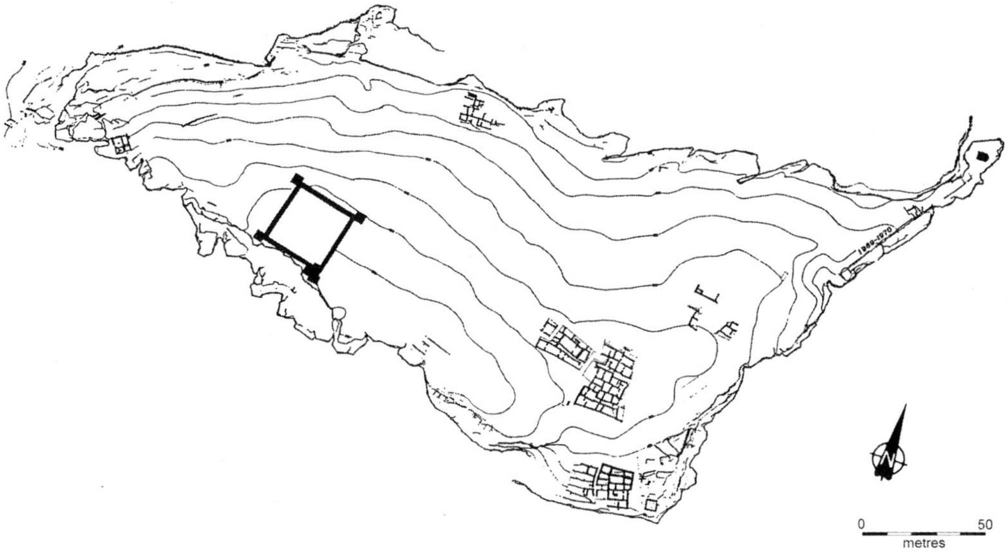

169. Plan of excavated areas at the Prinias settlement, showing location of Temples A and B (after Rizza 2000, Fig. 1, p. 161). By permission of G. Rizza.

out from other groups within the settlement. By Archaic, settlements are zoned to a greater extent than they had been in the twelfth to eleventh centuries, but this mostly involves the separation and development of public/civic spaces. This supports the evidence I have already presented for a relatively peaceful nucleation process, smoothly negotiated within strong existing frameworks of regional identity.

There is little evidence, either, for a wholly new conception or definition of domestic space in the enlarging settlements. This is perhaps unsurprising, since they continued, and literally built on, housing frameworks established in LM IIIC. We saw that domestic architecture at twelfth- to eleventh-century sites was characterised by regular rebuilding and alteration, often as part of an agglomerative process. This continued during PG-early Archaic, when residential areas at all sites seem to have been rebuilt at regular intervals: Azoria, Thronos, and Prinias demonstrate this for the nucleated sites, Vrokastro and Kavousi Kastro for the citadel sites (Figures 170 and 171).

The basic household unit seems to have operated in a roughly parallel form at both the large nucleations and small citadel settlements. For example, there is little sign of a diminishment in the relative status of the household, or of reduced levels of differentiation between households, at minor sites as a result of the shift of elites to major sites, as observable in some cases of state emergence elsewhere (Pauketat 2000: 26–7). Household-level storage, for example, continued to exist at both large and small continuing settlements, with few signs that particular large groups or institutions were starting to control the distribution of food at any level. Exceptional storage capacity does appear in possible public feasting buildings found at the nucleated settlements, which I will discuss later.

Though the larger settlement areas at nucleated sites theoretically allowed more room for expansion of individual houses, house sizes remain modest by comparison with those at large and prosperous LBA sites. The domestic complexes built up by extended families over time in the crammed settlement cores were not easy to expand in a unitary way at any point in these settlements' history. At the citadel sites (which comprise some of our best excavated sources,

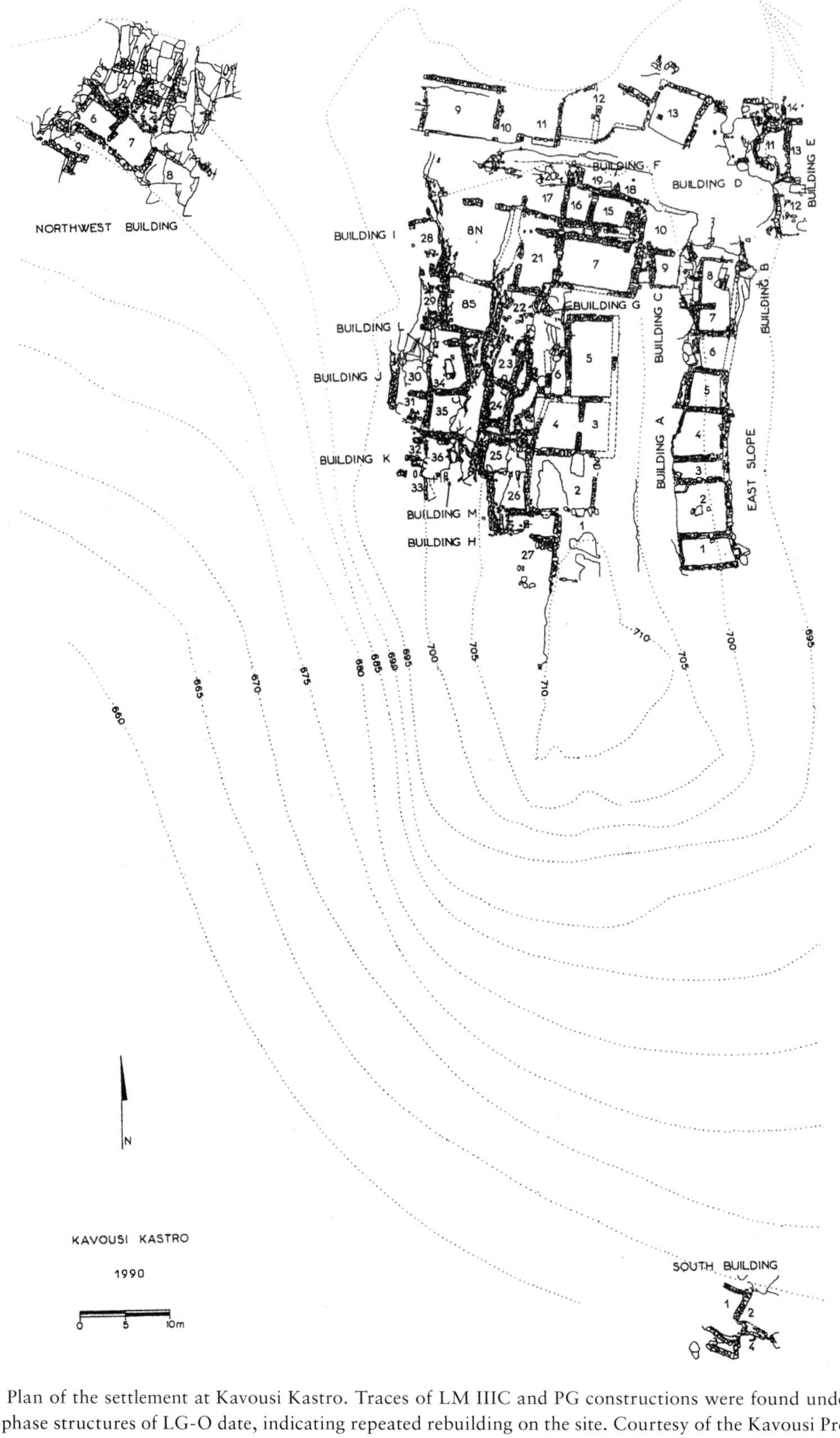

170. Plan of the settlement at Kavousi Kastro. Traces of LM IIIC and PG constructions were found under the final-phase structures of LG-O date, indicating repeated rebuilding on the site. Courtesy of the Kavousi Project.

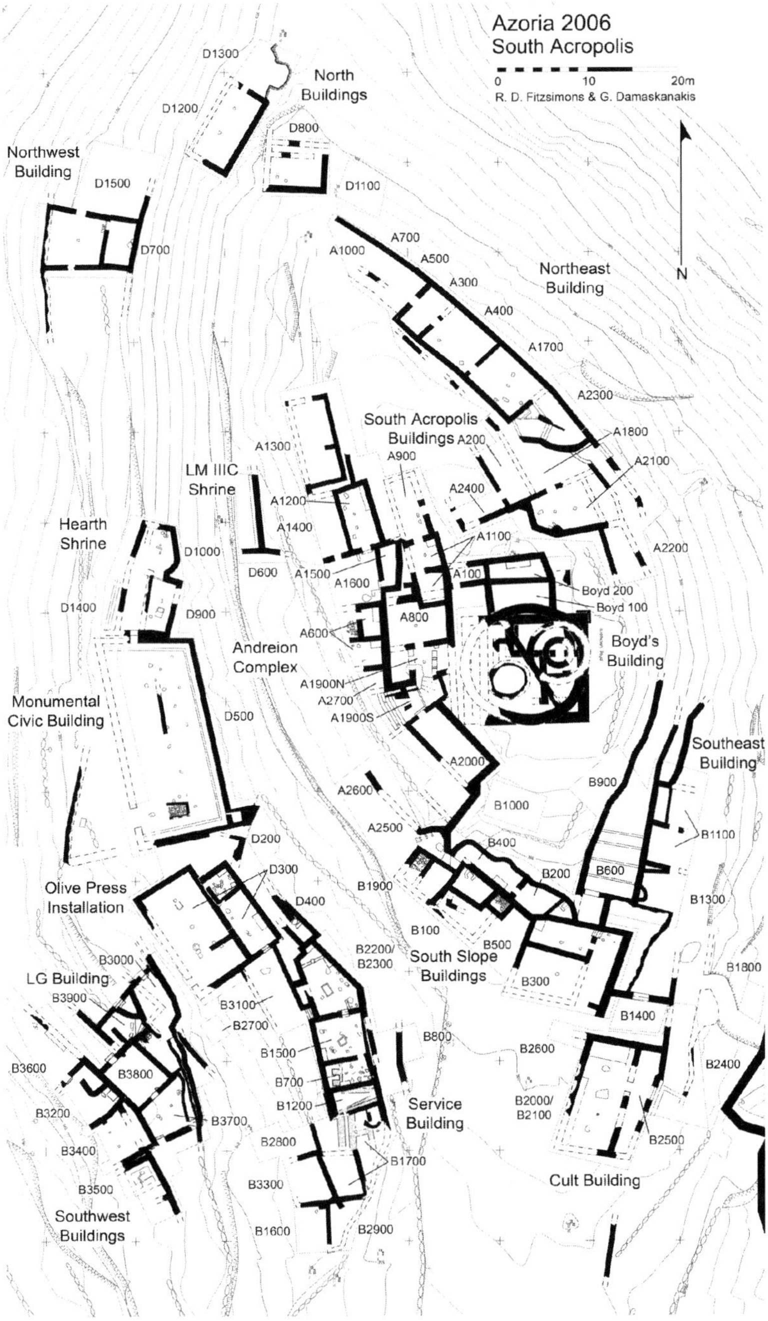

171. Plan of the Azoria settlement after excavation in 2006 (after Haggis et al. 2004). Structures and deposits of LM IIIC-G date were found under the Archaic settlement, with evidence of a major new building phase across the core of the settlement in the Archaic period. By permission of the Azoria Project.

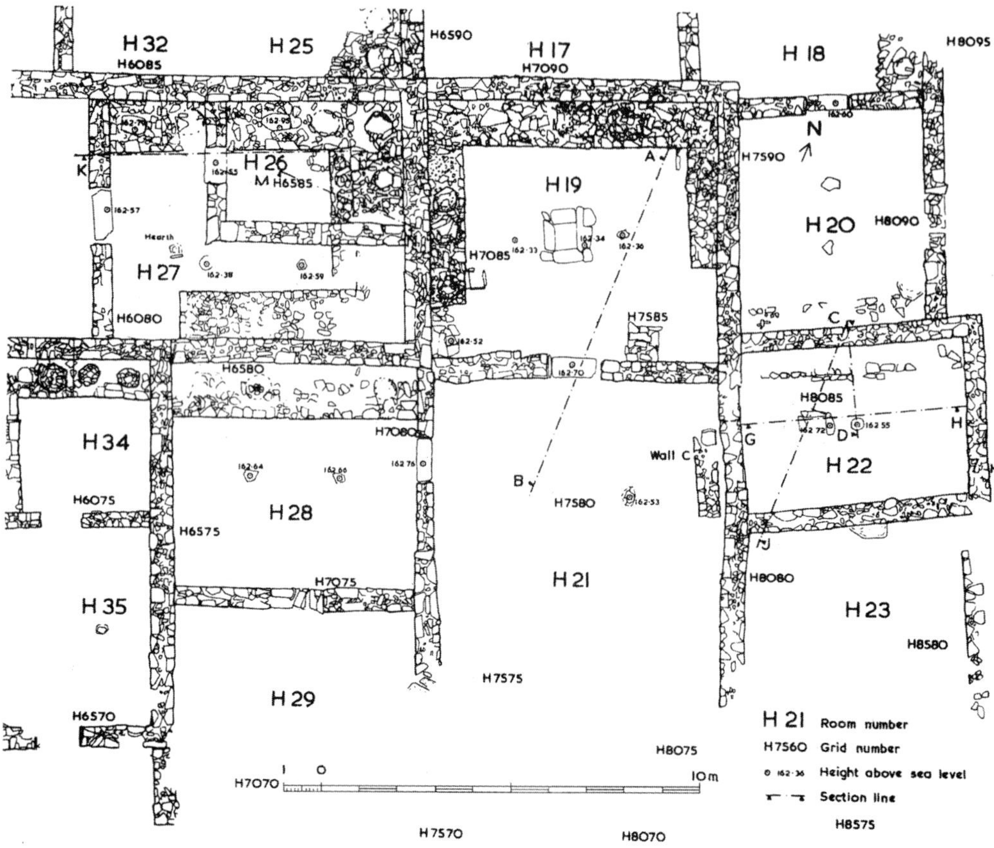

172. House at Zagora, extended before the abandonment of the settlement to include a former courtyard between two smaller houses (after Cambitoglou et al. 1988, Plate a). By permission of A. Cambitoglou.

yet are not widely representative of the period) space anyway remained at a premium. Some changes do appear, however. The citadel site of Kavousi Kastro, the larger nucleations at Azoria and Prinias, and the continuing and expanding site at Phaistos, in common with island sites like Zagora, all show a change of balance in household organization by LG/Archaic, with room sizes within a house tending to become more equal. More houses now incorporate two middle-sized 'main' rooms, one of which often seems to fulfil the functions of a kitchen (Cambitoglou et al. 1988: 79–107; Cucuzza 1998: 64–7; Gesell et al. 1985; Haggis et al. 2004: 352–64; Mazarakis Ainian 1997: 171–2; Morris 1998: 21–3; Rizza 2000, 2006; Figure 172). Houses at early Archaic Azoria are generally larger than their EIA predecessors at other sites (Figure 173). By the early seventh century, a single extended household group may often have come to own a whole large block operating as a single unit, as in the case of Phaistos Building AA or the North-West Building at Kavousi Kastro (Cucuzza 1998: 65–6, in press; Mook 1993, 1998; Figures 174 and 175). As we have seen, this had formerly only occurred in otherwise exceptional buildings, possibly in connection with feasting use. In the domestic arena, then, the kin group seems now to have been represented at a larger, more unitary scale, but also a more defined and standardised one.

Social ostentation and display via the house now seem less important than they had been in the early EIA, when even subtle enhancements of size and plan seem to have been socially significant. The display of a family's or clan's status seems to have been increasingly diverted into

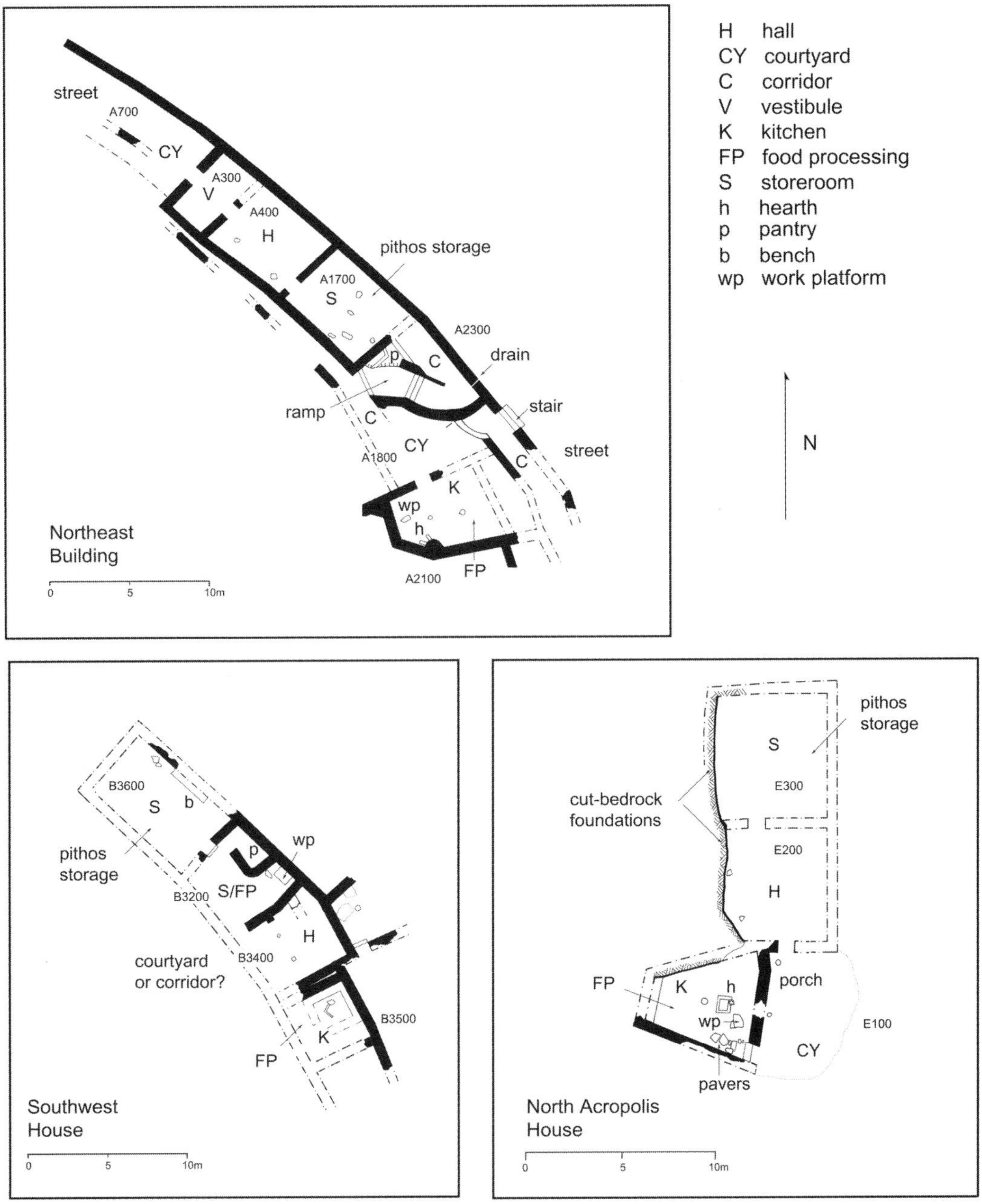

173. Plans of houses at Azoria (Azoria Project). By permission of the Azoria Project.

other spheres (those of cult and public feasting) as these became increasingly formalized, as well as into the burial arena, where the new access to high volumes of trade goods could be exploited. On the other hand, PG-early Archaic Crete shows little of the extreme egalitarianism in settlement planning hinted at by the seventh century in the central Aegean and colonial worlds, characterised by equally sized, almost identical house plots and standardised street plans (Nevett 1999: 80–154; Whitley 2001: 165–95). This is partly because of the earlier history of settlement development in Crete, which restricted the ability to replan at very large scales. But it may also

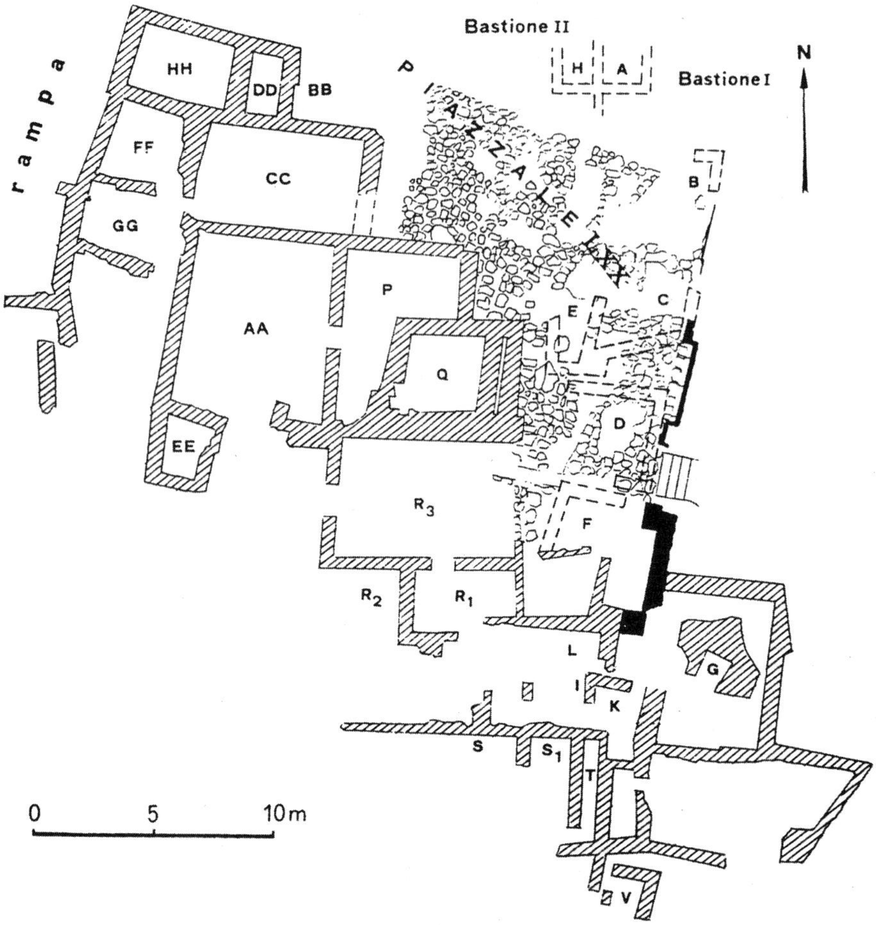

174. Plan of Geometric building complex at Phaistos (after Cucuzza 1998, Fig. 6.2, p. 64). By permission of N. Cucuzza.

reflect the less comprehensive, dominant, and strongly embedded nature of the equality principle in Cretan societies during the transition to the state, a point I shall return to later.

Overall, then, intra-settlement spaces seem to become generally more formalised and consolidated in this period, suggesting fewer opportunities now existed for their uncontrolled periodic appropriation by individual groups engaged in status-building activities. The slightly larger house sizes suggest that some formerly public space was being permanently split up and reallocated, as the extended kin group consolidated its standing within the emergent polity, but at the same time experienced new parameters on its power (Jameson 1990b; Pauketat 2000: 30–1). In the same connection, as the institution of public feasting developed, 'public' use of the house for hosting activities seems to have become more contained, and less volatile in character – even while household space generally expanded.

Feasting venues

Other social and political changes occurring in this period support the notion that public ceremonial feasting, sometimes incorporating a cult element but still separate from temple-based

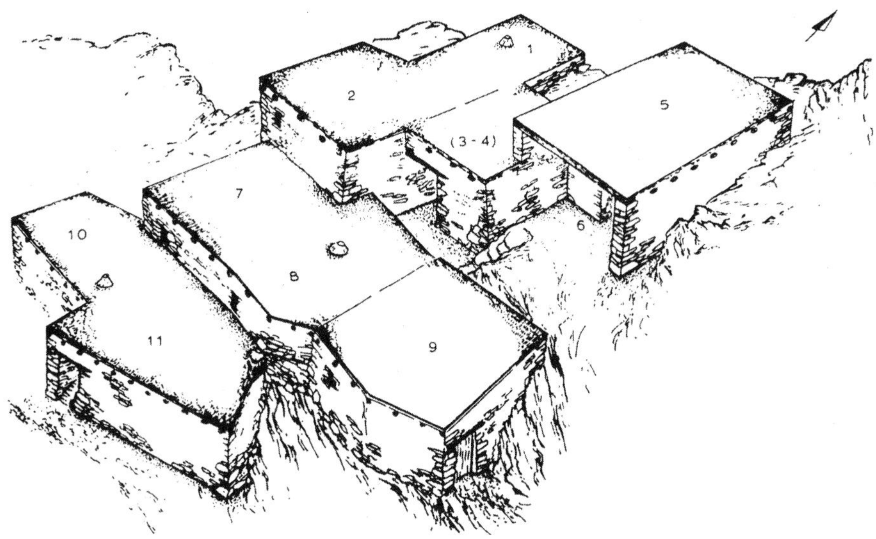

175. Reconstruction of the North-West Building at Kavousi Kastro (after Mook 1993, Fig. 4.2, p. 47). Courtesy of the Kavousi Project.

cult, played a significant role in the developing nucleations. By at least the Archaic period, but probably much earlier, it seems to have taken place in purpose-built structures of a more elaborate character than those I have tentatively identified in the earlier EIA. Recent work at Azoria, revealing a sixth-century building described by the excavators as an 'andreion', particularly supports this notion. As well as serving residents of the nucleations themselves, such buildings may have been important interaction points for people visiting from citadel sites or other small settlements in the wider territory of a nucleation, even if the latter preserved their own individual feasting or combined feasting/cult venues, as suggested above. Each of these levels of participation in feasting may have represented a different kind of community 'belonging'. At the nucleated sites, participation surely symbolised membership of the whole regional polity, with the nucleated settlement at its heart.

The growth of organised investment in feasting by the Archaic period prefigures the role of the common meal in Classical Cretan poleis and is itself rooted in the feasting practice of the earlier EIA, which sometimes seems to have moved in a rather volatile manner between private houses and purpose-defined public venues. We still have too few data from excavated PG-EA sites to know how far public feasting venues conformed to any kind of recognized template, as I argue to have been the case in the earlier EIA. On one hand, we might expect a growing concern with standardising the material culture of public life, as groups sharing very similar cultural histories physically came together and looked for common reference points. On the other hand, increasing emphasis on identity definition for the newly expanded settlements and their territories might promote deliberate differences in the design of such buildings from site to site. The Azoria 'andreion' complex incorporated specialised blocks of rooms for food storage (A1200, 1400, 1600), dining/cult (A800), and craft production (A1300), suggesting deliberate provision for public gatherings in a venue quite strongly distinguished from domestic houses (Haggis et al. 2004: 367–85; Figure 176). Like temples, however, feasting structures retained an overlap in form with the household sphere, of the kind that had helped enhance and ground their social role in the twelfth century: the Azoria 'andreion' had attached storerooms and kitchens like an expanded house of the period.

a

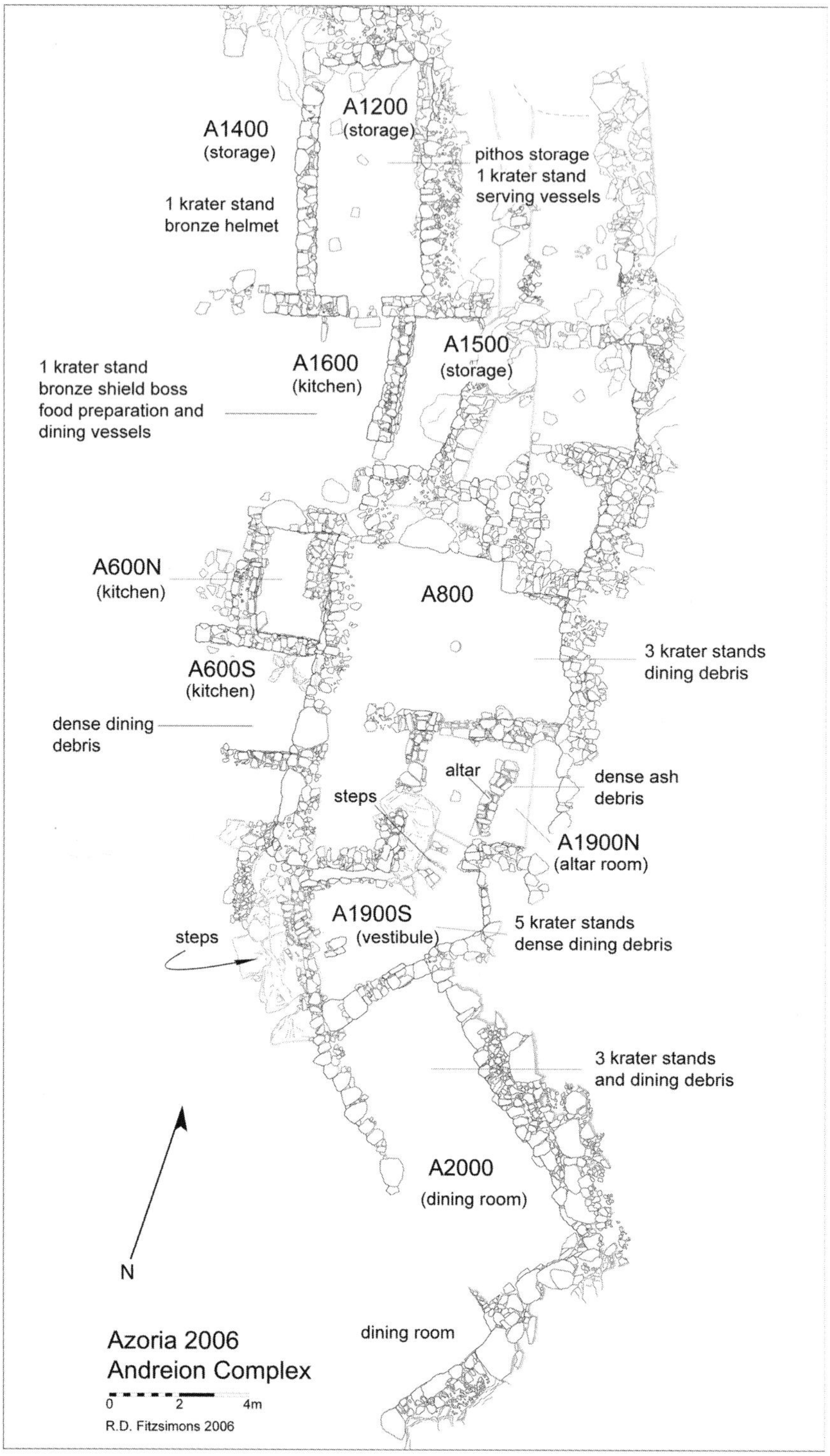

176a–b. Plan of the andreion complex at Azoria (Azoria Project). Unpublished images. By permission of the Azoria Project.

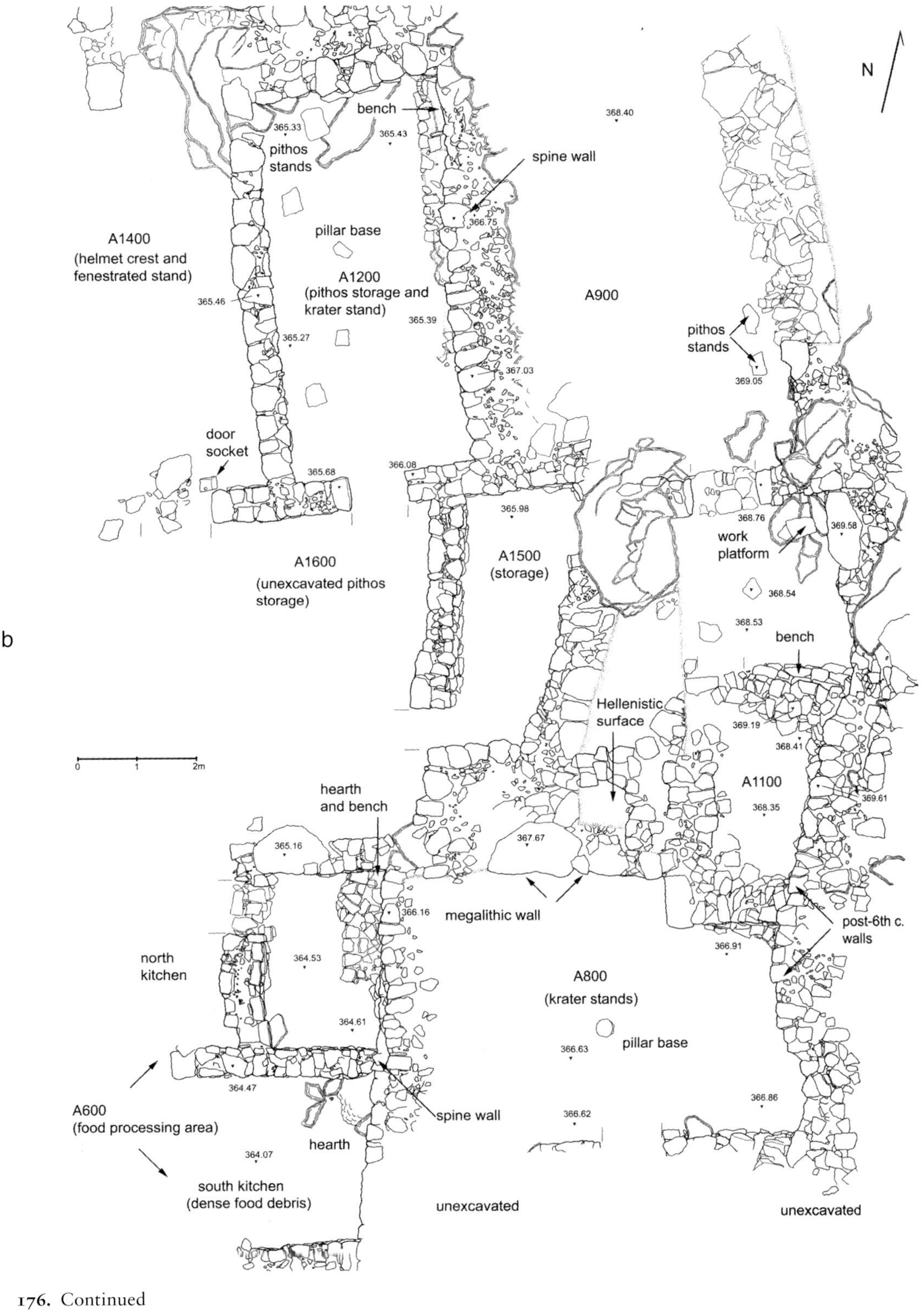

176. Continued

Civic zoning

By the seventh century, small states across the Aegean are distinguished by the emergence of distinct civic areas, increasingly formalized and monumentalised over time. At many of the Cretan PG-EA nucleated sites, summit areas (usually the location of the first occupation in the LM IIIC period) seem to be the zones chosen for concentrated public use, though we have limited evidence about this prior to the seventh century. Early Archaic Azoria provides the most detailed case study of the way a new degree of civic planning was combined with increased investment in building technology to distinguish these zones (Haggis et al. 2004: 349–51). A spine wall of massive blocks surrounded the summit, with structures built up against it on both sides. The wall blocked off the summit area for mostly public uses (including the andreion complex) though some apparently 'ordinary' houses were also located here. Recently a possible assembly building and temple have been found within the same zone (Haggis and Mook pers comm; Haggis et al. 2007a, 2007b). In view of the symbolically meaningful role held for residents of the expanding nucleations by the earliest settled parts of their sites (the latter were deliberately referenced when siting cult locales, as we have seen) and the general appeal of elevated locations for city cult in the Geometric to Classical Aegean, we might well expect to find the oldest-rooted town temple usually located on the hill summit and within a defined civic zone.

There is a frequent spatial association of legal inscriptions with cult buildings in Archaic Cretan settlements. This reinforces the notion that where space permitted, the main temples of PG-A Cretan towns stood in some kind of reserved public area (Bosanquet 1910; Marinatos 1936; Perlman 2002). However, because of the historical topography and often small sizes of the Cretan nucleations, such areas did not necessarily take on a regular 'agora' form, of the kind seen at Athens or Corinth, especially in their early stages of development. At Gortyn, a site of exceptional size that included large flat areas within its boundaries as it expanded, the Archaic temple of Apollo was able to be located on the spacious plain south of the earlier settlement ridge, in what may have resembled a mainland-type agora zone. Perlman notes that the term *agreion*, interpreted as referring to a place of assembly, is found in one of the sixth-century inscriptions from the temple (IC IV.9a and b; Perlman 2000: 61). A sixth-century inscription from the Chalara settlement area at Phaistos also refers to an agora (Watrous and Hadzi-Vallianou 2004a: 314–15). The late fourth- to third-century plan of Lato, a rugged hilltop site, shows a small agora area including a stoa and prytaneion, typical architectural features in mainland polis states. It seems that the agora template eventually became widespread in the island, notwithstanding the nature of settlement topography and history (Demargne 1903; Ducrey and Picard 1971, 1972; Figure 177). However, the relatively small size of the public zone and its relative proximity to residential areas in many PG-A Cretan polities might encourage particularly regular and widespread contact of the inhabitants with the civic apparatus. The strength of the common meal institution must also have promoted this.

In the wider cultural environment of this period, the definition of emergent state/ethnic identities was increasingly bound up with the physical morphology of a polity. The point is particularly highlighted by colonial settlements. At both site and landscape levels, whether in the cult, domestic, or civic sphere, recreating a particular cultural environment was seen as integral to the definition, survival, and success of these polities (de Polignac 1995: 89–128; Malkin 1987, 1998). The developments in Cretan civic zones show that Cretan communities subscribed to, and were aware of, prevalent ideas about the morphological features essential to every emergent state settlement. But their special history of development constrained the material reality: these states had a smaller-scale, and more crowded, cultural canvas on which to represent and define themselves than many of their central Greek or colonial contemporaries.

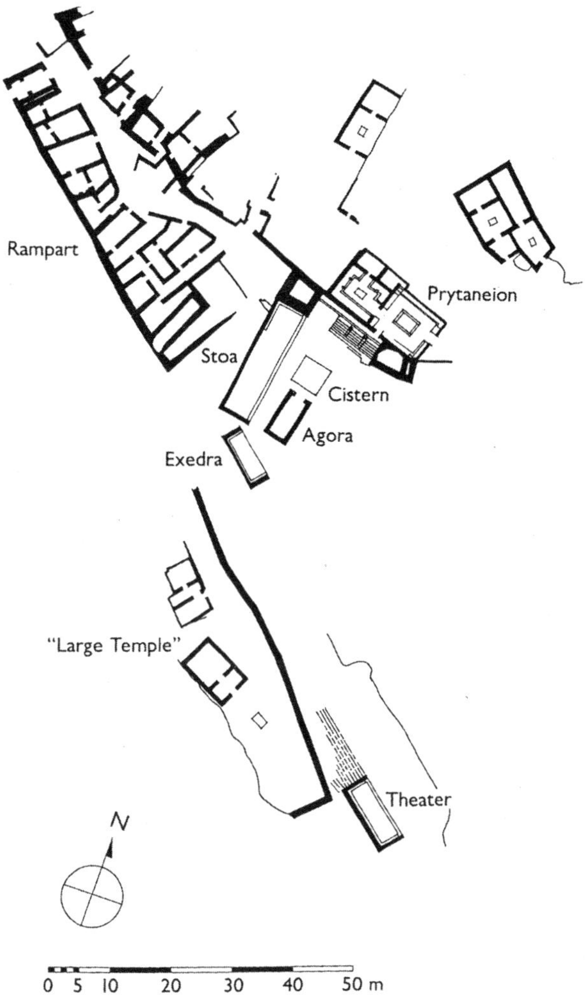

177. Plan of the Lato settlement by the Hellenistic period (after Picard 1992, Fig. 19.1, p. 154). By permission of the Ecole française d'Athens.

It is noteworthy that at the smaller continuing settlements of the PG-A period, civic zoning hardly appears at all. Though the single largest and most probably public building at Vrokastro (16–17) is located on the summit, this is otherwise a very cramped and built-up residential area. Kavousi Kastro preserves a set of large one-roomed houses on its summit, but with rather little evidence of any special function. The absence of civic zoning at these sites seems closely bound up with their lack of other developments towards the state form, and their eventual abandonment.

Fortification walls and interpolity conflict

Given the at least partly shared cultural framework among emergent Aegean states referred to previously, we might well expect PG-early Archaic Cretan polities to show attention to building fortification or perimeter walls – already important in physically and visually defining the polities of the early seventh-century Greek mainland and the colonial settlements (Whitley 2001: 165–95). However, other aspects of the historical and cultural background of Cretan polities suggest that town walls cannot be treated here as clear or expected diagnostic correlates of urban-level complexity.

By the Classical period, text sources refer to considerable interpolity conflict in Crete (especially central Crete). As I have noted, there are reasons to suppose the rise of this conflict might date back to the early Archaic period. In this light, large PG-Archaic settlements might be expected to have used defensive or boundary walls. Yet there is little evidence for them. Of course, most major sites in PG-A Crete already had naturally defensible and visually strategic positions that had promoted their selection as settlements in the twelfth century. Given that a general decline in the risk from coastal/maritime sources that seems to have encouraged the abandonment of extreme defensible sites from PG onwards, building walls is not likely to have been an immediate priority in the nucleation movement itself. Perhaps more reliance was now placed on sheer numbers of people, bound in new kinds of political and economic relations, to defend settlements.

Some limited traces of walls at nucleated sites by the Archaic period itself may represent growing levels of civic investment, increased intra-island tensions, or both. An explanation for their generally poor preservation may lie in historical reuse of the wall stones. Given the technical developments in architecture generally by this period, these are likely to have been more carefully shaped, and thus attractive for later reuse, than the rubble construction of LM IIIC fortifications. Traces of probably Archaic perimeter/fortification walls are preserved at Dreros, a site used only into the Early Archaic period; at Lato, where a late Classical wall may have an earlier Archaic phase; at Thronos, where there are perimeter/fortification walls on slightly different alignments in the Archaic and Classical periods; and at Anavlochos, where a potential perimeter or fortification of uncertain date has been noted (Belgiorno 1994: 204–11; Demargne 1903, 1931; Farnoux and Driessen 1991; Hayden 1988: 16–17). Parts of these structures might well date back into PG (or earlier), when the walls would probably have enclosed much smaller areas. Given significant settlement expansion over time, it is hardly surprising that these early incarnations do not survive well.

Notwithstanding these data, the overall lack of evidence for heavy walls on many nucleated sites, even those that survived as poleis into Classical times, is remarkable. We might view Cretan communities as having had a very long-term preference against fortifications, linked to the proximity of highly defensible topography always available for use in the inland core. This had served the population well in the most conflictful periods of the Bronze Age, and after the very successful, targeted, and strategic use of defensive topography circa 1200 BC, the tendency may have been again to avoid the use of artificially fortified sites, with this natural safety backup always in mind. Until the final abandonment of the citadel sites in the early Archaic period, these might have served as convenient refuges for at least some of the regional population.

Production zones

By the Archaic period there is some architectural evidence for the growth of specialised manufacturing production associated with nucleated sites – often located within the settlement itself. We also have, for the first time since 1200 BC, indications of extra-settlement production facilities. Processing of organic produce like oil and wine must surely have been boosted in volume from this time, as an international market for these products developed. There are various hints in the record at new levels of organization of production. At Azoria, a so-called industrial area existed in the core of the settlement for the pressing of wine (A1300). Though the increased range of types and higher quantities of metal goods in PG-EA Cretan graves suggest that a number of specialised metallurgical workshops must have existed in the island, we still have no single preserved example to study. At Azoria, Area A1200 had a hearth with remains of iron slag, but this was associated with storage jars and stone tools, as well as numerous grape remains suggesting wine production and storage – thus, it does not necessarily represent a highly specialised industrial area (Haggis et al. 2004: 373–9). A possible dyeing works (the identification is very uncertain) identified on the slopes below Ayios Georgios Papoura, in Lasithi, seems very likely to be connected with the large settlement above (Watrous 1980: 277–80). As in the earlier EIA, evidence for cloth-weaving and spinning remains widely scattered in domestic contexts, though one room at Kavousi Kastro does show a special concentration of loomweights (Gesell et al. 1985: 335).

Pottery production at a large, even centralized, scale, which we can already infer to have existed from evidence such as the standardised lekythos production mentioned in Part Three, begins to be indicated spatially. At Prinias, a kiln complex appears at Mandra di Gipari, an extra-settlement location. It produced both fine wares and the relief pithoi now becoming characteristic of the island (Rizza et al. 1992). Lato had a cluster of Archaic kilns within the main settlement area (Ducrey and Picard 1969). At Knossos, an individual seventh-century kiln within the settlement, used to produce small fine vessels, may represent specialisation at a district scale – so may the kiln found in Room G, an apparently domestic block in the southwest quarter at Phaistos (Levi 1958: 273, 1962: 397–418; Macdonald and Coldstream 1997). We need more regional studies using excavated pottery (coarse and fine) from several different types of settlement within a single PG-early Archaic territory to find out how regional systems of pottery production were changing and to elucidate the chronology of change. The grouping of Azoria, Vronda, and Kastro currently offers a good opportunity for such studies: another strong candidate region is that of Papoura and the Kera valley sites. The signs that the nucleated sites had very strong regionally referent political identities might lead us to expect that independent pottery workshops operated on the level of each nucleation, mainly serving the latter and a few smaller settlements nearby. This would allow each regional polity to assert and expand its status within the island by developing specialised styles, like the orientalising 'PGB' pottery styles of the ninth century at Knossos. However, in such a densely packed settlement environment, this is unlikely to have been very easily workable: markets and procurement networks must often have ranged across regional borders. Within polities, too, deliberately separated pottery manufacturing and consumption spheres might potentially have been developed in order to define clan groups and differentiate them from each other: this is certainly an increasing preoccupation in other areas of cultural practice at this period. So far, however, the evidence is too poor to identify such a pattern.

30 THE MORTUARY RECORD

Changes in mortuary practice in relation to state emergence

The regionally diverse and rapidly changing nature of the Cretan PG-EA mortuary record has generally discouraged analysis of its relationship to social structure (though see Whitley 1986, 2002, 2005). A recent study (Sjögren 2004) usefully brings together a large quantity of disparate data from across the island, yet its focus is on the period from Geometric onward, heavily restricting the insight it can offer on important trajectories of social development already well under way by this time.

Commentators have often been attracted to ethnicity-linked explanations in explaining aspects of this mortuary diversity and change, but almost always fail to discuss identity as a cultural construct in this regard – Whitley (1998b, 2002) is one of the few who have started to explore this topic. Mortuary data are reviewed selectively in most of the literature, with a focus mainly on analogies with grave goods or practices outside Crete. These are often explained using simplified concepts of immigration or 'influence', rather than broad-based, well-contextualised social and economic models (e.g., Hoffman 1997: 109–261; Kanta and Davaras 2004: 151; Kanta and Karetsou 1998; Kurtz and Boardman 1971: 173).

The poor chronological and quantitative resolution of much of the funerary data (thanks to poor or delayed publication, looting, and the very long-term, continuous tomb reuse characteristic of the PG-EA period) also limits meaningful interpretation. Of the several large cemeteries investigated, only one has been published to a standard that allows meaningful statistical analysis. Since this is Knossos, which we have already seen to have had a generally unrepresentative EIA history, strong caveats apply in extrapolating from these data to social organisation in the rest of the island. I will use Knossos extensively to support my arguments here but draw on other site records from across the island, analysed at consistent standards wherever possible, for essential comparison, just as I did in Part Two for mortuary data from the early EIA. Whitley's studies (Whitley 1986, 1991a) representing the most detailed analysis to date of Cretan PG-EA mortuary practices, focused almost entirely on Knossos (though the author lacked access to the full dataset from the North Cemetery, unpublished at the time of writing). It seems valuable, now that the cemetery has been fully published, to try to update and expand on this very useful work. My focus will be on interpreting mortuary practice in terms of broad developmental horizons, isolating individual temporal and spatial patterns in limited detail. Thus, my analysis is far from definitive and is mainly intended to support the larger set of arguments made in this chapter for the rise of a new degree of social complexity in Crete, with the emergence of institutions directly foreshadowing those of the polis state, from the tenth century onward.

From this period, Cretan burial practices suggest increasing concern to assert the power and status of the extended kin group. As the more complex social structures developing in large polities started to subsume, and potentially marginalise, the role of competitive individuals/small family units, lineages apparently felt the need to bolster their political salience by representing themselves as substantial, as internally coherent, and as embodying a historically established descent line. I have already noted changes in the representation of the extended kin unit in settlement pattern and in architectural organisation by the Late Geometric/early Archaic period, supporting the notion that this body took on a newly powerful role in PG-EA politics.

Comparisons with central Greek practice: an overview

As in the case of the settlement nucleation phenomenon, the major changes in mortuary practice identifiable from the PG period onward have limited parallels in the central Aegean. Here, after the significant changes of the twelfth century, no widespread and radical departures occur until the late eighth to early seventh century. One of the main shifts, the rise of the cremation rite to dominance, occurs gradually over time, just as in Crete (Snodgrass 1971: 140–213, 1980a: 54). When radical change does occur, its nature suggests that extreme competition for personal status based on individuals' consumption of prestige goods was being replaced by more inclusive, institutionalised structures based on a consensual ideology. For example, Morris has argued that widened social access to burial became available at Athens by circa 700 BC after a period of elite-restricted access operating from PG onwards (Morris 1987: 62–77). There are potential problems with the representativeness of the data behind this argument, as Morris himself points out. The generally increased number of LG burials at sites like the Athens Kerameikos may partly relate to the superior preservation of burials belonging to the cemetery's latest period – earlier graves were often disturbed by recutting within a limited area. The change may also be partly connected to a newly coherent, formalised level of cemetery organisation accompanying the more structured settlement planning that appeared at this period. Morris's notion that children only start to be buried at any representative rate from this date has been undermined by recent studies of earlier EIA child cremations from the Athens Agora (Morris 1987: 62, 78–9, 85–9; Liston pers comm). However, it is clear individual burial plot size does increase at just this time, suggesting an expansion of the number of people being allowed formal burial within loose kin-group boundaries. Along with these changes go an increasing use of inhumation and, in the first half of the seventh century, a new simplification and modesty in burial assemblages, with more emphasis turning to the grave marker and the burial ceremony rather than the grave contents. This reflects a developing stress on citizenship and cultural egalitarianism seen in other parts of the archaeological record, as wealth display moved to the better-insulated sphere of public cult. Making rich depositions in the latter arena bound the citizen into the community as a whole, while still allowing him to display his personal standing (de Polignac 1995: 11–89; Morgan 1990: 1–26; Snodgrass 1971: 416–37; Whitley 2001: 134–65).

As noted in Part Three, changes in other aspects of ritual behaviour suggest tendencies toward social institutionalisation in central Greece already from the PG period, perhaps stimulated by similar concerns about incipient social conflict. These include the growth of regional sanctuaries, the tighter symbolic manipulation of burial goods, and the increasing use of cultural references to the past to legitimate and promote small-group status (Antonaccio 1988, 1995; de Polignac 1995: 138–50; Lemos 2002: 151–84; Morgan 2003: 164–206; Morris 2000: 207–39). Clearly, though, none of these developments deeply restructured post-collapse mainland society. The very radical nature of the eighth-century mortuary changes described above reflects previous *failure* to develop the kind of stable, broad-based institutions established in Crete soon after the 1200 BC collapse horizon. Even the radically changed burial practices at Athens from circa 750 BC were themselves short lived (Morris 1987: 9, 125–40).

Crete's much smoother trajectory of social institutionalisation through the EIA (which I have argued to be directly tied into the planned nature of collapse in the island circa 1200 BC) allowed the quantities of wealth displayed in graves to remain uncontrolled. But in Crete, too, as states consolidated during the seventh century, status differentiation through burial good deposition became more subtle in nature, and more symbolically constituted. As in central Greece, alternative bases for social status, in law and in state-sponsored custom, partly took the place of wealth display and elaborate rites. We see both a general fall-off in grave good depositions, and an increased simplicity and uniformity between them, by the seventh century, with a modest new type of small individual burial becoming favoured, as I discuss below. This departure suggests the displacement of personal wealth–based competition to some degree. At the same time, inequalities of wealth and power continued to be asserted at the level of the large kin group until the end of the century, through the use of collective tombs and public cremation enclosures. Status inequality was thus still allowed to be represented at the level of the clan unit in Crete, even while Aegean-wide pressures were encouraging the rise of an egalitarian ideal and of a pre-eminent citizen class, incorporating multiple clan groups.

Consideration of the mortuary record alongside other aspects of the data discussed in this chapter suggests it would be wrong to portray developments toward the state in Crete as wholly smooth. Mortuary changes seen from PG suggest the existence of a new, strong clan-based contrapull to the institutionalising forces that supported large polity formation – even though, in the Cretan case, it was probably powerful clans themselves who had first enabled this process to get off the ground. Finding a balance between wider community/state interests and those of powerful *clans*, rather than elite individuals, was a problem particularly characteristic of the protostate transition in Crete, which applied, and had to start to be resolved, at an early date.

The kin unit and changes in burial from PG onwards

We have already seen that history and ancestry functioned as powerful political concepts in PG-EA Cretan societies, which seem to have recognised and honoured the collapse horizon circa 1200 BC as a formative period: I will turn to this theme again in the later discussion of cultural landscapes, below. The long continuity of cemetery and tomb use through the PG-early Archaic period at many sites founded in the twelfth to eleventh centuries confirms that a strong sense of place, linked to concepts of kin-group ancestry, was important in community self-conception during the state emergence period. The kin group already formed the basis of burial representation in LM IIIC, in a model persisting right through the period of community restructuring circa 1200 BC. It remained at the heart of burial practice throughout the EIA. From PG, though, there are several very important changes: a) a rise in the number of tombs with continuous long-term use and b) an increase in the number of burials per tomb and in the average number of goods interred with each burial. Representing the coherence, size, and wealth of the extended kin group, as well as the roots of the group in the 'origin' period of the LM IIIC-SM crisis, seems to

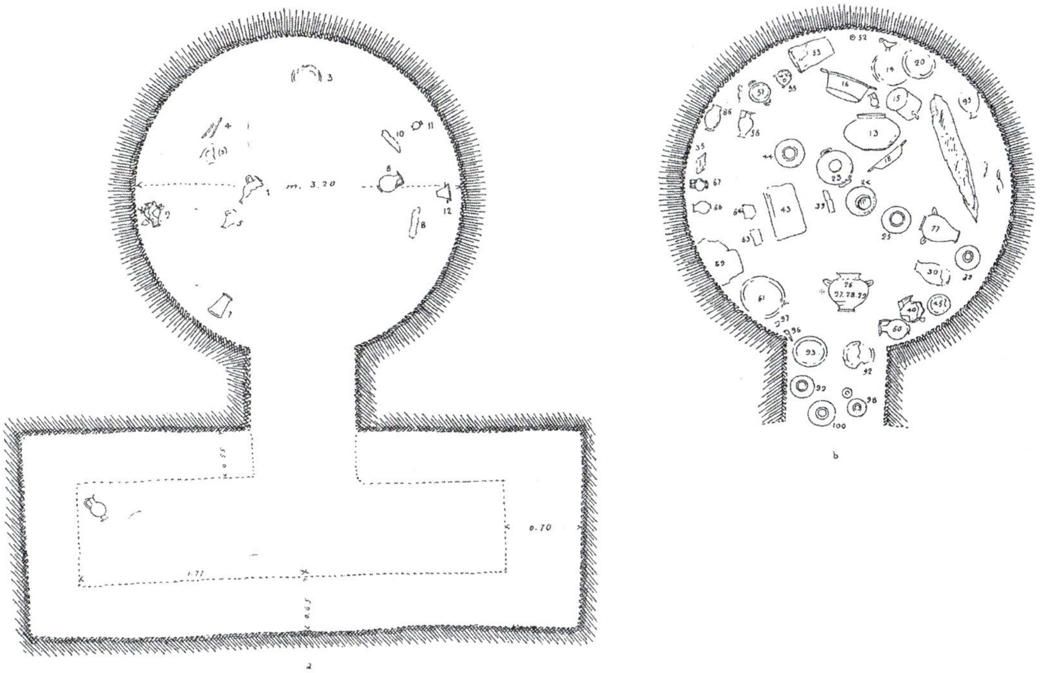

178. Plan of Arkades Tomb L (after Levi 1929, Fig. 411a–b).

have become increasingly important. It is essential to recognize the start date of these practices, and thus of the intentions and motivations behind them, as falling in the PG period, long *before* the eighth century BC (by which time many tombs had accumulated their largest concentration of burials). Seeing the practices as a feature of the eighth century misleadingly suggests they mark out a single major horizon of cultural and social change in Crete at roughly the same time as polis emergence on the mainland (Kurtz and Boardman 1971: 172).

The Knossos data provide the best opportunity to prove the above points statistically and to date the changes as first occurring from the PG period (at least LPG) onwards (see discussion below). But other burials from all over Crete lend support to the model. Tombs built between the PG and early Archaic periods are often appreciably larger than their LM IIIC-SM predecessors. This is especially true of those which first come into use well after the early PG period, once the new modes of representation had become fully established. Some large-group tombs take on a distinctive, quasi-monumental form by Geometric – an enlarged, round-based version of the stone-built tomb, usually referred to as a 'tholos' (though many LM IIIC-PG tombs had also used vaulting, it is the size of the burial group, more than the form of the tomb, that marks the new departure) (Figure 178). We also see continuations of the chamber tomb tradition (as at Knossos) as well as the use of natural caves and, rarely, tumuli, for multiple cremation burials in sizeable numbers. The feature common to all is the large size of burial group. Large tombs could end in the LG/O period by containing 80–100 burials or more (as in the cases, respectively, of Knossos Fortetsa Tomb P and Eleutherna Tomb A1K1: Agelarakis 2004, 2005; Brock 1957: 101–38). A group of smaller examples at Arkades includes Tombs L and M, both with a circular tholos form, and about thirteen and twenty-four burials, respectively (Levi 1929: 304–11, 312–80). By Geometric, the phenomenon of the large-group, long-lived tomb seems well established at nucleations like Gortyn, Phaistos, Knossos, Rotasi, Prinias, and Arkades (Alexiou 1967: 485–6; Boardman 1960, 1967a; Brock 1957; Coldstream 1963, 1979a: 49, 2002; Coldstream and

Catling 1996; Davaras 1968; Hood and Boardman 1961; Hutchinson and Boardman 1956; Hood and Coldstream 1958; Levi 1929: 78–380; Platon 1958b; Rizza 1978: 106–26; Vasilakis 1993, 1996: 334). As I shall discuss, it is also seen at some small continuing 'citadel' sites, suggesting that new kinds of concerns about status representation were emerging in both types of political unit. However, these smaller sites often have only a very few tombs of this type, with the majority of burials comprising small groups similar to those of the earlier EIA.

As early as the ninth century, and more widely from the early seventh century onward, we see hints at a new degree of social stratification emerging in Cretan societies, in the appearance, alongside the new large-group tombs, of very simple *individual* jar burials with few grave goods. At Arkades, for example, the simple pithos burials 102–3 may be contemporary with the first use of the built Tomb R in the same cemetery, which contained up to twenty-one burials dating from the late ninth century (Levi 1929: 202–304). The Kounavi cemetery in central Crete, where small PG pit burials containing few individuals appear in a cemetery that also has a large tholos dating in use from the late ninth century through the eighth, is another example (Rethimiotakis and Dimopoulou 1993; Figure 179). It seems, then, that new power dynamics started to be represented in cemeteries from fairly soon after the nucleation movement. Large lineage groups were becoming more firmly exclusive (only some people had the 'right' kind of lineage for large-group tomb burial), as well as more internally diverse (the most powerful lineages now defined themselves to include more people). A late variation on the large-group tomb, placing extreme emphasis on the cremation ritual, rather than grave good deposition, is the bone enclosure – seen, for example, at Eleutherna, Arkades, Prinias, and Vrokastro (Hall 1914: 154–72; Hayden 2005: 157–8; Levi 1929: 198–201; Rizza 1983: 50–1; Stampolidis 1990, 1994: 25–31, 2004: 61–8; Figure 180). At times some of these enclosures may have acted mainly as the cremation venue for bodies to be placed in the large tombs. In other instances they themselves seem to have formed the final resting place for the cremated dead.

By the early seventh century, a much stronger division line seems to have emerged in the cemeteries at nucleated sites – between large groups buried in extended-family tombs or enclosures with rich goods and the people buried individually and more simply in urnfield cemeteries (Figure 181). The evidence from the majority of urnfield burials presently known suggests that they represented lower-ranking groups, though not necessarily the entirety of the population excluded from group burial: much more extensive sampling across a range of sites would be needed to reach a judgement on this. Urn burials are often scattered around one or more large group tombs/enclosures, with the latter acting as focal points in a cemetery. Sites with urnfields include Arkades, Dreros, Aptera, Eleutherna, Falasarna, Itanos, and Oleros; one is currently being excavated at Ayia Roumeli in Sfakia (Andreadaki-Vlasaki 1991: 419; Apostolakou 1992; Englezou in press; Gondicas 1988: 97–108; Greco et al. 1997: 817; Kurtz and Boardman 1971: 171; Levi 1929: 78–173; Stampolidis 2004; van Effenterre 1948: 15–22). Knossos has its own version of the urnfield phenomenon, discussed below. This kind of regularised, formal distinction between categories of burial is *not* something widely seen in LG-early Archaic central Greece, with its growing emphasis on equality in burial form – though there are some echoes of it, as in the Corinth North Cemetery, where the eighth-century cemetery was dominated by cist graves but also had a central enclosure containing three graves set apart (Group A:15; Blegen et al. 1964: 21–3).

In Crete, simple urnfield-type burials of Archaic date appear in small clusters at the new small rural sites appearing in this period (discussed later). These are very poorly investigated and usually represent chance finds. Examples appear, for example, at Varypetros, near Chania, and Stamni and Alitsani in central Crete (Alexiou 1963b: 386; Gallet de Santerre 1952: 242; Platon 1952a, 1952b). In these very small settlements, large unified and prosperous clan groups may

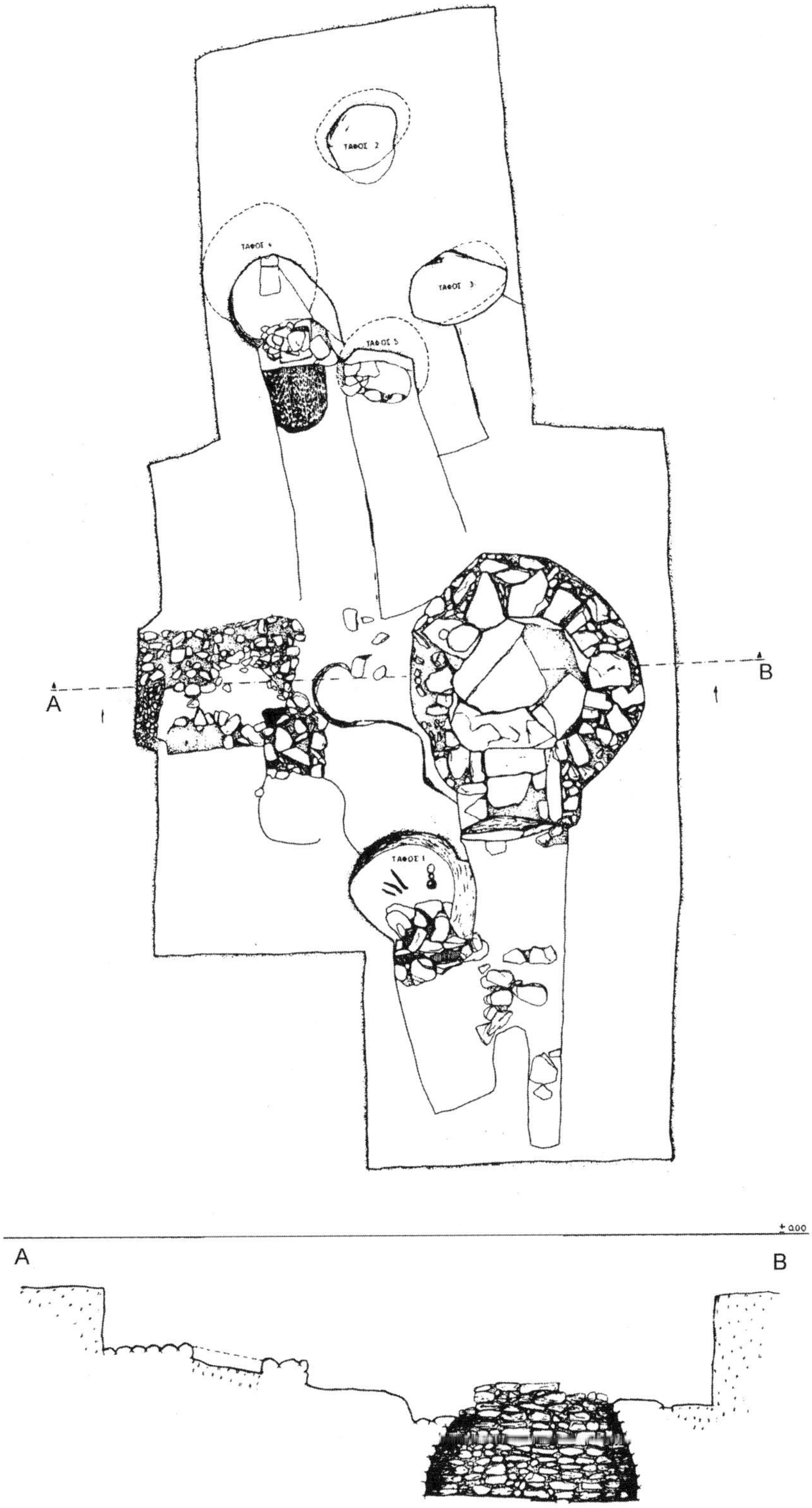

179. Plan of Kounavi cemetery (after Rethimiotakis and Dimopoulou 1993, Fig. 11, p. 464). By permission of G. Rethimiotakis.

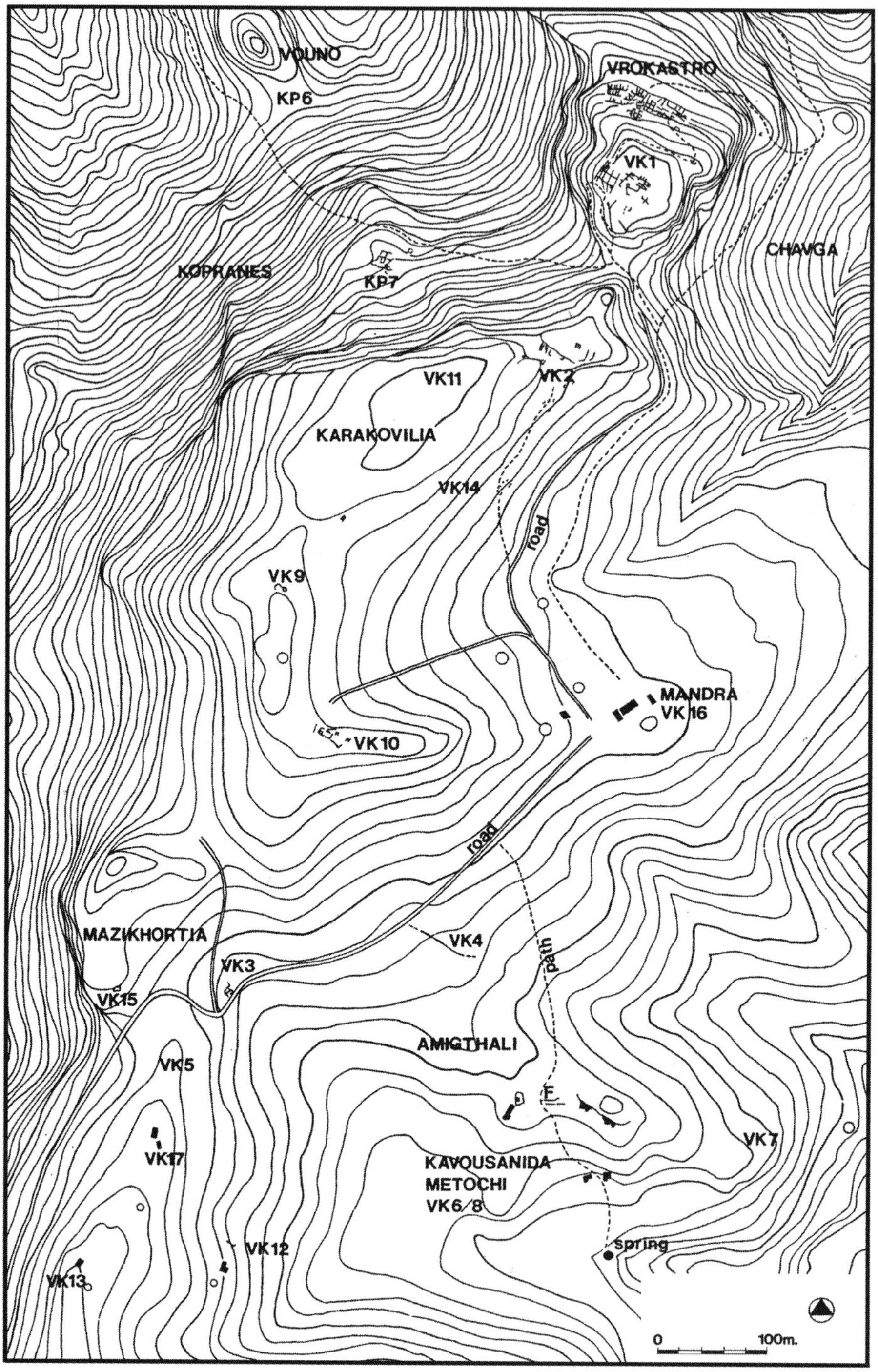

180. Map of tomb/bone enclosure clusters at Vrokastro (after Hayden 2005, Fig. 53). By permission of B. J. Hayden.

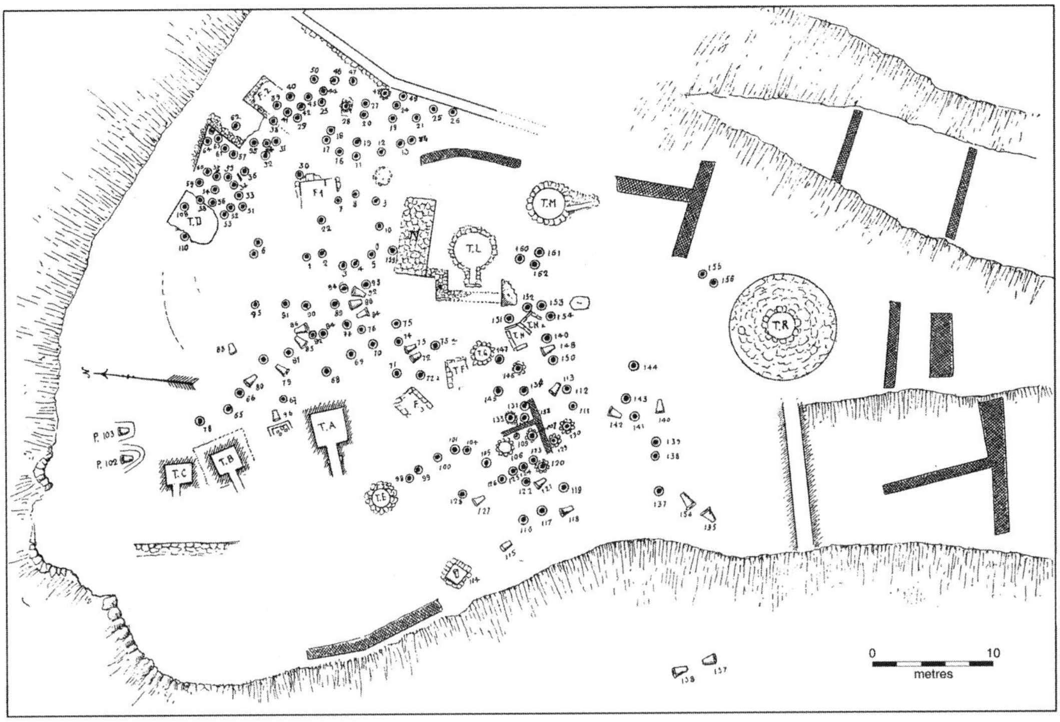

181. Plan of the Arkades cemetery (after Levi 1929, Tav. IV).

have been entirely lacking, with the residence, political activity, and burial monuments of such groups being focused at the main nucleations.

Burial group and burial form: contrasting traditions between Cretan sites and regions

Differences in mortuary practice between sites in the PG-A period often seem connected with individual earlier histories of settlement and cemetery development, outlined above. At Knossos, the late twelfth-century start of the Knossos Medical Faculty cemetery follows a transitional/restructuring period across the site, discussed in Part Two. The contraction and reorganisation of this large continuing settlement seem to have imposed a particular timescale for change in mortuary practice: it may have been resisted by a number of groups (combining to form a significant political force) on the basis of very long-standing local traditions and spatial associations. At some of the new sites established at the collapse period, also, we saw a certain reluctance to implement immediate change in the burial sphere, with a clinging-on to existing spaces for burial well into the twelfth century, one or two generations after the move. However, in this case the fact of relocation made continuing use of old cemeteries awkward in practical terms and challenged the very long-established Cretan tradition of burying near settlements. We have additionally seen that solid new community structures grew up rapidly to tie people into the new settlements and their landscapes. At the few large sites that continued in use right through the LBA-EIA transition, the cut-off did not apply so strongly; symbolic and pragmatic attachments to ancestral burial places could remain strong and valid, even while social and political relations changed significantly.

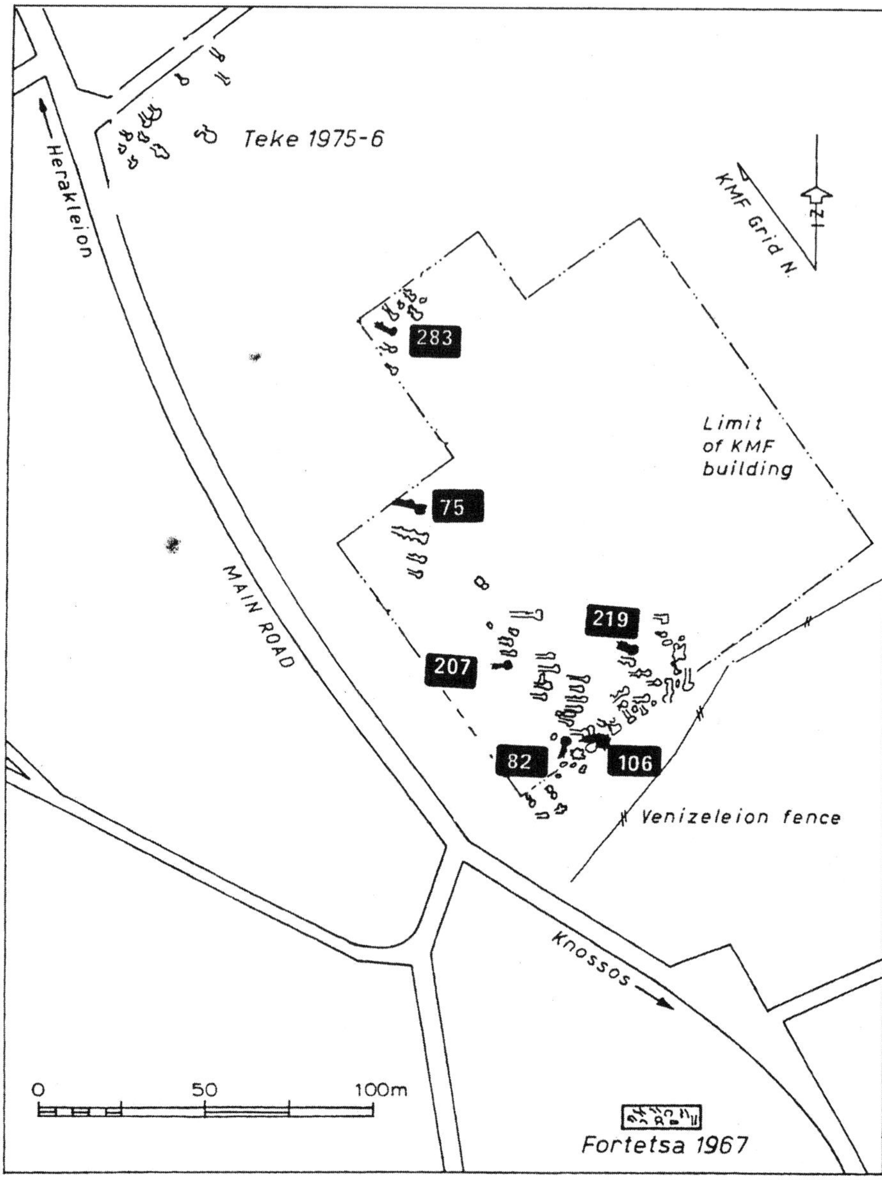

182. Plan of Knossos North Cemetery, showing tombs suggested to be of LM III origin (after Coldstream 1998b, Fig. 5.1, p. 59). By permission of Nicola Coldstream.

A slow or incomplete kind of social readjustment at Knossos may explain why the site maintained notable peculiarities in mortuary practice throughout the EIA, including adherence to the chamber tomb as the main burial form (this is also seen at Phaistos, though the tholos form does appear here from PG onward: Vasilakis 1996: 334). Some EIA tombs in the Knossos North Cemetery are so typical of the earlier tradition of Cretan chamber tombs that it has been suggested they *were* actually cleared and reused LBA tombs (Cavanagh 1996: 653–7; Coldstream 1998b: 58–9; Figure 182). If so, they are peculiarly well cleaned (few clearly LBA-dated objects were found in any of them, and those tombs most similar in construction to LBA predecessors lack concentrations of LBA finds). It is remarkable, too, if they are originally of LBA date and deliberately reused as such, that they do not differ in burial types or contents from other tombs within their clusters and are widely scattered enough among clusters to argue against any special status or significance being attributed to older tombs per se. It seems more likely that such tombs were deliberately constructed in the old tradition in order to lay claim to particular burial zones within the developing new cemetery. Indeed, the continuity of settlement use at Knossos through the crucial identity-forging period of the early EIA seems to have promoted several different types of reuse, adapted use, imitation, and archaising practice in the mortuary sphere – all helping to reground the community as a whole, and newly influential groups within it, in a prestigious heritage. We have already seen that these practices included the selective reuse of special or outstanding LBA tombs on the site (Isopata, Kefala) very soon after 1200 BC. The custom of continuing to make tombs in the chamber tomb tradition may have a similar framework of meaning. By the ninth century we see other kinds of references to the local Bronze Age past, which look more specific and targeted – in the styles of grave pottery in Knossian tombs and in the deliberate reuse of LBA larnakes in tombs at the same period, some of them associated with child burials (Coldstream 1994a, 1998b, 2000c). The assertion of ancestral links to place seems to have become especially important during the power shifts occurring in PG.

The continued use of the chamber tomb form throughout the whole EIA period reflects the fact that, just as at other sites, burials continued to be made within the general framework of the kin group. Musgrave's osteological study of the North Cemetery (the only extensive study of this type available for EIA Crete) confirms that real kin connections did bind the large groups buried in these tombs (Musgrave 1996). The especially dense pattern of large-group burials at PG-O Knossos suggests a particularly high number of similarly powerful extended-kin groups, engendered and sustained within an exceptionally large community in privileged contact with sources of value goods. The idea that the preeminent status of just a few kin groups was not easily consolidated is supported by the appearance of simplified, small-scale cremation burials at Knossos only in LG-O: in the PGB through G periods, nearly *all* those buried seem to be in large and wealthy collective tombs. When it does appear, the Knossian version of the modest single burial pattern reflected in the rise of urnfield burials at other large sites seems to be single or small-group interments of LG-'Orientalising' date, often placed in older EIA tombs following a gap or restriction in use (e.g., Tombs 34, 57, 59, 82, 123, 165; Fortetsa Tomb I [with a group found in the dromos of the earlier Tomb P]; Brock 1957: 98–100; Cavanagh 1996: 292; Coldstream and Catling 1996: 82–4, 98–9, 100, 126–7). The exact nature and meaning of this practice are still poorly investigated, due to subsequent looting and/or damage of the tombs. Because these burials were placed in existing large family tombs, they suggest that new kinds of selection may have been operating on who was given burial within the existing clan structure, alongside a general move away from elaboration in grave assemblages.

Other patterns of burial appear at the small continuing 'citadel' settlements. Here, *all* tombs often contain only relatively small groupings, right through into the Late Geometric period. The Fatsi-Droggara cemetery (associated with the settlement of Chamaizi Liopetra) and the Kavousi Aloni cemetery (used by some Kastro residents) provide examples (Boyd 1901: 15–16; Gesell et al. 1983: 410–12; Tsipopoulou 1997a). Limited scope for competition for – and consolidation of – status on the part of large clan groups probably existed in such communities (which were probably tied anyway into larger clan units based at nearby nucleations). On the other hand, by the LG period one or two moderately wealthy groups may in some cases have come to dominate these small communities, representing and building their power through large-group burial. This is suggested, for example, by the Skouriasmenos tholos and rich Plai tou Kastrou tomb at Kavousi (Boyd 1901: 143–9; Gesell et al. 1983: 412–13) and by Vrokastro Chamber Tomb II, which stands out from its peers for its high number of burials – twenty-four, instead of the six or so more typical of the other tombs (Hall 1914: 139–40). Unusually, though, these burials were inhumations, and the (badly looted) tomb does not show signs of a high level of wealth overall, so some other special factor may have linked the burial group. From the late eighth century, *both* the citadel sites and the large nucleations seem to take up the idea of bone enclosures, confirming that some consolidated and exclusive elite groupings did exist at citadel sites. However, the new level of stratification represented by the rise of the urnfield phenomenon is not seen at most of these sites: they are mostly abandoned by the time this tendency comes into its own.

I argued in Part Two that the basic similarity of twelfth- to eleventh-century burial practices across Cretan sites undermines Whitley's idea of intrinsically different social systems existing in the island in this period. It was really only once nucleation had taken place that contrasts in mortuary practice between sites developed to a degree suggesting the existence of different social systems – operating alongside, and connected with, one another within regional political units. This fact supports the point made earlier in this chapter: that settlement nucleation and the associated development of complexity did not occur *because* of intrinsic social structural differences between communities: rather, they helped develop them.

Spatial organisation of cemeteries

In twelfth-century Crete, we saw a tendency for several discrete tomb clusters or cemeteries to emerge around a site, as at Karfi and Vrokastro. In central Greek EIA cemeteries, such as Athens and Lefkandi, a kin-based clustering of individual tombs also seems indicated by the mixed gender/age structure of burials within separate plots from an early date (Lemos 2006; Morris 1987: 90; Popham et al. 1980). Clustering is seen at very many Cretan sites in the PG-EA periods, with the new types of large collective tomb being organised in dispersed clusters around the settlement, as well as forming clusters within a main cemetery. This suggests that even while individual kin groups continued to assert themselves in space, a strong identity nucleus for the polity as a whole was being consolidated. The main cemetery often had an LM IIIC-SM predecessor on the same site or nearby, but there are likely often to have been slight shifts in spatial focus during the phase of settlement nucleation starting in PG. At Arkades, for example, burials relocated in PG from the group of small LM IIIC/SM tholoi on the Kofinas ridge to a new main cemetery on the west slopes of the Profitis Elias hill, where a nucleated settlement was developing (Kanta and Karetsou 1998; Levi 1929: 78–380). At small citadel sites, too, we see changes in tomb/cemetery distribution from PG onwards, as if groups living here were redefining their relationships to each other in a changing political environment. At Vrokastro, the main focus from PG becomes the group of large built tombs on the Karakovilia ridge, probably already established from LM IIIC (Hall 1914: 144–74). But bone enclosures and other groups of tombs, like those at Chavga, are scattered at some distance around the settlement area, suggesting that a number of parallel clan units were defining themselves spatially (Figure 180). At Kavousi Kastro, a newly elaborate cluster pattern develops – a group of PG-EA tholos tombs of a moderate size were built on the plateau of Aloni, below the site, in a space distinct from that of the LM IIIC tombs at nearby Plai tou Kastrou, even though the latter area also continues in use into LG, with a large collective tomb. A rich large-group tholos also emerged by LG still farther away, at Skouriasmenos (Boyd 1901: 149; Coulson 1990b: 192; Gesell et al. 1983: 412–13; Figure 183). One or more of these clusters might potentially have been used by clans now resident at Azoria, yet still claiming links to their old territories by burying near the Kastro site. There was surely also a main Azoria cemetery (probably incorporating an urnfield by the EA period), as well as a number of clusters closer to the site, which have not yet been located.

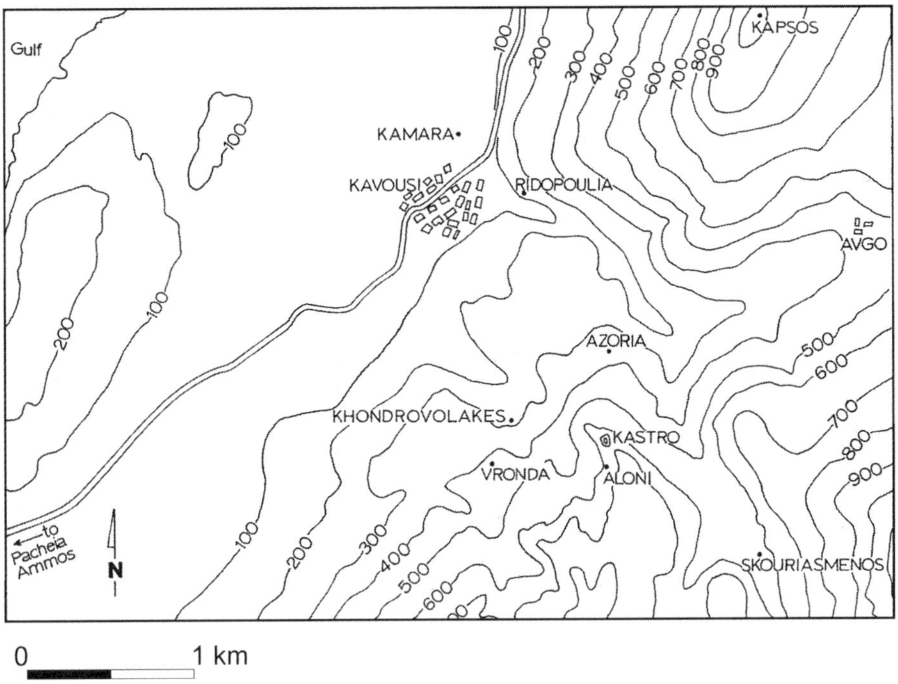

183. Map of EIA cemetery locations in the Kavousi area (after Gesell et al. 1983, Fig. 2). By permission of P. Day.

At least two different levels of kin belonging were seemingly being represented in these burial patterns – one in the tomb, the other beyond it, in the cluster. However, the relationship between them clearly altered over the course of the PG-A period in Crete: increasing emphasis was placed on the tomb unit, which became more elaborate and inclusive. The large main cemeteries developed strong elements of internal clustering and differentiation, perhaps related to emergent stratification. By LG, a central zone was often set aside for tombs distinguished by large size, numerous burials, great longevity, or distinctive form (and latterly for bone enclosures), while the simpler type of urnfield burials are scattered around. The latter may have clustered in their own subzones, with a kin-clan-related significance: more research on them is needed to establish this. The overall impression of complex, nested systems of identity and class relations by LG is supported by the use of burial spaces located in the wider landscape, beyond either the main cemetery *or* outlying tomb clusters. This notably occurs in the Azoria region, where one LG group reuses the abandoned Vronda settlement as a kind of bone enclosure (see below). The use of caves for PG-G collective burials also occurred at Ayios Spiridonas, near Praisos, and Piskokefala, near the citadel site of Sfakia Kastri (Platon 1952c; Tsipopoulou 1983, 1987, 2005a: 193–4, 233–5).

The best-documented example of a multiclustered cemetery pattern appears at Knossos (Figure 184). Phaistos seems to have a similar spread of burial places between the LM IIIC and G periods (Rocchetti 1970; Savignoni 1904; Watrous and Hadzi-Vallianou 2004a: 307–13) as do some of the large nucleations founded in LM IIIC, such as Prinias, Rotasi Kefala, and Gortyn (Biondi in press; Coldstream 1979a: 49; Galanaki 1993; Platon 1958b; Rizza 1978: 106–26). Many Knossian tomb clusters were first established in the late twelfth or eleventh centuries, scattered in different directions over a radius of up to circa two kilometres around the town. Major known clusters include Tekke, Ayios Ioannis, Kefala, Atsalenio, and Fortetsa (a cemetery in its own right), but the Knossos Medical Faculty (KMF) site remains by far the largest cemetery (Coldstream 1991). This itself comprises discrete clusters: three rows of tombs and a single

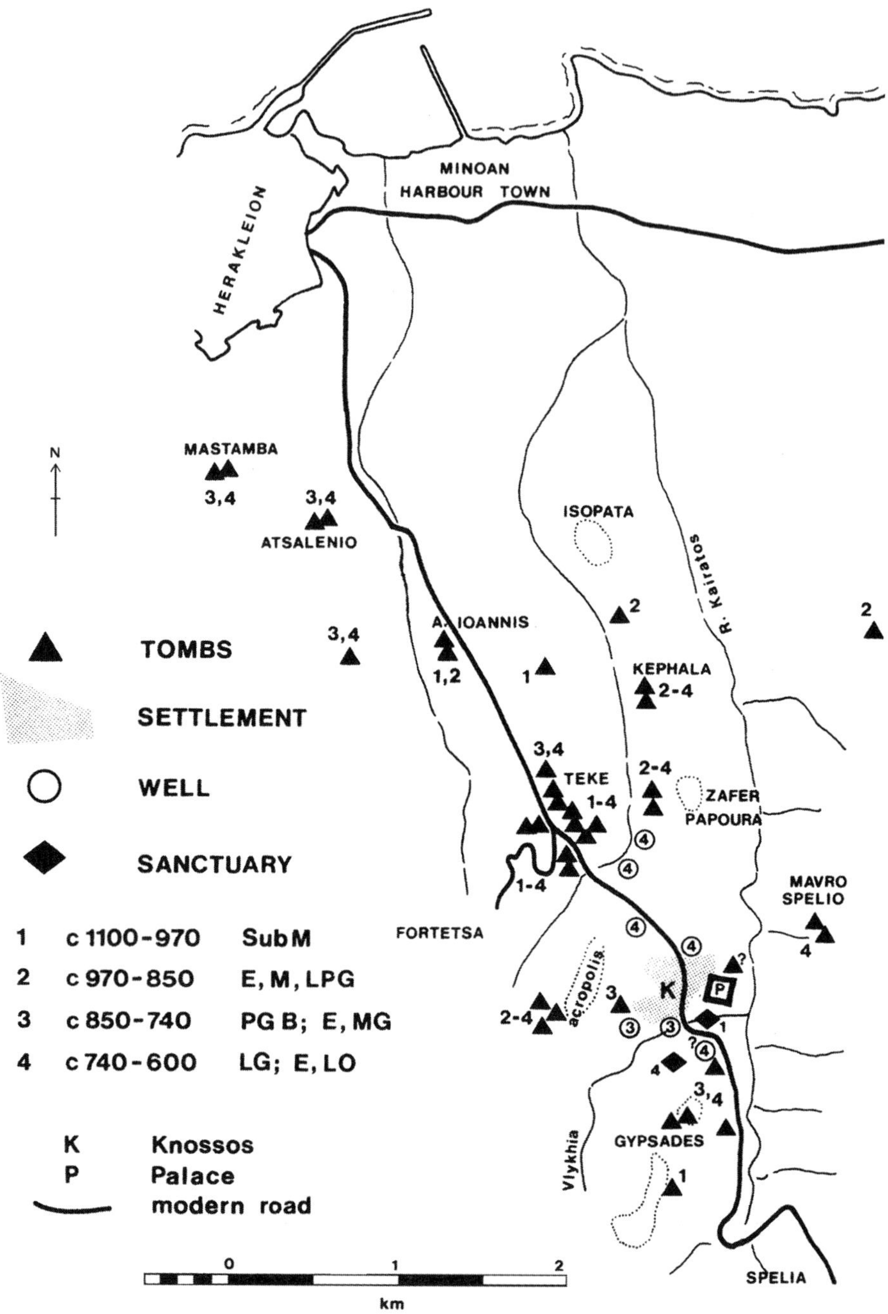

184. Locations of EIA tomb clusters around Knossos (after Coldstream 1991, Fig. 1, p. 107). By permission of Nicola Coldstream.

large complex tomb in the central area and four clusters of two to five tombs located, respectively, circa 13m to the southeast, 20m to the north, 50m to the north, and 120m to the north of the main cluster. The distances between the main cluster and the others, in this fairly flat and uniform landscape, suggest that decisions were already being made within the twelfth century (when most of the clusters started in use) about the representation of identity groups beyond the nuclear family level. Through the PG-A period the wealth, form, and size of tombs and the profile of the buried group (see below) never vary drastically between clusters, suggesting that the clustering represents kin linkages, rather than any other kind of ranking. As the size of the average burial group per tomb increased from PG onward, a proportion of the tombs in many Knossian cemetery clusters went out of use. At Fortetsa, for example, a number of tombs stopped being used by PGB, while others continued through to the seventh century. Most of the tombs in the central 'core' of the KMF cemetery were also abandoned by PG. Though new tombs were founded at Knossos during the course of the EIA, few new *clusters* seem founded later than PG. All these facts suggest that the clan structure was becoming increasingly dominant in burial, with fewer subdivisions of identity now being recognised as important within the extended kin group attached to a cluster,

The exceptionally wide scattering of the Knossian tomb clusters has sometimes been argued to reflect the dispersal of *residence* groups, as noted earlier. Yet the locations of the clusters do not suggest the kinds of concerns informing most EIA *settlement* cluster patterns – that is, defensible, strategic position combined with reasonable, if not ideal, access to arable land. At a site like Knossos, which continued directly from the LBA as a large population unit, it is difficult to see why the settlement would fragment so widely, yet still within a closely bounded area, during the collapse period. Communities like these were unprotected *except* by virtue of their size, and there is evidence against settlement fragmentation at both Knossos and Phaistos in the existence of a sizeable settlement core with use spanning the whole EIA (Coldstream 2000a; Hood and Smyth 1981: 16; Watrous and Hadzi-Vallianou 2004a: 311–13). In most cases there is no evidence for settlement adjacent to any of the tomb clusters: neither do clusters seem to concentrate together as the core settlement grows – that is, they do not follow the dominant pattern of nucleation affecting settlement in the PG-EA period. In view of all these facts, it seems more likely that scattered tomb clusters were sited with regard to the main subsistence territories, or other claimed lands, of specific clan units within the main settlement – whether these attachments were actually current or simply customary. The placing of tomb clusters in these areas, and their regular, continuous use over time, had a strong symbolic function in linking clan ancestry and identity to place. At the new sites established in LM IIIC, initial tomb clustering was probably also based on lineage. There were fewer existing attachments to place to build on here, however, so the positions of clusters may have been mostly linked to new claims and practices in land use.

Goods, rites, and status: variation over time and space

Thanks to the regular disturbance and clearing of collective tombs over time, and to the massing together of cremation urns in large-group tombs from PG onwards, we are able to retrieve little evidence on individual grave good associations. Sex and age evidence survives only poorly in the mainly cremated skeletal remains, making differentiation difficult to decode. Where the evidence is available, it does not indicate strongly polarised wealth differentiation between individuals in a tomb: much greater differentiation appears at the level of the group as a whole. It seems that most long-lived PG-O tombs contained mixed adult male and female interments of various ages, suggestive of extended family groups. Where individual grave good associations are clear, jewellery depositions seem mainly to accompany women, while weapons and some kinds of specialised feasting equipment appear most often with males. By the seventh century, new kinds of distinction may have been being made within tombs, as representational structures slowly changed to focus more on the individual, and emphasis grew on denoting status symbolically rather than through the sheer quantity of wealth goods. Whitley points out, for example, that Knossian polychrome cremation urns of this period seem most associated with females, and much more research might be done in this regard (Whitley 2005: 437–8).

Not all collective tombs represent this type of mixed sex/age group: burial practice was developing in other, new directions. The LG cemetery at Eleutherna included a collective tomb (A1K1) containing 113 burials. This had an overwhelming proportion of male interments (73.3% male and 7.8% female, with the rest undetermined), associated with a dense concentration of weapons (Agelarakis 2004, 2005). Male group tombs with military associations are found elsewhere in the Aegean at this time. At seventh-century Vroulia on Rhodes, one large tomb (Grave 18) set at the edge of the cemetery contained four males with weapons, in a pattern unique on the site (Kinch 1914: 50–1; Morris 1992: 181). The large bone enclosure at Halos in Thessaly (Voulokalyvas location j) also had concentrations of weapons, hinting at a male-dominated group (Malakasioti and Mousioni 2004: 359–63). These cases echo the set-apart group of elite male burials in the late eighth-century 'heroon' area at Eretria (Bérard 1982; de Polignac 1995: 130–2). The remarkable upper neck strength linking the males in A1K1 supports the notion that the men shared a certain type of regular activity – whether combat/combat training, athletics, or work. It seems that certain affinal groupings (which might overlap with extended kin groups in some respects) could be represented in burial at a status parallel to that of kin groupings.

Child burials are often marked out by rite, though remaining strongly associated with the wealth and prestige of the group to which they belonged, as they had been in the LBA and earlier EIA. In a tradition common in other insular and coastal Aegean regions, children are often inhumed, sometimes in jars. In the Cretan EIA, this usually occurred inside a collective or family tomb (for example, a young woman was inhumed together with her child in a moderately wealthy but small Late Geometric tholos tomb near Rotasi Kefala; Galanaki 1993). In many other regions during this period either children were buried individually, in adult fashion, or child burials were clustered in entirely separate groupings – as in the Alos cemetery in central Greece (Mousioti and Malakasioti 2004). At Knossos, the practice of jar burial is sometimes varied by burying children in reused LBA larnakes together with rich grave goods – a practice still placing them firmly within the kin group, but also linking them to a broader 'ancestral' tradition (Coldstream 2000c). From LG, however, child burials on Crete seem to become more physically separate from those of adults, as social statuses in general become more rigidly divided in a number of different ways.

There is significant evidence of food consumption or deposition in tombs during this period, perhaps especially during its latter part, though unevenness of data preservation means caution is needed in assuming this. We see it more commonly at Knossos in the long-lived large-group tombs of PG-O than those of SM-PG (Evely 1996: 635–6; Wall-Crowther 1996). The frequent appearance of animal bones in Geometric cremations at Eleutherna suggests offerings of meat and of fruit/cereal on the funeral pyre (Stampolidis 1990: 383–5, 2004: 62). The hint that the funerary feasting ritual took off (or became more elaborate or larger in scale) through this period supports the idea of a generally enhanced emphasis on membership of the larger social unit in death. Carried out on the occasion of each new burial in a tomb, it surely helped reinforce 'belonging' within a large and continuous kin group. In Cretan, mainland, and Cypriot rich tombs, the fact that spits become common grave accoutrements for wealthy males from PG onwards suggests increasing interest in/elaboration of the ritualised cooking and consumption of food during life, but also in funerary feasts (Stampolidis et al. 1998: 127–8). The mainland shows an even stronger tendency to emphasise the more public aspects of funerary ritual at the end of the EIA. In the so-called Opferrinnen burials appearing at Athens by the seventh century, trenches outside the grave were used to deposit feasting equipment and residues (Hägg 1988; Kistler 1998). Together with the rise of modest burials generally, this change seems to mark a dissociation of power display from individual wealth possession/consumption and a greater emphasis on shared, public display in marking the individual out as a member of the emergent citizen body. That Cretan communities seem to have developed the visible and public facets of burial at this time suggests that they were influenced by some of the same social pressures as their Aegean peers. In its Cretan form, however, the funerary feast remains most closely linked not to the status of individual citizens, but to the prominent and successful kin groups who used the large collective tombs. Any notion of citizenship that was being consolidated at this time seems to have been very tightly bound up with membership in an eminent local clan.

The concern with public aspects of burial moved to another level by the late eighth century, with the rise of bone enclosures, though these start as early as the end of ninth century at places like Vrokastro (Hayden 2003: 12–13, 2005: 157–8). They seem to represent a move away in funerary rites from a focus on the individual clan to a bringing together of a number of burying groups: participation at this level may have become core to defining membership in an emerging ruling class. The appearance of this kind of public enclosure for the funerary rite has parallels in other parts of the south central Aegean by LG-EA: examples appear on Thera and on Naxos, at Tsikalario (Kurtz and Boardman 1971: 179). As in Crete, these structures often seem to be deliberately sited as the focal point of a cemetery or of one subzone within a cemetery.

Within the enclosures, the dead were cremated in situ, in a process replacing the use of individual pyres in or beside the tomb, common in earlier EIA cemeteries (the cases of Arkades Tomb R, Veni, and Kounavi provide excellent examples). The remains are found mixed together with the funerary goods, with no very clear marking of status for groups or individuals, though the separate chambers may possibly have signified the boundaries of clan or sub-clan membership. The right to be cremated in the enclosures at all seems likely to have denoted a privileged status. Bone enclosures appear only in a few locations at each cemetery, and it is possible that these made reference to different traditional burial places for clans or groups of clans. At Vrokastro, one set of enclosures is sited adjacent to the large and long-lived built tombs of the earlier EIA on the Karakovilia ridge. They may have first been used as public pyres for the latest (LG-EA) interments in these tombs and have remained closely attached to the particular clan group or set of clan groups using the area, even while operating at a more inclusive scale than the earlier individual tombs. At Prinias, the positioning of at least one Geometric bone enclosure also seems to make deliberate reference to earlier burial monuments, while operating at a newly comprehensive level. It is built against a tumulus of PG date, which in turn overlies some relatively small and simple SM burials. The pattern suggests that one group's attachment to place survived many changes in burial customs and shifts in social self-conception (Rizza 1978: 106–26; Rizza and Rizzo 1984: 152–5; Tzanakis in press; Figure 185). At Eleutherna, scattered bone enclosures also seem linked to different groups. One particularly elaborate built complex (A), incorporating an enclosure and several cremation graves marked with monumental constructions, seems associated with some form of cult practice (figurines were found within the enclosure) as well as having a significant level of wealth (gold objects) associated with it. Tomb A1K1, closely adjacent to this complex, held an extraordinary concentration of male burials, discussed previously, and a rich assemblage of metal weapons and vessels (Stampolidis 1990, 1996: 25–91, 1998). Treatment of child burials in the same area suggests that a new generalised cut-off point between status in death as a child and as an adult – operating on a different level from either class or kin boundaries – was definitely in place by LG. A child in a pit grave found close to the complex appears from its grave goods to be of high-ranking status. But its separation from the main enclosure suggests

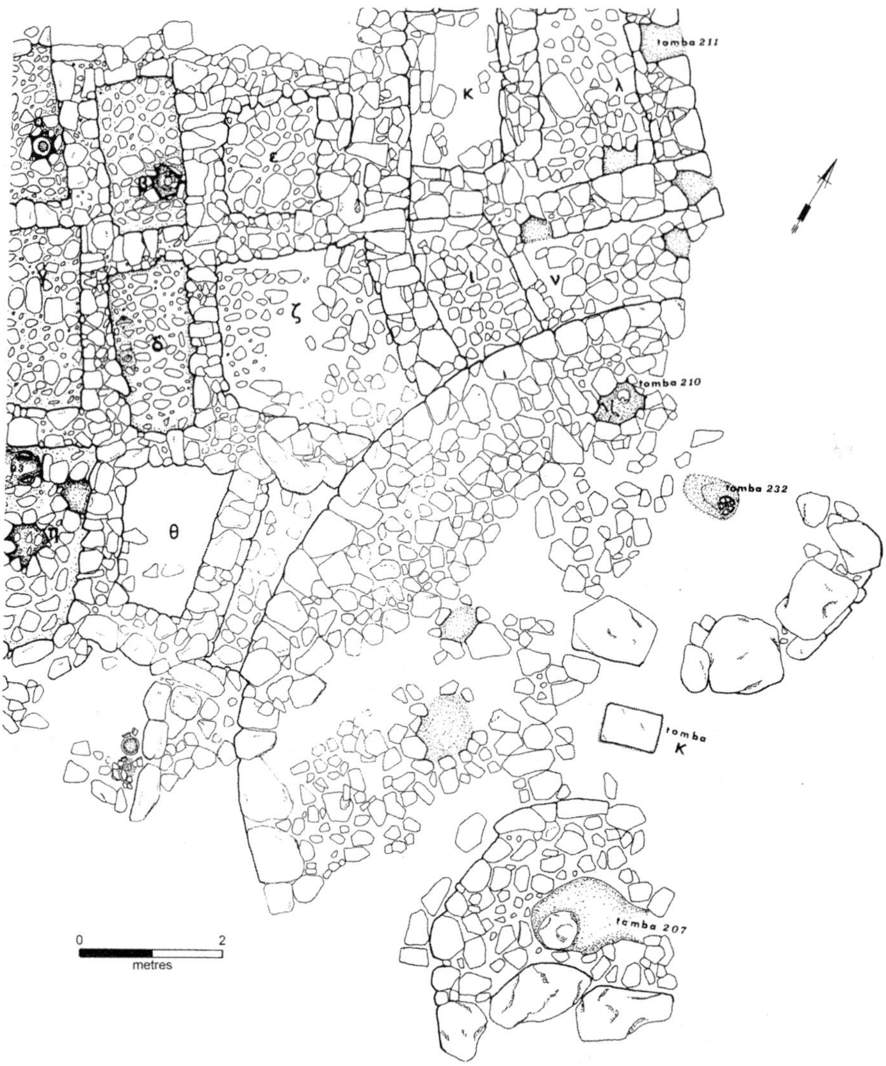

185. Plan of tumulus burial and bone enclosures at Prinias (after Rizza and Rizzo 1984, Fig. 444, p. 239).

that children (who had always been excluded from the adult rite of cremation) were now more firmly set apart from the adult members of their own clan group (Stampolidis 1990: 377). Though this child burial retained its family and wealth links through general spatial association with the elite funerary zone, it appears to have been excluded from the heart of the developing public bonding arena of the cremation enclosure. Knossos, which so far has produced no bone enclosures, may have its own variation on this aspect of social differentiation late in the EIA: examples of child inclusion seem lacking in the very latest large-group burials there (Musgrave 1996: 690). At some other sites, however, children's bones were included within bone enclosures, so this divide is not absolute or universal. Outside the zone of bone enclosures and associated monuments at Eleutherna, children's burials also continue to show signs of attachment to family groupings. Like adults outside this zone, they are treated on an extremely modest basis, within a developing urnfield cemetery.

Wider comparisons

We have already seen that some trends in Cretan burial rites and forms in the PG-EA period echo shifts in the wider Aegean. There are links to practices in other regions, too, and it should not surprise us, given Crete's broad contacts, that these are very diverse, and that they suggest travel in and close contact with the east Mediterranean as well as the Aegean sphere. In some Cretan collective tombs of this period (Arkades, Rotasi) a stone sarcophagus is found surrounded by cremation urns, suggesting that some group members – even if still cremated – were distinguished within their own wealthy kin group (Levi 1929: 207; Platon 1958b). The practice is also used by the sixth century in Corinth, Ionia, and the Dodecanese, again often apparently for wealthy or physically set-apart burials (Kurtz and Boardman 1971: 176–7). The type of tumulus seen at Prinias, covering multiple burials that probably formed parts of a single clan unit, is broadly paralleled at Alos in Thessaly. A markedly easternising practice seen in LG-EA Cretan burials is the use of bronze cauldrons over jar burials in the Arkades urnfield cemetery, reminiscent of contemporary north Syrian burials. Another such practice is the use of Phoenician cippi (stone burial markers) at Eleutherna and Knossos (Boardman 1970; Kourou 1991; Kourou and Karetsou 1998; Stampolidis 2004: 67–8).

The sixth-century and later hero cults of the mainland, and the Homeric tradition of heroes whose cremation mounds were the objects of contemporary reverence and later cult, may help us understand features like the elaborate tomb monuments, above-cremation mounds and cremation-related building complexes, some perhaps functioning in some ways as mortuary temples, as at Eleutherna Orthe Petra (Coldstream 1976; Hägg 1999; Stampolidis 1990: 396, 1998, 2004: 64–8). In general, though, Cretan EIA burial tends to remain markedly separate from cult activity (in the sense of clearly defined intra-settlement and extra-settlement spaces or buildings operating at a public level and associated with a specific set of cultic equipment). Though these spaces develop an increasing variety of formats, they are always separate and distinct from cemetery zones. By the eighth century, 'tomb cults' (ritual depositions of pottery or figurines separate from the original burial deposition) at Bronze Age tombs were a regular feature of central Greek society. These are often interpreted as representing the territorial assertion of local elites against emergent state bodies and the ideology of equality (Antonaccio 1995; Bérard 1982; de Polignac 1995: 138–43; Morris 1988, 2000: 195–309). In Crete, tomb cult of this type is not so widely apparent, though there are some hints at it, similarly concentrated in the later Geometric period (discussed later). The practice is not well understood but seems much more connected to private ritual than public cult as defined above.

An explanation of this divergence may be as follows. Early and strong social institutionalisation in Crete allowed mortuary practice to remain notably free and variable right through the EIA. For the same reasons, however, it never took a dominant role in the construction of community life. Though powerful groups in late PG-EA communities clearly saw the mortuary arena as of increasing political importance, they never focused the majority of their social and political energies there in the way seen in central Greece, where a marked competitive escalation in burial investment occurs in some areas prior to 700 BC. In the more balanced Cretan environment, and in the strongly clan-based state culture that was developing in the island, elite *individuals* and their mortuary monuments were never invested with the kind of mythical status and prestige seen in the mainland hero cults; nor, indeed, was the Bronze Age a major reference point in the identity definitions of clan-level groups, for reasons that I have already discussed. I consider further evidence for this latter statement in the discussion of cultural landscape change, below.

Mortuary practices in northeast central Greece show points of similarity to the Cretan pattern, in appearing to consolidate and build the role of clan status through burial. I looked earlier at the case of Alos, where a large bone enclosure dating from within the PG period almost certainly represents a powerful extended kin group. Indeed, the use of communal burials and tumuli in Thessaly generally is increasingly recognised as representing and reinforcing an early and strong political role for the clan here, though there was clearly considerable complexity in local social structures that is not yet properly understood. A number of different burial patterns appear alongside the use of tumuli in the Alos cemetery, and at Velestino, in the same region, exceptionally wealthy group burials in tholoi in at least two different locations coexist with modest single burials (Morgan 2003: 93–5, 138, 195). Notably, this area did not develop polis states based on a citizen class in the same way or at the same time as the central Aegean. Instead, a stronger social role for the clan emerged which in some ways echoes the oligarchical element of Cretan states – though the Thessalian *ethnos* states had a much larger, looser structure, not focused on a single nucleated settlement base (Morgan 2003: 4–16; Morris 1998: 37–40).

The sheer diversity of links between Cretan burial practices and those in other regions makes those links difficult to relate directly and specifically to ethnic identity. Like grave goods, rites used in burial recognised the standing of a particular group or individual in ways that were always embedded within generalised patterns of burial practice in the region, as well as in general beliefs about the meaning of death and about the afterlife, shared with other societies in the Aegean zone. Distinctive practices *may* reflect conscious ethnic associations/constructions within Cretan communities, as discussed in Part Three, but also relate to other types of status difference.

Proving the point: the Knossian data

I will conclude this discussion by turning to examine Knossian data specifically (as the best-published data set) to illustrate the points made above. In isolating the main features of mortuary change at PG-EA Knossos (covering all published tomb assemblages from all cemetery clusters) I will refer to Figures 186–97, which present some basic statistics: Table 3 shows the size of each sample used in compiling those statistics. The imperfect character of the record means that of 140 published tombs in the North Cemetery, fewer than that total, though never fewer than 100, have been used in each analysis. Confining analyses to intact tombs only would produce an unhelpfully small sample and a considerable bias towards the SM period (many tombs of this period were small, without many or rich grave goods, and went quickly out of use, contrasting with the dominant pattern of long-term reopening and reuse between the PG and G periods). The dating used here is usually that of the excavators (or those who have re-studied and published the material). Five main observations emerge as important, as I have indicated in the previous discussion:

1) CHANGES IN SIZE OF BURYING GROUP OVER TIME (FIGURES 186 AND 187)

The practice of burial in long-lived collective tombs covering this period gives rise to uncertainty as to the numbers of goods and bodies in the earliest interments, which were often pushed out into the *dromos* to accommodate later burials with larger assemblages of goods. It seems most useful to assess total interment numbers in broad size categories: classes of 'fewer than 3', '6 or

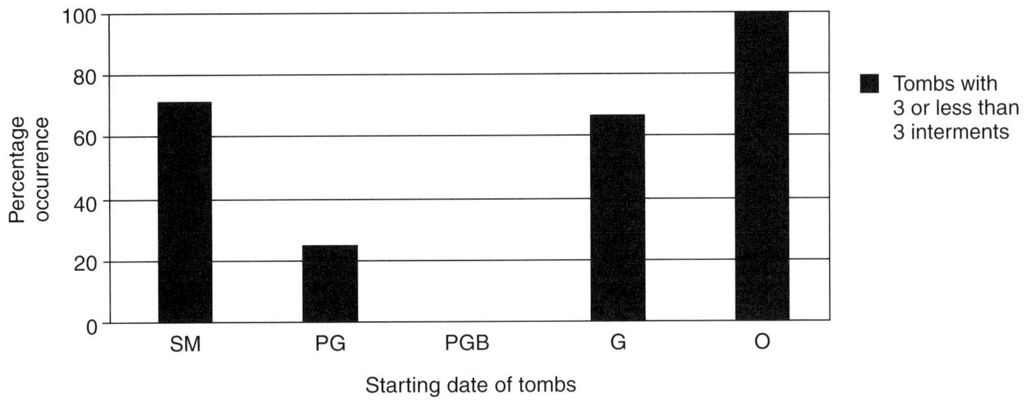

186. EIA Knossos: tombs with small groups of interments, as percentage of tombs with known interment numbers for each period. Image by the author.

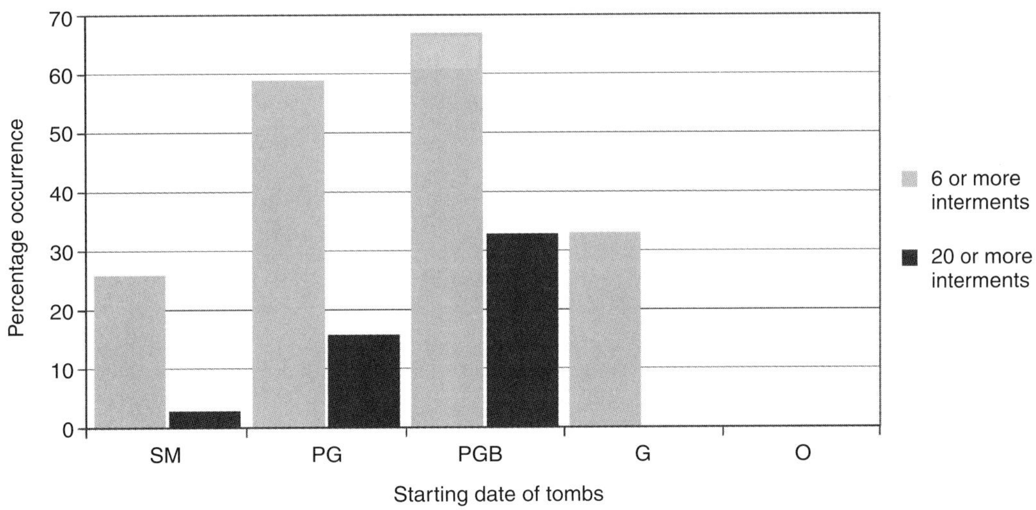

187. EIA Knossos: tombs with large groups of interments, as percentage of tombs with known interment numbers for each period. Image by the author.

more', '20 or more', and '40 or more' interments are selected as meaningful here. It is unsurprising (given the long-term use of tombs over the course of the EIA) that the highest numbers of interments recovered from most tombs appear to date to the latest (G-O) phase of their use. Nonetheless, a marked increase in burial group size from PG onward clearly goes together with increased tomb longevity from the same period (discussed below). The markedly low number of small burial groups (below 6 individuals) in tombs with use starting in PG clearly marks out the date of change (Figure 186). This point is supported by Figure 187, which shows that most large-group burials (above 20 people) start from the PG period. In the MG-O period, the appearance of smaller interment groups, whether in new tombs or in tombs with a gap in burials following an earlier EIA use, parallels the move towards more rigid, large-scale social divisions (identified above as involving the appearance of large numbers of modest single burials) seen in other Cretan cemeteries at the same date. The change is less obvious at Knossos because these small burials often reuse earlier tombs after a gap.

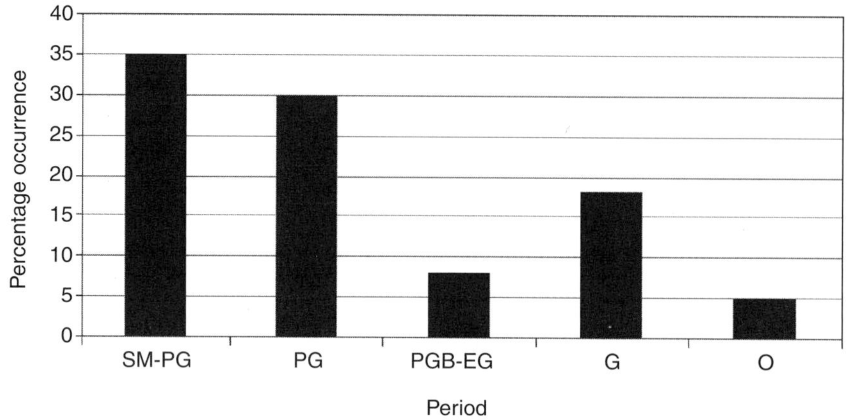

188. Knossos EIA tombs – start dates. Image by the author.

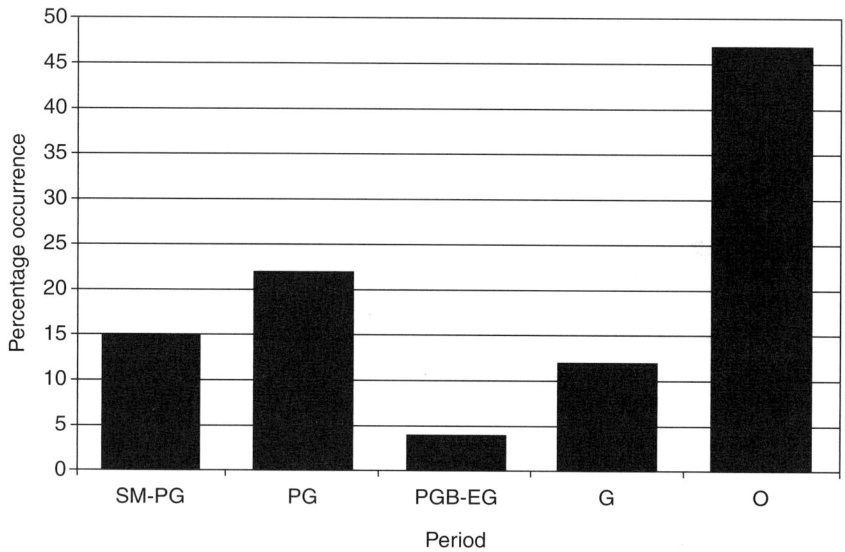

189. Knossos EIA tombs – finish dates. Image by the author.

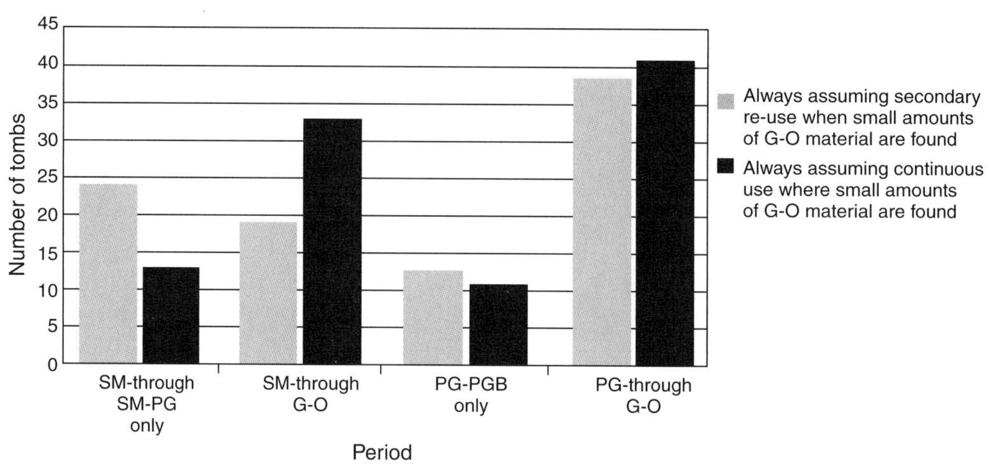

190. EIA Knossos: tomb longevity from the SM period onward. Image by the author.

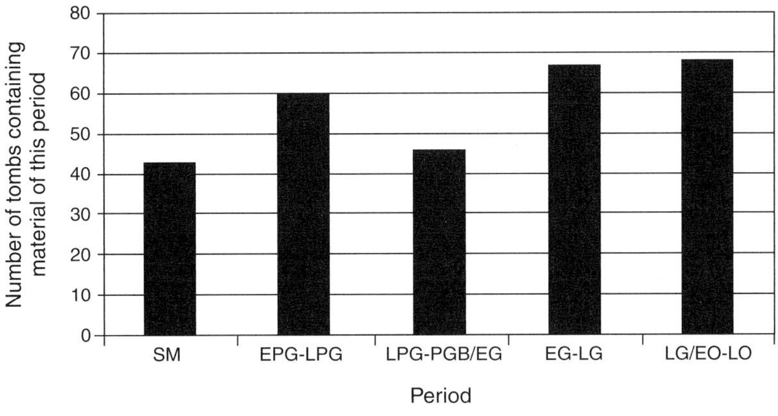

191. Summary: numbers of tombs representing different ceramic periods at EIA Knossos. Image by the author.

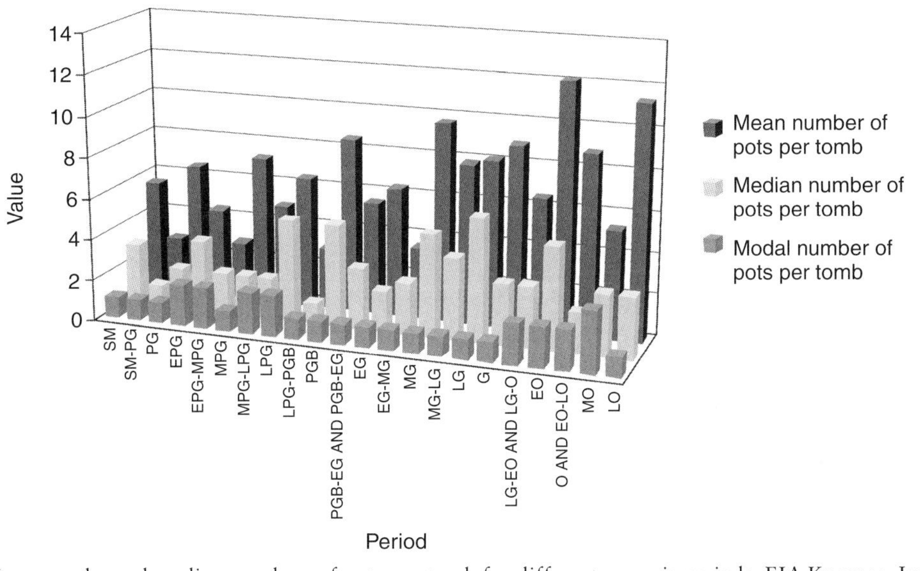

192. Mean, mode, and median numbers of pots per tomb for different ceramic periods, EIA Knossos. Image by the author.

A transitional/negotiational phase in mortuary practices before the use of really large-group burials took off in PG can be inferred from the record. At the Tekke and Ayios Ioannis cemeteries, which are dominated by tombs dating only between LM IIIC/SM and PG, the number of individuals per tomb is usually more than two but fewer than six, suggesting that burial groups were already tending to be slightly larger, and continuity of tomb use longer, than was typically the case in SM. The outlying cemetery clusters at Kefala and Fortetsa show the continuous use of a reduced number of tombs, by larger burying groups, from PG onwards. This contraction/concentration model is also seen at the KMF cemetery on a larger scale. Occasional *new* and subsequently long-lived tombs seem to come into use in that cemetery during exactly this period (EPG-PGB) forming part of the same phenomenon. New choices were clearly being made about representation of kin units, involving the symbolic amalgamation or demotion of some units in the interest of representing a group significantly larger than the nuclear family, and with a continuously defined identity, dating (symbolically or actually) from the earliest use of the cemetery.

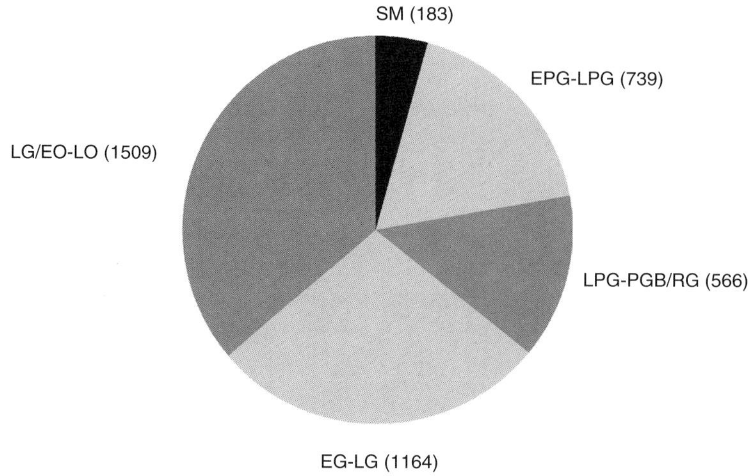

193. Summary: numbers of ceramics of different periods in tombs at EIA Knossos. Image by the author.

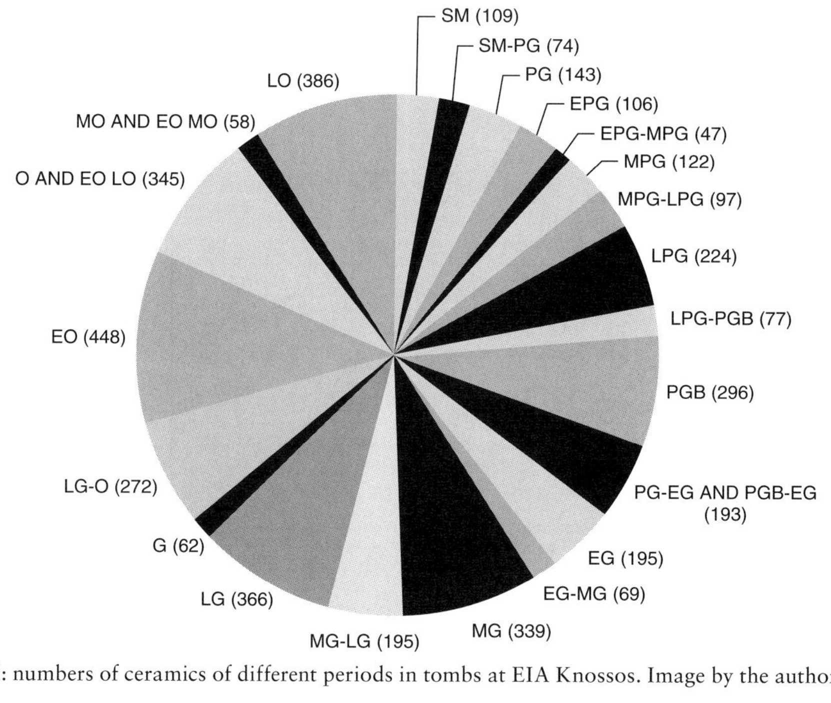

194. Detail: numbers of ceramics of different periods in tombs at EIA Knossos. Image by the author.

Against the dominant trends, a few tombs remain in use between PG and G-O yet keep only small numbers of burials, suggesting adherence to specific and bounded family and spatial ties.

II) CHANGES IN TOMB LONGEVITY OVER TIME (FIGURES 188–190)

Statistics on tombs' start dates highlight the rise of long-lived tomb use from PG onwards. The main peak for tomb start dates is in SM; for finish dates, peaks appear in both the SM/EPG and O periods. In combination, and taking into account the phenomenon of small-scale reuse of some tombs in the Orientalising period after a long gap, these statistics show that the main use

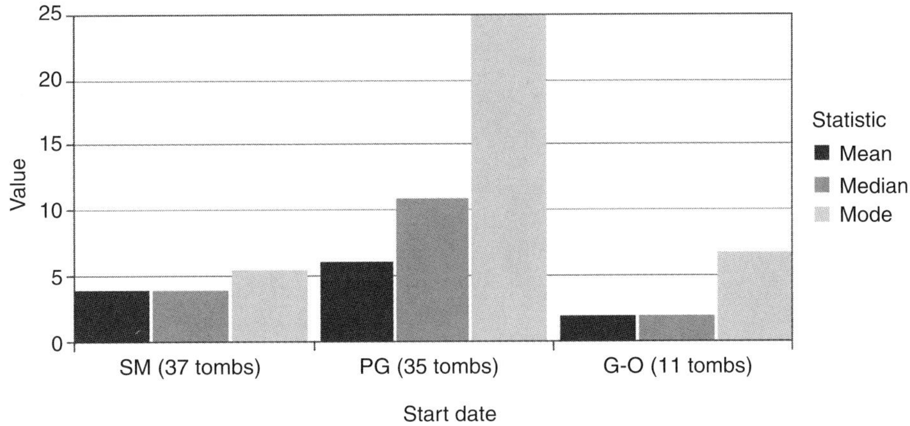

195. EIA Knossos: quantities of wealth items (including iron) in tombs of different start dates. Image by the author.

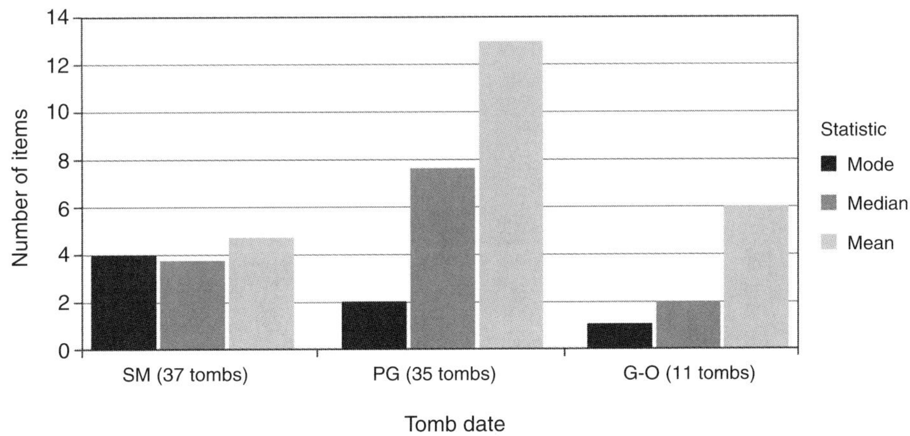

196. EIA Knossos: quantities of wealth items in tombs of different start dates, with iron included for SM tombs but excluded for those of the PG and O periods. Image by the author.

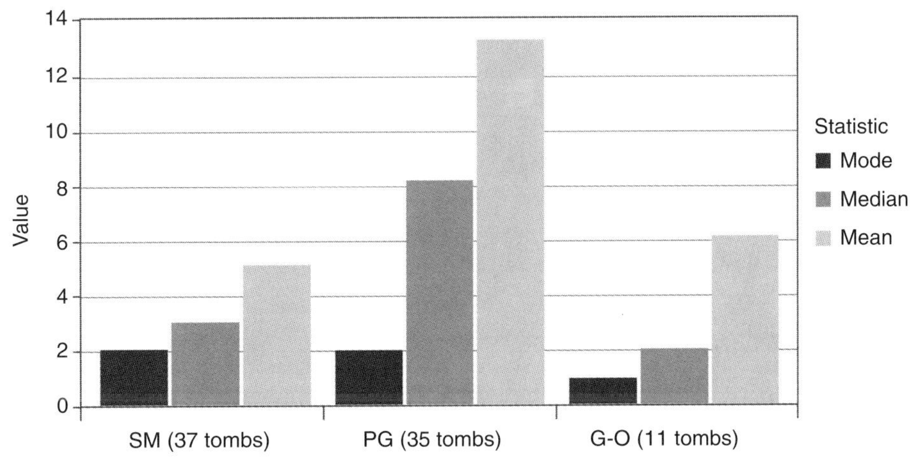

197. EIA Knossos: quantities of wealth items (excluding iron) in tombs of different start dates. Image by the author.

TABLE 3. *Quality of mortuary data from the Knossos North Cemetery*

Characteristics of interest	Tombs providing mainly complete and quantifiable data	Tombs providing *some* data usable in statistical analyses with a reasonable margin of error (including those with mainly complete data)
All of the following: interment numbers, date range, number of wealth goods, number of ceramics, burial rites (i.e., intact assemblage)	50	122
Number of interments	52	121
Burial rites	53	120

of large-group, long-lived tombs took off or commenced in PG, frequently continuing the use of SM tombs. The transition to long-term continuous use seems to have been fully complete by PGB, with hardly any new tombs founded between LPG and EG.

III) CHANGES IN THE NUMBER OF TOMBS IN USE OVER TIME (FIGURE 191)

The number of tombs in use overall appears to increase from PG, but this figure does reflect an overlap between the end of use of some SM-LPG tombs and the starting of new tombs in LPG-PGB (the PGB dip in tomb numbers illustrates this). The change is unlikely, then, to reflect *either* increased population *or* increased access to burial. The quality of preservation and the scattered pattern of tombs at Knossos do not allow us to say that the number of individual *burying groups* was really higher than that seen in SM. We would in fact expect it to be slightly lower, as the focus moved to large-group tombs used over long periods. This model is supported by the abandonment of tombs in many clusters during this period, as noted previously. The figure is important, though, in again reflecting the PG period as a horizon of change.

IV) CHANGES IN THE RELATIVE AMOUNT OF WEALTH DEPOSITED IN TOMBS OVER TIME (FIGURES 192–197)

Use of a number of different statistics prevents the production of misleading figures in this respect, given the disturbed nature of many tombs and the difficulties of dating metal objects in this period. Looking firstly at pots (Figure 192): in some periods the *modal* number of pots per tomb is as low as 1, simply because those periods see the use of widely different types of burial: for example, seventh-century burials include the new type of single interments as well as the last phase of use of wealthy collective tombs. The *mean* figure is more representative of the sizeable ceramic assemblages characterising the long-lived, multiple-burial tombs used into the seventh century. Significantly, it is much larger from LPG onwards than in the SM and E-MPG periods. Figures 193 and 194, which simply show the quantity of tomb pottery deposited by period across the site, reflect the same course of development. All these charts highlight the main boost in pot numbers as occurring from the LPG period. However, the statistics are affected by larger numbers of burials and the rising use of cremation burials *in* pots by PG, automatically producing higher numbers of pots per tomb, as well as being distorted by the use of the highest number of tombs overall in PG (discussed earlier).

Quantities of value goods, as well as interment numbers and pots, also undergo a shift upwards from LPG, giving an overall picture of an increased concentration of wealth in tombs that is not simply related to increased numbers of burials (Figures 195–97). For reasons discussed above, it became increasingly important and/or possible from this period onward to deposit larger amounts of such goods in graves. A problem arises, however, with defining wealth goods through all the periods under consideration here, since the social role of iron changed dramatically over the course of the Early Iron Age. This is partially resolved by producing three alternative statistics. Iron is treated as a 'wealth' item for all periods in one calculation (Figure 195), but for the SM-PG period only in a second one, given that after this period it becomes considerably more widespread in use (Figure 196). In a third calculation, iron is excluded from the category of prestige goods in all periods (Figure 197). In all three graphs, the average of wealth goods per tomb peaks in tombs that start in PG. This strongly supports the notion that deposition of concentrated amounts of wealth in tombs really takes off from this period. All three charts show lower average wealth for very late-starting tombs – reflecting the new pattern of small simple LG-O burials already mentioned. The figure would be much lower if it were not boosted by late deposits in some large new rich tombs of the same date (as the modal figure attests).

31 THE RITUAL LANDSCAPE AND THE CONSTRUCTION OF POLITICAL IDENTITY

Introduction: the changing ritual landscape

Earlier, I showed that in the early Cretan EIA, public cult and feasting ritual were clearly separated in spatial terms, and in some of their associated equipment, from each other and from everyday private household activity. At the same time, I noted that some aspects of practice and some associations overlapped between the two spheres. Each set of practices was also able to be partly borrowed into or referred to in the private sphere in certain circumstances.

We might expect some major changes in the way these spheres were viewed, and their associated practices carried out, to have accompanied settlement nucleation and the accompanying political readjustment. Small-scale feasting gatherings in adapted private houses or small specialised public blocks serving the whole community, alongside worship in small settlement temples, were surely no longer adequate to represent or unite the enlarged communities, with their new and stronger kinds of internal division. Both cult and feasting activities did indeed become elaborated and diversified within settlements, and more distanced from the domestic arena. They also moved out into the landscape at new scales. Extra-settlement ritual took on new significance as a way for each enlarged polity to interact with its peers, but also to negotiate relations with smaller groups in its expanded territory (including those living at the scattered 'citadel' sites). The marked changes now seen in ritual practice, just like those of the LM IIIC period, contradict the oft-cited notion of Crete's 'conservatism' or high degree of 'continuity' with Bronze Age ritual customs – indicating, instead, sensitive and rapid responses to changing political circumstances (Prent 2005b: 37–102).

During these changes, the feasting and cult sectors stayed linked in some respects. Food sacrifice and related feasting came to play an important part in almost *all* cult practice by the later EIA, both on Crete and elsewhere in the Aegean. The evidence from the andreion at Azoria suggests that a cult component was incorporated in formal public feasting in Archaic Crete; on the other hand, there is LG evidence for other kinds of feasting activity, divorced from any recognisable cult context and showing a spread into new landscape settings. I have already examined feasting's changing role in the mortuary and settlement arenas from PG on, suggesting it to have been a powerful, multivalent, and integral part of political life. Its increasing prominence in the cult sphere may reflect the emergence of a more inclusive, yet also more hierarchised, range of participation in cult in larger and more complex societies. Dedication of food and drink was one of the easiest ways for the mass of people to be active in worship, while elites and state bodies made use of higher-value, status-enhancing dedications of goods, as well as making food offerings.

The overlap with feasting practice, and general changes in the parameters of cult activity accompanying the rise of state polities, add to the difficulty of accurately identifying and understanding 'cult' in the later Cretan EIA. The artefact packages and spaces distinguishing settlement-level cult from extra-settlement cult in the LM IIIC–SM period are no longer valid. Small cult sites fitting neither of these categories appear in the landscape during PG-EA yet do not hang together in a class of their own. Many were of an open-air character, leaving ephemeral traces in the record, while others were built structures. Our knowledge of how space was organised within the landscape generally is much less complete as we enter the early Archaic period, when a new spread of human activity takes place into the valley floors and plains, a historically densely settled (and thus much-disturbed) landscape zone. Given the ongoing changes in settlement patterns and relationships between PG and Archaic, and the incomplete dating of many sites, we are often unable to 'match up' isolated cult places to single settlement units in any one period. Such matching is anyway questionable from an interpretative point of view. By LG-early Archaic, the political territories of many large nucleations included some very small residential rural sites, while sites of the 'citadel' type discussed previously were often still in use. Thus a single extra-settlement cult site might be 'attached' to a number of different settlements at different levels.

Another problem lies with bias in and quality of recording. Thanks to the appeal of cult-related remains to excavators (who have often tried to use the characteristics of EIA-Archaic cult buildings in a very direct way to 'explain' the origins of the Classical temple form), much of the excavated material is poorly recorded in terms of wider settlement context and thus difficult to date: it is the cult function of a building or site per se and its associated finds, not its wider context, that has often been seen as most interesting. Full stratigraphic and context information has not yet been made available from any major Cretan extra-settlement sanctuary, and information on small rural shrines has often only been acquired through chance finds or by rescue excavation.

Matters are complicated further by the increasing number and variety of symbolic reuse practices at this period, whether in the cult, 'secular' feasting, or mortuary spheres. Historically resonant places (whether or not originally associated with ritual) were reappropriated for ritual use in a number of different ways at this time. I shall pay special attention to these sites later. Thanks to two recently published works covering the subject of Cretan EIA cult in detail, however, this discussion does not need to offer a gazetteer of cult sites or an in-depth description or reevaluation of PG-A Cretan cult buildings (Prent 2005b; Sjögren 2004). Instead, building on these earlier discussions, I focus mainly on linking cult practice into the wider changes occurring in PG-EA society.

Comparisons with the wider Aegean

Cult formed a vital building block in the emergence of Aegean states by the late eighth century. The central mainland sees a major departure at exactly this time, with the widespread displacement of wealth-based competition from the mortuary into the cult sphere, and the marked expansion and elaboration of cult practice (de Polignac 1995: 11–89; Hägg 1983, 1996; Hägg et al. 1988; Morgan 1990). New developments included the founding of sanctuaries as territorial markers in the hinterlands of emergent poleis, and the establishment of temples within settlements, apparently for the first time. We also see (from as early as PG in some cases) the expanded and intensified use of open-air sanctuaries as important arenas for the negotiation of territorial and ethnic identity. Cult practice was becoming more complex, and more specific to particular times and places, within an increasingly formalised system of attachments of different gods and rites to specific sanctuaries. The material attributes of cult, as well as the abstract ones, became an important code about identity and power relations, able to be 'read' by people from many different Aegean regions, as well as by overseas communities now in regular touch with the Aegean and closely linked to its culture and politics (de Polignac 1995: 89–128; Malkin 1987). Investment in monumental cult architecture, particularly important in this regard, began by the seventh century. Though sanctuaries were becoming ever-better defined and hierarchised by the late eighth century, it can still be hard to distinguish '(inter)regional' from 'territorial' sanctuaries at this time. The concept of territorially 'owned' cult may have had little validity in the period prior to the emergence of state institutions. In some regions, such as Thessaly, where the main political unit was the *ethnos*, a number of small autonomous groups operating within this loose identity framework used a shared regional sanctuary as a defining reference point, as well as an interface zone. At the other extreme, a single powerful emergent *polis* was sometimes able to exert enough influence on a major regional sanctuary to give it a quasi-territorial status, as occurred in the case of Isthmia and Corinth (Morgan 1994).

As Cretan states emerged, in a process dating from PG onwards, we also see an increasingly strong, complex, and formalised political role for cult. Yet the change did not occur in the same ways as on the mainland – with regard either to the form of cult practice or to the way it was distributed through the landscape. Cretan communities did not adopt the typical Archaic temple plans of the central Aegean, which seem ultimately to have been rooted in the elite longhouses/feasting houses of this region (Mazarakis Ainian 1988, 1997). In Crete, the always-strong symbolic links of both cult and feasting buildings to the simple domestic template promoted a simpler plan, focused around a main room with hearth, for town temples. Built temples are very rare out in the Cretan landscape, even as they take off on the mainland: open-air ritual sites, often focused on natural places, remain strongly favoured, and where built structures do appear in this context they are often very small and simple. Developing Cretan states clearly used extra-settlement cult to establish and extend themselves, but perhaps never needed to rely on or invest in this activity as strongly as mainland polities, thanks to their relatively small size and the tight, historically rooted cohesion of their territories. Nonetheless, as I discuss later, they do seem to have been increasingly interested in annexing control of some old and traditionally shared major shrines in the landscape. We should bear in mind in this regard the interests of the powerful clan units of this period, which were competing with each other within large polities and some of which were continuing to live at the citadel sites. Depending on how it served their interests and affected their traditional territories, these units may either have powerfully contested or assisted the attachment of state centres to outlying territories through cult.

Cult equipment and rites of the PG-A period remain rooted in early EIA practices, but there are also changes over time – some shared with the mainland, others not. Small votive figurines in clay (human and animal) are now more concentrated in numbers and often mass produced and standardised in form. They are the main deposited artefact at small landscape shrines (the type of figurine used being linked to the individual cult) and are also represented in town shrines (Forster 1902, 1905; Hatzi-Vallianou 2000; Hayden 1997; Prent 2005b: 353–420, 503–8; Rizza and Scrinari 1968: 155–260; Sjögren 2004: 50–2). In contrast, bronze figurines and plaques and large bronze items like armour, weapons, vessels, and tripods are dedicated mainly at main town temples, and at the large regional long-rooted open-air sanctuaries, from the G period onward (Boardman 1961; Bosanquet 1902: 254–59, 1905; Halbherr 1901b: 375–84; Levi 1931; Prent 2005b: 353–424; Sakellarakis 1988). Despite the general lack of social restrictions in Crete on the personal possession of luxuries, by the end of the eighth century Cretans, like their central Greek peers, seem to have been under pressure to deposit more wealth in the cult sphere, as well as to expand that sphere in spatial terms. It is significant that these two classes of sanctuary – one closely linked to the state and lying within the state settlement itself, the other operating mainly at the level of interstate competition – saw the main wealth depositions. As elsewhere, the large public unit, the collectivity, was becoming the fulcrum of social power.

Small extra-settlement shrines

In the nucleated settlements, as extended kin groups came under new kinds of pressure to extend and assert their identity in order to retain political influence, small extra-settlement shrines (or shrines peripheral to the settlement) might be used by some of these groups to maintain territorial claims based on their original, prenucleation residence patterns and farming practices. There might be even stronger interest in such sanctuaries by the groups living at small citadel sites, concerned to keep a hold on relatively fragile, small-scale rights within a developing larger territory. On the other hand, state bodies themselves may have had strong interests in developing, taking over, or manipulating such shrines as tools in political relations.

Within the general category of small shrines, since we rarely know the exact boundaries of the nucleated settlements or their territories, it is hard to distinguish truly 'rural' sanctuaries, with their potentially more open political status, from peripheral sanctuaries, probably more closely controlled by a single polity. Some small shrines using distinctive natural locations distant from any large settlement may have had a relatively independent status. The Stravomyti cave, near Jouktas, and Megala Chorafia, also in central Crete, were used in the G period; the Ayiasmatsi and Melidoni caves in west Crete may have been used as early as Archaic after an EIA gap (Francis et al. 2000; Marinatos 1950: 248–57; Rutkowski and Nowicki 1996: 48–9, 65; Sakellarakis and Sakellarakis 1997: 224–91; Tyree 1974: 222; Tzedakis and Gavrilaki-Nikoloudaki 1987). These sanctuaries could well have been founded and developed by particular clans owning and working land in their vicinity. Other possibly 'clan-owned' sanctuaries of small open-air type are Stou Koukou tou Kefali and the spring sanctuary of Roussa Ekklesia, both in east Crete (Hogarth 1901: 148; Papadakis 1982; Platon 1954b: 511).

Other small isolated shrines in the countryside seem particularly likely to have had a close attachment to a large polity in their region. For example, the Smari summit temple came into use just as the site appears to have been subsumed within the Lyttos territory. The small open-air cult site of Ayia Triada probably became more fully and firmly attached to the expanding Phaistian polity by the eighth century (when the first built structure appeared on the site). Its use may originally have been shared with Gortyn, and conflict over its ownership have arisen somewhere in this period (D'Agata 1998: 24; Watrous and Hadzi-Vallianou 2004b: 325). Pachlitsani Agriada is a small shrine in the Kavousi region, probably in use as early as LM IIIC, which seems to have been most intensively used in PG-EA, almost certainly in connection with the rise of the Azoria nucleation nearby (Alexiou 1956; Gesell 1985: 57; Haggis et al. 2004: 344).

Small shrines in the closer vicinity of emergent nucleations, but still well outside the civic core, might have been attached to particular clans *within* the settlements. Possible examples of this type include several sites around Praisos – at Profitis Elias, Nea Praisos, and Masamvrysi – that need not all be contemporary. They are all one kilometre or more from the putative town centre (Forster 1902: 280, 1905: 243–59; Halbherr 1901b: 384–91; Whitley et al. 1999: 249–51). Still other small 'extra-settlement' sanctuaries lie so close to major nucleations that even if they were associated with particular clans, they were surely owned by, and functioned firmly within, the body of the polity. In both cases, the shrines seem to differ from either the town temples or the larger regional sanctuaries in the relatively simple character of their finds and architecture. Such cases include Thylakas, located on a peaktop just beside the Lato nucleation to its northwest (G-A); another small Archaic sanctuary appears at Sta Melissakia to the north of the site. Kato Plai, just below the Anavlochos ridge on the north (G), and Elounda Sta Lenika, below Elounda Oxa in the Mirabello region (PG), together with another small sanctuary near Elounda (late seventh through sixth centuries), are similar cases all founded between the PG and EA periods (Alexiou 1956; Bousquet 1938: 386–408; Faure 1967: 142; Demargne 1929, 1931: 379–407; Demerle 1937: 474, 1938: 482; Platon 1960c: 259–60; Reinach 1913: 278–300). Some of those shrines have simple built structures associated with them; others may have been open-air sites.

Whatever their exact political relationships and control structures, the date frame within which all these sites began to be used and their locations suggest they were closely bound up with the development of the newly complex polities. Their use might help to consolidate newly expanded territories by linking clans living at the main nucleated sites to their traditionally exploited lands. But it is not clear how far state interests overlapped with those of powerful clans in this regard. Cases like Smari highlight ambiguities concerning the exact ways in which kin units within a large nucleated polity kept up their claims to a distinct identity and territory through cult. Was the establishment of a cult here after the site's abandonment the initiative of a particular clan wishing to keep links to the site, or the marking out of territory through cult practice by the Lyttos state body? In this case I think it more likely that the state controlled the cult, in view of its nature: Athena cults in most parts of the Aegean tend to be strongly associated with the polis as a single entity (Schilardi 1988). We do not necessarily need to see state and clan units in opposition in such cases: the establishment of a state temple might easily be requested (and subsequently taken pride in) by particular clan groups after their incorporation within the state unit. However, we can certainly say that the widening range of sanctuary types offered more *opportunities* for the assertion of power and identity at the level of subgroups within the state, the authority of the state being, of course, itself deeply rooted in clan power.

Large regional/interregional shrines

In the new political environment of PG-Archaic Crete, we might expect changes to occur at large extra-settlement sanctuaries, with rights of access and worship passing into the hands of fewer, larger-scale players. Yet the high profile and very broad-based historical resonance of these sanctuaries, as well as their physical positioning, must have made real exclusivity of attachment difficult to achieve. The growth of such attachments was surely also discouraged by social codes developed during the collapse period. As we have seen, the social stability that characterised Crete in the early EIA seems to be linked to these sites' operation as *shared* identity reference and interaction points. Many of them, such as the Idaean, Psychro, Patsos, and Tsoutsouros caves and Kato Simi, flourished through the Geometric period and beyond without any hiatus or change in depositions suggesting radical shifts in control (Alexiou 1963a; Boardman 1961; Erickson 2002; Kanta 1991; Lebessi 1975; 1985; Rutkowski and Nowicki 1996: 1–45; Sakellarakis 1983, 1988, 1992; Watrous 1996: 101–11). The very densely packed map of PG-EA Cretan polities, and the wide-ranging external references of Cretan artistic production in this period, mean that we cannot easily identify the proportion of metal votives taken to a sanctuary from any one particular region/settlement within the island and thus gain insight into the origins of users, as we can on the mainland – though more work could be done on the provenancing of ceramic objects in this regard. Cults of Zeus, as at the Psychro and Psiloritis sanctuaries, tended to attract especially

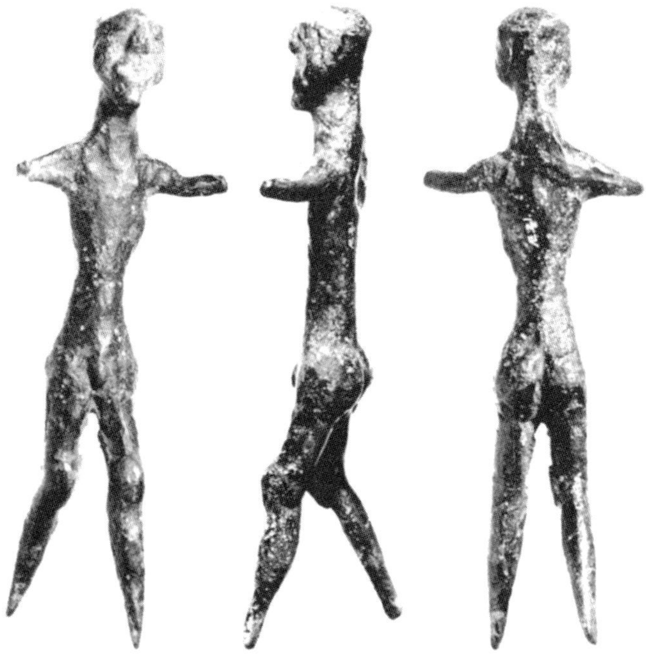

198. Bronze human figurine from Psychro cave (after Boardman 1961, plate III [21]). By permission of J. Boardman.

high quantities of metal, including large single pieces in the form of armour and weapons, as well as smaller metal items like figurines (Figure 198). This level of investment suggests that the sanctuaries were used in a different way from their smaller peers, at a level more closely linked to the state, without implying dominance of the cult by any one particular state. It is possible that some large bronze items were dedicated by elite individuals or powerful clans, especially when we consider the developed production and wide circulation of metal items in the island at this period. On the other hand, an increased investment in infrastructure at some of these sanctuaries by the Archaic period does seem most likely to be the work of state bodies. Kato Simi sees its greatest growth of value good deposits from Geometric onwards: the development of new building work there from circa 700 BC is notable (Kanta 1991; Lebessi 1975: 325; Prent 2005b: 343; Figure 199). The first shrine building at Ayia Triada was perhaps sponsored by Phaistos, as its links to the sanctuary became closer and more exclusive. Yet in contrast to mainland patterns, the long and continuing tradition of open-air shrines in Crete means that the appearance of built infrastructure (especially given its usually modest character in the early stages) is not a consistent basis on which to infer shifts in control/investment frameworks.

Sjögren has suggested a decline after 700 BC in the private use of large regional sanctuaries, citing reduced volumes of figurines, jewellery, and other small votives at these sites (Sjogren 2004: 58–66). This would support the notion that as state bodies consolidated their power, they moved to take control of the sites (or agreed to restrict their use to state level only). However, in an environment where multiple small and simultaneously expanding states were confined within a single island, retaining some level of shared use of major sanctuaries (whether between states or between different social groups within states) might act as a pressure release for developing tensions. This may even have encouraged the development of new sanctuaries formally shared by a number of polities. One possible example of this appears at Palaikastro – interestingly,

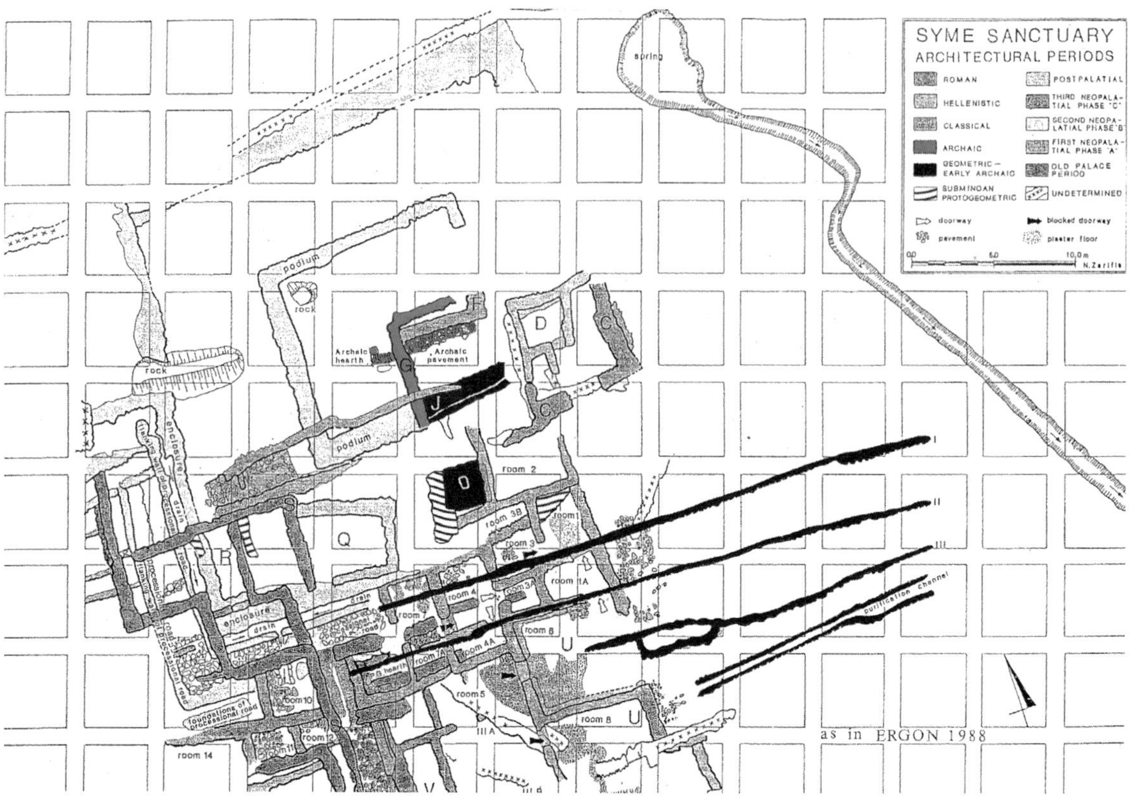

199. Plan of Kato Simi sanctuary, showing features constructed in the G-A periods (after Kanta 1991, Fold-out plan).

located on the coast rather than at a distinctive 'nature' site. A built temple of Diktaian Zeus was founded here in the LG-A period, at a considerable distance from any contemporary settlement in the region. Along with the investment in building, the site has remarkably rich finds – of the kind most typical of settlement temples or major regional sanctuaries – and thus seems unlikely to have been a shrine attached to any single small clan group (Bosanquet 1905, 1945; Thorne and Prent 2000). Yet from later texts, it seems always to have had a wide regional catchment of users, rather than being associated with a single polity: control of it was hotly disputed between east Cretan states as late as the Hellenistic period. The late establishment of such an isolated, yet important, shrine may reflect the particularly slow, awkward, and conflictful process of state formation in east Crete. The establishment of the sanctuary would facilitate the interaction of developing polities/regional communities without allowing any one of them to take control of this valuable harbour zone and the trade passing through it.

Trade sanctuaries and the island identity

The use of cult places/practice as a channel for trade and other kinds of external contacts (of great value to the newly expanding polities) is reflected in the growth of sanctuaries like Amnisos and Kommos during this period. A coastal sanctuary established on the Diktynnaion peninsula in west Crete may parallel the role of the Palaikastro temple as a trade gateway shared by several polities in the region (Savignoni and de Sanctis 1904). The coastal site at Amnisos, which had probably been used for cult throughout the EIA, has high volumes of Geometric to Archaic deposits, including imported figurines, and a built construction appears there by the late Archaic period. A new use of the Bronze Age cave site above the coast at Amnisos also appeared by Geometric times. In a newly complex arrangement, the harbour cult seems to have been dedicated to Zeus Thanatas, though the cave, which also had Geometric and Archaic material, was linked by Homer to the goddess Eilytheia (S. Marinatos 1929, 1930; N. Marinatos 1996; Schäfer et al. 1992: 159–85, 226–73). Kommos also saw new building between the late ninth and seventh centuries, with the construction of the Temple B structure and a growing density of deposits (Shaw and Shaw 2000: 14–37).

Though emergent states had a lot at stake in the coastal sanctuaries, individuals and small groups might also have had strong interests there under the relatively free exchange systems which were prevalent in the island. Given the physically open locations of the sites and the potentially broad economic interest in them, access would be difficult to restrict or monopolise. Finds at Kommos and Amnisos include *both* large, high-value luxury items – metals, imported figurines – and low-value votives, suggesting a broad variety of statuses among the worshippers. Though Kommos seems closely linked to the Phaistos polity by this period, more complex and varied levels of influence are likely to have operated here than at the much smaller and simpler Ayia Triada site, which seems only ever to have had the status of a territorial shrine (Watrous 1996: 101–2). Investment in substantial new built infrastructure at Kommos from the ninth century on suggests polity-level involvement; Phaistos almost certainly contributed heavily to this and was able in return to cream off a large proportion of the site's profits through provisioning and trade activities. On the other hand, the Phoenicianising design of the new shrine building suggest that complete symbolic appropriation, stressing tight and exclusive links to a particular polis or ethnic group, was neither possible nor desirable here. Symbolism at the major coastal sanctuaries had to be flexible and adaptable to sustain the very wide interregional participation on which profits were built. The case of Samos offers a parallel in the east Aegean. The success of this sanctuary as an interregional interaction point by at least the eighth century encouraged the nearby polis of Samos to allow considerable investment in infrastructure and in high-value dedications from outside powers, including the powerful Anatolian kingdoms (Freyer-Schauenberg 1974; Kyrieleis 1979, 1993).

Interestingly, tolerance and encouragement of diverse participation in the large Cretan sanctuaries did not always make for closer political links with the Aegean world, in which pan-Hellenic traditions were becoming central to identity structures: no large Cretan sanctuary ever took on pan-Hellenic status, for example. The architecture and format of many major sanctuaries in Crete stayed strongly attached to special local landscape features and traditions and made little use of the monumentalism typical of central Greek sites. The island's distinctive recent history (and the importance attached to this in community consciousness), along with its geographical position, mixed trade base, and peculiar outlook on trade, all contributed to ensuring that it was never viewed (either from within or from outside) as central to the cult interactions on which trans-Aegean political power was being constructed. While Cretans certainly participated in pan-Hellenic cults, they may have done so with a specially defined 'outsider' status similar to that of people originating from wealthy oriental states. At the same time, Crete's oldest and largest sanctuaries *did* come to hold a high status at a pan-Aegean level – the links of the Psychro and Idaean cave sanctuaries to the birth of Zeus suggest that the shrines would have drawn visitors from other parts of the Aegean and have been recognised as symbolising Crete's strong cultural and political ties to the wider region. An externally recognised affinity between Cretans and Apollo, patron deity of some early Cretan town temples like those of Gortyn and Dreros, may have led to the selection of Cretan priests to service one of the most important Aegean cults, at Delphi, by the later Archaic period, as the Homeric *Hymn to Apollo* tells us (Osborne 1996: 246). This choice may also have related to Crete's separation from the core of pan-Hellenic politics, helping to safeguard the nominal independence of the Delphi cult. I will return to discuss the peculiar identity status of Crete in the Aegean world in Part Five.

Symbolic reference to the past in the landscape: cult and other spheres

Hobsbawm (1975: 4) writes of 'invented tradition' that 'we should expect it to occur more frequently when a rapid transformation of society weakens or destroys the social patterns for which "old" traditions had been designed, producing new ones to which they are not applicable'. The fact that adapted, extended, or invented tradition played such a major part in EIA Aegean culture and society was undoubtedly linked to the fundamental disruption in social and political systems in many areas in the twelfth century. Given the particularly radical and permanent nature of this change in Crete and the island's previously complex and eventful history, it is unsurprising to find powerful references to the past, especially the recent past, appearing in a broad variety of ritual activities during the EIA. I have already addressed the nature and role of such references inside contemporary settlements and cemeteries. Now I turn to look at their appearance in the wider landscape during the PG-EA period.

1) REFERENCE TO NATURAL PLACES WITH HISTORICAL ASSOCIATIONS

We have seen how important a role was played by Crete's dramatic natural landscape in the radical, memorable horizon of cultural change associated with state collapse from circa 1200 BC. This new layering of meaning onto a landscape already long settled and rich in associations offered fruitful possibilities for emergent states in the PG-A period to legitimise themselves by reference to myth, tradition, and ancestry in the material dimension. By the same token, it provided opportunities for powerful clans within those states to place claims on the landscape – whether in parallel or contradistinction to those of the state – in the interests of promoting/defining their own identity and political strength. The diverse character and accessible scale of the Cretan landscape, and its long history of symbolic associations, meant that high-investment monumentalisation was often not necessary to lend weight and significance to a cult, leaving the way open for even small groups to develop powerful ritual foci in this way. Reuse practices often seem linked to the visual or experiential qualities of the landscape, as well as its historical resonance, with each aspect feeding into the others to enhance the experience.

As we have seen, harbour sites were regularly selected for cult use, partly because they provided access to the exterior world – but also, it seems, because visitors, even those from far away, had special familiarity with these spaces by repute and tradition. The Amnisos, Palaikastro, and Kommos coastal sanctuaries were all built in the middle of the clearly visible remains of Bronze Age harbour settlements. Given the latter's ruined state, a *knowledge* of local history and traditions and an established sense of the significance of the place were relied on to give weight to the rituals now conducted there and create a sense of shared privilege among the participants, however socially or ethnically mixed they actually were (Nixon 1990; Prent 2003, 2005b: 508–50).

Springs were also used for open-air cults by the Archaic period. Again, this sometimes occurred in ways thats linked these naturally special/memorable places with reference to the human past (Gesell 1985: 57). The large Kato Simi sanctuary was located close to a spring, channelled to run through the sanctuary precincts by Archaic times: the sanctuary's continuity of use right through the BA-EIA transition suggests this natural place had a fundamental resonance and entrenched place in social memory. Some other spring sanctuaries are located closer to settlements and seem to have more localised links: Roussa Ekklisia Anixi, in the Siteia mountains, has an Archaic settlement located quite close by (Papadakis 1982; Platon 1954b; Prent 2005b: 301–2). A small spring sanctuary was located at Vitsilovrysi just below Karfi, and probably used by groups living at Papoura after Karfi was abandoned (Pendlebury et al. 1938: 98–100). At least three layers of meaning operated here. Reference to a natural feature widely known by the local population was combined with reference to a visually striking location with a long history of ritual use (the peak of Karfi, which had been an MBA peak sanctuary) *and* to the history of an only recently abandoned settlement area, tied to the memorable twelfth-century period of upheaval and crisis. Some groups from the Papoura community are likely to have claimed ancestry at Karfi, and this small open-air shrine may have operated mostly at a clan level.

Peaktops were also often chosen for the siting of cult places, especially where these peaks had historical associations. We see this within settlements, as town cult diversified – in the cases of the Archaic temple on the Gortyn Acropolis and the Phaistos Acropoli Mediana temple, for example, which are both located on the original early EIA occupation areas of the sites (La Rosa 1996; Rizza and Scrinari 1968). The temple of Athena at Smari is an example of an *extra*-settlement shrine on a peak that had also housed an early EIA settlement.

At Knossos, a site that lacks any very distinctive internal topography, we see a direct reference back to the most prominent *built* element of the site – the palace – with the foundation of an open-air shrine in its ruins. This developed as a built temple – the 'Temple of Rhea' – in Archaic times but potentially started in use as early as the PG-G period – though the remains of this date, comprising ashy/burnt deposits and much fine pottery, could as well relate to feasting as to cult (Evans 1928: 5–7; Hartley 1931: 92–3, 108; Hood and Smyth 1981: 20; Prent 2005b: 261).

II) REFERENCES TO THE CULTURAL LANDSCAPE OF THE COLLAPSE PERIOD

Where ritual reuse of sites dating originally to the collapse period circa 1200 BC occurred, their often visually striking defensible topography seems likely to have been a very important additional point of reference, enriching their historical resonance. There are, however, cases of reuse at sites of this date where the topography was *not* particularly striking. They may have acted as proxies for more highly visible sites or dramatic settlements of the same period nearby. For example, the abandoned LM IIIC settlement of Monastiraki Chalasmeno shows evidence of clan-level feasting activity in the LG period (Tsipopoulou 2004a). Landscape setting seems very important here: the site's proximity to the striking Cha gorge, which had itself housed a defensible site of the collapse period, marked out the locality for great distances around. Within the site, reuse is highly targeted, limited to the central area of the settlement and to one of the most formerly impressive building complexes, the Megarons – perhaps itself originally a public feasting venue. Specific traditions about the site, as well as its setting, seem to have been built on to emphasise what was important in the new political conditions of the LG period. In this case, it seems to have been the integration and reinforcement, through feasting practice, of a particular group, perhaps a clan unit. The assemblage is not yet fully studied, but is certainly not of cult type, and a large number of drinking vessels are present. It is hard to believe that this complex alone was reoccupied as a normal dwelling. A repeated, specialised feasting use by a small group of people resident elsewhere, possibly at the Azoria nucleation, seems the best interpretation. The group may have claimed descent from the original inhabitants of the site, whether or not this was the case.

Symbolic reuse of a different kind at an abandoned LM IIIC settlement appears at Kavousi Vronda, in the same locality. Again, it occurred during the period of state consolidation in LG. The standing architectural remains had cist graves of mainly Late Geometric date cut into them (Day 1995; Day et al. 1986: 384–5, 387; Gesell et al. 1988: 297–8). The people using this cemetery may also have lived at Azoria, and the cutting of pyres and graves into abandoned buildings recalls the practice of interment in bone enclosures seen at other sites of this period. These features point, again, to an extended kin group or groups located within a large consolidating polity asserting themselves through claims to an 'ancestral' territory. Again, whether this group really had ancestral links to the original residents of Vronda is less relevant than the fact that the period of deep upheaval and planned restructuring at 1200 BC was perceived to have a core role in determining group identity (Haggis et al. 2004: 341). As with Chalasmeno, the Vronda site itself is not visually striking or memorable but offers excellent views of the landmark Kastro site, still occupied at this time.

We have learned from the mortuary record that the concept of ancestry was very important to kin groups concerned to assert their standing and their attachment to place under the changing political conditions, and that these groups were probably amenable to boosting the size and status of their lineages using fictive or tenuous ancestral links. We saw that they seem to have dated important origin or reference points in their ancestral lines to the twelfth century. The aspects of the PG-EA ritual landscape discussed above confirm this concern with the past as a source of symbolic power. But the types of site chosen for reuse, their original date, the types of reuse engaged in, and the agents involved reveal a remarkable variety and complexity in the way this concern operated. Emergent state bodies might choose to respect clan identities marked out in this way, but they could also manipulate, limit, and contest them using the same kinds of reference. Just as the line between the state body and the individual clans nested within that body are hard to distinguish in the archaeological record, so the boundary between collective and individual appropriation of the past is often obscure. One area that does seem more tied to the individual than to the public collectivity is small-scale reuse or cult at Bronze Age tombs (see below). Like many of the other reuses discussed here, these references mainly occur just at the period of state consolidation, suggesting a newly pressing need to assert individual or very small-group identity, as well as other levels of identity and belonging, in these changing political circumstances. Ultimately, state emergence is the linking thread of all the different types of reuse and reference mentioned here.

III) RITUAL LANDSCAPES AND REFERENCE TO THE PAST IN THE WIDER AEGEAN: COMPARISONS

Attention both to landscape setting and to the past was important in the siting of ritual practice on the mainland during the state emergence period. We saw that concerns of this type were already active in the earlier EIA, when abandoned LBA settlements were chosen as locations for regional sanctuaries, apparently because they offered secure and well-known regional reference points. Such considerations also applied within continuing settlements, as we saw in the case of Tiryns. The same sorts of concerns pertained to cult even as it changed its form and status by the late eighth century. As in Crete, certain visual/experiential characteristics seem to have enhanced the power of these references – hilltop locations were particularly important – and the EIA, as well as the BA, past could be referred to. At Eleusis, the summit area of the LBA town was reused for cult from at least LG, while contemporary settlement spread out in the near vicinity (Darcque 1981; Mylonas 1961: 56–63). At Corinth, a town sanctuary of Demeter and Kore developed by the eighth century in the ruins of the former LM IIIC settlement on the slopes of Acrocorinth, after the main occupation had moved down to the plain. This situation seems paralleled in the placing of town sanctuaries on the acropoleis of Athens and Aigeira as settlement moved onto the lower slopes (Blackman 2002: 36–7; Bookidis and Stroud 1997; Camp 2002: 21–6; Glowacki 1998).

During this same period of central Greek state emergence, small territorial sanctuaries closely attached to the emergent polities were sometimes also placed on old settlement locations, recalling the Smari case, which I have looked at above. Yet by far the greatest emphasis in this practice was on Bronze Age sites. There was a lack here of abandoned settlements dating to the early EIA – and as such, linked into a unified and dramatic historical horizon – that might have formed alternative reference points. Yet the practice has strong similarities of meaning with those adopted in Crete at this time. The choice of LBA sites for the new sanctuary locations was a way of firmly overwriting past territorial associations, which may have survived through much of the EIA, in order to consolidate or negotiate state ownership of the territory. Examples include the Argive Heraion, located on the LBA acropolis of Prosymna; the Mycenae temple (cult practice starts at this location by PG); and the erection of a shrine on the Menelaion site near Sparta (Antonaccio 1992; Hall 1995b; Klein 2002; Morgan and Whitelaw 1995). Again the visual qualities of the landscape were used to enhance these statements: all the preceding cult places are on prominences overlooking extensive flatlands and visible from major settlements nearby.

In contrast to Crete, there are few hints that clan-level groups were utilising the past to legitimate themselves in the landscape. I have already suggested the relative weakness or looseness of the clan unit in EIA mainland societies, and the much greater emphasis on individual status competition. However, there are a few cases that might represent activity at clan-group level. At the Pylos palace site in Messenia, PG-G reuse, showing concern with a fêted palatial past, may have taken the form of open-air feasting rather than cult, recalling the Chalasmeno case. Large areas of the palatial architecture were reused in a way that produced heavy burnt deposits, including remains of at least four iron spits together with numerous animal bones. No architecture except a small enclosure (reminiscent of the Ayia Triada shrine) dates to this period, and few pots have been found (Griebel and Nelson 1998; Popham 1991). No 'owner' of this activity at polity level can be clearly identified. Yet the history of the site seems too special, and the activity too widespread, to represent the claim of a few individuals or a single small clan unit. Instead, it suggests a possibly competitive activity, bringing together a number of powerful clans in a loosely organised format that could either prefigure or challenge the development of early state authority. The tendency to focus on Bronze Age remains, rather than those of the Early Iron Age, for symbolic reuse is likely to have directed traditions about the past in particular ways, making them more generic, remote, and glorious than specific and local. It perhaps encouraged the destructions and settlement changes of circa 1200 BC to be seen as almost entirely negative – the 'end of an era' – rather than, as in Crete, a creative horizon. In conjunction with the way settlement patterns were rebalanced, the emphasis on reference to a shared, generalised BA past from early in the EIA minimised opportunities to build and legitimise new strong local ties to land at the level of the small group, in the way seen in Crete. However, if references and claims of this type were relatively weak at the clan level, there is a belated attempt to make them stronger at the level of the individual in the growth of tomb cult during the eighth century, often seen as a last-ditch resistance to elites' incorporation within the state body. Some Bronze Age tombs became a focus for small ritual depositions (perhaps conceived as symbolic burials) at this time. As often isolated units in the landscape, they were fairly easily able to be appropriated by an individual or small group, and their remote, 'generic' history made them relatively easy to claim at this scale (Eder 1998: 175–6; Morris 2000: 195–309).

Though the contrasting landscape and social history of Crete drove reuse practices in a different way, references of the same type did also occur there in the late EIA, at places like Kamilari, where reference was made to a monumental EBA tomb; Mochlos (where an LM III chamber tomb was targeted) and Achladia, where deposits were made in an LM III tholos (Lefèvre-Novaro 2001; Soles 2001; Tsipopulou and Vagnetti 1995: 125; Wallace 2003b: 270–1). As elsewhere, these practices seem to concentrate in the crucial state consolidation horizon. It seems likely that they operated at the level of the kin group rather than that of the individual, given the context of contemporary mortuary practice in Crete. Since the placing of multiple interments over time in a shared tomb belonging to an extended kin group was still common here by the eighth century, actions of the same generic kind at much older tombs surely represented the literal inclusion of one's own *group* into a generic 'ancestral' family group. Thus, the practice seems to have represented a less radical and revolutionary agenda than on the mainland and one of perhaps more limited social importance. Given that the ancestry of powerful clans in PG-A Crete was so often tied to the 1200 BC horizon, these references to Bronze Age tombs may reflect attempts by peripheral or weaker clan groups to compete in the newly complex political environment.

In the Cyclades, EIA communities made their own kinds of cultural reference to the past, clearly related to those of other Aegean regions. The nature of practice changes over time here, too. As in Crete, the horizon of change circa 1200 BC seems to have formed a major social and political reference point as the state emerged. This is unsurprising, given the islands' history of dramatic and lasting cultural change at this period. I have already mentioned for Crete the practice of selective reuse or continued use of temples at otherwise abandoned EIA settlements as territorial shrines for states emerging in their regions. A very similar development seems to occur at Zagora, as noted earlier.

We see symbolic reuse practices within the emerging Cycladic polis settlements, too. On Naxos, PG tombs were placed close to one of the most prominent parts of the architecture of twelfth-century Grotta – the fortification wall that had been constructed in the crisis period, and nearby houses. From the Geometric period the tombs became the location of a cult involving circular stone platforms (of a type associated with burial cult at some mainland sites: Hägg 1988: 189, 191; Lambrinoudakis 1988; Mazarakis Ainian 1997: 122–2). As the Grotta settlement grew, the LH IIIC and PG pasts may have been interfused and conflated as decreasingly personalised, more inclusive layers of symbolism were attached to the place.

Conclusions

Close and subtle links in ritual show that the insular Aegean, Crete, and central mainland shared partly similar worldviews and traditions by the eighth century. At the same time, there were considerable and deep-rooted differences, connected to the different histories of the three areas at the collapse period circa 1200 BC and afterwards. Crete was marked out by particularly rich, diverse, and well-entrenched local traditions, closely tied to the special character of the island's landscape and able to be accessed at many different levels. Not only did the radical cultural changes of the recent past *physically* construct the core of the polis state (in terms of settlement pattern, settlement form, and institutional space); they also indirectly shaped (for example, via the visual connections between sites and the symbolic references able to be made to earlier EIA sites) the ways residents of the emergent states saw themselves at a number of different levels, from the extended kin group to the regional polity. At the same time, it is clear that the Bronze Age remained resonant in myth, tradition, and ritual practice. Exploitation of these rich and diverse symbolic resources was clearly instrumental in Crete's stable and early development towards the state – in maintaining the densely packed pattern of small states, each with a strongly defined identity; and in perpetuating the very strong role of the clan group within the state.

A recent case study in anthropology throws further light on these kinds of practices and their often vital role in the transition to complex societies. Study of tribal communities in Madagascar shows that where political identity is under pressure, reference is made to abandoned sites of various types in order to substantiate group authority, status, and land claims (Parker Pearson et al. 1999). The sites selected in this case – treated as ancestral burial places or cult locations – are

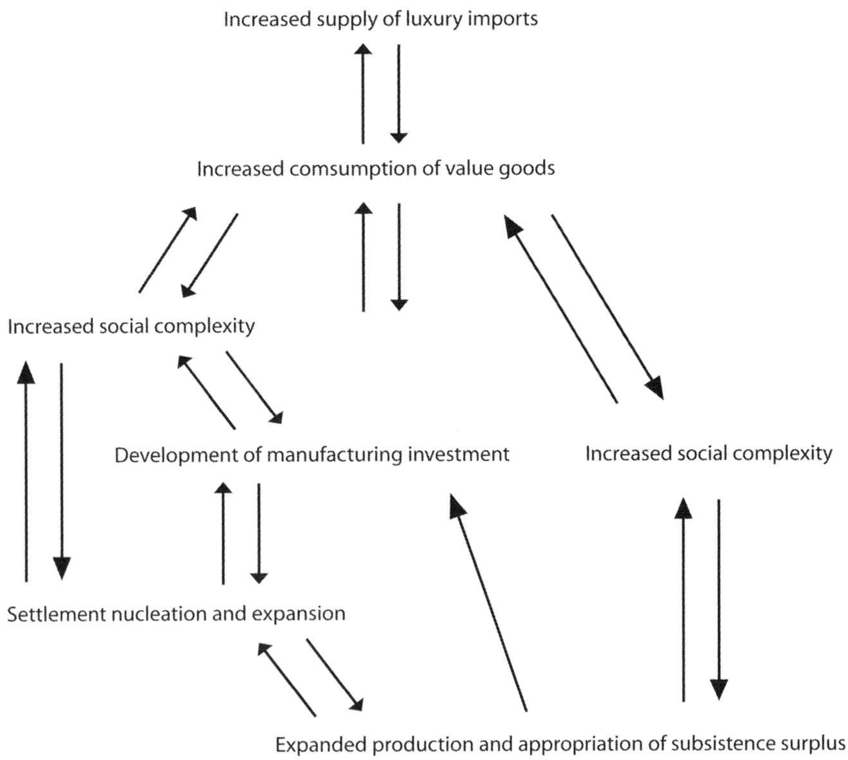

200. Diagram of connections between trade, settlement, and subsistence economy in PG-A Crete. Image by the author.

often actually *settlements* of relatively recent date – even though much earlier sites are still visible and available for reference in the landscape. As well as disregarding 'real' chronology, reference to the material past blurs the boundaries among the settlement, cult, and mortuary spheres in order to strengthen the connections of particular *topoi* with the identity and history of a particular group. Similarly, during a crucial period for the definition of community identities in EIA Crete, remains dating to the quite recent past were annexed in a variety of symbolic ways, helping to consolidate and develop newly important aspects of these identities. This does not suggest *actual* vagueness or confusion about which part of the past was referred to, but a creative selectivity in developing appropriate structures of reference. At trade sites and major gateway settlements, reference to generic Bronze Age traditions may have enhanced or guaranteed the value of social and economic transactions to the very mixed groups using these sites. But among the tightly knit proto-state communities forming the backbone of the island's settlement pattern by the early Archaic period it seems to have been local, Iron Age cultural roots that had the most direct salience in political life and were thus most valuable as points of material reference.

General conclusions on the PG-EA periods in Crete

Figure 200 summarises relationships among the different elements of growing socioeconomic complexity in PG-EA Crete. These include a developing value goods economy, stimulating increased specialisation and the rise of social inequality; a regionally based nucleation of settlement (with the new levels of political complexity that implies); and subsistence expansion. Settlement seems particularly prominent as the spine and engine of the island's social organisation over this period. It maintained, from its roots in the collapse era through the next 800 years, a form and distribution utterly different from anything seen in either the Neolithic-Bronze Age or the post-Roman periods in Crete, and in some ways contraindicated by the pattern of the island's natural resources. With significant modifications over time, closely linked to changing wider circumstances, this basic pattern directly structured the Cretan state as an economic and political unit. Crete's external trade relations expanded during the same period, playing an integral role in complexity growth by promoting subsistence expansion and specialisation. The (related) reduction of physical insecurity over time acted in a similar way, allowing the operation of much larger political and economic territories. These different processes and events cannot be shown to be exactly synchronous, but there seems no doubt that they came together to produce a major turning point in social and political life from the tenth century on.

32 THE EARLY ARCHAIC HORIZON: CORRELATES OF STATE CONSOLIDATION IN THE ARCHAEOLOGICAL RECORD

Assessing the reality of the 'Archaic gap'

The Archaic period proper marks a further turning point in Crete's sociocultural development. Some features of the record discussed previously, especially the spread of small shrines out into the landscape, may actually relate more to this set of changes than to those of the PG-earliest Archaic period, but are difficult to date precisely. My summary and interpretation of some other main features of change, presented below, marks the end of detailed archaeological synthesis in this book and is not intended to be comprehensive. The low quality of evidence for the period is one reason for this; the existence of Sjögren's recently published study of what data are available also precludes the need to produce a data summary, even though it leaves much to be said in interpretative terms (Sjögren 2004). The fact that dating of developments becomes much patchier, as a result of the very limited spread and detail of investigation carried out on sites of this period, contributes to making a synthetic approach unsatisfactory.

The impression of change in the archaeological record at this point, combined with the sketchiness of recorded evidence, has often led scholars to see the Archaic period, and specifically the sixth century, as some kind of hiatus or decline in the island's history (Boardman 1982; Coldstream and Huxley 1999; Morris 1998: 13, 66–8). Yet when the period is reviewed in the context of those before and after it, and at an islandwide scale, there is little to support the idea that the changes equate to a sudden widespread reduction of population, or any other catastrophic shift. As we have seen, the general patterns of change in mortuary representation from soon after circa 700 BC suggest that people were representing themselves more modestly in this arena while consolidating power elsewhere, in the developing political sphere. The monolithic wealthy kin group had, I think, by now become so well established within the state structure that it no longer needed to advertise or promote itself in burial in the same way. The tendency to simplification in burial has probably contributed to scholars' notion of a generalised population decline starting in the late seventh century, especially at Knossos, where the main cemeteries are suggested to have been abandoned after 630 BC. It is still not clear what typical burials of the sixth century here looked like, where they were located, or whether burial was a regular custom at all at this period. For the fifth century, too, a general lack of burial evidence at the site strongly suggests a permanent change in practice by this date, though some older tombs were reused in a very modest way (Coldstream and Huxley 1999). But the changing burial record is not enough of a basis on which to assume the abandonment of the site, or its intrinsic decline, in this period. In contrast to the Knossian picture, a review of accidental and surface finds across the rest of the

Cretan landscape points to plenty of burial activity going on through the sixth and fifth centuries, as Sjögren has shown. We should bear in mind here the notable differences between burial practices at Knossos and those in other parts of the island throughout the EIA, which I have attributed to the special social and economic history of the site.

The abandonment of many large nucleated settlements within the Archaic period, in a process of further nucleation probably related to the rise of friction and conflict among expanding polities, has sometimes given the same misleading impression of population decline (Figure 201). The very small number of excavations at large Archaic through Classical settlements outside Knossos has helped obscure the fact of widespread settlement continuity and expansion elsewhere in Crete. At an islandwide scale, the retention of a large number of settlement bases in continuous use is evident (on the basis of surface pottery and small-scale excavations) from 1200 BC right through into the Classical period, including examples examined earlier such as Praisos, Gortyn, Krousonas Koupo, Rotasi, Lyttos, and many others. Even at Knossos, excavators have found both seventh- and fifth-century occupation material stratified in a number of different areas, making it hard to believe there was minimal (or no) human presence here in the sixth century alone. It is worth noting that many of these deposits come from wells, or from sequences that show significant gaps within the EIA period, too. Regular rebuilding and related intrasite movement clearly took place at Knossos, as at many other large EIA-A settlements, undermining the validity of interpreting small gaps in sequences in particular locations as representing overall contraction of population. Extensive replanning of towns during Archaic times, including the creation of formal civic zones of the type seen at Azoria, should lead us to expect significant spatial readjustment at Knossos during this period. Recently Brice Erickson has suggested that a simple defeat in warfare led to the temporary abandonment of Knossos alone, perhaps resulting from an expansion of Gortyn (Erickson 2000: 142–6). Such a drastic and singular outcome remains, in my view, impossible to believe of a state that had such a very long and dominant role in earlier Cretan history and was so strong, prosperous, and powerful (according to both textual and archaeological sources) immediately before and immediately after this period. A phase of contraction and rebuilding at the site, linked to major shifts in the island's power balance during the Archaic period, seems a more likely explanation. We need to investigate further the nature of changes in social and political structures at the site in this period to explain better why, for example, burial practices do not return to any kind of status quo within the fifth century.

As we have seen, Cretan cult practice also seems to have undergone changes in the Archaic period, probably connected to large-scale territorial remodellings. Sanctuaries like Amnisos and Kommos fell partly out of use, adding further to the general impression of 'decline'. In the case of Kommos, this phase lasted from circa 600 BC to the early fourth century (Schäfer et al. 1992; Shaw and Shaw 2000: 36–7). Yet worship was apparently still taking place on the site, with two phases of altar building in this period and a large building, F, in use until 500 BC. We simply do not understand the nature of the change in practice, which again seems most likely to relate to power rebalancing among large political territories across the island, as they consolidated and expanded.

We have seen that new temple building took place within the sixth century, during urban expansion at continuing sites such as Phaistos and Gortyn. There are indications at Knossos, too, that temple construction, and ongoing use of temples, spanned the 'gap', with the presence of possible sixth-century antefixes near the Royal Road and the emergence of a new shrine at the locality named the 'Shrine of Glaukos' (which may have had a previous use for cult) after 500 BC. Monumental building also starts in this period at the previously established sanctuary of Demeter and the so-called Temple of Rhea (Callaghan 1976; Coldstream 1973; Coldstream and Huxley 1999: 297). Once again, it is almost inconceivable that these actions could take place

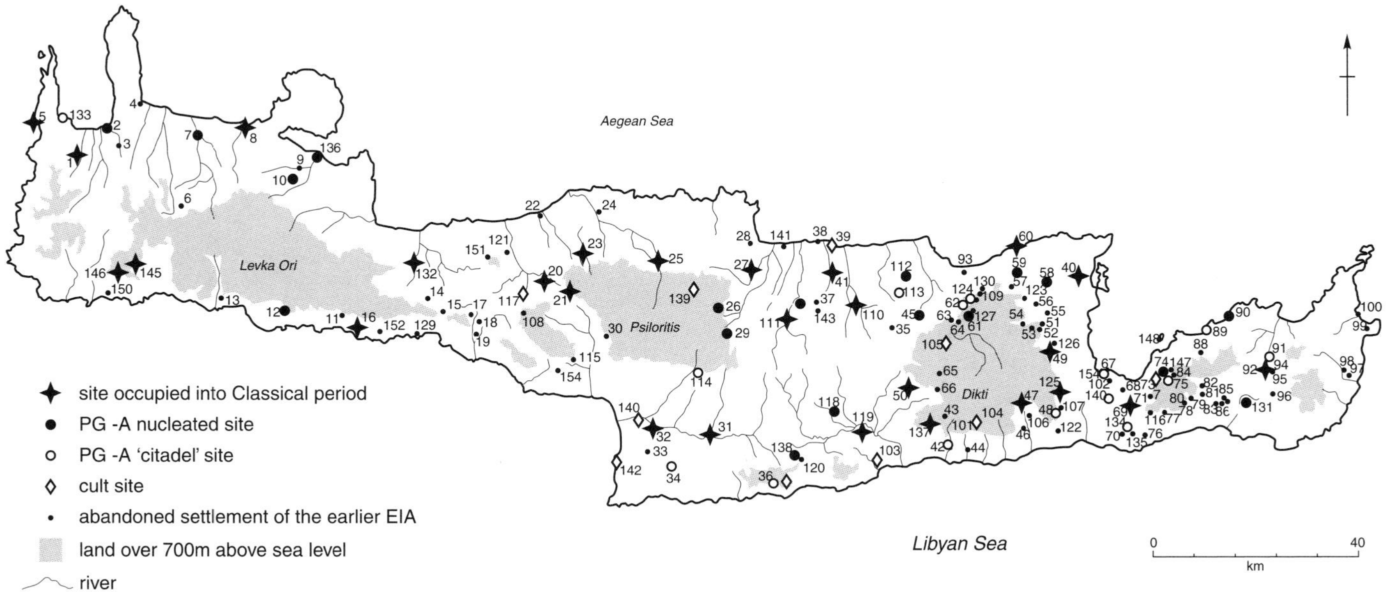

201. Significant Cretan settlement sites with EIA histories that were still in use in the late Archaic through Classical periods. Image by the author.

unless strong concepts of community identity and attachment to place persisted right through the sixth century. The nature of cult practice shows no sign of a major departure or divergence in form between the EA and Classical periods: indeed, by the early Classical period Cretan cult, like other areas of culture, seems to have ever-closer similarities with practice in the wider Greek world. This fact is related to continuous contact between the regions, but also, surely, to the continuous development of widely shared traditions across the perceived 'gap'. Those undertaking such activities clearly originated in the island and followed existing established cultural practices. Whatever political and cultural shifts occurred, a sizeable population continued to live in the island's established settlements and to carry on a cultural life well rooted in their traditions throughout the so-called gap period. Legal inscriptions on stone between the seventh and fourth centuries show that state-level institutions were continuously supported through the period by the use of writing, which had helped them first to consolidate.

The most recent scholarship on the period totally rejects the notion of an 'Archaic gap', on all of the preceding, and other, more detailed, grounds (Haggis et al. 2004: 344–6, esp. note 16). The excavation of Azoria, a site now shown to have had continuous occupation from the twelfth century onwards, experiencing destruction and rebuilding in the early fifth before its final abandonment, has particularly detracted from the notion. While revealing discontinuities in the stratigraphic record relating to the particular history of the site, the record has failed to show any 'black hole' matching up with the proposed 'gap' period.

In Part Five, I will explore how geopolitical changes on a large scale from the seventh century onwards may have especially encouraged Cretan communities to see themselves as 'different' and to be viewed as such by their external peers. These include increasing friction as the small Cretan states expanded, leading to regular conflict and the rise of powerful alliances between Cretan states and external powers, which hugely intensified and broadened the impact of actions at state level (including intra-island warfare, but also the development of connections to particular sanctuaries, markets, or products). As the colonial world boomed, Crete's lack of colonial connections, rooted in its unusual EIA trade profile, might increasingly have marginalised its political and economic standing, reducing the role of some of the coastal sanctuaries. On the other hand, an emerging bulk trade in subsistence goods by the sixth century offered new opportunities. The sixth century may represent a period of adjustment to these new conditions, sometimes disjointed and difficult in nature, while the fifth-century record reflects the island's settling-in to this new groove of development.

One aspect of change in the Archaic period: settlement pattern

One of the most important and visible types of cultural change in Archaic Crete is the reorientation of settlement, occurring at an islandwide scale. Although still poorly investigated, this seems able to tell us quite a lot about changes in society. Given the emphasis laid on settlement pattern change earlier in the book, it seems useful to consider it in detail here, though other aspects of the record cannot be covered in the same depth. The abandonment of a significant number of large nucleated sites occurs between the seventh and fifth centuries, while others continued and expanded – a process that, I will argue, is by now very likely to have involved conflict. This argument is made on the basis of a combination of features apparent in the island by this point, as well as the repeated references in the Classical texts to Crete as being characterized by internecine conflict. These features are site sizes and density across the island, which suggest maximally expanded local territories by the Archaic period; economic priorities increasingly tied to the production and trade of bulk agricultural products; making large territories ever more desirable, and the existence of very strong and well-entrenched regional identity structures by this period, allowing no further easy consolidation of different regional groups into larger polity units.

By the end of the seventh century, the final abandonment of most 'citadel' sites had taken place, suggesting, in view of the interpretation of these sites that I have given, above, a full consolidation of the state as a social unit by this date. Another important new feature is the development of ports for the continuing large polities, tied in to an expanding trade economy with a strong bulk trade component (Faure 1959: 184; Haggis 1993: 159–60; Hayden 2005: 168–9, 171–3). In some regions this is the first large-scale return to the coast since the Bronze Age. Below, I explore several main patterns of settlement change during the early Archaic period.

I) FURTHER NUCLEATION AT LARGE SITES

Nucleated settlements that were abandoned between the late seventh and early fifth centuries, despite having reached a considerable level of size and complexity, include Azoria, Dreros, Anavlochos, Kalo Chorio Maza, Ligortinos Kefala, and Prinias in central Crete and Kera Papoura in Lasithi. Those that continue into the Classical period include Axos, Eleutherna, Falasarna, Elounda Oxa, Gortyn, Krousonas Koupo, Polirinia, Praisos, Rotasi Kefala, Astritisi Kefala, Arkades, Lato, Lyttos, Milatos, Kalo Chorio Profitis Elias, Kalamafka Kastello, and others, including Chania, Knossos, and Phaistos (Bosanquet 1902, 1910; Di Vita 1984, 1991; Farnoux and Driessen 1991; Frost and Hadjidaki 1990; Gondicas 1988: 109–11; Mariani 1895: 244–6; Nowicki 2000: 173–4, 177–9, 190–1, 193–4, 221–2, 241–9; Sanders 1982: 161; Stampolidis 1996; Themelis 1992; Whitley et al. 1999: 253–6). Some, though not all, of the continuing sites can be identified with toponyms given in Classical inscriptions and literature.

There also are some possible cases of new inland nucleations being founded in this period, though in general the inland settlement distribution remained strongly conditioned by Iron Age patterns. Large and obviously important settlements without any very clear EIA history appear from Archaic onwards at the old Bronze Age site of Tylissos (which does have some EIA material) and at Irtakina in the far southwest of Crete: the role and history of a smaller site at nearby Elyros are also as yet unclear (Hatzidakis 1921: 59–63; Savignoni and de Sanctis 1901: 408–24; Kyriazopoulou in press). In the north Ierapetra isthmus, the population finally abandoned the Vrokastro site and other small villages between the coast and the mountainous hinterland to the south, to live during the seventh century in a tight cluster of semidefensible sites on the Meseleroi ridge, farther inland. The distribution of the sites indicates that they were strongly collaborative/interdependent in operation, suggesting that a single polity unit was now being defined, covering a larger territory than that formerly associated with Vrokastro. The populations of these small sites seem finally to have come together at the large settlement of Oleros, in the valley immediately to their south (Hayden 1995, 2005: 173–98). The late nucleation process here may reflect long-term difficulties in consolidating large political units in east Crete generally, which I have addressed above.

II) THE DEVELOPMENT OF PORT SITES

During the Early Archaic period a port settlement developed at Istron on the northwest coast of the Ierapetra isthmus, the traditional coastal hinterland of Vrokastro. It is interesting to consider how far the newly divergent focus of population in this region, between Oleros inland and Istron on the coast, reflects a pragmatic and permanent split of territorial interests and identity within an existing regional community, and how far an emerging partnership. Some collaborative element seems very likely in either scenario, and must also have applied in other cases where new coastal sites flourishing from Archaic seem closely linked to inland predecessors and contemporaries. Many questions arise here: for example, which particular groups within a regional community would be most likely to take the initiative to resettle on the coasts, and how much competition existed for the right to control the coastal zone? Alternatively, how far was this move made under pressure?

New growth of settlement around former Bronze Age sites near the coast is seen in the cases of Stylos and Aptera in west Crete (Andreadaki-Vlasaki 1988, 1990, 1999). Other coastal Bronze Age sites that now seem to have been taken into major use again are Gouves and Gournes near the north coast of central Crete and Nirou Chani and Ayia Pelagia, also in the busy north central region (Alexiou 1972: 230–44; Lebessi 1971b: 390; Marinatos 1935: 56; Pendlebury 1939: 324). It is hard to trace any EIA settlement history at or around these sites or to link them to any 'mother city' with EIA roots farther inland. A new or much-expanded pattern of near-coastal settlement appears in south Sfakia, at Tarrha, Araden, and Anopolis (the latter with EIA roots; Moody et al. 1998a, 2000a; Nixon et al. 1988, 1989, 1990). All these sites have limited agricultural hinterlands, in a region where mountains run almost down to the sea. The development of this pattern reflects the same rise of interest in coastal settlement seen elsewhere – perhaps connected in this case to the timber trade, which was certainly flourishing in this region by the Classical period (Rackham and Moody 1996: 128–31). Itanos is an east Cretan example of a coastal area booming from the same period with little EIA settlement background; Siteia, where a seventh-century sanctuary has recently been excavated, may have a similar history (Greco et al. 1997: 820–2; Kalpaxis et al. 1995: 734–6).

On the south coast of central Crete, the port at Keratokambos, developing from the eighth century, does have an EIA history of settlement nearby, but its political relations to the earlier-established settlements of Keraton Vigla and Viannos Korakias are unclear (Hood et al. 1964: 82; Nowicki 2000: 138–9; Platon 1957: 147). As the citadel site at Vigla declined in use in LG, how far were its inhabitants involved with the new coastal venture, and what support and profit links existed between the latter and the large and powerful inland Korakias settlement, with its EIA history? Though the political relationships between the three settlements are difficult to reconstruct, their inhabitants do seem very likely to have seen themselves as part of a single regional community unit at least within the LG/EA period, and probably well beyond.

All the preceding cases contribute to the impression that major political and economic rebalancing was taking place across the island in the EA period. The interest in coastal settlement continued and intensified into Classical times. In fourth-century texts such as Pseudo-Skylax, coastal sites like Olous and Chersonesos, little known archaeologically before the fifth century but with obvious EIA mother settlements (Elounda Oxa and Lyttos), are referred to in texts as 'poleis' in their own right. This confirms the notion that a largely independent status developed quickly for many ports between the Archaic and Classical periods (Baldwin Bowsky 1989; Perlman 1996). Other coastal cities well established by Classical times – perhaps originally attached to large inland nucleations but now clearly poleis in their own right – include Lebena (with Gortyn as mother city), Lato pros Kamara (Lato), Kissamos (Polirinia), and Matala (Gortyn).

III) THE SPREAD OF NEW SMALL VILLAGE OR FARMHOUSE SITES

Another very important change, closely related to the territorial expansion of nucleated settlements (and typical of developing states in many other contexts: e.g., Pauketat 2000: 28–9), is the appearance of small hamlets or farmhouses scattered through the landscape in growing densities from the seventh century onward; Sjögren's recent gazetteer (Sjögren 2004) has been exceptionally useful in identifying this pattern. The pattern of expansion of small rural sites also appears in central Greek areas by the sixth century at latest (Catling 2002: 155–87; Snodgrass 1991a, 1993). In Crete, it is important not to confuse this with the tail end of the EIA citadel-site phenomenon. All the small rural sites discussed below are newly established in LG-Archaic and have no earlier Iron Age history. There is often ambiguity about which particular nucleation these sites were linked to, particularly in central Crete, which has an especially dense pattern of large nucleated settlements with many small sites scattered between them. The exceptionally fertile landscape of the region and its well-established trade-based prosperity were surely major factors behind this density. In the Pediada area, for example, we see scatters of new small sites, seemingly related to the continuation and expansion of two major polities at Astritsi Kefala and Lyttos. Around Astritsi, small sites have been recorded dating between the late seventh and sixth centuries at Astraki, Houmeri, Kasanoi, and Klisidi (Ioannidou 1978: 570; Lebessi 1971a, 1973, 1976, 1978; Pariente 1991: 942; Pendlebury 1939: 314, 325, 342). The area around Lyttos shows the same pattern. Sites at Kastelli, Sta Koutsounaria, and Lakkoudia lie within the likely territory of this polity, which probably ran right up to the western Lasithi flanks by the Archaic period (Alexiou 1974: 901; Marinatos 1933: 313; Pendlebury et al. 1933: 80; Rethimiotakis 1987: 532, 1988). The smaller polity of Maza, located between Astritsi Kefala and Lyttos, may well have been taken over by one of them within the early Archaic period, when it goes out of use. A small rural unit at nearby Koxari may have been attached to Maza during the last stage of its independent existence, helping it control its territory, or else have been established after its demise, possibly to help mark a new border between Lyttos and Astritsi Kefala (Platon and Davaras 1960). In west central Crete, Ayios Myronas, located west of the large Profitis Elias polity and east of Krousonas Koupo, may have been a similar kind of border-marking site, founded by one polity but appropriated by another: Koupo did not continue in extensive use into Classical times (Mariani 1895: 228–31; Pendlebury et al. 1933: 91; Sjögren 2004: 117–18). There is also another small PG-A site near to, but separate from, the main Krousonas summit (Dimopoulou and Rethimiotakis 1987: 530–1). Profitis Elias Rokka remained a significant polity well into Classical times. Small agricultural settlements probably attached to it were scattered right up to the west slope of Jouktas, at Karnari and Karydaki, during the Archaic period (Karetsou 1974: 241–5; Pendlebury 1939: 12; Sjögren 2004: 120). Archanes, also located in this rich central region, sees use through the Geometric and Archaic periods, but the nature of this use is unclear, since it seems never to have become a major nucleated settlement or state-level polity, yet is more than a small agricultural outpost (Sakellarakis and Sakellarakis 1997: 36).

The Lasithi area shows a remarkably dense spread of small sites from the early Archaic period. This may originally have been because, in the changing circumstances of this period, the relatively small or scattered local nucleated polities (of which Papoura is the only one so far known) were unable to maintain a position of regional dominance in economic or political terms (Watrous 1982: 38–9, 42–5, 55–7, 61–4, 275–80). After the decline or conquest of this polity or polities at some time within the Archaic period, the whole Lasithi zone probably became shared between Lyttos and Lato – polities with much richer and more easily controlled hinterlands including good coastal access. By mutual agreement, a relatively large proportion of the Lasithi population may have maintained a scattered rural residence pattern, rather than move to the dominant large settlements a considerable distance away; the area is an especially large and useful fertile pocket and yet could not be easily managed from Lyttos or Lato, given its altitude and isolation.

The island's other main areas of prime fertile farmland also see a spread of small sites from this period. The Mesara shows dense rural site patterning around the very large nucleations of Phaistos and Gortyn from the seventh century, a pattern that continues right through the Classical period (La Torre 1989: 290–8; Watrous and Hadzi-Vallianou 2004a: 313–23;

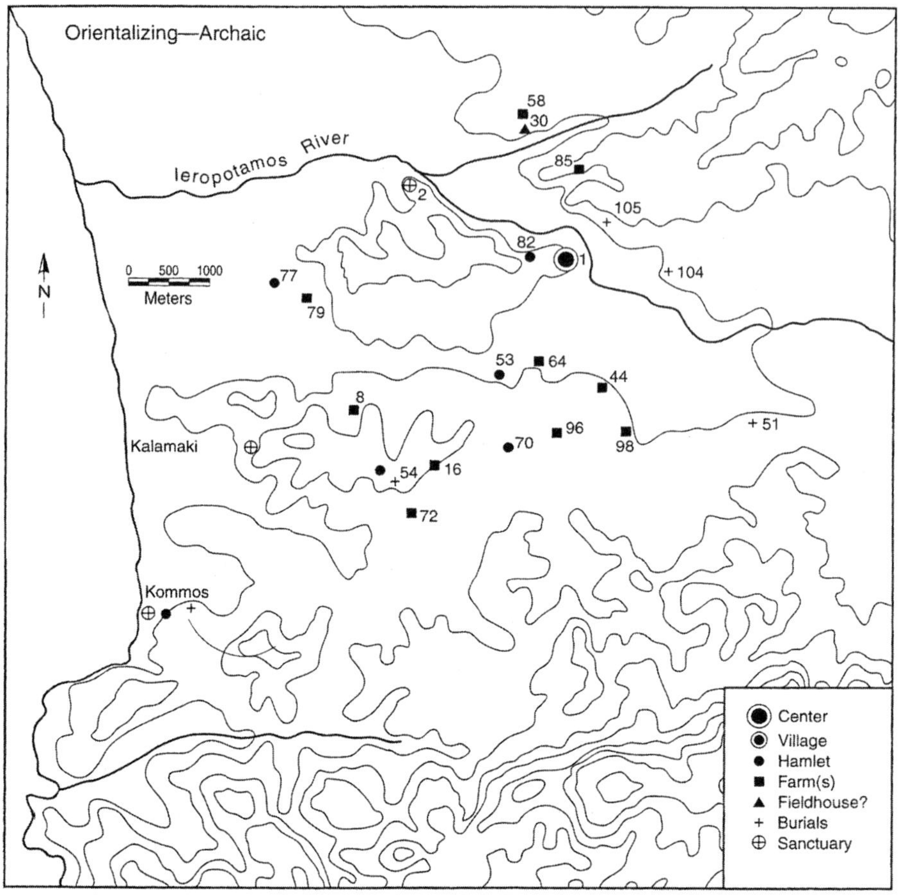

202. Map showing the spread of small rural sites around Phaistos (labelled 1 on map) in the Orientalising and Archaic periods (after Watrous et al. 2004, Fig. 11.5, p. 315). By permission of L. V. Watrous.

Figures 202 and 203). In the Phaistos region, Watrous and Hadzi-Vallianou note that these sites are located at an optimal distance from the Phaistos polity to allow its operation as a central place, and that they cluster most heavily in areas of easily workable dry marly soils. A spread of small rural settlement accompanies the further growth of the nucleated site at Thronos Kefala in the fertile Amari valley from Late Geometric onward (Belgiorno 1994: 211–24). The large building at Onithe Gouledianon, one of the very few excavated examples of a small rural site of Archaic date, looks like a high-investment structure for the use of a wealthy household/estate, demonstrating the variety of types of rural settlement in this period. It lies within the likely territory of the important Veni nucleation in the same region (Platon 1954c: 377–82, 1955b, 1956). Unfortunately the site is not published in any detail, so we can say little about its internal character or workings.

In east Crete, some small Archaic sites are seen in the Ziros plateau, a significant arable area (Schlager 1991: 23). These may have been within the outlying territory of Praisos, the major nucleation of this region: a spread of small sites may have been under way in the closer vicinity of Praisos, with the probable reuse of an LM IIIB farmhouse at Ayios Konstantinos at this time (Whitley et al. 1999: 235). In the Ierapetra isthmus a small settlement at Panagia Skali, perhaps founded as a field base in LM IIIC, was still in use by Archaic, probably as a satellite of Azoria

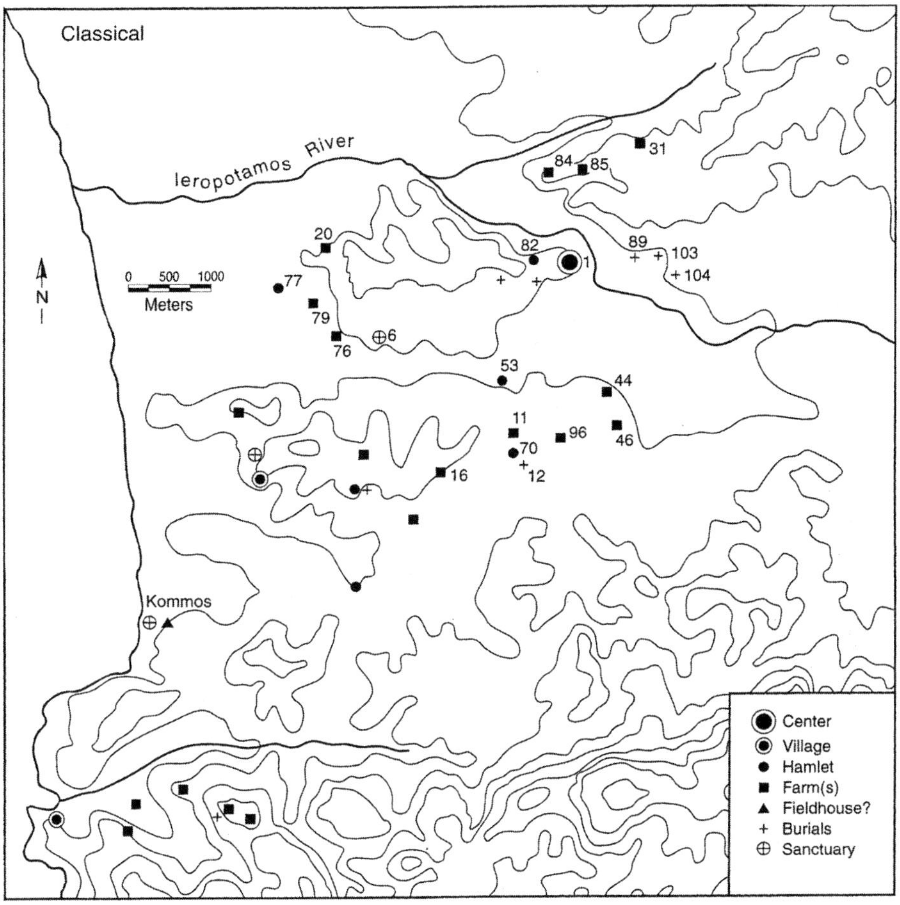

203. Map showing the spread of small rural sites around Phaistos (labelled 1 on map) in the Classical period (after Watrous et al. 2004, Fig. 11.10, p. 319). By permission of L. V. Watrous

(Haggis 2005: 131). The latter, like many of the other nucleated settlements that go out of use in Archaic, seems to have lacked the time or scope to develop many satellites of any size or permanence.

The phenomenon of rural spread suggests that state territories were becoming highly consolidated and more intensively exploited at this time – most probably through estate-based agriculture – with more labour permanently resident on the land. This labour must often have been of serf type: serfdom is already indicated textually by the sixth century and is discussed further in Part Five. Herding almost certainly expanded and specialised, too, as the territories of growing states drew in more mountainous and marginal land: grazing could help delineate and protect remote boundaries in an increasingly formalized environment of landownership (Wallace 2003a: 622–3). Expansion of production in this way must also be closely linked to changes in the wider economy, especially the rise of bulk subsistence trade.

The settlement change had strong political implications, as well as economic ones. As some existing nucleations were abandoned – after being conquered by, or otherwise politically amalgamated with, their neighbouring peers – it would be unrealistic and uneconomic for their entire populations to relocate to those peer settlements. On the other hand, severe political instability might have arisen if significant populations were allowed to remain at the old nucleation sites. A pattern of spread-out residence in the old territories, now ultimately controlled from the dominant large polity, formed one solution. In other cases, movement out into the territory may have reflected tensions or disputes about rights to territory of rival groups within an expanding polity. It is interesting to consider how residence at the new small rural bases might have affected kin-group identities, which I argued to have been very strongly attached to place through the EIA period, and to have had a central role in political change in PG-A Crete. During the first establishment of nucleated settlements as the political centres of their regions (from PG onwards) urban residence away from their lands seems to have been required of most prominent kin groups in the interest of building political coherence and economic growth. Now, after the consolidation of the state and with the new opportunities and pressures coming to bear on the state body, some residence out in the territory was acceptable, even advantageous, for the reasons I have suggested above. Still, the majority of rural residents do seem likely to have belonged to the least prosperous (indebted or conquered) and thereby least politically powerful classes of society. Urban living may increasingly have been considered a restricted privilege, mainly for full citizens. As territories expanded, then, each nucleated community was less closely linked to its territory in terms of the maintenance of practical connections between powerful kin groups and their traditionally exploited lands. Structures of authority and dominance now increasingly stood in for physical contact with or proximity to the land or the sense of attachment to it through lineage. If the new residents were serf labourers or residents of a conquered polity, then despite any historic attachment to the land they worked, they were politically subject to others' 'ownership' of that land, which new traditions may have been created to reinforce. The strong and direct links of identity, status, and land that had been created during the changes of the collapse period were now being permanently altered. References in Archaic texts to 'public' land provide further indications of developing territorial complexity, involving the social distancing of individual small groups from the land. Land designated in this way may have been acquired by conquest or reclaimed from the wild during the extensification of agriculture and/or territorial expansion, though some of it might date back to the tenth-century phase of nucleation and the associated enlargement of territories. Land with this designation seems to have been exploited on behalf of the state as a whole, being attached to no single clan or its ancestry.

It is very difficult to date the initial major spread of small rural sites, since nearly all are known only from survey or minimal excavation. Certainly the phenomenon is established by at least the early sixth century and very often probably starts within the seventh. Some small sites may not have stayed in use throughout the Archaic period: their falling out of use, like their foundation, mirrors the many and complex political changes connected to the expansion of, and friction between, large polities. Little can be said about the average size or internal layout of the small sites themselves, though examples like Onithe Gouledianon suggest that some were elaborate self-contained complexes, inhabited by extended and largely self-sufficient groups: the latter building had substantial storage and some production facilities (Platon 1954c: 377–82, 1955b, 1956).

A few sites of small 'citadel' type established in the earliest EIA but continuing directly through the Archaic period are difficult to interpret. These include Stavrochori Skalia in east Crete and Trachilos (Kastelli) Selli in west Crete (Nowicki 2000: 216–18, 218–19, 222). It is possible that we should continue to see these as independent clan strongholds that held out against the political changes involved in territorial expansion and conquest – existing under the (now very rare) tolerance of large polities and apparently with no significant independent political role. Without excavation, these sites remain hard to understand or properly date. It is possible that their status may have changed by this time to that of satellite hamlets similar to those discussed above.

IV) RELATIONSHIPS BETWEEN CULT SITES AND SETTLEMENTS

An obvious question arises about the relationship between the small rural settlements discussed above, and the small cult sites newly spread through the landscape. There are few obvious spatial links between these two types of site within any region. This fact may be partly due to the inadequacies of the record. It owes something, too, to the continuing use of small shrines in caves, often far away from any settlement, during the Archaic period. Coherent regional patterns do sometimes appear, incorporating a large nucleation, outlying small sites, and outlying cult places, all pretty clearly belonging within the same territory (for example, around Praisos and around Thronos Kefala/Sybrita). I argued earlier that rural cult sites might have represented points of power assertion for important clans based at the nucleated polities (but controlling far-flung territories) rather than for small subjugate farming groups actually resident on the land. Yet as the rural territory became settled, they might have become points where these increasingly divided classes could interact with each other and assert their bonds to the territory at different levels. This would help to keep the rural population of each region peacefully locked into a larger-scale political identity, even while excluding them from urban residence.

The spatial associations of the clan and the wider regional community must have become extremely complex by this period, as some nucleated settlements, themselves consisting of clan groups bonded within a single identity structure, became subsumed into other territories. In this process some individual clans might have lost their links with a specific residential location altogether, and their members have been spatially scattered, though elements of broad preexisting structures of community identity probably survived in the form of tribal units within the new larger state territory. Given the dense distribution of nucleated Cretan polities, many conquered nucleations undoubtedly contained some powerful clans that, until the conquest, had interacted as close equals with those in the victorious polity (and/or were related to them by blood). It is impossible to suppose that these groups were immediately or universally relegated to the status of serfs. Perhaps they took on the status of the perioikoi referred to in later texts (and discussed in Part Five), with the victorious polity adopting more subtle ways of appropriating their assets – by placing them on the land in a prosperous, yet still subjugate and heavily taxed position, and/or giving them some status in the polis that fell short of full citizenship. Allowing them to establish or continue dedicated rural cults with which they had special identity links might be one way of doing this.

V) THE *SYNOIKISMOS* MODEL AND THE ARCHAEOLOGICAL REALITY

The already described changes in settlement pattern in the LG-EA period do not match up very well to the model of political and physical integration (synoikismos) of separate small village communities into an urban core at the very end of the EIA or within the early Archaic, which I have referred to above (Perlman 1996: 238, 2000: 77). Studying the EIA history of sites like Gortyn, Phaistos, Lyttos, and Knossos shows they were already well established as settlement cores by Late Geometric and saw a clear process of spread over time. However, since few large settlements have been systematically surveyed and excavated with regard to remains from this period, this spread is often recorded as individual scattered units of Geometric-Archaic stratigraphy within a single large area. The impression that these units were entirely separate EIA settlements that 'came together' in LG-EA is unfortunately reinforced by descriptions like that of Sjögren (2004: 307), which identifies as separate 'sites' the scattered zones of known habitation remains within the mostly unexcavated urban areas at Knossos, Lyttos, Praisos, and others. Paula Perlman presents developments at Gortyn in a similar way. She presents the spread of Archaic material on the plain as a 'new village' despite the evidence for extensive Geometric settlement on the Ayios Ioannis and Armi ridges above – themselves an extension from the Acropolis hill, settled in LM IIIC (Allegro 1991; Di Vita 1991; Santaniello pers comm; see discussion in Part Two). On this basis Perlman goes on to ascribe different ethnic affiliations and foundations to the different 'sites' within the wider Gortyn area and finally to explain the eventual desertion of the 'villages' on the ridgetops as the result of an earthquake, rather than the process of settlement expansion onto lower-lying areas. These arguments are unconvincing given the wider context of settlement change discussed previously (Perlman 2000: 68–9, 77–8; Watrous and Hadzi-Vallianou 2004b: 342–4).

VI) EXPERIENCING THE NEW SETTLEMENT PATTERN

During the Archaic period, at least one portion of society lost the overarching perspective on the landscape obtained from the nucleated polities, as they went to live in small villages in the valleys and plains. As a result, their daily-experienced world probably became smaller and their loyalties, for this reason, perhaps more concentrated and restricted. Their life, except for visits to the dominant polity, increasingly located a considerable distance away as territories expanded, was now bounded by the locality they farmed, and by new kinds of border and authority indicators in the landscape. By Classical times, these included cult places, natural features like springs and hills, and inscribed boundary stones. This was increasingly a landscape of control, with the kinds of unequal experience described above feeding into the emergence of social inequalities. The past was still visibly present in the landscape and preserved within generalised traditions, but now less closely and strongly linked to individual groups and their ancestral territories, and more connected to the polis unit and its identity within the wider island and the greater Greek world.

33 THE POLIS AS PLACE AND AS CONCEPT IN CRETE

The meaning of the term 'polis' in ancient texts and modern usage and the earliest date at which we can use it to describe either a social or physical entity have been much discussed in the literature on early Greece (Demand 1996; Ehrenberg 1937; Flensted-Jensen 2000; Hansen 1993a, 1993b, 1996, 1997a, 1997b, 1997c, 1999d, 2004; Hansen and Nielsen 2004; Hansen and Raaflaub 1995, 1996; Lowells 1989; Morgan and Coulton 1997; Murray 2000: 234; Nielsen 2002; Perlman 1996: 233–4). Approaches mainly focused on textual evidence (as many of the preceding have been) without reference to the broader archaeological picture can become circular, overliteral, and sterile. Some scholars, notably Mogens Hansen, have looked meticulously for certain descriptive contexts and attributes in the texts associated with individual toponyms, then tried to tally these toponyms up to indicate the total numbers of polis states existing in different regions of Greece at particular points in time. Though this kind of work provides an invaluable reference resource, as an epistemology it ultimately fails to address the incomplete nature of the text record, the still fluid and developing nature of the state as a political and territorial entity through much of the Archaic period, and the changing nuances of meaning in texts, especially over an extended time period. It sidelines or ignores many important elements of the archaeological data, particularly in relation to settlement size, history, and regional context, and is undermined by the often very questionable identifications of text-referenced toponyms with sites on the ground. In general, notionally testable definitions of a polis that are isolated from any broader cultural and historical context are unsatisfactory – for example, that to be identifiable as a polis a site must have inscriptions/coins found in its vicinity, or have been still in use at a certain period with the Archaic-Hellenistic span, or have possessed certain of the physical features often connected in Classical times to the institutions of consensual politics, such as a *bouleuterion*: such approaches, given the unevenness of the archaeological evidence available and the very different regional histories of polis development across the Aegean, can only produce a deeply distorted picture (Sjögren 2004: 1).

Homer's references to Crete as having either one hundred or ninety 'poleis', a frequent focus for scholars trying to write the island's early history on the basis of texts alone, fit well with the dense, multi-noded character of the island's settlement pattern from PG onward, which was well entrenched by the eighth century (*Iliad* 2.644–51; *Odyssey* 19.172–4). But it makes little sense to try to match up these figures to the archaeological record and expect them to tally. Even if it could be taken to relate to eighth-century reality, Homer's word picture would be capturing a geography and society already in flux: the literary context suggests the numbers are impressionistic in any case. I return to discuss the Homeric texts further in Part Five. Some good examples of the problems in applying text-rooted approaches to investigating Cretan polis distribution appear in Paula Perlman's work, notwithstanding the fact that this author is one of the strongest authorities on the textual data from Archaic to Hellenistic Crete. The problems are broadly representative of text-centred approaches to defining the early 'polis' as both political and physical entity. To take only two examples, Perlman's identifications of the tiny site of Kounavi Ellenika as the polis of Eltynia (Perlman 1996: 282) and the very small Vryses Ayios Giorgios site in west Crete as the polis of Polichne are both highly doubtful, given the archaeological reality on the ground. Perlman completely ignores the large and important site of Pandanssa Veni as a potential polis, yet pays close attention to its contemporary neighbour at Thronos, simply because no inscription so far found provides an obvious name for Veni, while strong text evidence suggests that Thronos corresponds to ancient Sybrita. Elsewhere, Perlman has attempted to construct an inventory of Cretan poleis, which she suggests broadly matches the Homeric account of Crete as having either one hundred or ninety *poleis*. This is achieved by adding the number of textually referenced 'poleis' (assuming this to represent a constant between the Archaic and Classical period) to the number of textually referenced toponyms that are *not* directly described as poleis, and then adding these numbers to a (selected) number of archaeologically documented Archaic to Classical settlements that lack known ancient toponyms (Perlman 2004a: 1145). This method fails adequately to recognise the arbitrary nature of these categories – which are all heavily affected by data retrieval processes – and their potentially large overlap. When treating the archaeological evidence, little regard is paid to the wildly differing sizes, characters, or histories of the sites concerned. There is unfamiliarity either with the reality of the data on the ground or with the broader, long-term archaeological context. For example, Perlman lists Keratokampos Kastri, a small coastal site, together with 'Krousonas' (presumably Koupo, a major EIA-Classical polity) and 'Ellenika' (Zakros Ellenika, a typical 'citadel' site) without any differentiative comment, to arrive at a notional 'total' of 100 or so likely polis sites (Perlman 2004a: 1146–7).

Such approaches tend to use archaeological data in an inconsistent way. Sometimes they are cited as a supportive handmaiden to text-derived models like that of *synoikismos*, as in the Gortyn example above. At other times, when they inconveniently cannot be linked to text sources, those data are ignored or distorted. Ultimately, adopting over-narrow or rigid definitions of the polis, on one hand, *or* making loose and archaeologically ill-informed categorisations, on the other, can be very misleading.

I suggest that the most helpful kind of analysis focuses on categories of settlement or social organisation which are meaningful in terms of long-term historical narrative and explanation, using the whole range of available empirical data in a sophisticated, consistent, and contextualised way. Use of the term 'polis' seems to me most valid a) in denoting a level of social institutionalisation commensurate with a state-type organisation in anthropological terms (including social stratification, labour specialisation, multiple permanent public institutions, and a permanent, formal, and codified legal and governmental system) and b) in indicating a particular *type* of small state structure, peculiar to this period in the Mediterranean and based around a broadly consensual ideology and tight, small-scale ethnopolitical identity, on the lines I have presented in Part One and will discuss further in Part Five. When I use the term 'polis' for Crete it is in these senses (Davies 1997: 27–8; even while noting Demand's cogent argument [2006: 7–9] that ancient texts use the term in a much broader and more diverse sense, a point also dwelt on in much of Hansen's work). To be meaningful in the preceding senses, the 'polis' definition need not reflect permanent political independence: the frequent changes in territorial boundaries occurring in Archaic to Hellenistic Crete make any application of the term in this way across the period meaningless. But a well-defined, historically referent, and independent *identity* for the collective unit does seem a core feature. Focus on defining the polis as a particular type of settlement entity can also be misleading. Variations in the history and scale of settlement in different regions make using physical size as a standard criterion fraught with pitfalls: a long-established regional nucleation in Crete might be only a fraction of the size of a late Classical mainland polis and not have the same range of structural features, yet still have functioned over several centuries as a state body in the senses described above.

The nucleated Cretan sites that I have discussed above were without doubt the most complex type of political unit represented in the island, as well as the main spine of its settlement pattern, between the tenth and fifth centuries BC, and are therefore the best candidates for polis status – but from what point in their history, and to how many sites, should we apply the term? We do not at the moment have enough archaeological evidence to differentiate further or rank them at an islandwide scale. As a body, they directly prefigured the Classical states in their role as regional population bases with distinct individual identities, and in their increasingly formalised and complex economic, social, and political organisation. All over the Aegean by the early seventh century, the process of nucleation and the fact of living in a nucleated polity seem to have been tightly bound up with the emergence and functioning of early states (Morgan 2003: 45–85; Murray 2000: 236). In many ancient texts, however, the settlement name itself is less often referred to than an ethnic derived from that name, such as 'Spartiatiai' or 'Athinaioi' – stressing the close identity of the state body with its citizens even more than with its physical locale or form and highlighting the role of an extended ethnic/ancestral identity in binding the citizens in a single group. We have seen how the Cretan nucleations developing from PG onwards seem to represent well-grounded regional community structures embracing a number of disparate groups. But these groups were perhaps *never* all coresident at the main nucleated site, with the balance of minor settlement shifting considerably over time, as we have seen. Thus we might well expect 'polis' ethnics often to be used to cover whole regions in which small subgroups (such as those that had been resident at citadel sites until LG/EA) existed at a separate spatial level. This is a reason both not to focus the use of the term *polis* too literally at the level of an individual settlement, and, on the other hand, not to apply it to every settlement of this period. Rather, we have to strive to understand the full complexity of political and identity networks at regional level to get a feel for what a polis unit consists in at any particular stage of its development.

Though complex political and economic structures were already emerging in Crete from PG, given the further developments in political complexity from Archaic onwards, to what extent can we call the large sites occupied *only* up to the Archaic period polis states? Is their abandonment in fact the marker for the real emergence of 'the polis' in Crete? Though this model fits mainland patterns of state emergence with a seductive ease, it fits badly with the Cretan archaeological data viewed as a whole. The PG-EA polities undoubtedly did see major changes in their structure and organisation over time, but it seems unlikely that there were intrinsic structural differences between them that caused some to succeed as 'poleis' while others did not, given their extremely similar roots and development during the EIA. Instead, inequalities of scale, strength, population, prosperity, and alliance were probably the factors behind conflict, further nucleation, and territorial expansion from Archaic onward that reduced the overall number of such units. It appears there is no one clear point along the spectrum of these polities' development at which we can fix the crystallisation of 'the polis' in Crete, but we can at least give a *terminus ante quem* of the late seventh century. Early inscriptions like the one from Dreros dated circa 630 BC show a formalised and at least partly consensualist structure of governance already in place by the seventh century at latest and indicate that the large settlements were already referred to as 'poleis' even if (as in the Dreros case) they did not continue into the Classical period, being abandoned in Archaic. The teleological terms 'proto-poleis' and 'proto-state' can act as a compromise solution when discussing the formative period of these communities, between the tenth and seventh centuries. Yet we lack well-founded criteria in the presently available data to divide the notion of the 'proto-' from the 'true' polis meaningfully.

34 THE VALUE OF 'CLASSIC' STATE FORMATION MODELS FOR PG-EA CRETE, VIEWED IN ITS MEDITERRANEAN CONTEXT

Applying standard models

In concluding Part Four, I want to place all the developments discussed earlier in the context of state formation models generally, looking at a number of different strands of previous thinking on this subject and assessing how each can aid interpretation in this case. The uniquely limited way in which the island's communities chose to interact with the external world makes typical secondary state formation models inadequate: the developing Cretan states were *not* merchant states, orientated mainly towards the outside world in their economic relations; nor did they ever mirror in structure the Near Eastern societies with which they regularly interacted. They also stayed distinctly and consistently different in terms of history, culture, and social structure from their Aegean counterparts (as Part Five will emphasise), a fact that undermines very simple diffusion-based models. Other models of state formation also have restricted application here. Conflict – whether in the form of reaction against aggressive incoming settlers or the forceful takeover of weaker by (existing) stronger groups within the island – is unlikely to have been an initial motivating factor towards living in larger and more complex groups. The three-stage evolutionary model of EIA social development (from achieved-rank society to simple chiefdom to stratified state) is also problematic, as we have seen.

The special features of emerging complex societies in PG-A Crete – a precocious, smooth, and gradual process of institutionalisation; an early and marked degree of collective historical self-consciousness, with very strong political resonance at regional level; a consistently powerful role for multiple clan groups within the state body; and a highly active and profitable, yet curiously bounded, trade role – all suggest that other models are needed. Cross-cultural research has already highlighted the general inadequacy of models for the formation of large territorial states to describe the emergence of city-states accurately, and has in many ways argued against *any* single model for emergence of the latter kind of state. Crete's story highlights the role of contingent as opposed to predictable elements in small-state development, as well as the importance of self-consciousness and agency (whether individual or collective) in the process. Extreme generalising statements like Yoffee's (1997: 261) 'City-states grow from important pilgrimage sites, from market sites ... from defensive locations (into which people flock) ... from geographically favourable nodes in which one might control the distribution of water and access to prime agricultural land and trade routes, or (normally) from some combination of the above' apply to this case, as to many others. Yet studying Crete's EIA history in detail, as we have here, shows how much such statements miss or gloss over. Economic and environmental factors were *not* consistently determinative of Cretan communities' location or development but clearly altered their importance in relation to other imperatives through the emergence period. In the same way, considerations related to defensibility, cult locations and practice, production, and markets also changed hugely over time *in connection* to state emergence but did not determine or reflect it in simple or predictable ways. Models connecting state emergence to developing urbanisation and central-place function also leave much to be desired in this case. Though we do see elements of urbanisation, including the large-scale planning and zoning of public space, by the Archaic period (Haggis et al. 2004: 346; Sjögren 2004: 11), this process must be separated from the rise of complexity, which actually kicks off much earlier. We will probably never be able to retrieve a clear and extensive PG phase plan from a large continuously occupied settlement in order to trace in detail the ways in which developments in planning altered from this period. However, change seems likely to have been very subtle and limited at first, given the earlier history of settlement development. Major settlements do not seem to have taken on highly centralised or hierarchical economic or political relations, even at the level of the small region, until well after the state was consolidated.

Top-down or bottom-up?

State emergence in central Greece during the late eighth century has been previously described as a kind of 'social revolution' against resistant EIA elites (de Polignac 1995: 9; Morris 1987: 9, 22–3, 190, 1997b: 91, 1998: 12–13, 2000: 273–80). Yet dramatic intrasocietal conflicts seem minimally visible in the Cretan EIA, and complexity emergence here cannot easily be described as either bottom up *or* elite led. Rather, a number of broad-based clan groups, collaborating within tightly bound regional community units, supported and promoted the growth of complex institutions from PG onwards. Like central Greece, post-collapse Crete lacked a unified, consolidated single elite class for most of the period 1200–700 BC. Both areas seem characterised by a relatively volatile social environment, where a number of individual players or groups competed for wealth and power status (Raaflaub 1997b: 35). In the central Greek communities, I have suggested, this was an always very precarious and unstable process, with power continuously contested between a large number of individuals/small groups within each community through most of the period to 700 BC. In Crete, the extended kin-group unit seems to have become solidly enshrined and extended from a relatively early date – building on the stable institutions of the immediate post-collapse period in the island – and to have structured and insulated competition much more actively. The fact that the clan experienced such important growth in its strength and scale of operations during the process of complexity emergence in Crete suggests that its interests were heavily integrated with that process and that clan-based structures of inequality were well established here by the seventh century. Though central Greek communities also grew in prosperity through this period via participation in the burgeoning trade economy, the fact that this wealth was not circulated or consumed within the bounds of a similarly solid kin framework helps account for the generally undeveloped character of social institutionalisation/control structures prior to the eighth century.

Crete illustrates, then, not a totally separate, but a variant, route towards the broadly consensualist structures characterising Aegean states through the Archaic and Classical periods. These structures all seem ultimately rooted in a marked degree of social levelling and new social mobility opportunities following the collapse of 1200 BC. In all regions, the high density and broadly parallel strengths of competing groups under post-collapse conditions, including radically changed economic frameworks, prevented *either* the rapid emergence of wholly new kinds of stratification *or* the simple promotion of former subelite groups into elite roles. In Crete, however, the strong position for the extended family/clan embedded from very soon after collapse was maintained throughout the horizon of state emergence and consolidated via a range of cultural practices including burial, settlement, feasting, and cult, offering less chance for extreme social tensions to emerge. This kept the pressure towards egalitarian structures weaker and limited the opportunity or need for radically consensualist aspects to emerge within the new state form. In central Greece, where large kin-based groups had never built up the same coherence or degree of institutionalisation, there was much more continuous and extreme resistance to the rise of state authority by weakly enshrined elites (Morris 2000: 155–95). This seems to explain both the very radical shift to the cult and other public spheres as the main channel for growth and wealth display on the mainland, and the strongly consensualist political structures of early states in central Greece.

Diffusion

Diffusion and peer polity interaction are well-known explanatory models for state formation in ancient societies. We might well expect the regular EIA contact between different Aegean regions to promote diffusion of social concepts and cultural forms, and have seen that this did indeed occur in many different spheres (Raaflaub 1993: 74–5; Snodgrass 1986). Interaction with outside regions clearly played a role in building the state in Crete, but not a straightforward one. Booming external trade helped stimulate the rise of social and economic complexity in the island; on the other hand, Crete's peculiarly insulated economic outlook, created early and maintained throughout the EIA, blocked the potentially socially destabilising effects of trade, which might have encouraged a more radical kind of state form to emerge. At the same time, Crete's regular interactions with the wider Aegean world and the need to engage with the politics of that world, as well as the many shared aspects of social history mentioned, did encourage consensualist elements to become embedded in Cretan state structures.

Looking at diffusion from the opposite viewpoint, it is interesting that the kind of well-established and stable institutions appearing in the Cretan polities from the PG period were not paralleled in central Greece at such an early date. The fact shows the fallacy of assuming the direct transfer of political structures in any direction during state emergence. The nature of Cretan complexity was specific to Cretan history and conditions, while the specific social and economic pressures in central Greece caused it to develop a slightly different range of institutions, at a different time, and in more extreme circumstances. In Part Five, I will look at how awareness of major political and economic shifts in central Greece from the seventh century affected Cretan social outlooks, while showing that the latter continued to be shaped within the context of a different state structure and a slightly different geopolitical sphere.

Economic appropriation

Many existing state formation models focus on economic appropriation, particularly land appropriation, and the use of force to support it, as state-driving mechanisms. They sometimes take little account of changing concepts of attachment to land, or the role of individual or group agency, in this process (Carneiro 1970, 1981; Earle 1997: 67–105). These issues cannot be ignored in studying Crete – particularly the way in which the clan groups forming the bedrock of early Cretan states built their power. Settlement nucleation and the related emergence of more formalised landholding – which I have identified as turning points in the rise of proto-state structures from the tenth century on – both depended heavily on the existence of inclusive regional-scale identity structures closely attached to the landscape, rather than on the sheer strength or size of an emergent elite. When these structures were firm, a few strong clans could successfully mesh their territories and power bases at a nucleated core, with the marginalisation of weaker groups being peacefully rationalised by invoking their 'membership' of the regional collectivity. If the structures were weak, territorial integration would prove much more difficult, and aggrandising groups might regularly branch off from, or partly resist, incorporation in larger social systems. This may sometimes have been the case in particular areas of the island (such as east Crete) as noted above.

Economic aggrandisement was certainly going on in PG-EA Crete, at both individual and clan-group levels. But an unusual freedom in this respect, partly enabled by unrestricted social access to trade goods, seems to have prevented the exclusive concentration of wealth in the hands of either state bodies or powerful clans within the state. Most craft specialisation seems likely still in this period to have been supported through relatively small-scale investment by prosperous groups: truly large-scale market-based or state-funded specialised production was not yet in evidence. As overall economic growth continued to encourage social and economic mobility by broadening physical access to value good consumption, consolidating elites may have increasingly built up investment in other, more stable bases of growth, including the bulk production and exchange of subsistence goods – the latter sector was still strongly elite-controlled in the Aegean by the Classical period (Garnsey 1988: 107–19; Garnsey and Morris 1989: 100; Sallares 1991: 96–7; Sherratt and Sherratt 1993: 371–4; Small 1997a). However, there is no evidence for sudden newly circumscribed or monopolised growth in this or any other economic sector which corresponds to the horizon of change occurring in the tenth century. Economic growth in various dimensions clearly pushed forward the general rise of complexity in Cretan society but was not an engine able to move any single group into prominence: powerful structures of regional identity and authority and a sharing of power with other clan peer groups were central to building the state. Economic inequality consolidated gradually over the long term once this step had been made, but remained buffered by clan structures.

Physical coercion and warfare

Warfare also seems unconvincing as a main explanatory mechanism of state emergence or growth for Crete before the Archaic period. The contemporaneous development of such a high number of very similar settlement nucleations, and the strong historical and security-, economy-, and identity-related factors that determined their distribution, argue against coercive takeover of weaker by stronger groups as the mode by which early complex polities emerged from the tenth century, and against the notion that control of military force formed the main support of each emergent polity, either within or outside its borders.

Extreme nucleation, which I have noted to be one of the earliest correlates of increasing complexity in PG-A Crete, would be an unfavourable method for the exploitation of conflict-acquired territories, in a landscape where earlier EIA occupation had been so scattered. Security and productivity would be better maintained by letting local producers stay on the lands they worked, but in a subjugate position, as happened during the many conquest histories known from the island in the Classical and Hellenistic periods (Perlman 1996; van Effenterre and Bougrat 1969; Willetts 1977: 178–81, 211–16). If conflict *had* been a major factor in state formation, we would expect slower, less regular, and more asynchronous growth at the large sites and irregular abandonments of smaller communities nearby throughout the PG-EA periods. All the evidence here in fact suggests that collective identities for the emergent polities were still being carefully built and reinforced (still at a relatively small scale) in this period, and that conflict would be likely to fragment them and delay the full emergence and consolidation of states.

In some models, the motivating force for conflict-based state formation is 'economic circumscription', when a limited agricultural territory reaches the point of maximal exploitation. There is unrelieved pressure to produce more surplus, with growing indebtedness as a result on the part of some producers, who cannot splinter off into self-sufficient groups because there is no more agricultural land. Enlargement of the resource base then takes place through spatial expansion, involving forceful subjugation of weaker, economically dependent communities to more powerful ones and the rise of socioeconomic complexity in the newly expanded unit (Carneiro 1970, 1981; Earle 1997: 7–9; Giddens 1984: 254–6 contra these models). This kind of model seems inappropriate for the tenth century in Crete, when much less extensive territories were probably in use for agriculture than during the LBA, and the land that was in use (much of it previously treated as marginal) was probably being exploited much more intensively, thanks in part to the new patterns of settlement: there was plenty of room for expansion and growth at this stage. However, the model might be relevant *after* the main period of state consolidation in LG-EA, as significant territorial expansion occurred in a densely packed pattern of very similar settlements.

At a more general level, the links made by Earle between circumscription of resources in a looser social/macroeconomic sense (rather than in terms of subsistence only) and the strengthening of state power *do* provide a good model for Cretan state development in the Archaic to Classical periods (Earle 1997: 67–105, 133). The slow, attritive nature of state expansion at this time seems linked to the historical coexistence of so many similar polities, developing under similar conditions, as well as to the consensualist emphasis of the polis state form itself. Both factors prevented the easy expansion of governance and identity structures, and seem likely to have promoted the rise of interpolity conflict as a mode of developing and reinforcing the state from early Archaic.

Broad themes in the study of social change: how the Cretan case helps our understanding

It seems instructive that no single state formation model, or type of model, has proved satisfactory on its own to describe and explain the cultural changes occurring in PG-A Crete. In-depth and broad-ranging study of the material record of the type undertaken here reveals complex and special patterns that do not fit easily into cross-cultural generalising schemes. Classic questions about the priority of events, processes, and motivations in the rise of economic and political complexity have arisen throughout the preceding discussion (Gledhill and Rowlands 1982; Shanks and Tilley 1987: 58–9, 185; Trigger 1998: 179). In it I have highlighted the role of particular, contingent factors, as well as regionwide processes, in sociopolitical change and the role of cultural practice, particularly at a broad spatial scale, in conditioning social structures. In doing this it has proved extremely difficult to separate, or assign chronological priority to, different means and levels of power appropriation and institutionalisation. Whichever element we select for study is at least partly overdetermined by others, and archaeological dating is simply not good enough to allow confidence in any proposed hierarchy of developments. For example, did friction between nucleated communities engaged in territorial expansion from the tenth century onwards promote the emergence of more formally defined rights to land, and thereby push forward subsistence growth? Or did an increased focus on the control of larger land areas, as subsistence expansion occurred in order to support and balance increased prestige good production and consumption, stimulate the move into nucleated units in the first place? From yet another angle, how far did the changed economic base, supporting the growth of social inequality and promoting the production of large subsistence surpluses, itself increase the demand for and production of wealth goods? None of these questions is new in addressing the rise of states. But in Crete the unique clarity and richness of the archaeological record stimulate renewed discussion of them and shows more clearly than ever the difficulty (and irrelevance) of trying to map out a neat hierarchical predictive and determinative process.

Though conflict on its own did not create the state, Crete's history particularly highlights the important effects on sociopolitical development of conflict and insecurity at various different scales, ranging from external maritime threat, which drove permanent settlement change in the twelfth century, to organised interstate warfare. The consciousness of history/ancestry also emerges as an important force to be reckoned with in examining all the relationships mentioned above. Emphasis on ethnicity as directing and legitimising collective action (seen in the ancient texts and discussed in Part Five), reference to regionally based identity structures in settlement nucleation, representation of kinship and ancestral bonds in mortuary ritual, continuous use of long-established public sanctuaries through the collapse and state emergence period, and a variety of symbolic or ritual reuses, all indicate the core importance of ancestry- and history-focused *mentalités* in social transformations, rather than a role for them as merely superstructural adjuncts in sociopolitical change. Concerns with identity were inherent in complexity-driving factors including prestige good consumption, formal landholding, settlement nucleation, and territorial expansion. The important role of collective political consciousness and social 'memory' in complexity building encourages us to address the general issue of how 'society' is conceptualised and manipulated in basically nonliterate groups. Notions of 'society' seem to have been consistently important in Cretan worldviews during the disruptions of the collapse period, when whole communities, not just elites, undertook a considerable degree of ordered social restructuring in order to preserve their security and livelihood. They were still important during the PG-EA changes – and to a even greater degree, as a result of the strong new social frameworks created in the twelfth century.

It is clear from much of the foregoing discussion that lineage was a consistently powerful concept and a dynamic political unit in the emergent Cretan polis, but usually in the context of several peer lineages existing in parallel: the architecture of large settlements and cemeteries shows few signs of an exclusively dominant individual or group power at any polity. It does seem likely, however, that the sets of clans forming the major players in economic and political life in each region during the settlement nucleation process became increasingly entrenched as local ruling classes by the seventh century. Interestingly, some anthropological studies suggest that the emergence of territorial states can sometimes be held back by very strong lineage-based social structures (Allen 1984; Fried 1967: 173; Qviller 1981: 110–11, 146–7). The heavily clan-orientated form of small state that emerged in EIA Crete might seem to bear this out. Yet an apparently much weaker, less coherent political role for lineage in EIA central Greece produced something equally far from the 'classic' territorial state model – and, as I have argued, may actually explain the more disruptive, difficult nature and more radical outcome of polis state emergence in that region.

In this and the preceding chapters I have attempted to develop outline models of social developments in the wider Aegean and parts of the east Mediterranean by highlighting differences from and similarities with the Cretan record. This approach is further developed in Part Five on the basis of the textual record. Because these models are much more schematic and rely on a much less rich base of data than those I have developed for Crete, it is not possible to test them in detail against standard state formation models. However, it would be very surprising, in the light of the regional variability indicated in cultural developments across the Aegean in this period and the clear role of factors such as previous history, historical awareness/construction, and landscape form in affecting responses to collapse and post-collapse social development, if any of the preceding models were found to apply simply or precisely to large areas of the Aegean beyond Crete. Though the models have proved important tools for thinking with, I hope to have shown not only that we now have in Crete sophisticated enough data to move far beyond them, and towards writing a real and specific cultural history of the island, but that the potential exists to do the same in other Aegean regions, and to have raised stimulating and profitable lines of enquiry to follow up.

PART FIVE

Constructing difference: the history, structure, and context of Cretan states in the later Archaic through Classical periods

35 INTRODUCTION

Here, I examine a few distinctive ways in which Cretan state structures developed between the late Archaic and Classical periods, showing briefly how developments in other regions compare. In these comparisons, particular attention is paid to Athens and Sparta, for which most textual evidence is available, and each of which followed a distinctly different path of political development in this period. I will depart from the archaeologically centred approach used in earlier chapters and turn towards the textual record that becomes available in this period, while still drawing in archaeological data where possible to support the arguments made. The currently available archaeological evidence for this period in Crete is too patchy and unrepresentative to allow meaningful synthesis (Alcock 1999). Few large-scale systematic excavations of well-stratified urban sites covering this period have so far been undertaken, and the most recent, that of Azoria, has only recently been completed and awaits full publication. Selective investigation at Knossos, Thronos, Afrati, Lato, Praisos, and Itanos, among others, has retrieved isolated features and deposits: a large-scale excavation at Lato produced mostly late third- to early second-century material, along with some Archaic remains, but no good continuous stratigraphy. So far, Gortyn is the best-reported site covering the whole period, but some areas of the site are much better recorded and published than others. For many of the other regions with which Crete is compared here, the archaeological data have already been discussed at length by other scholars, and there is little point in revisiting them in detail when consistent comparisons with Cretan data cannot be made.

Inscriptional evidence for Crete is relatively rich – though far from consistently balanced in quality or retrieval across the island – and increases in quantity between the Archaic and Classical periods. As might be expected, I will make particular reference here to the Gortyn Law Code. Many of the earliest literary texts making reference to Crete date to the fourth century or later and must be viewed in that context, but I will also use them, in conjunction with the other data presented here, to suggest trends and features in Cretan society during the sixth and fifth centuries and to explore certain traditions in and about that society. I select particular aspects of society for attention here (identity structures, labour systems, feasting institutions, and other aspects of political machinery) because they are dealt with in most detail or most often by the texts – even though the relevant texts are often written by authors from outside Crete, with a variety of different agendas. Trade systems/orientations, on the other hand, are still most accessible through archaeological evidence, so I turn back to this source when considering them. The particular areas of study listed above have clear and broad relevance to the understanding of social and political developments as a whole, but it is not possible, given the scope of this book and the quality of the evidence, to map even their history in detail over the course of the Archaic and Classical periods, and my assessment will appear somewhat telescoped and general (Perlman 2005: 287). My overarching aim is to demonstrate the broadly formative role of EIA-Archaic sociopolitical and economic developments in the structure and operation of Classical Cretan states.

It is important to stress that in using texts to improve understanding of this period, the problems already identified in Part One in regard to the interpretation of texts are fully present – the more so because relevant text sources for Crete are relatively few, and often of specialised type. This makes it all the more important to include as wide as possible a range of archaeological evidence, where available, to support the arguments made, and to spend time looking at the context of production and consumption of each cited text, rather than taking it at face value. Within the scope of this book the archaeological evidence relevant to Athens, Sparta, and other compared areas cannot be covered in enough depth to give a fully secure base for the interpretation of texts relevant to these regions. For this reason, I rely on textual interpretations put forward by other scholars focusing on these areas, rather than revisiting the primary data myself.

Problems in generalisation and comparison

Crete's Archaic to Classical states shared many material and structural elements with those of the central Aegean, thanks to the common pressures operating by circa 700 BC towards state growth in a consensually orientated framework, the emergence of a generic 'Greek' cultural identity across the whole region from about the same period, and the existence of continuous and intense contacts within the Aegean throughout the EIA to Classical periods. Yet as we have seen, Cretan states also had their own special features, including a very important economic role for serf systems, a heavy vesting of political power in the clan unit, an especially important role for public dining as a social institution, and a lack of uptake of democratic politics. As I outlined in Part One, this distinctive profile has often been noted by previous scholars, but never related back to the island's earlier archaeologically documented social history in any properly contextualised way (pace Willetts 1955, 1965, 1977). Instead, as we have seen, there has been a tendency to make vague, generalising assertions about 'continuity' in Cretan culture and society without further investigation (Morris 1997b: 102, 1998: 49; Prent 2005b: 1–37).

Without a deep, historically grounded regional understanding, comparison of Crete with other regions can only ever be superficial, and conclusions from such comparisons must often be misleading. Ian Morris places Cretan state structures midway along a developmental spectrum between the extreme form of 'citizen state' existing by the Classical period at Athens and the *ethnos* states of north central Greece (Morris 1997b: 100). In fact, Cretan states seem to have incorporated elements found in both other types of state, not necessarily in balanced measure. Morris goes even further, in equating Sparta with Crete on this 'spectrum'; and Garnsey and Morris (1989: 101) categorise both these regions as having 'intermediate forms of state'. This approach echoes the kind of evolutionary model that I have already rejected for Crete and fails to consider the actual history and context of state development in each region. One of the reasons that modern scholars frequently make this kind of joint categorisation is that a number of ancient authors from the fourth century onward referred to shared or similar political institutions between Crete and Sparta. In the normal practice of the time, they often couched these links in terms of a shared ethnic heritage and/or a historical diffusion/colonisation process. Often the effect of both ancient and modern analyses is to lump the regions together as 'other', from a strongly Athenocentric viewpoint (Hodkinson 1997: 84; Morris 1997b: 105; Murray 1990b: 9; Perlman 1993, 2005: 286, 300–8).

Possible parallels between the Cretan and Spartan state structures are a subject of special interest in the present discussion. I will suggest that while they mainly reflect late (Classical) political links and agendas, they may also relate to partly similar regional histories, including histories of contact, between the two regions and that the only reliable way to assess the depth and significance of Spartan (or any other long-distance) political connections with, or influences on, Crete is to use detailed knowledge of Crete's earlier long-term cultural and social history. Parallels between Cretan states and the *ethne* of north central Greece are also worth investigation – these are hinted at, for example, in the ways that coinage was taken up and used in each region, in the strongly clan-based power structures they shared, and in the way they managed external interactions. Comparisons of Crete with Athens, on the other hand, highlight a number of stark structural differences, which again seem strongly rooted in earlier (EIA-Archaic) social and cultural histories.

In making comparisons, a problem arises with assuming we can talk about a single 'Cretan' state type in the same way as we can about, say, the Spartan state. The concept of 'the Cretan polis' does, as I shall show, seem to have some validity for use in comparative analysis but must always be used with reservations, since neither the EIA history nor the Archaic-Classical development of Cretan states was uniform across the island. Though ancient authors regularly referred to Crete as a single unit and conceptualized a standard, representative 'Cretan polis', the island contained numerous, differently identifying political entities right through this period (Perlman 2005: 282–3). Power *had*, though, become concentrated in much fewer, larger states by Classical times, and some very large-scale bonding structures, prefiguring the third-century Cretan political league, the 'Koinon', had started to emerge (Willetts 1977: 179–80). This tendency is hinted at by Crete's coinage (introduced on a shared standard, and in a few large states only, by the early fifth century), by the growing use of collaborative partnership (*sympoliteia*) agreements between Cretan states from the fifth century, and by formal *isopoliteia* treaties, offering reciprocal rights for the citizens of different states, which became popular from the late fourth through the second century in the island (Chaniotis 1996; Guizzi 1999; Le Rider 1966: 162–72; Stefanakis 1999: 249, 262–3; van Effenterre 1948: 154–6; Watrous and Hadzi-Vallianou 2004a: 325).

I also risk overgeneralising about other regions as I compare routes to political diversity in Thessaly, Athens, Sparta, Ionia, and the overseas Greek colonies. In the scope of this study I can offer only brief, simplified, and selective characterizations of state forms in many of these regions. The much greater amount of textual information available on Athens and Sparta than on other Greek states, and the particularly stark structural contrasts or similarities documented between these states and Crete, mean they receive most attention here, while other regions are mentioned at a more superficial and selective level. There remains a great need to explore diversity between, and diachronic changes within, Archaic to Classical states in general. Archaeology, considered alongside the existing texts, offers the best way to do this, in the absence of any new textual sources. Meanwhile, generalised comparison using both text sources and the available archaeological data can at least throw up interesting points to research (Alcock 1999: 178–9).

The central Greek polis structure over time: tensions between tyranny/kingship and participative governance

In all polis-type states, a governance structure of at least nominally consensual type, involving various forms of council and assembly, was rooted in the ideology of 'middling' citizen equality that had emerged by the late eighth century (Cartledge 1996; Finley 1999: 17–35; Morris 1996, 2000: 109–55). The move from this period onwards towards consumption of wealth goods in public contexts, especially cultic ones, was a permanent one in many regions, though by the fifth century there was a reduction of personally competitive wealth display even in the cult sphere and more emphasis on state-level investment (Whitley 2001: 294–329). The state framework seems increasingly to have been accepted as subsuming and supporting personal or small-group status roles, and the main sanctuaries, in particular, became dominated by mostly public-scale dedications, reinforcing the power of the state body. Still, however, regular enactment of the principles of participation in public life by individual citizens was felt necessary to reinforce state authority, through practices like the liturgy and *choregia*, involving mandatory or expected investment in public works by the rich (Davies 1967).

Landholding stayed linked to citizen status right through the Classical period: the ideal citizen held a literal 'share' of the state in this form. At the same time, acceptance of the alienability of land and its independent use in financial transactions had become ever more common by the fourth century (Descat 1995; Finley 1999: 95–123; Foxhall 2002; Osborne 1987, 1991; Thomas 1981: 47–8). Land was increasingly worked in the form of rural estates by noncitizens – slaves and serfs – on behalf of city-based landowners. Many central Greek poleis developed a heavy reliance on slavery after the early sixth century, and broad citizen participation in governance was in some cases kept practicable by the existence of a large chattel slave sector (Finley 1980: 67–93, 1999: 62–95; Fisher 1993: 1–3, 7, 16). Other areas, including Crete, continued to rely more heavily on a land-tied system of labour, alongside slavery.

The notional congruence of political identity between a single major regional settlement and its territory continued throughout expansions in the Classical period, during which whole states and their hinterlands were subsumed by other states or joined with them to form large political and military leagues. The latter became particularly important by the fourth century but were already developing as early as the sixth (Hansen 1993: 8; Hayden 1995: 93–4; Jeffery 1988: 350–64; Perlman 1996; Thomas 1981: 46–7). The distinctive ethnic/historical identity of each individual state was constructed and reinforced through material elements associated with it – cult, coinage, and colonies amongst them. Ethnicity, heritage, and mythic tradition played a vital role in guiding, legitimising, and defining the increasingly complex interactions between peer polities. State identity was tied into a mythic shared genealogy, which could be manipulated to serve changing wider political relations, as well as to reduce dissonance within the state (Hall 1997a; Malkin 1998; Osborne 1998). The importance of extended-kin or fictive-kin ties in power relationships at a more local level was embodied in institutions like the tribe (*phyla*) – membership of which determined proportional representation in citizen councils – and the smaller part kin-, part affinally based phratry, an important social unit in Athens from at least the sixth century (Lambert 1998; Murray 1983: 198). The reforms of Cleisthenes at Athens in 508/7 BC, often considered as marking the transition to full democracy, consolidated the role of tribal power, even while formally redefining the structure of the tribe to broaden and equalise political representation (Ostwald 1988). Laws kept marriage and property firmly within the extended kin group.

All poleis saw changes over time in internal power distribution. Such shifts are particularly well documented in Athens, which clearly shared features with a number of other Greek states, such as Corinth: Sparta followed a partly different path. From having a relatively small governing council complemented by a citizen assembly in the seventh century, the Athenian state came to incorporate a second, larger council (the Council of the Five Hundred), as well as a senior council and a probably enlarged assembly, by the early sixth (Hansen 1987). These institutions remained in place even though tyrants periodically took control of state affairs through much of the period to the end of the sixth century. The consistent ability of tyrant leaders to emerge *within* the structure of participative governance seems rooted in the very circumstances of state formation in central Greece. Person-centred competition was insulated, but never neutralised, by the entrenchment of a consensualist ideology. The importance of clan and tribal membership in power relations, and the restricted size of states, made the periodic appropriation of political control by powerful individuals from prominent families relatively easy (Salmon 1997). At the same time, the prevailing consensualist ideological framework meant that the strength of such leaders remained heavily dependent on day-to-day public support, which they maintained by demonstrating wealth and generosity in the form of public-sector investment. There are few examples of hereditary tyrannies beyond the third generation (Aristotle *Politics* 5.9.21–3). Democratic/consensualist 'swings', such as Cleisthenes' reforms, seem often to have occurred in reaction to extended periods of tyranny, with the two systems of rule thus feeding into each other, though other factors, particularly geopolitics, also played a role (Ober 1996, 1997; Raaflaub 1997b; Rhodes 1992b; Salmon 1997: 66, 70).

At Sparta, the Great Rhetra, a law code possibly dating back to the seventh century, indicates that a nonhereditary double kingship system was accompanied by the basic apparatus of a consensualist state (Cartledge 2001: 55–68, 2002a: 89–92, 113–17). The point at which this kingly leadership was first established is unclear. We have no more reason to date it right back through the Iron Age than we have for the tyrannies of Athens and Corinth, or for the oligarchies of Crete in their formalised Archaic-Classical forms. Late king lists nominally referring to the preliterate period simply recount the kind of mythical genealogies common to all Aegean states. Aristotle (in the context of a general comparison with Sparta) refers to a tradition of kingship in Crete, yet we have seen absolutely no archaeological evidence for such well-entrenched elite individuals in the Cretan EIA (*Politics* 1272a8–9). Only with the rise of the state is it likely that such ruler positions could have become fully institutionalised anywhere in the Aegean, and like those of tyrants, they always remained vulnerable to some extent within the consensualist structure of the polis state. Besides its kingship system, Sparta shows other aspects of divergence from other central Greek states. By Classical times an age-class system seems to have been particularly strongly enforced there, bounding consensual governance within strictly defined limits. Membership of the assembly, for example, was available only to those over thirty, and of the ruling council to those over sixty. The assembly was tightly controlled, in that the council could override assembly decisions. On the other hand, it also had considerable powers over the kings, able to suspend them and other officials if required. As in Athens, periodic social disruptions/rebellions at Sparta clearly pushed movement towards more participative government.

At Athens, the formal democracy established in 506/7 BC involved a radical new level of citizen participation, marking a powerful swing against the concentration of individual or small-group power (Ober 1996: 4). Further reforms were made in 460 BC, including the removal of the property qualification for council office and the award of further powers to the Council of Five Hundred and the lawcourts (Hornblower 1992: 10–11). Some extreme measures, such as ostracism, had by now been introduced: like the new lot-based selection system for council members, this extreme measure was intended to help knock down entrenched position and privilege (Aristotle *Politics* 1284a18–23; *Constitution of Athens* 22.i–iv). By the end of the century, though, the role of consensualism in the state was changing again. The events of the Peloponnesian War and a disastrous involvement in Sicilian campaigns in 415–413 BC weakened Athenian democracy considerably, and backswings towards oligarchy were seen in 411 and 404. Restrictions were placed on the assembly's power to legislate, while the tribal regions had less powerful representation (Andrewes 1992).

36 SPECIAL ASPECTS OF THE ARCHAIC TO CLASSICAL CRETAN POLIS

Political organisation

Classical Cretan states definitely lacked the kind of volatile political structure described for Athens and a number of other central Greek states: the absence of major 'swings' pushing the growth of radical participative structures is notable. They never developed large governing councils, and there was only ever a limited role for the general assembly – noted as meeting in the Gortyn agora by at least the fifth century (Perlman 2000: 72). Members of the council of *kosmoi* were elected from just a few powerful clans – contrasting with the lot-based selection from all citizens that applied to the Athenian Council of the Five Hundred by the sixth century, though membership in the latter was nonetheless subject to a property qualification (Aristotle *Politics* 1272a34–5; Ephorus cited in Strabo 10.4.18; Perlman 2000: 64–5; Willetts 1977: 184–5). As in many other Greek regions there was a second council, of elders (*gerontes*), operating alongside the council of *kosmoi* (Aristotle *Politics* 1271b41–2a12). The strongly clan-based system of governance persisted into the second century BC – when at Lato, for example, it was necessary to prove four generations' descent in one of certain clans, traceable through the male line, in order to hold a *kosmos* position (Baldwin Bowsky 1989). There were some boundaries on the concentration of power in this way: limits on how many times one man could serve as *kosmos* are already indicated in the Dreros inscription of the late seventh century, for example (Meiggs and Lewis 1989: 2–3). Important bureaucratic roles, like that of the scribe in the Spensithios decree, dating around 500 BC and probably relating to the Arkades polity, could also be inherited. The same decree shows that such inherited power could cross over into the religious sphere (Jeffrey and Morpurgo-Davies 1970).

This system of inequality was notably constant and well established – tyrannies are lacking in the history of the Cretan polis. Cretan societies seem to have been fixed so early on into systems of clan-based power that it was difficult for any single group or individual ever to gain a really preeminent position. This fact may also be linked to the strong grounding of wealth and power in land and land-tied labour, rather than the more flexible, but volatile, slave labour that financed the export commodity trade of central Greek polities. As a result, wealth and power were particularly difficult to transfer in Crete except by birth (Willetts 1969: 91).

Conflict

The internecine conflicts that I have suggested to have emerged in Crete from the Archaic period onward, on the basis of changes in settlement pattern and form, clearly intensified through

Classical and into Hellenistic times, as peer states with similar histories and aims continued to prosper and expand within a very tightly packed map. The expansion of Gortynian control across much of the Mesara occurred, almost certainly driven by the aim of garnering more agricultural territory (Perlman 1996: 258–70). By the mid-fourth century Pseudo-Skylax (47) notes that the Praisian territory extended from sea to sea. One of the longest-lived conflicts, drawing in major internal and external players, was between Knossos and Lyttos. It was well under way by the fourth century, when central Cretan states, as well as external players, lined up on either side: Gortyn with Lyttos, Lato with Knossos. In the fifth century Knossos allied itself with nearby Tylissos, in a treaty ratified by Argos, while Sparta came in on the side of Lyttos (Coldstream and Huxley 1999: 302; Viviers 1999: 221; *IC* I.VIII.4, I. XXX.1). These alliances raised the stakes of conflict hugely: the latter now constituted access both to the north and south coasts of Crete, plus a huge amount of prime arable territory.

Following such conflicts, abandonment or contraction of the main settlement centre of the losing side often seems to have been involved, explaining ongoing changes in Cretan settlement patterns all the way through Classical times. However, in a context of increasingly large territories and under a prevailing system of land-tied labour, these conflicts always probably left large parts of the conquered populations living on the land as serfs (rather than being taken as slaves to reside in the conquering polity) in order to allow efficient agricultural production to continue. This must have made large subjugated territories difficult ever to unite politically, and thereby have encouraged further conflict. Wars would also become more drawn-out and attritive, and more threatening to both sides, as states grew larger and more equally balanced in strength. By the late fourth century, *isopoliteia* agreements offered an alternative, more peaceful form of economic and political expansion but also effectively raised the stakes of conflict (Chaniotis 1996, 1999; Guizzi 1999; Perlman 1996).

Elizabeth Stone has used the example of second-millennium BC Mesopotamia to argue that warfare takes place between city-states only in the context of a higher-level hegemonic structure (Charlton and Nichols 1997: 8; Stone 1997). That this was apparently *not* the case in Archaic Crete cautions us again about the possibility of developing universal models for early state development. Alliances with mainland poleis – that is, in effect, incorporation within a broader political context – clearly helped stimulate and support aggression between Cretan communities by the fifth century, and we do see the growth of a powerful 'Greek' identity during this period. But there was no strong overarching political structure, either at an Aegean-wide or an islandwide scale, that included Cretan states. Nor did such a structure emerge *through* conflict, though the eventual emergence of large-scale leagues of poleis does show a tendency in this direction. Wars did produce greatly expanded territories, but these ultimately stayed focused around a single preeminent settlement and identity, rather than turning into true territorial states, in Classical times.

Class and lineage relations

Cretan states, like those of central Greece, increasingly used written law to represent their authority. The laws followed a widely standardised code format, linking Cretan polities closely to their Aegean peers (Hall 1997a: x; Osborne 1997: 78). The office of *poinikastas*, or scribe, became a publicly financed, high-status profession. The fact that this position is frequently referred to in the singular may reflect either the specific role of a particular scribe in recording the law in question or the existence of a single formal 'chief scribe' position within each state. In either case, evidence suggests that a number of high-ranking citizens in most states were able to read and write (Jeffery and Morpurgo Davies 1970; Stoddart and Whitley 1988; Whitley 1997, 1998c; Willetts 1977: 168–9, 186–90).

Many elements of the fifth-century Gortyn Law Code clearly go back to the early sixth century, or earlier (Perlman 2000: 60–1; Willetts 1965: 56–119, 1967, 1977: 216–44). The code tells us that much farmland was worked as rural estates: the systems of partible inheritance that it refers to suggest, on the basis of historical analogy, that these estates were fairly small and widely scattered (Guizzi 1999: 238; *IC* IV.72.IV). Serfs are shown to have had a consistently important role in agricultural production, and considerable rights in land and property (Guizzi 1999: 238–9; Harris 2002a: 419; Willetts 1967: 12–17). Tightly defined lineage relations, and the fictive extension of these into the sphere of bound labour, with the owner of serf-worked land standing in a 'paternal' relation to his serfs, controlled the movement of all kinds of wealth (Willetts 1955: 181–5, 1977: 216–23). For example, heiresses with children had to be married off within the wider clan, following a fixed ranking of relationships (*IC* IV.72.VII); serfs bound to the owner of a particular *klaros* or holding could inherit the property if he died without kin (*IC* IV.72.V); masters had a duty to protect the whole family of a male serf (*IC* IV.72.III); children of serfs could not be exposed without the permission of their master and belonged to that master if born in wedlock (*IC* IV.72.III–IV). As we might expect in a society so dominated by kinship bonds, adoption, whether of children or adults, into the citizen group was an issue of much political concern, constituting an officially sanctioned mode of social mobility and subject to very strong regulations (*IC*.IV.X–XI).

More complex stratification and greater mobility between social classes seem to have existed in Cretan society than in Athens and other central Greek poleis, yet lineage could transcend class relations and ultimately bounded social mobility in ensuring that political power remained within a small oligarchical group (Morris 1997b: 99–100). The fact that the large serf base existed alongside a slave class is one indicator of relatively complex stratification. Like their mainland peers, Cretan poleis also housed large numbers of 'foreigners' (*ksenoi*) – whether these originated from other Cretan poleis or from farther afield – as a separate class. Another hint of the relatively high opportunities for mobility in Cretan society is indicated by the appearance of a standard procedure for adoption of a 'foreigner' by a local citizen in the Gortyn code (*IC* IV.72.X.34–52, 72.XI.10–14). Social and economic circumscription in the relatively small Cretan states may have encouraged such flexibility from an early date. We have references to two official positions – the *mnamon ksenios* and *ksenios kosmos* – connected with the legal rights and status of foreigners at Gortyn, suggesting that foreigners constituted a relatively powerful (and potentially volatile) group (*IC* IV.72.XI.16–17, *IC* IV.14; Perlman 2002: 206–12). Another stratifying element was age-class membership, limiting and univeralising the activities of young people, including education and marriage, in a fairly rigid way. The strength of age-class systems in Crete was an oft-cited parallel with Sparta (Ephorus cited in Strabo 10.4.16, 10.4.20; Hornblower 1992: 2; Rhodes 2004: 469–70; Willetts 1967: 11, 1977: 184–5).

Trade and external relations

For Aegean states through the Archaic and Classical periods, trade was integrally linked to the growth of the 'pan-Hellenic' identity through writing, cult practice, oral tradition, and material culture (Hall 1997a: 45; Morris 2000: 257–61; Nagy 1996: 38–43). It was important to *live* in a particular way in order to interact securely and profitably with overseas client or partner groups: culture acted as a recognised and powerful force in the construction, as well as the representation, of shared identity. Crete had been historically involved enough with the Aegean world to be heavily tied into the same cultural identity framework. Yet its long-continued economic focus on a role as waystation and consumer and merchant base, rather than a specialised good exporter, clearly held back its ability to capitalise fully on this membership: for example, it controlled no colonies outright.

In the case of trade, texts tell us little in this period, partly because of social prohibitions on the open pursuit of commercial gain (Aristotle *Politics* 1.10; Finley 1999). It is necessary to turn back to the archaeological evidence. Across the Aegean world, trade in luxury goods was increasingly led by Attic pottery production: by the fifth century, consumption of eastern luxuries was proportionately less used to connote social prestige. The increasing strength and complexity of the state institution allowed status to be assured in a variety of other, abstract ways, including through the holding of public office. Even in Crete, where the uncontrolled consumption of easternising luxuries had particularly assisted prominent clans to develop and mark their status throughout the EIA, conditions were changing. Now Aegean-produced goods, with a rich local symbolic overlay (often alluding to myth and epic) in their form and decoration, were used to enhance prestige in a subtly coded manner, stressing membership in the wider Hellenic world. But though the *mode* of display changed, no serious restriction on personal display ever seems to have taken hold in long-stable Cretan social systems. At major Cretan sanctuaries after 600 BC there *is* a move away from the deposition of decorated ceramics and metalwork of any kind towards an emphasis on simple, plain fine ceramics. Elaborate, prestigious ceramic imports are now concentrated mostly in domestic or cemetery contexts (Erickson 2000, 2002, 2004). As in the rest of the Aegean world, private consumption and display of trade goods were still active, but used new types and formats of good, and became more firmly separated from the state/cult sphere as the latter grew in strength and influence.

In the increasingly Attic-dominated sphere of commodity exchange, Crete shows an idiosyncratic attitude. Even while some contacts with Attica continued, a general downturn in Attic pottery consumption in the island, especially after circa 500 BC, raises the question of how the new large-scale political allegiances in the Aegean in this period affected Crete's trade and consumption patterns (Erickson 2000: 385, 2004; Perlman 2004b: 127). Erickson has suggested that to fill the gap, Laconian products were more heavily taken up, at least in some parts of the island. Was Crete dissociating itself from the Attic political sphere, for reasons I will discuss further later, or were powerful groups in Athens holding back exports to make Cretan communities feel excluded? In either case, the generalised character of the change confirms that despite internal conflicts and diverse political alliances, Cretan states seem to have maintained strong binding interests with regard to external trade, which were not always congruent with individual states' off-island political linkages.

The picture of strong shared interests between Cretan states with regard to trade is supported by the fact that an independent coinage in Crete developed only from circa 470 BC. When it did appear, it was on a common standard and appeared only in a few most prominent states. Prior to this, use of other Aegean coinages appears to have served all the island's trade needs. The fact that when it did emerge, the coinage had internal circulation only and a very limited number of minting states reflects the continuing lack of a significant independent presence for Crete in the colonial and export trade sector (Stefanakis 1998, 1999: 248). Regions that did have such a presence, like Athens and Corinth, developed coinages much earlier, from the early sixth century. By the fourth century, Cretan coinages still shared the same reverse design – indicating close links between the coining states – and were distinguished by their obverse. Cities that were in a specially close, *isopolitieia*-type relationship, or that claimed to share ethnic genealogies, seem to have shared similar obverse designs, too – for example, in 425–420 BC an obverse design was shared by Gortyn and Phaistos. This suggests a close political relationship, in which Gortyn almost certainly had the upper hand (Stefanakis 1998; van Effenterre 1948: 154–6; Watrous and Hadzi-Vallianou 2004a: 324).

The circulation of bulk organic cargoes in the Aegean grew during the Archaic through Classical periods (Davies 1993: 45; Foxhall and Forbes 1982; Garnsey and Morris 1989: 100; Small 1997a). Crete, as an always-significant agricultural producer, probably found its markets rising in this environment; archaeological and textual evidence indicates that it became a major exporter of wine, oil, and probably cypress wood (Marangou 1999). A third-century decree indicates export of fish and murex from east Crete (Viviers 1999: 222–6) while a text of circa 330 BC records the sending of circa 5,252 hectolitres of grain to Crete from Cyrene (Watrous and Hadzi-Vallianou 2004a: 332–7). Though competition with other producer areas must have been significant, and the dense settlement of the island meant there was limited potential for major surplus production, Crete's strongly land-focused systems of labour may have served it particularly well in developing this trade.

It is very likely in this connection that we see a continuous growth of small rural settlements around Archaic to early Classical Phaistos, with each small site apparently controlling fairly large landholdings. At least one of these sites incorporated heavy agricultural equipment in the form of an oil press, suggesting the substantial investment of wealth in the countryside by this period. There is a further expansion of small sites onto marginal land in the same region from the fourth century; a related expansion of cultivation may be reflected in the changing pollen and charcoal profiles at Kommos (Shay and Shay 2000; Watrous and Hadzi-Vallianou 2004a: 318–19, 333–7). The fact that this and other port sites developed substantially during Classical times must surely have been connected with the developing bulk trade sector.

The changing trade pattern put Crete back as a player in the sphere of export competition, from which it had been absent for so long, and helps explain the eventual emergence of a local coinage. This shift must have changed perceptions of the island in the wider world, and exposed Cretan polities in new ways to the vagaries of the international market. Competition in this arena almost certainly contributed to intensifying interpolity conflict in Crete in late Archaic through Classical times, and export transactions and arrangements were certainly jealously guarded by each individual state (Alcock 1999: 177; Chaniotis 1999; Guizzi 1999: 242; Viviers 1999). For example, despite the existence of a long-term political alliance between Knossos and Tylissos, the latter had to pay duty if it exported goods through Knossos's ports. However, perhaps because of their small size (and related vulnerability in the market) and their historically oligarchical structures, Cretan polities do *not* exhibit regular internal tensions between the trade interests of elite and state, notable elsewhere within the Archaic to Classical Aegean. Instead, these interests seem to have mapped very closely onto each other (Small 1997b: 222, 1998: 283).

37 CRETAN IDENTITIES IN HISTORICAL PERSPECTIVE

State expansion and the accommodation of multiple-group identities

In order to understand the history, meaning, and outcome of the differences between Cretan societies and those of other Aegean areas in this period, we have to understand in detail how this difference was constructed and experienced in terms of identity, both from an internal and an external perspective. Across the Greek world, cultural and ethnic identity (closely tied into myth and history) had become highly complex and was being used in sophisticated ways for political and economic ends by Classical times. Nothing about its representation can be taken at face value.

Nearly all literary sources relating to Cretan identity structures offer external perspectives only. Some make reference to regional- or polis-level identity subgroupings within the island, but most mention 'Cretans' as a single homogeneous unit. This seems connected to the fact that almost all are written by non-Cretans and usually constitute fairly superficial mentions of the island within a much broader discursive context. The emphasis on a single 'Cretan' identity in these external perspectives partly echoes the case of the *ethnos* states of contemporary central Greece. Morgan (2003: 206–11) has noted that these large, loose groupings, containing a number of spatially scattered, lineage-based units of equal status, referred to a collective, state-level identity most often when interacting in the external arena, and much less so in local-scale operations, where the individual subunits were most important. The small size, high density, and very similar history and culture of individual polities in Crete may have made their individual identities of particularly low relevance to outsiders (Stefanakis 1999: 262–3). Crete also resembles the *ethnos* states in lacking any very strongly 'branded' export trade associated with individual poleis, which might raise the profile of this level of identity. At the intra-island scale, however, inscriptions show that polity-level identities were not only highly relevant, but well defined in territorial terms.

Considerable flexibility in state-level identity structures was required as political circumstances changed between the Archaic and Classical periods. These structures needed to represent and integrate many different groups scattered in the landscape around and between the expanding polities – including serfs and large conquered populations. Binding these groups securely and stably into the state was difficult, since 'legacy' identities for conquered poleis, built up over centuries, could not be easily wiped out. We have inscriptional evidence to indicate that newly subsumed polities did keep a strong hold on their names and their status as separate identity units. One route was for a conquered polity to take on a status as 'polis *υπηκοος*', or 'dependent' polis (Perlman 1996). For example, Perlman notes that inscriptional references to the polis of Rhittenia show it as having eventually become subjugated to Gortyn, yet continuing to use the name and the description of the entity as a polis after this event, indicating that the group that was once resident here still had some recognized separate identity or organization. One text even refers to the polity as having a *kosmos* council still in place (*IC* IV.80). Thus, however dispersed on the land, some parts of the conquered population (presumably the formerly dominant clans) retained social coherence and structure. Though subjugate, they were surely ranked differently than serfs born in the preexisting Gortynian territory. The class of *apetairoi*, mentioned in the Gortyn Law Code, may represent such groups (Larsen 1936; Perlman 1996: 241). We also have references to groups called *perioikoi*, apparently corresponding to communities with a similar dependent status but retaining a group identity and partial autonomy, whether living on their old settlements or scattered in the surrounding landscape. They seem to have paid tax or tribute to the ruling regional polity in return for this status. Dosiades directly equates Crete's *perioikoi* with subjugate poleis (Athenaeus *Deipnosophistae* 4.143), though Aristotle (*Politics* 1272b18–20) compares *perioikoi* in Crete directly to helots (serfs) at Sparta, not the Spartan *perioikoi*, which seem to have been politically independent tribute-paying settlements within Sparta's territory. The regular existence of a number of small, spread-out quasi-independent groups, retaining separate identities, within a single expanded political territory seems indicated in Crete by both terms. The relative status of such groups, and the terms applied to them, may well have varied between Cretan regions, according to the former standing and size of a conquered polity and the existing social divisions within it.

As polis territories became larger, we see references in inscriptions to tribal groups not closely integrated with any single polis or former polis identity, though they might be located within the territory of a large polity and partly affiliated with it. In an environment of vastly expanded territories, these groups may have proved difficult to control entirely by the locally dominant polity – perhaps being scattered across a territorial boundary and thus partly included within a neighbouring state's lands – and have continued to manage their affairs under their own loose identity structure while owing some kind of allegiance to one or more of the strongest local polities. Perlman notes that a group called the Kransopoeioi seem to be mentioned in inscriptions as *perioikoi* of both Knossos and Gortyn (Larsen 1936; Perlman 1996: 246). Tribes also existed as semiautonomous units wholly within very large territories like that of Gortyn, to the extent that they could sign political treaties and alliances on their own behalf. The Amyklaioi (possibly identified with Kommos or the coastal region) signed a treaty with Gortyn agreeing to pay tribute (*IC* IV.172). In another agreement concerning the rights of noncitizens at Gortyn, a group called the Latosioi appear, probably linked to a place called Latosion, which appears in another Gortyn inscription. This was clearly a separate settlement centre and identity focus within the wider Gortynian territory, yet does not appear to have had a subjugate-polis status (*IC* IV.78; Perlman 1996: 254, 261). In the Spensithios decree, a group called the Dattaloi separately authorizes the text, alongside the issuing polis authorities (probably those of Arkades); it is not clear whether these people are a prominent clan within the polis or a semiautonomous group in the wider region (Jeffery and Morpurgo-Davies 1970). By the fourth century some of these groups even had their own coinages, indicating a considerable degree of political and economic power; Perlman cites the case of the Oreioi or hill-tribes of the White Mountains. The existence of broadly shared coining standards across Crete facilitated such developments. There are again echoes of the mainland *ethne* in this pattern of spatially scattered autonomous lineages being firmly bound into a larger state structure. The difference was that in Crete these tribes were only ever minority components of states originally focused on a single polis settlement centre and its associated territory, however much this might expand over time to include subjugate settlements.

Even so, the marked fluidity and complexity in identity structures, as Cretan states expanded within such a crowded political environment, may have been factors in encouraging outsiders to lump the island's states together as one unit, or else to see it as being mainly represented by its most powerful polities.

External perceptions of Cretan identities: evidence from the earliest texts

In the earliest textual reference we have to ethnic identity structures in Crete, the *Iliad*'s Catalogue of Ships (2.647), the impression of a crowded number of poleis encapsulated in the description of Crete as 'hundred-citied' is well reflected in the Geometric to early Archaic archaeological record, even though the actual number of large nucleated sites with earlier EIA roots currently known or suspected is only about fifty (Boardman 1982: 22). The few towns mentioned by name in this source correspond to those where we know major EIA and later settlements existed, most of them with no clear BA predecessor: Gortyn, Lykastos (location unknown), Milatos, Phaistos, and Rhytion (usually considered to refer to the Rotasi Kefala site) are all referred to. The reference to Lykastos as 'white with chalk' strongly suggests a location in the marly landscape of central Crete, matching the other toponyms. This region, as we have seen, was a political and economic powerhouse containing many of the island's most important polities in the later EIA and very likely to have been the focus of greatest external attention and recognition.

The reference to Crete in the *Odyssey* repeats the idea of multiple similar polities, too many to name – but now offers ninety as the number, again showing the impressionistic quality of the description (*Odyssey* 19.172–7). Odysseus, disguised as a Cretan, does not speak of individual polities but describes the island's residents in terms of general ethnic groupings, some linked to contemporary mainland ethnic groups – Achaeans, Pelasgians, Eteocretans, Kydonians, Dorians. Odysseus is said to hail 'from Crete', but the 'Cretans' are never generalized as a category in this early text. None of the groups mentioned is directly associated with a particular region of the island: the audience/reader may have been expected to know their geographical associations. Nowhere is it indicated, either, that these groupings are the *only* ones comprising the island's population, though it does seem likely that they are being presented as the major players. The juxtaposition of the 'ninety cities' description with the small number of ethnic identity groupings strongly suggests that each ethnic unit covers a number of different polities.

The extreme vagueness of this description may well be an artistic device intended to add a sense of distance, romance, and mystery to the account, while still tying Crete into the framework of a broadly Greek identity through links to mainland ethnic groups. Placed in the mouth of Odysseus, it may also be intended to highlight the thinness of his disguise, revealing his limited knowledge of the island. It certainly lends great weight to a point we see hinted at in other elements of the textual record by the eighth century: understandings of the political world were deeply and inextricably embedded in concepts of ethnic identity; the ethnicity of the social/political unit *constituted* it and was an expected and typical way of describing or thinking about any region.

Of the five ethnic groups mentioned in the passage, two have no specific links to outside entities ('Eteocretans', translatable as '*echt*/old/true Cretans' and 'Kydonians'). Kydonians must surely be associated with the west and the region of Chania, because of the fact that the city bore the name of Kydonia by Classical times and almost certainly as early as the LBA (ku-do-ni-ja in the Linear B texts). An 'Eteocretan' identity for the inhabitants of Praisos specifically is dated before the period of the Trojan War by Herodotus, writing in the fifth century

(Herodotus 7.171). The term may possibly already have been used to distinguish some parts of Cretan society during the period of Mycenaean acculturation and have persisted (notwithstanding the transformation, restructuring, or disappearance of any actual group originally referred to) as an identity reference point through the collapse horizon circa 1200 BC and beyond the EIA. The 'Eteocretan' identity could be related to a phenomenon appearing in the seventh century in several east Cretan poleis – the use of a language not Greek, but written in Greek script, to duplicate legal inscriptions in Greek (Boardman 1982: 230; Bosanquet 1910; Duhoux 1982; Whitley 1998a). If we accept, as do a number of the aforementioned scholars, that the language does tie in somehow to this ethnic, it would suggest that already by Homer's time the latter had become attached to a particular regional unit in east Crete – but a broad one, much larger than any individual polis.

The term 'Pelasgians' is used elsewhere by Homer, as well as by later writers, to indicate a generic concept of a 'very old' Aegean population stratum. Its inclusion in this description contributes a sense of great antiquity to the history of Crete (reflected in later textual accounts) and ties Crete's history and identity into that of the wider Aegean at the most general level. Homer's references to 'Dorians' and 'Achaeans' also convey the sense of very large, general ethnic groupings, but these terms were more tied to one particular region of the Greek world (the Peloponnese) and had a more contemporary resonance. The term 'Achaeans', used throughout the epics to describe groups from all over the Aegean world massed under Peloponnesian leadership to fight at Troy, significantly comes first in the list, perhaps to stress that Cretans in the majority (or first and foremost) belonged to this politically charged identity grouping, the core of the pan-Hellenic identity. The use of 'Dorians' – a more specifically Peloponnesian subset of the 'Achaean' identity – suggests that Crete's links with the Peloponnese were already acknowledged as strong by Homer's time. We know of strong cultural links between the regions in both the LBA and the late EIA, either of which may be referred to here: west Crete has particular evidence of trade links with the Argolid, for example, from the eighth century. In contrast with later sources linking Cretan ethnicity *as a whole* to that of the Spartans (who claimed a 'Dorian' heritage), only one group *within* Crete is given this direct Peloponnesian association in Homer.

It is not clear whether any of Homer's listed identity groupings were associated with a tradition of migrations into Crete existing at the time of writing, or, if so, whether any such tradition had a basis in reality. The text dates to the beginning of the colonisation period, in which interregional contacts and links were regularly being explained or justified in ethnic terms. Referring to one group or region using the ethnic of another at this time could represent many different types of social and political connections and thus cannot be straightforwardly read in terms of a single 'original' datable migration from a single geographical area (Morgan 2003: 17). We have seen that at no point in the Cretan EIA do new large settlement foundations appear that stand out from widespread, consistent local patterns of settlement change. Nor do sizeable enclaves of divergent material culture become visible in any other aspect of the record. This argues against multiple major migration events during this period. Crete's pronounced openness to a very wide range of external contacts and trade throughout the EIA also suggests that any migrants who did arrive in the island were likely to have been already culturally/ethnically mixed groups of a small, highly entrepreneurial character, the members of which became well-integrated permanent or semipermanent residents in the island, very probably concentrated at its major gateway sites.

In sum, the ethnic designations in the Homeric account seem mainly to stress Crete's heritage of belonging (at different levels) to the wider Aegean world and to refer to broadly recognised traditional or contemporary identity distinctions between local groups. If they *do* reflect eighth-century traditions about migrations to Crete, any real events these traditions referred to would seem, on the basis of the archaeological record, much more likely to date to the Late Bronze Age (or earlier) than to the EIA (Perlman 2000: 77). In particular, there is no evidence to suggest that the Homeric references can be used as a *terminus ante quem* for a large-scale immigration of 'Dorian' people from the Peloponnese into Crete during the EIA. Yet all sorts of further assumptions have been predicated on this view, including the notion that the 'Dorians' stayed intact as a separately preserved stratum of Cretan society after their arrival and were responsible for importing major elements of social structure into the island, such as serfdom or the common meal (Catling 1996c: 646; Coldstream 1984b: 317; Coldstream and Catling 1996: 715; Demargne 1947: 93–8; Desborough 1964: 178–9, 192–5, 217–57; Willetts 1955: 250–4, 1965: 16–36, 1977: 143–215). Recently, Watrous and Hadzi-Vallianou (2004a: 310–15) have identified changes in EIA settlement in the Mesara with the advent of new ethnic groups, presenting the large nucleated settlements developing from PG onwards as those of incoming 'Dorians' and those of the more extreme defensible type, falling out of use by Geometric, as those of an oppressed Cretan population. This idea seems based on an overliteral reading of the textual sources and a single regional focus, rather than a consistent, wide-ranging analysis of archaeological data, and fails to explain islandwide patterns of settlement change at any period of the EIA. The same authors divide graves in the LM IIIC Phaistian cemeteries into two classes, rich and poor, which they suggest also to be linked into the same ethnic division. This interpretation is similarly uncontextualised with regard to wider patterns of EIA mortuary practice. Prent (2005b: 111, 123) reconstructs *two* waves of incomers – Mycenaeans in the early EIA, *followed* by Dorians – as explaining Crete's history in this period. Again, a hypothesis not supported by the wide-ranging evidence I have presented in Parts One to Four. As indicators of 'Dorian' immigration, Prent lists the following vaguely defined features of the Cretan EIA: 'interruption in the use of the cemeteries, changes in burial customs and pottery styles' (Prent 2005b: 123). Previously, I have shown that these features cannot be isolated in a single horizon, and that all of them can be explained using models other than that of mass migration.

In another part of the *Odyssey*, we see colony-type foundation myths with a Peloponnesian connection being applied to Crete. Menelaos, king of Sparta, is mentioned as being shipwrecked during the return from Troy at a place called Amyklai, near Gortyn: we know this toponym continued in the area into Classical times (*Odyssey* 3.293–4). Amyklai is often supposed to be the site of Kommos, and the shipwreck tradition, like the other Homeric accounts, could reflect either Bronze Age or late EIA links between Crete and the Peloponnese, specifically Laconia. It could also reflect the adoption by the eighth century of legitimising traditions linked to the heroic past by the emergent Gortyn state (Cucuzza 1997; Watrous and Hadzi-Vallianou 2004a: 310). The fourth-century source Konon (*FGrHist* 26.xxxvi, xlvii) links the Cretan toponym Amyklai directly to the Lakonian Amyklaion (a cult site for Sparta by at least the eighth century) in a more concrete way. 'People from Amyklai' are said to have 'settled Crete'. This reference must be seen in the later context of Crete's political alliances with Sparta, but the Homeric source does certainly suggest a tradition of strong central/west Cretan links with the Peloponnese generally, and Laconia especially, by the eighth century (Perlman 2000: 68–9, 77).

An account of Crete by Strabo in the first century AD still makes reference to broad historical divisions between ethnic groups in the island; I include it in this section because it borrows so heavily from Homer. In its own right, however, it suggests that some broad, conscious regional ethnic distinctions along these lines might have been claimed within the island in the more recent past (Strabo 10.4.6). Perhaps because Strabo's wider readership would be less familiar with Crete's geography, he adds slightly more detail and works systematically from west to east, tying the groups to named locations. He says that Achaeans and 'Laconians' collaborated to create the settlement at Polirinia in west Crete from preexisting small villages (10.4.13). The direct reference to Laconia, couched in the by-now-familiar terms of colonial foundation myth, echoes the references by Classical authors to close political parallels and ethnic connections between the two regions and reminds us of the specific archaeological evidence for contacts between Laconia and west Crete in Archaic to Classical times. Strabo places 'Dorians' – referred to separately from 'Laconians' as a much more generic group – in the 'east' of the island (perhaps simply referring to the main block of Crete beyond Psiloritis, after first discussing the far west) and 'Eteocretans' in the 'south' (notwithstanding Herodotus's account of a link between the Eteocretans and east Crete). Such vague and derivative references to ethnic groups and their geographic linkages give little or no more concrete information than Homer does.

Later sources and the validity of colonisation models for Crete

From the sixth century onward, just as long-distance interstate alliance building took off and the colonial movement flourished, text sources (which now include formal historical accounts) and archaeology both start to hint more specifically at a presence in, or links with, some Cretan regions on the part of other Aegean groups, with stronger overtones of colonial-type relationships. Kydonia/Chania, as a large and rich harbour state, became a focus of attention in this regard. While in the eighth century Homer had referred to the groups resident in this region using only a local ethnic ('Kydonians'), later authors link the area strongly to specific external groups. Accounts of Zakynthian and Samian interest in the site and of a short-lived Aeginetan settlement here in 524 BC, after the expulsion of the Samians with Aeginetan help, suggest that some of the most dynamic trading states of the Aegean viewed the use (and potentially the control) of this and other Cretan ports as a highly profitable exercise and may have tried to establish themselves there permanently in quite large numbers, in quasi-colonial operations (Erickson 2004: 207; Herodotus 3.44, 3.59; Stefanakis 1999: 254–5; Strabo 8.6.16). In the early fourth century, Plato (*Laws* 4.707) referred to 'people from Argos and Aegina' as resident in Crete – presumably referring either to a still-existent ethnic and cultural legacy from this period or to a tradition about the preexisting link. Strabo's late account uses direct 'colony' terminology to refer to the Aiginetan presence.

The account of Aegina as a party deeply interested in Crete, with long-established links to the island, ties in well with Aiginetan features in late Archaic to Classical Cretan material culture, including Aiginetan inscriptions on some local grave stelai at Chania, a hoard of Aiginetan coins at Matala, considerable numbers of Aiginetan pottery imports in the period around 500 BC, Aiginetan influence on early Cretan coinage styles, and the overstriking of some of the earliest Cretan coins on Aiginetan ones (Erickson 2004: 207; *IC* II.120–3; Stefanakis 1999). There seems little doubt that parts of west Crete at this period had strong contacts with Aegina, and that Aeginetans were frequently in the island, some of them even settling there. However, problems with the overgeneralised or overliteral application of the 'colony' model, especially in an intra-Aegean context, are highlighted here. The cultural history of Crete and its ethnic, social, and political relationships with central Greece, one of the core origin regions of colonising activity, contrast hugely with those of the main developing colonial areas of the period, such as Sicily and south Italy. They are very different also from those of the north Aegean, an area often referred to in ancient sources and modern scholarship as having been 'colonized' by central Greek polities: Papadopoulos (2005) has recently offered a cogent reevaluation of such arguments. The case of Crete reminds us that we should never accept at face value Archaic to Classical authors' use of colony-related terminology to indicate a uniform descriptive category or accurate historical analysis: it always needs to be placed in the context of the archaeological record, and of the political outlooks of the writers and readers concerned. If the term is applied only at a very general level, to signify a close, relatively stable (often trade-rooted) cultural and political linkage between groups in different regions, with a certain inequality of scale and prosperity usually involved, parts of Archaic to Classical Crete *might* well be designated as having a colonial or quasi-colonial relationship with the central Aegean. However, there is little trace of the kind of permanence or exclusivity of relationship with a mother city visible in the case of central Mediterranean colonies. Interests were too divergent, general power and wealth levels too evenly matched, and cultural history and contacts too close between Crete and central Greece to allow such relationships to be easily maintained.

'Cretan-ness'

The very large-scale expansion of some Cretan states during the Archaic to Classical period surely had a significant impact on contemporary conceptions of the island's identity as a whole. We have seen that polity-level identities in Crete were resilient, though flexible. Many clearly kept their integrity after conquest, unable to be fully or easily incorporated into the identity of the conquering state. Over time, however, broader *regional* community identities probably began to be appropriated directly by the island's strongest poleis, further reinforcing the cohesion of their increasingly sizeable territories. Such a process is suggested by Herodotus's account of the 'Eteocretan' identity group in Crete, which suggests a 'takeover' by the fifth century of this originally loose regional ethnic on the part of Praisos, one of few large states controlling the east Cretan region (Herodotus 7.171). These types of identity amalgamation at local level may have fed over time into the building of a more solid 'Cretan' identity, promoted by and vested in the few big state players that effectively controlled many of the island's affairs by the late Archaic period, such as Knossos, Phaistos, Gortyn, and Kydonia. These were historically front-runners in trade, had some of the best opportunities for agricultural expansion on the island, and were the first poleis to develop coinage, suggesting that a significant concentration of economic power lay in their hands.

As political and trade blocs consolidated across the Aegean in this period, such large-scale, cohesive identity structures would be increasingly useful in representing the still relatively small and numerous Cretan polities, with their historic lack of cultural 'branding'. As we have seen, Cretan states also benefited from building alliances with external groups and linking their identity structures closely to them. External perspectives on the island changed to reflect all these changes and, in doing so, contributed to building a concept of 'Cretan-ness' that was recognised both inside and outside the island, though this was never entirely cohesive (Perlman 2005: 282–3). We see this in fourth-century textual references to Crete's links with Sparta, where in most cases *the whole island* is associated with Sparta. The two regional identities are often bundled together to encapsulate the notion of 'other' state types within a complex political discourse centred on Athens. Another case in which the concept appears is that of the Gela colony in Sicily, developed in partnership with Rhodes. Whatever the individual polis origin of the Cretan traders who helped establish it (and the pottery there mostly suggests a west Cretan provenance for these groups), by the fourth century they were simply represented as 'Cretans' in Thucydides' foundation account, and perhaps in day-to-day business between the colony and the wider trade world (Thucydides 6.4). A similar level of generalisation applies to the developing tradition about Cyrene's colonisation, in which 'Cretans' were said to have been involved, again within a partnership (Herodotus IV.150–6). Indeed, Herodotus already consistently uses the term 'Cretans', rarely referring to a specific Cretan state unless a particular narrative or comment concerns it in particular. We need to understand properly how the 'Cretanness' concept operated when turning to another interesting aspect of identity construction and development in this period – the claimed links between Crete and Sparta (Perlman 2005: 300–8).

Exploring the Spartan link

1) THE TRADITIONS

The modification of identity concepts to support and accommodate new kinds of wide-ranging political and economic alliances is unsurprising in a context where myth and tradition had such huge political force (Davies 1993: 30–1; Herodotus 7.150.2). The general tradition of an ethnic or structural link between Crete and Sparta seen in the Archaic to Classical texts illustrates this well. Some texts place the link at the level of the individual Cretan polity, others at the pan-Cretan level. Most sources refer to the latter, though it is certain that a practical political connection never became generalised to include all Cretan polities, as the history of alliance in the Knossos-Lyttos conflict shows. This fact, the mostly late (fourth-century) date of the relevant sources, the divergent rationales they present for the link, the contemporary context of geopolitical alliance between the two regions, and the markedly different (archaeologically attested) timescales of state development for each region, all suggest that the texts mostly reflect changing angles of view on identity and political affiliation, rather than accurate historical accounts.

Though we have seen that traditions of close and long-term contact between Crete and Sparta/Laconia may be already referred to in Homer, the earliest overt linkage of the regions in terms of their having similarities in political structure is made in the fifth century by Herodotus, who recounts the tradition that Lykourgos, the legendary lawgiver of Sparta, took these laws from Crete (Herodotus 1.65). In the mid-fourth century Plato (*Laws* 1:3.682–3) closely linked the Cretan and Spartan constitutions and noted contemporary affinities between institutions in each region: 'Crete' is again characterised as a unit here, defined by reference to the tradition of Minos as lawgiver. Aristotle refers to the Lykourgos myth, and to Lyttos/'the Lyctioi' (known to have built formal links with Sparta by the time of writing and categorised by Aristotle here as a Spartan colony), when he introduces Cretan social and political systems in close association with those of Sparta (*Politics* 1271b20–32). All these texts show that the pragmatic political linkages we know to have existed between the regions by this period were strengthened by reference to a general tradition of similarity between Spartan and Cretan social systems. Since the illustrious antiquity of Cretan systems was often referred to in such contexts, this could reflect well on Sparta by association (Perlman 2005: 319). The Cretan historian Ephorus noted the close similarities, but also some differences, in political institutions in the two regions. Referring to Plato, whom he noted to hold the opposite view, Ephorus argued that Crete's characteristic institutions were exported to Crete *from* Sparta (cited in Strabo 10.4.17). But Plutarch (*Life of Lykourgos* 4) suggests again that Crete's laws were borrowed as a model for Lykourgos in making Sparta's laws, within a narrative of deliberate state design rather than one involving ethnic links. The flexibility inherent in the tradition is further shown by the account of Xenophon (a writer particularly familiar with the Spartan system and aiming to enhance its reputation in his text). He justifies the Spartan constitution entirely on objective grounds, suggesting it was independently 'designed', with no reference to Crete. The vagueness/superficiality in all these accounts and the contradictions between some of their claims suggest that they were mainly intended to reinforce or justify pragmatic long-distance linkages typical of the fourth-century and later political world and could also act as an intellectual shorthand or 'blueprint' for alternatives to the Athenian state structure, as Perlman has insightfully argued (Perlman 2005: 319).

What is most unconvincing in all these accounts is the notion of block transfer (and subsequent parallel development) of whole economic and sociopolitical 'packages' between the two regions in the pre-Classical period. Large-scale social change rarely occurs so smoothly, and the whole aim of this book has been to show how Cretan societies developed in *unique* ways over the course of the EIA, conditioned by particular material and historical factors. We have seen that state development in Crete was a gradual process, tied in strongly to preexisting social conditions, rather than any sudden event. State formation in Sparta does not seem to have occurred on a parallel timescale (though given the early emergence of the Sparta settlement itself as a major nucleation and the early annexation of Messenia, it does seem likely to have been fairly precocious in mainland terms). On the other hand, state emergence in this region is clearly much too close in time to the Cretan state emergence process to be able to represent the imitation of any finished, perfected Cretan state system. There clearly *were* major structural similarities and close links between Cretan and Laconian societies by Classical times, but these need to be analysed in historical context, and we must appreciate how far networks of formal alliance may have promoted and enhanced the links by representing them in broader, more deeply rooted terms. Much-referred-to parallels between the regions include the important role of serfdom and of the common meal, both of which I discuss at length later in the specific perspective of identity construction as well as that of broader social history. But there are also well-documented divergences. Apart from anything else, the contrast in scale between Sparta and any individual Cretan state suggests that fundamental differences in social organisation always prevailed between the two regions.

By the fifth century, the nature of their trade and colonial links highlights the regions' shared status as 'different' in the wider Greek world and their nonalignment with the aggressively expanding and democratically structured Athenian state (Erickson 2004, 2005). Direct trade connections between the regions may also have drawn them closer together politically, and I consider below exactly how these tied into political alliances and structural links by Classical times. Interestingly, the shared feature of lack of deep and proactive engagement in the foreign trade and colonial spheres is *not* highlighted in the texts comparing the two regions, a fact illustrating the often selective agendas of contemporary observers.

II) LANGUAGE CONNECTIONS AND 'DORIANISM'

An obvious focus for scholars (both ancient and modern) engaged in seeking or explaining parallels between the two regions has been the 'Doric' form of written Greek, used in both Cretan and Peloponnesian inscriptions from as early as the seventh century. Its distribution has been linked with the Classical myth of the 'return of the Heraklidae', in which the spread of tribes called *Doreioi* through the Peloponnese was said to have occurred following the end of the Trojan War (Cartledge 2002a: 46, 65–88; Hall 1995a, 1997a; Vanschoonwinkel 1991: 331–67). Legends tying Crete to this Peloponnesian descent tradition include, for example, the story that Phaistos was founded by a 'son of Herakles' named Ropalos (*IC* I.268, citing Stephanos of Byzantium). Such myths echo and extend the Homeric traditions linking Crete (especially central Crete) to a broadly Peloponnesian heritage, which I have discussed previously and which are hardly surprising in view of the two regions' proximity and demonstrably strong cultural connections in both the LBA and late LG-Classical periods. As polity-level identities in Crete became more amalgamated, and formal alliances with the Peloponnese developed, the notion of a 'Dorian' ethnic identity was frequently applied to Crete as a whole.

In fact, there is no overwhelming archaeological or linguistic evidence for a physical migration into the Peloponnese in the EIA, or of a single starting horizon for the spread of 'Doric' culture and language there or elsewhere in the Aegean (Hall 1997a: 114–28). Scholars who try to argue the case for Dorian migrations often rely on very shallow bases of archaeological evidence. For example, Cartledge has argued for the advent of PG pottery in Laconia as proof of 'Dorian' newcomers at this time. Yet the style appears here at the same time as elsewhere in Greece, whence it was transferred by trade from the Attico-Euboean region. The unusual *character* of PG Spartan pottery may be mostly connected to the region's isolation and Sparta's long-term status as the single dominant regional nucleation, concentrating production (Cartledge 2002a: 77–80; Snodgrass 1971: 246). Cartledge's argument suggesting Sparta's foundation by incomers also disregards evidence for use of the Sparta-Amyklai area through the LH IIIC period – it seems likely that extreme contraction of the regional population to this and a few other sites occurred at the end of the LBA, rather than total abandonment of the whole surrounding area, as he suggests (Cartledge 2002a: 58–63).

To understand its true significance, we need to recognise the long-term manipulation of the 'Dorian' concept in late EIA to Classical times as a political tool in defining a Peloponnesian identity loose enough to encompass a large number of poleis. Sparta was the most powerful among them and thus laid claim to the tradition most strongly (Cartledge 2002a: 65–6). The blanket Dorian origin myth developed, and was maintained, as a framework for more specific traditions that emerged over time to legitimate alliances or conflicts between developing states.

It is important also to recognise that language (especially in the form of written inscriptions) was an aspect of culture as susceptible as myth to manipulation in the interests of invented tradition – and thus cannot constitute direct evidence of any monolithic, generalised migration into Crete, either during the EIA or after. As a retrospective unitary category created by scholarship, the Doric dialect cannot, in any case, be pushed back to a single origin point (Hall 1995a, 1997a: 143–82). The Linear B script had had a very restricted class of users and represented a spoken language most similar to that of the later Arkado-Cypriot dialect, not the Doric of Archaic-Classical Crete and the Peloponnese. It seems most likely that a variety of dialects existed in Crete during the LBA period, linked up to different sets of internal and external relationships, including with the Peloponnese (Hall 1997a: 158–9; Perlman 2000: 65). In the post–1200 BC environment of multiple new contact systems, settlement dispersal, and the disappearance of literacy, the already-diverse regional dialects must have flourished and spread in new ways. By the time we see Cretan language written again, state bodies had already emerged and large-scale manipulations of identity through language and writing were already in play. The dual Eteocretan/Doric Greek inscriptions prove not only that Crete contained a variety of dialect groups right into Archaic times, but that dialects were actively manipulated and foregrounded politically during and soon after state emergence (Duhoux 1982; Hall 1995a, 1997a: 177–9; Whitley 1998c). As Cretan states expanded their territories at home and built important political and trade links abroad, especially with the Peloponnese, use of the wide-circulation Doric dialect would surely be strongly promoted at the level of formal trade or political arrangements, even while a number of dialect variations continued to be widely spoken at a colloquial or local level. Groups in central Crete, an area that since at least the tenth century BC had formed the island's developmental powerhouse and was a very active region of political alliance building by Classical times, may have especially promoted the use of a formal, widely shared Cretan script and dialect of Doric type, to help boost political bonds with the Peloponnesian region. In the east Cretan communities, which we have already seen to be divergent in various ways, there may have been greater ambivalence or dissent about these kinds of changes.

There is no doubt that the Doric dialect and its cultural associations were highly charged and manipulated in a political sense on the Peloponnesian mainland itself. The inclusion of deliberately archaising language elements in Classical Lakonian inscriptions was used to promote a conservative political agenda grounded in a claimed 'Dorian' heritage (Hall 1997a: 170–80; Hodkinson 1997: 92). Doric ancestry was also claimed for prestige-linked practices within the later Spartan polis: for example, the third-century kings Agis and Kleomenes justified the constitution by referring to its 'Lykourgan' origins (Hodkinson 1997: 84; Murray 1990b: 10), and some brigades in the Spartan army were classed as 'Dorian' units (Tyrtaios frag. 19.8). By the fifth century, then, the Doric linguistic status quo could be 'read backwards' into a number of different regional mythic histories (Hall 1997a: 170–9). Notably, given the close cultural links between Crete and Thera by Archaic times, Thera too shows use of a Doric dialect by the fifth century: the island claimed the status of a direct Spartan colony in the fifth century. This supports the idea that the physical proximity of areas like Crete and Thera to the south Pelopennese led to close cultural links over time, and that in Archaic to Classical times these linkages were, where possible, constructed within a colonial-type model centred on Sparta and promoted and reinforced through linguistic and other cultural forms (Hall 1995a: 85; Malkin 1994: 15–43, 67–115). While small Thera *was* appropriate for a colonial model, Crete was much less so, as we have seen. This fact is reflected in the always more ambiguous and/or divergent traditions of identity and language in the island. Distinctively Spartan political features appeared in Thera and its neighbours at a late date and probably *were* directly exported as a package, as a result of the political alliance: the governing council on Thera (and also on Melos, Knidos, and Kythera) by the fifth century was a council of ephors, for example. At exactly the same time, overtly Athens-aligned states in others of the Aegean islands were also deliberately adopting (or having imposed on them) various aspects of political culture, as well as language, from Athens in order to strengthen this link. As Greek polities started to align themselves within large leagues, 'Dorianism' provided a continuingly powerful trope by which to facilitate the process in the southwest Aegean, just as Ionianism did in the central and east Aegean. In Crete's case, at least, it seems that identity linkage with Sparta and Dorianism was not imposed upon a unitary allied population but was actively sought and assimilated at different levels by a number of different Cretan communities, being regularly reshaped and re-presented in the process (Erickson 2004: 210).

Crete's 'otherness' and its economic correlates

Despite increasingly formalized identity links with the Peloponnese in the Classical period, it seems that Crete continued, at one level, to be viewed as 'other' by much of the rest of the Greek world: it was noted by Aristotle, for example, as having no very active role in pan-Aegean affairs, a fact highly conducive to internal stability (*Politics* 1272b20–1). In Part Three, I observed that late EIA Crete had an unusual status in the world of trade, with a much weaker, more mixed, and more eastern-linked exchange identity than other Aegean areas. Interestingly, the *Odyssey* passage already quoted, touching broad ethnic groupings in Crete, lacks any reference to the deep-rooted and strong eastern connections reflected in the flourishing of sites like Kommos, in the growing import-substitution industry for orientalising products (surely involving some resident eastern workers), and in the high consumption of eastern trade goods. The general interest of this passage is in linking Crete to the *Aegean* world, in the context of emerging pan-Hellenic epic. Later texts reveal more about Crete's status as a partial outsider or exception within this world. Elsewhere in the Homeric epics, too, Sherratt has shown that these aspects of Crete's identity/associations *are* represented – and in a negative way. She notes that definition of 'Greek' identity within the epics as a whole is often against a symbolic 'other', personified in the Near Eastern/Phoenician trader/adventurer, whose characteristics of greed and cunning are presented as antithetic to 'Greek' heroic virtues (Morris 2000: 228–34; Sherratt 1994: 81–5, 1996: 90; Winter 1995). Sherratt argues that this antieastern definition of 'Greekness' was rooted in the recurrent economic instability linked to the circulation of eastern commodities prior to and during state formation. In this kind of polarised context, a decidedly ambiguous perception of Crete might well be expected to develop, and Sherratt notes in this regard the Cretan links of the negatively presented Phoenician trader with whom Odysseus travels and the symbolism of the untrustworthy Cretan character he impersonates.

In the late Archaic to Classical periods, with the growth of an export market in bulk subsistence products across the Aegean region in which Crete is likely to have been an active participant, the island's trade status may have become less extraordinary – yet it remained incompletely integrated into the core of the Hellenic identity. It was the home of a great many small feuding states, difficult to deal with individually in a political or economic sense. These lacked either the level of unitary cohesion or the kind of strong recent history of cultural 'branding' to become major players in the colonial or commodity export spheres. Central Greek states were variously willing to trade intensively with the island, ally themselves politically with parts of it, link their history and myth to it, and accord respect to its traditions. Their economic and political interest in the island as a market and provisioning point, and increasingly as a strategic military ally, was significant. But as neither a neat colonial unit nor a direct peer area, it remained set apart from all of them to some degree.

It is interesting to compare Crete in this respect with the northern Aegean and with Ionia. Like Crete, these areas had developed relatively complex societies long before the main take-off period of colonisation in the western Mediterranean and cannot be seen as colonial zones of the same type, notwithstanding the official colonial status of some of their polities during the Archaic to Classical period. Ionia shared with Crete the position of a gateway to the east Mediterranean commodity trade core. Yet like Crete's, its social and cultural systems had been so long tied into those of the Aegean that they could never be easily manipulated or annexed through access to 'Greek' culture. During the trade and colonial boom of the late EIA-Archaic period the Ionian communities (whether operating as a loose consortium of states, as at Naukratis, or at the level of individual regions or polities) developed a dynamic peer relationship with the central Aegean in political and trade terms, in a way Crete did not. The ultimate reasons for this seem to be Crete's unusual type of 'successful' collapse at 1200 BC (which allowed an exceptionally high number of strong, small, and complex political units to develop in the island from a very early date) combined with its consistently inwardly orientated position regarding the export commodity trade (which was also, as we have seen, related back to the conditions of its collapse circa 1200 BC).

The northern Aegean also contrasted with Crete in two important ways. It housed major raw material resources of its own, as well as routes for their trade through the Balkan region, and had very differently structured economic and political systems to those of the central Aegean, producing an environment in which the 'Hellenic' cultural identity package developing from the Geometric period onward was marketable (although more familiar, and accessible at closer range, than in most colonial areas). These facts, and the fact that the region suffered only limited collapse circa 1200 BC gave it a head start in developing autonomous prosperity during the EIA, and resulted in a distinctive variation on the colonial model.

Conclusions

Hall's comment that Classical origin myths should be 'viewed as the means by which ethnic communities "thought themselves" in the historical period' seems highly apposite for Crete, a region for which reading any of the identity-related traditions literally, or in isolation, proves extremely problematic (Hall 1997a: 2). We have seen how emphases in identity-related traditions altered, along with political outlooks, over time. In particular, the claims of long-established ethnic links between Crete and other Aegean regions appearing by the Classical period seem heavily developed and promoted to support the expanding scale of political and economic alliances. The number of individually identifying polities in the island reduced during the course of the Classical period, as state sizes and external alliances expanded. Yet polity-level identities never entirely disappeared within a uniform 'Cretan-ness': large states remained able to take up independent, often divergent positions in the wider political arena. By the third century, moves were made to mobilise 'Cretan-ness' in a pragmatic way, with a number of large poleis collaborating formally within a Cretan league, or *koinon* (Willetts 1977: 179–80). Yet this still excluded some important cities, and interpolity conflicts could still be fierce.

Despite its identity links with the wider Hellenic world, Crete retained clear differences from central Greece in geopolitical orientation – it never became embedded within the large mainland leagues or their conflicts, such as the Sacred and Peloponnesian Wars. Latterly it sought assistance and support as much from Egyptian or east Aegean states as from those of central Greece in its internal conflicts: Magnesia on the Maeander famously arbitrated in the Hierapytna-Itanos dispute in the late third century, and a Ptolemaic garrison was based at Itanos until 145 BC (Viviers 1999: 230).

The peculiar history of Cretan identity structures causes us once again to question generalising, processual-type models of ancient states' development and operation. Yoffee (1997: 258–9) notes that a common characteristic of city-states is a view of themselves as part of a wider collective/ethnic group, ultimately connected by genealogy. This model applies well to the pan-Hellenic cultural and ethnic framework, which helped promote many aspects of growth in the small states of Archaic to Classical Greece, such as colonial outreach and the formation of large political leagues. Crete's failure either to participate fully in this identity framework or to achieve its own unified identity held it back in these respects, yet it retained the city-state structure.

Interestingly, most Archaic to Classical ethnicity traditions about Crete did not clearly distinguish between LBA history prior to the disruptions circa 1200 BC and the period of crisis itself – though the 'Eteocretan' myth recounted by Herodotus refers to the Trojan War era (usually seen as corresponding best to the late LBA) as a distinct horizon of crisis and population shift. This lack of distinction contrasts strongly with the picture offered by the archaeological evidence for the construction of, and symbolic reference to, identity in the EIA-early Archaic period, where the two phases *are* distinguished. It may be connected to the late date of most relevant written sources. As the crisis horizon became further removed in time, and the pan-Hellenic identity, with its strong references to the epic tradition, became more powerful, generic Bronze Age narratives seem to have come more into play in representations of Cretan identity. Certainly, in the 'blueprint' for Crete that had come into circulation in literary, philosophical, and political spheres by the fourth century BC, the character of Crete's political structure is often linked to the rule of Minos (Perlman 2005).

38 SERFDOM AND SLAVERY IN THE CONSTRUCTION OF LATE ARCHAIC TO CLASSICAL SOCIETY: COMPARISONS BETWEEN CRETE AND OTHER AEGEAN AREAS

Introduction

Slave systems were characteristic of many ancient societies, typified as the latter were by high-risk, agriculturally based economies and authoritarian rulership and legal structures, with wage labour markets limited or absent (Andrewes 1982a; Cartledge 2002b; Cartledge et al. 2002; Finley 1980: 67–93, 1999: 62–123; Fisher 1993; Osborne 1995; Vernant and Vidal-Nauquet 1988; Vidal-Nauquet 1974). The Linear B record suggests that unfree (slave or bonded) labour systems had existed in the palatial states of the Late Bronze Age Aegean, but the twelfth-century collapse must have fragmented the resources needed to support these systems on any large scale (Chadwick 1976: 77–84; Ventris and Chadwick 1973: 123–5). In Crete, the wholly new settlement and territorial structure developing from circa 1200 BC would make it very difficult for most families to support large numbers of labouring dependents directly. Yet during the PG-A period, as complex institutions, including formalised landholding, emerged and territories enlarged, land-tied labour seems to have grown up as an important feature of the economy.

In Archaic to Classical Greece as a whole, we know that a number of different types of bound labour operated, described by a variety of terms. Alongside the term *doulos* (slave), appearing in texts from Archaic onwards and derived from Mycenaean Greek (*do-er-os*), *woikeus* is used to mean a serf, and *katakoimonos* a generic 'bondsman', in the Gortyn Law Code (Willetts 1967: 12–17). The term *apetairos*, also used in the Code, is not well understood but may indicate a standing between serf and citizen, perhaps applying to citizens of conquered poleis, as I have discussed earlier: *apetairoi* received privileges such as lower fines for rape (*IC* IV.72II.5). *Penestai* in Thessaly and *helotai* in Laconia also seem to correspond broadly to 'serfs', although each term represents something slightly different (Finley 1980: 69; Fisher 1993: 22–34). Thus, though land-bound labour was not characteristic of one type of state only, the different state forms within which it operated conditioned its precise structure in different ways.

In most regions, some form of chattel slavery had clearly begun to operate by the sixth century. Making slaves of war captives is a practice familiarly referred to by Homer (*Odyssey* 15.403–4, 17.320–3), and body-slavery for debt existed by the time of Solon's rule in Athens (Fisher 1993: 11; Harris 2002a). In the following discussion I will briefly compare labour systems in Athens, Crete, and Sparta, analysing the environmental, historical, social, and cultural factors that contributed to differences between these systems, and showing how these differences seem to have affected the fortunes of these regions in the long term.

Athens

Though their precise character is much debated, Solon's reforms of 597 BC helped map out a new course for bound labour in Athens (Andrewes 1982a; Foxhall 1997; Harris 1997; Wallace 1997). Plutarch describes *stasis*, or social disorder, prevailing in this period. Solon himself referred to his reforms as involving the 'removal of the boundary stones/borders [*horoi*] from the land', 'lifting of burdens' [*seisachtheia*], 'ending of enslavement of the poor', and 'restoring honour' (Aristotle *Constitution of Athens* 5–12; Harris 1997: 105–6; Plutarch *Life of Solon* 15.5, 16.3, 19). Membership of, and ranking within, the landowning classes seems to have been redefined by the state at this point, with significant administrative, political, and tax-raising implications. The same phase of reforms also included an enlargement of the state's governing council, though property qualifications still applied to membership in it.

The background to these changes seems likely to be as follows: by the end of the seventh century considerable amounts of land were probably being worked on a tied basis by people who had once owned them. Rising inequality in an agriculturally dependent economy, where landownership lay close to the core of political life, had promoted land-tied debt in the general way I suggested for Crete in Part Four. As a result, it seems that the territory of the polis was no longer felt to 'belong' to a suitably wide spread of citizen owners, in the spirit of the consensual ideology that had first consolidated the state and was still central to its existence (Cohen 2002: 101–2; Foxhall 1997: 220; Xenophon *Hellenica* 6.2.23). Citizens working their own or their recent ancestors' former holdings on others' behalf may have felt humiliated and disempowered, and growing imbalances in land control may have threatened the integrity of the citizen body as a group of nominal equals. Plutarch's account (*Life of Solon* 13.2) explains that 'the *demos*' was 'beholden' to the rich (ο δήμος ην 'ύπόχρεως των πλουσίων). A striking point about these developments, if Solon's law is a direct response to them, is that they had occurred so quickly after the state's emergence and consolidation, probably thanks to the very rapid growth of the economy in this period (Fisher 1993: 16, 38).

The proportion of produce paid over by those who farmed each indebted piece of land may have been relatively small. The amount of one-sixth, suggested by the use of the term *hektemoros* for these debtors, compares favourably to Venetian feudal arrangements, where up to a half of produce was paid to landowners (Fisher 1993: 15; Gasparis 1997: 115) and to what we might guess, by extension, about Mycenaean palatial sharecropping systems as hinted at in the Linear B tablets (Halstead 1999c, 2001). Perhaps alternative interpretations of this term – that the debtor *retained* only one-sixth of the produce or had the right to harvest only a sixth of any land plot – are more accurate. In any of these cases, the use of this standardised term to describe a large group of debtors hints that the amount due in such arrangements was already a standard one, perhaps regulated by law.

Solon's reforms appear to have been intended to 'free' the land and restore honour to indebted citizens by relieving the level of debt, though it is hard to know exactly how this was achieved (Harris 1997). The debt, or an equivalent land share, may have been purchased, perhaps at an artificially low price, by the state. If in land form, this was perhaps retained as public land. But such a solution would still leave the problem of future land- or person-tied debt arising. Direct personal enslavement for debt seems to have been abolished by the reforms, but land-tied labour and debt clearly continued to exist afterwards (Fisher 1993: 36; Harris 2002a: 420–1). To sustain confidence in borrowing transactions (essential to maintaining the integrity of the state and its status among its peers) yet discourage the same kind of crisis from arising again, new measures seem likely to have been put in place as part of, or alongside, the reforms (Harris 2002a: 429).

One of these may have been the promotion of completely non-landholding-based livelihoods to the poorest of the landowning classes – now defined legally as *thetes,* with access only to the minimum of citizen rights. These were the people most likely to become indebted again (Hornblower 1992: 4) and may now have been encouraged to take up work as paid labourers on others' land or turn to manufacturing or industrial tasks (Fisher 1993: 7, 12, 47; Hesiod *Works and Days* 441–72, 597–600). As such, they could easily be pushed to or beyond the margins of citizen status and permanently disenfranchised. Many new opportunities were arising in the manufacturing sector as a result of changing economic conditions. Athens, already a prosperous trading state and significant commodity-manufacturing centre, was on the cusp of a major export boom. In the absence of waged labour, large-scale involvement in the manufacture or exchange of export goods had hitherto probably been limited to individuals able to make a considerable financial investment or to small joint investor groups. Such investment was difficult for a large proportion of citizens, who held small-scale land-based capital in a high-risk environment (Hesiod *Works and Days* 689–94; Morris 2002: 35). The development of a wider, more complex patronage system to support these activities may now have been pursued under state encouragement. The steady rise of Athenian exports like fine pottery, lead, and silver during the course of the sixth and fifth centuries, as well as the city's monumental building programme, was clearly heavily supported through the use of chattel slaves. As Solon's reforms marked out bolder division lines between citizens deriving an adequate and comfortable maintenance from their land and the smallest marginal landowners, some of the latter may have been increasingly pressured to relinquish their grip on the land through total repurchase of their holdings by the state. As well as freeing them from debt, this might help push some of them towards participation in a patronage-based system of commodity production, while others became dependent landless labourers (Fisher 1993: 19). As a result, the commodity sector would become increasingly profitable for the very rich, making them less likely to complain about the loss of revenue from land-bound labour.

Over time, in the absence of a wage economy, highly unequal patronage relations could well turn into chattel slavery, and this process seems best to account for the changing class and wealth profile of Athens by the fifth century (Finley 1980: 90–2; Fisher 1993: 12; Ober 1989: 53–75, 198–289; Wood 1988). Pressure or encouragement to enter slavery as an alternative to low-rewarding and insecure independent or tied labour is not unknown in the historical record, including that of nineteenth-century America (Scheidel 2002: 178). The theoretical possibility of the slave's buying back his freedom always existed, making slavery appear to some extent an open-ended option (Fisher 1993: 58–79). An alternative notion long put forward about the chattel slave sector – that it was developed and sustained entirely by immigrants or war captives – cannot easily account for the rapid growth of such a large slave population and the eventual extreme dependence of the Athenian economy upon it (Cartledge 2002b: 162; Kyrtatas 2002). By the end of the fifth century Finley suggests Athens may have had sixty thousand slaves, and at the level of individual patronage, an indication of the wide-ranging reliance on slaves is given by such facts as that Demosthenes' father had fifty-two/fifty-three slave-craftsmen, or that Lysias inherited one hundred slaves (Finley 1980: 80). The building up of the slave class worked greatly to the advantage of the state body as a whole, in allowing investment in public works and gains in taxes levied on trade (Harris 2002b).

Foxhall (1997: 114) argues that Solon's reforms mostly benefited 'middling' citizen landlords, by restoring debt-ridden lands to them at little cost to them and restrengthening the ideals on which the polis had been founded. The drawing of new, stronger lines between economic classes seems likely to have strengthened and contracted the citizen class and made it more dynamic. The very rich lost out by debt repurchase/cancellation but may have been mollified by the fact that an increased number of small former landowners now started to become available as dependent labour. The latter lost any political influence but (at least at first) improved their subsistence security. Solon's conclusion that his reforms pleased either rich or poor only to a limited extent seems to reflect these various effects.

Crete

In Crete, land-tied labour seems to have retained a much more dominant and more stable role through the Archaic and Classical periods. The formalisation of land-tied indebted labour systems had probably started here longer ago and developed more gradually during a smoother process of settlement nucleation, territory expansion, and complexity growth, in which historically resonant identity structures were closely attached to particular territories (Figure 200). For these reasons, no concentrated, radical demand for debt redistribution ever seems to have developed at an influential level. By the Archaic period, in any case, governance structures had already become solidly dominated by oligarchical groupings, so the expectation of, and pressure for, notionally equal shares in the state and its land seen within a large citizen class like that of Athens was lacking. The fixed economic preeminence of a few clans produced a generally less competitive economic environment, involving less extreme and destabilising movements of subsistence resources through borrowing and lending. Because increased complexity in the trade economy had appeared after, or at the same time as, settlement nucleation and the related rise of complex, stable social institutions, there was little chance, either, for trade-related fluctuations to promote exaggerated, unstable borrowing and lending. The inward-orientated character of the Cretan trade in value goods meant citizens had few incentives to pledge or sell their land or its produce in order to finance investment in export manufacture. For this reason, too, there was less pressure to expand the landless slave population to support commodity manufacture. It is impossible to separate all these factors from each other in terms of chronology or causation, but together they go a long way to illuminate Crete's different trajectory.

Another feature of the Classical Cretan polis – long-lasting attritive warfare – is also likely to have helped maintain the role of serfdom, and vice versa. The risk of catastrophic economic loss or population displacement during the regular conflicts affecting Cretan states would be minimised by the spread-out patterns of serf residence and tight physical attachment to the land. Conquering states had little reason to try to dislodge this pattern: in fact, leaving serf systems in situ would aid social stability after annexation, allowing easy revenue gathering. What *was* sacrificed as a result of the general strength of serf systems was the absolutely secure control of a conquered territory. Given Crete's history of many densely packed very small states and strong regional identity structures, strong relationships between groups working the land in adjoining territories would surely persist, however often borders changed through conquest, making these borders always insecure to some extent (Aristotle *Politics* 1269a39–b3).

Yet again, attempts to model the Greek city-states' emergence and development as part of a predictable, standardised process fall rather flat when we look at Crete's attachment to serfdom. Stone's (1997) model, based on Bronze Age Mesopotamia, suggests that only large territorial states offer a permanent economic role for formal landholding, while city-state economies tend to rely more on a fluid labour system, often tied into lineage structures. This model is too polarised to be meaningful even for Archaic Athens. Landowning stayed important in distinguishing and maintaining the citizen class here, even *while* the labour market was becoming increasingly fluid. In Crete's small states we also see the importance of formalised landholding, but combined with a more static labour sector. In contrast to Mesopotamia, formalised mass labour control and highly centralised territorial state structures were never required to make large areas of land productive in the Aegean. A variety of labour/landholding relationships were thus available within the small state format, and their particular configuration was tied into the social history of each state. In Crete, friction between so many developing small state units, together with the strong lineage basis of social structures and the dominance of serf labour, prevented the emergence of very large territories ruled in a centralised way. Many central Greek states seem to have been able to expand more easily, thanks partly to their history, but perhaps also to their more flexible labour systems and the fact that more of their prosperity was based on value goods trade.

Laconia and Messenia

In Laconia, serf systems of a complex and varied nature clearly held a significant role into Classical times (e.g., Aristotle *Politics* 2.9; Herodotus 6.58. 2–3; Plato, *Laws* 6.776; Tyrtaios frag. 5; Cartledge 2002a: 138–79; Ducat 1990; Fisher 1993: 23–32; Hodkinson 1986, 1992, 2000: 65–151; Powell 1988: 248–52). In the study of the origins and historical impact of serfdom, Laconia's history provides an especially interesting comparison to Crete. The nature of collapse at circa 1200 BC, conditioned by each region's earlier history, seems likely to have encouraged especially strong small-scale attachments to land to develop in both areas, which were eventually formalised within state systems. However, differences in the scale of the systems involved, in the subsequent history of social institutions and identity construction, and in geopolitical outlook and standing, all contributed to giving serfdom a different role and structure in each region.

The extreme degree of nucleation from a spread of existing large and prosperous LBA settlements that probably occurred in Laconia from circa 1200 BC must have created a very large single territory incorporating multiple landowners, all with strong residual attachment to their traditional territories. Significant inequalities are likely to have existed between them from soon after the shift, based on the quality of these lands and their distance from the new centre of occupation. The serf relationships of the Spartan state seem to have emerged in this environment through a normal process of indebtedness, but to have developed at two or more different levels, as a result of this region's particular history and topography (Cartledge 2001: 82–3). While the inner Spartan territory contained serf holdings owned and controlled directly by the local residents, it seems holdings covering the more remote, poorer-quality arable land of the Helos plain were administered by Spartan citizens in plots allocated by the state, suggesting an early and generalized level of inequality between the inhabitants of this region and those of the inner Laconian area. At least some groups of helots seem to have been directly state managed and to have carried out public functions (Fisher 1993: 25; Hodkinson 2000: 113–51). The location of the plain, relatively close to Sparta and between the city and the sea, made its control an early, permanent, and unavoidable concern for Sparta residents as a body from an early date, giving the state a continuing interest in its management.

Subjugate or weak polities/groups within the wider Spartan region (*perioikoi*) also paid tithe or tribute by Classical times, but directly to the state, rather than to individual landowners, and in proportionally smaller amounts (Hall 2000). The tenor of these relationships seems to have been rooted in power balances negotiated during the course of the EIA-Classical period between the emergent Spartan polity and entire polities, rather than individuals, in outlying regions. This contrasts with the very long-established and direct control relationship with the Helos plain communities. The *perioikoi* were never fully conquered or otherwise integrally linked to the

Spartan state but controlled such extensive areas that they were an important component of the Spartan economy.

In yet another pattern of labour control, the Spartan state seems to have transferred the helotage system and its nomenclature into the neigbouring Messenian territory after its conquest in the seventh century, allocating to individual Spartan citizens the responsibility for supervision of each serf holding and the right to profits from it (Alcock 2002). With its history of functioning as a single political core for a very large territory, Sparta always differed in scale and ambition from any Cretan state. As well as expanding into Messenia, it was challenging Argos by the mid-seventh century. A second Messenian War occurred in the second half of the seventh century, and Sparta also led campaigns against Arkadian poleis, before being defeated at Tegea in the sixth century (Cartledge 2001: 102, 117; Hall 2000: 82; Tyrtaeus frag. 5.7). It effectively became a territorial state with very wide-ranging international influence, being asked by Croesus to ally itself with Lydia in the later sixth century (Herodotus 1.69). The powerful Corinth, long Sparta's gateway and proxy in trade, also became an ally in 525 BC, though battles with Argos continued. Many scholars have attributed this early and aggressive territorial spread to a search for land, and certainly the expansion is different from the trade-centred overseas colonisation of other central Greek states, in that it happened at close range and often took place through movement over land. As such, the expansion is closely bound up with issues of land-bound labour. I doubt that Sparta's early territorial expansion had much to do with overpopulation in subsistence terms. It seems, rather, to have been an alternative way of increasing economic and political standing in the absence of a dynamic export trade.

In Messenia, the mode of violent conquest and subjugation through which Spartan-controlled serf labour arrived seems to have created a subtly different, more overtly oppressive form of serfdom from that found in Sparta's closer hinterlands (Alcock 2002; Cartledge 2001: 148; Hammond 1982; Hodkinson 2000: 128–9). While the precise shares of produce paid over by Laconian serfs to landowners may have varied, Messenian serfs all seem to have had to offer a full half of their produce to Spartan masters. The physical format of serfdom was also different. Rather than being spread out in small landholdings, the population appears to have lived nucleated in sizeable villages of circa three hectares each and some much larger settlements, up to forty hectares – easier to collect contributions from, though more difficult to control politically.

Structural links between serfdom and political conservatism

The geopolitical relations of major mainland states, including Sparta, developed on a very different level from those of Crete, involving the emergence of very large territories with very long exposed borders and a massive scale of operations and resources during the Archaic period (Hall 2000: 81). The greater degree of hierarchy and complexity within Laconian serfdom seems to reflect this large scale of operations, and allowed/required serfdom to function as a context of repression at home, as well as abroad, in a way not seen in Crete. At the same time, it made the serf sector in general a less stable and controllable entity than was the case in Crete. One of the most important elements of Cretan serfdom by the sixth century was the fact that serfs had legal rights set well above those of slaves (Harris 2002a: 419; Willetts 1967: 12–17). It is not clear when these rights were attained, and how far they resulted from periodic rebellion or pressure to reform – these were not generally features of Cretan states' histories, as we have seen. The Gortyn Code shows serf entitlements as changing over time, suggesting that there *was* some need for continued and controlled concessions to this class in the interest of social order. Ultimately, though, the large size of the serf group and its always relatively high social standing, together with the well-established oligarchical rulership structures and rigid age-class system operating in the island, all seem to have contributed to the long-term stability of the Cretan state. Together, they discouraged the build-up of enough class cohesion to exert major pressure for change in governance, whether in the form of demands for more participative government or support for the rise of tyrants.

In the Laconian case, there seems to have been more pronounced social differentiation and mobility within a more complex serf class – opportunities to move in or out of it into the sub-citizen classes of *neodamodeis* and *hypomeiones* were relatively frequent (Bruni 1979; Ducat 1990: 155–73; Fisher 1993: 24; Hodkinson 1983; Talbert 1989). This offered more opportunities for pressures to build against the political status quo. Perhaps because of this volatility, it seems that the ultimate dividing line between the citizen class and the rest, including serfs, needed to be more aggressively drawn in Sparta than in Crete, with serfs in Sparta having fewer legal and social privileges than Cretan ones. In Sparta, participation in the common meal was the privilege of citizens. In Crete, 'slaves' (δούλοι) were also allowed to take part (though payment was required, suggesting that the slaves referred to in this case were in fact serfs: Athenaeus *Deipnosophistae* 4.143). We find no parallels in Crete for the forms of structured, state-sponsored ill treatment and oppression of serfs seen within Laconia and in the Messenian territory, or the apparently constant awareness of a need to keep the whole serf class under control (Ducat 1990: 107–27; Fisher 1993: 27; Plutarch *Life of Lykourgos* 20, 28; Powell 1988: 221–2). The preceding features are also likely to relate to the very highly centralised and long-distance operation of parts of the Spartan serf system: much of the serf class was literally and politically distant from the citizen core, in a way not seen in the relatively small Cretan states with their proportionally large serf classes – and thus was less controllable and more volatile. Ultimately, this large and geographically spread-out underclass could not be prevented from posing a threat to the state structure, and attempts at repression may even have hastened this. In the sixth century a Messenian serf revolt seriously weakened Sparta's control of the region, and there were other periodic attempts at organized rebellion, though the territory only became independent in the early fourth century (Ducat 1990: 129–53; Talbert 1989).

While Archaic Sparta was formally a monarchy, we have noted that its form of governance was in some ways more participatory than that seen in Cretan states. It developed further along this route in Classical times. The scale and structuring of serfdom here seem likely to have helped to bring pressure for change to bear. The economic support available to the single main core at Sparta from the very extensive territories under serf production freed a large citizen elite for participation in politics, as slavery and the commodity trade did in Athens. The military support offered by large blocs of serfs in the army allowed the Spartan state to undertake the major campaigns that made it a first-ranking Aegean power.

In Crete, serfdom's role as a powerhouse of political change was more limited. The greater economic and political risk, as well as the greater expansive potential, invested in Sparta's very large and mixed serf population was lacking. These differences are reflected in political and economic practice and custom. Spartan custom became notoriously concerned with blocking competitiveness among citizens in the form of luxury goods consumption. This stance seems to have been necessary to keep the large citizen class and complex, socially mobile serf sector coherent and stable. Cretan societies, in contrast, were able to permit much more of this kind of inequality within an ultimately more securely bounded and stable political framework. In both cases, it seems that the strength of serf systems ultimately limited the possibility of rapid change in the basis of political and social power, though to different degrees. On one hand, a large serf class in both areas allowed significant levels of social mobility. On the other, the presence of this large buffering class between the citizen and slave groups blunted any very dynamic or radical political action (whether of a top-down or bottom-up character) threatening the stability of the state body (Fisher 1993: 1, 7).

Like Crete and Sparta, the *ethnos* states tended to retain serfdom as a strong feature of their economy right through the Classical period. Here, too, it appears that there was very early and long-term attachment to particular land parcels (perhaps often at tribal rather than individual or family level) and that potential for the rise of extreme economic inequality may have been bounded by lineage structures. As in the case of Crete, there was no strong large-scale central authority or dynamic export sphere that could exert pressure to rebalance the whole basis of the economy. Again, the flourishing of serfdom seems closely tied into a political structure insulated from violent change, with limits on the growth of inequality (Garnsey and Morris 1989: 101).

39 THE PUBLIC FEASTING TRADITION AND ITS POLITICAL SIGNIFICANCE IN CRETE AND OTHER AREAS

The social role of feasting: a summary

The equalizing and bonding symbolism of the feast had an obvious public niche in all consensually structured states of the Archaic to Classical period, but the multiple subgroups within the state could also use this flexible mode of formal interaction as a distinguishing and internally bonding practice (Schmitt-Pantel 1990). There was never only one mode or level of commensality in any region of Archaic-Classical Greece, though substantial differences in emphasis by area do appear.

The public common meal and its venue (*syssition/andreion*) are noted by Classical authors as a particularly distinctive feature of the Cretan polis (Aristotle *Politics* 1271a26, 1329a40; Athenaeus *Deipnosophistae* 4.143; Plato *Laws* 1.625; Strabo, citing Ephorus, 10.4.18). In Part Two I presented evidence to suggest that secular communal feasting was an important binding institution for twelfth- and eleventh-century Cretan communities, while noting that aggrandising groups often seem to have used (and even to have tried to appropriate) public feasting as a means of status building. Ceremonial feasting continued to be used in both ways in Crete into the LG period, with a resonance strongly linked to that of public cult and of the past. As wealth and status relations became more fixed and represented in more abstract ways within the state, feasting took on an increasingly specialized and symbolic role: emphasis turned to its public, communal dimension, reinforcing the concepts of clan and polity coherence.

The common citizen meal (*phidition*) played a major role at Sparta; it was used by various writers to symbolise the peculiar structure of the Spartan state, and to link it with Crete in the generalised alternative 'blueprint' to Athens described by Perlman (2005), though in fact there were many differences in the role of feasting between the two regions (Aristotle *Politics* 1271a27–38, 1272a13–28; Hodkinson 1997: 90–2; Perlman 2005: 309–11; Xenophon *Spartan Constitution* III.5.1–7). Participation in the meal at Sparta was presented as a citizen's obligation, rather than a benefit provided by the state: contributions of rations were made directly by citizen participants. Xenophon attributed a moral and disciplinary function to the ceremony in controlling excessive personal ostentation through hospitality, as well as a practical role in supporting the citizen assembly (and thus participative government) in a literal sense. In Crete, with its low-participation politics, history of limited internal economic tensions, and general lack of need (because of its very well-entrenched oligarchic structure) to restrict competitive consumption, such issues seem less relevant. The Cretan common meal seems to have been financed more heavily by the state through tax and contributions from public land, though rich individuals could make substantial contributions: highly placed hereditary officials like the scribe/remembrancer Spensithios were required by law to supply fixed contributions of food to the *andreion* every year and received their salaries from the state partly in food. Such practices made a highly symbolic statement about the land- and produce-vested basis of the state's authority and the nature of membership in the state as a literal share in and responsibility for that base (Jeffery and Morpurgo Davies 1970). Serfs were allowed to take part in the meal, but they had to pay directly for this privilege, excluding them from the citizens' sense of entitlement (Athenaeus *Deipnosophistae* 1.143). Undermining this formal symbolism, the actual amounts of food that an individual or clan contributed or claimed in the feast, like their attendance, might vary depending on circumstances and need over time, being only notionally 'equal'.

In Athens and other central Greek states, feasting occurred in groups of various sizes and compositions, and within a number of different spaces (Cooper and Morris 1990; Lombards 1988: 263–86; Mazarakis Ainian 1997: 375–96; Murray 1983, 1990a, 1990c; Nevett 1999: 154–75; Whitley 2001: 296–300, 309–10, 341–65, 361–2). Several types of civic-zone building acted as venues for this activity at a number of different levels. They included the *stoa* (apparently used for everyday dining by private citizen groups) and the *tholos*, *prytanikon*, and *prytaneion*, buildings used by members of the governing councils, officials, and state guests. A 'public mess' (εν δημοσίω σιτήσεως) is additionally also referred to at Athens by the sixth century (Plutarch *Life of Solon* 24.3). Ritual dining also occurred in purpose-built complexes at major sanctuaries, and there were elaborate feasts at funerals. Small citizen groups dined formally together in the *symposion*, held in private houses. As public cult became the solid centre of civic life in the late eighth century, the *symposion*, with its ostentatious consumption and display of luxury products, seems to have helped balance and contain the kind of personal wealth display that had formerly been concentrated in funerary settings or uncontrolled semi-public feasting events. The ceremony took on an ever more elaborate form through the Archaic and Classical periods (Murray 1990a).

As we have seen, the need to constrain personal wealth competition and display was not a core feature in Cretan state emergence. In this light, it seems significant that we lack either text or archaeological evidence for the *symposion* in Crete, though given the limited nature of the studied archaeological record, the question remains open. The small number of houses it has been possible to study in Archaic to Classical Cretan towns seem to have lacked spaces dedicated to sympotic activity, even though the average house had apparently expanded in size since the EIA (Westgate in press). Yet the limited evidence we have suggests that public ceremonial dining in Crete did have other aspects than the *syssition* and was affected by similar considerations to those operating in central Greece. As on the mainland, large extra-settlement sanctuaries in Crete, such as Kato Simi, appear to have had some attached public dining facilities, facilitating the meeting and bonding of groups from different polities or different parts of a political territory. Within the Cretan polis settlements themselves, there is textual evidence for another kind of dining structure, the *koimetrion*, mentioned by Dosiades (Athenaeus *Deipnosophistae* 4.143) as used for state guests. A *prytaneion*, typically used for hosting state officials and guests, existed at Lato by the third century BC (Ducrey and Picard 1972: 577–9).

The character and use of feasting venues: evidence from texts and archaeology

The physical character of public feasting venues in Archaic to Classical Crete is obscure due to the lack of whole-site plans available for study. The evidence for EIA and early Archaic feasting areas discussed in Parts Two and Four, taken in conjunction with the textual evidence for Classical Cretan feasting, suggests that these always continued to exist as separate spaces. However, even following the find of a probable Archaic *andreion* at Azoria, huge problems remain in establishing exactly how such buildings were used.

A wish to bridge the gap between texts and archaeology has led some scholars onto rather thin ice in this regard. Some have hopefully reidentified Archaic cult buildings with central hearths, such as Kommos Temple A, the Prinias temples, and the Dreros temple, as *andreia* (Bergquist 1990: 41; Carter 1997: 89; Cooper and Morris 1990: 68; Schmitt-Pantel 1990). Prent (2005b: 417–18) has recently suggested an open-air feasting function for the so-called Temple of Rhea in the ruins of the Knossos palace. Somewhat confusingly, she wants to consider this use as of a *symposion* type, despite its isolation from any domestic context. While there is little doubt that food sacrifice and consumption took place in the buildings mentioned, such specialised reidentifications are mostly unconvincing and take us little further forward in interpretation. They fail to recognise that the close architectural and conceptual overlaps/shared frames of reference of the domestic, feasting, and cult spheres, well established in Crete from the early EIA, coexisted with *separately* defined spaces and activities related to each sphere, which also had a long history and had become increasingly formalised and elaborated by the Archaic period. Nor do they pay adequate attention to the site context, associated stratigraphy, and finds in each case. The Kommos temple area, for example, had a long prior history of identifiable cultic use typical of coastal sanctuaries across the Aegean in the EIA-Archaic periods. The site was not a residential settlement, so that whatever practice took place is unlikely to be related either to the domestic *symposion* or to the *andreion*-type public feast. At Dreros, the concentrations of figurines in the temple are completely sidelined in reidentifying it as a feasting building. In the Prinias case, it is clear from distinctive finds, including goddess figurines, that there was a settlement shrine in the location of Temples A and B from the LM IIIC period through to the settlement's abandonment in Archaic; additionally, the use of monumental stone reliefs by the EA period distinguishes this area from any other on the site and matches developments occurring in the cult sphere at about the same time across the Aegean world. Carter (1997: 87–96) suggests an *undifferentiated* cult/private feasting use of one of the final temple buildings at Prinias, or else the specialised feasting use of a nearby building to their east. The idea of a fully 'mixed' venue neglects the strong evidence for clear separation of these spheres in settlement architecture right through the EIA-Archaic periods that I have discussed above, which has been most recently reinforced by the finds of separate *andreion* and cult buildings within the civic zone at Azoria. The idea of a separate *andreion* somewhere in the close vicinity of the Archaic temple at Prinias is much more likely, given the existence of civic zoning in Cretan settlements by this period. On the basis of her assumptions about feasting use of the building, Carter goes further, in using the orientalising character of luxury goods and iconography in this part of the site to suggest that aspects of *sympotic* dining were in part introduced or borrowed to Crete from the east in the Archaic period. Not only is clear evidence for sympotic dining in a domestic context so far absent from the Archaic to Classical record in Crete, but we have seen that the roots of feasting at both public and private levels lie much further back in Cretan history, and that the practice was transformed over time to fit new social conditions. Given that the whole prestige culture, as well as the economic life, of Archaic Crete is tied up deeply with orientalising goods, it is simplistic to source the origins of either cultic or ceremonial feasting *practice* in the east.

Notwithstanding the limitations of the arguments reviewed above, it is worth noting that the Azoria *andreion* assemblage suggests cult practice formed a significant element in the use of public feasting buildings. Dosiades, cited in Athenaeus, records the pouring of a libation to the gods in the Cretan *andreion* before the feast took place. Texts suggest that other ceremonial features of the *syssition* were shared with *symposia* and public feasts on the mainland. Tales of battles and great deeds were recounted, and great men honoured with special dishes (Xenophon *Constitution of the Lakedaimonians* 5.6). At Azoria, a helmet fragment found in one of the *andreion*'s rooms suggests that armour and weapons were kept there, perhaps as badges of state honour and reference points for the tales (Haggis et al. 2004: 375, Figure 26). As elsewhere, then, public feasting in Crete called on cult, and on history/ancestry, as legitimizing, enhancing, and bonding forces and was, like the mainland *symposion*, to some degree symbolically linked to the feasts described in the epics (Hodkinson 1997: 90–1).

Turning to the physical character of the *andreion*, we have already seen that putative public feasting buildings in EIA Crete were unable to house very large groups of people at once (though at large sites they were irregularly supplemented by the use of private houses). By the Archaic period, we would expect feasting venues to have an expanded number of users, as polity size expanded, the role of public feasting was consolidated, and private hosting declined. Yet the buildings in question do not seem to have become proportionately large. The limits of the archaeological evidence and the vagueness of the texts covering this subject mean that the number of people normally using an *andreion* at one time is unclear. Was there more than one *andreion* in each polis settlement, and, if so, how was use divided between them? If large buildings designed for mass-group feasting did ever exist, it seems remarkable that they have not been found, at either excavated or surveyed sites. We cannot exclude that public dining sometimes occurred in the open air, at the council/assembly meeting place or somewhere else within the civic core, but protection against the elements would be desirable for much of the year, and the earlier history of many Cretan polis settlements meant that really large open areas often did not exist within the settlement centre, as we have seen. Using Azoria (a relatively small nucleation) as an example, the capacity to serve a citizen group numbering 1,000 or more individuals (based on a 14ha site size and maximal c. 5,000 population, estimating that up to 50% of the adult male population were citizens) on the daily basis suggested by the texts would have been extremely difficult to organize, even on a rotation schedule, in one building with a main room roughly equivalent in size to the main rooms of the larger houses of the earliest EIA. Within the civic zone, the *andreion* building is a singular feature, but unexcavated parts of the site could still reveal parallel or supplementary structures.

Texts tell us a small amount more about the physical character of feasting buildings. Dosiades (cited in Athenaeus *Deipnosophistae* 4.142) mentions an eventual decline of the principle of equality in the Spartan mess, with the space becoming smaller and more exclusive, and richer coverings beginning to be used for the couches. This suggests that in its heyday the mess was relatively large and simply furnished. Within *andreion* buildings in Crete (citing the case of Lyttos) Dosiades, cited in Athenaeus, notes two tables set apart for 'strangers' – presumably visitors to the polis belonging to ranks less exalted than those using the *koimetrion* or more closely bound into the local citizen body. The bonding role of the meal and the compact nature of the space are emphasised by the information that one cup of wine was shared by the whole participating group. This also suggests a relatively small and manageable group at each feast, even if the 'cup' referred to was a metaphorical one. Pyrgion (cited in Athenaeus *Deipnosophistae* 4.143) notes that the *syssition* was taken in a seated, rather than a reclining, position, distancing it from any luxurious symposion-type associations and linking it to the everyday sphere of public life. This arrangement also allowed the event to take place in a confined context, and the term *syssitikon oikou* used by Dosiades points to a relatively modest building or 'feasting *house*', formally or conceptually paralleling the ordinary domestic structure.

I suggest that relatively modest buildings like the Azoria *andreion* complex did in fact represent the main locales of secular public dining; that the concept of all citizens eating together, even in shifts, every day was an idealised and symbolic one, especially as community size increased; and that feasting buildings of normally relatively small size were used by different parts of the citizen group at different times (and not necessarily on a daily basis by all). If feasting was indeed broken down into small units, these were probably often congruent with extended kin groups or tightly knit groupings of extended kin and affines, like the phratries and sympotic groups of the mainland states. The crucial difference in Crete was that the use of the *syssition* concept and its state financing meant these smaller units embodied and/or contributed to the larger concept of the (oligarchic) state in a relatively seamless way, leaving little room for the *symposion* or any other kind of private feasting group to develop as a direct counterpoint to this important *habitus* of citizen equality. In other regions, the different types and scale of feasting within the state existed to some extent in a relationship of rivalry and tension with one another. The Cretan states show a restricted diversity in feasting practices, with less chance for social mobility through this means. Though extended kin groups might regularly feast together, they could not control the participation of others in the feast, in the way that symposiasts could. Because less exclusive, these dining groups could not wield such specific (and potentially socially disruptive) power as the mainland sympotic groups.

The common meal as political trait: Crete and Sparta compared

The more we learn about the shared features of the Cretan and Spartan states – serfdom, limited involvement in export trade, oligarchical government, and the relative importance of the common meal – the more it seems that all these elements were structurally linked, rather than individually or jointly representing ethnic features (exported or innate) or standard evolutionary stages. Like serfdom, the common meal seems partly related to the especially agriculturally orientated economic focus of both regions, which permanently facilitated (and focused attention on) the vesting of citizen status in land. As communities expanded and territories enlarged, involving potential disruption to land-tied identity structures, both these institutions (in consistently reinforcing the links of the citizen body to the land) had a powerful stabilising, conservatism-promoting role.

On the other hand, differences in the scale of the state, and in the general stability of the social base, affected the role and character of the common meal in each region. In Crete, the extreme dominance of the feasting scene by this form, and its practicability, were promoted by the small size of many poleis, and their consequent vulnerability to outside forces of political and economic disturbance. This encouraged maintenance of the well-rooted and strong internal cohesion that had existed within these states from their origins in the EIA. Spartan society allowed competitive *symposion*-type feasting to exist alongside the common meal and situated the two types of feast in sharp contradistinction to each other. As in other mainland states, it appears that the citizen meal could not easily be consolidated as the single main feasting institution within a large society kept together by relatively fragile citizen bonds and ideals, and that private feasting continued to act as a necessary outlet valve for tensions. However, the fact that Sparta had the ability to maintain the citizen meal as such a strong and characteristic institution does seem connected to the longevity and stability of other aspects of its political framework. In general terms the public meal institution embodied the consensualist ideology of most small Aegean states. However, as a part of political culture that was particularly able to help forestall or hold back extreme leveling swings, it seems to have been especially prominent and valued in those states with a conservative, oligarchic social system. In some ways it functioned as a vent for any pressure towards participative governance, enacting the ideal of citizen equality and participation in a stable and insulated context and symbolically counterbalancing any tendency for oligarchies to overreach the power they had over basic resources.

In many Aegean areas, we have seen that the trade boom occurring from the tenth century onward helped to displace many elements of personal competition and display into the sphere of public cult by the late eighth century. It may have been partly as a result of this very forceful shift that the role of communal dining as a socially insulating mechanism reduced in importance, and/or diversified, in some central Greek regions from at least the eighth century. In contrast, in both the Cretan and Spartan cases (though to different degrees) it seems that lack of full, proactive engagement in the export trade – producing lower social volatility and thus less need for radical displacement of wealth-based competition – helped perpetuate a singular importance for the public common meal into Classical times, as one of a number of stable insulating features. Another kind of link between the type of feasting institutions found in a region and the nature of its economic outlook relates to the role of the *symposion* as a cultural identity marker abroad. The process of market building through the promotion of a Hellenic cultural identity relied heavily on the appeal of this practice: versions of it were taken up with enthusiasm by communities abroad from the eighth century onward. The novel and prestigious equipment involved in the activity and the links of the practice to the Greek epic stories were clearly major factors in its popularity. The custom of feasting among a select group of peers must have helped bridge social gaps between Aegean entrepeneurs and their customers abroad (Leighton 1999: 245). Crete's limited participation in the export trade and colony-building world may have helped to keep the *symposion*'s role there relatively minor, and vice versa. For a major international player like Sparta, the situation was different. Notwithstanding the state's relatively limited role in export trade, the *symposion* clearly had a niche as both a diplomatic tool and a bonding mechanism, both within Sparta and in Spartan activities abroad.

In conclusion, the practice of ceremonial feasting tied states across the Aegean world closely together and linked them all into an illustrious shared mythic history – celebrated and recounted during feasts and through the practice of feasting itself. In many of its forms, it also reinforced (at different levels) the concept of consensual rule lying close to the heart of all these states. At the same time, emphasis on the community-wide common meal was singled out in some Classical texts as a diagnostic feature of states with an accepted degree of 'otherness' and was clearly considered a vitally distinguishing factor in this identity. Notably, however, it is never mentioned as characteristic of the *ethnos* states, which also belonged in the category of 'other' from the point of view of many ancient writers. The meal required central organization and storage and a central venue. As such, it seems ultimately linked to states centred on a single urban entity. Even if the practice took place in shifts or small groups, place (both at landscape and at settlement level) was core to its meaning – helping explain its significant role as a community-defining feature in Crete's densely packed environment of independent polities with similar histories and shifting territorial borders. The common meal concept also seems tightly linked, both notionally and pragmatically, into stable and conservative political systems, rather than those characterised by volatility, tension, and phases of radical change in political structures. If extreme forms of governance – either tyranny or democracy – *had* emerged in Crete or Sparta, their dominant forms of common meal might well have become redundant or marginalised. Democracy might have removed the need for the very regular and literal enactment of citizen equality that these meals represented by replacing them with more direct participation at the cutting edge of politics and an emphasis on diverse forms of small-group dining operating separately from state mechanisms. Tyrannies might have rejected or downsized the practice in favour of big hospitality or generosity gestures on behalf of the tyrant alone. The Cretan and Spartan oligarchies could manipulate state affairs to their advantage by consistently promoting the common meal as a tangible representation of consensualism, while knowing it was intrinsically unlikely to get out of control. In fact, Cretan states seem victims of their own early stable development in this regard. The smooth rise of the collective meal as institution probably held back the growth of diverse private interest groups of the type that stimulated growth, tension, and conflict in mainland polities. In Sparta, the potentially 'fossilising' role of the *phidition* may have been less of an issue, given the scale and variety of the state's interests, contacts, and political and economic base, which made it impossible to smooth out social tensions so easily.

It is interesting, finally, to consider how far collective dining practices on Crete affected women, traditionally barred from the mainland *symposion*. The Gortyn Law Code suggests that citizen women held considerable rights over inheritance and other kin-related matters. In a divorce case, for example, women kept their own property (even though the code generally placed women in a sexual sense under the 'ownership' of their husband; Di Lello-Finuoli 1991; *IC* IV.72.II.20–30, 72.III; Willetts 1977: 217). The generally less-rigid division between the citizen class and 'the rest' in Crete may have enhanced women's social mobility, even while excluding them from executive power. Notably, the Cretan *syssition* is said by Dosiades to have been hosted by a woman, with female assistants; Aristotle suggests (*Politics* 1272a19–24) that women and children of the citizen class also took part in the common meal, though under segregated conditions. These points reinforce how far Cretan communal feasting was from the typically closed, all-male *symposion* context (Athenaeus *Deipnosphistae* 4.143).

40 A FINAL COMPARISON: DEMOCRACY AND ITS ALTERNATIVES IN THE AEGEAN WORLD

Introduction

Classical democracy forms an interesting lens through which to conclude this review of the long-term outcomes of social change in the Aegean from circa 1200 BC. While a consolidation of the consensual ideal in terms of practical politics can be identified in many Aegean regions between the eighth and fifth centuries, most states never developed full democracy as their system of governance (Davies 1993: 24; Morris 1996: 46–7; Raaflaub 1997b: 32). A number of those that did do so consciously followed the model of the fifth-century democracy at Athens, in the direct interests of economic and military alliance with that polity. Democracy, then, was clearly not intrinsic to the viability of the polis state, and indeed some ancient authors presented it as a regrettable and temporary tendency. Its precise structure varied with time and place, but the comparisons I will draw here are mostly with the very broad-based, systematized, and direct type of citizen participation in governance seen at Athens, about which we know most (Davies 1993: 56; Hornblower 1992; Ober 1996; Raaflaub 1997b: 35).

The reasons for which democracy never took hold in Crete seem partly related to social and political trajectories already strongly marked out in the EIA. But developments between the seventh and fifth centuries also play an important role. Crete's structural divergence from central Greek polities, so consistently maintained even during this period of expanding alliances and ever-deeper and more complex connections between Aegean regions, reveals the depth of the gulf between consensualism as concept and structure, and democracy as conscious system and lived reality. Below, I will highlight what I think were the most important conditions preventing the development of democracy in Crete in this period: the previous history of local social systems, the particular orientation of economic frameworks in the island, the level and nature of conflict within and between Cretan states, the generally small scale of their political and economic operations, the broader geopolitical environment in which Crete functioned (and changes in it over time), and the particular structures of political and cultural identity pertaining to Crete and the Cretans in this period.

Issues of collective agency and choice are highly relevant here. The texts show that detailed analyses of political mechanisms, and awareness of the processes of diffusion and emulation that shaped them, were fully current in Aegean society by at least the fourth century. Many choices made about systems of governance were conscious and sophisticated ones, even while also being determined by historical parameters – indeed, as we have seen, 'history' itself was an actively manipulated and highly potent force in this regard. The colonization and empire-building phenomena show that Aegean states of the period were clearly able to adapt, borrow, and integrate elements of other political systems into their own in a conscious, overt, and formal way – though this must have been much less tidy or complete a process than a work like the *Politics* suggests. Ultimately, however, I argue that the historical parameters outlined earlier conditioned Crete's political path so heavily that a positive choice in favour of adopting democracy was never really available for its states.

I will end by using a conceit that returns us to issues in more recent history and politics – what did Crete theoretically *lose* by not developing democracy; how were its societies constrained by this fact? My argument is that it was the preconditions against democracy's emergence that mostly imposed the constraints, rather than the lack of democracy itself, but posing the question helps to clarify and extend this point. Athens flourished under democracy – expanding to dominate many areas of the Aegean in economic and political terms by the end of the fifth century. Did Crete, and other regions that did not develop democracy, suffer restrictions on economic and political growth as a direct or indirect result of this path, and, if so, how did Crete's 'alternative' state system suffer in this regard, in comparison to that of, say, Sparta?

Economy, geopolitics, and democracy: Athens and the Delian League

The operation of the interregional economy was closely bound up with the growth of democracy, just as it had been with the first emergence and consolidation of small consensualist states in the Aegean. For example, we saw previously that the rise of chattel slavery, closely linked to the burgeoning export trade, freed up Athenian citizens to participate in political life and, by increasing their prosperity, gave them a more pressing interest in direct participation. By the fifth century, trade had built the Athenian economy to a level allowing the cost of compulsory participation in politics to be reimbursed to poorer citizens – a difficult and rare achievement in the contemporary Greek world. As we have seen, the large slave sector also created a firmly fixed set of social and economic relations in Athens, limiting social mobility and giving democracy a relatively stable base from which to operate once it emerged. Societies with a greater reliance on serfdom (and a limited commodity export trade), like Crete and to some extent Sparta, seem to have lacked both this clear-cut social division and the fluidity of liquid resources to support mass participation in politics. The large serf sector produced relatively high social mobility, limiting class solidarity, and thus helped retain an uneven concentration of power even within the citizen unit.

Relationships in the trade arena were strongly bound up with wider geopolitical relations, which had their own political impacts, by the fifth century. Unlike Crete, the Ionian states – proactive in trade at an early date and long involved in close interaction with other major Aegean trading groups at home and abroad – became strongly aligned with Athenian political and military initiatives during and after the period of conflict with Persia, in the late sixth through fifth centuries. Given their proximity to the Persian heartland, Athens had a considerable interest in seeking the allegiances of Cycladic and Ionian states, offering them valuable protection in return. This resulted in the formation of the 'Delian League' with Athens at its head. After the victory against the Persians at Marathon, Athens undertook expansion of its influence, by means both of force and of diplomacy, into central mainland Greece and the Peloponnese, as well as the Aegean, eventually weakening even Sparta (Davies 1993: 38, 82–3; Powell 1988: 1–96; Rhodes 1992a).

In a paradigm echoing relations in the colonial world, mutual political interests and alliances were often felt to be best promoted by moulding the governance of the small Aegean ally states into a rough replica of Athens's democratic model, or even allowing Athens's courts and assemblies to overrule some aspects of local decision making (Davies 1993: 73–4; Hornblower 1992: 10; Isokrates 4.105–6). Notions of political identity in the allied regions, already lodged within a broader 'Greek' framework, were stable yet flexible enough to facilitate and rationalise this change as a proactive choice. A strong element of manipulation was clearly also often involved – Athens sometimes intervened to provoke and exploit local citizen revolts that pressured for the adoption of democratic systems, and settlers were sent out to promote Athenian structures and interests within the league even after formal alliances had been established. Contemporary text sources, particularly Herodotus, show that Athens's prominent trade and military status allowed Athenian-style democratic politics to be generalised as the most definably and desirably 'Greek' system of governance and symbolically opposed to 'Persian' despotism. In the vulnerable small Aegean states, being on the 'Greek' side in some cases became almost synonymous with having a democratic system and strong political links to Athens, despite Spartan attempts to counter this reality (Davies 1993: 64–9). Myths like that of the Ionian migrations, in which east Aegean states traced important aspects of their heritage back to Athens, legitimised the new political connections, and three concepts – Athens, political and economic power and prosperity, and democracy – became inextricably entwined in contemporary perception, lending each other enormous power.

In this context, Athenian alliance with Crete would have been generally desirable from a strategic point of view. But there was little potential in this case to develop the kind of close political integration that characterised the Athenian League, for a number of reasons. These included Crete's historically strong and 'different' identity structures and its political/trade alliances, both at the individual polity level and at the level of the island as a whole; the regularity of the island's internecine conflicts (but also the structurally similar and interdependent nature of its warring states); its physically isolated yet defendable position as an island region of substantial size, out of Athens's direct geographical orbit; and the nature of its existing political organisation. Cretan oligarchies, in contrast to the unstable tyrannies that periodically dominated many central and east Greek regions, had an entrenched authority and power base that made it hard for any externally 'marketed' or manipulated democratic movement to take hold. As we have seen, the peculiarly high level of internal conflict in the island had led by the fifth century to the formation of diverse alliances between Cretan polities and central Greek states – particularly those of the Peloponnese, a region often in conflict with Athens: I have looked earlier at the evidence for strong links of a structural, conceptual, and pragmatic kind with Sparta, Athens's direct rival. Complex identity traditions (often emphasising the antiquity of Cretan political structures), including that of Dorian descent, were used to give these alliances legitimacy and distinction and would be difficult to readjust rapidly. Where temporary alliance with Athens *was* made by Cretan states, it seems to have been of very close local interest – for example, when on the initiative of the poleis of Gortyn and Polichne Athens was persuaded to attack Kydonia in 429 BC (Thucydides 2.85) – rather than to develop any long-term strategic ambitions or political affiliation. Notably, Crete took no coherent or proactive role in the Persian wars, where it might have helped to strengthen or protect other Aegean states (Davies 1993: 39).

In this context, adopting a distinctive political system that directly followed that of Athens would be a huge and drastic step for any single small Cretan polity to take, cutting it off permanently, and riskily, from opportunities for integration with peers (whether within or beyond the island) with which it had much stronger historical and structural connections. This would have the effect of greatly increasing that state's political and economic vulnerability. From the Athenian point of view, too, the overall difficulty of introducing democratic systems, as part of a standard system of political ties, to just one or two Cretan states, and the limited gains likely to result, made the island a low priority for closer political integration in this vein.

Sparta's outlook

Considerable light is thrown on the role of geopolitics in the spread of democracy by the ultimately *different* trajectories of political development in Crete and Sparta, despite these regions' significant structural similarities, close practical political links, and strong connections in terms of identity-linked traditions. Neither region was a natural or easy ally for Athens – Crete for the reasons noted, Sparta because of its dominance of a large regional bloc that acted as a foil to Athens's expanding power. Yet by the Classical period Sparta did see the rise of a much more participative political system than existed in Crete, even while falling short of a full democracy. By the early fifth century, its weakened strength had placed it under regent government rather than kingship, and it could not isolate its large and (by comparison with Crete) relatively volatile society from the kind of popular pressure that had promoted successive Athenian reforms. In external relations, it often appeared as the traditional enemy of democracy, going to the lengths of intervening to undermine Cleisthenes' reforming rise to power in Athens (see below) – but the latter move was, more than anything, a strategic measure to put its own candidate in power and thus exert control in the region. Unlike Crete, Sparta had an interest in, and ability to undertake, large-scale aggressive expansion (supported by its conquered territories) from an early date, making it a major geopolitical player (Hammond 1982; Jeffery 1988: 350–3). As such, it was much more strongly bound into pan-Hellenic identity structures and operations. This may have helped push its identity and governance – concepts that were closely linked to each other everywhere in this period – further towards the overtly 'Greek' democratic mould as a matter of expediency, even while Spartan society and structures were still perceived as 'different' by other Greek states.

Democracy's links to conflict

Sparta's use of serfs and marginal citizen groups as soldiers in expansive campaigns may have helped push forward participative political systems there by expanding and strengthening the citizen class (just as the seventh-century rise to prominence of hoplite warriors has been argued to have promoted consensual politics in Athens, in a context where bearing of arms was seen as a core citizen qualification and duty; Aristotle *Politics* 1279b2–4; Cartledge 2001: 153–69; Hanson 1996; Morris 1987: 196–205; Raaflaub 1997a; Snodgrass 1991a: 18–19). The more that conflict on the state's behalf formed a regular part of everyday life, the more it seems likely that fighters would expect a stronger say in the governance of their state. The Persian wars, involving increased military activity across the Aegean, probably exacerbated this trend.

In this regard, it is notable that Crete took no part in the Persian wars, though it seems to have been active in the supply of mercenaries to the Archaic to Classical Mediterranean (Willetts 1977: 212–13). It may even have specialised in this activity, for some of the reasons already discussed: the long absence of a luxury export sector in the island, the narrow clan-focused power base and limited expansionary potential of its states, and the very wide-ranging contacts arising from its geographical position, could all help push potentially aggrandising groups, excluded from a role in governance, into this sphere. Specialisation in mercenary activity may have greatly diluted the conceptual link between fighting and participation in politics, and thus limited internal pressure towards democracy in Crete from this source. Though the Ionian states also supplied mercenaries, other geopolitical factors stimulated a trend to democracy there, as we have seen.

At very pragmatic levels, too, conflict was a significant factor in the emergence of democracy. The usually recognized 'birth' of formal Athenian democracy in 508/7 – after Cleisthenes' rise to power – was directly promoted by macroscale aggression between large states attempting strategic intervention in each other's internal politics, as well as by internal conflict. The sending of Spartan troops to Athens to support a coup by Isagoras stirred up powerful resentment among Athenian citizens: the latter turned to support the Cleisthenic agenda (which championed mass participation) as a direct result. The Athenian revolt also owed much to a strong reaction to a preceding phase of tyrannical rule. Though Cleisthenes' interests were probably not deeply different from those of any tyrant, he could only achieve power by espousing an extreme ideology that reflected the aggressive public mood at this moment (Davies 1993: 24). Another factor in the change was the increasing strength of factional interests in a booming economy and expanded city, causing yet another kind of conflict with which the unrepresentative structure of tyrant governance could no longer deal.

In Crete, the most prevalent types of conflict did *not* operate as a stimulus to democratic developments. As noted above, it was rarely worthwhile or productive for major Aegean polities to step in to shift the balance and system of power in any one Cretan state, and doing so was in any case made very difficult by the long-established and stable character of Crete's oligarchies, which offered few chances for foreign interests to support usurpers or proxies and thereby ferment revolt. Regular warfare between Cretan polities, combined with the strength of their cultural, historical, and political links in other respects, must also have discouraged this kind of intervention, because of the very uncertain outcomes involved in shifting the power base. It was surely recognised that there would be major problems in the assimilation and control of conquered peer states, or in the construction of interpolity alliances within the island, whether in a defensive or aggrandising framework, if markedly different systems of government came into use between states.

The potential for intrasocietal conflict as a creative force in democracy's emergence was also low in Crete. As we have seen, there was a limited potential for self-assertion on the part of competitive unstable factions through practices like the *symposion*. Clans were the main unit of organisation, and only a few of these held well-consolidated positions of power in each state. On the other hand, there was little incentive to political resentment and revolt in the form of tyrannies. Clan supremacy was so deeply and smoothly embedded that it offered little provocation to revolt. I have noted the masking, accommodating role played by institutions like the common meal in maintaining this balance. Thus, whether we look at democratic systems in terms of conscious willed adaptations, spontaneous or externally provoked social revolutions, or impositions/promotions by outside forces, we see how the particular types of conflict current in and absent from Crete worked against the kind of disruptive change associated with democracy's emergence in mainland central Greece.

Long-term causes and effects of divergence from the democratic path

Throughout this study I have noted the central roles of kinship, attachment to land, and specific kinds of labour system in forming and developing the Cretan state. In these respects, though, we should recognise the underlying similarities of all Aegean states of this period. Kin bonds were important in the Archaic to Classical poleis of central Greece, as the origins of archons and tyrants in powerful clan groups and the long persistence of intertribal conflicts tell us. Though tribal boundaries were becoming broader, more formalised, and more firmly geographically fixed by the time of Cleisthenes' reforms, they remained a very important basis of representation in governance, and power within the tribe stayed partly based on purity of lineage. The 'difference' of Cretan states lay in the narrow appropriation of power by a small group of clans at an early stage in state development, and in its consolidation into a permanent rulership structure. In conjunction with a luxury goods consumption sphere that always remained loosely controlled, and with early-established, strong, and stable public cult and feasting institutions, this helped permanently insulate social tensions. By contrast, radical consensualism in many central Aegean societies was born out of problematic levels of competition at a much larger, less coherent scale, rooted in the deep, unstructured kind of social fragmentation seen in these regions after the collapse circa 1200 BC.

With these factors behind it, we cannot say that Crete's road away from democracy was taken decisively at any single point in time. Several main horizons of development in the social framework do seem to have been important in ensuring this outcome. All have been studied in detail here – the highly structured collapse at circa 1200 BC, the tenth-century rise of complexity, and the period of state consolidation in early Archaic. Though all of these shifts were themselves linked into much broader interregional developments, they produced special conditions in Crete that made a full democratic transition by the fifth century appear not only difficult but deeply undesirable, despite the various advantages it might have generated. Crete's story shows how positive, proactive social adaptation to catastrophic circumstances at an early date can forestall much more radical and disturbing – even revolutionary – social change later on. But it also reminds us how much easier it is to make such adaptations at a relatively small scale than at a large one (where social environments are less easily controlled or cohered) and highlights the point that bypassing such upheavals can ultimately reduce opportunities for future societal growth. Indeed, we can now turn our perspective round to ask whether the lack of democracy *contributed* over time to promoting Crete's isolation and its special features – extreme levels of small-scale interstate conflict; a limited trade base; an agriculturally focused, serf-dominated economy; and a tight, stable, and conservative political structure.

Though the adoption of democratic systems certainly facilitated alliance and trade with the Aegean's major powers at this period, it did not determine it. For example, Athens was very willing to do business with nondemocratic states possessing a highly alien political structure (such as Lydia) where it was economically worthwhile. In this regard, Crete's lack of a flourishing export trade or major sphere of colonial dominance seems to have been more a cause than an effect of its rejection of democracy. There is no doubt, though, that the absence of a democratic governance system compounded Crete's already ambiguous standpoint with regard to the 'Greek' identity structure, helping explain continued limits on Cretan activity and influence in the Greek world at both political and economic levels – from the interregional sanctuaries to colonial industry and trade – as well as the perception of Crete as different and/or marginal by Classical authors. Such seemingly 'negative' outcomes, however, were not necessarily viewed that way by the people actually living in Cretan societies. They may have seen their states as remarkably successful in maintaining autonomy and stability while remaining active and prosperous in off-island networks – via trade in bulk subsistence goods, provisioning, intermediation in commodity trade, limited colonial involvement, and mercenary activity. Though Cretan polities lacked the export trading power of Athens, the east Aegean states, or the colonies, their inhabitants could always obtain the luxury imports they desired and securely export their agricultural produce. Despite oligarchic rule, access to wealth, if not power, remained relatively wide in Cretan societies: the island's social systems continued to allow more room for individual wealth-gathering and display than was possible under the tightly regulated consumption rules and ideologies of states like Sparta. At an everyday level, then, the Cretan citizen may have felt a more permanent sense of security, stability, prosperity, and social power than his peers in a contemporary democratic state. The central Aegean had undergone frequent and still-remembered periods of tyranny, probably leading to a strong impression of instability there, and democracy may well have been viewed from the perspective of the stable Cretan societies as a kind of temporary corrective – as it was by some analysts even within Athens itself. The history of more radical and rapid social change during the emergence and early development of the state in central Greece seems likely to have made revolts more expected and accepted there: in contrast, Crete's different history may have promoted social stability as an expectation by Classical times. It appears that only a major adjustment in the nature of the eastern trade connection and in regional political balance – as was seen with the rise of the Persian threat – was able to make divergence from the democratic path, and all that implied, seem more of a liability than a benefit. Yet even as Cretan states responded by aligning themselves more deliberately with central Aegean powers, they stayed strongly attached to their old institutions and maintained independent support links outside the Aegean political sphere.

The very long timescale over which I have suggested Crete's nondemocratic path to have been created suggests a relatively limited role for agent power in changing the status quo. Yet the fact that Cretan societies lacked democracy, as well as all their other special features, promoted regular examination of their history and politics by outsiders and by their own members, including the writing of specialist histories of the island, now lost to us. I have shown that the strong self-conscious identity structures of Cretan polities had deep historical roots, central to binding together post-collapse societies. *Conscious* conservatism and exceptionally rich access to historical awareness and reference (through material culture as well as other cultural forms) seem to have been important factors behind continued political stability: the state form was so firmly supported by solid traditions, and related enactments, of cohesion that there was little room for wholesale change. These traditions are likely, I believe, to have been widespread and organic, permeating every level of society. At the same time they remained able to be manipulated by ruling elites in their own interests to resist pressure to political change.

These outlooks would surely need to be adapted or subjugated to some degree as Crete's political and military ties with the central Aegean strengthened under the Persian threat, and we do have indications that this was the case. Yet fourth-century sources show that a firm sense of 'otherness' was still maintained on the part of the Cretan poleis, at both at an individual and a collective level, as well as by those viewing them from outside. This fact may have usefully reinforced political independence for the island's states in a context where Athens was using political parallelism and exploiting a common sense of threat from Persia to extend control across the Aegean. The rejection of democratic systems by Cretan states seems to have had the effect of emphasising their connections to each other and marking them to outsiders as a single unit. In masking or sidelining the regular antagonism between them, the nondemocratic trajectory surely became, over time, an important and consciously manipulated factor in orchestrating their joint political activity, foreshadowing their operation as a league during Hellenistic times.

Conclusions

I want to end this study with some fairly shallow 'what-if' scenario building (taking us briefly back to the issues surrounding modern democracy). What would Crete have gained from adopting democratic systems, and what was lost to the island by not doing so? It turns out that we cannot sensibly answer this question, simply because the appearance or nonappearance of democracy is tied into so many other factors and is itself not a finite division or boundary. Crete's history offers, more than anything, insight into the role of particular and contingent factors in social change, and into the way material conditions and practice heavily structure society – and the actions of agents – in the *longue durée*. Only some rather circular observations are possible with regard to the 'what-if?' question. For example, it is unlikely that democracy alone could have helped hasten or ease the attritive process of state expansion in Crete, in either an economic or a political sense, since restrictions on democratic developments were themselves rooted in the very long-term and widespread character of conflict between Cretan polities. The mode of expansion that Cretan states did follow – based in stable serf systems, long-drawn-out conflict, and small-scale treaties between poleis – might in fact have been hindered by the advent of democratic politics (especially at a single-state level), which would necessarily involve destabilisation of the whole social and economic framework in which this worked.

As for growth in the sphere of international trade activity, this was already limited by the long history of an inwardly orientated luxury goods trade, and a serf- rather than slave-supported agricultural economy, in Crete. Both facts themselves held back the advent of democracy, so that a scenario where democracy *was* taken up would have to assume they did not apply. Certainly, *not* taking up democratic systems did help to isolate Crete from the prosperity-boosting opportunities offered by the expanding Athenian empire and the colonial world. The absence of democracy as a finished system does seem connected to the fact that Crete became something of a backwater by the end of the Classical period – not unprosperous, but of relatively little political or economic importance at a regional scale, even while retaining its value as a pragmatic and conceptual bridge between the Aegean and parts of the east. Yet Sparta's case shows that the development of more democratic elements did not inevitably promote a major role in Athenian-style commodity trade when a state's previous history had marked out a different course. If the small Cretan states had bought into democracy at a late stage, they might well have been destabilised without seeing much of a reward.

How important was the presence or absence of democracy in Crete to the rest of the Aegean world, particularly in regard to the strength of the pan-Hellenic culture and political identity? If Crete had been very proactive in export trade; had possessed unstable internal social relations; had contained many fewer, and much larger, state bodies from an earlier date; had developed a fully 'Greek' identity; and yet had *still* not developed democracy, a very different flavour might have been imparted to Classical politics as a whole, with the status of democracy as a distinctively Hellenic bonding feature being markedly weakened. As it was, Crete's lack of democracy simply perpetuated its existing status as 'other' in the Hellenic world. While failure to take up democratic systems did not mean catastrophe for Crete, it did to some extent hold back Cretan societies' engagement with dominant understandings of the world and denied them membership of a historically influential cultural 'club'.

Contemporary perspectives are ambivalent on the advantages of democracy. Aristotle characterised it as representing the rule of the mob, failing to ensure that virtuous and wise men ruled, and thus as deviant from his ideal *politeia* (*Politics* 2,4), echoing some of Plato's views (*Laws* 3, *Republic* 8.558–62). Thucydides pointed out the poor historical outcomes linked to Athenian democracy (2.65); Aristophanes satirised the power of the citizen assembly in works like the *Ecclesiazusae*. Yet it is hard to find any commentator's deliberately promoting alternative existing systems as better. Plato, in particular, presents a utopia as the only more desirable alternative; despite Aristotle's critiques of Athenian democracy, he fails to hold up Crete as an example of an ideal oligarchy (*Politics* 2.10). Though the divergent systems of Cretan and Spartan poleis were treated with respect, they were seen as curiosities or unreachable ideals – not models for the future – by the fourth century, if not earlier (Hodkinson 1997: 84; Ober 1989: 153). Working consensualism and the 'middling' ideal still structured the thinking of most Classical Greeks, even as they critiqued democracy (Ober 1996: 144; Wolin 1996: 82–3). That prominent thinkers and politicians in Crete, as everywhere else in the Aegean, engaged with the reality of democratic practice is confirmed by the account of the seer Epimenides of Phaistos acting as adviser and arbitrator to the city of Athens in the seventh century (Plutarch *Life of Solon* 12.4). Whatever the perceived faults of democracy, it came to represent one of the most successful and influential political systems, and the encapsulation of 'Greek' culture and politics in the Classical period, in a complex variety of ways. It influenced both strategic and day-to-day economic and political decisions for every citizen living under it, or in contact with it. In this context, one way in which the lack of democratic structures deeply limited Crete's wider political influence, prosperity, and autonomy can be seen in the cultural sphere, as we move into the Hellenistic period. Here, too, we cannot separate the impact of democracy's reality as a finished system from that of the historical conditions which brought it into being. Substantial support, in terms of time, materials, and skills for arts, theatre, and rhetoric, was promoted both by the chattel slave economy – so closely tied into and promoted by the democratic system – and by the stimulus and freedom that the latter gave to citizen voices. This high-profile cultural development, together with the trade power and wealth of Athens, and the unique, extreme, and memorable features of democracy as a political system, all helped build the political and economic strength, fame, and influence of central Greek states abroad, including in the Macedonian world. Artistic and literary culture helped make the democratic zones of the Aegean, particularly Athens, influential power players as Macedonia extended its sphere of influence. Crete lost the chance of a strong foothold in the Hellenistic political world partly because of its lack of associations of the same type – closely linked to its lack of democracy, but also to the historical factors lying behind it. By analogy with the Ionian states – rich and influential not only thanks to their history of trade activity but through their strong and mutually beneficial symbioisis with Athens – a democratic Crete, given its valuable geographical position, might have built up a great deal more influence of this type.

Ultimately, the Aegean polis states declined thanks to the rise of a large territorial power in Macedonia that concentrated strength and resources at a level they could not. It was their particularly bounded nature, and the history behind this, that probably lay at the root of this failure (Davies 1997: 35; Runciman 1990). With or without democracy, Cretan states were in the same broad mould as other states of this type, so the lack of democracy per se did not play the decisive role here. However, Crete's conservative, stable, and narrow-based social systems, intensity of internecine conflicts, and lack of economic and cultural growth, all made it especially vulnerable to political marginalisation in the changing east Mediterranean world, limiting its ability to command alliance partners and keeping its interregional profile low. The states that prospered most during the changes of the Hellenistic period were those prosperous and powerful enough to move towards a large territorial structure or massive trade expansion – both features more closely connected historically with a democratic trajectory.

We have long known that the small states of Archaic to Classical Greece were structured differently, but scholarship has often failed to compare and analyse regional social histories when trying to explain the different structures, and/or taken textual/mythic histories too much at face value. Thanks largely to the quality and density of the archaeological data, the Cretan case, when studied carefully, highlights the crucial formative role of local history, especially cultural history, in the post-collapse Aegean.

REFERENCES

ABBREVIATIONS

Conference or anthology volumes where no editor is listed

Ancient Crete: 1984. *Ancient Crete: a hundred years of Italian archaeology: 1884–1984*. Rome: Italian School of Archaeology at Athens. Rome : De Luca Editione.

Peloponnesiakon Spoudon: 1997. *Praktika tou E' Diethnous Synedriou Peloponnesiakon Spoudon, 6–10 Septemvriou 1995* (*Πρακτικά του Ε'Διεθνούς Συνεδρίου Πελοποννησιακών Σπουδών, 6–10 Σεπτεμβρίου 1995*). Athens: Etaireia Peloponnesiakon Spoudon.

Pepragmena Z: 1995. Pepragmena tou Z' Diethnous Kritologikou Synedriou, Rethymnon, 1990 (*Πεπραγμένα του Z' Διεθνούς Κρητολογικού Συνεδρίου, Ρέθυμνο, 1991*). Rethymno: Iera Mitropolis Rethymnis kai Aulopotamouou.

Pepragmena H: 2000. *Pepragmena tou H' Diethnous Kritologikou Synedriou, Iraklion, 1996* (*Πεπραγμένα του Η' Διεθνούς Κρητολογικού Συνεδρίου, Ηράκλειω, 1996*). Iraklion: Etaireia Kritikon Istorikon Meleton.

Pepragmena I: in press. *Pepragmena tou I' Diethnous Kritologikou Synedriou, Chania, Octovriou 2006* (*Πεπραγμένα του Ι' Διεθνούς Κρητολογικού Συνεδρίου, Χανιά, 1–8 Οκτοβρίου 1996*).

Pepragmena ST: 1990. *Pepragmena tou ST' Diethnous Kritologikou Synedriou, Chania, 1987* (*Πεπραγμένα του ΣΤ' Διεθνόυς Κριτολογικόυ Συνεδρίου, Χανιά, 1987*). Chania: Filologikos Syllogos 'O Chrysostomos'.

Pepragmena Θ: 2006. *Pepragmena tou Th' Diethnous Kritologikou Synedriou, Elounta, 2001* (*Πεπραγμένα του Θ'Διεθνούς Κρητολογικού Συνεδρίου, Ελούντα, 2001*). Iraklion: Etaireia Kritikon Istorikon Meleton.

Pepragmena I: in press. *Pepragmena tou I' Diethnous Kritologikou Synedriou, Elounta, 2001* (*Πεπραγμένα του Ι'Διεθνούς Κρητολογικού Συνεδρίου, Xania, 2006*).

Praktika Theochari: 1992. *Praktika Diethnous Synedriou yia tin Arxaia Thessalia sti Mnimi tou D. P. Theochari.* (*Πρακτικά Θεοχάρη: Πρακτικά Διεθνούς Συνεδρίου για την Αρχαία Θεσσαλία στη μνήμη του Δ.Ρ.Θεοχάρη*). Athens: TAPA.

Thessalia: 1994. *Thessalia: dekapente chronia archaiologikis erevnas, 1975–1990, Apotelesmata kai prooptikes. Praktika synedriou Lyon, 17–22/04/1990* (Θεσσαλία : Δεκαπέντε χρόνια αρχαιολογικής έρευνας, 1975–1990. *Αποτελέσματα και προοπτικές, Πρακτικά Συνεδρίου Λυών, 17–22/04/1990*). Athens: Ministry of Culture.

Triantafyllou: 1990. *Tomos Timitikos K. N. Triantafyllou. Τόμος Τιμητικός Κ. Ν. Τριανταφύλλου.* Patras: G. Petraki.

Collections of ancient fragmentary/inscriptional written sources used

FGrHist: Jacoby, F., 1957. *Die fragmente der griechischen historiker.* Leiden: Brill.

IC: Guarducci, M., 1935–50 (translator). *Inscriptiones Creticae. Opera et consilio Friderici Halbherr collectae.* Roma: Libreria dello Stato.

1935. *Inscriptiones Creticae* I: *Titulae Cretae Mediae Praeter Gortynios.*

1939. *Inscriptiones Creticae* II: *Titulae Cretae Occidentals.*

1942. *Inscriptiones Creticae* III: *Titulae Cretae Orientalis.*

1950. *Inscriptiones Creticae* IV: *Tituli Gortynii.*

West, M. L., 2003 (translator). *Greek lyric poetry: The poems and fragments of the Greek iambic, elegiac, and melic poets (excluding Pindar and Bacchylides) down to 450 BC.* Oxford: Clarendon Press.

Main journal abbreviations

AAA	*Athens Annals of Archaeology*
ABSA	*Annual of the British School at Athens*
AD	*Archaiologikon Deltio n (Αρχαιωλογικόν Δελτίον)*
AE	*Archaiologiki Ephemeris*
AEMΘ	*Archaiologiko ergo sti Makedonia kai Thraki (Αρχαιολογικό έργο στη Μακεδονία και Θράκη)*
AR	*Archaeological Reports*
ASAtene	*Annuario di Scuola Archeologica Italiana di Atene*
AthMitt	*Mitteilungen des Deutschen Archaologischen Instituts Athenische Abteilung*
BCH	*Bulletin de Correspondance Héllenique*
CAJ	*Cambridge Archaeological Journal*
JFA	*Journal of Field Archaeology*
JHS	*Journal of Hellenic Studies*
KCh	*Kritika Chronika (Κρητικά Χρονικά)*
ÖJh	*Jahreshefte des Österreichischen Archäologischen Institutes in Wien*
PAE	*Praktika tis Archaiologikis Etaireias (Πρακτικά της Αρχαιωλογικής Εταιρείας)*
RDAC	*Report of the Department of Antiquities, Cyprus*
SMEA	*Studii micenei ed egeo-anatolici*

BOOKS AND ARTICLES

Adams, R. M., 1988. Contexts of civilizational collapse: a Mesopotamian view. In Yoffee and Cowgill: 20–44.

Adrimi-Sismani, V., 2006. The palace of Iolkos and its end. In Deger-Jalkotzy and Lemos: 465–83.

Agelarakis, A., 2004. Mnimes tis aristokratias apo tin Orthi Pertra tis Geometrikis Eleuthernas (Μνήμες της αριστοκρατίας απο την Ορθή Πέτρα της γεωμετρικής Ελεύθερνας). In Stampolidis and Giannikouri: 77–85.

2005. *The anthropology of Tomb A1K1 of Orthi Petra in Eleutherna. A narrative of the bones: aspects of the human condition in Geometric-Archaic Eleutherna.* Athens: University of Crete.

Agelarakis, A., A. Kanta, and J. A. Moody, 1992. Terraces, tombs, and the Early Argive Heraion, *Hesperia* 61: 85–105.

1995. *An archaeology of ancestors: tomb cult and hero cult in early Greece.* Lanham, MD: Rowman and Littlefield.

2001. Cremation burial in LM IIIC-Subminoan Crete and the cemetery at Pézoulos Atsipadhes. In Stampolidis 2001: 69–83.

Alcock, S., 1999. Three 'R's' of the Cretan economy. In Chaniotis 1999: 175–81.

2002. A simple case of exploitation – the helots of Messenia. In Cartledge et al.: 185–99.

Alcock, S., and J. F. Cherry, eds, 2004. Introduction. *Side-by-side survey: comparative regional studies in the Mediterranean world*. Oxford: Oxbow Books.

Alcock, S., and R. Osborne, eds, 1994. *Placing the gods: sanctuaries and sacred space in ancient Greece*. Oxford: Oxford University Press.

Alexiou, S., 1955. Anaskafi Katsamba Kritis (Ανασκαφή Κατσαμπά Κρήτης). *PAE*: 311–14.

1956. Ieron para to Kavousi Ierapetras (Ιερόν παρά το Καβούση Ιεράπετρας). *KCh* **10**: 7–19.

1963a. Tsoutsouros (Τσούτσουρος). In Archaiotites kai mnimeia (Nomoi Irakleiou kai Lasithiou: skafikai erevnai kai perisyllogi archaiotiton) (Αρχαιότητες και μνημεία (Νομοι Ηρακλείου και Λασιθίου: σκαφηκαί έρευναι και περισυλλογή αρχαιοτήτον)). *AD* **18B**: 310–11.

1963b. Chronika. *KCh* **17**: 362–412.

1967. Archaiotites kai mnimeia, kentrikis kai anatolikis kai anatolikis Kritis (Αρχαιότητες και μνημεία, κεντρικής και ανατολικής Κρήτης). *AD* **22**: 480–94.

1972. Archaiotites kai mnimeia kentrikis kai anatolikis Kritis (Αρχαιότητες και μνημεία κεντρικής και ανατολικής Κρήτης. Ανασκαφαί και περισύλλογη αρχαιοτήτον). *AD* **27B**: 619–24.

1974. Anaskafes – sostikes ergasies (Ανασκαφές – σοστικές εργασίες). *AD* **29B**: 899–901.

Allegro, N., 1991. Gortina: l'abitato geometrico di Profitis Ilias. In Musti et al.: 321–31.

Allen, M., 1984. Elders, chiefs and big men: authority legitimation and political evolution in Melanesia. *American Ethnologist* **11**: 20–41.

Amiran, R., 1982. *Ancient pottery of the Holy Land: from its beginnings in the Neolithic period to the end of the Iron Age*. Jerusalem: Biyalik Institute/Israel Exploration Society.

Amouretti, M.-C., 1986. *Le pain et l'huile dans la Grèce antique*. Paris: Belles Lettres.

1992. Oléiculture et viticulture dans la Grèce antique. In Wells: 77–87.

Andreadaki-Vlasaki, M., 1987. An early Greek child burial at Gavalomouri, Kissamos. *SMEA* **26**: 307–55.

1988. Aptera (Aptara). *Kritiki Estia* **2**: 280–2.

1990. Aptera (Aptara). *Kritiki Estia* **3**: 249–51.

1991a. The Chania area, ca. 1200–700 BC. In Musti et al.: 403–23.

1991b. Chamalevri. Agros Dim. Stratidaki (Χαμαλεύρι. Αγρος Δημ. Στρατιδάκι). *AD* **46B**: 426–29.

1996. Chamalevri (Χαμαλέυρι). *Kritiki Estia* **5**: 251–64.

1999. Stylos (Stylos). *Kritiki Estia* **7**: 175–7.

2004. I Kydonia tis dytikis Kritis sta proima chronia tou Sidirou (Η Κυδονία της δυτικής Κρήτης στα πρώιμα χρόνια του Σιδήρου). In Stampolidis and Giannikouri: 21–35.

Andreadaki-Vlasaki, M., and E. Papadopoulou, 2005. The habitation at Khamalevri, Rethymnon, during the 12th century BC. In D'Agata and Moody: 353–99.

Andrewes, A., 1982a. The growth of the Athenian state. In Boardman and Hammond: 360–92.

1982b. The tyranny of Pisistratus. In Boardman and Hammond: 392–417.

1992. The Peace of Nicias and the Spartan expedition. In Lewis et al.: 433–64.

Andriomenou, A. K., 1972. Discoveries and chance finds from the city of Chalkis and the surrounding area. *AD* **27A**: 170–84.

1990. From the earliest ceramic workshop at Chalkis (11th–8th century). In *Philia Epe: A tribute to George E. Mylonas, to commemorate his sixth year as an excavator*. Vol. 2. Athens: Archaeological Society at Athens: 71–98.

Antonaccio, C., 1992. Terraces, tombs, and the early Argive Heraion. *Hesperia* **61**: 85–105.

1995. *An archaeology of ancestors: tomb cult and hero cult in early Greece*. Lanham, MD: Rowman and Littlefield.

Apostolakou, B., 1992. Meseleroi Ierapetras: thesi Petrou Frameno (Μεσελέροι Ιεράπετρας – θέση Πέτρου Φραμένο). *AD* **47**, B2: 604.

Appadurai, A., ed, 1986. *The social life of things: commodities in cultural perspective*. Cambridge: Cambridge University Press.

Arapoyianni, Ch., 1996. Ayia Triada. *AD* **46**: 133.

1997. Ayia Triada. *AD* **47**: 116–18.

Aravantinos, V., A. Konecny, and R. Marchese, 2001. Plataiai: die Kampagne 2000. *ÖJh* **70**: 9–21.

Aschenbrenner, S. E., W. D. E. Coulson, W. P. Donovan, R. Hope Simpson, and N. C. Wilkie, 1983. Late Helladic settlement: stratigraphy and architecture. In McDonald et al.: 362–447.

Ashmore, W., and A. B. Knapp, eds, *Archaeologies of landscape: contemporary perspectives*: 253–69. Oxford: Blackwell.

Aubet, M. E., 1993. The Phoenicians and the west: politics, colonies and trade. Cambridge: Cambridge University Press.

Baldwin Bowsky, M., 1989. Portrait of a polis: Lato pros Kamara. *Hesperia* 58: 331–47.

Banou, E., and G. Rethemiotakis, 1997. Centre and periphery: new evidence for the relations between Knossos and the area of Viannos in the LM II-IIIA periods. In Driessen and Farnoux 1997: 23–59.

Barber, R. N., 1981. The late Cycladic period: a review. *ABSA* **76**: 1–23.

1987. *The Cyclades in the Bronze Age*. London: Duckworth.

Barnard, K., T. M. Brogan, and J. S. Soles, 2003. Conclusions: the decoration, character and relative chronology of the Neopalatial pottery. In Soles 2003b: 99–113.

Barrett, J. C., 1996. The living, the dead and the ancestors: Neolithic and Early Bronze Age mortuary practices. In Preucel and Hodder: 394–413.

1999. The mythical landscapes of the British Iron Age. In Ashmore and Knapp: 253–69.

Bartoloni, P., and L. Campanella, 2000. *La ceramica fenicia di Sardegna: dati, problematiche, confronti*. Roma: Consiglio Nazionale delle Ricerche.

Batziou-Efstathiou, A., 1992. Neoteres anaskafikes erevnes stin evryteri periochi tis Magoulas-Pefkakia (Νεότερες ανασκαφικες έρευνες στην ευρύτερη περιοχή της Μαγούλας-Πευκάκια). In *Praktika Theochari*: 279–85.

1994. Apotelesmata ton prosfaton anaskafikon erevnon sti Nea Ionia kai stin periochi Pefkakion (Αποτελάσματα τον Πρόσφατον ανασκαφικών έρευνων στη Ν. Ιωνια και στην περιοχή Πευκάκιων). In N. Koliou, *Neotera dedomena ton erevnon yia tin Archaia Iolko (Νεότερα δεδομένα των ερευνών γιά την αρχαία Ιωλκό)*. Volos: Demos Volou: 59–70.

2003. I Ysteroelladiki IIIG sto Kastro tou Volou (Η Υστεροελλαδική ΙΙΙΓ στο Κάστρο του Βόλου). In Kyparissi-Apostolika and Papakonstantinou: 253–63.

Baziotopoulou, E., and P. Valvanis, 1993. Deux acropoles antiques sur les montagnes de Galaxidi. *BCH* 117: 189–209.

Bedwin O., 1994. The animal bones. In Popham 1994c: 307–8.

Belgiorno, M. R., 1994. Ricognizione nel territorio di Sybrita. In Rocchetti 1994: 201–29.

Bendall, L. M., 2001. The economics of Potnia: palatial support for a Mycenaean deity. In Laffineur and Hägg: 445–52.

2004. 'Fit for a king'? Exclusion, hierarchy, aspiration and desire in the social structure of Mycenaean banqueting. In P. Halstead and J. Barrett, eds, *Food, cuisine and society in in prehistoric Greece*. Sheffield: University of Sheffield Press: 105–35.

Bender, B., 1993. *Landscape: politics and perspectives*. Oxford: Berg.

1999. Subverting the Western gaze: mapping alternative worlds. In Ucko and Layton: 31–45.

Bennet, J., 1985. The structure of the Linear B administration at Knossos. *AJA* **89**: 231–49.

1987a. The wild country east of Dikte: the problem of east Crete in the LM III period. In J. T. Killen, J. L. Melena, and J. P. Olivier, eds, *Studies in Mycenaean and Classical Greek presented to J. Chadwick*. *Minos* 20–22. Salamanca: Universidad de Salamanca: 77–88.

1987b. Knossos and LM III Crete: a post-palatial palace? In R. Hägg and N. Marinatos, eds, *The function of the Minoan palaces. Proceedings of the fourth international symposium at the Swedish Institute in Athens, 10–16 June, 1984*. Acta Instituti Atheniensis Regni Sueciae, Series in 40, XXXV. Stockholm: Swedish Institute at Athens: 307–12.

1990. Knossos in context: comparative perspectives on the Linear B administration of LM II-III Crete. *AJA* **94**: 193–211.

1992. 'Collectors' or 'owners'? An examination of their possible functions within the palatial economy of LM III Crete. In Olivier 1992: 65–103.

2001. Agency and bureaucracy: thoughts on the nature and extent of administration in Bronze Age Pylos. In Voutsaki and Killen: 25–38.

Benson, J., 1973. *The necropolis of Kaloriziki, excavated by J. F. Daniel and G. H. McFadden for the University Museum, University of Pennsylvania, Philadelphia.* SIMA XXXVI. Göteborg: Paul Åströms Förlag.

Bérard, C., 1982. Récupérer la mort du prince. In Gnoli and Vernant: 84–105.

Bergquist, B., 1990. Sympotic space: a functional aspect of Greek dining-rooms. In Murray 1990: 37–66.

Betancourt, P., 2003. Land use in LM III at the Chrysokaminou estate. In Kyparissi-Apostolika and Papakonstantinou: 555–61.

Betancourt, P., V. Karageorghis, R. Laffineur, and W. D. Niemeier, eds, 1999. *Meletemata. Studies in Aegean archaeology presented to Malcolm H. Wiener as he enters his 65th year.* Aegaeum 20. Liège: University of Liège.

Bikai, P. M., 1992. The Phoenicians. In Ward and Joukowsky: 132–42.

2000. Phoenician ceramics from the Greek sanctuary. In Shaw and Shaw 2000: 302–12.

Binford, L. R., 1972. Mortuary practices: their study and their potential. In L. R. Binford, ed, *An archaeological perspective.* New York: Seminar Press: 208–43.

Bintliff, J. L., 1977a. *Natural environment and human settlement in prehistoric Greece, based on original fieldwork.* Parts i–ii. Oxford: BAR.

1977b. Pedology and land use. In D. Blackman and K. Branigan, Survey of the lower catchment of the Ayiofarango Valley. *ABSA* 72: 24–30.

1991. The contribution of an *Annaliste*/structural history approach to archaeology. In Bintliff 1991a: 1–33.

ed, 1991a. *The Annales School and archaeology.* London: Leicester University Press.

1999. Introduction. In Chaniotis 1999: 1–15.

2007. Tanagra: la ville et la campagne environnante à la lumiere des nouvelles methodes de prospection. In *Tanagras: De l'objet de collection à l'objet archéologique.* Paris: Editions Picard, Musée du Louvre Editions: 101–15.

Bintliff, J. L., et al., 2002. The Leiden Ancient Cities of Boeotia Project: preliminary report on the 2001 season. *Pharos. Journal of the Netherlands Institute in Athens* **IX**: 33–74.

Biondi, G., in press. Recinto funerario in localita Dodeka Apostoloi. In *Pepragmena* X.

Blackman, D., 2002. Archaeology in Greece 2001–2. *AR* **48**: 1–53.

Blegen, C., R. S. Young, and H. Palmer, 1964. *Corinth XIII: The North Cemetery.* Princeton, NJ: American School of Classical Studies at Athens.

Blinkenberg, C., 1931. *1: fouilles et recherches 1902–1914.* Vol. I: *Les petits objets.* Berlin: de Gruyter.

Blitzer, H., 1993a. Olive cultivation and oil production in Minoan Crete. In M.-C. Amouretti and J. P. le Brun, eds, *Le production de vin et de l'huile en Mediterranéé de l'Age du Bronze a la fin du XVIème siècle.* Paris: Boccard: 163–75.

1993b. Ethnographic research on traditional life and land use during the late 19th and early 20th centuries. In Watrous et al. 1993: 240–3.

Blumler, M. A., 1993. Successional pattern and landscape sensitivity in the Mediterranean and Near East. In D. S. G. Thomas and R. J. Allison, eds, *Landscape sensitivity.* Chichester: Wiley: 287–309.

Boardman, J., 1957. Early Euboean pottery and history. *ABSA* 52: 1–29.

1960. Protogeometric graves at Ayios Ioannis near Knossos (Knossos Survey 3). *ABSA* 55: 128–49.

1961. *The Cretan collection in Oxford. The Dictaean Cave and Iron Age Crete.* Oxford: Clarendon Press.

1967a. The Khaniale Tekke Tombs, II. *ABSA* **62**: 57–75.

1967b. *Excavations in Chios, 1952–55. Greek Emporio.* London: British School at Athens.

1970. Orientalen auf Kreta. In *Dädalische Kunst auf Kreta im 7. Jahrhundert v. Chr.*: 14–25. Mainz am Rhein: von Zabern.

1982. Crete. In Boardman and Hammond, Part 1: 222–34.

1990. *The Greeks overseas.* London: Thames and Hudson.

1998. *Early Greek vase painting, 11th–6th centuries BC.* London: Thames and Hudson.

Boardman, J., and N. G. L. Hammond, eds, 1982. *The Cambridge ancient history: the expansion of the Greek world, eighth to sixth centuries BC.* 2nd ed. Vol. III. Cambridge: Cambridge University Press.

Boardman, J., N. G. L. Hammond, D. M. Lewis, and M. Ostwald, eds, 1988. *The Cambridge ancient history: Persia, Greece and the western Mediterranean c. 525–479 BC*. Vol. IV. Cambridge: Cambridge University Press.

Boardman, J., and J. Hayes, 1966. *Excavations at Tocra, 1963–65. Part 1: the Archaic deposits*. London: British School at Athens.

1973. *Excavations at Tocra, 1963–65. Part II: the Archaic and later deposits*. London: British School at Athens.

Bohannan, P., 1968. Some principles of exchange and investment among the Tiv. In E. E. LeClair and H. K. Schneider, eds, *Economic anthropology: readings in theory and analysis*. New York: Holt, Rinehart & Winston: 300–11.

Bonnefont, V. C., 1972. *La Crète: étude géomorphologique*. Unpublished PhD Dissertation, University of Lille.

Bookidis, N., and R. Stroud, 1997. *Corinth* XVIII.iii. *The sanctuary of Demeter and Kore: topography and architecture*. Princeton, NJ: American School of Classical Studies at Athens.

Borgna, E., 1997. Some observations on deep bowls and kraters on the 'Acropoli Mediana' at Phaistos. In Hallager and Hallager 1997: 273–305.

1999. Central Crete and the Mycenaeans at the close of the Late Bronze Age: the evidence of the 'Acropoli Mediana' at Phaistos. In Dakoronia 1999: 353–70.

2003a. Regional settlement patterns, exchange systems and sources of power in Crete at the end of the Late Bronze Age: establishing a connection. *SMEA* **XLV/2**: 153–83.

2003b. *Il complesso di ceramica tardominoico III dell'acropoli mediana di Festos*. Studia di archeologia cretese III. Padova: Centro di archaeologia cretese, Universita di Catania/Scuola Archeologica Italiana di Atene.

Bosanquet, R., 1902. Excavations at Praisos I. *ABSA* **8**: 231–70.

1905. Excavations at Palaikastro IV. The temple of Dictaean Zeus. *ABSA* **11**: 298–308.

1910. Inscriptions from Praesos. *ABSA* **16**: 281–9.

1945. Dikte and the temples of Diktaean Zeus. *ABSA* **40**: 60–77.

Bosanquet, R. C., R. M. Dawkins, M. N. Tod, W. L. Duckworth, and I. Myres, 1903. Excavations at Palaikastro II. *ABSA* **9**: 274–387.

Bottema, S., 1980. Palynological investigations on Crete. *Review of palaeobotany and palynology* **31**: 193–217.

Bourdieu, P., 1977. (translated by R. Nice) *Outline of a theory of practice*. Cambridge: Cambridge University Press.

Bousquet, J., 1938. Le temple d'Aphrodite et d'Ares a Sta Lenika. *BCH* **62**: 386–408.

Bowden, H., 1996. The Greek settlement and sanctuaries at Naukratis: Herodotus and archaeology. In Hansen and Raaflaub 1996: 17–39.

Boyd, H. A., 1901. Excavations at Kavousi, Crete, in 1900. *AJA* **5**: 125–57.

1905. *Gournia: report of the American Exploration Society's excavations at Gournia, Crete*. Philadelphia: University of Pennsylvania.

Boyd Hawes, H., B. E. Williams, R. B. Seager, and E. H. Hall, 1908. *Gournia, Vasiliki and other prehistoric sites on the isthmus of Hierapetra, Crete*. Philadelphia American Exploration Society, Free Museum of Science and Art.

Bradley, R., 2000. *The archaeology of natural places*. London: Routledge.

Braudel, F., 1979. (translated by S. Reynolds) *The Mediterranean and the Mediterranean world in the age of Philip the Second*. 2nd rev. ed. Vol. II. London: Fontana.

Brock, J. K., 1957. *Fortetsa: early Greek tombs near Knossos*. London: British School at Athens.

Brock, R., and S.Hodkinson, eds, 2000. *Alternatives to Athens. Varieties of political organisation and community in ancient Greece*. Oxford: Oxford University Press.

Broodbank, C., 2000. *An island archaeology of the early Cyclades*. Cambridge: Cambridge University Press.

Bruni, G. B., 1979. Mothakes, neodamodeis, Brasideioi. In *Schiavitu, manomissione e classi dipendenti nel mondo antico. Pubblicazione Istituto di Storia Antica* 13. Padova: Universita di Padova: 21–31.

Buckland, P. C., A. J. Dugmore, and K. J. Edwards, 1997. Bronze Age myths? Volcanic activity and human response in the Mediterranean and north Atlantic region. *Antiquity* 71: 581–93.
Burguières, A., 1982. The fate of the history of *mentalités* in the *Annales*. In *Comparative studies in society and history* 24: 424–37.
Burkert, W., 1998. (translated by E. Pinder and W. Burkert) *The Orientalizing revolution. Near Eastern influence on Greek culture in the Early Archaic Age*. Cambridge, MA: Harvard University Press.
Butzer, K. W., 1974. Accelerated soil erosion: a problem of man-land relationships. In I. R. Manners and M. W. Mikesell, *Perspectives on environment*. Washington, DC: Association of American Geographers: 57–77.
Cadogan, G., 1967. Late Minoan IIIC pottery from the Kephala tholos tomb near Knossos. *ABSA* 62: 257–65.
Cadogan, G., E. Hatzaki, and A. Vasilakis, eds, 2005. *Knossos: palace, city, state*. London: British School at Athens.
Callaghan, P., 1976. Excavations at a shrine of Glaukos, Knossos. *ABSA* 73: 1–30.
Callaghan, P. J., A. W. Johnston, P. M. Bikai, J. W. Hayes, and R. E. Jones, 2000. The Iron Age pottery from Kommos. In Shaw and Shaw 2000: 210–336.
Cambitoglou, A., A. Birchall, J. J. Coulton, and J. R. Green, 1971. *Zagora I: Excavation of a Geometric town on the island of Andros*. Athens: Archaeological Society of Athens.
1988. *Zagora 2: Excavation of a Geometric town on the island of Andros*. Athens: Archaeological Society of Athens.
Cambitoglou, A., J. K. Papadopoulos, and O. Tudor-Jones, 2001. *Torone* I: the excavations of 1975, 1976 and 1978. Athens: Greek Archaeological Society.
Camp, J., 2002. *The Archaeology of Athens*. New Haven, CT: Yale University Press.
Canuto, M. A., and J. Yaeger, 2000. *The archaeology of communities*. London: Routledge.
Carington-Smith, J., 2003. Echoes of a Mycenaean past at Koukos, Sykia. In Kyparissi-Apostolika and Papakonstantinou: 243–53.
Carington-Smith, J., and I. Βοκοτοπουλου, 1988. I anaskafi ston Kouko Sykias, 1988 (Η ανασκαφή στον Κουκο Συκιας, 1988). *AEMΘ* 2: 357–71.
1989. I anaskafi ston Kouko Sykias, 1989 (Η ανασκαφή στον Κούκο Συκιάς, 1989). *AEMΘ* 3: 425–39.
1990. I anaskafi ston Kouko Sykias, 1990 (Η ανασκαφή στον Κούκο Συκιάς, 1990). *AEMΘ* 4: 439–47.
1992. Excavation at Koukos, Sykias. *AEMΘ* 6: 495–503.
Carlier, P., 1992. Les collecteurs sont-ils des fermiers? In Olivier 1992: 159–67.
Carneiro, R., 1970. A theory of the origin of the state. *Science* **169**: 733–78.
1981. The chiefdom as precursor of the state. In G. Jones and R. R. Kautz, eds, *The transition to statehood in the New World*. Cambridge: Cambridge University Press: 37–79.
Carter, J., 1997. *Thiasos* and *marzeah*. In Langdon 1997: 285–312.
Carter, J. B., and S. P. Morris, eds, 1995. *The ages of Homer: a tribute to Emily Townsend Vermeule*. Austin: University of Texas Press.
Cartledge, P., 1996. Comparatively equal. In Ober and Hedrick 1996b: 175–87.
1998. Writing the history of Archaic Greek political thought. In Fisher and van Wees: 379–99.
2001. *Spartan reflections*. London: Duckworth.
2002a. *Sparta and Laconia*. 2nd ed. London: Routledge.
2002b. The political economy of Greek slavery. In Cartledge et al.: 156–74.
Cartledge, P., E. L. Cohen, and L. Foxhall, 2002. *Money, labour and land: approaches to the economies of ancient Greece*. London: Routledge.
Catling, H. W., 1964. *Cypriot bronzework in the Mycenaean world*. Oxford: Clarendon Press.
1977. The Knossos area, 1974–76. *AR*: 3–23.
1984. Workshop and heirloom: prehistoric bronze stands in the east Mediterranean. *RDAC*: 69–92.
1993. The bronze amphora and burial urn. In Popham et al. 1993: 81–97.
1994. Cyprus in the eleventh century B.C. – an end or a beginning?. In Karageorghis, ed 1979: 133–43.
1995. Heroes returned? Subminoan burials from Crete. In Carter and Morris: 123–39.
1996a. The Subminoan pottery. In Coldstream and Catling. Vol. II: 295–310.

1996b. The objects other than pottery in the Subminoan tombs. In Coldstream and Catling. Vol. II: 517–37.

1996c. The Subminoan phase in the North Cemetery. In Coldstream and Catling. Vol. II: 639–51.

1996d. The Dark Age and later bronzes. In Coldstream and Catling. Vol. II: 543–74.

1997. Minoan metalworkers at Palaikastro: some questions. *ABSA* **92**: 51–9.

Catling, H. W., J. F. Cherry, R. E. Jones, and J. T. Killen, 1980. The Linear B inscribed stirrup jars and west Crete. *ABSA* 75: 49–113.

Catling, R. W. V., 2002. The survey area from the Early Iron Age to the Classical period (c. 1050–c. 300 B.C.). In Cavanagh et al.: 153–256.

Caubet, A., 1992. Reoccupation of the Syrian coast after the destruction of the 'Crisis Years.' In Ward and Joukowsky: 123–31.

Cavanagh, W. G., 1996. The burial customs. In Coldstream and Catling. Vol. II: 651–77.

Cavanagh, W. G., and M. Curtis, 1998. *Post-Minoan Crete.* British School at Athens Studies 2. London: British School at Athens.

Cavanagh, W., and J. Crouwel, 2002. The survey area in the prehistoric periods. In Cavanagh et al.: 121–50.

Cavanagh, W., J. Crouwel, R. W. V. Catling, and G. Shipley, 2002. *The Laconia survey: continuity and change in a Greek rural landscape.* 2 volumes. London: British School at Athens.

Chadwick, J., 1976. *The Mycenaean world.* Cambridge: Cambridge University Press.

Chaffetz, D., 1981. *A journey through Afghanistan: a memorial.* Chicago: Regnery Gateway.

Chaniotis, A., ed, 1996. *Die Verträge zwischen kretischen poleis in der hellenistichen zeit.* Stuttgart: Steiner.

1999. *From Minoan farmers to Roman traders: sidelights on the economy of ancient Crete.* Stuttgart: Franz Steiner Verlag.

Charlton, T. H., and D. L. Nichols, 1997. The city-state concept: development and applications. In Nichols and Charlton: 1–15.

Chase-Dunn, C., and T. D. Hall, 1993. Comparing world-systems: concepts and working hypotheses. *Social Forces* 71 (4): 851–86.

Chatzi, G. E., 1982. I protogeometriki epochi sti Messinia (Η πρωτογεομετρική εποχή στη Μεσσηνία). In Praktika tou B' Diethnous Symderiou Peloponnesiakon Spoudon (*Πρακτικά του B'Διεθνούς Συνεδρίου Πελοποννησιακών Σπουδών*). Athens: Society for Peloponnesian Studies: 321–47.

Cherry, J. F., 1982. Register of archaeological sites on Melos. In Renfrew and Wagstaff: 291–310.

1988. Pastoralism and the role of animals in the pre- and protohistoric economies of the Aegean. In C. R. Whittaker, ed, *Pastoral economies in classical antiquity.* Cambridge: Cambridge Philological Society/ Cambridge University Press: 6–34.

Cherry, J. F., J. L. Davis, and E. Mantzourani, 1991. *Landscape archaeology as long-term history: Northern Keos in the Cycladic islands from earliest settlement until modern times.* Monumenta Archaeologica 16. Los Angeles: University of California Press.

Clark, J. A., 1990. *Soil and land use at an archaeological site: Pseira, Crete.* Unpublished PhD thesis, Queens University, Ontario.

Clark, J. E., and M. Blake, 1996. The power of prestige: competitive generosity and the emergence of rank societies in Lowland Mesoamerica. In Preucel and Hodder: 258–82.

Cline, E. H., 1994. *Sailing the wine-dark sea: international trade and the Late Bronze Age Aegean.* Oxford: British Archaeological Reports International Series 591.

1999. The nature of the economic relations of Crete with Egypt and the Near East during the Late Bronze Age. In Chaniotis 1999: 115–44.

Cline, E. H., and D. Harris-Cline, eds, 1998. *The Aegean and the Orient in the second millennium BC. Proceedings of the 50th Anniversary Symposium, Cincinnati, 18–20 April 1997.* Aegaeum 18. Liège: University of Liège.

Cohen, E. E., 2002. An unprofitable masculinity. In Cartledge et al.: 100–12.

Coldstream, J. N., 1963. Five tombs at Knossos. *ABSA* **58**: 30–44.

1973. *Knossos: the sanctuary of Demeter.* London: British School at Athens/Thames and Hudson.

1976. Hero cults in the age of Homer. *JHS* **96**: 8–17.

1979a. *Geometric Greece*. London: Methuen.

1979b. Some Cypriote traits in Cretan pottery, c. 950–700 BC. In Karageorghis, ed 1979: 257–64.

1983. Gift exchange in the eighth century BC. In Hägg 1983: 201–6.

1984a. Cypriaca and Cretocypriaca from the North Cemetery of Knossos. *RDAC*: 122–37.

1984b. Dorian Knossos and Aristotle's villages. In C. Nicolet, ed, *Aux origines de l'hellenisme: la Crète at la Grèce. Hommages á Henri van Effenterre*. Paris: Université de Paris: 311–22.

1986. Kition and Amathus: some reflections on their westward links. In V. Karageorghis, ed, *Acts of the international archaeological symposium 'Cyprus between the Orient and the Occident,' Nicosia, 8–14 September 1985*. Nicosia: Department of Antiquities: 321–9.

1988. Early Greek visitors to Cyprus and the eastern Mediterranean. In V. Tatton-Brown, ed, *Cyprus and the east Mediterranean in the Iron Age. Proceedings of the 12th British Museum Classical Colloquium*. London: British Museum Publications: 90–7.

1991. Knossos: an urban nucleus in the Dark Age? In Musti et al.: 287–99.

1994a. Urns with lids: the visible face of the Knossian 'Dark Age'. In Evely et al. 1994: 105–22.

1994b. Prospectors and pioneers: Pithekoussai, Kyme and central Italy. In Tsetskhladze and de Angelis: 47–61.

1996a. Knossos and Lefkandi: the Attic connections. In Evely et al. 1996: 133–46.

1996b. The Protogeometric and Geometric pottery. In Coldstream and Catling: 311–421.

1998a. Crete and the Dodecanese: alternative eastern approaches to the Greek world during the Geometric period. In Karageorghis and Stampolidis: 255–65.

1998b. Minos redivivus: some nostalgic Knossians of the ninth century BC (a summary). In Cavanagh and Curtis: 58–61.

2000a. Evans's Greek finds: the early Greek town of Knossos, and its encroachment on the borders of the Minoan palace. *ABSA* **95**: 259–301.

2000b. Early Greek and Classical Crete. In D. Huxley, *Cretan quests: British explorers, excavators and historians*. London: British School at Athens: 162–74.

2000c. Knossos: Minoan larnakes found in Early Iron Age contexts. In *Pepragmena H*: 271–83.

2002. Knossos: 'Geometric' tombs excavated by D. G. Hogarth, 1900. *ABSA* **97**: 201–17.

Coldstream, J. N., and H. W. Catling, 1996. *Knossos North Cemetery: early Greek tombs*. 2 vols. London: British School at Athens.

Coldstream, J. N., and E. Hatzaki, 2003. Knossos: early Greek occupation under the Roman Villa Dionysos. *ABSA* **97**: 279–306.

Coldstream, J. N., and G. L. Huxley, 1999. Knossos: the Archaic gap. *ABSA* **94**: 289–307.

Cook, J. M., 1959. Old Smyrna 1948–51. *ABSA* 53–4: 1–34.

1962. *Greeks in Ionia and the east*. London: Thames and Hudson.

Cook, J. M., and R. V. Nicholls, 1998. *Old Smyrna excavations: the temples of Athena*. London: British School at Athens.

Cook, R. M., 1937. Amasis and the Greeks in Egypt. *JHS* 57: 227–37.

Cook, R. M., and P. Dupont, 1998. *East Greek pottery*. London: Routledge.

Cooper, F., and S. Morris, 1990. Dining in round buildings. In Murray 1990: 66–85.

Coulson, W. D. E., 1983. The architecture. In McDonald et al.: 9–60.

1985. The Dark Age pottery of Sparta, I. *ABSA* 80: 29–84.

1988. The Dark Age pottery of Sparta, II: Vrondama. *ABSA* 83: 21–4.

1990a. *The Greek Dark Ages: a review of the evidence and suggestions for future research*. Athens: S. Vouyouka.

1990b. The Protogeometric period at Kavousi. In *Pepragmena ST*: 185–194.

1996. *Ancient Naukratis*. Oxford: Oxbow.

1997. The Late Minoan IIIC period on the Kastro at Kavousi. In Driessen and Farnoux 1997: 60–72.

1998. The Early Iron Age on the Kastro at Kavousi in east Crete. In Cavanagh and Curtis: 40–45.

Coulson, W., and M. Tsipopoulou, 1994. Preliminary investigations at Halasmenos, Crete, 1992–1993. *Aegean Archaeology* 1: 65–98.

Cowgill, G., 1988. Onward and upward with collapse. In Yoffee and Cowgill: 244–77.
Crielaard, J.-P., 1998. Surfing the Mediterranean web: Cypriot long-distance communications during the eleventh and tenth centuries BC. In Karageorghis and Stampolidis: 187–207.
1999. Early Iron Age pottery in Cyprus and North Syria: a consumption-oriented approach. In Crielaard et al.: 261–90.
Crielaard, J.-P., G.-J. van Wijngaarden, and V. Stissi, eds, 1999. *The complex past of pottery.* Amsterdam: Gieben.
Csapo, E., A. W. Johnston, and D. Geagan, 2000. The Iron Age inscriptions. In Shaw and Shaw 2000: 101–34.
Cucuzza, N., 1997. Considerazioni su alcuni culti nella Messará di epoca storica e sui rapporti territoriali fra Festós e Gortina. In *Rendiconti della Accademia Nazionale dei Lincei* 9/8: 63–93.
1998. Geometric Phaistos: a survey. In Cavanagh and Curtis: 62–9.
in press. Phaistos in the Geometric period. In Kaiser and Pilz.
Cullen, T., 1999. *Aegean prehistory: a review.* Princeton, NJ: Princeton University Press.
Cultraro, M., 2004. The northern Aegean in the Early Iron Age. In Stampolidis and Giannikouri: 215–27.
Cunningham, T., 2005. House, shrine, or house-shrine? Assessing cultic vs. domestic function in Late Bronze Age Crete. Unpublished paper given at the STEGA conference (Glowacki and Vogeikoff-Brogan in press).
D'Agata, A. L., 1997. Shrines on the Piazzale dei Sacelli at Ayia Triadha. The LM IIIC and SM material: a summary. In Driessen and Farnoux 1997: 85–100.
1998. Changing patterns in a Minoan and post-Minoan sanctuary: the case of Ayia Triada. In Cavanagh and Curtis: 19–26.
1999. *Haghia Triada II: statuine minoiche e post-minoiche dia vecchi scavi di Haghia Triada. Monografie della Scuola Archaeologica di Atene e delle missioni Italiane in oriente.* Padova: Scuola Archeologica Italiana di Atene.
2000. Public versus domestic? A Geometric monument building at Thronos/Kefala Amariou (Ancient Sybrita). In *Pepragmena Z*: 327–41.
2001. Religion, society and ethnicity on Crete at the end of the Late Bronze Age: the contextual framework of LM IIIC cult activities. In Laffineur and Hägg: 345–55.
2002. Ritual and rubbish in Dark Age Crete. The settlement of Thronos Kefala (ancient Sybrita) and the pre-Classical roots of a Greek city. *Aegean Archaeology* 4: 45–59.
2005. Central southern Crete and its relations with the Greek mainland in the post-palatial period. In D'Agata and Moody: 109–31.
2006. Cult activity on Crete in the early Dark Age: changes, continuities and the development of a 'Greek' cult system. In Deger-Jalkotzy and Lemos: 397–414.
D'Agata, A.-L., and J. A. Moody, 2005. *Ariadne's threads. Connections between Crete and the Greek mainland in Late Minoan III (LM IIIA2 to LM IIIC). Proceedings of the International Workshop Held at Athens, Scuola Archeologica Italiana, 5–6 April 2003.* Athens: Scuola Archeologica Italiana di Atene.
Dakoronia, F., 1991. Late Helladic III, Submycenaean and Protogeometric finds in the Sperchios valley. In E. W. Kase, G. J. Szemler, N. C. Wilkie, and P. W. Wallace, *The great isthmus corridor route, explorations of the Phokis-Doris expedition: 1.* Dubuque, IA: Kendall/Hunt: 70–3.
1992. Elateia (Ελάτεια). *Archaiologia (Αρχαιωλόγια)* 45: 20.
1993a. Homeric towns in east Locris. Problems of identification. *Hesperia* 62: 115–27.
1993b. Elateia (Ελάτεια). *Fokika Chronika (Φοκικά Χρονικά)* 5: 25–39.
ed, 1999. *A' Diethnes Dipestimoniko Symposio, Lamia 1994. I perifereia tou mykenaikou kosmou (Α' Διεθνές Διεπιστημονικό Συμπόσιο, Λαμία 1994. Η περιφέρεια του Μυκηναϊκού κόσμου).* Athens: Ministry of Culture/ID Ephorate of Prehistoric and Classical Antiquities.
2006. Early Iron Age elite burials in east Lokris. In Deger-Jalkotzy and Lemos: 483–504.
Darcque, P., 1981. Les vestiges mycéniens découverts sous le Telesterion d'Eleusis. *BCH* 105: 593–605.
1991. Pour l'abandon du terme 'megaron.' In Darcque and Treuil: 21–31.

Darcque, P., and R. Treuil, eds, 1991. *L'habitat égéen prehistorique. Actes de la Table Ronde internationale organisée par la Centre National de la Recherche Scientifique, l'Université de Paris I et l'Ecole française d'Athènes (Athènes, 23–5 juin 1987)*. Paris: Boccard.

Davaras, C., 1968. Two Geometric tombs at Atsalenio near Knossos. *ABSA* **63**: 133–46.

1972. Archaiotites kai mnimeia tis kentrikis kai anatolikis Kritis (Αρχαιότητες και μνημεία κεντρικής και ανατολικής Κρήτης). *AD* **27**, B: 650–1.

1973. Diaskari Siteias (Διάσκαρη Σιτείας). In Archaiotites kai mnimeia tis anatolikis Kritis (Αρχαιότητες και μνημεία ανατολικής Κρήτης). *AD* 28, **B2**: 591.

1974. Rock-cut fish tanks in Eastern Crete. *ABSA* **69**: 87–93.

Davenport, W. H., 1986. Two kinds of value in the Eastern Solomon Islands. In Appadurai: 95–110.

Davidson, D., 1980. Erosion in Greece during the first and second millennia BC. In R. A. Cullingford, D. A. Davison, and J. Lewin, *Timescales in geomorphology*. Chichester: Wiley: 143–59.

Davies, J. K., 1967. Demosthenes on liturgies: a note. *JHS* **87**: 33–41.

1993. *Democracy and Classical Greece*. Cambridge, MA: Harvard University Press.

1997. The 'origins of the Greek polis': where should we be looking? In Mitchell and Rhodes: 24–39.

Davis, J. L., ed, 1998. *Sandy Pylos: an archaeological history from Nestor to Navarino*. Austin: University of Texas Press.

Dawkins, R. 1914. Excavations at Plati in Lasithi, Crete. *ABSA* **20**: 1–18.

Day, L. P., 1995. The Geometric cemetery at Vronda, Kavousi. In *Pepragmena Z*: 789–810.

1997. The Late Minoan IIIC period at Vronda, Kavousi. In Driessen and Farnoux 1997: 391–407.

Day, L. P., W. D. E. Coulson, and G. C. Gesell, 1986. Kavousi, 1983–1984: the settlement at Vronda. *Hesperia* 55: 355–87.

1989. A new Early Iron Age kiln at Kavousi, Crete. *Rivista di Archeologia* **13**: 103–6.

Day, L. P., K. Glowacki, and N. Klein, 2000. Cooking and dining at LM IIIC Vronda, Kavousi. In *Pepragmena H:* 115–25.

Day, P. M., L. Joyner, V. Kilikoglou, and G. C. Gesell, 2006. Goddesses, snake tubes, and plaques: analysis of ceramic ritual objects from the LM IIIC shrine at Kavousi. *Hesperia* 75: 137–77.

Day, L. P., J. D. Muhly, and M. S. M. Mook, eds, 2004. *Crete beyond the palaces. Proceedings of a conference held at the American School of Classical Studies at Athens, 11–12 July 2000*. Philadelphia: INSTAP Academic Press.

Day, L. P., and L. Snyder, 2004. The 'Big House' at Vronda, Kavousi, and the 'Great House' at Karphi: evidence for social structure in LM IIIC. In Day et al. 2004: 63–79.

Day, L. P., L. Turner, and N. Klein, 2009. *Kavousi II. The Late Minoan IIIC settlement at Vronda: the buildings on the summit*. Philadelphia: INSTAP Academic Press.

De Fidio, P., 2001. Centralization and its limits in the Mycenaean palatial system. In Voutsaki and Killen: 15–25.

Deger-Jalkotzy, S., 1991. Zum Verlauf der Periode SH IIIC in Achaia. In Rizakis: 19–29.

1994. The post-palatial period of Greece: An Aegean prelude to the eleventh century BC in Cyprus. In Karageorghis 1994: 11–29.

1998. The Aegean islands and the breakdown of the Mycenaean palaces around 1200 BC. In Karageorghis and Stampolidis: 105–21.

1999. Military prowess and social status in Mycenaean Greece. In Laffineur: 122–34.

Deger-Jalkotzy, S., and F. Dakoronia, 1990. Elateia (Phokis) und die frühe Geschichte der Griechen. Ein österreichisch-griechisches Gräbungsprojekt. *Anzeiger der Österreichische Akademie der Wissenschaften Philosophische-Historische Klasse* **127**: 77–86.

Deger-Jalkotzy, S., and I. S. Lemos, eds, 2006. *Ancient Greece from the Mycenaean palaces to the Age of Homer*. Edinburgh : Edinburgh University Press.

Deger-Jalkotzy, S., and M. Zavadil, eds, 2003. *LH IIIC chronology and synchronisms: proceedings of the international workshop held at the Austrian Academy of Sciences at Vienna, May 7th and 8th, 2001*. Wien: Verlag der Österreichischen Akademie der Wissenschaften.

Demakopoulou, K., 1982. *To mykenaiko iero sto Amyklaio kai i YE IIIG periodos stin Lakonia (Το μυκηναικό ιερό στο Αμυκλαίο και η ΥΕ ΙΙΙΓ περίοδος στην Λακόνια)*. PhD dissertation, University of Athens.

Demand, N., 1996. *Poleis* on Cyprus and Oriental despotism. In Hansen and Raaflaub 1996: 7–17.
Demargne, J., 1901. Les ruines de Goulas ou l'ancienne ville de Lato en Crète. *BCH* **25**: 282–307.
1903. Fouilles a Lato en Crète, 1899–1900. *BCH* **27**: 206–32.
1929. Terres-cuites archaïques de Lato. *BCH* **58**: 382–429.
1931. Recherches sur le site de l'Anavlochos. *BCH* **55**: 365–407.
1947. *La Crète dédalique. Etudes sur les origines d'une renaissance.* Paris: Boccard.
Demerle, P., 1937. Chronique des fouilles et decouvertes archeologiques en Grece. *BCH* **61**: 440–76.
1938. Chronique des fouilles et découvertes archéologiques en Grèce. *BCH* **62**: 442–83.
Desborough, V. R. D'A., 1952. *Protogeometric pottery.* Oxford: Clarendon Press.
1964. *The last Mycenaeans and their successors.* Oxford: Clarendon Press.
1972a. *The Greek Dark Ages.* London: Ernest Benn.
1972b. Bird vases. *KCh* **24**: 245–77.
Descat, R., 1995. *L'economie antique* et la cité grècque. *Annales histoire, sciences sociales* **50**: 961–89.
Dever, W. G., 1992. The Late Bronze-Early Iron I horizon in Syria-Palestine: Egyptians, Canaanites, Sea Peoples and Proto-Israelites. In Ward and Joukowsky: 99–111.
Dickinson, O. T. P. K., 2006. *The Aegean from Bronze Age to Iron Age: continuity and change between the twelfth and eighth centuries BC.* London: Routledge.
Dietler, M., and B. Hayden, 2001. *Feasts: archeological and ethnographic perspectives on food, politics, and power.* Washington, DC: Smithsonian Institution.
Di Lello-Finuoli, A. L., 1991. Trasmissione della proprieta per successione ereditaria femminile e sistema di parentela nel 'Codice di Gortina.' In Musti et al.: 215–18.
Dimopoulou, N., and G. Rethimiotakis, 1987. Krousonas Malevision. *AD* **42**: 530–1.
Di Vita, A., 1984. Gortina. In *Ancient Crete*: 40–2.
1991. Gortina in etá geometrica. In Musti et al.: 309–21.
Donlan, W., 1994. Chiefs and followers in pre-state Greece. In C. M. Duncan and C. W. Tandy, *From political economy to anthropology: situating economic life in past societies.* Montreal/New York: Black Rose Books: 34–51.
1997. The relations of power in the pre-state and early state polities. In Mitchell and Rhodes: 39–49.
Donlan, W., and C. G. Thomas, 1993. The village community of ancient Greece: Neolithic, Bronze and Dark Ages. *SMEA* **31**: 61–71.
Donley-Reid, L. W., 1990. A structuring structure: the Swahili house. In Kent : 114–27.
Dothan, T., 1982. *The Philistines and their material culture.* New Haven, CT: Yale University Press.
1992. Social disolocation and cultural change in the 12th century BC. In Ward and Joukowsky: 93–99.
Doxey, D., 1987. Causes and effects of the fall of Knossos in 1375 BC. *OJA* **6**: 301–24.
Douglas, M., and B. Isherwood, 1980. *The world of goods: towards an anthropology of consumption.* Harmondsworth, UK: Penguin.
Driessen, J., 1992. 'Collector's items.' Observations sur l'élite mycènien de Cnossos. In Olivier 1992: 197–205.
1997. *An early destruction in the Mycenaean place at Knossos: a new interpretation of the excavation field-notes of the south-east area of the west wing.* Leuven: Katholieke Universiteit Leuven.
2001. Centre and periphery: some observations on the administration of the kingdom of Knossos. In Voutsaki and Killen: 96–113.
2005. *The scribes of the Room of the Chariot Tablets at Knossos: interdisciplinary approach to the study of a Linear B deposit.* Salamanca: Minos Supplement 15.
Driessen, J., and A. Farnoux, 1994. Mycenaeans at Malia? *Aegean Archaeology* **1**: 54–65.
eds, 1997. *La Crète mycènienne. Actes de la table ronde internationale organisé par l'Ecole française d'Athènes.* Paris: Boccard.
Driessen, J., and I. Schoep, 1999. The stylus and the sword: the role of scribes and warriors in the conquest of Crete. In Laffineur: 389–403.
Ducat, J., 1990. *Les hilotes.* Paris: Boccard.
Ducrey, P., and O. Picard, 1969. Recherches à Lato, I. Trois fours archaiques. *BCH* **93**: 792–822.
1970. Recherches á Lato. II. Le grand temple. *BCH* **94**: 567–90.

1971. Recherches á Lato IV. Le théatre. *BCH* **95**: 513–31.

1972. Recherches á Lato V. Le prytanée. *BCH* **96**: 567–92.

Duhoux, Y., 1982. *L'étéocretois. Les textes, la langue.* Amsterdam: J. C. Gieben.

Dunn, J., 1992. Preface. In Dunn, ed 1992: v–vii.

ed, 1992. *Democracy: the unfinished journey, 503 BC to AD 1993.* Oxford: Oxford University Press.

Durkheim, E., 1964. *The division of labour in society.* New York: Free Press.

Earle, T. K., 1997. *How chiefs come to power.* Stanford, CA: Stanford University Press.

Eder, B., 1998. *Argolis, Lakonien, Messenien vom Ende der mykenischen Palastzeit bis zur Einwanderung der Dorier.* Vienna: Verlag der Österreichischen Akademie der Wissenschaften.

1999a. *Late Bronze Age swords from ancient Elis.* In Laffineur: 443–7.

1999b. Ancient Elis in the Dark Ages. In Dakoronia 1999: 263–8.

2001a. Continuity of Bronze Age cult at Olympia? The evidence of the Late Bronze Age and Early Iron Age pottery. In Laffineur and Hägg: 201–9.

2001b. Die Anfänge von Elis und Olympia: zur Siedlungsgeschichte der Landschaft Elis am Ubergang von der Spätbronze-zur Früheisenzeit. In V. Mitsopoulos-Leon, *Forschungen in der Peloponnes. Akten des Symposions zur 100-Jahr-Feier des Osterreichischen Archaologisches Institut.* Athens: Osterreichischen Archaologisches Institut: 233–43.

2003. Patterns of contact and communication between the regions south and north of the Corinthian Gulf in LH IIIC. In Kyparissi-Apostolika and Papakonstantinou: 37–55.

2006a. The world of Telemachus: western Greece 1200–700 BC. In Deger-Jalkotzy and Lemos: 549–81.

2006b. Die spätbronze und früheisenzeitliche Keramik. In H. Kyrieleis, ed, *Anfänge und Frühzeit des Heiligtums von Olympia: die ausgrabungen am Pelopion 1987–1996.* Olympische 31. Berlin: de Gruyter.

Eder, B., and V. Mitsopoulos-Leon, 1999. Zur Geschichte der Stadt Elis vor dem Synoikismos von 471 v. Chr. *ÖJh* **68**: 1–39.

Ehrenberg, V., 1937. When did the *polis* rise? *JHS* **57**: 147–59.

Eliopoulos, T., 1998. A preliminary report on the discovery of a temple complex of the Dark Age at Kefala Vasiliki. In Karageorghis and Stampolidis: 301–3.

2004. Gournia, Vronda, Kephala Vasilikis: a triad of interrelated shrines of the expiring Minoan Age at the isthmus of Ierapetra. In Day et al. 2004: 81–91.

Erickson, B., 2000. *Late Archaic and Classical Crete: island pottery styles in an age of historical transition.* Unpublished PhD dissertation, University of Texas at Austin.

2002. Aphrati and Kato Syme: pottery, continuity and cult in Late Archaic and Classical Crete. *Hesperia* **71**: 41–90.

2004. Eleutherna and the Greek world ca. 600–400 BC. In Day et al. 2004: 199–211.

2005. The archaeology of empire: Athens and Crete in the fifth century BC. *AJA* **109**: 619–63.

European Union, 2003. *Preamble* to *draft treaty establishing a Constitution for Europe adopted by consensus by the European Convention on 13 June and 10 July 2003*, submitted to the President of the European Council in Rome on 18 July 2003. www.europa.eu.int/constitution/futurum/constitution/preamble.

Evans, A. J., 1906. The prehistoric tombs of Knossos. I. The cemetery of Zapher Papoura. II. The royal tomb of Isopata. *Archeologia* **LIX**: 1–171.

1928. *The palace of Minos at Knossos.* Vol. II. London: Macmillan.

Evely, D., 1996. The objects. In Coldstream and Catling. Vol. II: 621–36.

Evely, D., J. Crouwel, E. B. French, J. M. Musgrave, D. Reese, H. Sackett, E. Schofield, and S. Sherratt, 2006. *Lefkandi IV: the Bronze Age.* London: British School at Athens.

Evely, D., H. Hughes-Brock, and N. Momigliano, 1994. *Knossos: a labyrinth of history. Papers in honour of Sinclair Hood.* London: British School at Athens.

Evely, D., I. S. Lemos, and S. Sherratt, eds, 1996. *Minotaur and centaur: studies in the archaeology of Crete and Euboea presented to Mervyn Popham.* Oxford: BAR/Tempus Reparatum.

Farmakidou, E., 2004. Apo ta nekrotafeia tis archaias Ialysou. Dyo geometrikes tafes stin Kremasti Rodou (Απο τα νεκροταφεία της αρχαίας Ιαλυσού. Δυο γεωμετρικές ταφές στην Κρεμαστή Ρόδου). In Stampolidis and Giannikouri, eds: 165–77.

Farnoux, A., 1997a. Malia au Minoen Récent II-IIIA:1. In Driessen and Farnoux 1997: 135–48.

1997b. Quartier Gamma at Malia reconsidered. In Hallager and Hallager 1997a: 259–73.

Farnoux, A., and J. Driessen, 1991. Recherches sur l'Anavlochos. *BCH* 115: 749–50.

Fassoulas, C. G., 2000. *Field guide to the geology of Crete.* Iraklion: Natural History Museum of Crete/ University of Crete.

Faure, P., 1959. La Crète aux cent villes. *KCh* 13: 171–211.

1967. Nouvelles recherches sur trois sortes de sanctuaires crétoises. *BCH* 91: 114–50.

Febvre, L., 1938. History and psychology. In P. Burke, ed, 1973 *A new kind of history: from the writings of Lucien Febvre.* London: Routledge and Kegan Paul: 1–11.

Felsch, R., 1981. Mykenischer Kult im Heiligtum bei Kalapodi? In R. Hägg and N. Marinatos, eds, *Sanctuaries and cults in the Aegean Bronze Age.* Stockholm: Swedish Institute at Athens: 81–9.

1999. To mykenaiko iero sto Kalapodi – latreia kai teletourgiko (Το μυκηναϊκο ιερό στο Καλαπόδι – λατρεία και τελετουργικό). In Dakoronia, ed 1999: 163–71.

Felsch, M., K. Braun, A. Palme-Koupa, and P. Armstrong, 1996. *Kalapodi I.* Mainz am Rhein: Verlag Philipp von Zabern.

Ferrarese Ceruti, M. L., L. Vagnetti, and F. Lo Schiavo, 1987. Minoici, micenei e ciprioti in Sardegna alla luce delle piu recente scoperte. In M. S. Balmuth, *Nuragic Sardinia and the Mycenaean world: papers from a colloquium in Rome, September 1986.* Studies in Sardinian Archaeology 3. Oxford: BAR: 7–39.

Feuer, B., 1983. Mycenaean Thessaly: our present state of knowledge. *Praktika Theochari*: 286–7.

1994. Mycenaean Thessaly. *Thessalia*: 211–14.

Finley, M. I., 1979. *The world of Odysseus.* Harmondsworth, UK: Penguin.

1980. *Ancient slavery and modern ideology.* London: Chatto and Windus.

1999. *The ancient economy.* 3rd ed. Sather Classical Lectures v. 43. Berkeley: University of California Press.

Fisher, N., 1993. *Slavery in Classical Greece.* Bristol: Duckworth/Bristol Classical Press.

Fisher, N., and H. van Wees, 1998. *Archaic Greece: new approaches and new evidence.* London: Duckworth/Classical Press of Wales.

Flannery, K., 1972. The cultural evolution of civilizations. *Annual Review of Ecology and Systematics* 3: 339–426.

Flensted-Jensen, P., ed, 2000. *Further studies in the ancient Greek polis. Copenhagen Polis Centre Papers* 5. Stuttgart: Franz Steiner Verlag.

Flensted-Jensen, P., T. H. Nielsen, and L. Rubinstein, 2000. *Polis and politics: studies in ancient Greek history.* Copenhagen: University of Copenhagen.

Forbes, H., 1992. The ethnoarchaeological approach to ancient Greek agriculture. In Wells: 87–102.

Forster, E. S., 1902. Praisos. The terracottas. *ABSA* 8: 271–81.

1905. Terracotta plaques from Praesos. *ABSA* 11: 243–57.

Fossey, J. M., 1988. *Topography and population of ancient Boeotia.* Chicago: Ares.

Fotou, V. 1993. *New light on Gournia: unknown documents of the excavation at Gournia and other sites on the isthmus of the Ierapetra by Harriet Ann Boyd. Aegaeum* 9. Liège: Aegaeum.

Foxhall, L., 1995. Bronze to iron: agricultural systems and political structures in Late Bronze Age and Early Iron Age Greece. *ABSA* 90: 239–50.

1997. A view from the top: evaluating the Solonian property classes. In Mitchell and Rhodes: 113–37.

1998. Cargoes of the heart's desire? In Fisher and van Wees: 295–311.

2002. Access to resources in Classical Greece: the egalitarianism of the polis in practice. In Cartledge et al.: 209–21.

Foxhall, L., and H. A. Forbes, 1982. *Sitometreia*: the role of grain as a staple food in Classical antiquity. *Chiron* 12: 41–90.

Francis, E. D., and M. Vickers, 1984. Green goddess: a gift to Lindos from Amasis of Egypt. *AJA* **88**: 68–9.

Francis, J., S. Price, J. Moody, and L. Nixon, 2000. Agiasmatsi: a Greek cave sanctuary in Sphakia, SW Crete. *ABSA* **95**: 427–73.

Freyer-Schauenberg, B., 1974. *Samos XI: Bildwerke der archaischen Zeit und des strengen Stils.* Bonn: Rudolf Habelt Verlag.

Fried, M. H., 1967. The evolution of political society: an essay in political anthropology. New York: Random House.

Friedman, J., 1975. Tribes, states and transformations. In M. Bloch, ed, *Marxist analyses and social anthropology.* London: Malaby: 161–202.

Frost, F. J., and E. Hadjidaki, 1990. Excavations at the harbor of Phalasarna in Crete: the 1988 season. *Hesperia* **59**: 513–27.

Galanaki, K., 1993. Rotasi (archaio Rytion) – thesi Embasos (Ροτάσι (αρχαίο Ρύτιον) – θέση Εμπασος). *AD* **48**, B2: 466–7.

Galaty, M. L., and W. A. Parkinson, eds, 1999. *Rethinking Mycenaean palaces: new interpretations of an old idea.* Monograph 41. Los Angeles: Cotsen Institute of Archaeology, UCLA.

Gallet de Santerre, H. G., 1952. Chronique des fouilles en 1951. Trouvailles fortuites. *BCH* **76**: 242.

Garnsey, P. 1988. Mountain economies in southern Europe: thoughts on the early history, continuity and individuality of Mediterranean pastoralism. In C. Whittaker, ed, *Pastoral economies in Classical antiquity.* Cambridge: Cambridge University Press: 196–210.

Garnsey, P., and I. Morris, 1989. Risk and the *polis*: the evolution of institutionalised responses to food supply problems in the ancient Greek state. In P. Halstead and J. O 'Shea, eds, *Bad year economics: cultural responses to risk and uncertainty.* Cambridge: Cambridge University Press: 98–106.

Gasparis, Ch., 1997. I gei kai oi agrotes stin mesaioniki Kriti (*Η γη και οι αγρότες στη μεσαιωνική Κρήτη*). Athens: Institute of Byzantine Studies.

Gauss, W., and F. Ruppenstein, 1998. Die Athener Acropolis in der frühen Eisenzeit. *AthMitt* **113**: 1–60.

Gell, A., 1986. Newcomers to the world of goods: the Muria Gonds. In Appadurai: 110–41.

Gellner, E., 1983. *Nations and nationalism.* Oxford: Blackwell.

1988. *Plough, book and sword.* Chicago: University of Chicago Press.

Gesell, G. C., 1985. *Town, palace and house cult in Minoan Crete.* Göteborg: Paul Åströms Förlag.

Gesell, G. C., L. P. Day, and W. D. E. Coulson, 1983. Excavations and survey at Kavousi, 1978–1981. *Hesperia* **52**: 389–420.

1985. Kavousi 1982–1983: the Kastro. *Hesperia* **54**: 327–55.

1988. Excavations at Kavousi, Crete, 1987. *Hesperia* **57**: 279–301.

1991. Excavations at Kavousi, Crete. *Hesperia* **60**: 145–78.

1995. Excavations at Kavousi, Crete, 1989 and 1990. *Hesperia* **64**: 67–120.

Giddens, A., 1984. *The constitution of society: outline of a theory of structuration.* Berkeley: University of California Press.

Gill, D., and L. Foxhall, 1997. Early Iron Age and Archaic Methana. In C. Mee and H. Forbes, eds, *A rough and rocky place: the landscape and settlement history of the Methana peninsula, Greece. Results of the Methana Survey project sponsored by the British School at Athens and the University of Liverpool.* Liverpool: Liverpool University Press: 57–62.

Gitin, S., A. Mazar, and E. Stern, 1998. *Mediterranean peoples in transition.* Jerusalem: Israel Exploration Society.

Gledhill, J., and M. Rowlands, 1982. Materialism and socioeconomic process in multi-linear evolution. In Renfrew and Shennan, eds: 144–49.

Glowacki, K. T., 1998. The acropolis of Athens before 566 BC. In K. J. Hartswick and M. C. Sturgeon, eds, *ΣΤΕΦΑΝΟΣ. Studies in honour of Brunilde Sismondo Ridgway.* Philadelphia: University of Pennsylvania Museum: 79–88.

2002. Digging houses at LM IIIC Vronda (Kavousi), Crete. *Pallas: revue d'etudes antiques* **58**: 33–49.

2004. Household analysis in Dark Age Crete. In Day et al., 2004: 125–36.

2007. House, household and community at LM IIIC Vronda. In R. Westgate, N. Fisher, and J. Whitley, eds, *Building communities: house, settlement and society in the Aegean and beyond*. London: British School at Athens: 129–39.

Glowacki, K., and N. Vogeikoff-Brogan, in press. *STEGA: the archaeology of houses and households in ancient Crete from the Neolithic period through the Roman era. Proceedings of a conference at Ierapetra, Crete, 26–28 May 2005*. Princeton, NJ: American School of Classical Studies at Athens.

Gnoli, G., and J.-P. Vernant, eds, 1982. *La mort, les morts dans les societés antiques*. Cambridge: Cambridge University Press/Maison des Sciences de l'Homme/.

Godart, L., 1972. Les tablettes de la série Co de Knossos. In M. Ruiperez, ed, *Acta Mycenaea: Proceedings of the Fifth International Colloquium on Mycenaean Studies*. Salamanca: Universidad de Salamanca: 418–24.

1992. Les collecteurs dans le monde égéen. In Olivier 1992: 257–85.

Godart, L., and Y. Tzedakis, 1994. Les necropoles d'Apodoulou et d'Armenoi au MR IIIB. In Rocchetti 1994: 61–6.

1997. Les royuames mycèniens de Crète. In Driessen and Farnoux 1997: 153–62.

Gondicas, D., 1988. *Recherches sur la Crète occidentale*. Amsterdam: Hakkert.

Greco, E., T. Kalpaxis, A. Schnapp, and D. Viviers, 1997. Itanos. *BCH* **121**: 809–24.

Griebel, C. G., and M. C. Nelson, 1998. The Ano Englianos hilltop after the palace. In Davis: 97–101.

Grove, A. T., 1992. Climatic reconstruction in the eastern Mediterranean with particular reference to Crete. In Grove et al.: 16–20.

Grove, A. T., J. A. Moody, and O. Rackham, eds, 1992. *Petromarula 1. Stability and change in the Cretan landscape: a colloquium at the Orthodox Academy of Crete, Kolymbari, April 1990*. Cambridge: University of Cambridge, Department of Geography.

Guizzi, F., 1999. Private economic activities in Hellenistic Crete: the evidence of the isopoliteia treaties. In Chaniotis 1999: 235–47.

Hadjimichali, V., 1971. Récherches à Lato, III: Maisons. *BCH* **95**: 167–222.

Hägg, R., 1988. Funerary meals in the Geometric necropolis at Asine? In Hägg et al.: 189–93.

ed, 1983. *The Greek renaissance of the eighth century BC: tradition and innovation. Proceedings of the Second International Symposium at the Swedish Institute in Athens, 1–5 June, 1981*. Stockholm: Swedish Institute at Athens.

ed, 1996. *The role of religion in the early Greek polis. Proceedings of the third international seminar on ancient Greek cult, organized by the Swedish Institute at Athens, 16–18 October 1992*. Stockholm: Swedish Institute at Athens.

1997. *The function of the "Minoan Villa": proceedings of the Eighth International Symposium at the Swedish Institute at Athens, 6–8 June 1992*. Stockholm: Swedish Institute at Athens.

1999. *Ancient Greek hero cult: proceedings of the fifth international seminar on ancient Greek cult, organized by the Department of Classical Archaeology and Ancient History, Göteborg University, 21–23 April 1995*. Stockholm: Paul Åströms Förlag.

Hägg, R, N. Marinatos, and G. C. Nordquist, eds, 1988. *Early Greek cult practice*. Stockholm: Swedish Institute at Athens.

Haggis, D. C., 1993. Intensive survey, traditional settlement patterns, and Dark Age Crete: the case of Early Iron Age Kavousi. *JMA* **6/2**: 131–74.

1999. Some problems in defining Dark Age society in the Aegean. In Betancourt et al.: 303–8.

2001. A Dark Age settlement system in east Crete, and a reassessment of the definition of refuge settlements. In Karageorghis and Morris: 41–61.

2005. *Kavousi I. The archaeological survey of the Kavousi Region*. Prehistory Monographs 16. Philadelphia: INSTAP Academic Press.

Haggis, D. C., and M. Mook, 1993. The Kavousi coarse wares: a Bronze Age chronology for survey in the Mirabello area, east Crete. *AJA* **97**: 265–93.

Haggis, D. C., M. S. Mook, C. M. Scarry, L. M. Snyder, and W. C. West, 2004. Report on the Azoria excavations 2002–3. *Hesperia* **73**: 339–400.

2007a. Excavations at Azoria, 2003–2004. Part 1. *Hesperia* **76**: 243–421.

2007b. Excavations at Azoria, 2003–2004, Part 2. The Final Neolithic, Late Prepalatial, and Early Iron Age occupation. *Hesperia* **76**: 665–717.

Haggis, D. C., and M. S. Mook, in press. The Early Iron Age-Archaic transition in Crete: the evidence from recent excavations at Azoria, Eastern Crete. In Mazarakis Ainian in press.

Haggis, D. C., and K. Nowicki, 1993. Khalasmeno and Katalimata: two Early Iron Age settlements in Monastiraki, east Crete. *Hesperia* **62**: 303–37.

Halbherr, F., 1901a. Three Cretan necropoleis: report on the researches at Erganos, Panaghia, and Courtes. *AJA* 5: 259–93.

1901b. Cretan expedition XVI. Report on the researches at Praisos. *AJA* 5: 371–92.

Hall, E., 1914. *Excavations in eastern Crete: Vrokastro.* Philadelphia: University of Pennsylvania.

Hall, J. M., 1995a. The role of language in Greek ethnicities. *Proceedings of the Cambridge Philosophical Society* (NS) **41**: 83–100.

1995b. How Argive was the 'Argive' Heraion? The political and cultic geography of the Argive plain, 900–400 BC. *AJA* **99**: 577–613.

1997a. *Ethnic identity in Greek antiquity.* Cambridge: Cambridge University Press.

1997b. Alternative responses within polis formation: Argos, Mycenae and Tiryns. In H. Damgaard Andersen, H. W. Horsnaes, S. Houby-Nielsen, and A. Rathje, eds, *Urbanization in the Mediterranean in the ninth to sixth centuries BC.* Danish Studies in Classical Archaeology, Acta Hyperborea 7. Copenhagen: Museum Tusculanum Press: 17–45.

2000. Sparta, Lakedaimon and the nature of perioikic dependency. In Flensted-Jensen: 73–89.

Hall, J. A., M. Atherden, O. Rackham, and D. Grove, 1992. A pollen diagram from the White Mountains: a preliminary interpretation. In Grove et al.: 40–1.

Hallager, B. P., 1985. Crete and Italy in the Late Bronze Age III period. *AJA* **89**: 293–305.

2000. The Late Minoan IIIC pottery. In Hallager and Hallager 2000: 135–75.

2003. The Late Minoan IIIB:2 pottery. In Hallager and Hallager 2003: 197–266.

Hallager, B. P., and P. J. P. McGeorge, 1992. *Late Minoan III burials at Khania: the tombs, finds and deceased in Odos Palama.* Göteborg: Paul Åströms Förlag.

Hallager, E., 1977. *The Mycenaean palace at Knossos: evidence for final destruction in the IIIB period.* Stockholm: Medelhavsmuseet.

1988. Khania and Crete ca. 1375–1200 BC. In W. Balder, C. Davaras, R. Willetts and A. Hakkert, eds, *Cretan Studies.* Amsterdam: Hakkert: 115–23.

1999. Nodules and LM IIIB Kydonian pottery from the Little Palace at Knossos. In Betancourt et al.: 309–19.

Hallager, E., and B. P. Hallager, eds, 1997. *The Greek-Swedish excavations at the Agia Aikaterini Square, Kastelli, Khania 1970–1987.* Vol. I: *From the Geometric to the Modern Greek period.* Acta Atheniensis Regni Susciae Series in 4, XLVII. Stockholm: Svenska Institut Athen.

eds, 1997a. *Late Minoan III pottery chronology and terminology: acts of a meeting held at the Danish Institute at Athens, August 12–14, 1994.* Danish Institute at Athens Monograph 4. Aarhus: Aarhus University Press.

eds, 2000. *The Greek-Swedish excavations at the Agia Aikaterini Square, Kastelli, Khania, 1970–1987.* Vol. II: *The Late Minoan IIIC settlement.* Acta Atheniensis Regni Susciae Series in 4, XLVII. Stockholm: Svenska Institut Athen.

eds, 2003. *The Greek-Swedish excavations at the Agia Aikaterini Square, Kastelli, Khania, 1970–1987.* Vol. III: *The Late Minoan IIIB: 2 settlement.* Acta Atheniensis Regni Susciae Series in 4, XLVII. Stockholm: Svenska Institut Athen.

Halstead, P., 1987. Traditional and ancient rural economy in Mediterranean Europe: plus ça change? *JHS* 107: 77–87.

1992. Agriculture in the Bronze Age Aegean: towards a model of Bronze Age economy. In Wells: 105–19.

1996. Pastoralism or household herding? Problems of scale and specialization in early Greek animal husbandry. *World Archaeology* **28** (1): 20–42.

1999a. Missing sheep: on the meaning and wider significance of O in Knossos sheep records. *ABSA* **94**: 145–67.

1999b. Towards a model of Mycenaean palatial mobilization. In Galaty and Parkinson: 35–43.

1999c. Surplus and share-croppers: the grain production strategies of Mycenaean palaces. In Betancourt et al.: 319–27.

2001. Mycenaean wheat, flax and sheep: palatial intervention in farming and its implications for rural society. In Voutsaki and Killen: 38–51.

Halstead, P., and G. Jones, 1989. Agrarian ecology in the Greek islands: time stress, scale and risk. *JHS* 109: 41–55.

Halstead, P., and J. O'Shea, 1982. A friend in need is a friend indeed. In Renfrew and Shennan: 92–100.

Hamilakis, Y., 1996. *Strategies for survival and strategies for domination. Wine, oil and 'social complexity' in Bronze Age Crete.* Unpublished PhD dissertation, University of Sheffield.

1999. Sacralising the past: cults of archaeology in modern Greece. *Archaeological Dialogues* **6**: 115–59.

Hamilakis, Y., and E. Yalouri, 1996. Antiquities as symbolic capital in modern Greek society. *Antiquity* 70: 117–29.

Hammond, N. G. L., 1982. The Peloponnese. In Boardman and Hammond: 321–60.

Hansen, J. M., 1988. Agriculture in the prehistoric Aegean: data versus speculation. *AJA* **92**: 39–52.

Hansen, M. H., 1987. *The Athenian assembly in the age of Demosthenes.* Oxford: Blackwell.

1993a. The *polis* as a citizen-state. In Hansen 1993b: 7–30.

ed, 1993b. *The ancient Greek city-state: symposium on the occasion of the 250th anniversary of the Royal Danish Academy of Sciences and Letters. July 1–4, 1992.* Copenhagen: Munksgaard.

ed, 1996. *Introduction to an inventory of poleis: symposium, August 23–6 1995.* Copenhagen: Munksgaard.

1997a. Πολις as the generic term for state. In Nielsen 1997: 9–17.

1997b. A typology of dependent *poleis.* In Nielsen 1997: 29–38.

1997c. The Copenhagen inventory of *poleis* and the *Lex Hafniensis de civitate.* In Mitchell and Rhodes: 9–24.

ed, 1997d. *The polis as an urban centre and as a political community: symposium August 29–31, 1996.* Copenhagen: Munksgaard.

2004. Introduction. In Hansen and Nielsen: 3–150.

Hansen, M. H., and T. H. Nielsen, eds, 2004. *An inventory of archaic and classical poleis: an investigation conducted by the Copenhagen Polis Centre for the Danish National Research Foundation.* Oxford: Oxford University Press.

Hansen, M. H., and K. Raaflaub, eds, 1995. *Studies in the ancient Greek polis.* Stuttgart: Franz Steiner Verlag.

1996. *More studies in the ancient Greek polis.* Stuttgart: Franz Steiner Verlag.

Hanson, V. D., 1992. Practical aspects of grape-growing and the ideology of Greek viticulture. In Wells: 161–7.

1996. Hoplites into democrats: the changing ideology of Athenian infantry. In Ober and Hedrick 1996b: 289–313.

Harding, A. F., 1984. *The Mycenaeans and Europe.* London: Academic Press.

Harris, E., 1997. A new solution to the riddle of the *seisachtheia.* In Mitchell and Rhodes: 103–13.

2002a. Did Solon abolish debt-bondage? *Classical Quarterly* **52.2**: 415–30.

2002b. Workshop, market place and household: the nature of technical specialisation in Classical Athens and its influence on economy and society. In Cartledge et al.: 67–100.

Harrison, A., and N. Spencer, 1998. After the palace: the early 'history' of Messenia. In Davis: 147–62.

Harrison, R. J., 1988. *Spain at the dawn of history.* London: Thames and Hudson.

Hartley, M., 1931. Early Greek vases from Crete. *ABSA* **29**: 56–114.

Haskell, H., 1997. Mycenaeans at Knossos: patterns in the evidence. In Driessen and Farnoux 1997: 187–93.

2005. Region-to-region export of transport stirrup jars from LM IIIA2/B Crete. In D'Agata and Moody: 205–23.

Hatzaki, E., 2005. Postpalatial Knossos: town and cemeteries from LM IIIA2 to LM IIIC. In D'Agata and Moody: 65–97.

Hatzi-Vallianou, D., 1980. Smari Pediadas: ena apomonomena kentro Isterominoikou-Protoellenikou politismou stin Kriti (Σμάρι Πεδιάδας: ένα απομονομένα κέντρο Υστερομινοικού-Πρωτοελληνικού πολιτισμού στην Κρήτη). *AAA* 13: 20–60.

2000. I latreia tis Athinas stin Akropoli Smariou (Η λατρεία της Αθήνας στην Ακρόπολη Σμαριού). In *Pepragmena H*: 71–82.

2004. Omirikia stoicheia stin Akropoli Smariou (Ομηρικά στοιχεία στην Ακρόπολη Σμαριού). In Stampolidis and Giannikouri: 105–27.

Hatzi-Vallianou, D., and O. Evthimiou, 2000. Κεραμεική απο την Ακρόπολη Σμαριού. In *Pepragmena H*: 537–57.

Hatzi-Vallianou, D., and S. Parchapidi, 1999. The acropolis of Smari (Crete). An approach to the planning and construction of the external wall enclosure. In Betancourt et al.: 873–82.

Hatzidakis, J., 1921. *Tylisos a l' époque minoenne*. Paris: P. Geuthner.

Hayden, B. J., 1983. New plans of the Early Iron Age settlement of Vrokastro. *Hesperia* **52**: 367–87.

1987. Crete in transition. LM IIIA-B architecture: a preliminary study. *SMEA* **26**: 199–234.

1988. Fortifications of postpalatial and Early Iron Age Crete. *Archäologischer Anzeiger* **1**: 1–21.

1991. Terracotta figures, figurines, and vase attachments from Vrokastro, Crete. *Hesperia* **60**: 103–44.

1995. Rural settlement of the Orientalising through Early Classical period: the Meseleroi Valley, eastern Crete. *Aegean Archaeology* **2**: 93–144.

1997. Evidence for 'megalithic farmsteads' of Late Minoan III through Early Iron Age date. In Driessen and Farnoux 1997: 195–204.

2001. Elias to Nisi: a fortified coastal settlement of possible Late Minoan IIIC date in the Vrokastro area, eastern Crete. In Karageorghis and Morris: 61–65.

2003. *Reports on the Vrokastro area, eastern Crete*. Vol. 1: *Catalogue of pottery from the Bronze and Early Iron Age settlement of Vrokastro in the collections of the University of Pennsylvania Museum of Archaeology and Anthropology and the Archaeological Museum, Herakleion, Crete.* Philadelphia: University of Pennsylvania Museum of Archaeology and Anthropology.

2004. (with contributions by H. Dierckx, G. W. M. Harrison, O. Rackham, J. Moody, G. Postma, and A. B. Stallsmith) *Reports on the Vrokastro area, Eastern Crete*. Vol. 2: *The settlement history of the Vrokastro area and related studies*. Philadelphia: University of Pennsylvania Museum of Archaeology and Anthropology.

2005. (with contributions by H. Dierckx, M. Hahn, G. W. M. Harrison, O. Rackham, J. Moody, O. Postma, M. K. Risser, and A. B. Stallsmith). *Reports on the Vrokastro area, eastern Crete*. Vol. 3: *The Vrokastro Regional Survey project: sites and pottery*. Philadelphia: University of Pennsylvania Museum of Archaeology and Anthropology.

Hayden, B. J., J. A. Moody, and O. Rackham, 1992. The Vrokastro Survey Project, 1986–1989: research design and preliminary results. *Hesperia* **61**: 293–354.

Helms, M. W., 1988. *Ulysses' sail: an ethnographic odyssey of power, knowledge and geographical distance*. Princeton, NJ: Princeton University Press.

Heltzer, M., 1988. Sinaranu, son of Siginu, and the trade relations between Ugarit and Crete. *Minos* **23**: 7–15.

Hemingway, S., 1996. Minoan metalworking in the postpalatial period: a deposit of metallurgical debris from Palaikastro. *ABSA* **91**: 213–52.

Hiller, S., 1982. Amnisos in den mykenischen texten. *Kadmos* **21**: 33–63.

1997. Cretan sanctuaries and Mycenaean palatial adminstration at Knossos. In Driessen and Farnoux 1997: 207–12.

Hirsch, E., and M. O'Hanlon, 1995. *The anthropology of landscape: perspectives on place and space.* Oxford: Clarendon Press.

Hodder, I. ed, 1982a. *Symbolic and structural archaeology*. Cambridge: Cambridge University Press.

1982b. The identification and interpretation of ranking in prehistory: a contextual perspective. In Renfrew and Shennan: 150–5.

1987. The contribution of the long term. In Hodder 1987a: 1–8.

ed, 1987a. *Archaeology as long-term history*. Cambridge: Cambridge University Press.

Hodges, R., 1982. The evolution of gateway communities: their socioeconomic implications. In Renfrew and Shennan: 117–24.

Hodkinson, S., 1983. Social order and the conflict of values in Classical Sparta. *Chiron* 13: 378–406.

1986. Land tenure and inheritance in Classical Sparta. *Classical Quarterly* 36: 378–406.

1992. Sharecropping and Sparta's economic exploitation of the helots. In Y. M. Sanders, ed, *Filolakon: Lakonian studies in honour of Hector Catling*. London: British School at Athens: 123–34.

1997. The development of Spartan society and institutions in the Archaic period. In Mitchell and Rhodes: 83–103.

2000. *Property and wealth in Classical Sparta*. London: Duckworth/Classical Press of Wales.

Hoffman, G., 1997. *Imports and immigrants: Near Eastern contacts with Iron Age Crete*. Ann Arbor: University of Michigan.

Hogarth, D. G., 1900. The Dictaean Cave: preliminary report. *ABSA* 6: 94–116.

1901. Excavations at Zakro, Crete. *ABSA* 7: 121–49.

Holloway, R., 2000. *The archaeology of ancient Sicily*. London: Routledge.

Hood, M. S. F., 1952. *Excavations in Chios 1938–65: Prehistoric Emborio and Ayia Gala*. 2 vols. London: Thames and Hudson/British School at Athens.

Hood, M. S. F., and J. Boardman, 1961. Early Iron Age tombs at Knossos. *ABSA* 56: 68–81.

Hood, M. S. F., and N. Coldstream, 1968. A Late Minoan Tomb at Ayios Ioannis near Knossos. *ABSA* 63: 206–18.

Hood, M. S. F., G. L. Huxley, and N. Sandars, 1959. A Minoan cemetery on Upper Gypsades. *ABSA* 53–4: 194–262.

Hood, M. S. F., and D. Smyth, 1981. *Archaeological survey of the Knossos area*. 2nd ed. London: British School at Athens/Thames and Hudson.

Hood, M. S. F., and P. M. Warren, 1966. Ancient sites in the province of Agios Vasilios, Crete. *ABSA* 61: 163–91.

Hood, M. S. F., P. M. Warren, and G. Cadogan, 1964. Travels in Crete, 1962. *ABSA* 59: 50–100.

Horden, P., and N. Purcell, 2000. *The corrupting sea: a study of Mediterranean history*. Oxford: Blackwell.

Hornblower, S., 1992. The creation and development of democratic institutions in ancient Greece. In Dunn, ed 1992: 1–17.

Humphreys, S. 1978. *Anthropology and the Greeks*. London: Routledge and Kegan Paul.

Hunt, L., ed, 1989. *The new cultural history*. Berkeley: University of California Press.

Hutchinson, R. W., 1956. A tholos tomb on the Kephala. *ABSA* 51: 74–81.

Hutchinson, R. W., and J. Boardman, 1954. The Khaniale Tekke tombs. *ABSA* 49: 215–30.

Iakovidis, S., 1962. *I mykenaiki akropoli ton Athinon* (Η μυκηναϊκή ακρόπολη των Αθηνών). Athens: Archaeological Society of Athens.

1969. *Perati: to nekrotafeion* (*Περατή: Το νεκροταφείον*). 3 vols. Athens: Archaeological Society of Athens.

1983. *Late Helladic citadels on mainland Greece*. Leiden: Brill.

1989. *Glas. I. I anaskafi 1955–61* (*Γλάς, I. Η Ανασκαφή 1955–61*). Athens: Archaeological Society of Athens.

2001. *Gla and the Kopais in the 13th century BC*. Athens: Archaeological Society of Athens.

Ioannidou, A., 1978. Perisyllogi archaion – tychaia evrimata (Περισυλλογή αρχαίων – τυχαία ευρύματα). *AD* 28: 569–74.

Isager, I., and J. E. Skydsgaard, 1992. *Ancient Greek agriculture: an introduction*. London: Routledge.

Jameson, M. H., 1990a. Domestic space in the Greek city-state. In Kent 1990: 92–113.

1990b. Private space and the Greek city. In Murray and Price: 171–99.

1997. Women and democracy in fourth-century Athens. In P. Brule and J. Outhen, eds, *Esclavage, gene, economie en Grèce ancienne*. Rennes: Presses Universitaires de Rennes: 95–107.

Jameson, M. H., C. N. Runnels, and T. van Andel, 1994. *A Greek countryside: the southern Argolid from prehistory to the present day*. Stanford: Stanford University Press.

Jeffery, L. H., 1988. Greece before the Persian invasion. In Boardman et al.: 347–67.

Jeffery, L., and A. Morpurgo Davies, 1970. ΠΟΙΝΙΚΑΣΤΑΣ and ΠΟΙΝΙΚΑΖΕΝ: BM 1969. 4–2.1. *Kadmos* IX. 2: 118–54.

Johnannowsky, W., 2002. *Il santuario sull'acropoli di Gortina*. Vol. II. Athens: Scuola Archaeologica Italiana di Atene.

Johnston, A. W., 2005. Kommos: further Iron Age pottery. *Hesperia* 74: 309–93.

in press. Cretan writing in the Greek world. In Kaiser and Pilz.

Jones, D. W., 1999. The archaeology and economy of Homeric gift exchange. *Opuscula Atheniensa* 24: 13–24.

2000. *The external relations of Early Iron Age Crete, 1100–600 BC*. Philadelphia: Archaeological Institute of America.

Jones, G., 1994. Appendix 1. The LM II plant remains. In Popham 1994c: 303–6.

Kaiser, I., and O. Pilz, in press. *Greece in the Geometric to Archaic periods: proceedings of a conference at the Deutsches Archäologisches Institut Aten, January 2006*.

Kalligas, P. G., 1992. Thessalia kai Euboia kata tin Primi Epochi tou Sidirou (11os–9os ai, p. Ch.) (Θεσσαλία και Εύβοια κατά την Πρώιμη Εποχή του Σιδήρου (11ος–9ος αι. π. Χ.)). In *Praktika Theochari*: 298–307.

Kallitsaki, H., 1997. The Mycenaean burial enclosure in Phourni, Archanes. In Driessen and Farnoux 1997: 213–27.

Kalpaxis, T., A. Schnapp, and D. Viviers, 1995. Itanos. *BCH* 119: 713–76.

Kanta, A., 1980. *The Late Minoan III period in Crete: a survey of sites, pottery and their distribution*. Göteborg: Paul Åströms Förlag.

1991. Cult, continuity and the evidence of pottery at the sanctuary of Syme Viannou, Crete. In Musti et al.: 479–505.

1994. The post-palatial period in the area of Amari: trade and communication between the north and south coasts of Crete. In Rocchetti 1994: 67–75.

1997. LM IIIB and LM IIIC pottery phases. Some problems of definition. In Hallager and Hallager 1997a: 83–111.

2001a. The cremations of Olous and the custom of cremation in Bronze Age Crete. In Stampolidis 2001: 59–69.

2001b. Cretan refuge settlements: problems and historical implications within the wider context of the eastern Mediterranean towards the end of the Bronze Age. In Karageorghis and Morris: 13–23.

2003a. The acropolis of Kastrokefala and its pottery. In Deger-Jalkotzy and Zavadil: 146–65.

2003b. The citadel of Kastrokefala and the date of the Minoan refuge citadels. In Deger-Jalkotzy and Zavadil: 167–82.

2005. Response to Haskell. In D'Agata and Moody: 223–5.

Kanta, A., and K. Davaras, 2004. The cemetery of Krya, district of Seteia: developments at the end of the Late Bronze Age and the beginning of the Early Iron Age in east Crete. In Stampolidis and Giannikouri: 149–59.

Kanta, A., and A. Karetsou, 1998. From Arkadhes to Rhytion: interactions of an isolated area of Crete with the Aegean and the East Mediterranean. In Karageorghis and Stampolidis: 159–75.

Kanta, A., and N. Stampolidis, 2001. The Orne aipy. In Karageorghis and Morris: 95–115.

Karageorghis, V., 1967. Relations between Cyprus and Crete during the 11th century BC. In *Pepragmena tou B' Diethnous Kritologikou Synedriou (Πεπραγμένα του Β' Διεθνούς Κρητολογικού Συνεδρίου, 1987)*. Athens: Etaireia Kritikon Istorikon Meleton: 180–5.

1979. Some reflections on the relations between Cyprus and Crete during the Late Minoan IIIB period. In Karageorghis, ed 1979: 199–204.

ed, 1979. *Acts of the international archaeological symposium 'Cyprus and Crete, c. 2000–500 BC', Nicosia, 16–22 April 1978*. Nicosia: Department of Antiquities.

1983. *Palaepaphos-Skales: An Iron Age cemetery in Cyprus (Ausgräbungen in Alt-Paphos auf Cypern)*. Konstanz: Universitätsverlag Konstanz.

1990a. *Tombs at Palaepaphos. 1. Eliomylia 2. Teratsoudhia*. Nicosia: A. G. Leventis Foundation.

1990b. *The end of the Late Bronze Age in Cyprus*. Nicosia: Pierides Foundation.

1992. The crisis years: Cyprus. In Ward and Joukowsky: 79–87.

1994. *Cyprus in the eleventh century BC*. Nicosia: A. G. Leventis Foundation.

1998. Mycenaean 'acropoleis' in the Aegean and Cyprus: some comparisons. In Cline and Harris-Cline: 127–37.

2001. Patterns of fortified settlements in the Aegean and Cyprus c. 1200 BC. In Karageorghis and Morris: 1–13.

Karageorghis, V., and C. E. Morris, eds, 2001. *Defensive settlements of the Aegean and the eastern Mediterranean after c. 1200 BC. Proceedings of an international workshop held at Trinity College Dublin, 7th–9th May, 1999*. Nicosia: Trinity College Dublin and the A. G. Leventis Foundation.

Karageorghis, V., and N. C. Stampolidis, eds, 1998. *Eastern Mediterranean: Cyprus-Dodecanese-Crete 16th-6th cent. BC. Proceedings of the International Symposium, Rethymnon, 13–16 May 1997*. Athens: University of Crete/A. G. Leventis Foundation.

Karantzali, E., 2005. The Mycenaeans at Ialysos: trading station or colony? In Laffineur and Greco: 141–51.

Kardulias, P. N., and M. T. Shutes, eds, 1997. *Aegean strategies: studies of culture and environment on the European fringe*. Lanham, MD; Oxford: Rowman and Littlefield.

Karetsou, A., 1974. Skafikai erevnai kai perisyllogi archaion eis kentriki Kriti (Σκαφηκαί έρευναι και περισυλλογή αρχαίων εις κεντρική Κρήτη). *PAE*: 240–6.

Karetsou, A., and G. Rethimiotakis, 1990. Kofinas. Iero korifis (Κόφηνας. Ιερό κορηφής). *AD* 45: 429–30.

Kent, S., ed, 1993. *Domestic architecture and the use of space: an undisciplinary cross-cultural study*. Cambridge: Cambridge University Press.

Kerschner, M., 1997. Ein stratifizierter Opferkomplex des 7. Jhs. v.Chr. aus de Artemision von Ephesos, *ÖJh* 66: 85–226.

Killen, J. T., 1964. The wool industry of Crete in the Late Bronze Age. *ABSA* 59: 1–15.

1985. The Linear B tablets and the Mycenaean economy. In A. Morpurgo-Davies and Y. Duhoux, eds, *Linear B: a 1984 survey*. Louvain: Peeters: 242–305.

Kinch, K. F., 1914. *Vroulia: fouilles de Vroulia (Rhodes)*. Berlin: Georg Reimer.

Kistler, E., 1998. *Die 'Opferinne-Zeremonie'. Bankettideologie am Grab, Orientalisierung und Formierung einer Adelgesellschaft in Athen*. Stuttgart: Franz Steiner Verlag.

Klein, N., 1997. Excavation of the Greek temples at Mycenae by the British School at Athens. *ABSA* 92: 247–323.

2004. The architecture of the Late Minoan IIIC shrine at Vronda, Kavousi. In Day et al. 2004: 91–103.

Klippel, W. E., and L. M. Snyder, 1991. Dark Age fauna from Kavousi, Crete: the vertebrates from the 1987 and 1988 excavation. *Hesperia* 60: 179–86.

Knapp, A. B., 1986. *Copper production and divine protection: archaeology, ideology and social complexity on Bronze Age Cyprus*. Göteborg: Paul Åströms Förlag.

1992a. Archaeology and *Annales:* time, space and change. In Knapp 1992b: 1–23.

ed, 1992b. *Archaeology,* Annales, *and ethnohistory*. Cambridge: Cambridge University Press.

Knapp, A. B., and E. Blake, 2005. Prehistory in the Mediterranean: the connecting and corrupting sea. In Knapp and Blake, eds 2005: 1–24.

eds, 2005. *The archaeology of Mediterranean prehistory*. Oxford: Blackwell.

Kolonas, L., 1991. Mykenaikes enkatastaseis stin Oreini Dymaia chora (Μυκηναϊκές εγκαταστάσεις στην Ορεινή Δυμαία χώρα). In Rizakis: 93–104.

1997. Neoteri mykenaiki topografia tis Achaias (Νεότερη μυκηναϊκή τοπογραφία της Αχαϊας). In *Peloponnesiakon Spoudon*: 468–96.

Konsolaki, E., 2003. I mykenaiki enkatastasi sto nisaki Modi tis Troizinias (Η μυκηναϊκή εγκατάσταση στο νησάκι Μόδι της Τροιζηνίας). In Kyparissi-Apostolika and Papakonstantinou: 417–33.

Kopcke, G., 1990. What role for Phoenicians? In G. Kopcke and I. Tokumaru, eds, *Greece between east and west: 10th–8th centuries BC. Papers of the meeting at the Institute of Fine Arts, New York University*. Mainz: von Zabern: 103–14.

Kopytoff, I., The cultural biography of things: commoditization as process. In Appadurai: 64–90.

Kotsonas, A., in press. Orientalizing ceramic styles and wares in Early Iron Age Crete. In Kaiser and Pilz.

Kourou, N., 1991. A funerary *cippus* at Eleutherna – evidence of Phoenician presence? *BICS* 37: 99–106.

2001. Tenos-Xobourgo: a new defensive site in the Cyclades. In Karageorghis and Morris: 171–91.

2004. I Tinos kata tin Promi Epochi tou Sidirou (Η Τήνος κατά την Πρώιμη Εποχή του Σιδήρου). In Stampolidis and Giannikouri: 427–37.

Kourou, N., and A. Karetsou, 1994. Το ιερό του Ερμού Κραναίου στο Πατσώ Αμαρίου. In Rocchetti 1994: 81–164.

1998. An enigmatic stone from Knossos. A re-used cippus? In Karageorghis and Stampolidis: 243–55.

Koutsidou, E., and N. S. Margaris, 1992. The recovery of plant communities in grazing exclosures in the island of Chios. In Grove et al.: 60–4.

Kraay, C., 1976. *Archaic and Classical Greek coins.* Berkeley: University of California Press.

Kuniholm, P., 1990. Archaeological evidence and non-evidence for climatic change. *Philosophical Transactions of the Royal Society of London* A330 : 645–55.

Kurtz, D., and J. Boardman, 1971. *Greek burial customs.* London: Thames and Hudson.

Kyparissi-Apostolika, N., and M. Papakonstantinou, eds, 2003. *Proceedings of the 2nd International Interdisciplinary Colloquium 'The Periphery of the Mycenaean World,' 26–30 September 1999.* Athens: Greek Ministry of Culture/14th Ephorate of Prehistoric and Classical Antiquities.

Kyriazopoulou, A., in press. Elyros. I physiognomia mias polis ton istorikon chronon sti notiodytiki Kriti ('Ελυρος. Η φυσιογνομία μίας πόλης των ιστορικών χρονών στη νοτιοδυτική Κρήτη). In *Depragmena I.*

Kyrieleis, H., 1979. Babylonische bronzen im Heraion von Samos. *Jahrbuch des Deutschen Archäologisches Instituts* 94: 32–48.

1988. Altorientalischer pferdeschmuck aus dem Heraion von Samos. *AthMitt* Band 103: 36–75.

1993. The Heraion at Samos. In Marinatos and Hägg: 125–53.

2002. Zu den Anfänge des Heiligtums von Olympia. In H. Kyrieleis, ed, *Olympia 1875–2000: 125 Jahre Deutsche Ausgrabungen: Internationales Symposion, Berlin, 9–11 November 2000.* Mainz am Rhein: von Zabern: 221–39.

Kyrtatas, D. J., 2002. Domination and exploitation. In Cartledge et al.: 140–56.

La Rosa, V., 1996. Per la Festós di etá arcaica. In M. G. Picozzi and F. Carinci, eds, *Vicino Oriente, Egeo-Grecia, Roma e mondo romano: tradizione dell'antico e collezionismo di antichitá: studi in memori di Lucia Guerrini.* Rome: Erma di Bretschneider: 68–87.

La Torre, G. F., 1989. Contributo preliminare alla conoscenza del territori di Gortina. *ASAtene* 66–7: 277–32.

Laffineur, R., ed, 1999. *Polemos: le contexte guèrrier en Egeé a l'age du Bronze. Actes de la 7e rencontre égéenne internationale.* Aegaeum 19. Liège: Universite de Liège.

Laffineur, R., and E. Greco, 2006. *Emporia: Aegeans in the central and eastern Mediterranean. Proceedings of the 10th International Aegean Conference, Italian School of Archaeology at Athens 14–18 April 2004.* 2 vols. Liège: Universite de Liège.

Laffineur, R., and R. Hägg, eds, 2001. *Potnia: deities and religion in the Aegean Bronze Age. Proceedings of the 8th International Aegean Conference, Göteborg, Göteborg University, 12th–15th April 2000.* Liège: Université de Liège.

Lambert, S., 1998. *The phratries of Attica.* Ann Arbor: University of Michigan Press.

Lambrinoudakis, V., 1988. Veneration of ancestors in Geometric Naxos. In Hägg et al.: 235–46.

Lambrinoudakis, V., and O. Philaniotou-Hadjianastasiou, 2001. The town of Naxos at the end of the Late Bronze Age: the Mycenaean fortification wall. In Karageorghis and Morris: 157–71.

Lane, P., 1987. Reordering residues of the past. In Hodder 1987a: 54–67.

Langdon, S., 1995. The pottery of the Early Iron Age and Geometric periods. In Runnels et al.: 57–73.

1997. *New light on a dark age: exploring the culture of Geometric Greece.* Columbia: University of Missouri Press.

Larsen, J. A., 1936. Perioeci in Crete. *Classical Philology* 31: 11–22.

Leach, E., 1954. *Political systems of highland Burma. A study of Kachin social structure.* London: London School of Economics and Political Sciences.

Lebessi, A., 1969. Afrati (Αφρατί). In S. Alexiou, Archaiotites kai mnimeia tis kentrikis kai anatolikis Kritis (Αρχαιότητες και μνημεία της κεντρικής και ανατολικής Κρήτης). *AD* 24, B2: 415–818.

1970. Afrati (Αφρατί). In S. Alexiou, Archaiotites kai mnimeia tis kentrikis kai anatolikis Kritis (Αρχαιότητες και μνημεία της κεντρικής και ανατολικής Κρήτης). *AD* 25, B2: 455–60.

1971a. Anaskafikai erevnai kai perisyllogi arxaion eis Kentrikin Kritin (Ανασκαφηκαί έρευναι και περισυλλογή 'αρχαίων εις Κεντρικήν Κρήτην). *ΠAE* 287–300.

1971b. Eis tafos tou 70 p.ch. aionos (Εις τάφος του 7ο π.χ. 'αιωνος). *AAA* 4: 384–92.

1973. Houmeri (Χούμερι). *AD* 28, B: 567.

1975. Ieron Ermou kai Afroditis eis Simi Viannou (Ιερόν Ερμού και Αφροδίτης εις Σήμη Βιάννου). *PAE* 322–39.

1976. Astraki (Αστράκι). *AD* 31: 351–3.

1978. Houmeri (Χούμερι). *AD* 33: 567.

1985. *To iero tou Ermi kai tis Afroditis sti Simi Viannou. I. Chalkina kritika toremata* (*Το ιερό του Ερμή και της Αφροδίτης στη Σύμη Βιάννου. I. Χάλκινα κρητικά τορέματα*). Athens: Archaeological Society of Athens.

1996. The relations of Crete and Euboea in the tenth and ninth centuries BC: the Lefkandi centaur and his predecessors. In Evely et al. 1996: 146–55.

Lefevre-Novaro, D., 2001. Les offrandes du VIIIe-VIIe siecle av. J-C deposés dans la grande tombe de Kamilari (Messara): problèmes et hypothèses. Unpublished paper given at the Cretological Congress, Elounda, 2001 (*Pepragmena Θ*).

Leighton, R., 1999. *Sicily before history: an archaeological survey from the Palaeolithic to the Iron Age.* London: Duckworth.

Lemos, I. S., 1994. Birds revisited. In Karageorghis 1994: 229–36.

2002. *The Protogeometric Aegean.* Oxford: Oxford University Press.

2006. Athens and Lefkandi: a tale of two sites. In Deger-Jalkotzy and Lemos: 505–31.

Le Rider, G., 1966. *Monnaies crétoises du Ve au Ier siecle av. J-C.* Paris: P. Geuthner.

Levi, D., 1929. Arkades. Una citta cretese all'alba della civilita ellenica. *ASAtene* 10–12: 15–710.

1931. I bronzi di Axos. *ASAtene* 13–14: 43–146.

1955. Cronaca d'Arte. Attivitá della Scuola Archeologica Italiana di Atene nell'anno 1954. *Bollettino d'Arte* 40: 141–64.

1958. Gli scavi a Festós nel 1956 e 1957. *ASAtene* 35–6: 193–361.

1962. Gli scavi a Festós negli annni 1958–60. *ASAtene* 39–40: 377–504.

Lewis, D. M., J. Boardman, J. K. Davies, and M. Ostwald, eds, 1992. *The Cambridge ancient history: the fifth century BC.* 2nd ed. Vol. V. Cambridge: Cambridge University Press.

Liverani, M., 1987. The collapse of the Near Eastern regional system at the end of the Bronze Age: the case of Syria. In Rowlands et al.: 66–74.

1990. *Prestige and interest: international relations in the Near East c. 1600–1100 BC.* Padova: Sargon Press.

Lolos, Y., 2001. Dark Age citadels in southern Salamis. In Karageorghis and Morris: 115–37.

Lombards, M., 1988. *Annali della Scuola Superiore di Pisa* (3rd series): 263–86.

Lo Schiavo, F., 1982. Copper metallurgy in Sardinia during the Late Bronze Age: new prospects on the Aegean connections. In Muhly et al.: 271–85.

1995. Cyprus in Sardinia in the Mediterranean trade routes toward the west. In V. Karageorghis and D. Michaelides, eds, *Cyprus and the sea: proceedings of the international symposium.* Nicosia: University of Cyprus: 45–59.

Lo Schiavo, F., E. Macanamara, and L. Vagnetti, 1985. Late Cypriot imports to Italy and their influence on local bronzework. *Papers of the British School at Rome* 53: 1–71.

Lowells, R., 1989. Critique of Hansen. *Classical Philology* 84: 322–34.

Lowenthal, D., 1985. *The past is a foreign country.* Cambridge: Cambridge University Press.

Macdonald, C., 1986. Problems of the twelfth century BC in the Dodecanese. *ABSA* 81: 125–51.

Macdonald, C., and J. N. Coldstream, 1997. Knossos: area of the southwest houses: early Hellenic occupation. *ABSA* 92: 191–247.
MacGillivray, U. A., 1997. Late Minoan II and III pottery and chronology at Palaikastro: an introduction. In Hallager and Hallager 1997a: 193–209.
Maddin, R., 1982. Early iron technology in Cyprus. In Muhly et al.: 303–12.
Malakasioti, Z., and A. Mousioni, 2004. Nea evrimata tis Isteris Epochis tou Chalkou kai tis Epochis tou Sidirou stin Alo (Νέα ευρήματα της Υστερης Εποχής του Χαλκού και της Εποχης του Σιδήρου στην 'Αλο). In Stampolidis and Giannikouri: 353–69.
Malkin, I., 1987. *Religion and colonization in ancient Greece*. Leiden: Brill.
1994. *Myth and territory in the Spartan Mediterranean*. Cambridge: Cambridge University Press.
1998. *The returns of Odysseus: colonisation and ethnicity*. Berkeley: University of California Press.
Manning, S. W., 1999. *A test of time*. Oxford: Oxbow Books.
Manning, S. W., and L. Hulin, 2005. Maritime commerce and geographies of mobility in the Late Bronze Age of the eastern Mediterranean: problematisations. In Knapp and Blake, eds 2005: 270–303.
Maran, J., 1999. Political and religious aspects of architectural change on the Upper Citadel of Tiryns. The case of Building T. In Betancourt et al.: 113–23.
2005. Late Minoan coarse ware stirrup jars on the Greek mainland. A postpalatial perspective from the 12th century BC Argolid. In D'Agata and Moody: 415–33.
2006. Coming to terms with the past: ideology and power in Late Helladic IIIC. In Deger-Jalktozy and Lemos: 123–50.
Marangou, A., 1999. Wine in the Cretan economy. In Chaniotis 1999: 269–78.
Marangou, L. I., 1989. Teichismenoi oikismoi ton geometrikon chronon (90s–80s p. Ch. aionas) (Τειχισμένοι οικισμόι των γεωμετρικών χρόνων (9ος–8ος π.Χ. αιώνας)). *Praktika tis Akademias Athenon* 63: 80–92.
2002. *Amorgos I. I Minoa* (*Αμοργος* I. *Η Μινώα*). Athens: Archaeological Society of Athens.
Margaris, N. S., 1990. Effects of recent agricultural changes on the landscapes of Mediterranean Europe. In Grove et al.: 26–8.
Mariani, L., 1895. Antichita cretesi. *Monumenti Antichi* 6: 135–348.
Marinatos, N., 1996. Cults by the seashore: what happened at Amnisos? In R. Hägg 1983.
Marinatos, N., and R. M. Hägg, eds, 1993. *Greek sanctuaries: new approaches*. London: Routledge.
Marinatos, S., 1929. Anaskafai en Kriti (Ανασκαφαί εν Κρήτη). *PAE*: 94–104.
1930. Anaskafai en Kriti (Ανασκαφαί εν Κρήτη). *PAE*: 91–9.
1933. Funde und Forschungen auf Kreta. *Archäologischer Anzeiger*: 287–314.
1935. Enati kai dekati archaiologiki periferia Kritis (Ενάτη και δεκάτη αρχαιολογική περιφέρεια Κρήτις). *AD* 15: 49–83.
1936. Le temple géometrique de Dreros. *BCH* 60: 214–84.
1950. To spilaion tis Lykastou (Το σπήλαιον της Λύκαστου). *ΠAE*: 248–57.
Markoe, G., 1998. The Phoenicians on Crete: transit trade and the search for ores. In Karageorghis and Stampolidis: 233–43.
Mastrokostas, E., 1962a. Achaia Teichos Dymaion (Αχαϊα Τείχος Δυμαίον). *Εργον*: 171–5.
1962b. Anaskafi tou Teichos Dymaion (Ανασκαφή του Τείχους Δυμαίων). *ΠAE*: 127–33.
1963. Anaskafi tou Teichos Dymaion (Ανασκαφή του Τείχους Δυμαίων). *ΠAE*: 93–8.
1964a. Anaskafi tou Teichos Dymaion (Ανασκαφή του Τείχους Δυμαίων). *AD* 18, B1: 111–14.
1964b. Anaskafi tou Teichos Dymaion. Architektonika leipsana, stromatografia (Ανασκαφή του Τείχους Δυμαίων. Αρχιτεκτονικά λείψανα, στρώματογραφία). *ΠAE*: 60–7.
1965. Anaskafi tou Teichos Dymaion (Ανασκαφή του Τείχους Δυμαίων). *ΠAE*: 121–36.
Matsas, D., 2004. I Samothraki sti Proimi Epochi tou Sidirou (Η Σαμοθράκη στη Πρώιμη Εποχή του Σιδήρου). In Stampolidis and Giannikouri: 227–59.
Matthäus, H., 1988. Heirloom or tradition? Bronze stands of the second and first millennium B.C. in Cyprus, Greece and Italy. In E. B. French and K. A. Wardle, eds, *Problems in Greek prehistory*. Bristol: Bristol Classical Press.
1998. Cyprus and Crete in the early first millennium BC. A synopsis with special reference to new finds from the Idaean Cave of Zeus. In Karageorghis and Stampolidis: 127–59.

Mazarakis Ainian, A., 1988. Early Greek temples: their origin and function. In Hägg et al.: 105–19.

1997. *From rulers' dwellings to temples: architecture, religion and society in Early Iron Age Greece (1100–700 BC)*. Jonsered: Paul Åströms Förlag.

1998. Oropos in the Early Iron Age. In M. Bats and B. d 'Agostino, eds, *Euboica: l'Eubea e la presenza euboica in Calcidica e in Occidente: atti del convegno internazionale di Napoli, 13–16 novembre 1996*. Centre Jean Berard: Istituto Universitario Orientalio, Dipartimento del mondo classico e del Mediterraneo antico: 179–215.

ed, in press. *The Dark Ages revisited. Proceedings of a conference in honour of W. D. E. Coulson, Volos, 14–18 June 2007*.

McDonald, W. A., 1983. The Dark Age at Nichoria: a perspective. In McDonald et al.: 316–32.

McDonald, W. A., W. D. E. Coulson, and J. Rosser, eds, 1983. *Excavations at Nichoria in south-west Greece*. Vol. III: *Dark Age and Byzantine occupation*. Minneapolis: University of Minnesota Press.

McDonald, W. A., and G. R. Rapp, 1972. *The Minnesota Messenia expedition: reconstructing a Bronze Age regional environment*. Minneapolis: University of Minnesota Press.

McDonald, W. A., and R. Hope Simpson, 1961. Explorations in southwestern Peloponnese. *AJA* 65: 221–60.

1969. Further explorations in southwestern Peloponnese, 1964–8. *AJA* 79: 123–77.

McDonald, W. A., and N. C. Wilkie, eds, 1992. *Excavations at Nichoria in south-west Greece*. Vol. II: *The Bronze Age occupation*. Minneapolis: University of Minnesota Press.

McFadden, D., 1954. A Late Cypriot tomb from Kourion, Kaloriziki: No. 40. *AJA* 58: 131–42.

Mee, C., 1982. *Rhodes in the Bronze Age*. Warminster, UK: Aris and Phillips.

Meiggs, R., and D. Lewis, eds, 1989. *A selection of Greek historical inscriptions to the end of the fifth century BC*. Rev. ed. Oxford: Clarendon Press.

Mitchell, L. G., and P. J. Rhodes, 1997. *The development of the polis in Archaic Greece*. London: Routledge.

Möller, A., 2001. *Naukratis: trade in Archaic Greece*. Oxford: Oxford University Press.

Moody, J. A., 1987. *The environmental and cultural prehistory of the Khania region of West Crete: Neolithic through Late Minoan III*. Unpublished PhD dissertation, University of Minnesota.

1992. Continuity of settlement and land-use systems in west Crete. In Grove et al.: 52–9.

1997. The Cretan environment: abused or just misunderstood? In Kardulias and Shutes: 61–79.

2004. Western Crete in the Bronze Age: a survey of the evidence. In Day et al. 2004: 247–65.

2005. Unravelling the threads: climate changes in the Late Bronze III Aegean. In D'Agata and Moody: 443–71.

Moody, J., L. Nixon, O. Rackham, and S. Price, 1998a. Surveying *poleis* and larger sites in Sphakia. In Cavanagh and Curtis: 87–95.

Moody, J., A. Peatfield, and S. Markoulaki, 1998b. Ayios Vasilios Valley Survey. In D. J. Blackman, ed, Archaeology in Greece 1997–98. *AR* 1997–98: 120–1.

2000b. Report from the Ayios Vasilios Valley Survey. In *Pepragmena H*: 359–73.

Moody, J., O. Rackham, and G. Rapp, 1996. Environmental archaeology of prehistoric NW Crete. *JFA* 23: 273–97.

Moody, J. A., H. L. Robinson, J. Francis, L. Nixon, and L. Wilson, 2000a. Ceramic fabric analysis and survey archaeology: the Sfakia survey. *ABSA* 98: 37–105.

Mook, M. S. M., 1993. *The Northwest Building: houses of the Late Bronze and Early Iron Ages on the Kastro at Kavousi, east Crete*. Unpublished PhD dissertation, University of Minnesota.

1998. Early Iron Age domestic architecture: the Northwest Building on the Kastro at Kavousi. In Cavanagh and Curtis: 45–57.

2000. Subminoan pottery and cultural identity in Protogeometric Crete. Unpublished paper given at the conference *Lighten our darkness: cultural transformations from the Alps to Anatolia in the first millennium BC*, Birmingham University, January.

2004. From foundation to abandonment: new ceramic phasing for the Late Bronze Age and Early Iron Age on the Kastro at Kavousi. In Day et al. 2004: 163–81.

2005. The Kavousi fabrics: a typology for coarse pottery in the Mirabello region of eastern Crete. In Haggis 2005: 167–77.

Mook, M., and W. D. E. Coulson, 1997. Late Minoan IIIC pottery from the Kastro at Kavousi. In Hallager and Hallager 1997a: 337–71.

Moran, W. L., ed and trans, 1992. *The Amarna letters.* Baltimore: Johns Hopkins University Press.

Moreland, A., 1992. Restoring the dialectic: what can archaeologists learn from Annalistes? In Knapp 1992b: 112–31.

Morgan, C. A., 1986. *Settlement and exploitation in the region of the Corinthian gulf, ca. 1000–700 BC.* Unpublished PhD thesis, University of Cambridge.

1990. *Athletes and oracles.* Cambridge: Cambridge University Press.

1994. The evolution of a sacral 'landscape': Isthmia, Perachora, and the early Corinthian state. In Alcock and Osborne: 105–43.

1997. The archaeology of sanctuaries in Early Iron Age and Archaic *ethne:* a preliminary view. In Mitchell and Rhodes: 168–99.

1998. Ritual and society in the Early Iron Age Corinthia. In R. Hägg, ed, *Ancient Greek cult practice from the archaeological evidence: proceedings of the fourth international seminar on ancient Greek cult, organised by the Swedish Institute at Athens, 22–24 October 1993.* Stockholm: Paul Åstroms Förlag: 73–90.

1999. *Isthmia* VIII. *The Late Bronze Age settlement and Early Iron Age sanctuary.* Princeton, NJ: American School of Classical Studies at Athens.

2003. *Early Greek states beyond the polis.* London: Routledge.

Morgan, C., and J. J. Coulton, 1997. The *polis* as a physical entity. In Hansen 1997d: 87–144.

Morgan, C., and T. M. Whitelaw, 1995. Pots and politics: ceramic evidence and the rise of the Argive state. *AJA* **95**: 79–108.

Morris, I., 1986. Gift and commodity in Archaic Greece. *Man* (NS) **21**: 1–17.

1987. *Burial and ancient society: the rise of the Greek city-state.* Cambridge: Cambridge University Press.

1988. Tomb cult and the Greek renaissance: the past in the present in the eighth century BC. *Antiquity* **62**: 750–61.

1989. Circulation, deposition and the formation of the Greek Iron Age. *Man* (NS) **23**: 502–19.

1991. The early polis as city and state. In Rich and Wallace-Hadrill: 25–59.

1992. Death-ritual and social structure in Classical antiquity. Cambridge: Cambridge University Press.

1993. The Kerameikos stratigraphy and the character of the Greek Dark Age. *JMA* **6**: 207–21.

1994. Archaeologies of Greece. In I. Morris, ed, *Classical Greece: ancient histories and modern archaeologies.* Cambridge: Cambridge University Press: 8–49.

1996. The strong principle of equality and the Archaic origins of Greek democracy. In Ober and Hedrick 1996b: 19–48.

1997a. The art of citizenship. In S. Langdon, *New light on a Dark Age: exploring the culture of Geometric Greece.* Columbia: University of Missouri Press: 9–43.

1997b. An archaeology of equalities? In Nichols and Charlton: 91–107.

1997c. Introduction. In Morris and Raaflaub 1997: 1–11.

1997d. Archaeology as a kind of anthropology. In Morris and Raaflaub 1997: 229–41.

1998. Archaeology and Archaic Greek history. In Fisher and van Wees: 1–91.

1999. Foreword. In Finley 1999: ix–xxxii.

2000. *Archaeology as cultural history: words and things in Iron Age Greece.* Oxford: Blackwell.

2002. Hard surfaces. In Cartledge et al.: 8–44.

Morris, I., and K. Raaflaub, eds, 1997. *Democracy 2500? Questions and challenges.* Dubuque, IA: Kendall/Hunt.

Morris, M. W., 1994. *A pedological investigation of catchment basins below Late Minoan period archaeological sites in eastern Crete, Greece.* Unpublished PhD dissertation, University of Tennessee.

2003. *Soil science and archaeology: three test cases from Minoan Crete*. Philadelphia: INSTAP Academic Press.

Morris, M. W., J. T. Ammons, M. E. Timpson, and J. E. Foss, 2005. A pedological investigation and soil survey of the Kavousi region. In Haggis 2005: 153–67.

Moschonisioti, S., 2004. Evchoria diakosmimeni keramiki apo to nekrotafeio tis archaias Mendis (Ευχώρια διακοσμημένη κεραμική απο το νεκροταφείο της αρχαίας Μένδης). In Stampolidis and Giannikouri: 277–95.

Mountjoy, P., 1986. *Mycenaean decorated pottery: a guide to identification*. Göteborg: Paul Åstroms Förlag.

Muhly, J. D., 1982. The nature of trade in the Late Bronze Age eastern Mediterranean: the organisation of the metals trade and the role of Cyprus. In Muhly et al.: 251–71.

1999. The Phoenicians in the Aegean. In Betancourt et al.: 517–27.

Muhly, J. D., R. Maddin, and V. Karageorghis, eds, 1982. *Early metallurgy in Cyprus. Acta of the International Archaeological Symposium*. Nicosia: Department of Antiquities.

Murray, O. 1983. The symposion as social organization. In Hägg 1983: 195–9.

1990a. Sympotic history. In Murray, ed 1990: 3–14.

1990b. Cities of reason. In Murray and Price: 1–29.

ed, 1990c. *Sympotica: a symposium on the symposion (Symposium held at Balliol College, Oxford, 4–8 September 1984)*. Oxford: Clarendon Press.

2000. What is Greek about the polis? In Flensted-Jensen et al.: 231–49.

Murray, O., and S. Price, eds, 1990. *The Greek city from Homer to Alexander*. Oxford: Clarendon Press.

Musgrave, J. H., 1996. The human bones. In Coldstream and Catling: 677–702.

Musti, D., A. Sacconi, L. Rocchetti, M. Rocchi, E. Scafa, L. Sportiello, and M. E. Gianotta, eds, 1991. La transizione dal miceneo all'alto arcaismo. Dal palazzo alla cittá. Atti del Convegno Internazionale, Roma, 14–19 Marzo 1988. Rome: Instituto per gli Studi Micenei ed Egeo-Anatolici, Consiglio Nazionale delle Ricerche.

Myers, J. W., E. E. Myers, and G. Cadogan, 1992. *The aerial atlas of ancient Crete*. Los Angeles: University of California Press.

Mylona, D., 1999. The bones of suckling animals. In Tzedakis and Martlew: 64–7.

Mylonas, G., 1961. *Eleusis and the Eleusinian mysteries*. Princeton, NJ: Princeton University Press.

Nagy, G., 1996. *Homeric questions*. Austin: University of Texas Press.

Negbi, O., 1992. Early Phoenician presence in the Mediterranean islands: a reappraisal. *AJA* **96**: 599–615.

Nevett, L., 1999. *House and society in the ancient Greek world*. Cambridge: Cambridge University Press.

Newton, M., K. A. Wardle, and P. I. Kuniholm, 2003. Dendrochronology and radiocarbon determinations from Assiros and the beginning of the Greek iron Age. *AEMΘ* **17**: 173–90.

2005. Troy VIIB2 revisited: the date of the transition from Bronze to Iron Age in the northern Aegean. In H. Todorova and M. Stefanovich, eds, *The Struma/Strymon river valley in prehistory: in the steps of J. H. Gaul*. Sofia: James Harvey Gaul Foundation: 501–17.

Nicholls, R. V., 1959. Old Smyrna: the Iron Age fortifications and associated remains on the city perimeter. *ABSA* **54**: 35–138.

Nichols, D. L., and T. H. Charlton, eds, 1997. *The archaeology of city-states: cross-cultural approaches*. Washington, DC: Smithsonian.

Nielsen, T. H., ed, 1997. *Yet more studies in the ancient Greek polis. Papers from the Copenhagen Polis Centre 4*. Stuttgart: Franz Steiner Verlag.

ed, 2002. *Even more studies in the ancient Greek polis. Papers from the Copenhagen Polis Center*. Stuttgart: Franz Steiner.

Niemeier, W.-D., in press. The sanctuary of Kalapodi (ancient Phokis). New evidence for the continuity of cult from the Mycenaean to the Archaic period. In Mazarakis Ainian, in press.

Nixon, L., 1990. Minoan settlements and Greek sanctuaries. In *Pepragmena ST*: 59–67.

Nixon, L., J. A. Moody, V. Niniou-Kindeli, S. Price, and O. Rackham, 1990. Archaeological survey in Sphakia, Crete. *Echos du Monde Classique* **34** (NS 9): 213–20.

Nixon, L., J. A. Moody, S. Price, and O. Rackham, 1989. Archaeological survey in Sphakia, Crete. *Echos du Monde Classique* 33 (NS 8): 201–15.

Nixon, L., J. A. Moody, and O. Rackham, 1988. Archaeological survey in Sphakia, Crete. *Echos du Monde Classique* 32 (NS 7): 159–74.

Nowicki, K., 1987a. Topography of refuge settlement in Crete. *Jahrbuch des Römisch-Germanischen Zentralmuseums* 34: 213–34.

1987b. The history and setting of the town at Karphi. *SMEA* 26: 235–56.

1988. Investigations in the Cretan Mountains. *Archeologia* (Warsaw) 39: 189–98.

1990. The West Siteia Mountains at the turn of the Bronze and Iron Ages. *Aegaeum'* 6: 161–80.

1991. Report on investigations in Greece. VII. Studies in 1990. *Archeologia* (Warsaw) 42: 137–45.

1992a. Report on investigations in Greece. VIII. Studies in 1991. *Archeologia* (Warsaw) 43: 113–19.

1992b. Fortifications in Dark Age Crete. In S. van Maele and J. M. Fossey, eds, *Fortificationes Antiquae*. Amsterdam: J. C. Gieben: 53–76.

1993. Report on investigations in Greece. IX. Studies in 1992. *Archeologia* (Warsaw) 44: 95–101.

1994a. A Dark Age refuge centre near Pefki, east Crete. *ABSA* 89: 235–68.

1994b. Katalimata. In Coulson and Tsipopoulou: 94–97.

1994c. Some remarks on the pre- and protopalatial peak sanctuaries in Crete. *Aegean Archaeology* 1: 31–48.

1995a. Report on Investigations in Greece. X. Studies in 1993–1994. *Archeologia* (Warsaw) 46: 63–70.

1995b. To Flechtron and other Dark Age sites near Kera Karfi. *Pepragmena Z*: 693–702.

1996. Arvi Fortetsa and Loutraki Kandilioro. *ABSA* 91: 253–85.

1998. Lasithi (Crete): One hundred years of archaeological research. *Aegean Archaeology* 3: 27–48.

1999a. The historical background of defensible sites on Crete: LM IIIC versus Protopalatial. In Laffineur: 575–81.

1999b. Economy of refugees: life in the Cretan mountains at the turn of the Bronze and Iron Ages. In Chaniotis 1999: 145–73.

2000. *Defensible sites in Crete, c. 1200–800 BC (LM IIIB/C through Early Geometric)*. Liège: Université de Liège.

2001. Sea raiders and refugees: problems of defensible sites in Crete c. 1200 BC. In Karageorghis and Morris: 23–39.

2002. From Late Minoan IIIC refuge settlements to Geometric acropoleis: architecture and social organization of Dark Age villages and towns in Crete. *Pallas: revue d'etudes antiques* 58: 149–74.

2004a. East of Kavousi, west of Mochlos. The west Siteia mountains at the end of the Bronze Age. In Day et al. 2004: 265–80.

2005. Report on investigations in Greece. XI. Studies in 1995–2003. *Archeologia* (Warsaw) 55: 75–100.

2006. The end of the Neolithic in Crete. *Aegean Archaeology* 6: 7–72.

2008. *Monastiraki Katalimata: excavation of a Cretan refuge site 1993–2000*. Philadelphia: INSTAP Academic Press.

Ober, J., 1989. *Mass and elite in democratic Athens*. Princeton, NJ: Princeton University Press.

1996. The Athenian revolution of 508/507 BC. Violence, authority and the origins of democracy. In J. Ober, ed, *The Athenian revolution: essays on Greek democracy and political theory*. Princeton, NJ: Princeton University Press: 34–52.

1997. Revolution matters: democracy as demotic action (a response to Kurt A. Raaflaub). In Morris and Raaflaub 1997: 67–87.

Ober, J., and C. Hedrick, 1996a. Democracies ancient and modern. In Ober and Hedrick 1996b: 3–19.

eds, 1996b. *Demokratia: a conversation on democracies, ancient and modern*. Princeton, NJ: Princeton University Press.

Olivier, J.-P., ed, 1992. *Mykenaika: Actes du IXe Colloque International sur les textes mycéniens et égéens, organisé par le Centre de l'Antiquité Grecque et Romaine de la Fondation Hellénique des Récherches Scientifiques et l'Ecole française à Athènes (Athènes, 2–6 octobre 1990)*. Paris: Boccard.

1997. La collecte et la circulation de l'information économique dans la Crete mycénienne. In Driessen and Farnoux 1997: 391–407.

2001. Les 'collecteurs': leur distribution spatiale et temporelle. In Voutsaki and Killen: 139–60.

Osborne, R., 1987. *Classical landscape with figures: the ancient Greek city and its countryside.* New York: Sheridan House.

1991. Pride and prejudice, sense and subsistence: exchange and society in the Greek city. In Rich and Wallace-Hadrill: 119–47.

1995. The economics and politics of slavery at Athens. In A. Powell, ed, *The Greek world.* London: Routledge: 27–43.

1996. *Greece in the making, 1200–479 BC.* London: Routledge.

1997. Law and laws: how do we join up the dots? In Mitchell and Rhodes: 74–83.

1998. Early Greek colonization? The nature of Greek settlement in the West. In Fisher and van Wees: 251–69.

Østby, E., 1997. Early Iron Age in the sanctuary of Athena Alea at Tegea. Recent excavations. *Acta ad archaeologiam et artium historium pertinentia* 9: 79–107.

Østby, E., J.-M. Luce, G. Nordquist, C. Tarditi, and M. E. Voyatzis, 1994. The sanctuary of Athena Alea at Tegea: first preliminary report (1990–1992). *OpAth* 20: 89–141.

Ostwald, M., 1988. The reform of the Athenian state by Cleisthenes. In Boardman et al.: 303–47.

Palaima, T. G., 1989. Perspectives on the Pylos oxen tablets: textual and archaeological evidence for the use and management of oxen in Late Bronze Age Messenia (and Crete). *Studia Mycenaea*: 85–124.

1992. The Knossos oxen dossier: the use of oxen in Mycenaean Crete. Part I. General background and scribe 107. In Olivier 1992: 463–75.

Palmer, L., 1963. *On the Knossos tablets.* Oxford: Clarendon Press.

Palmer, R., 1992. Wheat and barley in Mycenaean society. In Olivier 1992: 475–99.

Panayiotakis, N., 2004. L'evolution archéologique de la Pediada (Crete centrale): premier bilan d'une prospection. *BCH* 127: 327–40.

2005. Contacts between Knossos and the Pediada region in central Crete. In Cadogan et al.: 177–86.

Papadakis, N., 1982. Roussa Ekklisia. *AD* 37: 389.

Papadimitriou, A., 1998. Η οικιστική εξέλιξη της Τίρυνθας μετά την Μυκηναϊκη εποχή. In A. Pariente and G. Touchais, eds, *Argos et l'Argolide. Topographie et urbanisme (Actes de la Table Ronde Internationale Athenes-Argos 28/4–1/5 1990.* Athens: Ministry of Culture/Goulandris Foundation: 117–30.

2002. Argos, Odos Papalexopoulou, oikopedo M. Kampaniari (Αργος, οδός Παπαλεξοπούλου, οικόπεδο Μ. Καμπανιάρι). *AD* 52: 135–8.

2006. The Early Iron Age in the Argolid: some new aspects. In Deger-Jalkotzy and Lemos: 531–47.

Papadopoulos, J., 2005. *The Early Iron Age cemetery at Torone.* 2 vols. Los Angeles: Cotsen Institute of Archaeology, University of California at Los Angeles.

Papadopoulou, E., 1997. Une tombe à tholos 'intra muros': le cas du cimitière MR d'Armenoi. In Driessen and Farnoux 1997: 316–40.

Papagiannopoulos, K., and G. Zachos, 1991. Entatiki epifaniaki erevna stin dytiki Achaia – mia alli prosengisi (Εντατική επιφανειακή έρευνα στην δυτική Αχαϊα – μια άλλη προσέγγιση). In Rizakis: 139–53.

Papapostolou, I., 2003. To telos tis Mykenaikis epochis ston Thermo (Το τέλος της Μυκηναϊκής εποχής στον Θέρμο). In Kyparissi-Apostolika and Papakonstantinou: 135–47.

Pariente, A., 1991. Chronique des fouilles en 1990. *BCH* 115: 942–6.

Parker Pearson, M., 1982. Mortuary practices, society and ideology: an ethnoarchaeological case study. In Hodder 1982a: 99–113.

Parker Pearson, M., Ramilisonina and Retsihisatse. 1999. Ancestors, forests and ancient settlements: Tandroy readings of the archaeological past. In Ucko and Layton, eds: 397–410.

Parlama, L., 1974. Mykenaika Eleias (Μυκηναϊκά Ελείας). *AD* 29: 25–58.

Paschalidis, K., 2006. Stoicheia mykenaikou charaktira stin Anatoliki Kriti kata to telos tis epochis tou Chalkou: nea megara sto Chalasmeno Ierapetras (Στοιχεία μυκηναϊκού χαρακτήρα στην Ανατολική

Κρήτη κατά το τέλος της εποχής του Χαλκού; νέα μέγαρα στο Χαλασμένο Ιεράπετρας). In *Pepragmena Θ*: 219–33.

Pauketat, T. R, 2000. Politicisation and community in the pre-Columbian Mississipi valley. In Canuto and Yaeger: 16–44.

Peatfield, A., 1990. Minoan peak sanctuaries: history and society. *Opuscula Atheniensia* 18: 117–32.

Peltenburg, E., and S. Pickles, 1998. Metallurgy, society and the Bronze-Iron transition in the east Mediterranean and the Near East. *RDAC*: 67–100.

Pendlebury, H. W., J. D. S. Pendlebury, and M. B. Money-Coutts, 1938. Excavations in the plain of Lasithi III. Karphi. A city of refuge of the Early Iron Age in Crete. *ABSA* 38: 57–148.

Pendlebury, J. D. S., 1939. *The archaeology of Crete*. London: Methuen.

Pendlebury, J. D. S., E. Eccles, and M. B. Money-Coutts, 1933. Journeys in Crete, 1934. *ABSA* 33: 80–101.

Perlman, P., 1993. One-hundred-citied Crete and the 'Cretan politeia'. *Classical Philology* 87: 193–207.

1996. Polis ηπηκοος. The dependent *polis* and Crete. In Hansen 1996: 233–88.

2000. Gortyn. The first seven hundred years. Part I. In Flensted-Jensen et al.: 59–90.

2002. Gortyn. The first seven hundred years. Part II. The laws from the Temple of Apollo. In Nielsen 2002: 187–228.

2004a. Crete. In Hansen and Nielsen: 1144–96.

2004b. Tinker, tailor, soldier, sailor: the economies of Archaic Eleutherna, Crete. *Classical Antiquity* 23/1: 95–137.

2005. Imagining Crete. In M. H. Hansen, ed, *The imaginary polis*. Copenhagen: Copenhagen Polis Centre: 282–335.

Perna, K., 2004. Karphi: Soltanto un sito di refugio? *Creta Antica* 5: 155–79.

Pernier, L., 1914. Templi arcaici sulla Patella di Prinias. *ASAtene* I: 18–111.

1934. New elements for the study of the archaic temple at Prinias. *AJA* 38: 171–7.

Petrie, W. M. F., 1886. *Naukratis* I. London: Trübner.

Petropoulos, M., 1988. Triti anaskafiki periodos sto Ano Mazaraki (Rakita) Achaias (Τρίτη ανασκαφική περίοδος στο Ανω Μαζαράκι (Ρακίτα) Αχαϊας. In *Praktika tou G'Diethnous Synedriou Peloponnesiakon Spoudon II (Πρακτικά του Γ'Διεθνούς Συνεδρίου Πελοποννεσιακών Σπουδών II)*. Athens: Etaireia Peloponnesiakon Spoudon: 165–92.

1990. Αρχαιολογικές έρευνες στην Αχαϊα. In *Triantafyllou*: 495–537.

Petroulakis, E., 1915. Kritikis Atsipadas tafoi (Κρητικής Ατσιπάδας τάφοι). *AE*: 48–50.

Pfaff, C., 1999. The Early Iron Age pottery from the sanctuary of Demeter and Kore at Corinth. *Hesperia* 68: 55–134.

Picard, O., 1992. Lato. In Myers et al.: 155–9.

Pierart, M., 1991. Aspects de la transition en Argolide. In Musti et al.: 133–44.

Piteros, X., 2003. I mykenaiki akropoli tis Larisas tous Argous (Η μυκηναϊκή ακρόπολη της Λάρισας τους 'Αργους). In Kyparissi-Apostolika and Papakonstantinou: 369–97.

Platakis, E., 1970. Isterominoika-ypominoika ktismata eis Kastrokefala Almyrou Irakleiou (Υστερομινοικά-υπομινοικά κτίσματα εις Καστροκεφάλα Αλμυρού Ηρακλείου). *KCh* 22: 511–14.

Platon, L., 1997. Caractère, morphologie et datation de la bourgade postpalatiale de Kefali Chondrou Viannou. In Driessen and Farnoux 1997: 357–73.

Platon, N., 1952a. Anaskafi YM III laxevton eis tin periochi Episkopis kai Stamnion Irakleiou (Ανασκαφή ΥΜ ΙΙΙ λαξευτών εις την περιοχή Επισκοπής και Σταμνίων Ηρακλείου). *ΠΑΕ*: 619–28.

1952b. Geometrikai tafoi tis perioxis Episkopis kai Stamnion Pediadas (Γεωμετρικαί τάφοι της περιοχής Επισκοπής και Σταμνίον Πεδιάδας). *PAE*: 628–30.

1952c. Tafikon spilaion protogeometrikon chronon eis Berati (Perati) Piskokefalon (Ταφικών σπήλαιον πρότογεωμετρικών χρονών εις Μπερατί (Περατί) Πισκοκεφάλον). *PAE*: 639–43.

1954a. I archaiologiki kinesis en Kriti kata to etos 1954 (Η αρχαιολογικη κινησης εν Κρητη κατά το ετος 1954). *KCh* 8: 499–517.

1954b. Anaskafai periochis Siteias (Ανασκαφή περιοχής Σιτείας). *PAE*: 361–8.

1954c. Anaskafi Onithe Gouledianon Rethymnis (Ανασκαφή Ονυθέ Γουλεδιανών Ρεθύμνης). *PAE*: 377–82.

1955a. I archaiologiki kinesis en Kriti kata to etos 1954 (Η αρχαιολογική κήνησης εν Κρητη κατά το έτος 1955). *KCh* 9: 553–69.

1955b. Anaskafi Onithe Gouledianon Rethymnis (Ανασκαφή Ονυθέ Γουλεδιανών Ρεθύμνης). *PAE*: 298–305.

1956. Anaskafi Onithe Gouledianon Rethymnis. (Ανασκαφή Ονυθέ Γουλεδιανών Ρεθύμνης). *PAE*: 226–8.

1957. Anaskafi Chondrou Viannou (Ανασκαφή Χόνδρου Βιάννου). *PAE*: 136–47.

1958a. I archaiologiki kinesis en Kriti kata to etos 1958 (Η αρχαιολογική κίνησης εν Κρήτη κατά το έτος 1958. *KCh* 12: 454–83.

1958b. Anaskafi geometrikon tholoton tafon Rotasiou (Ανασκαφή Γεωμετρικαί θολοτών τάφων Ροτασίου). *KCh* 12: 468.

1960a. Mirsini (Μυρσίνη). *BCH* 84: 820–1.

1960b. Anaskafai periochis Praisou (Ανασκαφαί περιοχής Πραισού). *PAE*: 302.

1960c. Anatoliki Kriti (Ανατολική Κρήτη). *AD* 16: 259–62.

Platon, N., and C. Davaras, 1960. I archaiologiki kinesis en Kriti kata to etos 1960 (Η αρχαιολογική κίνησης εν Κρητη κατά το έτος 1960). *KCh* 14: 514–15.

1962. Archaiotites kai mnimeia Kritis – kentriki kai anatoliki Kriti (Αρχαιότητες και μνημεία Κρήτης – κεντρική και ανατολική Κρήτη). *AD* 17B: 281–91.

de Polignac, F., 1995. *Cults, territory and the origins of the Greek city-state*. Trans. Janet Lloyd. Chicago: University of Chicago Press.

Polunin, O., and A. Huxley, 1987. *Flowers of the Mediterranean*. London: Chatto and Windus.

Pope, K., 1993. Geology and soils. In Watrous et al. 1993: 197–205.

2004. Geoarchaeology of the western Mesara. In Watrous et al. 2004: 39–59.

Popham, M. R., 1979. Connections between Crete and Cyprus between 1300–1100 BC. In Karageorghis, ed 1979: 178–92.

1991. Pylos: reflections on the date of its destruction and on its Iron Age reoccupation. *Oxford Journal of Archaeology* 10: 315–24.

1992. The Subminoan pottery. In Sackett et al. 1992: 59–66.

1994a. Precolonisation: early Greek contact with the east. In Tsetskhladze and de Angelis: 11–34.

1994b. Late Minoan II to the end of the Bronze Age. In Evely et al. 1994: 59–102.

1994c. *The Minoan Unexplored Mansion at Knossos*. 2 vols. London: Thames and Hudson/British School at Athens.

Popham, M. R., P. G. Calligas, and L. H. Sackett, eds, with J. Coulton and H. W. Catling, 1993. *Lefkandi II. The Protogeometric building at Toumba. Part 2: Excavation, architecture and finds*. London: Thames and Hudson/British School at Athens.

Popham, M. R., and I. S. Lemos, 1996. *Lefkandi III. The Toumba cemetery: excavations of 1981, 1984, 1986, 1992–4. The plates*. London: Thames and Hudson/British School at Athens.

Popham, M. R., and E. Milburn, 1971. The Late Helladic IIIC pottery of Xeropolis (Lefkandi): a summary. *ABSA* 66: 333–52.

Popham, M. R., L. H. Sackett, and P. G. Themelis, 1980. *Lefkandi I. The Iron Age: the settlement and the cemeteries*. London: Thames and Hudson/British School at Athens.

Poursat, J.-C., 1997. La fin des arts 'palatiaux' dans la Crete mycénienne. In Driessen and Farnoux 1997: 387–90.

Powell, A., 1988. *Athens and Sparta*. London: Routledge.

Prent, M., 2003. Glories of the past in the past: ritual activities at palatial ruins in Early Iron Age Crete. In van Dyke and Alcock: 81–104.

2005a. Cult activities at the Palace of Knossos from the end of the Bronze Age: continuity and change. In Cadogan et al.: 411–19.

2005b. *Cretan cults and sanctuaries*. Amsterdam: Brill.

in press. Orientalising imagery in Crete : the example of Gortyn. In Kaiser and Pilz.

Preston, L., 1999. Mortuary practices and the negotiation of social identities at LM II Knossos. *ABSA* 94: 131–45.

2005. The Kefala tholos at Knossos: a study in the re-use of the past. *ABSA* 100: 61–125.

Preucel, R. W., 2000. Making Pueblo communities: architectural discourse at Kotyiti, New Mexico. In Canuto and Yaeger: 58–78.

Preucel, R. W., and I. Hodder, eds, 1996. *Contemporary archaeology in theory: a reader.* Oxford: Blackwell.

Prokopiou, N. M., 1991. Sybrita Amariou: first indications for a new LM IIIC site. In Musti et al.: 371–400.

1994. Syvritos Amariou. I metávasi apo to télos tis epochís tou chalkoú stin proimí epochi tou síderou (Σύβριτος Αμαρίου. Η μετάβαση απο το τέλος της εποχής του Χαλκού στην πρώιμη εποχή του Σιδήρου). In Rocchetti 1994: 249–54.

1997. Late Minoan III pottery from the Greek-Italian Excavations at Sybritos Amariou. In Hallager and Hallager 1997a: 371–401.

Qviller, B., 1981. The dynamics of the Homeric society. *Symbolae Osolenses* 56: 109–55.

Raaflaub, K., 1988. Homer and the beginnings of political thought in Greece. In J. J. Cleary and D. C. Shartin, eds, *Proceedings of the Boston Area Colloquium of Ancient Philosophy* 4. Boston: University Press of America: 1–25.

1993. Homer to Solon: the rise of the *polis*. The written sources. In Hansen 1993b: 41–106.

1997a. Soldiers, citizens, and the evolution of the early Greek *polis*. In Mitchell and Rhodes: 49–60.

1997b. Power in the hands of the people: foundations of Athenian democracy. In Morris and Raaflaub: 31–67.

Rackham, O., 1973. The vegetation of the Myrtos region and charcoal and plaster impressions. In P. M. Warren, *Myrtos: an Early Bronze Age settlement in Crete.* London: Thames and Hudson/British School at Athens: 283–304.

1982. Land-use and the native vegetation of Greece. In M. Bell and S. Limbrey, *Archaeological aspects of woodland ecology*. Oxford: BAR: 177–98.

1992. Vegetation history of Crete. In Grove et al.: 29–39.

1996. Ecology and pseudo-ecology: the example of ancient Greece. In G. Shipley and J. Salmon, *Human landscapes in Classical antiquity: environment and culture.* London: Routledge: 16–44.

Rackham, O., and A. T. Grove, 2001. *The nature of Mediterreanean Europe: an ecological history.* New Haven, CT: Yale University Press.

Rackham, O., and J. A. Moody, 1996. *The making of the Cretan landscape.* Manchester: Manchester University Press.

Raftopoulou, S., 1997. Tafes tis Epochis tou Sidirou sti Sparti (Ταφές της Εποχής του Σιδήρου στη Σπάρτη). In *Peloponnesiakon Spoudon*: 272–82.

Rahmstorf, L., 2003. Clay spools from Tiryns and other contemporary sites: an indication of foreign influence in LH IIIC? In Kyparissi-Apostolika and Papakonstantinou: 397–415.

Rapp, G., 1978. The physiographic setting. In G. Rapp, Jr., and S. E. Aschenbrenner, *Excavations at Nichoria in southwest Greece.* Vol. I: *Site, environs, and techniques.* Minneapolis: University of Minnesota Press: 26–9.

Rasmussen, T., 1991. Corinth and the Orientalising phenomenon. In T. Rasmussen and N. J. Spivey, *Looking at Greek vases.* Cambridge: Cambridge University Press: 57–78.

Reese, D., ed, 1996. *Pleistocene and Holocene fauna of Crete and its first settlers.* Madison, WI: Prehistory Press.

with contributions by M. J. Rose and D. Ruscillo, 2000. The Iron Age fauna. In Shaw and Shaw 2000: 415–647.

Rehak, P., and J. Younger, 1999. Neopalatial, final palatial, and postpalatial Crete. In Cullen: 383–475.

Rehder, J. E., 2000. Ironworking in the Greek sanctuary. In Shaw and Shaw 2000: 80–9.

Reinach, A., 1913. L'autel rustique de Mont Phylakas. *Revue archéologique* 21: 278–300.

Renfrew, C., 1980. The Great Tradition versus the Great Divide: Archaeology as anthropology. *AJA* 84: 287–98.

1982. Bronze Age Melos. In Renfrew and Wagstaff: 35–45.

1985. *The archaeology of cult: the sanctuary at Phylakopi.* London: British School at Athens/Thames and Hudson.

1986. Varna and the emergence of wealth in prehistoric Europe. In Appadurai: 141–69.

Renfrew, C., and Shennan, S., eds, 1982. *Ranking, resource and exchange: aspects of the archaeology of early European society.* Cambridge: Cambridge University Press.

Renfrew, C., and J. M. Wagstaff, eds, 1982. *An island polity: the archaeology of exploitation in Melos.* Cambridge: Cambridge University Press.

Rethimiotakis, G., 1987. Kastelli. *AD* **42B**: 531–2.

1988. Kastelli. *Kritiki Estia* **2**: 327–8.

1997a. LM III pottery from Kastelli Pediada. In Hallager and Hallager 1997a: 305–37.

1997b. A chest-shaped vessel from Kastelli Pediada. In Driessen and Farnoux 1997: 407–21.

Rethemiotakis, G., and N. Dimopoulou, 1993. KG' Eforeia proistorikon kai Klassikon Archaiotiton – anaskafikes ergasies. Kounavoi Pediados (KG' Εφορεία προιστορικών και Κλασσικών Αρχαιοτήτων – ανασκαφικές εργασίες. Κουνάβοι Πεδιάδος). *AD* **48**: 445–72.

Rhodes, P. J., 1992a. The Delian League to 449BC. In Lewis et al.: 34–62.

1992b. The Athenian revolution. In Lewis et al.: 62–96.

2000. Who ran democratic Athens? In Flensted-Jensen et al.: 465–77.

Rich, J. and A. Wallace-Hadrill, eds, 1991. *City and country in the ancient world.* London: Routledge.

Ridgway, D. W., 1992. *The first western Greeks.* Cambridge: Cambridge University Press.

Rizakis, A. D., ed, 1991. *Achaia und Elis in der Antike – Akten des 1. internationalen Symposiums Athen, 19–21 Mai, Athen 1991.* Athens: Kentron Ellenikes kai Romaïkes Archaiotitos tou Ethnikou Idrimatos Erevnon: 19–29.

Rizza, G., 1978. Gli scavi di Prinias e il problema delle origine dell'arte greca. In *Quaderni di La Ricerca Scientifica* **100**: 85–137.

1983. Prinias nelle fasi geometrica e orientalizzante. *ASAtene* **61**: 45–51.

1991. La citta arcaica sulla Patela. In Musti et al.: 331–49.

2000. Scavi e ricerche a Prinias dal 1992 al 1996. In *Pepragmena H*: 159–60.

2006. Scavi e ricerche a Prinias dal 1997 al 2000. In *Pepragmena Θ*: 55–63.

Rizza, G., D. Palermo, and F. Tomasello, 1992. *Mandra di Gipari, una officina protoarcaica di vasai nel territorio di Priniás.* Catania: Scuola archeologica italiana di Atene.

Rizza, G., and G. Rizzo, 1984. Prinias. In *Ancient Crete*: 227–56.

Rizza, G., and V. S. M. Scrinari, 1968. *Il santuario sull'acropoli di Gortina.* Roma: Istituto Poligrafico dello Stato, Libreria.

Roberts, N., 1979. The location and environment of Knossos. *ABSA* **74**: 231–41.

1981. The physical environment of the Knossos area. In Hood and Smyth: 5.

Rocchetti, L., 1970. Depositi sub-micenei e protogeometrici nei dintorni di Festos. *ASAtene* 31–32: 41–70.

1974. Materiali ceramici a Festos fra il XIII ed il X sec. A. C. In *Antichita Cretesi. Studi in onore di Doro Levi* 2: 149–52.

1975. La ceramica dell'abitato geometrico di Festos a occidente del palazzo minoico. *ASAtene* 52–53: 169–300.

1989. La ceramica della necropoli di Curtes. *ASAtene* **66–67**: 173–257.

1990. La necropoli di Curtes. In *Pepragmena ST*: 261–5.

ed, 1994. *Sybrita: la valle di Amari fra bronzo e ferro.* Roma: Gruppo Editoriale Internazionale.

2000. Scavi greco-italiani a Sybrita. In *Pepragmena H*: 811–14.

2006. Scavi greco-italiani a Sybrita. In *Pepragmena Θ*: 165–70.

Rocchetti, L., N. Prokopiou, and A.-L. D'Agata, 1994. Missione greco-italiana a Sybrita, Campgne di scavo 1993 e 1994. *SMEA* **34**: 141–2.

1995. Campagna di scavo 1995. *SMEA* **36**: 147–8.

Roebuck, C., 1959. *Ionian trade and colonisation.* New York: Archaeological Institute of America.

Rougemont, F., 2001. Some thoughts on the identification of the 'collectors' in the Linear B tablets. In Voutsaki and Killen: 129–39.

Rowlands, M., 1987. Centre and periphery: a review of a concept. In Rowlands et al.: 1–11.

Rowlands, M., M. T. Larsen, and K. Kristiansen, eds, 1987. *Centre and periphery in the ancient world.* Cambridge: Cambridge University Press.

Runciman, W. G., 1990. Doomed to extinction: the polis as evolutionary dead-end? In Murray and Price: 347–67.

Runnels, C., and J. Hansen, 1986. The olive in the prehistoric Aegean: the evidence for domestication. *OJA* 5: 299–308.

Runnels, C., D. J. Pullen, and S. Langdon, 1995. *Artifact and assemblage: the finds from a regional survey of the southern Argolid, Greece.* Vol. 1: *The prehistoric and Early Iron Age pottery and the lithic artifacts.* Stanford, CA: Stanford University Press.

Rutkowski, B., 1986. *The cult places of the Aegean.* New Haven, CT, and London: Yale University Press.

1987. The temple at Karphi. *SMEA* **26**: 257–80.

Rutkowski, B., and K. Nowicki, 1985. Report on investigations in Greece III. *Archeologia* (Warsaw) **36**: 119–29.

1986. Report on investigations in Greece IV. *Archeologia* (Warsaw) **37**: 159–70.

1987. Report on investigations in Greece V. *Archeologia* (Warsaw) **38**: 177–83.

1990. Report on investigations in Greece VI. *Archeologia* (Warsaw) **41**: 113–25.

1996. *The Psychro Cave and other sacred grottoes in Crete.* Warsaw: Art and Archaeology.

Rutter, J. B., 1974. *The Late Helladic IIIB and IIIC periods at Korakou and Gonia in the Corinthia.* Unpublished PhD thesis, University of Pennsylvania.

1992. Cultural novelties in the post-palatial Aegean world: indices of vitality or decline? In Ward and Joukowsky: 61–79.

Sackett, L. H., M. R. Popham, and P. M. Warren, 1965. Excavations at Palaikastro VI. *ABSA* **60**: 248–308.

Sackett, L. H., et al., 1992. *Knossos, from Greek city to Roman colony. Excavations at the Unexplored Mansion at Knossos II.* London: British School at Athens.

Sakellarakis, Y., 1983. Anaskafi Idaio Antro (Ανασκαφή Ιδαίω 'Αντρω). *PAE*: 415–500.

1987. Ekato chronia erevnas sto Idaio Antro (Εκατώ χρώνια έρευνας στο Ιδαίω 'Αντρω). *AE* **126**: 239–63.

1988. Some Geometric and Archaic votives from the Idaean Cave. In Hägg et al.: 173–93.

1992. The Idaean Cave ivories. In J. L. Fitton, ed, *Ivory in Greece and the eastern Mediterranean from the Bronze Age to the Hellenistic period.* London: British Museum Publications: 113–40.

1993. Ivory trade in the Aegean in the eighth century BCE. In A. Biran and J. Avram, *Biblical archaeology today. Proceedings of the international congress on Biblical archaeology, Jerusalem April 1990.* Jerusalem: Israel Academy of Sciences and Humanities/American Schools of Oriental Research: 345–66.

Sakellarakis, Y., and E. Sakellarakis, 1997. *Archanes: Minoan Crete in a new light.* Athens: Eleni Nakou Foundation.

Sallares, R., 1991. *The ecology of the ancient Greek world.* London: Duckworth.

Salmon, J., 1997. Lopping off the heads? Tyrants, politics and the *polis*. In Mitchell and Rhodes: 60–74.

Sanders, I. F., 1982. *Roman Crete.* Warminster: Aris and Phillips.

Santaniello, E., in press. Lekythoi from Gortyn. In I. Kaiser and O. Pilz, eds, *Geometric Crete. Proceedings of a conference at the Deutsches Archaölogisches Institut Aten.*

Sapouna-Sakellarakis, E., 1990. Archanes a l'époque mycénienne. *BCH* **114**: 67–102.

Sarpaki, A., 1992. The palaeoethnobotanical approach: the Mediterranean triad or is it a quartet? In Wells: 61–77.

1999. The archaeobotanical study of Tzambakis House, Rethymnon, Crete. In Tzedakis et al.: 40–41.

Sarpaki, A., and G. Jones, 1990. Ancient and modern cultivation of *Lathyrus clymenum L.* in the Greek islands. *ABSA* **84**: 363–8.

Savignoni, L., 1904. Scavi e scoperte nelle necropoli di Phaestos. *Monumenti antichi* **14**: 501–666.

Savignoni, L., and G. de Sanctis, 1901. Esplorazione archeologica delle provincie occidentali di Creta. *Monumenti antichi* 11: 281–472.

Savvopoulou, T., 2004. I periochi tou Axiou stin Proimi Epochi tou Sidirou. (Η περιοχή του Αξιού στην Πρώιμη Εποχή του Σιδήρου). In Stampolidis and Giannikouri: 307–17.

Saxe, A. A., 1970. *Social dimensions of mortuary practices.* Unpublished PhD dissertation, University of Michigan.

1971. Social dimensions of mortuary practices in Mesolithic populations from Wadi Haifa, Sudan. In J. A. Brown, ed, *Approaches to the social dimensions of mortuary practice.* New York: Academic Press.

Schäfer, J., 1991. Das problem ser Kultkontinuität im Falle des Heligtums des Zeus Thenatas. In Musti et al.: 349–59.

Schäfer, W., et al., 1992. *Amnisos: nach den archäologischen, historischen und epigraphischen Zeugnisse des Altertums und Neuzeit.* 2 vols. Berlin: Deutsches Archaologisches Institut, Abeteilung Aten.

Scheidel, W., 2002. The hireling and the slave: a transatlantic perspective. In Cartledge et al.: 175–84.

Schilardi, D. U., 1973. A fortified acropolis on the Oikonomos island of Paros. *AAA* **6**: 260–5.

1975. Paros, Report II: the 1973 campaign. *JFA* **2**: 82–96.

1976. Ανασκαφαί Πάρου. *PAE*: 287–94.

1983. The decline of the Geometric settlement of Koukounaries at Paros. In Hägg 1983: 173–83.

1984. The LH IIIC period at the Koukounaries Acropolis, Paros. In J. A. MacGillivray and R. L. N. Barber, eds, *The prehistoric Cyclades: contributions to a workshop on Cycladic chronology.* Edinburgh: Department of Classical Archaeology, University of Edinburgh: 184–204.

1986. Paros. *Εργον της Αρχαιολογική Εταιρείας* **88**: 109–13.

1988. The temple of Athena at Koukounaries. In Hägg et al.: 41–50.

Schlager, N., 1991. *Archaölogische Geländeprospektion Südostkreta: erste Ergebnisse.* Wien: Schindler.

Schmitt-Pantel, P., 1990. Sacrificial meal and *symposion*: two models of social institutions in the Archaic city. In Murray, ed 1990: 14–37.

Schoep, I., 1998. Towards an interpretation of different levels of administration in Late Minoan IB Crete. *Aegean Archaeology* 3: 75–87.

Schoinas, Ch., 1995. Ayia Triada. *AD* **45**: 113–19.

Schwab, K. A., 2000. Bronze, lead and faience vessels. In Shaw and Shaw 2000: 395–8.

Seager, R., 1906. *Excavations at Vasiliki.* Philadelphia: University of Pennnsylvania Museum.

Seiradaki, M., 1960. Pottery from Karphi. *ABSA* **55**: 1–37.

Sfikas, G., 2000. *Wild flowers of Crete.* Athens: Efstathiadis Group.

Sgouritsa, N., 2006. The Aegeans in the central Mediterranean: the role of western Greece. In Laffineur and Greco: 515–27.

Shanks, M., 1996. *Classical archaeology of Greece: experiences of the discipline.* London: Routledge.

Shanks, M., and C. Tilley, 1987. *Social theory and archaeology.* Cambridge: Polity Press.

Shaw, J. W., 1980. Excavations at Kommos (Crete) during 1979. *Hesperia* **49**: 207–51.

1989. Phoenicians in southern Crete. *AJA* **93**: 165–84.

1998. Kommos in southern Crete: an Aegean barometer for east-west interconnections. In Karageorghis and Stampolidis: 13–29.

Shaw, J. W. (with contributions by L. Costaki and C. Murphy), 2006. History and functions of the monumental Minoan buildings at Kommos. In Shaw and Shaw 2006: 1–117.

Shaw, J. W., and M. C. Shaw, 1997. Mycenaean Kommos. In Driessen and Farnoux 1997: 423–4.

2000. *Kommos: an excavation on the south coast of Crete by the University of Toronto and the Royal Ontario Museum under the auspices of the American School of Classical Studies at Athens.* Vol. IV: *The Greek sanctuary.* Princeton, NJ: Princeton University Press.

2006. *Kommos: an excavation on the south coast of Crete by the University of Toronto and the Royal Ontario Museum under the auspices of the American School of Classical Studies at Athens.* Vol. V: *The monumental Minoan buildings at Kommos.* Princeton, NJ: Princeton University Press.

Shaw, J. W., M. C. Shaw, J. B. Rutter, and A. van de Moortel, 2006a. The architecture and stratigraphy of the civic buildings. In Shaw and Shaw 2006: 845–79.

Shaw, J. W., A. van de Moortel, and J. B. Rutter, 2006b. The harbour town and its international connections. In Shaw and Shaw 2006: 854–63.

Shaw, M. C., 1990. Late Minoan hearths and ovens at Kommos, Crete. In Darcque and Treuil: 231–54.

2000. The sculpture from the sanctuary. In Shaw and Shaw 2000: 135–210.

Shay, C. T., and J. M. Shay, 1999. Review of Aegean prehistory VI: the palatial Bronze Age of the Greek mainland. In Cullen: 329–81.

2000. The charcoal and seeds from Iron Age Kommos. In Shaw and Shaw 2000: 647–69.

2004. Environment, land capability, and botanical studies in the western Mesara. In Watrous et al. 2004: 59–11.

Shelmerdine, C., 1999. The palatial Bronze Age of the central and southern Greek mainland. In Cullen: 329–81.

Shennan, S., 1993. After social evolution: a new archaeological agenda? In Yoffee and Sherratt: 53–9.

Sherratt, A., 1992. What can archaeologists learn from Annalistes? In Knapp 1992b: 135–42.

Sherratt, E. S., 1981. Patterns of contact: manufacture and distribution of Mycenaean pottery, 1400–1100 BC. In J. G. P. Best and N. M. W. de Vries, *Interaction and acculturation in the Mediterranean. Proceedings of the Second International Congress of Mediterranean Pre- and Proto-history, Amsterdam 19–23 November, 1980*. Amsterdam: B. R. Grüner: 179–85.

1994. Commerce, iron and ideology: metallurgical innovation in 12th–11th century Cyprus. In Karageorghis 1994: 59–106.

1996. With us but not of us: the role of Crete in Homeric epic. In Evely et al. 1996: 87–100.

1998. Sea Peoples and the economic structure of the late second millennium in the eastern Mediterranean. In Gitin et al.: 292–307.

2001. Potemkin palaces and route-based economies. In Voutsaki and Killen: 214–39.

2003. Bronze Age and Early Iron Age Crete. *Antiquity* 77: 858–61.

Sherratt, A., and S. Sherratt, 1991. From luxuries to commodities: the nature of Mediterranean Bronze Age trading systems. In N. Gale, ed, *Bronze Age trade in the Mediterranean*. Oxford: BAR: 351–87.

Sherratt, S., and A. Sherratt, 1993. The growth of the Mediterranean economy in the early first millennium BC. *World Archaeology* **24**/3: 362–78.

1998. Small worlds: interaction and identity in the ancient Mediterranean. In Cline and Harris-Cline: 329–43.

Simandiraki, A., 2004. Minopaidies: the Minoan civilisation in Greek primary education. *World Archaeology* **36**/2: 177–88.

2005. Minoan archaeology in the Athens 2004 Olympic Games. *European Journal of Archaeology* 8(2): 157–81.

Sjögren, L., 2004. *Cretan locations: sites, settlements and early poleis in Crete (800–500 BC)*. Oxford: BAR.

Skerlou, E., 2004. Ena iero tis Geometrikis kai Archaikis periodou stin periochi Iraklis tis Ko. Mia proto parousiasi (Ένα ιερό της Γεωμετρικής και Αρχαϊκής περιόδου στην περιοχή Ηρακλής της Κω. Μια πρότη παρουσιάση). In Stampolidis and Giannikouri: 177–89.

Skon-Jedele, N. J., and M. K. Dabney, 2000. Scarabs. In Shaw and Shaw 2000: 351–2.

Small, D. B., 1997a. City-state dynamics through a Greek lens. In Nichols and Charlton: 107–18.

1997b. An archaeology of democracy? In Morris and Raaflaub: 217–28.

1998. Surviving the collapse: the *oikos* and structural continuity between Late Bronze Age and later Greece. In Gitin et al.: 283–92.

1999. Mycenaean polities: states or estates? In Galaty and Parkinson: 43–48.

Smith, R. A., 2005. Minoans, Mycenaeans and Mokhlos: the formation of regional identity in Late Minoan III Crete. In D'Agata and Moody: 185–205.

Snodgrass, A. M., 1971. *The Dark Age of Greece*. Edinburgh: Edinburgh University Press.

1980a. *Archaic Greece: the age of experiment*. London: J. M. Dent.

1980b. Iron and early metallurgy in the Mediterranean. In T. Wertime and J. Muhly, eds, *The coming of the age of iron*: New Haven, CT: Yale University Press, 335–74.

1982a. Cyprus and the beginnings of iron technology in the eastern Mediterranean. In Muhly et al.: 285–97.

1982b. Les origines du culte des heros dans la Grèce antique. In Gnoli and Vernant: 89–105.

1983. Two demographic notes. In Hägg 1983: 167–71.

1986. Interaction by design: the Greek city state. In A. C. Renfrew and J. F. Cherry, *Peer polity interaction and sociopolitical change*. Cambridge: Cambridge University Press: 47–59.

1987. *An archaeology of Greece: the present state and future scope of a discipline*. Berkeley: University of California Press.

1989. The coming of the Iron Age in Greece: Europe's earliest bronze/iron transition. In M. L. Sorensen and R. Thomas, *The Bronze Age–Iron Age transition in Europe: aspects of continuity and change in European societies c.1200–500 BC*. Oxford: BAR: 22–35.

1991a. Archaeology and the study of the Greek city. In Rich and Wallace-Hadrill: 1–25.

1991b. Structural history and Classical archaeology. In Bintliff 1991a: 57–72.

1993. The rise of the *polis*. The archaeological evidence. In Hansen 1993b: 30–41.

1996. Iron. In Coldstream and Catling: 575–97.

Snyder, L. M., and W. E. Klippel, 1994. The vertebrate faunal material. In Coulson and Tsipopoulou: 92–3.

1996. The Cretan badger (*Meles meles*) as a food resource at the Iron Age village of Kastro, East Crete. In Reese 1996: 283–93.

1999. Dark Age subsistence at the Kastro Site, east Crete: exploring subsistence change and continuity during the Late Bronze Age–Early Iron Age transition. In S. J. Vaughan and W. D. E. Coulson, eds, *Palaeodiet in the Aegean*. Oxford: Oxbow Books: 65–83.

Sofianou, X., and E. Saliaka, in press. Καύσεις στη νεκρόπολη της αρχαίας Ιτάνου (Kavseis sti nekropoli tis archaias Itanou). In *Pepragmena* I.

Soles, J., 2001. Reverence for dead ancestors in prehistoric Crete. In Laffineur and Hägg: 229–37.

2003a. Conclusions on Chalinomouri. In Soles 2003b: 127–30.

2003b. *Mochlos IA. Period III. The Neopalatial settlement on the coast. The Artisans' Quarter and the farmhouse at Chalinomouri*. Philadelphia: INSTAP Academic Press.

Soles, J. S., and C. Davaras, 1992. Excavations at Mochlos 1989. *Hesperia* **61**: 413–45.

Soles, J. S., D. Mylona, D. S. Reese, A. Sarpaki, R. A. K. Smith, and W. Schoch, 2003. Chalinomouri farmhouse. In Soles 2003b: 103–27.

Souaref, K., 2004. H proimi epochi tou Sidirou stin anatoliki parathermaiki zoni. Faseis tis proimis epochis tou sidirou stin trapeza tis Toumbas Thessalonikis (Η πρώιμη εποχή του Σιδήρου στην ανατολική Παραθερμαϊκη. ζόνη. Φάσεις τησ πρώιμις εποχής του Σιδήρου στην τράπεζα της Τούμπας Θεσσαλονίκης). In Stampolidis and Giannikouri, eds: 317–29.

Sperling, A., 1942. Explorations in Elis, 1939. *AJA* **46**: 77–89.

Stampolidis, N., 1990. Eleutherna on Crete: an interim report on the Geometric-Archaic cemetery. *ABSA* **85**: 375–405.

1994. *Archaia Eleutherna III.2. Apo ti Geometriki kai archaiki nekropoli. Tafikes pyres kai omirika epi (Αρχαία Ελεύθερνα III.2. Απο τη Γεωμετρική και αρχαϊκή νεκρόπολη. Ταφικές πύρες και ομηρικά έπη)*. Rethymnon: University of Rethymnon.

1996. *Eleutherna Antipoina (Ελευθερνα Αντιποινα)*. Eleutherna: University of Crete Publications.

1998. Imports and amalgamata: the Eleutherna experience. In Karageorghis and Stampolidis: 71–95.

ed, 2001. *Praktika tou Symposiou 'Kavseis stin Epoxi tou Chalkou kai tin proimi epoxi toy sidirou', Rodos, 29 Apriliou–2 Maiou 1999 (Πρακτικά του Συμπόσιου 'Κάυσεις στην Εποχή του Χαλκού και την Πρώιμη Εποχή του Σιδήρου', Ρόδος, 29 Απριλιου–2 Μαιου 1999)*. Athens: Panepistimiou Kritis.

2003. On the Phoenician presence in the Aegean. In Stampolidis and Karageorghis: 217–32.

2004. I Eleutherna tis proimis epochis tou Sidirou. Skeseis me to Aigaio kai tin anatoliki Mesogeio (Η Ελεύθερνα της πρώιμης εποχής του Σιδήρου. Σκέσεις με το Αιγαίο και την ανατολική Μεσόγειο). In Stampolidis and Giannikouri: 51–77.

Stampolidis, N. K., and A. Giannikouri, eds, 2004. *To Aigaio stin Proimi Epochi tou Sidirou. Praktika tou Diethnous Symposiou, Rodos, 1–4 Noemvriou 2002 (Το Αιγαίο στην Πρώιμη Εποχή του Σιδήρου.*

Πρακτικά του Διεθηνούς Συμπόσίου, Ρόδος, 1–4 Νοεμβρίου 2002). Athens: University of Crete/ Ministry of Culture/Archaeological Institute of the Aegean.

Stampolidis, N., A. Karetsou, and A. Kanta, 1998. *Cyprus, East Mediterranean and Crete, 1600–600 BC*. Iraklion: National Museum.

Stampolidis, N. Chr., and V. Karageorghis, eds, 2003. *Sea routes: interconnections in the Mediterranean 16th-6th c. BC. Proceedings of the International Symposium held at Rethymnon, Crete, in September 29th–October 2nd 2002*. Athens: University of Crete/A. G. Leventis Foundation.

Steel, L., 1996. Transition from bronze to iron at Kourion: a review of the tombs from Episkopi-*Bamboula* and *Kaloriziki*. *ABSA* **91**: 287–300.

2004. *Cyprus before history: from the earliest settlers to the end of the Bronze Age*. London: Duckworth.

Stefanakis, M., 1998. A mid-fourth-century BC alliance coinage on Crete? The case of Kytaion reassessed. In Cavanagh and Curtis: 96–104.

1999. The introduction of coinage in Crete and the beginning of local minting. In Chaniotis 1999: 248–65.

Stoddart, S., and J. Whitley, 1988. The social context of literacy in Archaic Greece and Etruria. *Antiquity* **62**: 761–2.

Stone, E., 1997. City-states and their centres: the Mesopotamian example. In Nichols and Charlton: 15–27.

Stos-Gale, Z., N. H. Gale, and D. Evely, 2000. An interpretation of the metal finds, using lead isotope and chemical analytical procedures. In Hallager and Hallager 2000: 206–15.

Tainter, J., 1990. *The collapse of complex societies*. 2nd ed. Cambridge: Cambridge University Press.

Talbert, R. J. A., 1989. The role of the helots in the class struggle at Sparta. *Historia* **38**: 22–40.

Taramelli, A., 1899. Richerche archeologiche cretesi. *Mounmenti Antichi* **9**: 285–448.

Tegou, E., 2001. Tholotos tafos tis proimis epochis tou Sidirou stin Pantanassa Amariou, N. Rethymnis (Θολοτός τάφος της πρώιμης εποχής του Σιδήρου στην Παντάνασσα Αμαρίου, Ν Ρεθύμνης). In Stampolidis 2001: 121–55.

Televantou, C. A., 2001. Ayios Andreas on Sifnos: a Late Cycladic III fortified acropolis. In Karageorghis and Morris: 191–215.

2004. I Andros kata tin proimi epochi tou Sidirou (H 'Ανδρος κατά την πρώιμη εποχή του Σιδήρου). In Stampolidis and Giannikouri: 421–7.

Themelis, P., 1992. Eleutherna. In Myers et al.: 91–6.

Thomas, C. G., 1981. The Greek polis. In R. Griffeth and C. G. Thomas, eds, *The city-state in five cultures*. Oxford: Clio Press: 31–69.

Thorne, S. M., and M. Prent, 2000. The sanctuary of Diktaean Zeus at Palaikastro: a re-examination of the excavations by the British School in 1902–1906. In *Pepragmena H*: 169–79.

Tilley, C., 1982. *A phenomenology of landscape: places, paths and monuments*. Oxford/Providence: Berg.

2004. *The materiality of stone: explorations in landscape phenomenology: 1*. Oxford: Berg.

Tiverios, M., 2004. Oi panepistimakes anaskafes sto Karabournaki Thessalonikis kai i parousia tob Foinikon sto voreio Aigaio (Οι πανεπιστιμιακές ανασκαφές στο Καραμπουρνακι Θεσσαλονίκης και η παρουσία τον Φοινίκων στο βόρειο Αιγαίο). In Stampolidis and Giannikouri: 295–307.

Tomlinson, R. A., 1972. *Argos and the Argolid. From the end of the Bronze Age to the Roman occupation*. London: Routledge and Kegan Paul.

Touchais, G., and N. Divari-Valakou, 1998. *Argos du néolithique a l'epoque geometrique: synthèse des données archeologiques*. Paris : Ecole française d'Athènes.

Traxasopoulou-Salakidou, E., 2004. I Akanthos stin Proimi Epochi tou Sidirou (H Ακανθος στην Πρώιμη Εποχή του Σιδήρου). In Stampolidis and Giannikouri: 265–77.

Triandaphyllidou Baladie, Y., 1988. To emboriko kai i oikonomia tis Kritis (*Το εμπορικό και η οικονομία της Κρήτης*). Iraklion: Vikelaia Library.

1992. The Cretan rural landscape and its changes in late-medieval and modern times. In Grove et al.: 47–51.

Trigger, B., 1998. *Sociocultural evolution*. Oxford: Blackwell.

Trölle, S., 1978. An Egyptian head from Camirus, Rhodes. *Acta Archaeologica* **49**: 139–50.

Tsetskhladze, G., and F. de Angelis, 1994. *The archaeology of Greek colonization: essays dedicated to Sir John Boardman*. Oxford: Oxford University Press.

Tsipopoulou, M., 1983. Tafiki spilaia ston Ayio Spiridona Siteias (Ταφική σπήλαια στον Αγιο Σπυρίδωνα Σιτείας). *AD* 38: 78–104.

1987. Tafoi tis proimis epochis tou siderou stin anatoliki Kriti (Τάφοι της Πρώιμης Εποχής του Σιδήρου στην ανατολική Κρήτη). *AD* 39: 232–45.

1997a. Phatsi Droggara: Un dépôt de céramique de la fin de l'Âge du Bronze et du début de l'Âge du Fer provenant de Crète orientale. In Driessen and Farnoux 1997: 455–84.

1997b. LM III reoccupation in the area of the palatial building at Petras, Siteia. In Hallager and Hallager 1997a: 209–59.

2001. A new late Minoan IIIC shrine at Halasmenos, East Crete. In Laffineur and Hägg: 99–103.

2004a. Mia periptosi proimon symposion i aplos iroolatreias - Geometriki symposion sto Xalasmeno Ierapetras (Μια περίπτωση πρώιμων συμποσίων η απλός ήρωολατρείας – Γεωμετρική συμπόσιων στο Χαλασμένο Ιεράπετρας). In Stampolidis and Giannikouri: 127–43.

2004b. Halasmenos: destroyed but not invisible. New insights on the LM IIIC period in the isthmus of Ierapetra. First presentation of the pottery from the 1992–1997 campaigns. In Day et al. 2004: 103–25.

2005a. *H anatoliki Kriti stin Proimi Epochi tou Sidirou (Η Ανατολική Κρήτη στήν Πρώιμη Εποχή του Σιδήρου)*. Iraklion: YPPO/Archaeological Institute of Crete.

2005b. Mycenoans at the isthmus of Ierapetra. In D'Agata and Moody: 303–35.

Tsipopoulou, M., and L. Little, 2001. Kavseis tou telos tis epochis tou Chalkou stin Kritsa Mirabellou, anatoliki Kriti (Καύσεις του τέλους της εποχής του Χαλκού στην Κριτσά Μιραμπέλου, Ανατολική Κρήτη). In Stampolidis 2001: 83–99.

Tsipopoulou, M., and K. Nowicki, 2003. Μινοίτες και μυκηναίοι στο τέλος της εποχής του Χαλκού στην Ανατολική Κρήτη. In Kyparissi-Apostolika and Papakonstantinou: 561–81.

Tsipopoulou, M., and L. Vagnetti, 1995. *Achladia: scavi e ricerche della Missone greco-italiana in Creta orientale 1991–1993*. Roma: Gruppo Editoriale Internazionale.

2006. Late Minoan III evidence from Kritsa, Mirabello. In *Pepragmena Θ*: 201–11.

Tsipopoulou, M., L. Vagnetti, and M. A. Liston, 2003. New evidence for the Dark Ages in eastern Crete: an unplundered tholos tomb at Vasiliki. *SMEA* 45/1: 84–119.

Tsoukala, E., 1996. The animal bones from Smari: a preliminary report: In Reese 1996: 273–7.

Tsoukala, D., and D. Hatzi-Vallianou, 2000. Panida kai diatrofikes synetheies stin Akropoli Smariou (Πανίδα και διατροφικές συνεθείες στην Ακρόπολη Σμαριού κατά τη Γεομετρική/Ανατολίζουσα και παλαιοανακτορική εποχή). In *Pepragmena H*: 396–420.

Turland, N. J., L. Chilton, and J. R. Press, 1993. *Flora of the Cretan area*. London: HMSO.

Tyree, L., 1974. *Cretan sacred caves: archaeological evidence*. Unpublished PhD dissertation, University of Missouri, Columbia.

Tzanakakis, M., in press. Αγια Ρουμέλι (Τάρρα) 1970: οι πρωιμότερες ταφές (Ayia Roumeli (Tarra) 1970: oi proimoteres tafes). In Kaises and Pilz.

Tzedakis, Y., 1969. L'atélier ceramique postpalatiale á Kydonia. *BCH* 93: 396–418.

1976. Archaiotites kai mnimeia dytikis Kritis. Archaiologikes erevnes. Gavalomouri. (Αρχαιότητες και μνημεία δυτικής Κρήτης. Αρχαιολογικές έρευνες. Γαβαλομούρι). *AD* 31: 364–72.

1977. Eforeia proistorikon kai Klassikon archaiotiton Chanion. Nomos Chanion – archaiologikes erevnes. Gavalomouri. (Εφορεία προϊστορικών και Κλασσικώναρχαιότητων Χανιών. Νομός Χανιών – αρχαιολογικές έρευνες. Γαβαλομούρι). *AD* 32: 330–1.

1978a. Eforeia proistorikon kai Klassikon archaiotiton Chanion. Nomos Chanion – archaiologikes erevnes. Gavalomouri Kissamou (Εφορεία προϊστορικών και Κλασσικών αρχαιότητων Χανιών. Νομός Χανιών – ανασκαφικές εργασίες. Γαβαλομούρι Κισσάμου). *AD* 33, B2: 376–7.

1978b. Eforeia proistorikon kai Klassikon archaiotiton Chanion. Nomos Chanion – anaskafikes ergasies. Vouves Kissamou (Εφορεία προϊστορικών και Κλασσικών αρχαιότητων Χανιών. Νομός Χανιών – ανασκαφικές εργασίες. Βούβες Κισσαμου). *AD* 33, B2: 374–5.

1978c. Nomos Rethymnis. Anaskafikes ergasies Armenoi (Νομος Ρεθήμνης. Ανασκαφικές εργασίες Αρμένοι). *AD* 33, B2: 378–81.

1979. Cypriote 'influences' on the Geometric pottery of western Crete. In Karageorghis, ed 1979: 192–99.

1980. Nomos Rethymnis. Anaskafikes ergasies Armenoi (Νομός Ρέθημνης. Ανασκαφικές εργασίες Αρμένοι). *AD* 35, B2: 512–17.

Tzedakis, Y., S. Chryssoulaki, S. Voutsaki, and Y. Venieri, 1989. Les routes minoennes: rapport préliminaire. Defénse de la circulation ou circulation de la défense? *BCH* 113: 42–75.

Tzedakis, Y., S. Chryssoulakis, Y. Venieri, and M. Avgouli, 1990. Les routes minoennes. Le poste de Xiromandres et le contrôle des communications. *BCH* **114**: 44–65.

Tzedakis, I., and E. Gavrilaki-Nikoloudaki, 1987. Spilaio Melidoniou (Σπηλαιο Μεληδονιου). *AD* **42B**: 576–8.

Tzedakis, Y., and H. Martlew, 1999. *Minoans and Mycenaeans: flavours of their time*. Athens: National Archaeological Museum.

Ucko, P. J., and R. Layton, eds, 1999. *The archaeology and anthropology of landscape: shaping your landscape*. London: Routledge.

Vagnetti, L., 1998. Variety and function of the Aegean derivative pottery in the central Mediterranean in the LBA. In Gitin et al.: 69–75.

van Andel, T. H., and C. Runnels, 1987. *Beyond the acropolis: a rural Greek past*. Stanford, CA: Stanford University Press.

van Andel, T. H., C. Runnels, and K. Pope, 1986. Five thousand years of land use and abuse in the southern Argolid, Greece. *Hesperia* 55: 103–28.

van Andel, T. H., E. Zangger, and A. Demitrack, 1990. Land use and soil erosion in prehistoric and historical Greece. *JFA* 17: 379–96.

van de Moortel, A., and E. Zachou, 2006. 2004 excavations at Mitrou, east Lokris. *Aegean Archaeology* 7: 39–49.

van Dyke, R., and S. E. Alcock, eds, 2003. *Archaeologies of memory*. Oxford: Blackwell.

van Effenterre, H., 1948. *Nécropôles du Mirabello*. Paris : Ecole française d'Athènes.

1991. Dévéloppements territoriaux dans la Crète post-minoenne. In Musti et al.: 197–206.

van Effenterre, H., and M. Bougrat, 1969. Les frontières de Lato. *KCh* 21: 9–53.

van Wees, H., 1992. *Status warriors: war, violence and society in Homer and history*. Amsterdam: Gieben.

van Wijngaarden, G.-J., 1999. The complex past of pottery: an introduction. In Crielaard et al.: 1–19.

Vanschoonwinkel, J., 1991. *L'Egée et la Méditeranée orientale à la fin du deuxième millénaire: témoignages archéologiques et sources écrites*. Providence: Brown University Center for Old World Archaeology and Art.

Vasilakis, A., 1993. Ayios Ioannis (Agros Pelagias Fasoulaki – Katsamba). (Αγιος Ιωάννης (άγρος Πελαγίας Φασουλάκη – Κατσαμπά)). ***AD*** **48**, B2: 445.

1996. Ag. Ioannis Faistou (Αγιος Ιωάννης Φαιστού). *Kritiki Estia* 5: 334–6.

2004. Protogeometrikos oikismos sti Gria Vigla Moiron sti notia Kriti (Πρωτογεωμετρικός οικισμός στη Γριά Βίγλα Μοιρών στη νότια Κρήτη). In Stampolidis and Giannikouri: 93–105.

Vavouranakis, G., 2000. Unpublished paper given at the conference *Lighten our darkness: cultural transformations from the Alps to Anatolia in the first millennium BC*, Birmingham University, January.

Ventris, M., and J. Chadwick, 1973. *Documents in Mycenaean Greek*. Cambridge: Cambridge Universtiy Press.

Vernant, J.-P., and P. Vidal-Nauquet, 1988. *Travail et esclavage en Grece ancienne*. Brussels: Complexe.

Vidal-Nauquet, P., 1974. Reflexions sur l'historiographie grecque de l'esclavage. In *Actes du colloque 1972 sur l'esclavage*. Paris: Belles Lettres: 25–44.

Vita-Finzi, C., 1969. *The Mediterranean valleys: geological changes in historical times*. Cambridge: Cambridge University Press.

Viviers, D., 1999. Economy and territorial dynamics in Crete from the Archaic to the Hellenistic period. In Chaniotis 1999: 221–35.

Vlachopoulos, A., 2003. O Ysteroelladikos IIIG oikismos tis Grottas Naxou. Sto kentro i stin periferia tou mykenaikou Aigaiou (Ο Υστεροελλαδικός ΙΙΙΓ οικισμός της Γρόττας Νάξου. Στο κέντρο η στην περιφέρεια του μυκηναϊκού Αιγαίου). In Kyparissi-Apostolika and Papakonstantinou, eds: 493–513.

Vokotopoulou, I., 1987. Anaskafikes erevnes sti Chalkidiki (Ανασκαφικές έρευνες στη Χαλκιδική). *AEMΘ* 1: 279–85.

1988. Ανασκαφή Μένδης 1988 (Anaskafi Mendis 1988). *AEMΘ* 2: 331–45.

1989. Ανασκαφή Μένδης 1989 (Anaskafi Mendis 1989). *AEMΘ* 3: 409–23.

1990. Μένδη-Ποσειδι 1990 (Mendi-Poseidi 1990). *AEMΘ* 4: 399–410.

1991. Poseidi 1994 (Ποσειδι 1994). *AEMΘ* 8: 269–74.

Vokotopoulos, L., 1998. Kato Kastellas, Lenika (Κάτο Κάστελλας, Λενικά). *Kritiki Estia* 1997–1998: 237–70.

Voutsaki, S., 2001. Economic control, power and prestige in the Mycenaean world: the archaeological evidence. In Voutsaki and Killen: 195–214.

Voutsaki, S., and J. Killen, eds, 2001. *Economy and politics in the Mycenaean palace states: proceedings of a conference held on 1–3 July 1999 in the Faculty of Classics, Cambridge.* Cambridge: Cambridge University Press/Cambridge Philological Society.

Wagstaff, M., 1981. Buried assumptions: some problems of the interpretation of the 'Younger Fill' raised by recent data from Greece. *Journal of Archaeological Science* 8: 247–64.

Waldbaum, J., 1978. From bronze to iron: the transition from the Bronze Age to the Iron Age in the eastern Mediterranean. Göteborg: Paul Astroms Förlag.

1982. Bimetallic objects from the eastern Mediterranean and the question of the dissemination of iron. In Muhly et al.: 325–49.

Walker, S., 1996. Bones from Palaikastro Building 1: a preliminary report. In Reese: 277–83.

Wallace, R., 1997. Solonian democracy. In Morris and Raaflaub: 11–31.

Wallace, S. A., 2001. *Socioeconomic change and the meaning of settlement in the Early Iron Age of Crete, 12th–7th centuries BC.* Unpublished PhD dissertation, University of Edinburgh.

2002. Case studies of settlement change in Early Iron Age Crete (c.1200–700 BC): economic interpretations of cause and effect assessed in a long-term historical perspective. *Aegean Archaeology* 4: 61–99.

2003a. The changing role of herding in Early Iron Age Crete: implications of settlement shift for economy. *AJA* 107: 601–29.

2003b. The perpetuated past – re-use and continuity in material culture as evidence for the growth of community identity structures in the Early Iron Age of Crete, 12th to 7th centuries BC. *ABSA* 97: 251–77.

2004. I diataxi ton oikismon kai oi koinoniko-oikonomikes allayes stin Kriti kata tin Proimi Epochi tou Sidirou (Η διάταξη των οικισμών και οι κοινωνικο-οικονομικές αλλαγές στην Κρήτη κατά την Πρώιμη Εποχή του Σιδήρου). In Stampolidis and Giannikouri: 1–10.

2005a. Bridges in the mountains: issues of structure, multi-vocality, responsibility and gain in filling a management gap in rural Greece. *JMA* 18.1: 55–85.

2005b. Last chance to see? New research at 21st-century Karfi: presentation of new architectural data and their analysis in a wider context. *ABSA* 98: 1–60.

2006a. The gilded cage? Settlement and socioeconomic change after 1200 BC: a comparison of Crete and other Aegean regions. In Deger-Jalktozy and Lemos: 619–65.

2006b. Natural and cultural landscapes in Bronze to Iron Age Crete. Review article on Morris, M. W., 2002, *Soil science and archaeology: three test cases from Minoan Crete* (Prehistory Monographs 4, INSTAP Academic Press). *Aegean Archaeology* 7: 80–4.

2006c. Subsistence and hinterland as factors in settlement location and sociopolitical change through the Early Iron Age of Crete. In *Pepragmena Θ*: 161–79.

2007. Why we need new spectacles. Mapping the experiential dimension of prehistoric Cretan landscapes. *CAJ* 17/3: 249–70.

2008. Review of O. T. P. K. Dickinson, 2006, *The Aegean from Bronze Age to Iron Age; continuity and change between the twelfth and eighth centuries BC. AJA* 112: 187–8.

in press a. Building societies in post-collapse Crete: tradition, status competition and the templates of domestic and special buildings at Karfi and other sites, 1200–1000 BC. In Glowacki and Vogeikoff-Brogan.

in press b. Citadel *and* city-state: studying complexity in Cretan EIA communities using new surface ceramic data. In Kaiser and Pilz.

in press c. The roots of the Cretan polis: surface pottery and the archaeology of central Crete, 1200–500 BC. In *Pepragmena I*.

in press d. Formative landscapes: regional experiences of collapse and their long-term impacts in different Aegean areas. In Mazarakis-Ainian in press.

Wall-Crowther, S., 1996. The animal bones. In Coldstream and Catling: 703–11.

Walsh, V. A., and W. A. McDonald, 1983. House construction and town layout. In McDonald et al.: 455–67.

Ward, W. A., and M. S. Joukowsky, 1992. *The crisis years: the 12th century BC from beyond the Danube to the Tigris*. Dubuque, IA: Kendall/Hunt.

Wardle, K. A., 1980. Excavations at Assiros, 1975–9. *ABSA* **75**: 229–67.

1989. Assiros Toumba. *ABSA* **84**: 447–63.

Wardle, K., and Wardle, D., 2003. Prehistoric Thermon: pottery of the Late Bronze and Early Iron Age. In Kyparissi-Apostolika and Papakonstantinou: 147–57.

Warren, P. M., 1983. Knossos. Stratigraphical Museum Excavations, 1978–82. Part II. *AR* **29**: 63–87.

1997. Late Minoan III pottery from the city of Knossos: Stratigraphical Museum extension site. In Hallager and Hallager 1997a: 157–93.

2005. Response to Eleni Hatzaki. In D'Agata and Moody: 97–103.

Warren, P. M., and V. W. Hankey, 1989. *Aegean Bronze Age chronology*. London: Bristol Classical Press.

Wason, P., 1994. *The archaeology of rank*. Cambridge: Cambridge University Press.

Waterhouse, H., and R. Hope Simpson, 1960. Prehistoric Laconia: Part I. *ABSA* **55**: 67–107.

1961. Prehistoric Laconia: Part II. *ABSA* **56**: 114–75.

Watrous, L. V., 1977. Aegean settlements and transhumance. *Temple University Aegean Symposium* **2**: 3–6.

1980. J. D. S. Pendlebury's excavations in the plain of Lasithi. The Iron Age sites. *ABSA* **75**: 269–83.

1982. *Lasithi. A history of settlement on a highland plain in Crete*. Princeton, NJ: Princeton University Press.

1992. *Kommos III: An excavation on the south coast of Crete. The Late Bronze Age pottery*. Princeton, NJ: Princeton University Press.

1993. Cretan relations with the Aegean in the Late Bronze Age. In C. Zerner, P. Zerner, and J. Winder, eds, *Proceedings of the international conference 'Wace and Blegen: pottery as evidence for trade in the Aegean Bronze Age 1939–89,' held at the American School of Classical Studies at Athens, December 2–3, 1989*. Amsterdam: J. C. Gieben: 81–90.

1996. *The cave sanctuary of Zeus at Psychro. A study of extra-urban sanctuaries in Minoan and Early Iron Age Crete*. Liège: Université de Liège.

1998. Crete and Egypt in the seventh century BC: Temple A at Prinias. In Cavanagh and Curtis: 75–9.

1999. Review of Aegean prehistory III: Crete from earliest prehistory through the protopalatial period. In Cullen: 157–215.

2001. The isthmus of Ierapetra in east Crete and the Dark Age 'refuge settlement' of Profitis Elias: diaspora or local population change? In Karageorghis and Morris: 85–95.

Watrous, L. V., and D. Hadzi-Vallianou, 2004a. The polis of Phaistos: development and destruction (Late Minoan IIIC-Hellenistic). In Watrous et al. 2004: 307–39.

2004b. Creation of a Greek city-state (Late Minoan IIIC-Orientalizing). In Watrous et al. 2004: 339–51.

Watrous, L. V., D. Hadzi-Vallianou, and H. Blitzer, 2004. *The plain of Phaistos: cycles of social complexity in the Mesara region of Crete*. Los Angeles: Cotsen Institute of Archaeology, University of California.

Watrous, L. V., et al., 1993. A survey of the Western Mesara Plain in Crete: preliminary report of the 1984, 1986 and 1987 field seasons. *Hesperia* **62**: 191–248.

Webb, V., 1978. *Archaic Greek faience.* Warminster: Aris and Phillips.

1996. Faience and glass. In Coldstream and Catling. Vol. II: 599–611.

Wells, B., 1992. *Agriculture in ancient Greece. Proceedings of the Seventh International Syposium at the Swedish Institute at Athens, 16–17 May, 1990.* Stockholm: Swedish Institute at Athens.

Westgate, R., in press. House form and social structure in Classical and Hellenistic Crete. In Glowacki and Vogeikoff-Brogan.

Whitley, A. J. M., 1986. *Style, burial and society in Dark Age Greece: social, stylistic and mortuary change in the two communities of Athens and Knossos between 1100–700 BC.* Unpublished PhD dissertation, University of Cambridge.

1988. Early states and hero cults: a reappraisal. *JHS* **108**: 173–82.

1991a. *Style and society in Dark Age Greece: the changing face of a pre-literate society 1100–700 BC.* Cambridge: Cambridge University Press.

1991b. Social diversity in Dark Age Greece. *ABSA* **86**: 341–65.

1993. Response to Papadopoulos (ii): woods, leaves and trees in the Early Iron Age of Greece. *JMA* **6/2**: 223–9.

1997. Cretan laws and Cretan literacy. *AJA* **101**: 635–61.

1998a. From Minoans to Eteocretans: the Praisos region 1200–500 BC. In Cavanagh and Curtis: 25–39.

1998b. Review of Coldstream and Catling 1996, *Knossos North Cemetery: Early Greek tombs. AJA* **102**: 611–13.

1998c. Literacy and law-making: the case of Archaic Crete. In Fisher and van Wees: 311–31.

2001. *The archaeology of ancient Greece.* Cambridge: Cambridge University Press.

2002. Objects with attitude: disentangling biographical myth from cultural reality in Early Iron Age warrior burials. *CAJ* **12.2**: 217–32.

2005. Style wars: towards an explanation of Cretan exceptionalism. In Cadogan et al.: 433–42.

in press. The Cretan orientalizing: a comparative perspective. In Kaiser and Pilz.

Whitley, J., K. O'Conor, and H. Mason, 1995. Praisos III: a report on the architectural survey undertaken in 1992. *ABSA* **90**: 405–28.

Whitley, J., M. Prent, and S. Thorne, 1999. Praisos IV: a preliminary report on the 1993 and 1994 survey seasons. *ABSA* **94**: 405–28.

Whittaker, C., ed, 1988. *Pastoral economies in Classical antiquity.* Cambridge: Cambridge University Press.

Wilkens, B., 1996. The fauna from Italian excavations on Crete. In Reese: 241–63.

Willetts, R. F., 1955. *Aristocratic society in ancient Crete.* London: Routledge and Kegan Paul.

1965. *Ancient Crete: a social history from early times until the Roman occupation.* London: Routledge and Kegan Paul.

1967. *The law code of Gortyn.* Berlin: De Gruyter.

1969. *Everyday life in ancient Crete.* London: Batsford.

1977. *The civilization of ancient Crete.* London: Batsford.

1982. Cretan laws and society. In Boardman and Hammond 1982: 234–49.

Winter, I., 1995. Homer's Phoenicians: history, ethnography, or literary trope? A perspective on early orientalism. In Carter and Morris: 274–71.

Wolin, S. S., 1996. Transgression, equality and voice. In Ober and Hedrick 1996b: 63–91.

Wood, E. M., 1988. *Peasant-citizen and slave: the foundations of Athenian democracy.* London: Weiss.

Wright, J., 2005. *The Mycenaean feast.* Princeton, NJ: Princeton University Press.

Xanthoudides, S. A., 1904. Εκ Κρήτης: οι τάφοι τον Μουλιανών. *AE*: 1–56.

1918. Archaiologiki Periferia (Kritis). Erevnai, skafai kai evrimata kata to etos 1918. (Αρχαιολογική περιφέρεια (Κρήτης). Ερευναι, σκάφαι. και ευρύματα κατά το έτος 1918). *AD* **4**: 23–32.

1921. Archaiologiki Periferia (Kritis). Erevnai, skafai kai evrimata kata to etos 1919. (Αρχαιολογική περιφέρεια (Κρήτης). Ερευναι, σκάφαι. και ευρύματα κατά το έτος 1919). *AD* **6**: 154–7.

Yaeger, J., 2000. The social construction of communities in the Classic Maya countryside: strategies of affiliation in western Belize. In Canuto and Yaeger: 123–43.

Yalouri, E., 2001. *The Acropolis: global fame, local claim.* Oxford: Berg.

Yasur-Landau, A., 2006a. Halasmeno fagito: burnt dishes and scorched pots: some preliminary observations on LM IIIC cooking ware. In *Pepragmena Θ*: 233–53.

2006b. The last *Glendi* in Halasmenos: social aspects of cooking in a Dark Age Cretan village. *Aegean Archaeology* 7: 49–67.

Yoffee, N., 1997. The obvious and the chimerical: city-states in archaeological perspective. In Nichols and Charlton: 255–65.

Yoffee, N., and G. Cowgill, 1988. *The collapse of ancient states and civilizations.* Tucson and London: University of Arizona Press.

Yoffee, N., and A. S. Sherratt, eds, 1993. *Archaeological theory: who sets the agenda?* Cambridge: Cambridge University Press.

Yon, M., 1992. The end of the kingdom of Ugarit. In Ward and Joukowsky: 111–22.

Zaccagnini, C., 1977. The merchant at Nuzi. *Iraq* 39: 171–91.

1987. Aspects of ceremonial exchange in the Near East during the late second millennium BC. In Rowlands et al.: 57–66.

Zapheiropoulou, F., 2004. Oi Kyklades stiv proimi epochi tou Sidirou os tiv isteri Archaiki epochi (Οι Κυκλάδες στην πρώιμη εποχή του Σιδήρου ώς την ύστερη Αρχαϊκή εποχή). In Stampolidis and Giannikouri: 413–21.

Zerner, C., P. Zerner, and J. Winder, eds, 1993. *Proceedings of the international conference 'Wace and Blegen: pottery as evidence for trade in the Aegean Bronze Age, 1939–89', held at the American School of Classical Studies at Athens, December 2–3, 1989.* Amsterdam: J. C. Gieben.

INDEX